Simple Business Process Model

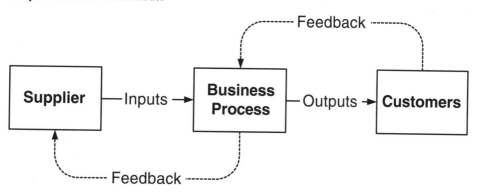

Process Analysis and Improvement

Tools and Techniques

THE MCGRAW-HILL/IRWIN SERIES in Operations and Decision Sciences

OPERATIONS MANAGEMENT

Bowersox, Closs, and Cooper
Supply Chain Logistics Management
First Edition

Chase, Jacobs, and Aquilano
**Operations Management for
Competitive Advantage**
Tenth Edition

Davis and Heineke
**Operations Management: Integrating
Manufacturing and Services**
Fifth Edition

Davis and Heineke
Managing Services
First Edition

Dobler and Burt
Purchasing and Supply Management
Sixth Edition

Finch
OperationsNow.com
First Edition

Fitzsimmons and Fitzsimmons
Service Management
Fourth Edition

Flaherty
Global Operations Management
First Edition

Gehrlein
Operations Management Cases
First Edition

Gray and Larson
Project Management
Second Edition

Harrison and Samson
Technology Management
First Edition

Hill
Manufacturing Strategy: Text & Cases
Third Edition

Hopp and Spearman
Factory Physics
Second Edition

Jacobs and Whybark
Why ERP?
First Edition

Knod and Schonberger
Operations Management
Seventh Edition

Lambert and Stock
Strategic Logistics Management
Third Edition

Leenders and Fearon
**Purchasing and Supply
Chain Management**
Twelfth Edition

Melnyk and Swink
Value-Driven Operations Management
First Edition

Moses, Seshadri, and Yakir
HOM Operations Management Software
First Edition

Nahmias
Production and Operations Analysis
Fifth Edition

Nicholas
Competitive Manufacturing Management
First Edition

Olson
**Introduction to Information Systems
Project Management**
Second Edition

Pinto and Parente
**SimProject: A Project Management
Simulation for Classroom Instruction**
First Edition

Schroeder
**Operations Management:
Contemporary Concepts and Cases**
Second Edition

Seppanen, Kumar, and Chandra
Process Analysis and Improvement
First Edition

Simchi-Levi, Kaminsky, and Simchi-Levi
**Designing and Managing the
Supply Chain**
Second Edition

Stevenson
Operations Management
Eighth Edition

Vollmann, Berry, Whybark, and Jacobs
**Manufacturing Planning &
Control Systems**
Fifth Edition

Zipkin
Foundations of Inventory Management
First Edition

BUSINESS STATISTICS

Aczel and Sounderpandian
Complete Business Statistics
Fifth Edition

ALEKS Corporation
ALEKS for Business Statistics
First Edition

Alwan
Statistical Process Analysis
First Edition

Bowerman and O'Connell
Business Statistics in Practice
Third Edition

Bowerman, O'Connell, and Orris
Essentials of Business Statistics
First Edition

Bryant and Smith
**Practical Data Analysis: Case Studies in
Business Statistics, Volumes I, II, and III**

Cooper and Schindler
Business Research Methods
Eighth Edition

Delurgio
Forecasting Principles and Applications
First Edition

Doane
LearningStats CD Rom
First Edition, 1.2

Doane, Mathieson, and Tracy
Visual Statistics
Second Edition, 2.0

Gitlow, Oppenheim, and Oppenheim
Quality Management
Third Edition

Lind, Marchal, and Wathen
**Basic Statistics for Business
and Economics**
Fourth Edition

Lind, Marchal, and Wathen
**Statistical Techniques in Business
and Economics**
Twelfth Edition

Merchant, Goffinet, and Koehler
Basic Statistics Using Excel for Office XP
Third Edition

Kutner, Nachtsheim, Neter, and Li
Applied Linear Statistical Models
Fifth Edition

Kutner, Nachtsheim, and Neter
Applied Linear Regression Models
Fourth Edition

Sahai and Khurshid
Pocket Dictionary of Statistics
First Edition

Siegel
Practical Business Statistics
Fifth Edition

Wilson, Keating, and John Galt
Solutions, Inc.
Business Forecasting
Fourth Edition

Zagorsky
Business Information
First Edition

QUANTITATIVE METHODS
AND MANAGEMENT SCIENCE

Hillier and Hillier
Introduction to Management Science
Second Edition

Process Analysis and Improvement

Tools and Techniques

Marvin S. Seppanen
Productive Systems

Sameer Kumar
University of St. Thomas

Charu Chandra
University of Michigan—Dearborn

McGraw-Hill Irwin

Boston   Burr Ridge, IL   Dubuque, IA   Madison, WI   New York   San Francisco   St. Louis
Bangkok   Bogotá   Caracas   Kuala Lumpur   Lisbon   London   Madrid   Mexico City
Milan   Montreal   New Delhi   Santiago   Seoul   Singapore   Sydney   Taipei   Toronto

McGraw-Hill
Irwin

PROCESS ANALYSIS AND IMPROVEMENT: TOOLS AND TECHNIQUES

Published by McGraw-Hill/Irwin, a business unit of The McGraw-Hill Companies, Inc., 1221 Avenue of the Americas, New York, NY, 10020. Copyright © 2005 by The McGraw-Hill Companies, Inc. All rights reserved. No part of this publication may be reproduced or distributed in any form or by any means, or stored in a database or retrieval system, without the prior written consent of The McGraw-Hill Companies, Inc., including, but not limited to, in any network or other electronic storage or transmission, or broadcast for distance learning.

Some ancillaries, including electronic and print components, may not be available to customers outside the United States.

This book is printed on acid-free paper.

1 2 3 4 5 6 7 8 9 0 CCW/CCW 0 9 8 7 6 5 4

ISBN 0-07-285712-9

Editorial director: *Brent Gordon*
Executive editor: *Scott Isenberg*
Editorial assistant: *Lee Stone*
Senior marketing manager: *Douglas Reiner*
Lead producer, Media technology: *Beth Cigler*
Project manager: *Bruce Gin*
Senior production supervisor: *Rose Hepburn*
Lead designer: *Matthew Baldwin*
Lead supplement producer: *Cathy L. Tepper*
Senior digital content specialist: *Brian Nacik*
Cover design: *Allison Traynham*
Cover Image: *@Getty Images*
Typeface: *10/12 Times New Roman*
Compositor: *Cenveo*
Printer: *Courier Westford*

Library of Congress Cataloging-in-Publication Data

Seppanen, Marvin S.
    Process analysis and improvement : tools and techniques / Marvin Seppanen, Sameer Kumar, Charu Chandra.
        p. cm. — (The McGraw-Hill/Irwin series Operations and decision sciences)
    Includes bibliographical references and index.
    ISBN 0-07-285712-9 (alk. paper)
    1. Reengineering (Management) I. Kumar, Sameer, II. Chandra, Charu, III. Title. IV. Series.
HD58.87.S47 2005
658.4'063—dc22
                                                                2004055207

www.mhhe.com

Preface

EXHIBIT 1 Four Basic Tasks for Process Analysis and Improvement

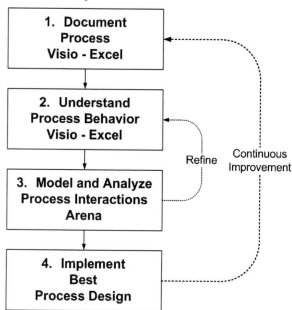

All businesses in the 21st century are facing ever-increasing consumer expectations. This is true whether the manager or engineer is in charge of a fast-food operation, a call center, a health care clinic, a university, or an automotive assembly plant. The consumer wants and expects the product or service to have better quality, more ease of use, and lower cost than ever before. The consumer has learned that the marketplaces can deliver more for less and is increasingly demanding it with every purchase decision. The same is true on the business-to-business level, where suppliers are increasingly becoming partners with their customers.

Every business process is sought to be improved or reinvented in order to remain competitive in today's global environment. New business processes must be designed using the best practices of the past while incorporating the flexibility needed to keep pace with an ever-changing world. A structured approach is required to effectively understand the present processes and then to search for and implement process improvements. The paper, pencil, and file cabinet technology of the past century is being replaced using the personal computer found on the manager's and engineer's desks. Unfortunately, the personal computer has yet to become fully integrated into this process analysis and improvement function. This textbook has been developed to start bridging this gap.

Exhibit 1 illustrates the four basic tasks that are fundamental to any structured process analysis and improvement approach.

The personal computer with currently available software can be central to accomplishing these four tasks. In the past, Management Information Systems were thought to be the solution for the data side of the process management issue. Even after the introduction of the personal computer to the business world in the 1980s and networks and Enterprise Resource Planning (ERP) systems in the 1990s, most business processes are still waiting for an effective solution. This textbook takes the approach of using software currently available on many desktops and using those tools to develop solutions for today. In the future, these tools and techniques are likely to be integrated into more comprehensive systems; however, the power of desktop computers will still be a key component in that evolution.

Target Audience

This textbook is meant to fulfill the needs of senior undergraduates as well as beginning graduate students and practitioners in technical and managerial fields who are interested in analytical approaches to process analysis and improvement. The text is designed for a course with a title such as "Process Analysis and Improvement," "Business Process Redesign," or "Process Mapping and Improvement." This course could be an introductory graduate-level course in business administration, industrial engineering, management of technology, engineering management, or a senior design course in industrial or manufacturing systems engineering undergraduate programs. We assume that students understand business or engineering statistics, production and operations management, and have a moderate-level proficiency in Microsoft Excel or similar personal computer software.

Our primary audiences for this text are students taking an introductory graduate course in management science, operations management, and industrial engineering programs, where students will gain the necessary personal computer application skills for business process analysis, design, and improvement. Students completing this course will have a high level of Excel application knowledge, a moderate proficiency in Visio, and a basic understanding of simulation using Arena. Students will also be exposed to an interchange of data between applications using Visual Basic for Applications (VBA). This is not a computer programming course. This text will enable students to solve complex business problems using popular software tools and solution templates included on the CD-ROM provided with the text.

Secondary audiences are students taking the Process Analysis and Design course for undergraduate programs in industrial engineering, engineering management, manufacturing systems engineering, and management of technology. We use a case study/project approach in this text so that it also is appropriate for senior engineering design courses.

This course could be a prerequisite to an advanced course in discrete-event simulation titled "Manufacturing System Simulation," "Simulation Software Design," or "Application of Process Simulation in Service Operations."

Subject and Approach

The primary purpose of our textbook is to describe and illustrate how to create an integrated business process analysis and improvement capability using the popular software tools Excel, Visio, Arena, and Visual Basic for Applications (VBA). This textbook is designed for students to learn by doing. A comprehensive CD-ROM accompanies this textbook containing all of the Visio drawings, Excel workbooks, and Arena models covered. Although a quick reading of the textbook can give the reader an appreciation of the material, learning to use computer-based tools and techniques requires considerable practice. The Visio drawings, Excel workbook, and Arena models illustrated in the textbook and contained on the accompanying CD-ROM have been carefully designed by practitioners with more than 30 years of experience in using computer-based tools. All exhibits illustrated in this textbook are direct copies of the supporting material from the appropriate software source. The textbook CD-ROM provides the student with complete solution templates using the appropriate software tools. Students will use these templates to formulate their own problem solutions. Exercises at the end of each chapter encourage readers to extend their knowledge and skills in using the tools and techniques presented.

Textbook Features

This textbook demonstrates integrated applications of Excel, Visio, Arena, and VBA for modeling business applications. We use Excel for the analysis and organization of data using spreadsheets, graphs, charts, statistical analysis, and linear/nonlinear optimization. Visio is used for process mapping and other graphical applications including office layout and organizational charts. The Arena process simulation software is used to model and understand the operational behavior of complex business systems. Finally, we introduce VBA to provide a method for the automation of applications and the transfer of data between applications. Other salient features of this textbook are described below.

Project Orientation

This textbook offers techniques to apply the tools—Excel, Visio, Arena, and VBA—to a process analysis and improvement project, a natural outcome of integration of various topics covered in the entire textbook. We provide the project team with a number of tools and accessories such as a Gantt chart for a typical one-semester student project, examples of successfully completed process analysis and improvement projects, application templates, two service case studies, and a number of applicable manufacturing operations models developed in Arena.

Exhibits

All the illustrations in the textbook are called *exhibits* as they represent either an Excel worksheet, a Visio drawing, an Arena model, or VBA editor display. The source worksheets, drawings, and models are included in the textbook CD. As the emphasis of the textbook is computer-based applications, illustrations in the textbook are drawn from Excel, Visio, and Arena software. For maximum benefit the reader must utilize these software tools.

Source Worksheets, Drawings, and Models

For each chapter we have developed an Excel workbook named **Chapter *X* Worksheets.xls** and also a Visio drawing file called **Chapter *X* Drawings.vsd**. The first sheet in each Excel workbook is named *Exhibits*. This sheet is an index that links textbook exhibits to Visio pages and Excel worksheets and also lists Arena models and other related files included on the CD for each chapter.

Challenge Levels

Some sections of this textbook have been marked as a challenge. Those sections may not be of interest to all readers or be appropriate for some coursework applications. They can be skipped or skimmed over without missing the main flow of the textbook.

Learning Objectives

Each chapter starts with an overview, followed by a concise set of student learning objectives. The chapter provides necessary instructional material including the appropriate computer-based applications to achieve the student's learning objectives. Exercises at the end of each chapter are meant to reinforce understanding of the learning objectives.

Instructional Support

The textbook CD-ROM provides PowerPoint transparencies for each chapter to enhance the effective dissemination of topics covered and demonstrate applications utilizing various software tools.

Software Tools

The textbook uses Microsoft Excel XP (Version 10) and Visio 2003 (Version 11), and Arena (Version 8.0). A demonstration/academic version of Arena 8.0 is provided on the textbook CD courtesy of Rockwell Software. The Visio drawings will function with Visio 2002 or later.

Case Studies

This textbook provides a number of case studies and industry examples from service and manufacturing sectors where various functions and features of these tools are used. These business system case studies and examples reflect the reality of service and manufacturing operations to form the backbone of process modeling and analysis. These case studies demonstrate how to successfully analyze and improve a business process. We use the above-mentioned software tools with an applications perspective to develop business solutions using concepts and techniques from process management, process flow analysis, and process integration.

Textbook Organization

This textbook is organized in a 12-chapter format for use in a semester-long course. Exhibit 2 illustrates the organization of textbook chapters and suggests some potential paths of study.

One chapter might be covered each week with adequate time for examinations and project presentations. The chapters track a general format of how it works (Chapters 3, 5, and 7) followed by how it is used (Chapters 4, 6, and 8). Two introductory case studies are pre-

EXHIBIT 2
Textbook Chapters with Suggested Teaching Flow

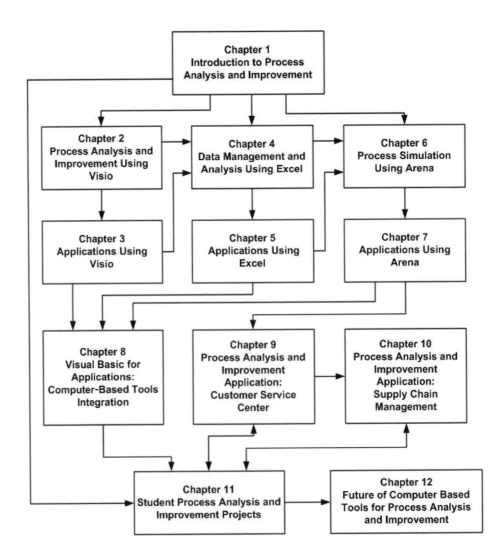

sented in Chapters 1 and 2. The case study in Chapter 2 has sufficient depth to be used as a prototype for a student course project. Chapter 10 presents applications in supply chain management. Chapter 11 presents summaries of student projects taken from their actual work experience as practicing managers and engineers. Visio is the focus of Chapters 2 and 3, Excel is the focus of Chapters 4 and 5, and Arena is the focus of Chapters 6 and 7, while VBA is extensively covered in Chapter 8. Because we are attempting to integrate these computer-based tools, some applications of each tool are included in every chapter. Chapter 12 completes the textbook by looking into the future. Some instructors may wish to skip certain material such as Chapter 8, Visual Basic for Applications: Computer-Based Tools Integration. Other instructors may wish to cover Visio or Arena in more depth using the textbook material provided as part of those software packages or widely available in major bookstores. Where appropriate, the textbook also references additional material that may be available on the Web or as part of supporting materials provided with the software.

Chapter 1: Introduction to Process Analysis and Improvement introduces readers to the dynamics of a "new business game," which is shaping organizations. This chapter explains how market forces are pushing businesses toward vertical and horizontal alignments. It describes opportunities for process analysis and improvements in various types of business operations. It also outlines how the redesign of existing business processes should be approached, starting from understanding the components of a simple business process model to process life cycle, identifying opportunities for process improvements, process mapping and analysis, and utilizing computer-based tools. A simple but comprehensive example of analysis, design, and optimization of a fast-food drive-through operation is presented to demonstrate the application of the computer-based tools and techniques.

Chapter 2: Process Analysis and Improvement Using Visio describes how business processes can be improved using process mapping and how to construct a process map using Visio. This chapter outlines the main features and functions of Visio. We also review the history of process mapping and various process mapping symbols. The goal of this and the following chapter is to introduce the reader to the Visio software and to move the reader with reasonable computer skills to an intermediate proficiency level for using Visio to analyze processes graphically.

Chapter 3: Applications Using Visio presents a wide range of graphical process analysis and improvement applications that can be accomplished using Visio. These applications include cause and effect diagrams, process improvement using value analysis, building an organization chart, and creating an office layout, all using Visio.

Chapter 4: Data Management and Analysis Using Excel presents the history of data management and analysis. It also describes how to design functional Excel worksheets, use statistical data analysis and optimization tools, build pivot tables, and develop Excel macros using VBA. The goal of this and the following chapter is to move the reader with a basic skill level in using Excel or similar software to an expert proficiency level. The example worksheets and templates are designed to make the reader an everyday expert Excel user.

Chapter 5: Applications Using Excel provides templates and detailed examples for using Excel to improve business processes. These applications include quality function deployment (QFD), technology function deployment (TFD), Six-Sigma, and equipment operating/repair cycles for developing simulation models.

Chapter 6: Process Simulation Using Arena covers a brief overview of queueing system theory and demonstrates how simple calculations can be made using either Excel or Arena. The basic structure of the Arena simulation environment is introduced by covering a simple queueing system model in detail. Sources of additional information are reviewed using the material from the Arena software CD-ROM examples and Smart files. The chapter concludes with a review of the basic information required to conduct a successful simulation project. The goal of this and the following chapter is to introduce the reader to the Arena software and move the motivated reader with reasonable computer skills to a beginning proficiency level in developing and using discrete event simulation tools.

Chapter 7: Applications Using Arena presents an extensive set of simulation examples based primarily on manufacturing systems but with relevance to a broader range of applications. This example set begins with a simple single unit and batch production systems and extends those models to include staff scheduling, equipment failures, inspection—rejection—rework, and material handling equipment. The transfer of data to and from worksheets is also demonstrated. We present the modeling of multiple product flows along with several alternative approaches supported by Arena. The size limitations presented by the Arena academic edition are reviewed along with two modeling techniques that can be used to minimize the impact of those limitations.

Chapter 8: Visual Basic for Applications: Computer-Based Tools Integration introduces the student to VBA applications, including how VBA provides integration between Excel, Visio, and Arena applications. VBA macros are recorded from both Excel and Arena. A VBA-based simulation example is presented to read variable data from an Excel workbook.

Chapter 9: Process Analysis and Improvement Application: Customer Service Center introduces readers to a case study dealing with a customer service call center. This chapter lays the groundwork by showing an application of the computer-based tools and techniques in a popular real-life service operation. The process is defined, documented, and improved using computer-based tools in a step-by-step manner. Collection and organization of data is accomplished by using Excel. Mapping the process is achieved by invoking Visio, and process modeling is demonstrated using Arena discrete event simulation. In addition to the standard Arena edition, the special purpose Arena Contact Center Edition is also demonstrated. This chapter has sufficient depth to be used as a prototype for a student course project.

Chapter 10: Process Analysis and Improvement Application: Supply Chain Management introduces readers to extended enterprises as companies form global alliances that result in global supply chains. Competition is now between supply chains rather than between companies. This chapter presents a brief review of supply chain theory, provides examples of prominent supply chains, and gives the beer game case study to demonstrate building a supply chain model using Excel, Visio, and Arena.

Chapter 11: Student Process Analysis and Improvement Projects offers summaries of student projects taken from their actual work experience as practicing managers and engineers. This textbook has been designed to support a course where the students spend considerable time analyzing, documenting, and improving an existing business process or designing a new process. Past student case studies are included to demonstrate how others have used the computer-based tools and techniques to solve real-life problems.

Chapter 12: The Future of Computer-Based Tools for Process Analysis and Improvement provides a perspective on tools such as enterprise knowledge base, vendor-supplied virtual objects, and seamless integration of various computer-based tools in a collaborative environment to facilitate process modeling and optimization.

Course Organization

In order to help instructors plan a course delivery, Exhibit 3 illustrates a sample syllabus for a semester course based on this textbook. Similarly, Exhibit 4 illustrates a sample outline for a 16-hour short course based on this textbook.

EXHIBIT 3
Semester Course Syllabus Using the Textbook

Week	Text Chapter	Topics Covered
1	1	1. Introduction to Process Analysis and Improvement
		a. Introduction to Computer-Based Tools: Excel, Visio, and Arena
		b. Drive and Eat Case Study
2	11	1. Application of Computer-Based Tools and Techniques: Student Case Studies
		2. Course Project Requirements & Software Problems
3	2	1. Process Improvement Using Visio
		a. Seven Process Improvement Tasks
		b. Process Mapping Symbols and Visio Stencils, Templates, and Shape Sheets
4	3	1. Applications Using Visio
		a. Cause and Effect Diagram
		b. Process Improvement Using Value Analysis
		c. Building an Organization Chart
		b. Creating an Office Layout
5	4	1. Data Management and Analysis Using Excel
		a. Basic Excel Concepts
		b. Advanced Excel Techniques: Data Filters, Pivot Tables, Optimization
6	5	1. Applications using Excel
		a. Quality Function Deployment (QFD)
		b. Technology Function Deployment (TFD)
		c. Six-Sigma
		b. Operating/Repair Cycle
7	6	1. Mid Term Exam
		2. Queuing System Analysis and Process Simulation Using Arena
8	7	1. Applications Using Arena
		a. Manufacturing Simulation Models
		b. Arena Academic Edition Limits
9	7	1. Applications Using Arena Continued
		a. Inspection – Rejection – Rework
		b. Material Handling Equipment
		c. Multiple Product Flows
10	8	1. Computer-Based Tools Integration using VBA
11	9	1. Application of Computer-Based Tools and Techniques
		a. Customer Service Center Case Study
		b. Arena Contact Center Edition
12	10	1. Application of Computer-Based Tools and Techniques: Supply Chain Management
13	12	1. Future Computer-Based Tools for Process Analysis and Improvement
		2. Course Evaluation
14		1. Final Project Presentations

EXHIBIT 4
Sixteen-hour Short Course Outline Using the Textbook

Hour	Text Chapter	Topics Covered
	1	**Introduction to Process Analysis and Improvement**
1		Introduction to Computer Based Tools: Excel, Visio, & Arena
2		Drive & Eat Case Study
	2	**Process Improvement Using Visio**
3		Seven Process Improvement Tasks
4		Process Mapping Symbols and Visio Stencils
Office Assignment 1		Create a Process Map and Process Analysis Template for an element of your job
	3	**Applications Using Visio**
5		Visio review and other applications
	4	**Data Management and Analysis Using Excel**
6		Basic Excel Concepts
7		Advanced Excel Techniques: Data Filters
8		Advanced Excel Techniques: Pivot Tables
Office Assignment 2		Create a Advanced worksheet for an element of your job
	4	**Data Management and Analysis Using Excel**
9		Visio and Excel review: Organizational Chart
	5	**Applications using Excel**
10		Advanced Excel Techniques: Statistics (Descriptive, Regression, ANOVA)
11		Advanced Excel Techniques: Optimization (Solver - Transportation)
12		Operating/Repair Cycle
Office Assignment 3		Create a Operating/Repair Cycle worksheet for an element of your company
	6	**Process Simulation Using Arena**
13		Queuing System Analysis using Excel
14		Queuing System Analysis using Arena
	7	**Applications Using Arena**
15		Manufacturing Simulation Models
16		Multiple Product Flows
Office Assignment 4		Create an Arena model for a critical process at your company

Acknowledgments

We gratefully acknowledge all those who helped us in bringing this textbook to publication. First and foremost we have greatly benefited from the wealth of a vast array of published materials on the subject of process analysis and improvement.

We would like to thank Professors Carol Romanowski, SUNY Buffalo; Ryan Underdown, Lamar University; Ranga Ramasesh, Texas Christian University; and Patrick A. Thompson, University of Florida, for carefully reviewing the manuscript of the textbook at various stages. The content has benefited immensely from their valued insights, comments, and suggestions.

Our sincere thanks to our students whose foresight, ingenuity, and professional knowledge is reflected in various case studies adopted in the textbook, particularly in Chapter 11.

We offer our grateful appreciation to our families who have shown their enormous patience and showered their encouragement and unconditional support throughout the long process of completion of this textbook project.

Finally, we wish to thank our editor, Scott Isenberg, and his able assistant, Lee Stone, and the entire McGraw-Hill/Irwin production team led by Bruce Gin for their assistance and guidance in the successful completion of this textbook.

About the Authors

Marvin S. Seppanen   *Winona, Minnesota*

is the founder and principal consultant of Production Systems, Winona, Minnesota, a company specializing in the design, analysis, and development of industrial strength simulation models for more than 20 years. His process simulation has included the modeling of high-volume printing, electrical and mechanical fabrication, high-speed automated packaging, jet engine overhaul, airline baggage transfer, just-in-time receiving, automotive assembly, underground coal mines, army personnel, and military inventories. He is a registered professional engineer and is active in several professional organizations. Dr. Seppanen has taught engineering at the University of St. Thomas, General Motors Institute, and the University of Alabama. He received his undergraduate and master's degrees in industrial engineering and his Ph.D. in operations research from the University of Minnesota. When not helping students and clients improve their processes, he attempts to improve the process of grape growing in southeast Minnesota with the goal of starting a small commercial winery.

Sameer Kumar   *Minneapolis, Minnesota*

is a professor and Qwest Endowed Chair in global communications and technology management in the College of Business at the University of St. Thomas, Minneapolis, Minnesota. Prior to this position he was a professor of engineering and technology management at St. Thomas. Before joining St. Thomas, Dr. Kumar was a professor of industrial engineering in the Department of Industrial Management, University of Wisconsin-Stout. His major research areas include optimization concepts applied to design and operational management of production and service systems. He has been actively involved in a wide variety of challenging industry projects for more than 23 years in the United States and India. He has published and presented articles in various research journals and conferences. He is a registered professional engineer, certified manufacturing technologist, certified manufacturing engineer, and certified plant engineer and has earned masters degrees in mathematics (University of Delhi), computer science (University of Nebraska), and industrial engineering and operations research (University of Minnesota). He received his Ph.D. in industrial engineering from the University of Minnesota.

Charu Chandra   *Dearborn, Michigan*

is an associate professor in industrial and manufacturing systems engineering at the University of Michigan-Dearborn. Prior to this, Dr. Chandra was a postdoctoral fellow at Los Alamos National Laboratory and at the University of Minnesota. He has worked in the industry as an information technology manager and systems analyst. He is involved in research in supply chain management and enterprise integration issues in large complex systems. He has also consulted extensively in the areas of supply chain management and information systems design and development. He teaches courses in information technology, operations research, and supply chain management. His master and Ph.D. degrees are in industrial engineering and operations research from the University of Minnesota and Arizona State University.

Brief Contents

Contents

Introduction to Process Analysis and Improvement

Summary and Learning Objectives

This chapter introduces *Process Analysis and Improvement* by briefly reviewing the concepts, techniques, and computer-based tools used to analyze and improve processes. We first define, describe, and illustrate the concept of a *process.* The simple process example of preparing a meal illustrates the importance of process context. We next survey a range of techniques used in process analysis and improvement activities. The chapter will develop the relationship between the computer-based tools Visio, Excel, and Arena. Finally, we use the complete set of computer-based tools to present a simple process analysis case study involving fast-food delivery.

The learning objectives for this chapter are

1. Use a process map to describe a process.
2. Analyze a simple process considering process life cycle and optimization.
3. Use process mapping to improve an existing process.
4. Understand the role of computer-based tools in process analysis and improvement.
5. Explain the interactions between drive and eat customers and crew members using the Visio drawings.
6. Explain sources of variability in drive and eat process.
7. Use Arena to develop an optimized drive and eat process.

Introduction

All businesses in the 21st century are facing ever-increasing consumer expectations. This is true whether the manager or engineer is in charge of a fast-food operation, a call center, a health care clinic, a university, or an automotive assembly plant. The consumer wants and expects the product or service to have better quality, ease of use, and lower cost than ever before. The consumer has learned that the marketplaces can deliver more for less and are increasingly demanding it with every purchase decision. The same is true at the business-to-business level, where suppliers are increasingly becoming partners with their customers.

Managers of every business process constantly seek to improve or reinvent the business in order to remain competitive in today's global environment. New business processes must be designed using the best practices of the past while incorporating the flexibility needed to keep pace with an ever-changing world. A structured approach is required to effectively understand the present processes and then to search for and implement process improvements. The paper, pencil, and file cabinet technology of the past century can be replaced using the personal computer now found on the desk of nearly every manager and engineer. However, the personal computer has yet to become fully integrated into this process design and improvement function. This textbook has been developed to start bridging this gap. We start with a brief history of process analysis and improvement.

Brief History of Process Analysis and Improvement

It is difficult to pinpoint exactly when we started to analyze and improve the processes that impacted human activities. We may point to some stories in the Bible as evidence of its early beginnings; certainly our hunting-and-gathering forebearers used some meaning to improve their food supply. Starting in the 16th century, worldwide ship operators and traders certainly showed a high degree of planning and organization to outfit ships with sufficient crew and supplies to journey around the globe, make trades, and then return to their home ports after as much as a year with enough goods to generate a profit. Other examples of organized processes can be gleaned from our industrial and military development.

The early part of the 20th century is marked by several well-documented examples of people concerned with process analysis and improvement. As industrial engineers, we look back to the founders of the scientific management concept—Frederick Taylor, Henry Gantt, and Frank and Lillian Gilbreth. We introduce the process mapping symbols developed for the Gilbreths in chapter 2 and the Gantt chart in chapter 3. At about the same time, Dr. Walter A. Shewhart of the Bell Telephone Laboratories first applied statistical techniques to the analysis and control of manufacturing processes.

The field of quality presents an interesting case study in the evaluation of process analysis and improvement. Shewhart, Harold F. Dodge, and Harry G. Romig, all Bell System employees, were early developers of statistically based sampling and inspection. These techniques became widely applied particularly in industries that supported U.S. efforts in World War II. Following the war, U.S. industries were too busy meeting domestic demand and rebuilding the war-damaged countries to be overly concerned with quality and process improvement. Efforts to help rebuild Japan included the introduction of quality techniques by American statisticians Drs. W. Edwards Deming and Joseph M. Juran. As a strong industrial country, the United States took little notice of these activities until the 1970s when cars being built in Japan greatly increased their total share of the world market, based both on price and quality advantages. This flood of low-priced and high-quality products from Japan finally awoke leaders of industries worldwide to the need of improving processes or be forced out of business. Exhibit 1–1 provides a rough time line for the evolution of quality-based initiatives or movements applied in the United States.

The Zero Defects movement relied heavily on posters, slogans, and inspection to improve process quality. Its success was limited and typically short-lived. The Quality Circles movement was based on the U.S. perception of how the Japanese were producing such low-cost, high-quality automobiles. This movement empowered groups of employees to meet on company time to analyze and improve the processes they worked with on a daily basis.

EXHIBIT 1–1
Quality Movement Timeline
Page quality timeline |
Chapter 1
Drawings.vsd

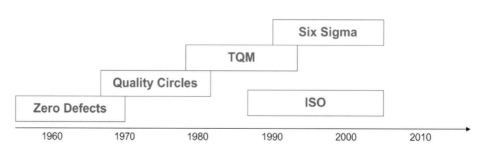

Limited training on a few of the techniques included in this textbook and field of quality improvement was provided by management, often through the industrial engineering department. Often these Quality Circles found that the source of their problems lay outside the scope of their workspace. This shortcoming of Quality Circles often led to finger-pointing and few real breakthroughs. The need for broader, higher level support process quality improvement lead to the Total Quality Management (TQM) movement, which required participation from the leadership of the organization's top management. TQM included an expanded tool set reflecting the development of the TQM Visio stencil, which we introduce in chapter 2.

The three quality methods discussed so far focused on process analysis and improvement in a rather ad hoc structure. They placed considerable effort on empowering employees or those closest to process to make improvements. Limited training and support was provided, but the movements lacked sustainable focus and were often eliminated when business downturns required capacity reduction. International Organization for Standardization (ISO) and Six Sigma represent more recent and organized quality movements. ISO is a European-based movement intended to document and standardize the product design and production process. ISO certification relies heavily on tools such as process maps to document the current process. It is less focused on the improvement of process and because of its extensive documentation requirements might tend to discourage continuous process improvement. The Six Sigma movement intends to build upon and improve the prior quality movements. In chapter 5, we introduce the statistical calculation using Excel for estimated process capability and note the expected number of defects per million produced by a process. Six Sigma implementations involve a wider focus more closely aligned with this textbook. Six Sigma relies on the training and certification of belts (green, black, black master) or individuals who are then required to conduct process analysis and improvement projects within their organizations. The training of these individuals includes a heavy emphasis on statistics and many of the techniques we cover in this textbook. We'll discuss the issue of *process selection* for analysis and improvement later in this chapter, but it is central to the development and maintenance of successful Six Sigma programs.

As illustrated in Exhibit 1–1, the field of quality improvement has seen the continuous evolution of new movements, but is also based more or less on the implementation of statistical methods and process analysis and improvement. In this textbook, we briefly cover a few of the statistical techniques but concentrate more on the tools and techniques for process analysis and improvement.

Another side field of development which gained considerable notice in the 1990s was business process reengineering. Basically this movement used the tools and techniques covered in this textbook to analyze a wide variety of processes and suggest improvements.

Whereas this review of the recent history of process analysis and improvement is no doubt colored by the background and biases of the authors (all of whom are trained in industrial engineering), it does indicate that there is a great deal of overlap between a number of fields of endeavor. What we bring to the table is a set of templates or examples of how to use widely available personal computer–based software tools to analyze and improve real-world processes.

We first define what a process is, and then investigate the task of process analysis and improvement.

What Is a Process?

A *process* can be defined as a series of value-added tasks that are linked together to convert inputs into a product or service to an output. It must have one or more activities that serve a useful purpose for an organization or individual. Processes can be defined at many different levels and with various boundaries, including

- Processes must have a beginning and an end (boundaries).
- Processes are coordinated activities that involve people, procedures, technology, and infrastructure.
- Processes constitute a significant portion of organizational costs.
- An organization is only as effective as its processes.
- All work is part of a process that starts and ends with a customer.

Processes are an effective way to manage an organization at any level and eventually support its overall goals. By improving processes, a business or organization can improve internal efficiencies, effectiveness, adaptability, and customer service levels.

An ideal process reflects three main attributes:

1. Making processes *efficient* means minimizing the resources used.
2. Making processes *effective* means producing the desired results.
3. Making processes *adaptable* means being able to adapt to changing customer and business needs.

Documenting processes involving people, particularly employees, can lead to insights and changes that can help improve an area or operation. One way to understand a process is to start thinking about its major elements: inputs, outputs, activity steps, decision points, enablers, and functions.

This text is dedicated to introducing the reader to a variety of personal computer–based tools to assist in analyzing and improving processes.

Production Process

The production process is any process or facility designed to transform a set of input elements into a specified set of output elements. Any production process can be broken down into three components: inputs, outputs, and production function. Another way of looking at the input-output process model is shown in Exhibit 1–2, illustrating the way in which various ingredients are brought together and transformed to accomplish the objectives for which the process was designed.

Outputs Specification of the desired output(s) is the usual starting point for designing a production operation. Financial considerations may dictate that managers search for some activity that will produce a satisfactory return on the invested capital. The possession of extra capital is frequently the prime motivation for a search to discover desirable outputs. Other motivational means include a new product or service introduction by a competitor

EXHIBIT 1–2
Production Process Model
Page production process model | Chapter 1 Drawings.vsd

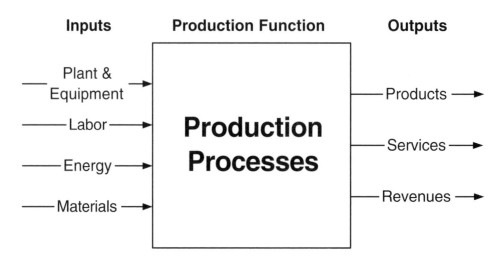

that is receiving strong consumer acceptance or a market survey that uncovers a consumer need that is not being satisfied. Also a creative employee in the organization may come up with an output that will achieve an economically satisfying level of demand.

Because of the dynamic character of the marketplace, new output opportunities are continually developing. A previously unwanted product or service can unexpectedly shift into a situation where it is under substantial demand. Of course, the converse is also true: An accepted product can begin to lose popularity. This can be traced, sometimes, to the activities of a competitor, but it can also be explained as a shift in consumer needs. It is the job of production management to set up and run the system that can produce a desired output.

Production Function   The production function can be very complicated; many kinds of inputs can be required and a variety of outputs can emerge. But the idea of transforming a set of inputs to yield a set of outputs is not complex. The design of an input-output process to accomplish specific objectives is another matter. It can be very difficult.

Inputs   In a typical manufacturing process, plant and equipment constitute uncontrollable input, whereas the three elements materials, energy, and labor constitute the primary controllable inputs. The uncontrollable inputs represent primarily fixed costs. These are costs that do not vary as a function of the output rates. For the most part, fixed costs arise as a result of investments in plant, equipment, and so forth. Most of these are depreciated as a function of time and not as a function of production volume. The controllable inputs primarily represent variable costs for operating the process. Such costs are paid out on a per-unit (of volume) basis. Direct labor and material costs can be charged to each unit of production. Variable costs, as a system of input classification, also create certain anomalies. For instance, indirect labor charges are associated with office work. Such costs are difficult to assign to a particular unit of output on a cost per piece basis. These are assigned to a cost category called *overhead costs.* Similarly, salaries that are paid to supervisory personnel fall outside the specific definition that is being used.

Managers exercise most of their day-to-day control over outputs through inputs to the production process. It is harder to make changes in the process than in the inputs, once the process is in place.

Simple Process Example

We often encounter the term *process* in our day-to-day social or business interactions. Let us first explore the meaning of process by a simple example, preparing a meal. Exhibit 1–3 illustrates a simple process model.

EXHIBIT 1–3
Food Preparation Process Model
Page food preparation process model |
Chapter 1
Drawings.vsd

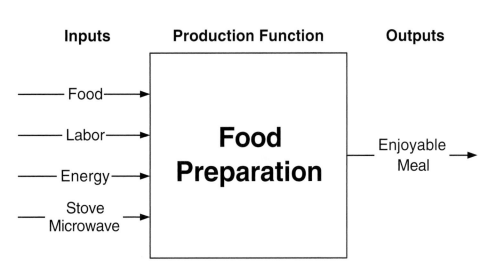

EXHIBIT 1–4 **Breakfast Process Map**

Page breakfast process map | Chapter 1 Drawings.vsd

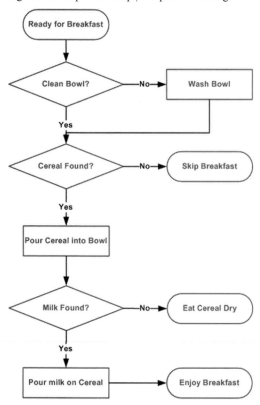

The process model illustrated in Exhibit 1–3 should raise several important process context questions:

- Who prepares the meal?
- Who eats the meal?
- What foods are available?
- What food preparation facility is available?

To illustrate the importance of these context questions, consider the following potential range of situations for which this process might apply:

- College student cooking breakfast for self.
- College student cooking dinner for a new date.
- White House chef cooking a state dinner for 500 guests.

In the first case, the student may simply pour a bowl of breakfast cereal, add milk, and eat. Of course, problems can arise if some of the key inputs cannot be found. A possible process map for this first case is illustrated in Exhibit 1–4. The second situation is a bit more complex and might require some special shopping to get the right combination of foods. The reader should modify the Visio process map illustrated in Exhibit 1–4 to fit this more complex situation.

The third case, preparing a White House state dinner, is far more complex than either of the two prior situations. This process may require several months and a staff of hundreds to perform. We'll skip the details of developing a process map for the White House chef, but it is likely to include decisions related to determining the guest of honor, regional dishes that might be served, and the President's likes and dislikes, among other decisions. An experienced White House chef will develop process in great detail in order to maximize staff effectiveness during the dinner planning, preparation, and serving stages. In addition, after the dinner has been completed, the White House chef will debrief the staff to determine what went well and what did not. This latter stage is critical to process improvement for future state dinners. Our college student, likewise, might incorporate a plan for process improvement to assure that critical ingredients are available tomorrow morning.

Business Process Feedback Model

A business process is the way in which work is done in an organization. It is a blending and transformation of a specific set of inputs into a more valuable set of outputs. Inputs to the process may include entities, such as people, materials, supplies, semifinished products, equipment, services from others, and information. A simplified business process model is shown in Exhibit 1–5.

Models are widely used in many fields to understand, teach, test, and visualize how business process performs. Most readers are familiar with the periodic table of chemical elements or historical time lines. These models graphically illustrate a great deal of complex information in a relatively compact format. Similar graphical models have a wide application in mathematics and physical sciences. A visual model often makes a complex concept easier to understand than descriptive text. The axiom that a picture is worth a thousand words is very much supported by many types of business models.

Business process models can be used to document how an organization functions and can serve as a starting point for improving process performance. Such models can be used

EXHIBIT 1–5
Simple Business Process Model
Page simple business process model | Chapter 1 Drawings.vsd

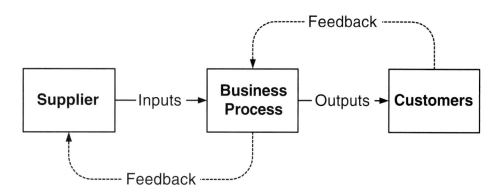

to teach new personnel how a process works or what is expected from a particular activity. Business process models can be used to show how a process

1. Functioned in the past.
2. Should function today.
3. Can be improved in the future.

The simplified business process model is a closed system with feedback mechanisms linking suppliers and customers to the process, where both suppliers and customers may be external or internal.

Process inputs can also be thought of as resources. Inherently, resources are required at various stages in a process in order to keep the process moving forward. When resources are not immediately available, delays will result. Process speed is dependent on having the right resources at the right place at the right time.

Process Analysis and Improvement Opportunities

In the wake of increasing global competition, the manufacturing environment has to change continuously in order for businesses to remain productive and efficient. A growing number of businesses are becoming multinational to strategically position themselves in global markets with worldwide manufacturing operations. Dornier, et al. (1998) indicate that changing business conditions have prompted manufacturers to design equipment to accommodate new products without expensive retooling. This has enabled manufacturers to move into new markets and leave them just as quickly. These new markets impose demands for products to match specific consumer needs requiring the customization of products or even the alteration of an entire product line. Facilities are now being utilized whereby manufacturers can create prototypes for new products in remarkably short periods of time. Flexible manufacturing systems techniques are being utilized and are enabling companies to offer lower costs, faster turnaround time, and quality levels that meet or exceed customer expectations. Quality of products is more uniform and predictable with low waste of scrap and rework, and manufacturers are reaping the benefits of greater flexibility and optimum utilization of production facilities and equipment. (Bisson and Folk, 2000; Savory and Olson, 2001). Consequently, opportunities for improvement need to be identified to deal with issues such as product quality, material handling, product design time, service facilities, manufacturing setups, and factory and office overhead.

In addition to the process analysis approach described earlier, we propose integration and standardization to facilitate these improvements.

Integration

Many manufacturing and service systems are currently being run on an informal basis. In an informal system, a feeling prevails that information cannot be used properly in planning and decision-making functions. An informal production or service system is a method of work that, in most instances, has evolved over time and become habitual. It is performed by one or, at most, a handful of employees in a given function or discipline; runs counter to or bypasses standard operating procedure; and appears superficially to be functional. Within an organization, the informal system can present difficult choices for managers. Certain telltale signs indicate the presence of an informal system in an operation. We may look for informal systems if (1) confusion erupts when an individual moves from one function to another; (2) someone takes a brief or extended leave of absence, and his or her replacement cannot step in and perform the absent worker's duties; or (3) a person leaves the organization and the functioning of the area where he or she worked suddenly declines.

Tolerating informal systems represents a dangerous abdication of fundamental responsibility on the part of the managers and engineers assigned to run manufacturing enterprises (McCann, 1999; Zygmont, 1988; Jones and McLeod, 1986). A formal system, however, is run with data, coming from the same database. These data differ in the level of their details depending on macro decisions such as new production operation policies where fewer details are required, or micro decisions such as day-to-day production scheduling where more details are needed for operational decisions (Finn, 2002; Wilbur 1999; Goddard, 1986). Integration of business functions such as marketing, design, manufacturing, purchasing, and product distribution within a company to have cross-functional business operation is achievable through common policies, a common action plan, and most importantly, through shared information used in various decisions, based on common knowledge bases (Kesner, 2001; Ravichandran and Rai, 2000).

Standardization

Decision making in a typical company is hierarchically distributed. Detailed decisions are generally made at lower levels while macro decisions are made at higher levels. For the operational level, in many cases the goal is to achieve more standardization and automation of operations, whereas for the strategic level, it is to outline policies for smooth functioning of operational activities (Labovitz and Rosansky, 2000). Consumers are demanding that companies increase product diversity. In order to remain competitive, companies respond with many specialized versions of a product. This is leading to modularized products in the marketplace. Modularization of product designs enables assembly of products from a set of standardized constituent units. Different assembly combinations from a given set of design effectively wed flexibility of the end product with standardization of constituent parts amenable to automation. Modularization also provides opportunities for exploiting economies of scope and scale from a product design approach. We achieve standardization in a manufacturing or service environment by identifying commonalities within operations, processes, and services.

Standardizing operations results in common manufacturing strategies and techniques for similar operations. For example, a sheet metal fabrication operation performed at different locations may be based on a common methodology, while allowing the flexibility to recognize unique needs of different markets. Similarly, process standardization should be carried out on a corporate basis allowing flexibility to recognize differences in markets. In the sheet metal fabrication example, the process of shearing would require cuts made with the same geometry, stress, and tolerances while using automated shearing equipment (as opposed to using specialized fixtures and jigs) and break press would minimize set-up time, thereby increasing production scheduling flexibility (Gander, 2002).

A knowledge base for a manufacturing enterprise should be developed to meet companywide needs for standardization. Such a system should be developed from the bottom up within a top-down planning design configuration. The development of the knowledge base will occur in incremental steps. One of the reasonable ways to schedule development is to select among current problems; maximize incremental benefits to cost ratio locally, if there are choices available, and undertake smaller projects initially. The optimal design would require a common database with preplanned tools to convert data into information, ready for use as input to various operational procedures and other decision support systems.

Any process change initiated should be intended to improve specifically stated outcome(s). In the absence of outcome measures, a company is strictly focusing on things its managers care about internally within its business organization. A company may believe it is achieving success while its customers notice no change. Customers care most about the results they obtain by working with their suppliers. A company stays in business if its products are best at satisfying desired outcomes within the customer's acquisition constraints. Customers care about a company's processes only to the extent they have to deal with them. In general, the less process they experience to acquire a company's products and achieve the outcomes they want, the better. Typically, organizational systems and culture are commonly built around process. The challenge in creating alignment with customers is in establishing better balance between process, product, and outcome emphasis.

Process Analysis Approach

The process analysis approach allows an analyst or team to account for, in an orderly manner, the multiplicity of factors that affect a process. Further, the process analysis approach provides both an action plan and a visible display or template. Exhibit 1–6 illustrates a process analysis template that can be used to structure the development of an effective process.

EXHIBIT 1–6
Process Analysis Template
Page process analysis template | Chapter 1 Drawings.vsd

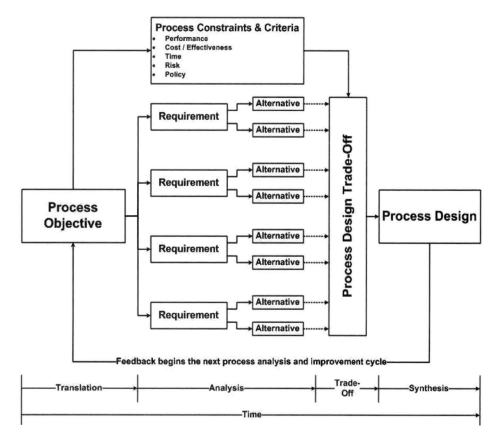

Three steps are fundamental to any structured process analysis and improvement approach:

1. **Translation and understanding** Determine a common language (or terminology) for the statement of the process objective and the criteria and constraints that are acceptable and understandable.
2. **Analysis and trade-off study** Determine as many alternative approaches as possible to solve the problem as a whole or to solve portions of the problem. Apply selection criteria and constraints to choose the best combination of alternatives to meet the objective.
3. **Synthesis** Achieve a "best" process.

The selection of process criteria and constraints (physical, fiscal, timing, and policy) that are used to control the trade-off of alternatives are either imposed by the political, physical, and economic environment in which the process must operate or be established by the process analyst or team. It should also be understood that this process logic must be repeated in a cyclic manner as a process is developed from the initial concept to the final functioning process. The process analysis and improvement steps—translation, analysis and trade-off, and synthesis—are carried out in cycles. The steps may be repeated several times, each adding more detail or concentrating on a particular process requirement. Feedback exists between cycles as well as between phases within a cycle. Each succeeding cycle gives more detail to the developing process improvement strategy or solution.

The practitioner of the process analysis approach methodology need not necessarily be a highly trained person, but he or she must exhibit common sense. An orderly approach and a logical manner of reasoning are desirable characteristics of the process analyst. We hope to instill these characteristics in the reader of this text. Let's begin by reviewing the typical process life cycle.

Process Life Cycle

Many organizations have processes in place that evolved over the years without careful planning and thought. Such processes, while functional, are not efficient or effective. Such processes present opportunity for analysis and improvement. One can use the process development life cycle approach to come up with the improved design of business processes. Steps involved in completing the life cycle and their respective outcomes are illustrated in Exhibit 1–7.

Process development life cycle is an ongoing practice. Competition (both national and international) usually necessitates the continuing study of a given product so that the associated business processes can be improved and a part of the gains passed on to the consumer in the form of a better product at a reduced selling price. Once this is done by a given business organization, competitors invariably introduce similar improvement programs, and it is only a matter of time until they have produced a more sellable product at a reduced price. This starts a new cycle in which the given organization reviews its business processes and improves them. Conditions in industry cannot be static; otherwise, bankruptcy would result. Progress in productivity and quality improvement is the only key to continued profitable operation.

EXHIBIT 1–7
Process Life Cycle
Page process life cycle | Chapter 1 Drawings.vsd

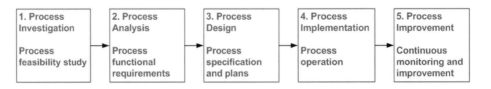

1. Process Investigation	2. Process Analysis	3. Process Design	4. Process Implementation	5. Process Improvement
Process feasibility study	Process functional requirements	Process specification and plans	Process operation	Continuous monitoring and improvement

Process Analysis and Improvement

All processes are in need of continuous improvement to stay competitive in an ever-changing world. Process improvement activities can include the following:

- Eliminating entire processes or subprocesses that are unnecessary.
- Automating manual activities.
- Combining steps.
- Outsourcing elements of the process.
- Changing the location where steps are done or where the people perform them.
- Altering or modifying how activity steps are done.

Let's review how we carry out a process analysis and improvement project using a seven task approach.

Process Analysis and Improvement Tasks

Our process analysis and improvement approach includes the seven tasks illustrated in Exhibit 1–8 and detailed in this section.

Task 1. Select Process and Define Its Boundaries

While we assert that all processes are in need of continuous improvement, an organization with limited resources must use some method to determine which processes are most critical to the success of the overall organization. The first task is to identify which process will be analyzed and eventually improved. Essentially in this task, we realize a general familiarity of the process and also finalize the selection of metrics and the type of process analysis.

The level of detail and overall scope of the process should also be identified. These factors are often defined by the availability of resources and the span of authority for implementation of potential process improvements.

The most important criterion to use in order to select a process for analysis, that is, to identify a process to improve its impact on customer-perceived value. We should select processes that most contribute to customer-perceived value to be world class or at least competitively superior. These are processes that should be benchmarked, reengineered, or improved, depending on the current level of process performance as compared to customer expectations and perceptions of outputs of the process.

EXHIBIT 1–8
Seven Process Improvement Tasks
Page seven tasks |
Chapter 1
Drawings.vsd

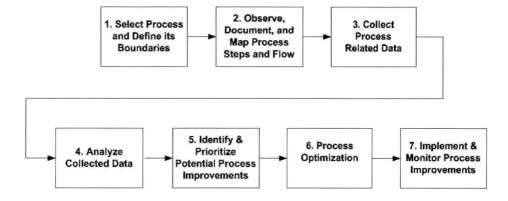

Additional criteria that can be used to decide which process to first analyze include:

- Process as part of a core competency
- Cost reduction
- Cycle time reduction
- Defect reduction
- Bottlenecks
- Obsolete or changing technology, especially information technology
- Competitive reasons
- Mergers or acquisitions

Jeff Rich, a Six Sigma Master Black Belt at the Trane Corporation in LaCrosse, Wisconsin, has developed a structured approach to identify, select, and monitor processes being analyzed and improved. He typically looks for projects that can be completed by Six Sigma Green or Black Belts within a four- to six-month time frame. As the overall manager of Six Sigma projects at his location, Jeff tries to maintain a backlog of projects to be assigned to available personnel. He maintains a prioritized list of potential process analysis and improvement projects. This priority is based in part on the expected return on investment or effort required to accomplish each projects. Each potential process analysis and improvement project must be defined in terms of how its success will be measured. Further, those measures and metrics must be aligned with the corporation's mission, values, and goals.

Once a process has been identified for analysis and improvement, we must carefully identify where the process begins and ends. This can be categorized as establishing process boundaries. The case study that we present at the end of this chapter has a process boundary that is relatively simple to define. That boundary is limited to the physical location and time (from 11:30 AM to 12:30 PM) of the fast-food process.

One word of caution, most process analysis and improvement projects tend to suffer from expanding or creeping boundaries. Only the skill and experience of the project manager can be counted on to limit this expansion of scope. We leave the task of project management to other sources.

Students using this textbook in a classroom setting will be using different constraints and criteria for selecting a suitable process for analysis and improvement. Chapter 11 outlines our approach for conducting such a project in a classroom setting and provides examples of work completed by graduate-level students working in corporate settings.

Task 2. Observe, Document, and Map Process Steps and Flow

The second task is to observe and map each process step and the overall process flow. In this task, we record process-related information such as time, cost, required resources, and other information. Special note should be made of when and how decisions are made that alter the flow path. This task is used to develop the process flow or process sequence map. The use of Visio software for this task is developed later in this chapter. We start by illustrating two types of process maps developed using Visio. We then cover some of the ways in which the information contained in the process map might be developed within an organization.

Simple Process Maps

Exhibit 1–9 illustrates a simple process map developed using Visio, based on a traditional Christmas poem. The traditional structure for process mapping is a general flow from top to bottom with arrowheads indicating the specific flow direction. Rectangular shapes are used to indicate process steps, while diamonds are used to indicate decision steps. Process

EXHIBIT 1–9

Holiday Process Map

Page holiday process map | Chapter 1 Drawings.vsd

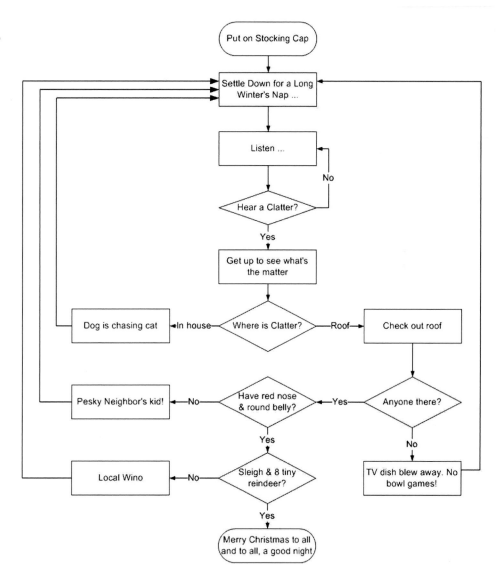

steps may have multiple entry points but only a single exit. Decision steps may also have multiple entry points and two or more exit points, depending on the complexity of the decision being made. The flow lines leaving the decision step are labeled with the criteria for selecting each path.

The process map should begin and end with at least one terminator symbol shaped as an elongated circle. The process map illustrated in Exhibit 1–9 begins with the subject "Put on Stocking Cap" and terminates with the subject saying, "Merry Christmas to all and to all, a good night." The intermediate steps are traced by following the flow arrows or connectors.

Exhibit 1–10 illustrates a logic process map developed using Visio for planning computer code required by an industrial application. The logical process map has one starting point, Case Enters Gantry Control Point, and two possible end points, "Case Bypasses Gantry" and "Gantry Attempts to Take Case," which are selected based on 10 decision

EXHIBIT 1–10
Logic Process Map
Page logic process
map | Chapter 1
Drawings.vsd

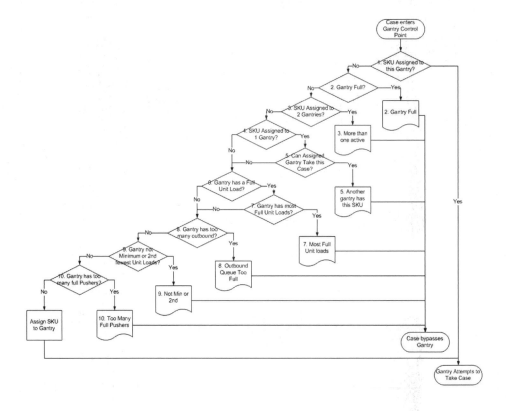

points contained in the logic flow. In order to make the process map easily understood, all yes decisions move toward the right, while no decisions move left.

Process Observation and Documentation

The method used to collect the necessary information depends on the knowledge level of the analyst, the total available timeframe, and availability of other individuals who are familiar with the process. There are three basic information collection methods:

1. **Self-generate** If the analyst personally knows the process, he or she can draw a preliminary process map and ask others who work or interact with the process to react to it. This method produces a map faster than the other two ways, but its usefulness is limited by the amount of process knowledge possessed by the analyst.

2. **One-on-one interviews** A series of one-on-one interviews with suppliers, performers, and customers of the process will enable the analyst to create a straw model of the process map. The interviewer can then route the map to those interviewed and others who are knowledgeable of the process, and ask them to review it for completeness and accuracy. This method works best when the interviewer has good questioning and listening skills and is able to synthesize information rapidly. It also helps to be familiar with the part of the business the analyst is mapping before starting the interviews.

3. **Group interview** The third method available to create a process map is to arrange for the relevant individuals to participate as a group to generate the map. This method provides the greatest direct interaction among the suppliers, performers, and customers of the process. A high degree of participation increases the sense of ownership that the group feels regarding the map and, more importantly, the process. This method works best when a skilled facilitator works with the group to help them identify and lay out the inputs, outputs,

and steps of the process. The facilitator does not need to be familiar with the process. However, he or she should possess strong questioning and listening skills as well as a sound knowledge of the following mapping conventions. The facilitator should

- Use the group interview method and a skilled mapping facilitator whenever possible.
- Select the right people to create the map. Generally speaking, the right people are those who are
  - knowledgeable of the process;
  - interested in improving the process;
  - available and willing to stay in the room for the duration.
- Establish ground rules at the start and post them on a flip chart. Group participants must
  - record creation method and conventions;
  - agree that no team member's comings and goings will be allowed;
  - turn off cell phones and pagers;
  - think rough draft—"first get it down; then get it good!";
  - encourage communication;
  - discourage finger-pointing (no-fault rule applies);
  - go for quantity of information (breadth versus depth);
  - keep a bin list (a list of outstanding or unresolved issues).
- Use a room large enough that people can easily move around.
- Have plenty of paper to write on.
- Use self-stick notes to generate the initial steps, then categorize information by steps, output, input, measure, function, and so on.
- Sequence and rearrange the steps based on the self-stick notes.
- Use a notebook computer to record information directly into Visio and project the display on a large screen.
- Do not let a particular technology or software package hinder your group process or progress. The analyst can clean up the details later.
- Keep the energy flowing. The project is successful when other people start spontaneously adding or changing items on the map themselves.
- Respect everyone's contribution.

Finally, the facilitator should act as a catalyst to jump-start the group and help participants when they stray or start to slow down.

Process Mapping Pitfalls

Exhibit 1–11 lists some pitfalls and possible remedies when creating process maps.

We are now ready to discuss briefly the computer tools used in this textbook for process analysis and improvement and outline the integrated problem-solving framework utilizing these tools.

Task 3. Collect Process-Related Data

This task collects the quantitative data associated with each process step previously identified. In task 2, process is observed and in task 3 data is collected for each process step. Tasks 2 and 3 are parallel or simultaneous activities. Excel workbooks (see chapters 4 and 5) are an effective means to collect, organize, analyze, and illustrate these collected data.

Subsequent process analysis most often requires the collection of process performance data, such as cost, time, or defect data. The type of project selected to be mapped or

EXHIBIT 1–11

Process Mapping Pitfalls

Sheet process mapping pitfalls | Chapter 1 Worksheets.xls

Pitfall	Possible Remedy
"Unbalanced" process map (too much detail in some areas, not enough in others)	Compare to other parts of the map; ask, Does this step contain roughly the same amount of effort as that step?
Process map gaps (missing or uncertain steps).	Ensure that those who help create the map are knowledgeable of the process, or have others review the draft for completeness and accuracy
Process map too "busy"	Use additional paper and plenty of white space, or use expanded maps cross-referenced to base map.
Process map takes too long, or people get bogged down	Establish ground rules, such as outstanding items list move on after five minutes follow rough draft principle; first get it down, then get it good use facilitator
Unclear terminology, or cannot remember what was said about a particular step	Take notes while mapping. Use Excel to create a glossary of terms
Mixed group (some upper level, some lower level) or defers to designated decision	Stress that firsthand knowledge of the work process is what matters Strive for equal participation, even if it means redefining the group Try to prevent this problem by staffing the group with the right mix up front and explaining to management that they should select those closest to the work

improved usually dictates type of analysis and required level of detail. For example, a quality improvement project was selected because of customer complaints regarding errors in the process output. In this case, the analyst might collect and analyze defect data in order to determine and eliminate the root causes of defects. Alternatively, if the customer complained that the output took too long to receive, the analyst would concentrate on cycle time analysis, rather than defects, assuming that outputs are defect free.

Task 4. Analyze Collected Data

This task involves summarizing all collected process-related observations. Initial analysis of a process begins with interpreting the completed process maps. The important thing to remember is that maps are a means not an ends. Often, but not always, one or more steps of the process that the analyst mapped will require a more detailed breakdown before improvements are recommended.

Reviewing the Process Map

Exhibit 1–12 shows how process maps can be used in a variety of process analysis and improvement applications. The exhibit contains the information listed below for each process analysis and improvement application.

- **Typical analysis questions** This is a "thought-starter" list of the questions to be answered as part of the analysis. These are representative and by no means the only questions that will arise.
- **Additional data requirements** Generally speaking, process maps do not provide the performance data needed for subsequent analysis. This section lists the type of data required for a particular application.
- **Analysis methods** These are the methods of analysis that are likely to be most useful for the specific application, and for which the process maps provide the foundation.

Value Analysis

Regardless of any other analysis subsequently performed, once the analyst has reviewed and interpreted a completed map or flowchart, the group should be asked to classify each

EXHIBIT 1–12
Process Mapping Applications
Sheet Process Mapping Applications | Chapter 1 Worksheets.xls

Application	Cost Reduction	Cycle Time Reduction	Quality Improvement (Defect Reduction)	Measurement System Design or Evaluation
Typical analysis questions	What does it cost to operate the process? Which steps cost the most? Why? Which steps add value and which do not? What are the causes of cost in this process?	Which steps consume the most time? Why? Which steps add value and which do not? Which steps are redundant, bottlenecks, or add complexity? Which steps result in delays, storage, or unnecessary movement?	How should the process be changed to reduce or eliminate variation? Is variation due to common or special causes? What are the causes of defects? Which variables must be managed to have the desired effect on the relevant quality characteristics?	Based on customer expectations data, what are the requirements for inputs and outputs of this process What should our measures be to assure that the requirements are met? Do our current measures assess what is important to our customers? What happens to the measurement data we currently collect?
Additional data requirements	Cost for each input, output, and step Determination of whether the step is value-added or non-value-added	Bottleneck Complexity Delays Elapsed time Redundancy Storage Transportation Whether the step is value-added or non-value-added	Common or special causes of variation Defect categories and descriptions Desired quality characteristics Process requirements	Process requirements
Process map type	Cross-functional process map Flowchart	Cross-functional process map Flowchart	Cross-functional process map Flowchart	Cross-functional process map Flowchart Relationship map

step as value-added or non-value-added. Elimination of non-value-added steps generally reduces cycle time and cost, and increases productivity.

Mangelli and Klein (1994) indicate that a value-added step usually has three characteristics:

1. It accomplishes something the customer cares about and is willing to pay for.
2. It transforms (physically changes) an input.
3. It is important to do it right the first time.

Selander and Cross (1999) take the understanding of the existing process through the process map to the next stage, which is conducting a value analysis as described in their article "Process Redesign." Using the process map, the percentage of value a given process is providing to the customer can be estimated. Each process step is categorized into value-added and non-value-added steps. The categorized process steps are evaluated for individual process time and the percentage of workflow through each process step. Such analysis provides comparison of total process time yield to actual cycle time estimates. This data comparison gives a fairly accurate estimate of delay time, which can be used as a basis for improvement.

Once the customer value of a process is estimated, that value can be used as a goal in seeking process improvements. It all depends on the process, and each category of activities (moves, setups, failures) has its own characteristics and responds to improvement efforts differently. This necessitates reviewing each category of activities separately.

Value-Adding Process Steps   Prior to a redesign, value-added content can range from 10 percent to 25 percent of the total process cycle time. Generally speaking, very good performance requires that the value-added content be increased to around 40 percent to 60 percent of the total process time. But the higher the value-added content in the current state, the larger the improvements will be. Value increases from steps designed to increase customer satisfaction. There are many things a business can incorporate to enhance the customer–client relationship.

Non-Value-Adding Process Steps Moves and Setups   As many as two-thirds of the move and setup steps can be designed out of a process and will disappear when a business implements the redesigned process. The reason lies in the legacy nature of moves and setups. Typically, these types of work activities evolve within a process over time. Proper process mapping and value analysis expose these types of legacy activities so organizations can take them out or change them to fit the goals of the process, business, and customer more closely.

Internal/External Failures and Control Steps   Internal and external failures are more difficult to reduce because they usually involve activities inherent in the process. These are quality issues, such as product or assembly errors caught internally or defective products returned from customers. These can also be rework issues, such as the rerouting of calls to a call center that would require extensive employee retraining over time to correct.

Process Cycle Time

Many organizations have not documented or calculated their cycle times, real or theoretical. This implies that they have never attempted to systematically map and measure any of their processes. It is, however, important to keep key performance variables in any process somewhat in balance. These performance variables pertain to effectiveness, reliability, safety, cost, and time. The goal should be to optimize all of these performance variables and not to sub-optimize one at the expense of the others. For a typical process, key elements of performance include productivity, timeliness, customer satisfaction, safety, market share, utilization, and throughput. It is therefore important to create effective, reliable processes first and then make them faster.

Process cycle time is a significant and vital performance characteristic of a process. *Total cycle time* refers to the amount of time required to progress from the beginning to the end of the entire process. For example, total cycle time may refer to the amount of time to design, manufacture, and deliver a new product from beginning to end. *Cycle time* may refer to a portion of a process.

Process steps could be value-adding or non-value-adding. As such, cycle time is the sum of all value-adding steps and all non-value-adding steps. To identify whether a step is value-adding or not, answers to any of the following questions provide rationale:

- Is the step actually moving the process forward?
- Is the customer willing to pay money for this particular process step?
- Would the value of final output be negatively affected by eliminating a process step?

In setting specific goals in their cycle time reduction initiatives, many organizations use theoretical cycle time. The *theoretical cycle time* is defined as the amount of time consumed by only value-adding process steps. For example, a total cycle time of 10 days containing 10 percent total value-added steps has a theoretical cycle time of $10\% \times 10$ days $=$ 1 day. We can say that current process is 10 times theoretical cycle time.

In chapter 2 we provide a set of worksheet templates to structure your process value analysis. We also demonstrate the use of Visio in developing the appropriate process maps.

Task 5. Identify and Prioritize Potential Process Improvements

This task is based on gathering information relating to the following issues when looking for areas to improve:

- Determine the real purpose or function of the process step.
- Determine how this step directly adds value to the process output.
- Determine if this process step can be eliminated, minimized, or combined with another value-adding process step.

Some of the obvious areas for process improvement may include the following:

- Redundant and unnecessary transportation, storage, delay, or inspection process steps.
- Recurring sequences of delay-transportation-delay process steps.
- Major chokepoints that constrict process throughput rates and create significant delays.
- All rework process steps.
- Inefficient process layouts, sequences, or flows.
- Inefficient or redundant transportation routings.
- Redundant material handling or packaging and unpackaging.

Process simulation is one way to assess dynamic process behavior. In chapters 6 and 7 we introduce the Arena simulation software, which has been widely applied for the testing of process alternatives

Task 6. Process Optimization

This task develops process changes that can actually result, for instance, in reduced cycle times, such as,

- Reducing process complexity through process simplification.
- Changing linear process flow to parallel flow.
- Using decision-based, alternative process flow paths.
- Changing the sequence or layout of a process.
- Using technology as a time reduction means.
- Letting customers do some of the process work.

As part of an improvement effort, it is critical to calculate time savings and potential cost savings with any improvement prior to its development. Cost savings need to be compared to the cost of implementing the proposed process analysis changes. Before and after process maps are a good approach to document expected gains from a proposed process improvement. The Excel templates presented in chapter 2 also can help summarize the expected process improvements.

Process optimization also involves the determination of process parameters that best meet the overall objectives of the process. First, optimum target values are established for each critical process parameter. Then, the nature of variation around these target values is determined to help maintain consistent process performance. Statistically based experimental techniques are used to establish optimum parameter values and to understand the nature of variation in the process. Collectively, these techniques are called *experimental designs,* and their application to process optimization is referred to as *design of experiments.*

Process optimization usually requires a number of experimental cycles to optimize a process. These cycles will tend to progress through three stages, exploring the nature of process parameters at an increasing level of detail at each stage. The three stages of process optimization are

1. Screening experiments.
2. Focused experiments.
3. Process modeling and simulation.

Screening experiments involve taking a rough look at a large number of variables in order to determine those that have a significant effect on process results. Focused experiments involve looking at fewer variables in more detail than in a screening experiment. Process modeling and simulation involves developing precise mathematical models of the process, which can be used to accurately predict process results under various process conditions. There is not a perfectly clear distinction between the three stages of process optimization. However, by considering these classifications, it may be easier to choose and apply one of the many techniques of experimental design that best suits your current situation. Each experimental cycle should be conducted and documented in a systematic fashion. The five activities of an experimental cycle are to plan, design, conduct, analyze, and apply. These five activities are illustrated in Exhibit 1–13 and are described below.

Plan the Experiment

Planning the experiment involves activities that are necessary to provide the foundation for conducting the experiment in an orderly, efficient manner. A team should be formed that includes representatives from all appropriate disciplines required to conduct the experiment. A team leader should guide the team in developing a precise statement of the objective of the experiment. The team must then obtain management support of their objective and establish detailed guidelines for conducting the experiment. These should include defining the quality characteristics to be studied, selecting the independent variables and their values, determining measurement requirements, and selecting an overall experimental strategy.

Design the Experiment

Designing the experiment involves the selection of the most efficient experimental techniques and the construction of the resulting experimental layout. A wide range of experimental techniques are available to choose from. Screening designs are used at the beginning of an investigation. Here the primary objective is to reduce the initial set of factors that may affect the result to a small set of factors that together have the dominating influence. Response surface designs are used later in an investigation for the final optimization. They are also used when one wishes to develop a model relating the dominating factors to the response variables that quantify the results (performance, yield, quality). Sometimes simplex designs and steepest ascent approaches are used to achieve optimal conditions in problems where experiments can only be done one at a time in a sequence. They should then be preceded by a screening. In addition, special designs are needed in mixture problems. This type of problem is common in the chemical, food and beverage, cosmetics, and drug industries. They arise because here the factors express the percentages of constituents and add up to 100 percent. This introduces a constraint on the design and must be handled with special tools and models.

The process analyst should choose a technique based on the overall objective of the experiment. For example, one may begin by choosing a technique to screen many variables. Then the process analyst chooses to conduct either a full-scale experiment or to construct a

EXHIBIT 1–13
Experimental Cycle
Page experimental cycle | Chapter 1 Drawings.vsd

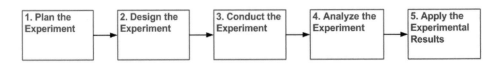

1. Plan the Experiment → 2. Design the Experiment → 3. Conduct the Experiment → 4. Analyze the Experiment → 5. Apply the Experimental Results

graphical or mathematical simulation model of a process. It is important to choose experimental methods with well-understood ways of analyzing the data, preferably using the computer to perform most of the calculations. Regardless of the techniques one chooses, it is important to use good experimental methods such as replication, randomization, and blocking to help remove experimental bias. *Replication* implies conducting the same experiment multiple times to reduce the chance variation in the results. *Randomization* is the use of chance to divide subjects into groups. *Blocking* means forming a group of subjects before an experiment starts.

Conduct the Experiment

Conducting the experiment involves execution of the experiment as developed in the planning and design stages. Much preparation and coordination is often necessary to ensure that the experiment is conducted according to plan. Have a well-documented plan and provide clear instructions to all those who assist with the experiment. Include a written schedule to guide the progress of the experiment. Take extra time to make sure that all resources will be available when needed. Develop a method of collection of experimental data that helps ensure the accuracy of the data and its traceability to experimental conditions. These preliminary efforts are essential for executing the experiment smoothly, with the least effort and in the shortest amount of time. Failure to consider these aspects of conducting an experiment can lead to erroneous measurements and biased results.

Analyze the Experiment

Analyzing the experiment involves making calculations that convert raw data into meaningful information. It also involves interpreting the experimental results using numerical or graphical methods. Analysis includes determining the most important factors, selecting the optimal levels for those factors, understanding the nature and degree of variation in the process, and predicting expected results at the recommended factor settings. During analysis one should compare the actual experimental results with those believed to be true before the experiment. Possibly, new theories will be required to explain the experimental results, or additional experimentation will be necessary to address unanswered questions.

Apply the Experimental Results

The final goal of process optimization is to use the knowledge gained from the experiment to improve a process. Experimental results may be used to develop more appropriate product and process limits, to modify how certain steps of the process are performed, or to choose the best materials and equipment. Any changes in the process will require changes in documentation, which support the process. A new and improved process baseline may be the outcome. With a better understanding of process variation, a process analyst can establish a positive control plan to control the variation of all inputs to the process. After optimization, the analyst can apply an effective control program to the process.

Process Modeling and Simulation

The task of process modeling and simulation is covered in detail in chapters 6 and 7. Process modeling and simulation is also demonstrated by the process analysis and improvement case studies beginning in this chapter and continued in chapters 9, 10, and 11.

Task 7. Implement and Monitor Process Improvements

The final task provides the payoff for the entire process analysis and improvement activity. Process improvements associated with such redesigns are usually implemented either as a pilot run, in which the improvement is tested either over a specified time period, or a complete switchover, in which the improvement is initiated instantly, or as a gradual phase-in, whereby the new process gradually replaces the old one. The strategies for implementing process improvements have been left to others.

Before introducing our techniques for process analysis and improvement, we first review the software tools used throughout this text.

Computer-based Tools

The computer software tools used in this book to analyze a business process, design a new business process, and improve an existing business process include the popular software: Microsoft's Excel and Visio, and Rockwell Software's Arena. Exhibit 1–14 illustrates a potential information flow of data between computer tools and how they interface with each other. Each of these tools supports Visual Basic for Applications (VBA) that can be used to move data between applications. Microsoft Visio presents process logic as a visual diagram with necessary flows from one entity to the next. Excel is a repository of process data and Arena software analyzes the process performance through simulation model.

Exhibit 1–15 shows the proposed integrated problem-solving framework utilizing these tools. The process improvement cycle starts with creation of a process map and collection of data for the process as part of developing process documentation. The next step in this cycle deals with the project team's understanding of the process logic described in the Visio process flow diagram and also analyzing process data using various statistical analysis tools (such as regression, ANOVA, Optimizer, etc.) in Excel. Following this step, Arena simulation software is utilized for process modeling in order to refine critical process parameters. Finally, best process improvement solution identified is implemented. The appropriately chosen performance measures are used to monitor the process continuously. As part of continuous improvement, the four-step integrated problem-solving framework is revisited when the existing process functionality become degraded or when additional improvements are desired.

Short descriptions for these tools are provided in the following paragraphs.

EXHIBIT 1–14 Computer-based Tools
Page computer-based tools | Chapter 1 Drawings.vsd

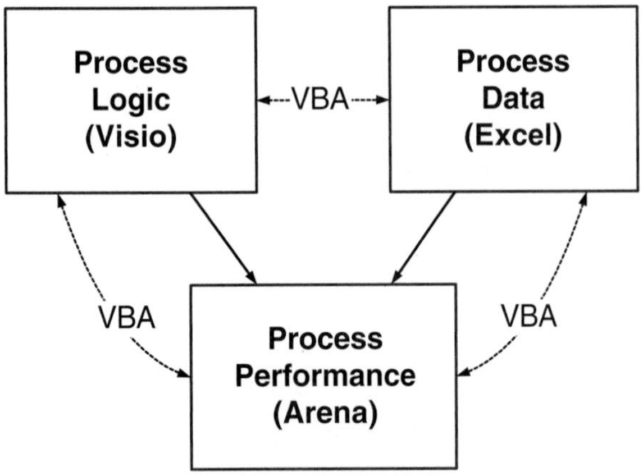

EXHIBIT 1–15 Four Basic Process Analysis and Improvement Steps
Page four basic steps | Chapter 1 Drawings.vsd

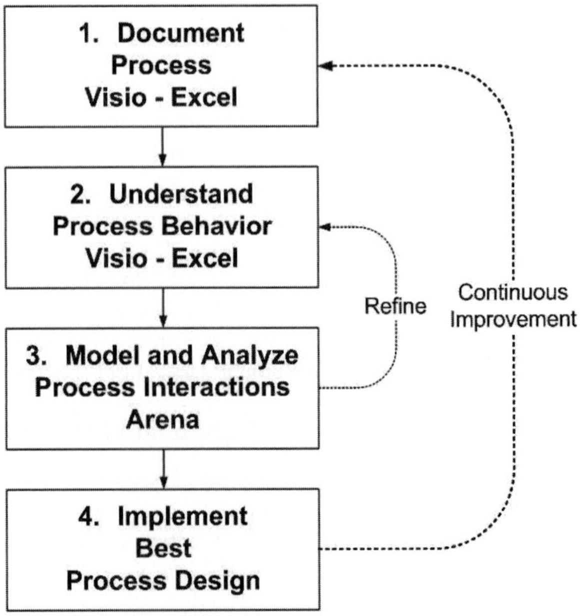

Microsoft Visio

Visio is a powerful Microsoft tool for creating and sharing business process diagrams. Primarily these diagrams are used to document process logic. Different editions of Visio provide a set of intelligent diagramming tools and a common graphics engine that helps in conveying ideas graphically by easily creating drawings and diagrams. Visio works seamlessly with other Office programs including Microsoft's Word, Excel, and PowerPoint. Chapter 2 covers how to use Visio for process improvement, while chapter 3 provides additional Visio applications for process analysis and improvement.

Microsoft Excel

Microsoft Excel is part of the Microsoft Office suite. With these programs users can access, analyze, and organize process data wherever it resides in the organization, which can greatly reduce the dependence on the information technology department to produce custom reports. Chapter 4 covers how to use Excel for data management and analysis, and chapter 5 provides additional Excel applications for process analysis and improvement.

Arena

The Arena simulation system by Rockwell Software provides a flexible modeling environment combined with an easy-to-use graphical user interface. It is designed for building computer simulation models that accurately represent an existing or proposed business process. These models are used to evaluate the potential process performance under a variety of dynamic conditions. Arena integrates all simulation-related functions—animation, input data analysis, model verification, and output analysis—into a single simulation-modeling environment. Its flexible flowcharting objects can capture the essence of various types of processes. Chapter 6 covers the building of process models using Arena, while chapter 7 provides additional Arena applications for process analysis and improvement.

Visual Basic for Applications (VBA)

Although the object orientation of the software tools may not be directly apparent to the beginning user, it becomes very critical in advanced applications using Visual Basic for Applications (VBA). VBA can be used to record macros for transferring data between Excel, Visio, and Arena applications. Chapter 8 covers VBA programming in more detail.

Software Objects

The three software tools used throughout this text—Visio, Excel, and Arena,—each use an object-oriented design strategy. The user of these software tools works with objects and their associated properties. In Visio, the basic object is the Shape, while in Excel it is the Cell, and in Arena it is the Module. Each of these objects has certain properties associated with them. It is these properties and the user's ability to change them that make these software tools flexible for process analysis and improvement. Let us consider each of these software tools in a bit more detail to understand their object structure. Exhibit 1–16 illustrates the general object structure of each software tool used in this text.

A Visio drawing page is a collection of shapes. Of course, the order, position, and linkage of shapes add

EXHIBIT 1–16 **Software Object Model**
Page software object model | Chapter 1 Drawings.vsd

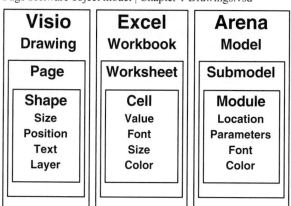

the meaning of the drawing. Actually in Visio, the drawing file itself is also an object with its own set of properties, as are the individual drawing pages. Visio shapes automatically carry a large number of properties as they are dragged from a stencil or toolbar to the drawing page. Some of these properties, such as size and position, are visually apparent as the shape is dragged into position. Other properties, such as text content and format, color, and line characteristics, can typically be adjusted using Visio toolbar icons. Even more exacting and detailed Visio shape properties can be controlled using the Visio Shapesheet. The Visio page is typically unlimited in size but is often scaled to fit the standard printing format of 8.5 by 11 inches. Chapter 2 covers Visio Objects in more detail.

An Excel workbook represents the highest object set and, of course, has its associated set of properties. An Excel workbook can comprise up to 256 worksheets, again each with its own set of properties. Each Excel worksheet comprises 256 rows by 65,536 columns, or a total of 16,777,216 cells. Each of these cells can have its own individual properties, however, for convenience we usually allow most cells to take on the default set of properties. The most obvious cell property is its value or textual contents. Most Excel users simply type numeric values or text strings into cells. Cells may also contain formulas, which calculate and display a number value or text string based on information contained elsewhere in the worksheet, workbook, or another workbook somewhere in the reach of the computer system. Owing to the World Wide Web, this other workbook could be located almost on any computer on the planet. Other cell properties include font size and type, text color, background color, border, and more. Another major Excel object type is the chart. More complex than a single cell, an Excel chart has a set of properties almost as extensive as a Visio shape. Chapter 4 covers Excel objects in more detail.

Arena's highest object set is the model or doe extension file. The model, in turn, is composed of various submodels and modules. The properties of the Arena module are typically defined through a series of dialog boxes. These boxes are often nested to provide increased levels of detail. Many Arena modules automatically generate an associated module that contains related information in a default format. The complexity of the Arena module can be on the order of the Visio shape, but unfortunately Arena does not support a Shapesheet that contains all pertinent information in a single format. Similar to Visio, many Arena modules are linked together to indicate the flow of entities through the process model. Arena submodels are the means for reducing the apparent complexity of the overall model. Chapter 6 covers Arena Objects in more detail.

Process Analysis and Improvement Case Study: Drive & Eat

In order to demonstrate the application of the computer-based tools and techniques proposed in this text, we present an analysis of process in detail. The reader is encouraged to suggest and test improvements to the initial process concept that we present in the remainder of this chapter. The focus of this case study is the process analysis of a fast-food drive-through operation: Drive & Eat. We will analyze the process only during its period of maximum demand, the noon-hour rush. The Drive & Eat operator would like to maximize profit by minimizing the labor input and meeting a reasonable level of customer service. Specifically, the operator would like to determine if a staff of two could handle the expected volume of 60 customers between 11:30 AM and 12:30 PM. We will use the full set of computer-based tools to analyze the Drive & Eat process.

Exhibit 1–17 illustrates the process analysis template for the proposed Drive & Eat process.

The process objective is simple: to maximize Drive & Eat profits. The Drive & Eat owner has specified several process constraints and criteria. These include the following:

- The average customer must spend fewer than five minutes in the system.
- At least 80 percent of arriving customers must be served.
- Profit equals $0.30 per item delivered.
- The order queue size (waiting line) must be limited.

The Drive & Eat process has four requirements to be satisfied to complete the service for each customer:

- Receive the customer's order.
- Collect the customer's money.
- Make the food that has been ordered.
- Deliver the food to the customer.

The proposed process assigns the one Crew.Type.1 staff member to handle the first two tasks. The one Crew.Type.2 staff member will be assigned the remaining two requirements. Several alternatives to this initial process concept could be considered, including

- Assigning additional staff members.
- Cross-training the staff members to share duties.
- Incorporating automation, such as a credit or debit card payment.

In this example, we present analysis related only to the number of staff members used and maximum queue size for the order speaker. Other alternatives are left as exercises for the reader.

EXHIBIT 1–17
Drive & Eat Process Analysis Template
Page D&E process analysis | Chapter 1 Drawings.vsd

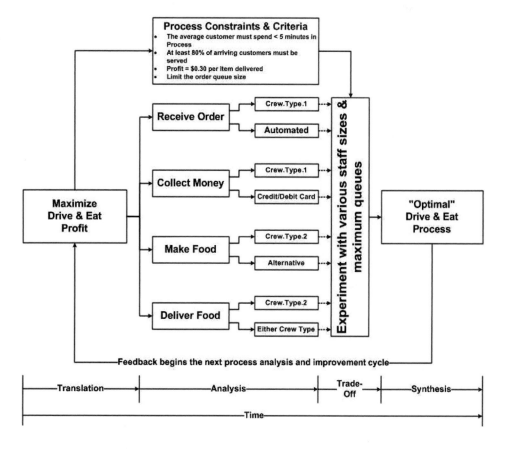

EXHIBIT 1–18
Drive & Eat Visio
Process Flow
Diagram
Page D&E process
flow diagram |
Chapter 1
Drawings.vsd

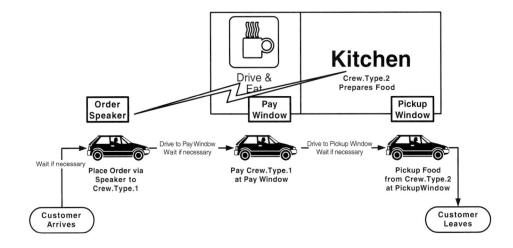

EXHIBIT 1–19 Drive & Eat Visio Process Map
Page D&E process map | Chapter 1 Drawings.vsd.

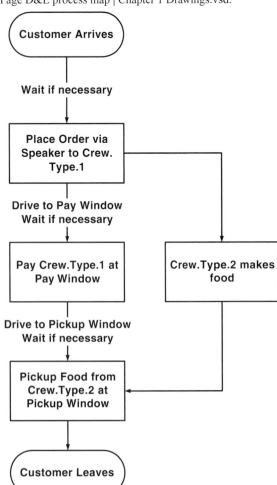

Visio Process Flow Diagram and Process Map

We start the analysis of the Drive & Eat operation by developing the Visio process flow diagram shown in Exhibit 1–18 and the process map shown in Exhibit 1–19. The process flow diagram is based on the rough layout of the process, while the process map, which we discuss later, illustrates the process operating plan or logic. Arriving customer vehicles join a queue or waiting line in front of the order speaker station used to place orders by talking with a Crew.Type.1 member. After placing the food order, the customer drives forward to the pay window and the food order is dispatched to the kitchen for preparation. At the pay window, a Crew.Type.1 member collects the customer's payment. The customer then drives forward to the food pickup window. When a Crew.Type.2 member has prepared the food order, it is delivered to the customer at the pickup window. Because it is a drive-through operation, the customer leaves the system after receiving the food order.

Exhibit 1–19 illustrates the process map for the Drive & Eat facility. Although not directly apparent from the process flow diagram and map, we assume in this analysis that the Drive & Eat facility has a single line of traffic flow, one order speaker, one pay window, and one pickup window. The kitchen has adequate space for more than one staff member to prepare the food. From a practical standpoint, the kitchen is at some point likely to become too crowded for efficient operation, but this aspect is beyond the scope of our current investigation.

For our initial investigation we placed no limit on the number of customers that could wait at any of the service points: order speaker, pay window, and pickup window. This assumption proved unworkable with as many as 25

EXHIBIT 1–20
Drive & Eat Excel Data Analysis—Processing Times
Sheet D&E processing times | Chapter 1 Worksheets.xls

	A	B	C	D	E	F	G
2					Expected Customers per Hour		60
3		Process Times in Seconds					Expected
	Customer Process	Minimum	Most	Maximum		Crew	Crew
4	**Steps**	(a)	Likely (c)	(b)	Mean	Type	Utilization
5	Enter Order Station		10		10.0		
6	Place Order Station	30	45	70	48.3	1	81%
7	Enter Pay Window		10		10.0		
8	Pay for Food	15	20	30	21.7	1	36%
9	Enter Pick Up Window		10		10.0		
10	Pick Up Food	15	20	22	19.0	2	32%
11	Make Food Time	Process Times in Seconds					Expected
		Minimum	Most	Maximum		Crew	Crew
12	Items Ordered	(a)	Likely (c)	(b)	Mean	Type	Utilization
13	1	15	25	35	25.0	2	42%
14	2	20	35	50	35.0	2	58%
15	3	25	45	65	45.0	2	75%
16	4	30	55	80	55.0	2	92%
17	5	35	65	95	65.0	2	108%
18	6	40	75	110	75.0	2	125%

customers waiting to place an order. Instead, the process simulation model presented later in this chapter limits the number of customers who will wait to place an order.

Excel Data Management and Analysis

Some initial process time estimates were available from a similar fast-food operation. We organized the available data into the Excel worksheet illustrated in Exhibit 1–20.

The time required for the customer to drive from one station or window to the next was estimated to be a constant 10 seconds plus any delays created while waiting for other customers to move forward. The observed minimum, most likely value or mode, and observed maximum processing times were available for the three customer processing steps: Place Order Station, Pay for Food, and Pick Up Food. For example, the time to place an order ranged from 30 to 70 seconds with a most likely value of 45 seconds. These processing times are assumed to follow the triangular distribution. For the triangular distribution, the mean time is the average of the minimum, mode, and maximum parameters. We automated the calculation for the mean of these three values using the Excel formula:

$$E6 = SUM (B6:D6) / 3 = (30 + 45 + 70) / 3 = 48.3$$

The time to prepare the food for a particular order was found to depend on the order size, which ranged from 1 to 6 items. Sheet Drive & Eat processing times indicate that the Make Food time is based on the order size. The Make Food time varies from 15 to 110 seconds depending on the order size and random variability.

Based on the data illustrated in Exhibit 1–20, the owner of the proposed Drive & Eat facility became concerned that two staff members might not be adequate to handle the 60 customers expected to arrive during the noon-hour rush. Two columns were included in worksheet Drive & Eat processing times to indicate which Crew Type is assigned to each processing step, and the Expected Crew Utilization was calculated as follows using the Excel formula:

$$G6 = E6 * Expected\_Customers\_per\_Hour/3600 = 48.3 * 60/3600 = 81 \text{ percent}$$

where Expected_Customers_per_Hour = 60 as input in cell G2. Note that 3,600 is the number of seconds per hour.

The information presented in Exhibit 1–20 can be used to estimate the expected crew utilization for all tasks. Crew.Type.1 has been assigned two tasks: Place Order Station and Pay for Food for total expected work content of

$$81\% + 36\% = 117\%$$

Clearly one Crew.Type.1 staff member will not be able to serve 60 customers per hour. Unless the Crew.Type.2 staff member can help out, we have a problem with the original assumption of two staff members serving 60 customers per hour. Crew.Type.2 has also been assigned two tasks. The first task, to pick up the food, is expected to utilize 32 percent of the staff member's time. The expected crew utilization for the second task, make the food, is more difficult to calculate because of the variable order size. If most of the orders were for one or two items, a single Crew.Type.2 with a total utilization between 74 percent (= 32 percent + 42 percent) and 90 percent (= 32 percent + 58 percent) may be able to help out Crew.Type.1. On the other hand, if most of the orders were for two or more items, a single Crew.Type.2 with a minimum total expected utilization of 90 percent (= 32 percent + 58 percent) will not be able to help Crew.Type.1. In such a case, we may need two Crew.Type.2 crew members to perform the two tasks: pick up food and make food.

Exhibit 1–21 shows a histogram generated by Excel for the number of items included in a customer order. Sheet Drive & Eat order size contains the original 100 observations used to generate the histogram. Eleven of the 100 orders, or 11 percent, were for a single item. The most frequent order size was for four items. The average order size was 3.54 items.

Arena Process Simulation

We developed an Arena simulation model for the proposed Drive & Eat process to help determine just how large a crew is needed to meet the noon rush hour. Exhibit 1–22 illustrates the basic structure of that model. The Arena model tracks the flow of customers and their food orders through the Drive & Eat operation. After the order has been placed, the food order is sent to the kitchen while the customer drives forward to the pay window and then to the pickup window. We included in the Arena model a customer sequence number to assure that each customer receives the food he or she ordered. The reader should verify that because of the wide range in Make Food times, it is possible that when two Crew.Type.2 staff members are working, an order for a single item might be ready before the large order placed by the prior customer. Because of the model complexity, three model processes were developed in more detail using Arena submodels: Order at Speaker, Pay for Food, and Pick Up Food.

The reader should install the Arena demonstration version and model file, D&E.doe from the text CD-ROM, to develop a better understanding of how we constructed this model. Notice that the Arena simulation model includes a clock to show the current simulation time and a plot to show the Work in Process (WIP) for the number of customers and food orders in the Drive & Eat operation.

In Arena, like most Microsoft Windows applications, double-clicking on an object brings up an additional window for entering more information. Double-clicking the Arena process module labeled *Pickup* in the Pickup Food submodel generates the dialog box illustrated in Exhibit 1–23. We used this window to specify the detailed information of the pickup process step. The oper-

EXHIBIT 1–21   **Drive & Eat Excel Data Analysis—Items Ordered Histogram**

Sheet D&E order size | Chapter 1 Worksheets.xls

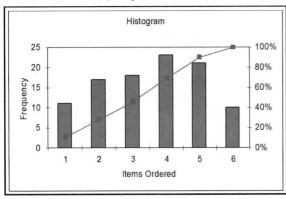

EXHIBIT 1–22
Model D&E.doe
Logic Network Flow

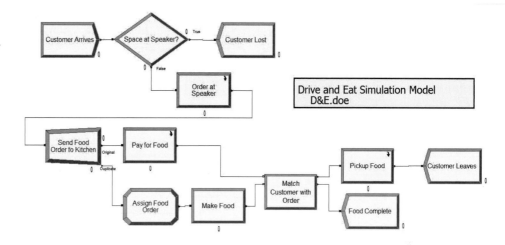

ation will be performed by the Arena resource name Crew.Type.2. The delay or processing time will be a random variable drawn from a triangular distribution with parameters of 15, 20, and 22 seconds as specified in row 10 of the worksheet Drive & Eat processing times shown in Exhibit 1–20.

We used similar Arena modules to develop the complete Drive & Eat model. Details of the Arena modeling process will be covered in chapters 6 and 7.

Arena Model Execution

Exhibit 1–24 illustrates the Arena model in the run mode. The top part of the screen illustrates the Arena logical modules from Exhibit 1–22. The current contents or the number of entities processed in the current replication are shown below or to the right of most modules displayed. At the time Exhibit 1–24 was captured, 12:00:00, 28 customers or entities had entered the Drive & Eat system, while 20 had left after being served. No customers were lost because they found the queue too long (>5). The remaining eight customers were at various stages of processing: five at the Order Speaker, two at Pay for Food, and one at Pick Up Food. Those customers are illustrated as vans on the lower part of Exhibit 1–24. The small boxes represent the four in-process food orders: one waiting to be delivered and three in the Make Food process. The green boxes indicate that all of Drive & Eat Resources, including Crew.Type.1, Crew.Type.2, Order.Speaker, Pay Window, and Pickup Window, are currently busy.

The plot at the upper right of Exhibit 1–24 illustrates the number of customers (upper line) and food orders (lower line) in the Drive & Eat system for the current simulation replication. The number of customers had a maximum of 10 but had more typically been in the range of four to nine. The number of food orders had a maximum of three, but had more typically been in the range of zero or one.

Model Results

After the initial simulation model was validated, it became apparent that two staff members were not able to

EXHIBIT 1–23 Model D&E.doe Pickup Process Module Dialog Box

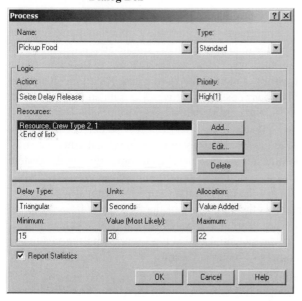

EXHIBIT 1–24
Model D&E.doe
Execution Screen

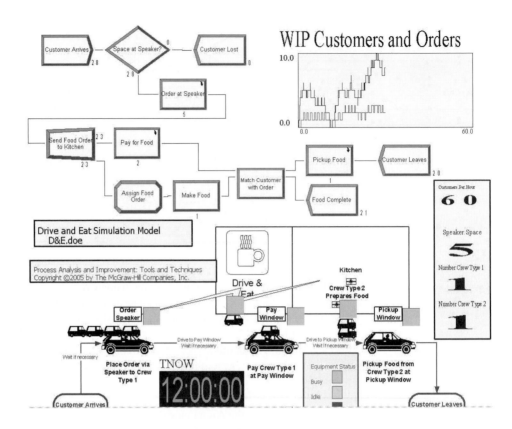

keep up with the customer flow generated when an average of 60 customers per hour arrived at the Drive & Eat system. This condition caused a large number of incoming customers to back up or be queued at the Order Speaker. Rather than reducing the expected customer arrival rate, management decided to limit the maximum number of customers waiting for the order speaker. This limitation would be directly related to the physical layout of the Drive & Eat facility. The operator wished to track the number of customers lost because of inadequate waiting space.

The Arena simulation software includes a Crystal Reports database system for reviewing the simulation results. Exhibits 1–25 through 1–29 illustrate a sampling of the available report formats. Exhibit 1–25 illustrates the total cost summary for the 50 replications, each covering the rush hour period. Each of the Crew.Type.1 staff members cost the owner of the Drive & Eat system $7.50 per hour while the more skilled Crew.Type.2 staff members cost $8.50 per hour. The average utilized or busy cost per hour was $15 with an idle cost of $1. We have modeled the Drive & Eat system to consider all staff service time as Value Added (VA) activities.

Exhibit 1–26 illustrates the Drive & Eat system entity or Customer Total Time statistics. The average customer spent 7.17 minutes in the system. The customer time in the system ranged from 1.67 to 13.89 minutes. These statistics do not include the time spent by the customers still in the system at 12:30 PM, the end of each simulation replication. The data for the Food Order entity type represents the processing of the food order from receiving until delivery. On an average, food orders were in the system 2.20 minutes with a range of 0.59 to 6.24 minutes. The data for the potential entity type represents the customers dropped when more than five customers were already waiting for the order speaker. The average times are also illustrated graphically. The terms *Minimum Average* and *Maximum Average* require some explanation. They represent the minimum and maximum values of

EXHIBIT 1–25
Model D&E.doe
Crystal Reports—
Costs

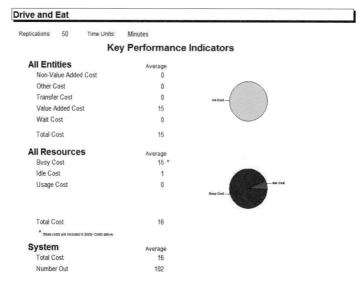

Drive and Eat

Replications: 50   Time Units: Minutes

Key Performance Indicators

All Entities	Average
Non-Value Added Cost	0
Other Cost	0
Transfer Cost	0
Value Added Cost	15
Wait Cost	0
Total Cost	15

All Resources	Average
Busy Cost	15 *
Idle Cost	1
Usage Cost	0
Total Cost	16

* these costs are included in Entity Costs above.

System	Average
Total Cost	16
Number Out	102

EXHIBIT 1–26
Model D&E.doe
Crystal Reports—
Customer Entity
Times

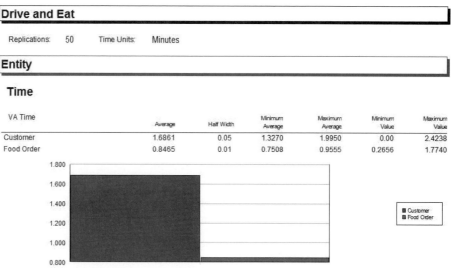

Drive and Eat

Replications: 50   Time Units: Minutes

Entity

Time

VA Time	Average	Half Width	Minimum Average	Maximum Average	Minimum Value	Maximum Value
Customer	1.6861	0.05	1.3270	1.9950	0.00	2.4238
Food Order	0.8465	0.01	0.7508	0.9555	0.2656	1.7740

the average calculated for each of 50 model replications. Thus in one of the 50 replications, the average Customer Total Time was 4.55 minutes. Another replication had an average Customer Total Time of 9.68 minutes. The other 48 replications had values within these extremes.

One of the Drive & Eat owner's constraints was that the average customer should spend five minutes or less at the Drive & Eat operation. Clearly this initial model does not consistently meet this constraint and therefore must be considered as infeasible.

Exhibit 1–27 illustrates the Drive & Eat system queues or waiting line statistics. Most of the customers were forced to wait to get in the Get Order Speaker queue. The queue averaged 2.63 customers with a maximum of 5, which was the limit originally tested. Similar statistics are presented for the other system queues.

Exhibit 1–28 illustrates the Drive & Eat system resource statistics. Crew.Type.1 was busy 95.2 percent of the time, whereas Crew.Type.2 was busy 91.8 percent of the time. The other Drive & Eat system components or resources were busy 80.5 percent to 95.1 percent of the one-hour period.

EXHIBIT 1–27 **Model D&E.doe Crystal Reports—Queues**

Drive and Eat

Replications: 50   Time Units: Minutes

Queue

Other

Number Waiting	Average	Half Width	Minimum Average	Maximum Average	Minimum Value	Maximum Value
Get Order Speaker.Queue	2.6340	0.19	0.8144	3.6879	0.00	5.0000
Get Pay Window.Queue	0.2664	0.01	0.1340	0.3123	0.00	1.0000
Get Pickup Window.Queue	0.4690	0.13	0.02993815	1.9668	0.00	5.0000
Make Food.Queue	0.6260	0.14	0.05630942	2.2179	0.00	5.0000
Match Customer with Order.Queue1	0.00469899	0.00	0.00	0.04058363	0.00	1.0000
Match Customer with Order.Queue2	0.4757	0.02	0.3007	0.6638	0.00	2.0000
Order.Queue	0.1492	0.01	0.07362689	0.1762	0.00	1.0000
Pay.Queue	0.4803	0.02	0.2426	0.5586	0.00	1.0000
Pickup.Queue	0.4250	0.03	0.1963	0.5707	0.00	1.0000

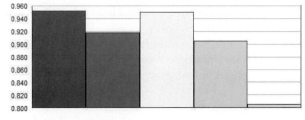

Exhibit 1–29 illustrates the Drive & Eat system output statistics. The number of customers lost because of the queue wait for the order speaker was 5, averaged 8.86. The fraction of customers entering the system who are being served within the one-hour replication period averaged 0.76 with a range of 0.60 to 1.00. The number of items delivered to customers ranged from 140 to 190 with an average of 164.16. The half width indicates the 95 percent confidence level half-width value. Thus, we can say that the true average number of items delivered lies in the range

$$164.16 \pm 3.11$$

or between 161.01 and 167.27 with 95 percent confidence. We expect to be correct 19 out of 20 times with such a statement. The percent of arriving customers served ranged from 60.5 percent to 100.0 percent with an average of 75.6 percent, which does not meet the owner's constraint of 80 percent served. The Drive & Eat system profit is generated by multiplying the number of items delivered by $0.30, the profit per item, and subtracting the labor cost, in this case $7.50 + $8.50 = $16.00 dollars per hour. In this scenario, the profit ranged for $26.21 to $41.15 with an average of $33.35 ± $0.93.

Results based on 50 replications of the rush hour period found the following:

1. Of the desired 60 customers, 75.6 percent were served during the one-hour noon rush period.
2. An average of 2.6 customers waited to place orders at the speaker.
3. The average customer spent 7.2 minutes at Drive & Eat system.
4. The average Drive & Eat system profit is $33.36 for the rush hour period.

While the Drive & Eat system is profitable, two conclusions can be drawn from the results highlighted above:

1. The constraint of serving 80 percent of the arriving customers was not met.
2. The constraint of limiting the average customer time to five minutes was exceeded.

EXHIBIT 1–28 **Model D&E.doe Crystal Reports—Resources**

Number Busy	Average	Half Width	Minimum Average	Maximum Average	Minimum Value	Maximum Value
Crew.Type.1	0.9521	0.02	0.7463	0.9944	0.00	1.0000
Crew.Type.2	0.9183	0.01	0.7592	0.9843	0.00	1.0000
Order.Speaker	0.9506	0.02	0.6876	1.0000	0.00	1.0000
Pay.Window	0.9046	0.03	0.5860	0.9869	0.00	1.0000
Pickup.Window	0.8051	0.03	0.5439	0.9612	0.00	1.0000

EXHIBIT 1–29
Model D&E.doe
Crystal Reports—
Outputs

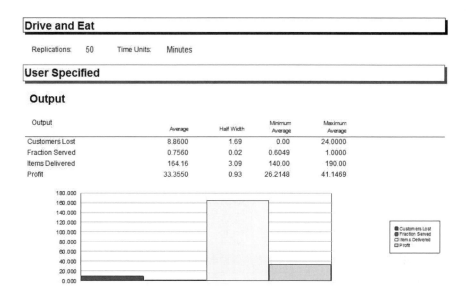

Drive and Eat

Replications: 50   Time Units: Minutes

User Specified

Output

Output	Average	Half Width	Minimum Average	Maximum Average
Customers Lost	8.8600	1.69	0.00	24.0000
Fraction Served	0.7560	0.02	0.6049	1.0000
Items Delivered	164.16	3.09	140.00	190.00
Profit	33.3550	0.93	26.2148	41.1469

Certainly some additional staffing would be required to meet the noon rush hour and to achieve the owner's constraints. The Drive & Eat owner would like to know if only one additional staff member would be adequate, and, if so, what type should be added. If one additional staff member is not adequate, will the additional sales cover the additional staffing costs? In addition, the owner of the proposed Drive & Eat may want to know at what customer volume level the two-staff crew would be adequate.

Challenge

Model Experimentation

The Arena simulation software provides two tools to assist the model user in seeking the best or optimal solution. The first is the Process Analyzer (PAN) that manually executes a set of user-specified model scenarios. The second is OptQuest, which automatically seeks an optimal solution based on the objective and parameters specified by the model user. We will demonstrate the Process Analyzer in this chapter while OptQuest will be covered in chapter 9 in conjunction with a service application.

Process Analyzer

We used the Arena Process Analyzer to conduct a series of simulation experiments with varying crew sizes and the maximum capacity of the queue or waiting line before the order speaker. The number of members of each crew type was varied from the original one to two. The speaker queue space was varied from two to six. This resulted in the testing of

$2 * 2 * 5 = 20$

scenarios. Once the Process Analyzer has been set up (see file D&E.pan), it automatically conducts the 20 simulation runs of 50 replications each.

The results of this experiment are illustrated in Exhibit 1–30 after being copied to an Excel worksheet. The data has been sorted by profit and by the conditional formatting used to indicate which scenarios meet the system owner's constraints.

The Arena Process Analyzer reported six statistics:

- Profit — Items Delivered * $0.30 − labor cost
- Fraction Customers Served — Customers served ÷ Total arriving customers
- Customer Minutes — Average
- Customers Lost — Average
- Items Delivered — Average
- Customers Served — Average

EXHIBIT 1–30
Model D&E.doe
Process Analyzer
Results
Sheet D&E process
analyzer | Chapter 1
Worksheets.xls

Number of Crew Members			Simulation Results 50-Day Averages							
Type 1	Type 2	Speaker Queue Space	Max Profit	> 80% Faction Customers Served	< 5 Customer Minutes	Customers Lost	Items Delivered	Customers Served	Profit per Item	Items per Customer
1	1	6	$33.45	78.2%	7.6	6.5	164.5	46.6	$0.203	3.53
1	1	5	$33.35	75.6%	7.2	8.9	164.2	46.3	$0.203	3.55
1	1	4	$33.14	75.0%	6.6	9.9	163.5	45.7	$0.203	3.57
1	1	3	$32.49	73.8%	5.8	11.7	161.4	45.1	$0.201	3.58
1	1	2	$30.84	71.8%	4.8	14.4	155.8	43.7	$0.198	3.56
2	1	6	$27.45	77.9%	8.1	3.5	169.5	47.2	$0.162	3.59
2	1	5	$27.21	78.7%	7.4	4.6	168.7	47.3	$0.161	3.57
2	1	4	$26.92	77.7%	6.9	5.8	167.8	46.9	$0.160	3.57
2	1	3	$26.69	79.0%	6.3	6.4	167.0	46.8	$0.160	3.56
1	2	4	$26.39	77.9%	5.4	9.3	169.3	46.9	$0.156	3.61
2	2	6	$26.32	87.7%	4.4	3.1	194.0	54.0	$0.136	3.59
1	2	5	$26.20	79.1%	5.9	7.6	168.6	47.3	$0.155	3.56
1	2	6	$26.12	78.0%	6.5	7.4	168.4	47.7	$0.155	3.53
2	1	2	$25.79	75.5%	5.3	10.7	164.0	45.8	$0.157	3.58
1	2	3	$25.69	76.4%	4.8	10.9	167.0	46.5	$0.154	3.59
2	2	5	$25.16	87.6%	4.1	3.5	190.2	53.6	$0.132	3.55
2	2	4	$24.40	85.8%	3.8	5.2	187.6	52.8	$0.130	3.55
2	2	3	$23.52	82.7%	3.4	7.6	184.7	51.3	$0.127	3.60
1	2	2	$22.09	74.6%	4.0	12.3	155.0	44.1	$0.143	3.52
2	2	2	$19.45	80.2%	3.0	9.7	171.2	48.3	$0.114	3.55

The following data elements were calculated directly on the worksheet.

- Profit per item   Profit ÷ items delivered
- Items per customer   Items delivered ÷ customers served

The 20 scenarios were sorted by descending profit. The scenario profit ranges from $33.45 to $19.45. Blue values in the columns marked Fraction Customers Served and Customer Minutes indicate infeasible scenarios based on the owner's original constraints. When those scenarios were eliminated, the highest profit scenario was found to be

- Crew.Type.1 members = 2
- Crew.Type.2 members = 2
- Speaker Queue Space = 6

with the following results:

- Profit $26.32
- Items delivered   194.0
- Fraction customers served   87.7 percent
- Customer minutes   4.4
- Items delivered   194.0
- Customers served   54.0
- Profit per item $0.136
- Items per customer   3.59

All feasible solutions involved increasing the crew size beyond the original one of each type.
    Based on the analysis just presented, it seems that the owner of Drive & Eat has two options:

1. Staff the rush hour period with a crew of more than two staff members.
2. Attempt to reduce the estimated processing times.

One option for reducing processing time might be a credit card swiping unit at the order station to eliminate the need for all charge customers to stop at the pay window. Other measures might also be incorporated to reduce the Make Food time.

In the exercises at the end of this chapter the reader is encouraged to expand the basic D&E.doe model to include limits on the number of customers waiting and to utilize flexible crew management.

Exercises

1. Install and test software.

   a. Microsoft Excel with add-in Data Analysis and Solver. Load workbook file Chapter 1 Worksheets.xls.

   b. Microsoft Visio Standard Edition. Load drawing file Chapter 1 Drawings.vsd.

   c. Arena Academic Edition. Run the D&E.doe model and review its output.

2. Describe and document a business process with which you are familiar. Include at least the following elements:

   a. History

   b. Product or service provided

   c. Current operation

   d. Improvement potential

   Use the Process Analysis template as a guide for organizing your information.

3. Draw process maps for these processes:

   a. Getting a book from the public library.

   b. Process used to keep your checkbook up to date.

   c. Course registration in a university.

4. A company currently uses an inspection process to check the material it produces. Management wants to institute an overall cost reduction system. One possible reduction is to eliminate one inspection position. This position tests material that has a defective content on the average of 4 percent. By inspecting all items, the inspector is able to remove all defects. The inspector can inspect 40 units per hour, and the inspector's hourly rate including benefits is $20.00. If the inspection position is eliminated, defects will go into product assembly and will have to be replaced later on at a cost of $27.50 each when they are detected in the final product testing.

   a. What is the cost to inspect each unit?

   b. Is there a benefit or loss from the current inspection process? How much?

   c. Should the inspection position be eliminated?

Challenge

5. Contrast the Drive & Eat model to fast-food systems with which you are familiar. What advantages and disadvantages might the proposed Drive & Eat process have over existing fast-food outlets? Suggest three potential improvements to the Drive & Eat process.

6. One limitation on the Drive & Eat simulation model presented in this chapter is a lack of limits on queues or waiting line length. In practice, the number of customers waiting for service will be self-limiting. Potential customers finding a long queue waiting to order will select another fast-food place or take the opportunity to start that much-needed diet. Likewise, the physical layout of the facility will limit the number of vehicles (customers) that can wait between service locations: the order speaker, pay window, and pickup window. Modify the original simulation model to limit the maximum number of customers waiting between the order speaker and the pay window to two, and the maximum number of customers waiting between the pay window and the pickup window to one. (*Hint:* Use Arena resources to control the number of customers in the waiting areas. This will make it easy to test different values. Test how this modification alters the results presented in Exhibit 1–30.)

7. It has been suggested that cross-functional staff training might be a method for increasing the throughput capacity of the Drive & Eat system with a smaller crew size. Use Arena Resource Sets to permit the assignment of alternative crew types, whenever the primary type is not available. For example, use a Crew.Type.2 staff member to answer the order speaker if no Crew.Type.1 staff member is available. Test the revised model with different staffing levels and customer arrival rates. Does cross-functional training improve customer service level or system throughput? Why or why not?

8. It has been suggested that credit card sales might increase sales and reduce the crew processing time for the Drive & Eat system. Modify the original model to apply a random fraction (*hint:* use a variable) to each incoming customer. Selected customers will use a credit card for payment. Credit card customers increase the time to enter the order station from 10 to 30 seconds, order one additional food item, and must pass through the pay window but skip the actual payment process. Cash customers increase the time to enter the order station from 10 to 15 seconds to account for the additional step of selecting the payment method. Remember to increase the Make Food time to handle up to seven items. Test the revised model with different staffing levels and customer arrival rates. Does accepting credit cards appear to make sense? What system modifications might make this work even better?

9. Use the Arena Input Processor (see chapter 9 for assistance) to determine a reasonable statistical distribution fit for each of the following Drive & Eat processing steps:

   a. Enter order station

   b. Place order station

   c. Enter pay window

   d. Pay for food

   e. Enter pickup window

   f. Pick up food

   Comment on the relative degree of fit or statistical validity of this analysis. How does the coefficient of variation impact this analysis?

10. Use the **Excel Tool**>**Data Analysis**>**Regression** (see chapter 5 for assistance) to analyze the relationship between the number of items ordered and the prepare food time. Comment on statistical validity of this analysis. Propose an alternative method for modeling the prepare food time and incorporate that into Arena model D&E.doe. How did that change impact the simulation results?

11. Modify the Arena model D&E.doe to incorporate the significant findings from exercises 9 and 10. How did these changes impact the simulation results?

Process Analysis and Improvement Using Visio

Summary and Learning Objectives

This chapter provides an overview of process mapping tools used over the past 100 years and illustrates how a modern computer software tool such as Visio can greatly enhance the task. We cover the basic steps to develop a Visio drawing. Two business processes are used to demonstrate the potential for process improvement using Visio. The Visio application of process mapping is continued from chapter 1. We also introduce the concept of Process Value Analysis using an Excel template and supplemented with Visio process maps.

The learning objectives for chapter two are

1. Familiarity with the history of process mapping tools and associated symbols.
2. Ability to create a simple drawing using Visio.
3. Ability to locate and modify existing Visio application.
4. Ability to create a new drawing using an appropriate Visio template.
5. Ability to conduct a detailed process improvement study using Visio.

Evolution of Process Mapping Tools

A number of techniques for mapping processes have been used over the past 100 years. Until recently, these tools were manual (paper and pencil) and were difficult to maintain and update as the underlying processes changed. These techniques range from traditional tools such as flow diagrams, time lines, and Program Evaluation and Review Technique (PERT) charts to quite complex simulation software models requiring a lot of expertise.

Computer-based tools such as Visio are powerful object-oriented tools, which can provide a standardized tool for rapidly constructing and maintaining process maps.

Most users believe that the more intelligence built into the process map, the greater its usefulness. By intelligence, we mean the effective use of symbols to represent what actually takes place in the process. Most users of process maps tend to rely on very few symbols and thus limit the tool's usefulness. It is not the number or variety of symbols that makes the process map useful; the important point is to include enough symbols to help recognize where waste, delays, and rework occur in a process.

Each new business analysis method has tended to develop and use its own set of symbols for developing flowcharts or process maps. A historical review of these may help readers develop their own personal set of symbols for process mapping. The exact symbol used

EXHIBIT 2–1
Gilbreth Process Mapping Symbols
Sheet ASME symbols | Chapter 2 Worksheets.xls

Source: Gilbreth, 1921

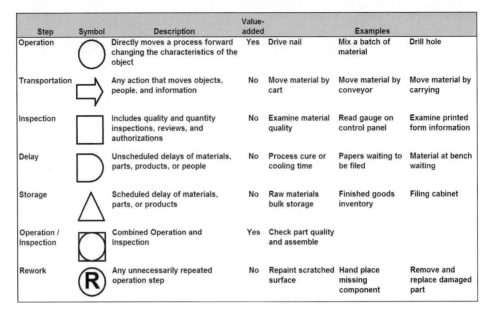

Step	Symbol	Description	Value-added	Examples		
Operation		Directly moves a process forward changing the characteristics of the object	Yes	Drive nail	Mix a batch of material	Drill hole
Transportation		Any action that moves objects, people, and information	No	Move material by cart	Move material by conveyor	Move material by carrying
Inspection		Includes quality and quantity inspections, reviews, and authorizations	No	Examine material quality	Read gauge on control panel	Examine printed form information
Delay		Unscheduled delays of materials, parts, products, or people	No	Process cure or cooling time	Papers waiting to be filed	Material at bench waiting
Storage		Scheduled delay of materials, parts, or products	No	Raw materials bulk storage	Finished goods inventory	Filing cabinet
Operation / Inspection		Combined Operation and Inspection	Yes	Check part quality and assemble		
Rework	(R)	Any unnecessarily repeated operation step	No	Repaint scratched surface	Hand place missing component	Remove and replace damaged part

is not important for common understanding of the symbol's meaning by all users. We suggest that the actual equipment photo or icons might also make meaningful symbols for process mapping.

Gilbreth Process Mapping Symbols

In 1921, Frank and Lillian Gilbreth published a set of process symbols that have become a worldwide standard in the Transactions of the ASME (now Society of Manufacturing Engineers). Exhibit 2–1 illustrates the basic Gilbreth symbols and some typical applications. The original symbol set did not include the combined Operation/Inspection or the Rework symbol included in Exhibit 2–1. Exhibit 2–1 also includes a column labeled Value Added. Only the Operation symbols are used to indicate process steps that add value to the object. Thus, process steps using other symbols add nothing to the final value of the object and should be considered for elimination. The original storage symbol used by the Gilbreths was rotated 180 degrees from that shown in Exhibit 2–1. The shapes illustrated in Exhibit 2–1 can be found in the Visio Total Quality Management (TQM) Diagram Shapes stencil.

Commonly Used Process Mapping Symbols

Exhibit 2–2 illustrates many of the commonly used flowcharting symbols, which we have collected as a Visio stencil file **Process Analysis.vss**. We designed the Process Analysis.vss stencil file to be used to support most general process mapping tasks. Visio permits mixing shapes from many stencils to develop a complete process map or other drawing.

IBM Flowcharting Template

The widespread adoption of computerized data processing in the mid 1900s led IBM to develop and widely distribute the plastic flowcharting template illustrated in Exhibit 2–3. This template used symbols, which conformed to the International Organization for Standardization (ISO) but also contained extensions used by IBM. The template is somewhat dated in the 21st century with the almost total elimination of data cards and magnetic tape. The general set of symbols is still widely used and available in the Visio stencil **Basic Flowchart Shapes.vss** (see Exhibit 2–4).

EXHIBIT 2–2
Commonly Used Process Mapping Symbols
Stencil Process Analysis.vss

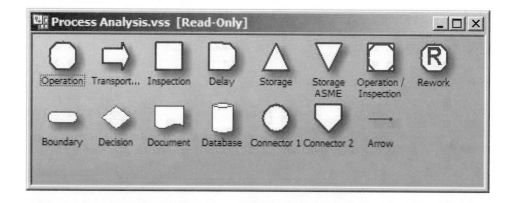

EXHIBIT 2–3
IBM Flowcharting Template

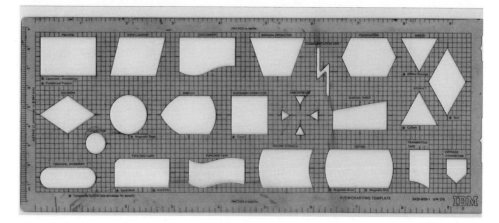

EXHIBIT 2–4
Stencil Basic Flowchart Shapes.vss

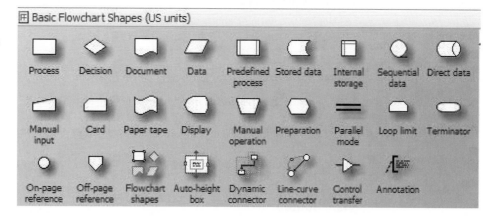

Quality Improvement Tools Symbols

The choice of process mapping tool depends on whether the selected tool provides enough detail for the business needs. Once the process map is drawn, it is easy to identify main problems and analyze and derive solutions to problems. The as-is process map is the start to design a new process, and further steps include systematic process diagnosis, process analysis, process implementation, and process maintenance. Getting good data from the manufacturing process or the supply chain process that is being mapped is vital to coming up with a good process map and the identification of problems and bottlenecks in the process. Visio standard edition includes the TQM Diagram Shapes, shown in Exhibit 2–5, and the Visio Cause and Effect Diagram Shapes stencil for their use in quality improvement

EXHIBIT 2–5
Stencil TQM
Diagram Shapes.vss

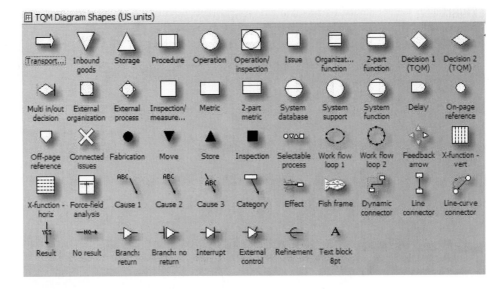

efforts. (See Exhibit 2–25 for a complete list of stencils provided by Visio 2003 standard edition).

Process Mapping Software

Microsoft Visio is one of several graphical tools that can be applied to the task of process analysis and improvement. Graphical software tools with similar capabilities to Visio are

- allClear by Proquis
- ARIS PPM by IDS Scheer
- AllFusion by Computer Associates
- FlowCharter by iGrafx
- Smartdraw by Smartdraw.com

We have chosen to use Visio in this textbook because of its close integration with other Microsoft Office products and its ability to incorporate VBA code (see chapter 8). Let's begin by covering some of the Visio basics.

Visio: The Visual Language of Business

Visio Startup

Like all Windows programs, Visio can be started either by selecting a previously saved file such as **Chapter 2 Drawings.vsd** from the Windows Explorer or by clicking on the Visio icon 🗔. When the Visio icon is selected, Visio displays some recent files and solution options. The format of these options depends on the version of Visio being used. Exhibit 2–6 illustrates the Visio 2003 opening dialog box. The left side of Exhibit 2–6 illustrates the standard edition Visio solution templates. Notice that moving the cursor over the templates causes a brief description to appear in the lower left corner of the display. The lower right side indicates the most recently used drawing or stencil files. This window might change slightly with other versions of the Visio software. We'll discuss the various Visio solution templates later in this chapter.

EXHIBIT 2–6
**Visio Opening
Dialog Box**

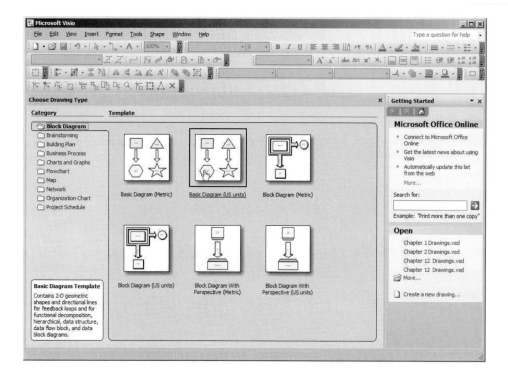

EXHIBIT 2–7

Visio Workspace
Page improved flow
process map |
Chapter 2.vsd

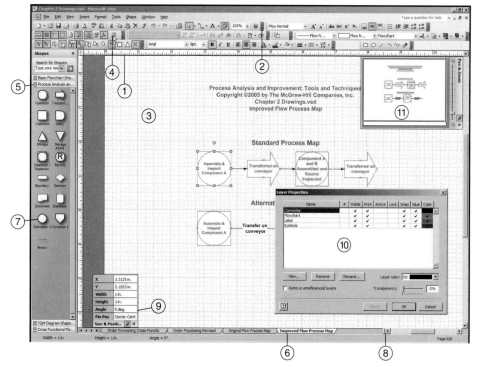

Visio Workspace

Each Visio drawing type opens with stencils, shapes, and toolbars appropriate to that drawing type. Exhibit 2–7 illustrates a typical Visio workspace with some of its major components identified.

1. The drawing page opens with size, orientation, scale, grid, and measurements appropriate for the drawing type.
2. Find additional related tools by clicking the arrows next to the button.
3. Use the drawing page grid to align shapes to each other.
4. Screen tips appear when the mouse pointer is paused over a toolbar button.
5. Stencils, or collections of masters, dock to the left of the drawing page, by default.
6. Page tabs are used to quickly insert new pages, navigate multiple-page drawings, delete pages, rename pages, and reorder pages.
7. Masters are shapes that can be added to drawings. To view information about a shape, pause the cursor over the shape of interest.
8. When a drawing has multiple pages, move the horizontal scroll bar to view all of the page tabs.
9. Use the Size and Position dialog to size shapes exactly.
10. Use the Layout Properties dialog to define drawing layers.
11. The Zoom window provides a quick method to navigate a complex page.

Visio Toolbars

Like any Windows product, Visio permits the user to select the level of detail for the icons shown at the top of the active windows. Users with a relatively small computer display or limited resolution may wish to keep the number of icons to a minimum. However, when learning a new software tool, it is helpful to display a relatively complete set of icons, and then with experience remove those icons that are less commonly used or can be conveniently invoked by keystrokes such as **Ctrl-C** for copy.

Visio Tools or icons are functionally grouped on the toolbar at the top of the Visio window. The user can specify which toolbar groups are displayed by choosing **View > Toolbars** (see Exhibit 2–8) and selecting the desired toolbar group to be displayed or not displayed. The same set of options can be viewed by right-clicking on any current Visio icon. The Toolbar groups checked in Exhibit 2–8 were displayed in Exhibit 2–7.

Exhibit 2–9 identifies the Visio toolbar groups along with their typical buttons or icons. For example, the icons available in the standard group are illustrated in Exhibit 2–10. These standard group icons are common to most Windows applications and are used for opening and closing drawing files, printing, spell checking, and other functions. The type of drawing tool can also be selected. We will introduce these tools in the next section.

The other icon groups listed in Exhibits 2–8 and 2–9 will become more evident as we develop Visio application skills. New Visio users are encouraged to test various Visio icons. If your drawing has been saved and backed up, there is little chance of completely losing your work. It is better to experiment when learning than when attempting to meet a critical deadline.

The Customize option in Exhibit 2–8 permits the advanced Visio user to add or delete icons from the toolbar groups or to move icons between groups. The look and

EXHIBIT 2–8 Visio View > Toolbars

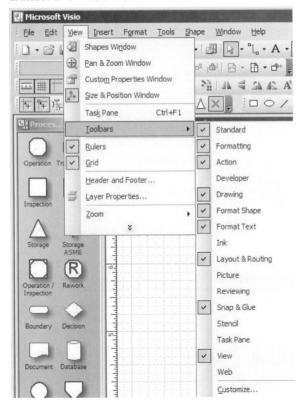

EXHIBIT 2–9

Visio Toolbars

Sheet Visio toolbars |
Chapter 2
Worksheets.xls

Toolbar	Typical Toolbar Buttons
Standard	Primary tools for dragging, dropping, and drawing shapes, as well as standard Windows-program tools for opening, closing, saving, and printing files
Formatting	Buttons for changing the text style, font, text formatting, color, and line style
Action	Buttons to align, rotate, connect, change the stacking order, and group shapes
Developer	Tools for running macros, displaying the ShapeSheet window, opening Microsoft VBA, and switching to design mode while working in VBA
Format Shape	Style lists for lines and fills along with tools for shadows, layout, grouping, stacking order, and rotation
Format Text	Style lists for text along with tools for choosing format, alignment, size, color, and bullets
Ink	Buttons for freehand drawing with ballpoint and felt-tip pens
Layout & Routing	Buttons for changing how connector routing behaves
Picture	Buttons for inserting or editing pictures
Reviewing	Buttons for controlling the reviewing of the drawing
Snap & Glue	Buttons for turning snap or glue off or on
Stencil	Buttons for opening, creating, and changing stencils
Task Pane	Turns on the Task Pane at the right side of the display, Ctrl-F1
View	Buttons for showing or hiding the grid, guides, and connection points, and for displaying particular layers or layer properties
Web	Tools for inserting hyperlinks, paging forward or back on the Web, opening Microsoft Internet Explorer, and starting Shape Explorer

EXHIBIT 2–10

**Visio Standard
Group Toolbar**

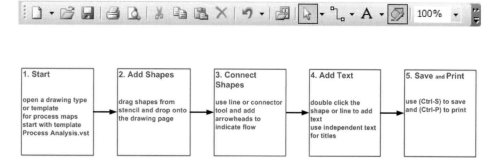

EXHIBIT 2–11

Five Visio Steps

Page five Visio steps |
Chapter 2
Drawings.vsd

1. Start	2. Add Shapes	3. Connect Shapes	4. Add Text	5. Save *and* Print
open a drawing type or template for process maps start with template Process Analysis.vst	drag shapes from stencil and drop onto the drawing page	use line or connector tool and add arrowheads to indicate flow	double click the shape or line to add text use independent text for titles	use (Ctrl-S) to save and (Ctrl-P) to print

feel of Visio can be highly customized to meet your needs or your organization's requirements. Toolbar groups can be dragged to different locations based on user preference. Your
layout most likely will not exactly match Exhibit 2–7.

Let us learn and explore Visio software by starting with the basic concepts.

Visio Concepts

A few basic concepts are required to understand how the Visio software has been designed
and how to get the maximum benefit from its application. Exhibit 2–11 illustrates the five
steps that are common for developing all Visio drawings. We now cover those basic steps
in more detail.

Category	Operation	Step	Operation Steps	Comments	Tips
Connecting shapes	Change a connection from point-to-point to shape-to-shape	1	Drag a red (glued) connector endpoint into the shape's center and release		
		2	If desired, repeat for the second connector endpoint		
Connecting shapes	Change a connection from shape-to-shape to point-to-point	1	Drag a red (glued) connector endpoint away from the shape and then back to one of the shape's connection points	When dragging the endpoint back to the shape, a box appears only around the connector endpoint	
		2	If desired, repeat for the second connector endpoint		
Connecting shapes	Point-to-point, on drawing page	1	From the Standard toolbar, click the connector tool		Point-to-point connections: Visio maintains the original connection between the connection points
		2	Drag from the connection point on the first shape to a connection point on the second shape	The connection points turn red and the shapes are connected point-to-point	Point-to-point connectors endpoints are small red boxes
Connecting shapes	Shape-to-shape, automatic	1	Click the connector tool on the Standard toolbar		Shape-to-shape connections: Visio maintains the most direct connection between the connection points
		2	Drag a shape from a stencil onto the drawing page		When moved shapes have shape-to-shape connections, the connector attaches at the closest point between the shapes
		3	While the shape is still selected, drag another shape from a stencil onto the drawing page	The shapes are automatically connected shape-to-shape	
Connecting shapes	Shape-to-shape, on drawing page	1	From the Standard toolbar, click the connector tool		Shape-to-shape connections: Visio maintains the most direct connection between the connection points
		2	Position the connector tool over the center of the first shape until a red box appears around the entire shape Hold down the mouse button and drag to draw a connector		Shape-to-shape connectors end points are large red boxes
		3	While holding the mouse button, position the connector tool over the center of the shape to be connected until a red box appears around the entire shape, and then release the mouse button	The shapes are connected shape-to-shape	

EXHIBIT 2–12 **Visio Basic Operations**
Sheet Visio basic operations | Chapter 2 Worksheets.xls

Visio includes a large number of potential commands or operations. Exhibit 2–12 summarizes those operations in an easy-to-search worksheet. The reader is encouraged to utilize worksheet Basic Operations by selecting the desired operations or categories using the filter arrows in row 2. Much of the same information is available directly from the Visio Help system, by pressing the **F1**, the Help key and searching for the desired information. Being Windows based, Visio has a feel similar to most Microsoft Office applications.

Drawing Files

When Visio is activated, it creates or loads a Drawing File that has the **vsd** file extension. Visio may have multiple drawing files active at any one time. A Visio drawing file may contain one or more drawing pages.

Drawing Page

The page is the basic Visio drawing window. Only one Visio drawing page is active at a time. Visio drawing pages can be inserted, named, reordered, and deleted. Visio includes tabs for quickly moving between drawing pages. Visio drawing pages have properties, which can be viewed and modified on a Shapesheet. Shapesheets will be introduced later for advanced Visio users.

Each Visio drawing page is printed as a single entity. If the drawing page scale does not match the print page, several pages will be printed from a single drawing page. As a cautionary note, by default, Visio prints the entire drawing file. Individual drawing pages can be selected for printing.

Material on a single drawing page should be limited to 50 shapes. Complex drawings can be developed by linking pages with off-page reference shapes.

Grid Origin Each Visio drawing page has a grid origin at (0, 0) points. By default, the grid origin is in the lower left corner of the drawing page. All object locations are measured

EXHIBIT 2–13   Visio Page Properties Setup (Defining Background Page)

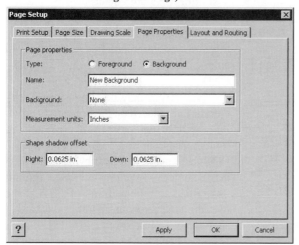

EXHIBIT 2–14   Visio Page Properties Setup (Assigning Background Page)

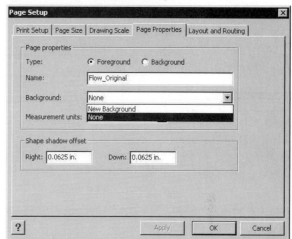

relative to the grid origin. The X values increase to the right while the Y values increase in the vertical direction. The grid or ruler scale is shown at the top and left of the drawing window. The ruler display can be turned on or off by selecting **View > Ruler** from the toolbar. Try this and also notice the other viewing options. What is the impact of each option? The Grid Origin can be moved to any location on the drawing page by pressing the **Ctrl** key and dragging the ⊞ symbol from the upper left corner to the desired location. This trick can sometimes be useful when sizing or locating a shape on a Visio drawing page.

Foreground and Background Pages   Each Visio drawing contains at least one foreground page and may also contain one or more background pages. A *background* is a page that appears behind another page. Background pages are used to repeat a common element on several drawing pages. For example, the organization name or graphic display can be repeated on all drawing file pages. Only one background page can be assigned to each foreground page, but each background page can also have a background page. Therefore, background pages can be used to create a layered effect.

When a background is assigned to a foreground page, the shapes on the background are visible when the foreground page is displayed, but the background shapes cannot edit them from the foreground page. To edit the shapes on a background, display the background in the drawing window by clicking the background page tab, and then editing the shapes.

A foreground page can be converted to a background page using the following step (see Exhibit 2–13):

1. Display the foreground page you want to convert to a background.
2. Choose **File > Page Setup**, and then click the **Page Properties** tab.
3. For Type, select **Background**.
4. Click **OK**.

When a background page is created, it is added to the list of available backgrounds (see Exhibit 2–14).

For practice, use any available multiple-page Visio drawing and make a selected page the background; then apply it to some of the other pages. The impact can be great or a total mess. How was your first attempt?

EXHIBIT 2–15
Visio Box Shape with
Text Added

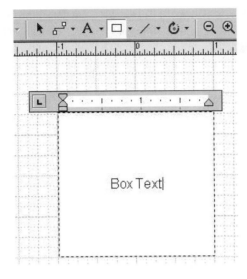

EXHIBIT 2–16
Visio 1-D Connector

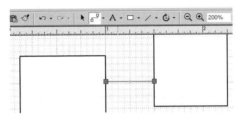

Shapes

Visio drawings are constructed by placing shapes or objects onto the drawing page. This use of shapes or objects as Visio drawing tools differentiates this software from simple line-based software such as Auto-CAD.

Visio shapes may be simple boxes, circles, or lines placed on the drawing page using the drawing tools from the Standard toolbar (see Exhibit 2–9). Text can be added to almost any Visio shape by double-clicking the object on the drawing page. Exhibit 2–15 illustrates the addition of a box shape to a drawing page and adding text to that shape. Notice in Exhibit 2–15 that the box tool has been selected from the standard toolbar group. The new shape was first located by clicking the desired location for the upper left corner and then sized by dragging its lower right corner. When the new shape is double-clicked, text can be added by typing it in. Notice the text scale located above the shape. The properties of these basic shapes can be modified in terms of size, position, orientation, and color. Text placement, size, and color can also be modified later following standard Windows techniques.

Each Visio shape has an underlying ShapeSheet that permits the shape's properties to be modified in spreadsheet format. The ShapeSheet for a selected shape or the drawing page can be viewed by using the menu command **Window > Show ShapeSheet**.

Shape Types

Visio shapes are of two general types: 1-D (one-dimensional) shapes and 2-D (two-dimensional) shapes. The 1-D shapes are used to connect the 2-D shapes, which make up major components of a Visio drawing. Currently, Visio is strictly a two-dimensional tool that does not support three-dimensional graphics. Limited 3-D effects can be incorporated into your Visio drawing using shadows focused on a vanishing point.

1-D Shapes The 1-D shapes are connectors (lines, arcs, or splines) that can only be lengthened, repositioned, and rotated. When selected, 1-D shapes have a small green box at both ends. These boxes change in color from green to red when they are connected to a 2-D shape. The box at the starting line end contains a cross, while the terminating line end contains a plus sign. Exhibit 2–16 illustrates the addition of a line connecting two existing shapes using the connector tool.

1-D shapes are typically used to indicate flows or movement. Line or connector end points can be formatted with a variety of arrowheads or line end effects: **Format > Line** (see Exhibit 2–17) or select the **Line Ends** ⛢ icon from the Format toolbar group.

Notice that the Visio Line Format Dialog permits a different symbol and size for each end of the line or connector. Proper use of these characteristics required identification of the implied line flow direction. Visio marks the beginning of the connector with a multiplication sign and the end with a plus sign.

EXHIBIT 2–17 **Visio Line Format Dialog**

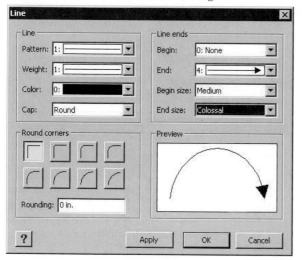

The 1-D shapes or connectors are used to link 2-D shapes. Visio connectors are of two types: shape-to-shape (dynamic) connector or point-to-point (nondynamic) connector.

Shape-to-Shape (Dynamic) Connector   With shape-to-shape connections, Visio automatically maintains the most direct connection between the connection points. When shapes having shape-to-shape connections are moved, the connector attaches at the closest point between shapes. Shape-to-shape connector end points are large red boxes. Dragging the connector end point inside the shape being connected creates a dynamic connector.

Point-to-Point (Nondynamic) Connector   With point-to-point connections, Visio maintains the original connection between the connection points. Point-to-point connector end points are small red boxes. Dragging the connector end point to the edge shape being connected creates a nondynamic connector.

2-D Shapes   Most Visio shapes are 2-D shapes, which have corner selection handles that can be dragged to resize the shapes proportionally and side selection handles that can be dragged to resize the sides of the shapes that the handles are on. The small green boxes on the corners and sides of each shape are that shape's selection handles. [ ] The center point of the rectangle or Pin Position is used for locating the shape on the drawing page.

Shape Handles

Visio shapes have a variety of handles that can be dragged to modify a shape's appearance, position, or behavior. For example, handles can be used to glue one shape to another, to move a shape's text, or to change the curve of an arc.

Selection Handles and End Points   Selection handles (2-D shapes) and end points (1-D shapes) appear when a shape is selected using the pointer tool on the Standard toolbar. To resize a shape, drag its selection handles or end points. Selection handles are used to resize shapes. When the pointer tool on the Standard toolbar is used to select a 2-D shape, selection handles appear. Dragging the selection handles resizes the shape. Two-dimensional shapes can be resized proportionally or in either the vertical or horizontal direction unless those features have been locked. The 2-D shapes can also be rotated or inverted. Additionally, the Pin Position can be used for rotating 2-D shapes.

Connection Points   Some 2-D shapes have connection points (blue X symbols), where the end points of a 1-D shape can be glued to the 2-D shape. [ ] New connection points can be created using the connection point tool on the Standard toolbar. [ ]

Control Handles   Some master shapes have control handles that allow functions not available with standard 1-D and 2-D shapes. A control handle looks like a selection handle with darker shading. Each control handle has a function unique to the shape on which it appears. For example, a control handle might be used to adjust the roundness of a shape's corners, to reshape an arrow, or to adjust the line spacing. This behavior is programmed into the shape's ShapeSheet spreadsheet. Pausing the pointer over the control handle displays a tip that explains what the control handle does.

Control Points   Control points appear on lines, arcs, and freeform curves when the shape is selected using the pencil tool on the Standard toolbar. Control points are round green handles that appear between two vertices. Drag control points to change the curve or symmetry of a segment. Vertices appear as green diamond-shaped handles. Control points appear as round handles.

Eccentricity Handles   Eccentricity handles are used to adjust the angle and magnitude of an elliptical arc's eccentricity. To display eccentricity handles, select an arc, click the pencil tool on the Standard toolbar, and then click the control point at the center of the arc. Eccentricity handles appear as circles on each end of a dashed line.

Padlocks   Padlocks may appear in place of corner selection handles to indicate that the shape is locked against specific changes. For example, some shapes are locked against flipping, rotating, sizing, or other changes that would destroy their specially programmed behavior. Choosing the **Format > Protection** menu command can lock shapes. Padlocks appear only when a shape is locked against sizing or rotating. When a shape is locked against repositioning, deleting, or selecting, no padlocks appear, but those actions are nevertheless blocked. When selecting a shape that is locked against sizing or rotating, its selection handles appear as padlocks.

Rotation Handles   Rotation handles appear when a shape is selected using the rotation tool on the Standard toolbar. Rotation handles are indicated by round green corner handles and by a pin, which marks the center of rotation. To rotate a shape, drag a corner handle. To change the center of rotation of a shape, move the rotation pin. Rotation handles appear as round corner handles. The rotation pin appears as a circle that has a small plus sign in the center.

Vertices   Vertices appear when a shape is selected using the pencil, line, arc, or freeform tool on the Standard toolbar. A green diamond-shaped handle indicates a vertex. To change the form of a shape, the tool used to create the shape is used to drag a vertex. The vertex turns magenta to indicate that it's selected. Add or delete line segments by adding or deleting vertices using the pencil, line, arc, or freeform tool on the Standard toolbar.

Layers

Visio layers are used to organize related shapes on a drawing page. Pressing the layers  icon from the View toolbar group displays the Layers Properties dialog illustrated in Exhibit 2–18. The Layers Properties dialog is used to define and change layer properties. A *layer* is a named category of shapes. Visio layers do not determine how shapes appear on the page. The way shapes overlap is determined by their stacking order and whether or not backgrounds are assigned to the page. For example, in an office layout, the walls, doors, and windows can be assigned to one layer, electrical outlets to another layer, and furniture to a third layer. That way, when planning the electrical system, the Visio user does not have to worry about accidentally rearranging the walls.

Drawing layers can be selectively viewed and/or printed by checking or unchecking the columns labeled *Visible* and *Print* in the Layer Properties dialog box. This allows the Visio user to show, hide, or lock shapes and guides on specific layers to permit editing without viewing or affecting other shapes.

EXHIBIT 2–18   **Layer Properties Dialog Box**

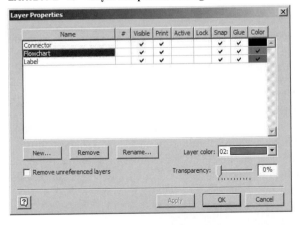

A shape can be assigned to one or multiple layers or to no layers, and every page in a drawing can have a different set of layers. Many Visio stencil masters are already assigned to layers, so when they are dropped onto the page, the layer is added as well.

New layers can be created to organize custom categories of shapes, and individual shapes must then be assigned to the new layer. When a new layer is created, it is added only to the current page, not to all pages in the drawing file. Similarly, when a new page is created, the new page does not inherit layers from the previous page.

However, when a shape with a layer assignment is copied from one page to another, the layer is added to the new page. If the page already has a layer with the same name, the shape is added to the existing layer.

When a shape that does not already have a predefined layer assignment is created, it is automatically assigned to the active layer. The active layer can be changed to ensure that new shapes are added to the appropriate layer. For example, when adding electrical wiring shapes to a drawing of an office layout, the user must first make the electrical layer active.

In a drawing with many shapes and layers, it may be more efficient to designate one or more active layers so that all new shapes are automatically assigned to those layers.

Challenge

ShapeSheet

Every Visio shape is described in its own ShapeSheet spreadsheet, which contains information about the shape's geometry and its other properties (see Exhibit 2–19). For example, the ShapeSheet spreadsheet contains a shape's dimensions and the *x*- and *y*-coordinates of each of its vertices. Exhibit 2–20 illustrates the selection of the ShapeSheet spreadsheet for the currently chosen shape using the **Window > Show ShapeSheet** command or icon.

EXHIBIT 2–19 **ShapeSheet Spreadsheet**

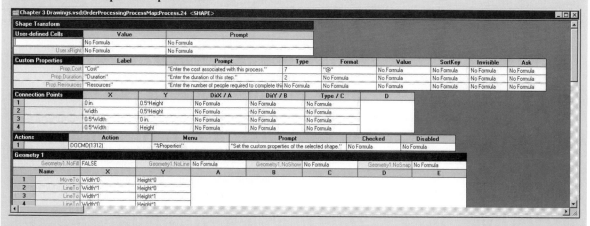

EXHIBIT 2–20
ShapeSheet
Spreadsheet Menu

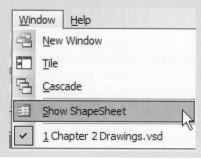

EXHIBIT 2–21
Custom Properties
Dialog Box

Custom Properties	✕
Cost:	
Duration:	
Resources:	
┌ Prompt ───────────────────────
Enter the cost associated with this process.
?	Define...	OK	Cancel

ShapeSheet Sections

The ShapeSheet data for the selected shape is divided into a number of specific sections. Each section controls the behavior and appearance of some aspect of a shape. Exhibit 2–19 illustrates the User-defined Cells, Custom Properties, Connection Points, Actions, and Geometry sections.

Each ShapeSheet spreadsheet can contain only one of each type of section, except for Geometry sections. The Geometry section lists the coordinates of the vertices for the lines and arcs that make up the shape. If the shape has more than one path, it has a Geometry section for each path. The user can add Geometry sections to modify a shape.

ShapeSheet Cells

Within the ShapeSheet, individual data elements are stored in cells. The Visio user can define much of this information by using formulas rather than hard-coded numbers. This is important because formulas make a shape smart: They allow a shape to behave differently depending upon how it's used. A formula can include standard mathematical and comparison operators, as well as a full set of mathematical, trigonometric, statistical, and date and time functions.

Custom Properties

A Visio drawing is more than a picture—it's a valuable medium for storing data. A shape can act as a visual database field that stores data that you can retrieve in a report. For example, a shape in a flowchart can store data about the cost, duration, and resources involved in the process the shape represents.

Custom properties are stored in their own section of the shape's ShapeSheet spreadsheet. The Visio user can add custom properties using the Define Custom Properties dialog box. To store data with a Visio shape, add custom properties to shapes so that other users can enter custom-property data. Many Visio masters already include custom properties. For example, the Flowchart stencil masters include custom properties, which include cost, duration, and resources. Office layout stencil masters include fields for inventory number and owner. Exhibit 2–21 illustrates a typical Custom Properties dialog box.

Visio Editions and Samples

Visio is available in two editions, standard and professional. Both Visio editions share a core set of features. This means that the common methods and concepts described above work with both Visio editions. The Visio software is identical for both editions; these differ in the content of the stencils provided with each edition. The standard edition provides diagramming solutions that help such business professionals as project managers, marketers and salespeople, HR personnel, and administrative staff. The professional edition is designed for the advanced user or technical professionals, including IT specialists, developers, and engineers. The professional edition is designed to visualize existing ideas, in-

EXHIBIT 2–22
Visio Applications
Sheet Visio
applications |
Chapter 2
Worksheets.xls

Solutions	Stencils, *.vss	Areas of Application			
		Management	Operations	Sales and Marketing	Finance / Accounting / Banking
Business Process	Arrow Shapes	Cost/benefit analysis	Human resources processes	Information flow	Accounting processes
	Audit Diagram Shapes	Cross-functional diagrams	Benefits handling	Marketing collateral materials	Annual reports
	Basic Flowchart Shapes	Process analysis	Information flow	Order processing	Audit and work flow
	Cause and Effect Diagram Shapes	TQM / business process re-engineering	Recruiting processes	Work flow diagrams	Cross-functional diagrams
	Cross-functional Flowchart Shapes Horizontal		Web Diagramming		Fiscal management
	Cross-functional Flowchart Shapes Vertical				TQM/process analysis
	EPC (Event-driven Process Chain) Diagram Shapes				
	Fault Tree Analysis Shapes				
	TQM Diagram Shapes				
	Work Flow Diagram Shapes				
Building Plan	Cubicles	Office Expansion Layout	Manufacturing Cell Layout	Customer Proposal Layout	Bank Layout
	Office Accessories				
	Office Equipment				
	Office Furniture				
	Walls, Doors and Windows				
Organization Charts	Organization Chart Shapes	Hierarchy of management and departments	Hierarchy of human resources	Departmental hierarchy for managing commissions	Hierarchy of signing authority
		Organizational design	Hierarchy of information services	Hierarchy of sales contacts within the company	
			Organizational design		

EXHIBIT 2–23
Visio 2003 Web Samples
Sheet Visio web
samples | Chapter 2
Worksheets.xls

Drawing Filename, *.vsd	Sample Application
ActvDir	Active directory diagram
BFLowcht	Basic flowchart
BldgPlan	Block diagram
BlkDiagm	Building floor plan
BNetwork	Basic network diagram
Brainstm	Brainstorming mind map
Calendar	Calendar
Database	Database diagram
DNetwork	Detailed network diagram
EECtrl	Electrical engineering control diagram
FluidPwr	Fluid power diagram
MeetRoom	Meeting room layout
OrgChart	Organization chart
ProcEng	Process engineering diagram
Rack	IT rack diagram
Timeline	Timeline diagram
UML	UML diagram
WebDsgn	Web design diagram
WebSite	Web site diagram
WinUI	Window UI diagram

formation, and systems, and to prototype new ones. This textbook focuses only on the standard Visio edition.

Visio Standard Edition Applications

Exhibit 2–22 outlines the wide range of business drawing and diagram types that can be created using Visio standard edition. Potential business categories are listed at the top of the table. The first column lists the type of solutions provided by Visio standard edition with the corresponding stencils in the second column. The remaining columns of the table list a few potential applications.

Visio Web Samples

Microsoft has included a set of Visio 2003 samples, which demonstrate some potential Visio application. Search office.microsoft.com for Visio samples. Exhibit 2–23 lists these Visio sample drawings.

The next section reviews the Visio concept of stencils and templates.

Visio Stencil Files

The true power of Visio comes from the ability to store and reuse shapes as stencil masters. Visio uses the **vss** file extension when saving stencil files. Exhibit 2–24 lists some of the

EXHIBIT 2–24
Visio Standard
Edition Stencils
Sheet Visio stencils |
Chapter 2
Worksheets.xls

Stencil Category	Typical Master Shapes		
Stencil Name, *.vss			
Block Diagram			
Basic Shapes	Triangle	Square	Pentagon
Blocks	Box	Diamond	Circle
Blocks Raised	Up arrow	Right arrow	Circle
Blocks with Perspective	Hole	Shallow block	Block
Brainstorming			
Brainstorming Shapes	Main topic	Topic	Association line
Legend Shapes	Good	To do	Done
Building Plan			
Cubicles	Straight workstation	Panel post	Round corner
Office Accessories	Small plant	Coat rack	Paper tray
Office Equipment	Telephone	Terminal	Tower PC
Office Furniture	Table	Bookshelf	Desk
Walls, Doors and Windows	Room	Door	Window
Business Process			
Arrow Shapes	45 degree double	Fancy arrow	Flexi-arrow 1
Audit Diagram Shapes	Tagged process	Decision	Tagged document
Basic Flowchart Shapes	Process	Data store 3	Document
Cause and Effect Diagram Shapes	Effect	Category 1	Fish frame
Cross-functional Flowchart Shapes Horizontal	Functional band	Separator	
Cross-functional Flowchart Shapes Vertical	Functional band	Separator	
EPC (Event-driven Process Chain) Diagram Shapes	Event	Function	Process path
Fault Tree Analysis Shapes	AND gate	OR gate	Inhibit gate
TQM Diagram Shapes	Transport	Inbound goods	Storage
Work Flow Diagram Shapes	Accounting	Bank	Copy

stencil files provided with Visio standard edition along with the names of some typical master shapes. Exhibit 2–24 is organized like Visio with the stencil files grouped by type of application. Each edition of Visio is supplied with a specific set of stencil files; other Visio editions augment this basic set of stencils. Many third parties have developed specialized Visio stencils for particular applications and industries. You'll find that it is relatively easy to develop your own stencils. Custom stencils are one way an organization can standardize the look and feel of their graphical applications.

Each stencil file is a collection of one or more stencil master shapes. When a stencil file has been attached to a Visio drawing (use **File > Shapes >** to select the desired stencil from the list; see Exhibit 2–25), master shapes can be dragged to the drawing. Any number of stencils can be opened for use with a particular drawing file. Each stencil master contains a specific set of properties, which are maintained in the drawing.

Visio 2003 also introduced a shapes search feature. Enter the word *desk,* and Visio will find all shapes on your computer that contain the word *desk.*

In addition to standard stencils, the Visio user can create custom stencil masters having properties associated with a specific application. Exhibit 2–26 illustrates how a drawing shape is dragged to a new stencil. If the **Ctrl** key is pressed during the dragging, the original shape is retained on the drawing. Shapes added to a stencil are automatically named **Master.n** where *n* is a sequential number. Right-clicking and selecting **Master Properties** can change the master name. Exhibit 2–27 illustrates the Master Properties dialog box, where the master name and characteristics can be changed. The user must be careful to save and safeguard customized stencil files.

The Visio user can create a special document stencil, which contains all masters in the active page: **Windows > Show Document Stencil**.

Visio Solution Template Files

When Visio is initially opened, the first display (shown in Exhibit 2–6) permits the user to select a drawing template provided by Microsoft. The Visio standard edition's predefined templates are listed in Exhibit 2–28, along with the specific stencil that each opens. The default drawing page size for each solution is also indicated.

EXHIBIT 2–25
File Stencil Menu Selection

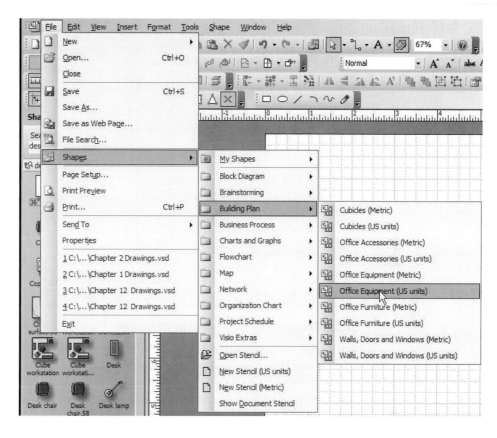

EXHIBIT 2–26
Creating a New Stencil

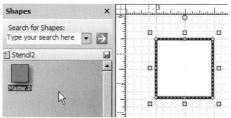

The Visio user can also create Template Files by saving a drawing with a **vst** file extension. The template drawing page is typically blank but contains page properties such as size, orientation, and other details. The template file also includes a selected set of stencils. A customized template can also contain a corporate label or other standard feature used in a set of drawings.

We now have some conceptual and working understanding of how Visio software can be used to develop a drawing. We now put Visio to use as a process improvement tool.

Using Visio as a Process Improvement Tool

Visio graphical software can be used to create a flowchart or map of the business process. The Visio user selects and positions shapes, colors, arrows, and other elements from a preexisting suite of drawing tools or stencils. Visio has a large number of licensed users worldwide and has a library of more than 1,000 business shapes, each of which has behind it a formula describing how the shape behaves.

Flowcharting or process mapping using Visio provides a visual baseline for business process improvements. Process mapping defines the present process as the first step to finding and defining problems that become the basis for change. Being visual, it is understandable across multiplant and multinational environments. The process improvements may reduce costs, streamline inspection, increase throughput, reduce inventories, reduce

EXHIBIT 2–27
Master Properties
Dialog Box

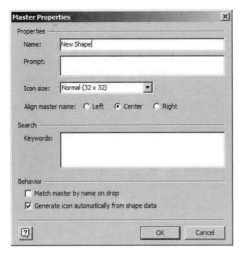

the time-to-market cycles, or provide other competitive attributes.

In process mapping using Visio, the system creates a drawing that rigorously defines the existing process. The diagramming of a process makes visible previously hidden redundant efforts, duplicate documentation, and other non-value-adding activities. Inefficient methods may include procedures that are no longer needed, duplicate checking or testing, inefficient processes, confusing forms or work instructions, poor data-gathering methods, and other unnecessary practices. In addition to flowcharting an existing process, a business may need to flowchart a process when it launches a new product or plans a major change in its manufacturing capacity.

Order Processing System Improvement

To illustrate the construction and use of a process map for process improvement, consider a typical order processing system. Some form of order processing system is used by nearly any business selling a product from an inventory. Often this is a sideline business, such as providing spare parts or documentation. Even sideline businesses are important for maintaining customer confidence and goodwill.

Customer orders are received, credit and inventory are checked, and, if everything is correct, the ordered product is shipped and the customer is invoiced. In this case, the Process Product or Object Analysis method is used to track the movement of the order through the process. If the customer's credit is inadequate or the ordered product is not in stock, the customer must be recontacted to resolve the problem (cash on delivery shipment or backordering).

The method of communication or order movement is likely to vary, often as a function of the organization's size. In a new or small business, information can travel by direct personal contact, that is, walk and talk. Larger or growing organizations may use the telephone for this information. This method is typically applied when functions are at separate locations.

EXHIBIT 2–28 **Visio Standard Edition Solution Templates**
Sheet Visio templates | Chapter 2 Worksheets.xls

Template Category	Page Size			Block Diagram				Brain stor ming	Building Plan					Visio Extras							Process Analysis and Improvement: Tools and Techniques Copyright ©2005 by The McGraw-Hill Companies, Inc.
Template Name, *.vst	8.5" x 11"	11" x 8.5"	22" x 17"	Basic Shapes	Blocks	Blocks Raised	Blocks with	Brainstorming	Legend Shapes	Cubicles	Office Accessories	Office Equipment	Office Furniture	Walls, Doors and	Backgrounds	Borders and Titles	Callouts	Connectors	Embellishments	Symbols	Template Application
Block Diagram																					
Basic Diagram	x			x											x	x					Contains 2-D geometric shapes and directional lines for feedback loops and functional decomposition, hierarchical, data structure, data flow block, and data block diagrams.
Block Diagram	x				x	x									x	x					Contains 2-D and 3-D shapes and directional lines for feedback loops and annotated functional decomposition, data structure, hierarchical, signal flow, and data flow block diagrams.
Block Diagram with Perspective	x					x									x	x					Contains 3-D geometric shapes, directional lines, and a vanishing point for changing depth and perspective. Use for functional decomposition, hierarchical, and data structure diagrams.
Brainstorming																					
Brainstorming Diagram	x							x	x						x	x					Create brainstorming diagrams (graphical representations of thought processes) for planning, problem solving, decision making, and brainstorming.
Building Plan																					
Office Layout		x								x	x	x	x	x							Create floor charts, floor plans, and blueprints for facilities management, move management, office supply inventories, assets inventories, office space planning, and cubicles.

EXHIBIT 2–29
First-Cut
Process Map
Page order processing
process map |
Chapter 2
Drawings.vsd

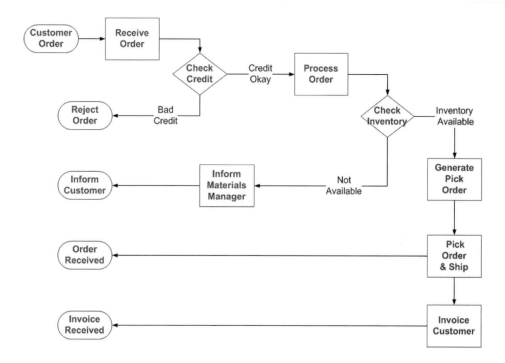

Verbal messages tend to be forgotten, thus either of the first two methods may also in-volve a paper-based message system. In some cases, a single set of paperwork is started with each incoming order and moved through the process. In other cases, separate paper trails may start with a phone call from other functional areas.

In today's business environment much of this information transfer is done electronically. Although this raises new questions about traceability and backup, electronic transfer can greatly speed up the entire process.

First Cut Process Map

Exhibit 2–29 illustrates a first-cut process map for order processing system. The general di-rection of the flow in most process maps is from the top; in this case, it all starts when the customer generates the order. The desired outcome of the process is the delivery of the or-dered product to the customer along with the invoice. Two events can stop this process, poor customer credit or lack of inventory. The current process map indicates that some time may pass before the customer is informed of these conditions. While this process map fol-lows the flow of a customer order through its processing steps, it lacks some critical infor-mation needed to evaluate potential process improvements. Knowing the time required and the cost to perform each step in the process would be of considerable benefit for further analysis.

Another missing component is who does the work associated with each operation step. The cross-functional process map illustrated in the next section is one method for address-ing this shortcoming.

Cross-Functional Process Map

The placement of symbols in a process map is typically left to the developer. The normal convention is to flow from top to the bottom of each drawing page. Cross-functional process mapping adds a formal element to process mapping. The drawing page is either vertically or horizontally divided into columns or rows. Each column or row is then labeled

EXHIBIT 2–30
Cross-Functional
Process Map
Page order processing
cross-functional |
Chapter 2
Drawings.vsd

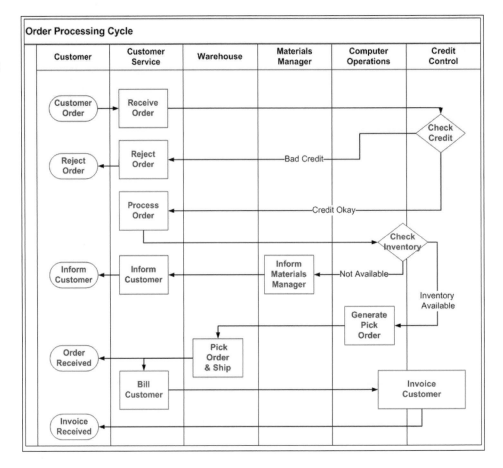

by process function or organization. Symbols are placed in the appropriate row or column to match those functions.

The cross-functional process map illustrated in Exhibit 2–30 indicates who does each operation with the separate columns provided for six functional groups: Customer, Customer Service, Warehouse, Materials Manager, Computer Operations, and Credit Control. In most cases the Customer is external to the primary organization. The roles of the various functional groups are clearly delineated in Exhibit 2–30.

The number of process steps and the delay to inform the customer of problem conditions represents opportunities for process improvements. Some potential improvements are presented in the next section.

The process maps illustrated in Exhibits 2–29 and 2–30 offer several potential avenues for process improvements. These include the ability to

- Combine functional groups to reduce cross-group information transfers, for example, Customer Service and Credit Control.
- Develop a Web-based system to permit immediate online checking of credit and inventory status.
- Use an automated credit or debit system to eliminate the need for invoicing.
- Allow direct customer order picking, for example, a supermarket or department store model.

The process maps offer a good starting point for the generation of improvement ideas. The key point is that the current system has been documented. When we know what we are doing, we start to improve.

EXHIBIT 2–31   Revised Process Map

Page order processing revised | Chapter 2 Drawings.vsd

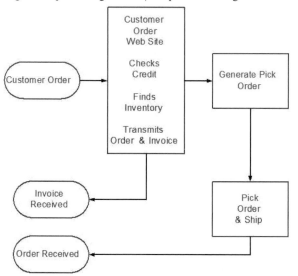

Revised Process Map

Exhibit 2–31 illustrates one potential revised process map based on the Customer Order Web site, which has been designed to handle the customer order entry, credit check, inventory check, and order process—all in a single customer interaction. Of course, the developer of the Web site would require a more detailed process map to define the internal logic of that process step.

As of 2003, none of the large online retailers, Amazon.com and bn.com, seem to have fully implemented such a complete customer service system. These vendors still confirm the availability of inventory after the initial order has been placed. This seems like a good opportunity for a creative software developer.

Process Improvement Using Value Analysis

Jeffrey Selander and Kelvin Cross (1999) take the understanding of the existing business process gained through the process map to the next stage, conducting a value analysis. Using the process map, the percentage of value a given process is providing to the customer can be estimated. First, each process map activity or step is listed and evaluated individually and placed into the appropriate category using the Process Value Analysis Template, illustrated in Exhibit 2–32. The reader will note that when using the template worksheet, each cell contains a comment to assist the user in providing the proper information. The last row of the template worksheet automatically provides the appropriate totals and counts.

Using the Process Value Analysis Template, first list each process step and then classify the process category as one or more of the following:

Operation
Transportation
Delay
Inspection
Storage
Rework

Five of the six categories are classified as non-value-added steps. Only the first, Operation, is considered value added. Each process step is categorized using the following value-added

EXHIBIT 2–32

Process Value Analysis Template
Sheet process value analysis template | Chapter 2 Worksheets.xls

	A	B	C	D	E	F	G	H	I	J	K
1	**Process Value Analysis Template**			**Process Mapping Symbols**					Process Analysis and Improvement: Tools and Techniques Copyright ©2005 by The McGraw-Hill Companies, Inc.		
2	**Process Name/Description**		◯	⇨	◗	▢	△	®			
3	Step Number	Step Description	Operation	Transportation	Delay	Inspection	Storage	Rework	Time (Units)	Required Resources	Notes
4	1										
5	2										
6	3										
7	4										
8	5										
9	5	**Process Totals**	0	0	0	0	0	0	0.000		

EXHIBIT 2–33

Process Improvement Summary Template

Sheet process improvement template | Chapter 2 Worksheets.xls

		Process Mapping Symbols	Value-Added	Suggested Improvements	Before Improvements		After Improvements		Net Improvement Losses in Red			
Process Improvement Summary Template					**Process Steps**				Process Analysis and Improvement: Tools and Techniques Copyright ©2005 by The McGraw-Hill Companies, Inc.			
Process Name/Description					Before Improvements		After Improvements		Net Improvement Losses in Red			
Step Type		Process Mapping Symbols	Value-Added	Suggested Improvements	# of Steps	Time (Units)	# of Steps	Time (Units)	# of Steps		Time (Units)	
Operation		○	Yes	Optimize					0	-	0.000	-
Transportation		⇨	No	Reduce or eliminate					0	-	0.000	-
Delay		◗	No	Reduce or eliminate					0	-	0.000	-
Inspection		☐	No	Combine with Operation					0	-	0.000	-
Storage		△	No	Reduce or eliminate					0	-	0.000	-
Rework		Ⓡ	No	Reduce or eliminate					0	-	0.000	-
Process Totals					0	0.000	0	0.000	0	-	0.000	-
Value-Added Percentage					-	-	-	-				

test. The categorized process steps are evaluated for individual process time and the required resource. The number of template worksheet rows can be adjusted to match the process being evaluated.

Such analysis provides a comparison of total process time yield to actual flow time estimates. This data comparison gives a fairly accurate estimate of delay time, which can be used as a basis for improvement.

After the customer value of a process is estimated, that value can be used as a goal in seeking process improvements. It all depends on the process. Each category of activities (moves, setups, failures) has its own characteristics and responds to improvement efforts differently. This necessitates reviewing each category of activities separately.

After the initial process value analysis is completed, a careful review should be made using the process improvement techniques presented in this chapter.

Finally, after process improvements have been made and mapped using the Process Value Analysis Template illustrated in Exhibit 2–32, improvements are evaluated using the Process Improvement Template illustrated in Exhibit 2–33.

Summarize the number of steps and the corresponding flow times for both the original (before) and the improved (after) process. The template automatically sums and generates the percentage improvements. The last row of Exhibit 2–33 calculates the percentage of steps and flow times attributable to value-added or operation steps. The value-added approach is illustrated using the following example.

Using the various step symbols shown in Exhibit 2–33, a process can be mapped at any level of detail, from a macro to a micro level. For instance, a two-operations subassembly of components A and B without inspection is illustrated as a four-step process map in Exhibit 2–34.

The four-step processes illustrated in Exhibit 2–34 are summarized using process value analysis, illustrated in Exhibit 2–35. Notice that the process step flow times and required resources have been included in Exhibit 2–35. The total four-step process time is 45 minutes.

EXHIBIT 2–34 **Four-Step Process Map**

Page original flow process map | Chapter 2 Drawings.vsd

Four-Step Process Map

EXHIBIT 2–35
Four-Step Process Value Analysis
Sheet 4-step process value analysis | Chapter 2 Worksheets.xls

| Process Value Analysis Template | | Process Mapping Symbols | | | | | | Process Analysis and Improvement: Tools and Techniques Copyright ©2005 by The McGraw-Hill Companies, Inc. | | |
| Four-Step Process Value Analysis | | ○ | ⇒ | D | ■ | ▲ | Ⓡ | | | |
Step Number	Step Description	Operation	Transport ation	Delay	Inspection	Storage	Rework	Time (Minutes)	Required Resources	Notes
1	Assemble component A	X						15.0	Assembly	
2	Transfer on conveyor		X					5.0		
3	Assemble components A and B	X						20.0	Assembly	
4	Transfer on conveyor		X					5.0		
4	**Process Totals**	2	2	0	0	0	0	45.0		

The four-step process illustrated in Exhibit 2–34 turns into a fourteen-step process if we allow for mistakes in the process. The complete fourteen-step process is illustrated in Exhibits 2–36 and 2–37. The total fourteen-step process time is 127 minutes, or about three times that of the four-step process.

By introducing source inspections to the two operations, we are able to eliminate 10 process steps. Our new process now looks like Exhibit 2–38, which is summarized in Exhibit 2–39. The total time for the revised four-step process is 51.5 minutes.

The time and steps saved in the process redesign are shown in Exhibit 2–40. The redesign eliminates 10 of the 14 process steps. Such combined operation and inspection steps are called Source Inspections, since they occur right at the source (that is, at the Operation itself).

Exercises

1. Develop a basic flowchart or process map for any business process. Start with the Block Diagram template. Add appropriate shapes and connectors. Also add text to the drawing.

2. Use the Visio drawing created in exercise 1.

   a. Create a new stencil for holding existing shapes and new shapes.

   b. Create a new master shape by modifying an existing shape. Include properties, move the shape to your stencil, and specify how the shape's stencil icon appears.

   c. Create a new template that includes your stencil.

3. Create a simple two-page flowchart named **FirstnameLastnameFlowChart.vsd** with two linked pages named "Patient and Prescription" and "Call Doctor."

   a. The title of the flow chart is "Patient and Prescription."

   b. The process starts when a patient brings in a prescription to the clerk, who takes the prescription.

   c. The clerk checks for validity of the prescription.

   d. If the prescription is not valid, the clerk calls the doctor.

EXHIBIT 2–36
Fourteen-Step Process Map
Page original flow process map | Chapter 2 Drawings.vsd

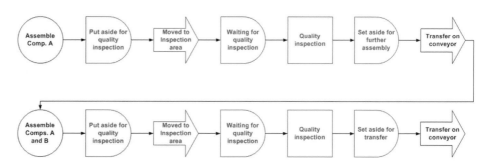

Fourteen-Step Process Map

EXHIBIT 2–37
Fourteen-Step
Process Value
Analysis
Sheet 14-step process
value analysis |
Chapter 2
Worksheets.xls

| Process Value Analysis Template | | | Process Mapping Symbols | | | | | | Process Analysis and Improvement: Tools and Techniques   Copyright ©2005 by The McGraw-Hill Companies, Inc. | | |
| Fourteen-Step Process Value Analysis | | ⬤ | ➡ | ⬭ | ◼ | ▲ | Ⓡ | | | |
Step Number	Step Description	Operation	Transportation	Delay	Inspection	Storage	Rework	Time (Minutes)	Required Resources	Notes
1	Assemble component A	X						15.0	Asembly	
2	Put aside for quality inspection			X				10.0		Wait for Move
3	Moved to Inspection area		X					5.0		New Move
4	Waiting for quality inspection			X				10.0		Wait for Inspection
5	Quality inspection				X			6.0	Inspection	
6	Set aside for further assembly			X				10.0		Wait for Move
7	Transfer on conveyor		X					5.0		
8	Assemble components A and B	X						20.0	Asembly	
9	Put aside for quality inspection			X				10.0		Wait for Move
10	Moved to Inspection area		X					5.0		New Move
11	Waiting for quality inspection			X				10.0		Wait for Inspection
12	Quality inspection				X			6.0	Inspection	
13	Set aside for transfer			X				10.0		Wait for Move
14	Transfer on conveyor		X					5.0		
14	**Process Totals**	2	4	6	2	0	0	127.0		

EXHIBIT 2–38
Improved
Process Map
Page improved flow
process map |
Chapter 2
Drawings.vsd

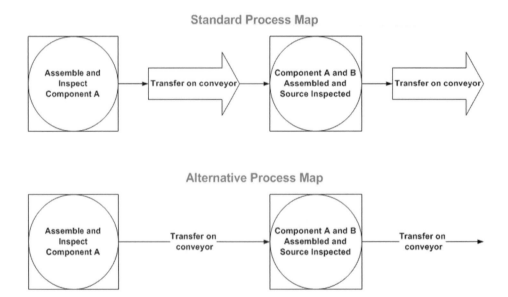

e. In turn, the doctor validates the prescription.

f. If the prescription is not valid, the doctor rejects the prescription.

g. If the prescription is valid, the clerk enters the prescription information.

h. Next, the clerk initiates a check stock activity.

i. If the drug is in stock, the clerk fills the prescription; otherwise, the clerk orders the drug from the distributor.

j. The Call Doctor activity is linked to a new page connector named "To Call Doctor."

k. This connector in the second page is connected to Call Doctor activity.

EXHIBIT 2–39
Improved Process Value Analysis
Sheet improved process value analysis | Chapter 2 Worksheets.xls

Process Value Analysis Template		Process Mapping Symbols							Process Analysis and Improvement: Tools and Techniques Copyright ©2005 by The McGraw-Hill Companies, Inc.		
Combined Four-Step Process Value Analysis		◯	⇒	D	▢	△	Ⓡ				
Step Number	Step Description	Operation	Transport ation	Delay	Inspectio n	Storage	Rework	Time (Minutes)	Required Resources	Notes	
1	Assemble and Inspect component A	X			X			18.0	Assembly/Inspection	Combination
2	Transfer on conveyor		X					5.0		
3	Assemble and Inspect components A and B	X			X			23.5	Assembly/Inspection	Combination
4	Transfer on conveyor		X					5.0		
4	**Process Totals**	2	2	0	2	0	0	51.5		

EXHIBIT 2–40
Process Improvement Summary
Sheet process improvement summary | Chapter 2 Worksheets.xls

Process Improvement Summary Template				Process Steps				Net Improvement Losses in Red			Process Analysis and Improvement: Tools and Techniques Copyright ©2005 by The McGraw-Hill Companies, Inc.
Process Improvement Example				Before Improvements		After Improvements					
Step Type	Process Mapping Symbols	Value-Added	Suggested Improvements	# of Steps	Time (Minutes)	# of Steps	Time (Minutes)	# of Steps		Time (Minutes)	
Operation	◯	Yes	Optimize	2	35.0	2	41.5	0	No Change	-6.500	-19%
Transportation	⇒	No	Reduce or eliminate	4	20.0	2	10.0	2	50%	10.000	50%
Delay	D	No	Reduce or eliminate	6	60.0			6	100%	60.000	100%
Inspection	▢	No	Combine with Operation	2	12.0			2	100%	12.000	100%
Storage	△	No	Reduce or eliminate					0	-	0.000	-
Rework	Ⓡ	No	Reduce or eliminate					0	-	0.000	-
			Process Totals	14	127.0	4	51.5	10	71%	75.500	69%
			Value-Added Percentage	14%	28%	50%	81%				

4. Study the process map found on the page "Shop Job Flow" of the Visio drawing file Chapter 2 Exercises.vsd found on the text CD and displayed in Exhibit 2–41. Develop revised process maps with the following objectives:

   a. General flow improvements.

   b. Continuous product flow improvements.

   c. Automated quality checking implementation.

5. Perform the following operation in Visio:

   a. Drag the Process shape from the Basic Flowchart Shapes Stencil into the drawing area.

   b. Type a short string of text or sentences into the Process shape and then rotate the text counter-clockwise by 90 degrees.

   c. Type a short string of text or sentences somewhere in the drawing area and then rotate the text counterclockwise by 90 degrees.

   d. Modify the text properties such as color, font, and effects.

   e. Adjust the text by setting such paragraph properties as alignment, bullets, and tabs.

   f. Run spell-checker on the text.

6. Exhibit 2–42 illustrates a process used to assemble an upholstered loveseat. Stations A, B, and C fabricate the upholstery; stations P, Q, and R assemble the loveseat frame; station W is where the two assemblies are brought together; and some final tasks are completed in stations X and Y. One worker is assigned to each of the stations. Typically, there is no inventory kept anywhere in the

EXHIBIT 2–41

Job Shop Work Order Processing

Page shop job flow | Chapter 2 Exercises.vsd

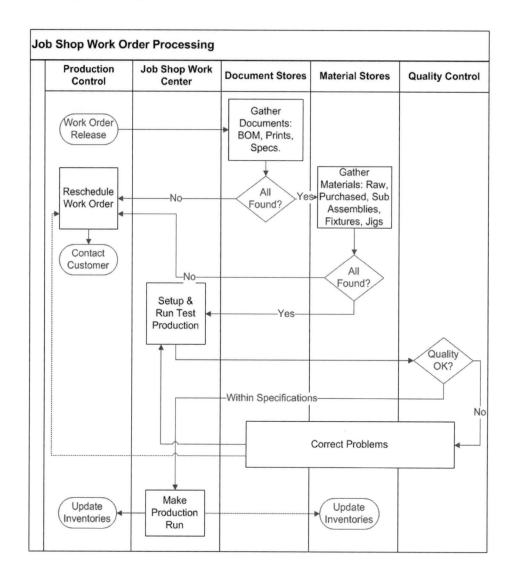

process, although there is room for one unit between each of the stations that might be used for a brief amount of time. The numbers associated with each station indicate the expected time to complete the required tasks.

a. What is the possible daily output of this process if eight hours of processing time is available each day?

b. Given the output rate in A, what is the efficiency of the process?

c. What is the throughput time of the process?

EXHIBIT 2–42
Loveseat Assembly
Process
Page assembly |
Chapter 2
Exercises.vsd

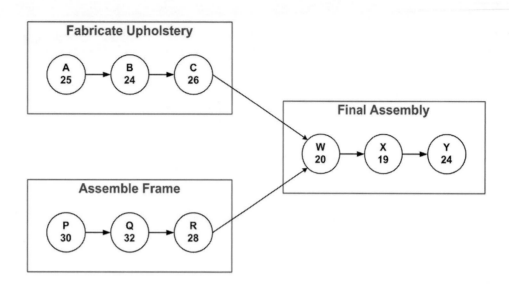

Applications Using Visio

Summary and Learning Objectives

This chapter demonstrates several business applications using Visio including organization charts, office layouts, Gantt charts, and cause and effect diagrams. All of these examples rely on stencils and templates provided as part of Visio 2003 standard edition. In most cases, it is better to start a new drawing file by opening a Visio template file. See Exhibit 2–28 or open workbook Chapter 2 Worksheets.xls, worksheet Visio templates to find a complete cross-listing of Visio templates and stencils.

The learning objectives for this chapter are the

1. Ability to build or modify an organization chart using Excel and Visio.
2. Capability to create or modify an office or simple facility layout using Visio.
3. Ability to build or modify a cause and effect diagram using Visio.
4. Capability to generate or modify a Gantt chart using Visio.

Building an Organization Chart

Most organizations that consist of more than a few people have an organization chart that shows the structure of the company. Although it is certainly possible to build an organization chart using Visio (a template is included for just that purpose), it is usually more efficient to maintain organization information in an Excel workbook file or similar database. It is easier to update a file, especially since you don't have to worry about laying out the chart on a piece of paper or learning a new tool—even an easy tool like Visio. Now you have the best of both worlds: the ability to maintain your organization information in a file and the ability to create a Visio organization chart automatically from the contents of that file. This section shows you how to build a Microsoft Excel workbook file and use it to create an organization chart.

We will go through the following three tasks:

1. Building the Excel Workbook file.
2. Using Visio Organization Chart Wizard.
3. Modifying the Organization Chart.

Task 1. Building the Excel Workbook File

Although the Visio Organization Chart Wizard can build an organization chart from a variety of file types, the easiest way to maintain and use a file is to create an Excel workbook file. With the proper column identification (detailed in this section), creating an organization chart from a worksheet is very straightforward. Exhibit 3–1 illustrates the general worksheet format.

EXHIBIT 3–1
Organizational Chart Data
Sheet organizational chart data | Chapter 3 Worksheets.xls

	A	B	C	D	E
1	Name	Position	Reports_To	Department	Telephone
2	Jim Collier	Controller	Pete Young	Finance	x299
3	Chris Young	Mkt Mgr - Mkt Dev	Geri Cooper	Marketing	x269
4	Dave Bolin	Customer Svc Mgr	Pete Young	Finance	x301
5	Eric Meyer	VP Sales	Susan Emerson	Sales	x250
6	Geri Cooper	VP Marketing	Susan Emerson	Marketing	x255
7	Jason Jacobs	Executive Assistant	Susan Emerson	Operations	x260
8	Karl Cameron	Dir. Channel Sales	Eric Meyer	Sales	x270

EXHIBIT 3–2
Organization Chart Wizard Menu Path

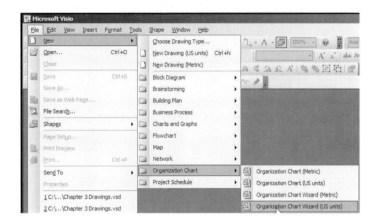

1. To create the file, open a new, blank Excel workbook or copy the worksheet Organizational Chart Data to be used as a template and skip to step 4.
2. Enter the following column headings in the first row of the worksheet:
   a. Name
   b. Position
   c. Reports_To
   d. Department
   e. Telephone
3. Add some sample data to your worksheet using Exhibit 3–1 as a guide or fill it out with your own organization's information. Notice that relationships between organizational positions are defined in the column labeled "Reports_To." Sheet **Organizational Chart Data | Chapter 3 Worksheets.xls** could be used for this exercise by moving a copy of the worksheet to a new workbook, thus saving the new workbook (see Chapter 4 for Excel operation details).
4. When your worksheet is complete, save your file as **Organizational Chart.xls** workbook file. Note that the saved Excel workbook may contain only a single worksheet. When done, close Excel.

Task 2. Using Visio Organization Chart Wizard

Once you have defined and saved your data file, you can use the Visio Organization Chart Wizard to build an organization chart from that data.

1. Start the Visio Organization Chart Wizard by selecting the menu command **File > New > Organization Chart**, and choose **Organization Chart Wizard** using Exhibit 3–2 as a guide.
2. The first panel of the Organization Chart Wizard opens (see Exhibit 3–3). Select the radio button labeled **Information that's already stored in a file or database**.

EXHIBIT 3–3 Organization Chart Wizard Dialog Step 1

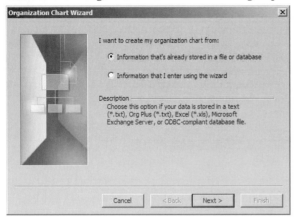

EXHIBIT 3–4 Organization Chart Wizard Dialog Step 2

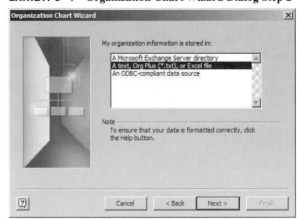

EXHIBIT 3–5 Organization Chart Wizard Dialog Step 3

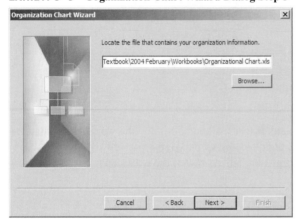

EXHIBIT 3–6 Organization Chart Wizard Dialog Step 4

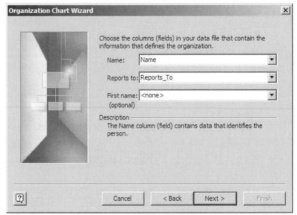

3. Click on the Next button to display Exhibit 3–4. In this panel, select the radio button labeled **A Text, Org Plus (*.txt), Or Microsoft Excel File**.

4. Click on the Next button to display Exhibit 3–5. In this panel, choose the Excel file that contains the organization data, **OrganizationalChart.xls**, created earlier in task 1. Click on the Browse button to select the file from the standard Windows open file dialog box. You may find that Visio must open the source data file.

5. Click on the Next button to display Exhibit 3–6. In this panel, choose the worksheet column that corresponds to the person's name (Name) and to whom they report (Reports_To) from the drop-down menus. Notice that Visio automatically selects the correct worksheet columns based on the column headings in row one of the worksheet. Visio is able to do this because of the way you named the columns.

6. Click on the Next button to display Exhibit 3–7. In this panel, use the drop-down menus to choose the fields to display on the first line Name and second line Position of each box in the organization chart.

7. Click on the Next button to display Exhibit 3–8. In this panel, choose the information you want added to the organization chart shapes as custom properties. In this example, choose **Department** and **Telephone**, then click on the Add button. Name and Position are

EXHIBIT 3–7   **Organization Chart Wizard Dialog Step 5**

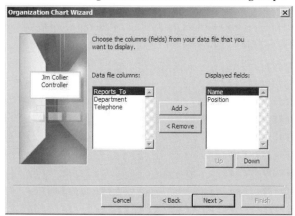

EXHIBIT 3–8   **Organization Chart Wizard Dialog Step 6**

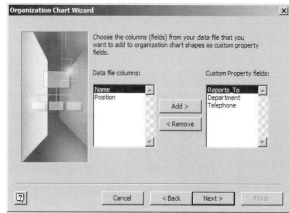

EXHIBIT 3–9   **Organization Chart Wizard Dialog Step 7**

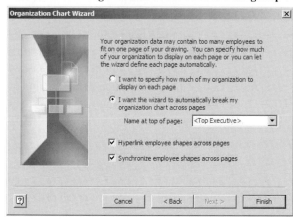

already displayed, and the Reports-To relationship will be shown by the structure of the diagram.

8. Click on the Next button to display Exhibit 3–9. In this panel, let the wizard decide how to break your organization across multiple pages by selecting the second radio button.

Click on the Finish button. Visio generates the organization chart for you as illustrated in Exhibit 3–10. Notice on the left of the Visio display that the Organization Chart Wizard has automatically opened three stencils, which you may find helpful in updating or modifying your organization chart. These are

• Organization chart shapes—Used to add new shapes and structures.

EXHIBIT 3–10
Organizational Chart
Original
Page organizational
chart | Chapter 3
Drawings.vsd

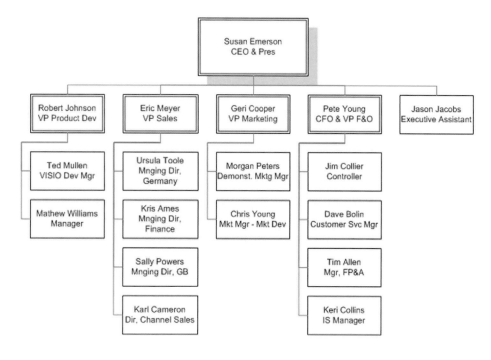

EXHIBIT 3–11
Organizational Chart Toolbar, Stacked Shapes

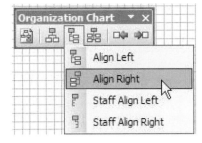

EXHIBIT 3–12
Organizational Chart Stacked Shapes

EXHIBIT 3–13
Organizational Chart Arrange Subordinates Selection

EXHIBIT 3–14
Organizational Chart Arrange Subordinates Dialog Box

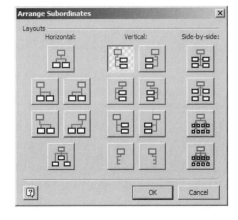

• Backgrounds—Used to add a colorful background page.
• Borders and titles—Used to make your drawing look professional.

Task 3. Modifying the Organization Chart

Visio does a good job of laying out an organization chart, but you may wish to customize the results yourself. Visio provides plenty of tools for changing an organization chart.

This section demonstrates some of those tools.

1. To improve the layout of the organization chart on the page, you will use the Organization Chart toolbar, as shown in Exhibit 3–11.

2. Click on the box for Pete Young. Choose the drop-down menu on the Organization Chart toolbar that controls stacked shapes.

3. Choose the combination illustrated in Exhibit 3–11 and click on it. This stacks the subordinates of Pete Young in a different pattern, which is depicted in Exhibit 3–12. Do you like this one better? If not, use the Undo icon to return to the original layout. Or you may want to type a few other combinations.

4. Select Eric Meyer, and right-click on the shape to display the shortcut menu, shown in Exhibit 3–13. Choose **Arrange Subordinates**.

5. Choose the top-left button in the Vertical section (see Exhibit 3–14). This stacks the subordinates of Eric Meyer in a slightly different pattern from the one used earlier.

6. Next, add subordinates to Mathew Williams. First promote him to a manager by right clicking on **Mathew Williams** and choose **Change Position Type . . .** from the shortcut menu, illustrated in Exhibit 3–15. Then choose the Manager shape (see Exhibit 3–16). Notice the shape change as he is promoted to manager.

7. Be sure that Mathew Williams is still selected, and choose the Connector tool from the Standard toolbar. Then click on the Position shape in the Organization Chart Shapes stencil, and drag it

EXHIBIT 3–15
Organizational Chart
Change Position
Type Menu

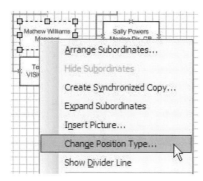

onto the page and onto the shape for Mathew Williams.

8. Repeat this action to give Mathew two subordinates. Fill in their names and titles: Jane Smith, Assistant Manager, and Judy Simpson, Assistant Manager. You do this by right-clicking and selecting **Properties** as is shown in Exhibit 3–17.

9. Notice how this action pushed poor Ted Mullen clear off the page! To fix this, click on **Mathew Williams**, and choose the Stacked Shape button on the Organization Chart toolbar. Choose the bottom-left shape.

The shapes are now rearranged so everything fits on the page once again. Exhibit 3–18 illustrates a completely revised Organization Chart with a border from the Borders and Titles stencil. At this point, it may be useful to revise the original Excel workbook **OrganizationalChart.xls** to include the new information for Mathew Williams. This will make it possible to again automatically regenerate the organizational chart using the Visio Organization Chart Wizard.

EXHIBIT 3–16
Organizational
Change Position Type
Dialog Box

You may have noticed that when the Visio Organization Chart Wizard was complete, a new item was added to the Visio toolbar, **Organization Chart**. Select the new item to generate the drop-down menu illustrated in Exhibit 3–19 and then select **Export Organization Data**. A windows file save dialog box is opened to select the filename and format for the exported data. Exhibit 3–20 illustrates the workbook generated by Visio. In addition to lacking the formatting of the original workbook, shown in Exhibit 3–1, the exported workbook contains several additional columns: UniqueID, Reports_To_2, and Master_Shape. Those new columns provide a symbolic means to link organizational relationships. Also, notice that the new assistant managers, Jane Smith and Judy Simpson, have been added but that their information is not complete.

The reader is encouraged to check out other features in the Organizational Chart Drop-Down menu, depicted in Exhibit 3–19.

EXHIBIT 3–17
Organizational Chart
for Mathew Williams

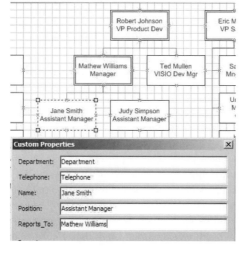

EXHIBIT 3–18
Organizational Chart
Revised

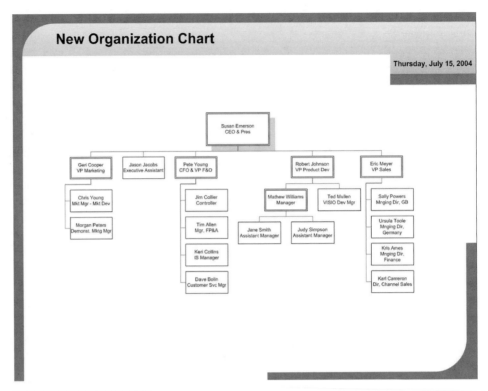

EXHIBIT 3–19
Organizational Chart
Drop-Down Menu

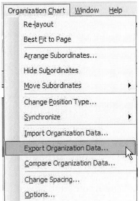

EXHIBIT 3–20
Organizational Chart
Export Workbook

	A	B	C	D	E	F	G	H
1	Unique_ID	Department	Name	Reports_To	Telephone	Title	Reports_To	Master_Shape
2	ID1		Susan Emerson		x350	CEO & Pres		0
3	ID2	Sales	Eric Meyer	Susan Emerson	x250	VP Sales	ID1	1
4	ID3	Sales	Karl Cameron	Eric Meyer	x270	Dir, Channel Sales	ID2	2
5	ID4	Sales	Kris Ames	Eric Meyer	x280	Mnging Dir, Finance	ID2	2
6	ID5	Sales	Sally Powers	Eric Meyer	x320	Mnging Dir, GB	ID2	2
7	ID6	Sales	Ursula Toole	Eric Meyer	x359	Mnging Dir, Germany	ID2	2

Creating an Office Layout

One of the many useful things you can do with Visio is to plan the furniture layout of a room or office. This becomes necessary when you plan to purchase new furniture because you need to evaluate the number of pieces that will fit in the room. It can be an expensive mistake to purchase furniture, spend days assembling it, and then discover that you cannot fit it all into the room. A few hours spent working with Visio can save you time, money, and

EXHIBIT 3–21
Office Layout
Drawing
Page office layout |
Chapter 3
Drawings.vsd

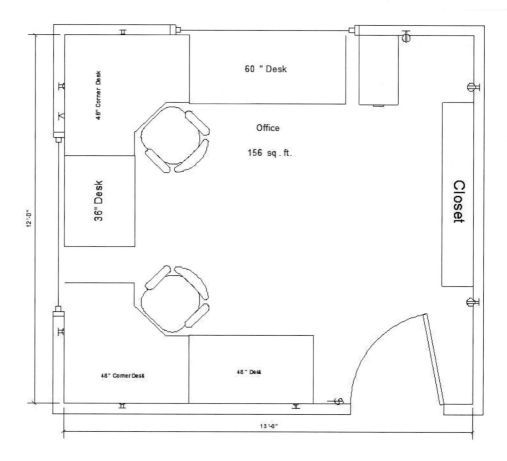

headaches later. As a guide in this exercise, a completed example is illustrated in Exhibit 3–21.

We will go through the following three tasks:

1. Specifying the office size.
2. Creating new furniture stencil.
3. Adding furniture to the office layout.

Task 1. Specifying the Office Size

The first task in planning a furniture layout is to set up the dimensions of the room. This effort includes not only specifying the room's shape and size, but also adding important structural elements, such as doors, windows, and closets. It is not a good design to place a desk in front of the closet or to cut off all the light in the room by placing a big hutch in front of a window.

EXHIBIT 3–22 **Office Layout Menu Selection**

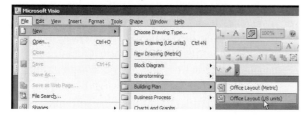

1. To start working on the room design, you need to use the office layout feature. Select **File > New > Building Plan > Office Layout (US units)** (see Exhibit 3–22).

2. This opens a new Office Layout Template; complete with these stencils:

Cubicles.vss

Office Accessories.vss

EXHIBIT 3–23 Visio Page Step Dialog

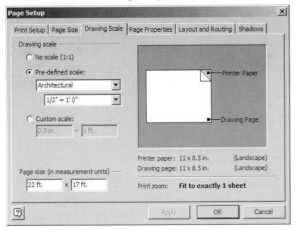

Office Equipment.vss

Office Furniture.vss

Walls, Doors and Windows.vss

You need these for laying out the room and adding furniture. Notice that the rulers are calibrated in feet, and the scale is set to display a reasonably sized room (22 feet × 17 feet) about right for the student learning Visio. The drawing scale can be changed by selecting **Page Step** from the File menu (see Exhibit 3–23), and clicking on the **Drawing Scale** tab. Click on the **Page Properties** tab and enter "My Office" in the Name field. Click on **OK** to close the Page Setup dialog box and view the new settings. Save your new drawing at this point, and name the file **My Office Layout.vsd**.

EXHIBIT 3–24
Office Layout Sizing

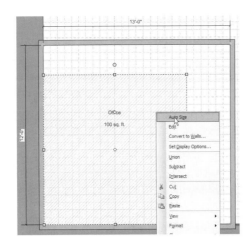

3. Drag the rectangular room shape ▦ onto the drawing page from the stencil **Walls, Doors and Windows.vss**. Position the lower left corner of the shape at the zero point of both rulers. Click and drag the upper vertical blue guide to resize the vertical room dimension to 12 feet. This action moves the upper horizontal wall and redraws the dimensions for the vertical walls. Click and drag the right blue guide to resize the horizontal room dimension to 13 feet. This action moves the right vertical wall and redraws the dimensions for the horizontal walls. Add Controller dimension and Space shapes from the Walls, Doors and Windows stencil. Right-click on the hatched area that displays the area of the room (in square feet), and choose **Auto Size** from the shortcut menu, as is done in Exhibit 3–24. This expands the area to fill the room.

4. Resize the drawing page by selecting **Size to fit Drawing contents** on the **File > Page Setup > Page Size Dialog box**, as shown in Exhibit 3–25. Move the zero-zero point of the grid to the layout by pressing the **Ctrl** key and dragging the origin crosshairs ⊞ to the lower left corner of the layout.

5. Drag the door shape ▱ from the Walls, Doors and Windows stencil until it is close to the bottom right corner, making sure that the door itself overlaps the right wall. When you release the mouse button, the door should "snap" into the corner. Right-click on the door and choose **Properties** from the shortcut menu. Select a 36-inch door width from the drop-down menu in the Custom Properties dialog box, shown in Exhibit 3–26.

6. Now you will add some windows to allow light into the office. The first window will be on the left wall

EXHIBIT 3–25 Office Layout Sizing

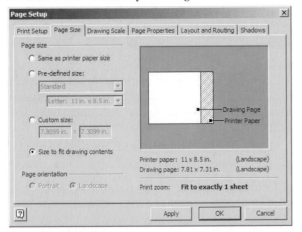

EXHIBIT 3–26
Office Layout Door
Shape Custom
Properties Dialog Box

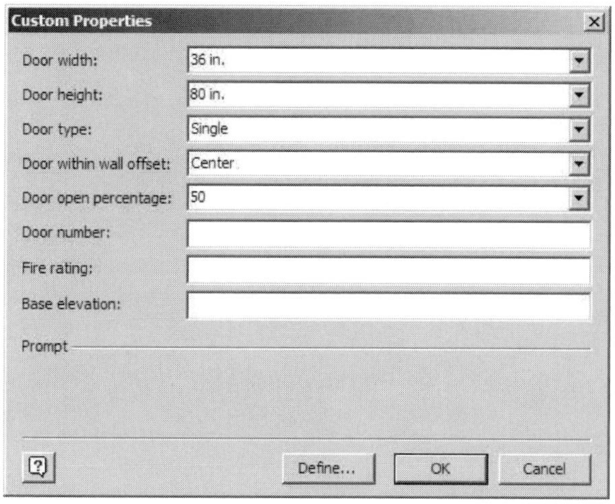

(12-foot vertical wall). Click and drag the window shape ⊟ from the stencil **Walls, Doors and Windows.vss** and position it so it is overlapping the left wall. The window automatically pivots to align with the wall. Click and drag the window until its center point is even with the 6-foot mark on the vertical ruler. Notice the dotted line that appears in the ruler as you drag the window. This line helps you position the window correctly. Click on the small green rectangle at the lower end of the window shape, and drag it until it is even with the 3-foot mark on the vertical ruler. Notice how the upper edge of the window also moves, keeping the window centered. Drag another window shape onto the upper horizontal wall centered on the 6.5-foot mark on the horizontal ruler. Right-click on the window shape and choose **Properties** from the shortcut menu. Choose 72 inch from the Window Width drop-down menu to increase the size of the window.

7. Now you are going to add a closet. Because there is no closet shape in the template, you will have to build one. Choose the Rectangle drawing tool from the toolbar, and drag a rectangle on the right vertical wall that extends from the 10-foot mark down to the 3-foot mark in the vertical ruler. Make sure the rectangle extends a foot into the room. Type the word *Closet* to label the shape and increase the font size to 18 points. Rotate the text by selecting the text block tool 🔄 from the Standard toolbar to make it fit the object. Click the shape, and then do one of the following:

   a. To rotate the shape's text block, drag a rotation handle.
   b. To move the shape's text block, drag the rotation pin.
   c. To resize the shape's text block, drag a selection handle.

8. It would not do to place furniture in front of the light switch, so you need to mark it. Drag the light switch shape 🔲 from the stencil **Office Equipment.vss** and drop it on the wall by the door.

9. Drag some electrical outlets onto the walls around the room as well, and place them according to the diagram. Because the outlet shapes ⊖ are so small, use the sizing handles to increase their size and make them more visible.

10. Add a phone jack 🔲 to the left vertical wall at the 9.5-foot mark.

We now have our basic office, as illustrated in Exhibit 3–27.

Task 2. Create a New Furniture Stencil

Obviously an empty room would be difficult to work in, so let us add some furniture. You will want to try various layouts before finding one you really like. First we will create a stencil with furniture of the size that you already own or would like to purchase. Each

EXHIBIT 3–27
Office Layout
without Furniture

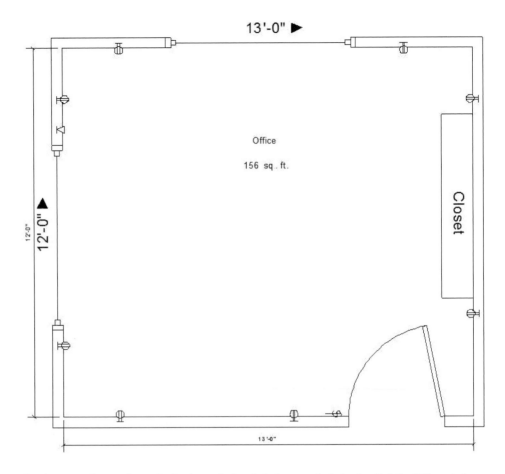

furniture vendor produces desks, laterals, bookshelves, and chairs in slightly different sizes. To modify the size, drag a shape, for example, a desk, from the stencil **Office Furniture.vss** onto the drawing, size it to match the piece supplied by the vendor of your choice, and then drag that custom piece onto your new stencil, adding it to the stencil. That way, the next time you need a desk, you will have one, all sized and ready to go.

EXHIBIT 3–28
New Stencil Menu

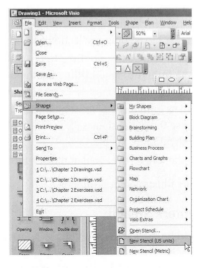

1. To create a new stencil, select **File > Stencil > New Stencil** (see Exhibit 3–28). This adds a blank stencil to your template. Click in the upper left corner of the new stencil, and choose **Properties** from the menu. This opens the stencil's Properties dialog box. The disk icon in the upper right corner of the stencil title bar indicates that a change has been made to the stencil that needs to be saved. Click on the disk icon. Enter the name **My Furniture.vss** for the File Name in the Save As dialog box, and click on **Save**. Then click on the title bar of the Office Layout Shapes stencil to make the stencil visible. You are now ready to start adding your furniture to the blank stencil.

2. To create a 60-inch desk, drag the Desk shape onto the drawing, but put it outside the room. Right-click on the desk shape and choose **View >**

EXHIBIT 3–29
Sixty-inch Desk
Stencil Master

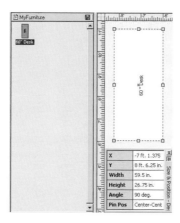

EXHIBIT 3–30
Forty-eight-inch Desk
Stencil Master

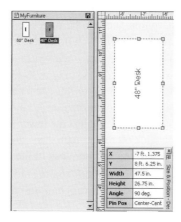

EXHIBIT 3–31
Forty-eight-inch
Corner Desk Shape
Development

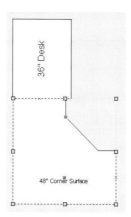

EXHIBIT 3–32
Office Layout Stencil,
My Furniture.vss

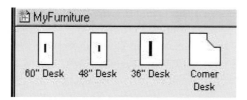

Size & Position from the shortcut menu. In the Size & Position window, enter the height as 26.75 inches and the width as 59.5 inches. These values correspond to the dimensions of the standard 60-inch desk. Add the name **60″ Desk**. Hold down the Ctrl key and drag the new desk onto the stencil **My Furniture**. This adds the desk to the stencil without deleting it from the drawing. Right-click on the new stencil shape, and choose **Master Properties** from the shortcut menu. Enter the new name **60-inch Desk**. Exhibit 3–29 illustrates the final result.

3. To create a 48-inch desk, return to the desk shape, and adjust the width to 47.5 inches. Hold down the Ctrl key and drag the new desk onto the stencil **My Furniture**. Right-click on the new stencil shape, and choose **Master Properties** from the shortcut menu. Enter the new name **48-inch Desk**. Exhibit 3–30 illustrates the final result.

4. To create a 36-inch desk, follow the previous tasks with a width of 35.5 inches. Then delete the desk shape from the drawing by not holding the Ctrl key when moving the shape to the stencil.

5. To create a corner surface, drag the Corner Surface 1 shape from the stencil onto the drawing, once again placing it outside the room area. Adjust both the width and height to 47.25 inches. Next, you need to adjust the dimension where the corner surface joins the desk because this dimension should match the width of the desk (see Exhibit 3–31). Drag the 36-inch desk onto the work area and align it with the corner surface. Grab the segment-sizing handle and drag it to match the corner surface edge dimension of the desk width. Drag the corner surface onto the stencil **My Furniture** and adjust the name to read **Corner Desk**.

Save the new stencil for safekeeping. Delete any extraneous shapes (such as the 36-inch desk) remaining on the drawing. The completed stencil is also illustrated as Exhibit 3–32 and has been stored as **My Furniture.vss**.

Task 3. Add Furniture to the Office Layout

1. To add two corner surfaces, drag and drop the corner desk shape near the lower left corner of the office. Click on one of the electrical outlets in that corner, then Shift-click on the other one to select them both. Choose **Shape > Bring to Front** to ensure they will be visible when you move the corner desk all the way into the corner. Then drag the corner desk flush with the walls in the corner of the room. Drag another corner desk from the stencil and place it near the upper left corner of the room. Right-click on the shape, and choose the menu

EXHIBIT 3–33
Positioning
Corner Desk

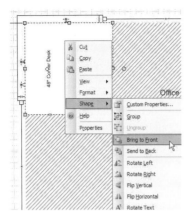

command **Shape > Rotate Right**. This aligns the shape with the corner of the room. Click on the two electrical outlets and the phone jack in the upper left corner, and choose the menu command **Shape > Bring to Front** or **Ctrl-f**. Then bring the corner desk into the upper left corner, see Exhibit 3–33.

2. To add a 36-inch desk and two 60-inch desks, drag a 36-inch desk onto the screen and align it with the corner desk located in the upper left corner of the room. Then drag a 60-inch desk onto the drawing area. Right-click on the desk, and choose the menu command **Shape > Rotate Right**. Bring over the desk against the lower wall, and align it with the corner desk. Hold down the Ctrl key, click on the 60-inch desk, and drag a copy of it to the upper wall under the window. Align it with the corner desk in the upper left corner.

3. To add two desk chairs and a file, drag two desk chairs onto the drawing, one at each corner desk. Click on the rotation handle of the lower chair and drag it around to face the corner desk. Repeat this action with the other chair.

4. Drag a file shape from the Office Layout Shapes stencil into the upper right corner. Rotate the file (**Shape > Rotate Right** from the shortcut menu), and align it with the end of the desk.

This completes your office layout. Compare your results to Exhibit 3–21.

Other Layout Applications Using Visio

Visio is not limited to office layout. It also does a great job on any type of facility design, even your new home. When developing a layout design for a facility such as a manufacturing plant, you should start as we did by developing a stencil of equipment to be included in the facility. This stencil may include machines, storage racks, and mobile equipment such as forklift trucks. Use the Visio Shape tools such as **Flip Vertical**, **Flip Horizontal**, **Rotate Left**, and **Rotate Right** to create stencil masters of equipment in different configurations to speed the process of layout development. Using Visio layers is also extremely helpful when developing facility layouts using Visio. A key point is that the Visio drawing can be done in scale. The other advantage is that the final layout can be quickly copied to other programs such as Word or Arena.

Exhibit 3–34 illustrates a Visio layout drawing prepared for an industrial application showing a scaled drawing of a warehouse cross section. This drawing was developed using standard Visio shapes such as boxes. Visio Dimensions were also added to provide a reference scale. The Controller Dimension shape is found on the stencil **Walls, Doors and Windows.vss**.

EXHIBIT 3–34
Warehouse Cross-Section Scale Layout Drawing
Page warehouse layout | Chapter 3 Drawings.vsd

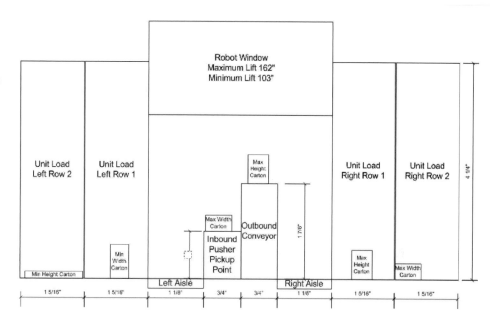

Cause and Effect Diagram

The cause and effect diagram is used to identify, explore, and display the possible causes of a specific problem or condition. The cause and effect diagrams were developed by Kauro Ishikawa of Tokyo University in 1943 and thus are often called *Ishikawa diagrams.* Professor Ishikawa pioneered quality management processes in the Kawasaki shipyards, and in the process became one of the founding fathers of modern management.

The cause and effect diagram is used to explore all potential or real causes (or inputs) that result in a single effect (or output). The effect or problem is stated on the right side of the chart and the major influences or "causes" are listed to the left. Causes are arranged according to their level of importance or detail, resulting in a depiction of relationships and hierarchy of events. This can help you search for root causes, identify areas where there may be problems, and compare the relative importance of different causes. A cause and effect diagram can aid in identifying reasons why a process goes out of control.

A well-detailed cause and effect diagram will resemble the skeleton of a fish and hence the alternate name *fishbone diagram.* The main causal categories are drawn as "bones" attached to the spine of the fish.

Cause and effect diagrams are drawn to clearly illustrate various causes affecting a process by sorting out and relating these causes. For every effect, there are likely to be several major categories of causes. Causes in a cause and effect diagram are frequently arranged into four major categories. Whereas these categories can be anything, for manufacturing operations we might use

- 4Ms: Manpower, Methods, Materials, and Machines,

or for administration and service application we may find to be more useful

- 4Ps: People, Policies, Procedures, and Plant (equipment).

Don't be afraid to mix these major categories or to try the conventional

- Who, What, Where, When, Why, and/or How.

EXHIBIT 3–35
Manufacturing
Quality Cause and
Effect Diagram
Page cause and effect
template | Chapter 3
Drawings.vsd

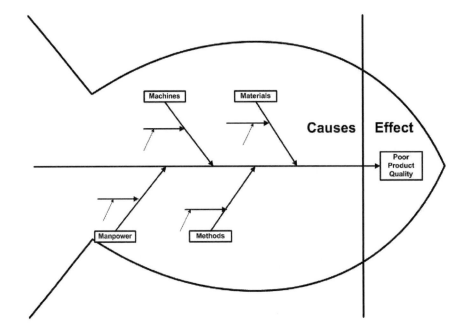

EXHIBIT 3–36 **Stencil Cause and Effect Diagram**
Shapes.vss

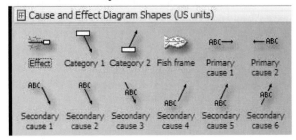

From this list of possible causes, the most likely are identified and selected for further analysis. When examining each cause, look for things that have changed, that is, deviations from the norm or patterns. Look to cure the cause and not the symptoms of the problem. Push the causes back as much as is practically possible. You may use any major cause category that emerges or helps people think creatively. Exhibit 3–35 illustrates the starting point for the cause and effect diagram to study a manufacturing quality problem. This drawing was developed using the stencil **Cause and Effect Diagram Shapes.vss**, as illustrated in Exhibit 3–36.

Identifying Causes of Problems

When a team engages in problem-solving activity, team members analyze a process to identify the symptoms causing the problem and to identify the conditions under which the problem seems to occur. In that sense, process analysis is akin to identifying the symptoms of a disease. The medical team discovers where and when it hurts. But treating symptoms isn't the same as curing a disease. A team has to identify and verify the deep causes behind the symptoms in order to develop effective solutions.

The cause and effect diagram is a very attractive tool. On the face of it, it is easy to learn and apply. The cause and effect diagram helps teams to organize their ideas, theories, and possible explanations for the symptoms it discovers. Through brainstorming and clustering, a team builds layers of possibilities by continuously asking Why? The team then lays out their responses in the shape of a fishbone.

However, it is a mistake to approach it without mastering at least some organizational learning skills, such as working together with others, seeking the truth, being open to different ideas, seeing others who might oppose you as colleagues with different ideas. Without such skills, internal politics can dominate the process (e.g., the most powerful opinion dominates; team members bring to the diagram construction process a political agenda).

The cause and effect diagram, like other problem-solving techniques, is a heuristic tool. As such, it helps users organize their thoughts and structure the quality improvement process. Of course, the diagram does not provide solutions to quality problems. The final cause and effect diagram does not rank causes according to their importance. Cause and effect diagrams can reveal important relationships among various variables and possible causes and provide additional insight into process behavior.

Cause and Effect Diagram Construction

The following tasks are typically used to create a cause and effect diagram:

1. Clearly state the problem or situation you are addressing. This can be very broad, such as "the team goal was to improve the internal approval process" or much more specific, such as "Reduce errors on Transmittal Forms by 20%." The key is that the team is in agreement on the problem statement or Effect.
2. Generate the causes needed to build a cause and effect diagram in one of two ways:
   a. Structured brainstorming about possible causes without previous preparation.
   b. Ask members of the team to spend time between meetings using simple Check Sheets to track possible causes and to examine the production process steps closely.
3. Construct the actual cause and effect diagram by
   a. Placing problem statement in the box on the right.
   b. Drawing the traditional major cause category steps in the production process, or any causes that are helpful in organizing the most important factors.
   c. Placing the brainstormed ideas in the appropriate major categories.
   d. Asking for each cause, Why does it happen? and listing responses as branches off the major causes.
4. Interpretation: To find the most basic causes of the problem
   a. Look for causes that appear repeatedly.
   b. Reach a team consensus.
   c. Gather data to determine the relative frequencies of the different causes.

Cause and Effect Diagrams Using Visio

There are many possible applications of cause and effect diagrams. Four main applications are as follows:

1. **Cause enumeration** is one of the most widely used graphical techniques for quality control and improvement. It usually develops through a brainstorming session in which all possible types of causes (however remote they may be) are listed to show their influence on the problem (or effect) in question. Cause enumeration facilitates the identification of root causes because all conceivable causes are listed.

2. **Dispersion analysis** is used when each major cause is thoroughly analyzed by investigating the subcauses and their impact on the quality characteristics (or effect) in question. The key to this diagram's effectiveness lies in the reiteration of the question, why does this dispersion occur?

This diagram helps us analyze the reasons for any variability, or dispersion. Unlike cause enumeration where smaller causes that are considered insignificant are still listed, in dispersion analysis, causes that don't fit the selected categories are not listed. Sometimes small causes are not isolated or observed. Consequently, it is possible that some root causes will not be identified in dispersion analysis.

3. **Process analysis** is where the emphasis is on listing the causes in the sequence in which the operations are actually conducted. The advantage of this diagram is that since it follows the sequence of the production process, it is easy to assemble and understand. The

disadvantage is that similar causes appear again and again, and causes due to a combination of more than one factor are difficult to illustrate.

4. **Quality function deployment (QFD)** is used to identify what the customer (internal or external to the organization) wants. Questions such as *what*, *when*, *where*, *why*, and *how* will the customer use the product? may help in identifying his or her needs.

To illustrate a complete cause and effect diagram we present the customer QFD in Exhibit 3–37, requirements for a coffee maker. This drawing was developed using the Visio stencil **Cause and Effect Diagram Shapes.vss**.

The cause and effect diagram illustrates the options available when developing the design for a coffeemaker. In this example, we identify the important design features for a coffeemaker. The customer is clearly an external consumer who would make and drink the coffee. The customer could be a restaurant operator or an individual consumer. Since we propose to market the product to a large population, we interview many consumers to determine what they want. To keep things simple for this example, we decided to concentrate on the home and office use of the coffeemaker. Typical answers are shown here.

The product (coffeemaker) will be used for the following:

What: To make coffee in the amount I want, two to eight cups, to keep coffee warm, no burns, easy to clean.

When: Anytime, immediately when I get up, several times during the day.

Where: In office, home, car, recreational vehicle, campsite.

Why: Satisfying beverage, to dampen hunger, to perk up.

How: Hot, right taste, right concentration, with sugar, cream, or powdered cream, no grounds.

Clearly, the power source for heating the water plays an important part in the decision. Homes and offices use 110-volt power supplies, whereas cars and recreational vehicles

EXHIBIT 3–37
Coffee Maker QFD Cause and Effect Diagram
Page cause and effect QFD | Chapter 3 Drawings.vsd

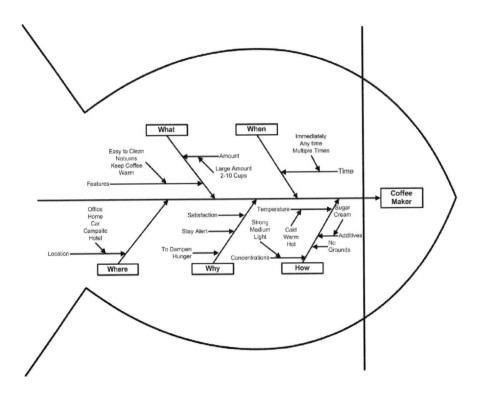

work with 12-volt batteries. A campsite may lack power, so a wood fire is needed to warm the water. Thus, we must first decide which market to serve. It is possible to develop a power supply (perhaps using a transformer) to serve more than one type of user, but the resulting cost of the product may be prohibitive.

Chapter 5, "Applications Using Excel," presents a QFD relationship matrix between Customer Wants and Design Features and determines the priorities of various design features associated with this coffeemaker example.

Other Visio Applications

As an easy-to-use, general-purpose business graphical tool, Visio can find many applications related to process analysis and improvement. In this section we will suggest a few of these applications.

Maps

Visio standard edition provides several stencils useful for developing maps used for such purposes as showing the location of a new store or research facility. These stencils include

Directional map shapes 3D
Landmark shapes
Metro shapes
Recreation shapes
Road shapes
Transportation shapes

Unfortunately some of the later versions of Visio have eliminated some stencils that were useful for drawing maps on a larger scale. Exhibit 3–38 illustrates a map of the United States developed from a previously available Visio stencil. The reader could regenerate that stencil by drawing individual states to a new stencil and then saving that stencil with a name like States.vss. We'll use this map again to illustrate a transportation problem in chapter 10.

Gantt Charts

Another Visio application related to process analysis and improvement are Gantt charts, which are used for illustrating a project schedule. Exhibit 3–39 illustrates a potential schedule for a project associated with this textbook. This drawing was developed using

EXHIBIT 3–38
USA Map Drawing
Page USA Map |
Chapter 3
Drawings.vsd

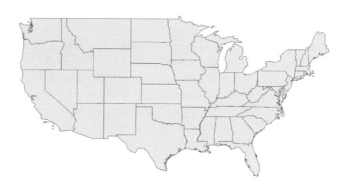

EXHIBIT 3–39   **Process Analysis and Improvement Project Gantt Chart**

Page project Gantt chart | Chapter 3 Drawings.vsd

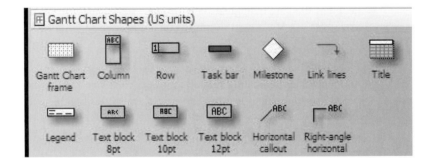

							Sep 2004				Oct 2004				Nov 2004			Dec 2004
ID	Task Name	Text Chapter	Resource Names	Start	Finish	Duration	9/5	9/12	9/19	9/26	10/3	10/10	10/17	10/24	10/31	11/7	11/14	11/21	11/28	12/5

Process Analysis and Improvement Project

ID	Task Name	Text Chapter	Resource Names	Start	Finish	Duration
1	Define Process Analysis and Improvement Project	1 & 11	Instructor	9/8/2004	9/8/2004	1d
2	Indentify Process Analysis and Improvement Project		Student	9/9/2004	9/12/2004	4d
3	Interview Project Personnel		Student	9/13/2004	9/15/2004	3d
4	Present Project Proposal		Student	9/15/2004	9/15/2004	1d
5	Refine Project Proposal		Joint	9/16/2004	9/22/2004	7d
6	Visio Instruction	2 & 3	Instructor	9/15/2004	9/28/2004	14d
7	Develop Visio Process Maps & Layouts		Student	9/16/2004	9/27/2004	12d
8	Present & Review Process Maps		Joint	9/28/2004	9/28/2004	1d
9	Excel Instruction	4 & 5	Instructor	9/29/2004	10/12/2004	14d
10	Collect & Organize Process Data		Student	9/30/2004	10/13/2004	14d
11	Analysis Process Data		Student	10/14/2004	10/26/2004	13d
12	Present and Review Process Data		Joint	10/27/2004	10/27/2004	1d
13	Arena Instruction	6 & 8	Instructor	10/13/2004	11/1/2004	20d
14	Develop Preliminary Arena Process Model		Student	10/14/2004	10/20/2004	7d
15	Develop Detailed Arena Process Model		Student	10/21/2004	10/26/2004	6d
16	Model Verification & Validation		Joint	10/27/2004	10/27/2004	1d
17	Develop Model Experimentation Plan		Student	10/28/2004	11/3/2004	7d
18	Conduct Simulation Experiments		Student	11/4/2004	11/17/2004	14d
19	Develop and Refine Conclusions & Recommendations		Student	11/18/2004	11/24/2004	7d
20	Document Project Findings & Results	11	Student	11/25/2004	11/30/2004	6d
21	Present Project Findings & Results		Student	12/1/2004	12/1/2004	1d
22	Evaluate Project		Instructor	12/2/2004	12/8/2004	7d

EXHIBIT 3–40

Stencil Gantt Chart Shapes.vss

Gantt Chart Shapes (US units)

Gantt Chart frame | Column | Row | Task bar | Milestone | Link lines | Title

Legend | Text block 8pt | Text block 10pt | Text block 12pt | Horizontal callout | Right-angle horizontal

stencil Gantt chart shapes (see Exhibit 3–40). More project details are included in Chapter 11 "Student Process Analysis and Improvement Projects."

We will illustrate the development of a Gantt chart using the Process Analysis and Improvement Project shown in Exhibit 3–39, where various tasks are carried out by the instructor, the student, and jointly by the instructor and the student. The project follows a time line with tasks performed according to a schedule. A start date and a finish date for each task establish the parameters for the schedule. This schedule assumes a class meeting date starting on Wednesday, September 8, 2004.

To develop a new Gantt chart in Visio, take these steps:

1. Use the menu commands **File > New > Project Schedule > Gantt Chart**, referring to Exhibit 3–41 as a guide.

EXHIBIT 3–41   **Gantt Chart Selection Menu Sequence**

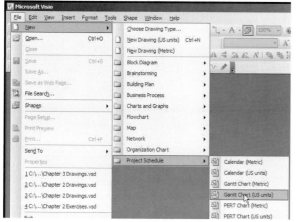

EXHIBIT 3–42   **Gantt Chart Options Dialog**

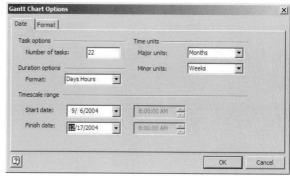

EXHIBIT 3–43
Blank Gantt Chart

ID	Task Name	Start	Finish	Duration
1	Task 1	9/6/2004	9/6/2004	1d
2	Task 2	9/6/2004	9/6/2004	1d
3	Task 3	9/6/2004	9/6/2004	1d
4	Task 4	9/6/2004	9/6/2004	1d
5	Task 5	9/6/2004	9/6/2004	1d
6	Task 6	9/6/2004	9/6/2004	1d
7	Task 7	9/6/2004	9/6/2004	1d
8	Task 8	9/6/2004	9/6/2004	1d
9	Task 9	9/6/2004	9/6/2004	1d
10	Task 10	9/6/2004	9/6/2004	1d
11	Task 11	9/6/2004	9/6/2004	1d
12	Task 12	9/6/2004	9/6/2004	1d
13	Task 13	9/6/2004	9/6/2004	1d
14	Task 14	9/6/2004	9/6/2004	1d
15	Task 15	9/6/2004	9/6/2004	1d
16	Task 16	9/6/2004	9/6/2004	1d
17	Task 17	9/6/2004	9/6/2004	1d
18	Task 18	9/6/2004	9/6/2004	1d
19	Task 19	9/6/2004	9/6/2004	1d
20	Task 20	9/6/2004	9/6/2004	1d
21	Task 21	9/6/2004	9/6/2004	1d
22	Task 22	9/6/2004	9/6/2004	1d

2. The first panel of Gantt Chart Options opens, as can be seen in Exhibit 3–42. Input following the parameters: Number of tasks **(22)**, Start date **(9/6/2004)**, Finish date **(12/17/2004)**, Major units **(Months)**, and Minor units **(Weeks)**. The blank Gantt chart illustrated in Exhibit 3–43 soon appears.

We are now ready to start entering the Task Name and Duration information. In this example we are using the normal student workweek of seven days (select the menu commands **Gantt Chart > Configure Working Time . . .**). A start date and finish date must be assigned to each task. This can be done in one of three ways, by

1. Changing the text contents of these fields.

2. Manipulating with the blue task bar in the last column, as shown in Exhibit 3–44. The size of the task bar can be changed by holding one edge with the cursor, then dragging

EXHIBIT 3–44 Changing the Task Duration Using the Task Bar

9/16/2004	10/5/2004	20d	

EXHIBIT 3–45 Linking Gantt Chart Tasks

EXHIBIT 3–46 Preliminary Gantt Chart

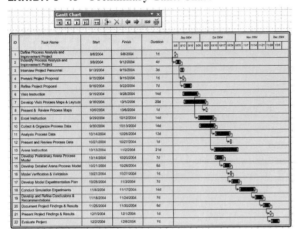

EXHIBIT 3–47 Inserting Gantt Chart Column

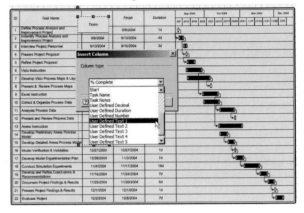

and dropping it to the desired place. The place can also be changed. All changes are reflected in the Start and Finish columns.

3. Linking the start of a second task to the finish of the first task. Exhibit 3–45 illustrates the linking of task 9 and task 13. First click on the row labeled as *Task 9,* then press the shift key and click on the row labeled as *Task 13.* Next right-click to get the menu displayed in Exhibit 3–45 and select **Link Tasks**. Task 13 will now be forced to start after the completion of task 9.

Exhibit 3–46 illustrates the Gantt chart to this point.

To add a new row, drag and drop the ROW control from the stencil Gantt Chart shapes shown in Exhibit 3–46. In order to indicate the creation of a task, drag and drop the Column control from the left panel to the place right after the ID column. A window will appear to ask the type of the column to be inserted. Select **User defined text 1** type from the various options provided, as shown in Exhibit 3–47. We label this new column *Text Chapter* and provide the desired information. We also add a column labeled *Resource Names.*

The Title shape is used for adding a title to the chart. It can be done by dragging and dropping this shape to the workplace. Use caution when entering text in the chart; the cell size is not automatically adjusted. Cell size should be changed manually by clicking on the cell, dragging one of its borders (upper or lower), and changing its size.

A Gantt chart, as any other chart in Visio, can be drawn page by page. The number of tasks is thereby adjusted to fit the chart on one page.

Exercises

1. Use Visio to draw an organization chart for your university department or your workplace.

2. Use Visio to develop a layout of the room in which you sleep. Develop an alternative layout of the available furniture.

3. One of the most useful things you can do with Visio is to plan the furniture layout of a room. This is especially true if you are going to purchase new furniture; you need to calculate the cost and evaluate the number of pieces that will fit in the room. It can be an expensive mistake to purchase furniture, perhaps spend days assembling it, and then discover that you cannot fit it all into the room. A few hours working with Visio can save you time, money, and headaches later.

   a. You are given a room with the dimensions 15 feet × 15 feet. The name of the page where you will lay out the office will be called **MyOffice**. The name of the file that you will create will be called **LastnameFirstnameOfficeLayout.vsd**. There will be windows on the west and north walls and a door 36 inches wide on the corner of the south wall adjacent to the east wall. There will be six electrical outlets on the walls and a long closet on the west wall. Of course, an empty room is pretty difficult to work in, so let us add some furniture to the room.

   b. First you need to add a new, empty stencil to this diagram. The reason for this is the furniture in the Office Layout Shapes stencil is not the right size. Each furniture vendor produces desks, bookshelves, and chairs in slightly different sizes. To modify the size, drag a shape (for example, a desk) from the Office Layout Shapes stencil onto the drawing, size it to match the piece supplied by the vendor of your choice, and then drag that custom piece onto your new stencil, adding it to the stencil. That way, the next time you need a desk, you will have one all sized and ready to go. Call this stencil by the name **Furniture** and the name of the file where you are saving it as **Lastname Firstname Furniture.vss**.

   c. We need to add two corner desks, one on the lower left corner and the other on the upper left corner of the office. Include a desk against the left wall and align it with the two corner desks. Align the two desks, one against the upper wall, next to the upper corner desk, and the other against the lower wall, next to the lower corner desk. Also, bring two desk chairs into the drawing—one at each corner desk.

   d. Next use Visio to calculate the cost to equip your office. Assume the following costs:

      i. Corner desk—$400 each

      ii. Desks against the left wall and upper and lower wall—$600 each

      iii. Desk chairs—$250 each

   e. Generate the total layout cost.

4. Give an example of a service process layout designed to maximize the amount of time the customer is in the process. Draw the layout of such a process in Visio showing multiple departments and the possible flows of customers through the process.

5. Describe the food delivery process employed at a fast-food restaurant using Visio.

   a. Provide a rough-cut layout of the food delivery process. Use Visio to diagram the basic flow through the process. Critique the layout. Are there any unnecessary steps? Can failure points be eliminated?

   b. Can the customer/provider interface be changed to include more technology? More self-service?

   c. Develop the revised Visio flow diagram.

Challenge

6. In this exercise you will set up a manufacturing process for a Ping-Pong paddle.

   a. Specify the type of equipment and raw material you will need to manufacture the Ping-Pong paddle—from the receipt of seasoned wood to packaging for shipment.

b. Assume that one unit of each type of equipment is available. Also assume that you have a stock of seasoned wood and other materials needed to produce and box 50 paddles. Using reasonable assumptions about times and distances where necessary,

    i. Develop an assembly drawing for the paddle.

    ii. Prepare an assembly chart for the paddle.

    iii. Develop a process flowchart for the paddle.

Supply chain management is the management of the activities that transform raw materials into intermediate goods and final products, and then deliver those final products to the customers. For most companies, supply chain management requires operating a network of manufacturing and distribution facilities that are often scattered around the world. The activities of the supply chain range from purchasing, manufacturing, logistics, distribution, and transportation to marketing. Usually, different companies own the various links in the supply chain.

A company in Seattle manufactures printers in a two-stage production process that involved the following activities:

1. Assembly and testing of printed circuit boards.
2. Final assembly and testing (FAT), which involved the assembly of other subassemblies (motor, cables, keypad, gears, etc.) and printed circuit boards from Printed Circuit Assembly and Test (PCAT) to produce a working printer, including the final testing of the printer.

The components needed for PCAT and FAT were sourced from other company divisions, as well as from external suppliers worldwide. The printers for different countries had been customized to meet the language and power supply requirements of the country of sale. This customization process involves assembling the appropriate power supply module and plug for the correct voltage requirements (110 V or 220 V), and packaging it with the working printer and a manual written in the appropriate language. The finished products of the factory consist of printers destined for different countries. These products are then sorted into three groups bound for three distribution centers in North America, Europe, and Asia Pacific. Outgoing products are shipped to the three distribution centers by ocean. The total factory cycle time through the PCAT and FAT stages is about a week. The transportation time from Seattle to the distribution center in San Jose, California, is about a day, whereas it takes four to five weeks to ship the printers in Europe and Asia.

Also relevant are the locations of suppliers, manufacturing facilities, distribution centers, and dealers for the Inkjet printer. The manufacturing facility for the Inkjet printer is in Seattle, Washington. The U.S. distribution center is in San Jose, California. The U.S. suppliers are in Denver, Colorado (for integrated circuit manufacturing), Los Angeles, California (for PCAT), Austin, Texas (for Print Mechanism Manufacturing) and Dallas, Texas (for FAT). Major U.S. customers (dealers) are in Boston, New York City, Los Angeles, Seattle, Miami, and Dallas.

Problems 7, 8, and 9 are based on the supply chain for the Inkjet printer described above.

7. Draw the supply chain network (U.S. portion) of an Inkjet printer manufactured by a U.S. company. Essentially, you will have to draw the network of suppliers, manufacturing sites, distribution centers, dealers, and customers for the Inkjet printer on page **USA Map | Chapter 3 Drawings.vsd**. Draw a cause and effect diagram to identify customer requirements for an Inkjet printer manufactured by this company.

8. Gantt charts are bar charts that show activities and their durations. Gantt charts are used for scheduling, planning, and managing projects. Using Visio and the **Project Schedule\Gantt Chart.vsd** drawing from the Visio Samples folders draw a Gantt chart for designing and production ramp-up of an Inkjet printer. The Gantt chart for the development and ramp-up efforts will show task dependencies; milestones; major product development phases; and also show tasks under each phase; start date; end date; and duration for each task. Include a title for the Gantt chart with the creation date.

9. Draw a cause and effect diagram to identify customer requirements for an Inkjet printer manufactured by this company.

Data Management and Analysis Using Excel

Summary and Learning Objectives

This chapter describes the need for data management and analysis, using computer-based tools such as Excel. It traces the history of tools used for data management and analysis. We assume the reader has a basic understanding of Excel concepts. In this chapter, we present the step-by-step use of the intermediate and advanced features of Excel such as data filtering, data auditing, and pivot tables.

The learning objectives for this chapter are to

1. Describe the need for data management and analysis.
2. Trace the historical perspective on business tools for data management and analysis.
3. Use Excel data auditing to trace formulas in a complex worksheet.
4. Develop a variety of Excel-based graphs.
5. Develop a worksheet using filtering.
6. Analyze a large dataset with Pivot tables.

Data Management and Analysis

Data management involves storing, accessing, transforming, and distributing data and information. Data analysis methodologies can range from simple visual approaches to sophisticated statistical techniques. Process analysis and improvement relies on the collection, organization, and analysis of operating data. We have chosen to use Excel for this task because of its widespread availability and the fact that nearly every personal computer user has at least a basic understanding of the tool. Other data management tools such as Access have widespread application but are not as readily adaptable to the casual user. In this chapter, we introduce many of the advanced Excel techniques that are not as widely used as they could be by individuals or teams responsible for process analysis and improvement. In chapter 5, we introduce additional Excel-based techniques for data analysis and optimization.

Spreadsheet Application Software

Spreadsheet programs are among the most commonly used personal computer-based software programs in the industry. Microsoft Excel and Lotus 1-2-3 continue to be the main data manipulation tools of the operations managers, although Microsoft Excel appears to have taken over the dominant market share for this type of software.

Microsoft Excel essentially enhances the operations manager's ability to perform such tasks as

Comprehensive math functions

Data manipulation

Data transfer or linking functions

Analytical and statistical procedures

Microsoft Excel provides additional analytical power to an operations manager involved in planning and decision making. Excel's widespread availability and ease of use make it the tool of choice for this chapter.

History of Data Management and Analysis

The following section presents a brief history illustrating how different devices and computer-based tools have evolved for data management and analysis.

Mechanical, Electromechanical, and Tape Calculators

Early devices used to aid in data management and analysis include the *abacus* and the counting rods, or "bones," of the Scottish mathematician John Napier. The *slide rule,* invented in 1622 by William Oughtred, an English mathematician, was widely used to make approximate calculations, but starting in about 1970 the electronic or battery-operated calculator replaced it. In 1642, Blaise Pascal devised what was probably the first simple adding machine using geared wheels.

In 1671, an improved mechanism for performing multiplication by the process of repeated addition was designed by Gottfried W. von Leibnitz. A machine using the Leibnitz mechanism was the first to be produced successfully on a commercial scale; devised in 1820 by the Frenchman Charles X. Thomas, it could be used for adding, subtracting, multiplying, or dividing. A mechanism permitting the construction of a more compact machine than the Leibnitz mechanism was incorporated into a machine devised later in the 19th century by the American inventor Frank S. Baldwin. Later, Baldwin and another American inventor, Jay R. Monroe, redesigned the machine. At about the same time, W.T. Odhner of Russia constructed a machine using the same device as Baldwin's. Charles Babbage, an English mathematician, and William S. Burroughs, an American inventor, also made important contributions to the development of the calculating machine.

Early mechanical adding machines were equipped with a keyboard on which numbers to be added were entered, a lever to actuate the addition process, and an accumulator to display the results. A full keyboard consisted of 10 columns of keys with nine keys in each column, numbered 1 through 9. Each column could be used to enter a figure in a particular decimal place so that a number up to 10 digits long could be entered; if no key was pressed in a given column, a zero was entered in that decimal place. The lever was pulled in one direction when a number was to be added and in the opposite direction when it was to be subtracted. The accumulator was a set of geared wheels, each corresponding to a decimal place and having the digits 0 through 9 printed on its circumference. When a given wheel made a complete rotation, the next wheel was advanced by one digit. The mechanical adding machine remained essentially the same until the mid-1960s, when improvements were made consisting of motors to actuate additions and subtractions and mechanisms to print out results on a paper tape.

Post-It Notes

In the early 1970s, Art Fry, a 3M chemist, was in search of a bookmark for his church hymnal that would neither fall out nor damage the hymnal. Fry noticed that a colleague at 3M, Dr. Spencer Silver, had developed an adhesive that was strong enough to stick to surfaces but left no residue after removal. Fry took some of Dr. Silver's adhesive and applied it along the edge of a piece of paper. His church hymnal problem was solved.

Fry soon realized that his "bookmark" had other potential functions when he used it to leave a note on a work file, and coworkers kept dropping by seeking bookmarks for their offices. This bookmark was a new way to communicate and to organize. 3M crafted the name Post-it Note for Fry's bookmarks and began production in the late 1970s for commercial use.

In 1977, test markets failed to show consumer interest for the self-stick removable notes. However, in 1979, 3M implemented a massive consumer sampling strategy, and the Post-it Note took off. Today, we see Post-it Notes peppered across files, computers, desks, and doors in offices and homes throughout the country. From a church hymnal bookmark to an office and home essential, the Post-it Note has colored the way we work. Large-sized Post-it Notes are also available for direct posting to walls for group decision-making sessions.

Paper and Electronic Worksheets

The accounting profession used paper worksheets since at least 1900. The paper format made it difficult to add or rearrange information. Of course all calculations had to be made manually and required frequent updating and rechecking.

In the late 1970s, the advent of the personal computer and the IBM personal computer (PC) in particular changed the way data is stored, retrieved, and displayed in almost every organization. Once loaded into a computer, a worksheet is a simple way to automatically calculate amounts for business purposes, such as developing a budget for the coming year or summarizing the past year's expenses. Worksheets are also useful for decision-making support in areas such as investment analysis, capital equipment replacement, and sales projections. Worksheets are like pencil and paper worksheets, except that they appear on a PC screen. They can be customized in the same fashion that paper and pencil worksheets can, and almost any task that is a repetitive administration function can be relegated to a computer worksheet, if totals and calculations are required.

VisiCalc   VisiCalc was the first computer worksheet program, which was created and marketed in 1979 by Harvard students Dan Bricklin and Bob Frankston. It computed in ways that no worksheet ever had and accountants everywhere fell in love with it.

As financial worksheets evolved, they began to do more things and do them faster. Worksheet software has become known for formulaic calculations, graphic visualization (charts, and graphs), what-if analysis, and long-term planning and forecasting in a financial environment. Now it is possible to talk to a worksheet, making data entry even easier with verbal commands. These days, worksheet software is so packed with features that it might appear almost magical to an early VisiCalc user.

Lotus 1-2-3   Lotus 1-2-3 from IBM's Lotus Development Corporation claims to have been the second worksheet product in the marketplace after Excel. Lotus 1-2-3 has been in the market since 1984 although the first versions of Lotus 1-2-3 were really VisiCalc for the IBM PC. Because of the fast rise of the PC during the later 1980s, Lotus 1-2-3 rapidly became the worksheet standard. It is sold either individually or as part of Lotus SmartSuite, a desktop productivity package that includes a word processor, a database, presentation graphics, and time-management and multimedia software. In the mid-1980s, Lotus Development introduced Symphony as an integrated office tool based on Lotus 1-2-3. Although Symphony had many new features it never became a marketplace success.

Excel   At one time, Lotus 1-2-3 was the industry-standard worksheet; Excel now holds that distinction. With a market share estimated at 60 percent to more than 90 percent, Excel is the leader in the worksheet market. Microsoft Office, a software package which includes a version of Excel, has more than 120 million licensed users worldwide. The worksheet is also sold separately as Excel. Originally developed for the Macintosh, Excel for Windows was introduced in October 1987; seven major versions have been released since.

Intermediate-Level Excel Concepts

Before introducing advanced Excel features, some review of workbook concepts will help bring all readers to a reasonable starting point. Many organizations have purchased the rights to use computer-based training tools for most Microsoft Office products. If the reader feels unfamiliar with much of the material in the next few pages, a few hours spent on those training tools or in any of the Excel books listed in the reference section of this textbook might be of help.

The descriptions and examples in this section are based on sheet **Order Book** illustrated in Exhibit 4–1. Although the sheet Order Book may not have direct application to process analysis and improvement, many of the advanced Excel techniques may prove valuable when organizing and analyzing the data association with most process analysis and improvement projects. The techniques illustrated in the sheet Order Book are of particular value when designing a worksheet on which data will be entered by someone other than the worksheet designer. Worksheet Order Book has been constructed to include many advanced Excel features, such as Conditional Formatting, AutoFiltering, and an extensive application of formulas.

One feature built into all workbooks supplied with this textbook are Excel macros that execute computer code written for Visual Basic for Applications (VBA). Excel tasks that are frequently repeated are good candidates for automation using a VBA macro. Exhibit 4–1, the worksheet Order Book, contains two buttons in range H1:L1 linked to VBA macros for sorting the order data. Test those macros by clicking on each. Notice how the sort order of the data is "magically" sorted. Excel supports VBA that can be used to automate tasks performed frequently and to control or exchange information with other tools, such as Visio and Arena. Chapter 8 covers VBA in more detail and illustrates how a sheet Order Book is sorted.

EXHIBIT 4–1
Worksheet Order Book
Sheet order book | Chapter 4 Worksheets.xls

CurrentDate ▾ fx 2/22/2005

	A	B	C	D	E	F	G	H	I	J	K	L	M
1		Order Book	Process Analysis and Improvement: Tools and Techniques Copyright ©2005 by The McGraw-Hill Companies, Inc.			To enter data using Form, Press F5, select Orders, and Data > Form ...		Sort by Due Date	Filtered Quantity	Filtered Backlog	Sort by Order Date	Filtered Shipments	Filtered Backorders
2		Current Date	2/22/2005			Right Click to Select from List		Sums	113,400	$435,000		13,000	3,000
3	Sequence	Order Date	Due Date	Lead Time Days	Slack Days	Customer	Product	Unit Price	Order Quantity	Outstanding Order Value	Shipped Date	Shipped Quantity	Backorder Quantity
4	1	1/11/2005	2/1/2005	21	-21	Interstate	Standard	$2.50	5,000	$0	2/1/2005	5,000	Shipped
5	2	1/9/2005	2/8/2005	30	-14	Acme	Improved	$4.50	6,000	$13,500	2/1/2005	3,000	3,000
6	3	1/18/2005	2/8/2005	21	-14	Xsell	Widget	$5.00	6,000	$30,000			Active
7	4	1/7/2005	2/20/2005	44	-2	Ajax	Widget	$5.00	5,000	$0	2/22/2005	5,000	Shipped
8	5	1/30/2005	2/27/2005	28	5	Ajax	Improved	$4.50	10,000	$45,000			Active
9	6	1/23/2005	3/6/2005	42	12	Ajax	Widget	$5.00	6,000	$30,000			Active
10	7	2/8/2005	3/6/2005	26	12	Xsell	Widget	$5.00	10,000	$50,000			Active
11	8	1/14/2005	3/13/2005	58	19	Best	Beta	$10.00	500	$5,000			Active
12	9	1/21/2005	3/13/2005	51	19	Modern	Beta	$10.00	200	$2,000			Active
13	10	1/25/2005	3/13/2005	47	19	Xsell	Improved	$4.50	6,000	$27,000			Active
14	11	2/1/2005	3/13/2005	40	19	Interstate	Standard	$2.50	10,000	$25,000			Active
15	12	2/13/2005	3/13/2005	28	19	Best	Beta	$10.00	100	$1,000			Active
16	13	1/16/2005	3/20/2005	63	26	City Wide	Widget	$5.00	4,000	$20,000			Active
17	14	1/28/2005	3/27/2005	58	33	Modern	Beta	$10.00	600	$6,000			Active
18	15	2/11/2005	3/27/2005	44	33	Interstate	Widget	$5.00	5,000	$25,000			Active
19	16	2/15/2005	3/27/2005	40	33	Acme	Widget	$5.00	10,000	$50,000			Active
20	17	2/4/2005	4/3/2005	58	40	Best	Standard	$2.50	10,000	$25,000			Active
21	18	2/18/2005	4/3/2005	44	40	Modern	Standard	$2.50	5,000	$12,500			Active
22	19	2/6/2005	4/10/2005	63	47	City Wide	Improved	$4.50	4,000	$18,000			Active
23	20	2/20/2005	4/10/2005	49	47	Ajax	Widget	$5.00	10,000	$50,000			Active
24		Excel Expressions:		C4 - B4	C4 - CurrentDate			VLOOKUP (G4, PriceTable, 2)		IF (L4>0, IF (L4<I4, (I4-L4)*H4, 0), I4*H4)			IF (L4>0, IF (L4<I4, I4-L4, "Shipped"), "Active")
26							Beta	$10.00	Order Quantity Statistics				
27							Improved	$4.50	5,670	Average			
28							Standard	$2.50	100	Minimum			
29							Widget	$5.00	10,000	Maximum			

Workbooks and Worksheets

The standard Excel file format has the extension **xls** and is referred to as the *Excel workbook*. Excel may have several workbooks opened at any time. The only requirement is that each workbook have a unique filename. For this chapter, that workbook filename is **Chapter 4 Worksheets.xls**. Each Excel workbook is made up of one or more worksheets. Only one worksheet from a given workbook can be displayed at any time.

The number of worksheets within a single workbook is limited by the amount of available computer RAM. By default, each new Excel workbook is initiated with three worksheets or viewing pages, named *Sheet 1, Sheet 2,* and *Sheet 3.* Double-clicking on the tab at the bottom of the window and typing the new name can change the worksheet name. Dragging the tab to a new location changes the order in which worksheets are displayed. Worksheets can be copied or moved between or within a workbook using the **Edit > Move or Copy Sheet . . .** command.

Unlike the open page format of Word or Visio, Excel divides the workspace into rows and columns. Excel worksheets may have up to 65,536 rows and 256 columns. Each Excel worksheet row and column intersection is described as a worksheet cell, for example, cell **E3** of worksheet Order Book contains the text: **Slack Days**. Each cell has its own content and formatting. Cell content may be a blank, a number, a string of text, or an equation, which is displayed as either a number or a string of text.

Width of columns and height of rows can be adjusted. The maximum column width is 255 characters; the maximum row height is 409 points. Columns, rows, and even worksheets can be hidden to make the layout less confusing. An individual cell may contain up to 32,767 characters of text. Only 1,024 characters of text are displayed in a cell, but all 32,767 characters of text are displayed in the formula bar. The formula bar appears to the right of the = sign at the bottom of the Excel icons. A cell's content can be edited by moving the cursor over the content of the formula bar and typing new content.

Range Names

Excel Range Names are a technique to make the worksheet easier to use. Rather than refer to a worksheet cell C2, we can instead use a name **CurrentDate**. Cell ranges are named using **Insert > Name > Define . . .** and using the Define Name dialog box illustrated in Exhibit 4–2. Collections of worksheet cells are identified as ranges and can be named. In this example, case cell C2 has been named **CurrentDate**.

Range names can be used in formulas and for moving around an entire workbook by pressing **F5** (GoTo) and selecting the desired range name from the dialog box illustrated in Exhibit 4–3. This same feature is available by clicking the selection arrow just to the right of the formula bar. This window typically indicates the currently selected cell or range.

EXHIBIT 4–2   Define Name Dialog Box

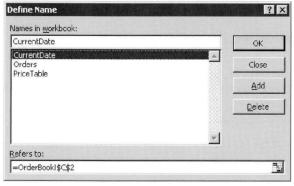

Absolute Referencing

The cell identified in Exhibit 4–2 used a format of **OrderBook!$C$2**. **OrderBook** is the worksheet name. Named ranges can be referenced from any worksheet in the current workbook. The $ signs in cell reference **$C$2** have special meanings in Excel and are referred to as *absolute referencing*.

When a formula is moved in an Excel worksheet, the cell references within the formula do not change. When a formula is copied, the cell references may change based on the type of reference used. After moving or copying cells containing formulas, verify that the cell references used in the formula produce the result that

EXHIBIT 4–3 Go To Dialog Box

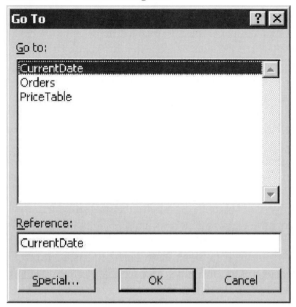

EXHIBIT 4–4 Worksheet Order Book Cell E4 Formula

Sheet order book | Chapter 4 Worksheets.xls

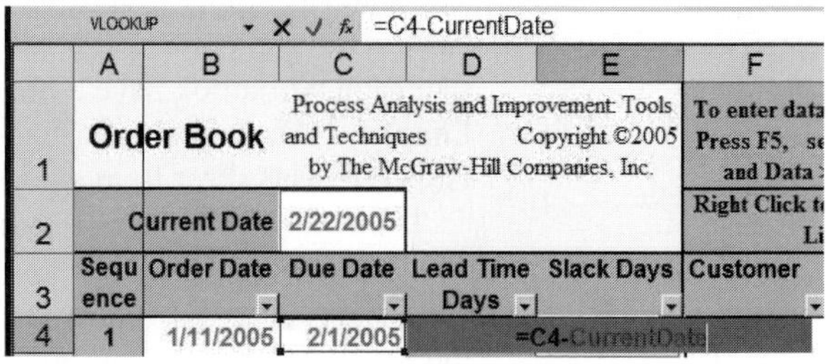

you want. Switch to the type of reference you need. For example, the formula for cell E4 illustrated in Exhibit 4–4 uses a reference to the value in the range **CurrentDate = $C$2**, which was defined using an absolute reference illustrated in Exhibit 4–2. This means that the formula in cell E4 can be copied to anywhere in the range E4:E24 with the formula remaining valid.

The reference to cell C4 in Exhibit 4–4 is relative and will change if the formula is copied to another worksheet column. For example, if cell E4 is copied to cell G4, the invalid formula illustrated in Exhibit 4–5 will occur. Notice the change in reference from C4 to F4. This problem could be corrected by changing the formula in cell F4 to **= C4-CurrentDate** prior to copying it to another column. Notice, we have not made the row reference absolute. Why?

Copy and Paste

Excel uses the standard windows **Ctrl-C** (copy) and **Ctrl-V** (paste) keystroke combination to copy and paste the contents and formatting of cells, ranges, rows, and columns. When copying and pasting multiple cells, care must be taken to assure that the target is of the same size as the original source. Cell or range contents can also be dragged to a new location. Keystroke **Ctrl-X** cuts data ready to be pasted to a new location. Note the selected range is highlighted with a dashed border.

EXHIBIT 4–5 Worksheet Order Book Invalid Cell F4 Formula

Sheet order book | Chapter 4 Worksheets.xls

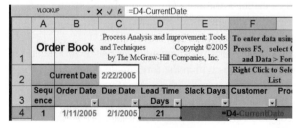

Paste Special

One powerful Excel feature is the **Edit > Paste Special . . .** , which can be used instead of the default **Ctrl-V** (paste). The dialog box illustrated in Exhibit 4–6 then appears. Some of the options found to be particularly useful are as follows:

• Values—All formulas are calculated and the results pasted in the new cells.

EXHIBIT 4–6   Paste Special Dialog Box

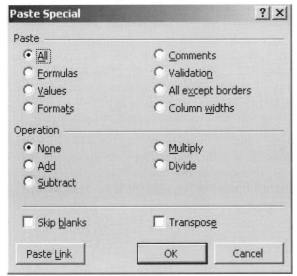

EXHIBIT 4–7   Fill Series Dialog Box

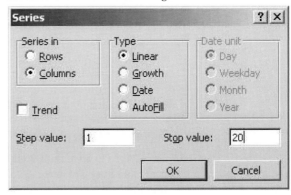

- Formats—Only the formats (colors, fonts, etc.) are pasted.
- Transpose—The range is transposed or flipped along the diagonal and then pasted.

Fill Series

Often the Excel user needs to insert a set of sequential numbers in a range, as has been done in column A of Exhibit 4–1, the worksheet Order Book. This can be done automatically by typing the first number and selecting the range to be filled or the stop value. The menu commands **Edit > Fill > Series** . . . generates the Fill Series dialog box illustrated in Exhibit 4–7. The illustrated dialog box options fill range A4:A23 with the values 1, 2, . . . , 20. Other options can be selected to fill ranges with dates and trend lines.

Number Formats

Numeric Excel data can be formatted using the following major types: General, Number, Currency, Accounting, Date, Time, Percentage, Fraction, Scientific, Text, Special, and Custom. To apply a format or other property, such as color, font, and so forth, select the desired range, right-click the mouse, and select **Format Cells** . . . . The dialog box illustrated in Exhibit 4–8 should appear when the Number tab is selected. The other tabs of the Format Cells dialog box can be used to select fonts, colors, border, and more.

EXHIBIT 4–8   Format Cells Dialog Box

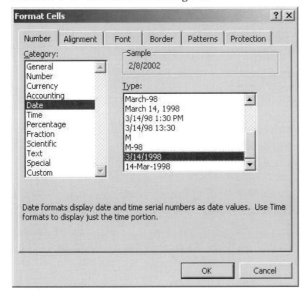

Dates and Times Formats

Excel stores dates as sequential numbers, known as *serial values*. Excel supports two date systems: the 1900 and 1904 date systems. The default date system for Microsoft Excel for Windows is 1900. The first Excel date, January 1, 1900, is stored internally as serial value 1. The last Excel date, December 31, 9999, is stored internally as serial value 2,958,465. The current date in Exhibit 4–1, worksheet Order Book cell C2, is February 22, 2005. Excel stores that serial value as 38,405, the number of days since January 1, 1900.

Time values are stored as decimal fractions. Dates and times are values that can be added, subtracted, and included in other calculations. For example, to determine the difference between two dates, simply subtract one date from the other. Time is the fractional part of the date and time value. For example, $0.25 = 6:00$ AM, whereas $0.75 = 6:00$ PM.

The Excel user can view a date as a serial value and a time as a decimal fraction by changing the date or time cell format to a General or Number format.

Advanced Operations

Let's return to Exhibit 4–1 and examine some of the features built into the worksheet Order Book. First, notice the colors used in the worksheets throughout this text. In general, all user input data is color-coded as red text on a white background. All data calculated by Excel is color-coded as black text on a rose background. Typically, the formulas or expressions used by Excel are also illustrated near the calculated values color-coded as blue text on a white background. In the worksheet Order Book in Exhibit 4–1 (page 90), the Excel expressions are illustrated in worksheet row 24.

Formatting

Worksheet Order Book columns B, C, and K have been formatted as date. Excel offers many potential date formats. The reader can experiment with other formats to find those that fit their requirements. Worksheet Order Book columns H and J have been formatted as currency.

Cell Formula Calculations

Surprisingly, some Excel users manually enter all data into their worksheets. Excel's real power is in its ability to calculate values and in its rich selection of functions to support those calculations.

Worksheet Order Book columns D and E illustrate calculations based on Excel dates. Worksheet Order Book column D, labeled **Lead Time Days**, is calculated using the following expression:

$$D4: = C4 - B4$$

Lead Time Days is the difference between the Due Date (C4) and the Order Date (B4).

Worksheet Order Book column E, labeled **Slack Days**, is calculated using the following expression:

$$E4: = C4 - \text{CurrentDate}$$

Slack Days is the difference between the Due Date (C4) and the CurrentDate, and is a named range equivalent to cell C2.

The equations in range D4:E4 have been copied to range D4:E23. To do this, select **D4:E4**, **copy** (Ctrl-C), select **D4:D23**, and **paste** (Ctrl-V).

Excel IF Function

Worksheet Order Book column J, labeled **Outstanding Order Value**, is calculated using a nested IF function in the following expression:

$$J4: = \text{IF } (L4 > 0, \text{IF } (L4 < I4, (I4 - L4) * H4, 0), I4 * H4)$$

The basic IF function works as follows:

$$= \text{IF } (A, B, C)$$

EXHIBIT 4–9
Order Book Cell J4 and M4 Operations
Sheet order book detail | Chapter 4 Worksheets.xls

Condition	Definition	OrderBook Displayed Formula Cell J4	Cell M4
L4 >0 and L4 < I4	Partial order shipped	(I4 - L4) * H4	I4 - L4
L4 >0 and L4 >= I4	Complete order shipped	0	"Shipped"
L4 <= 0	None yet shipped	I4 * H4	"Active"

The value of B is displayed if A is true or, if false, the value of C is displayed. The expressions for worksheet Order Book columns J and M are a bit complex. Exhibit 4–9 defines the logical operations for cells J4 and M4.

The combined result of this logical function is the unit price (H4) times the outstanding order quantity (I4-L4). Notice what happens when the shipped quantity is greater than the order quantity. Can this happen in practice?

Worksheet Order Book column M, labeled **Backorder Quantity**, is calculated using a nested IF function in the following expression:

$$M4: = IF (L4>0,IF(L4<I4,I4-L4,"Shipped"),"Active")$$

Other Excel Functions

The order quantity statistics, average, minimum, and maximum are calculated by

$$I27: = AVERAGE(I4: I23)$$

$$I28: = MAX(I4: I23)$$

$$I29: = MIN(I4: I23)$$

Advanced Calculations Using Excel Functions

Worksheet Order Book columns H, J, and M each demonstrate some of the many available Excel functions. Worksheet Order Book column H, labeled **Unit Price**, is calculated using the Lookup function in the following expression:

$$H4: = VLOOKUP(G4,PriceTable,2)$$

The VLOOKUP function can be located by selecting menu commands **Insert > Function**, or by clicking the Paste function icon *fx*. The dialog box illustrated in Exhibit 4–10 appears along with appropriate help and definitions.

EXHIBIT 4–10   Paste Function Dialog Box

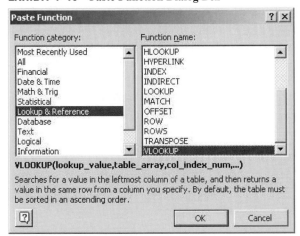

The VLOOKUP function compares the value in cell G4 with those in the first column of the named range PriceTable, G26:H29. The value displayed in cell H4 is taken from the second column of range PriceTable. In the case of cell H4, the value in cell G4 is Widget; its price of $5.00 is displayed in cell H4.

Lookup tables are a great way to eliminate the need to have to reenter repeated data. For example, to change all prices, only the values in range H26:H29 need to be altered. If a new product is added, insert a new row at 28 using the following menu commands: Select row 28 by clicking on the **28** on the left margin, **Ctrl-+** or **Insert > Rows**. Add the new product name and price in range I28:H28. It might be useful to sort the product name alphabetically. To do this select range **PriceTable** and click the Ascending Sort icon *2↓*.

Exhibit 4–10 also lists some of the potential mathematical, statistical, and financial functions available in Excel. Rather than listing all those functions in this text, it is best to search the Excel online (F1) help. Go to the Help Contents tab and select

- Creating formulas and auditing workbooks
- Worksheet functions
- Engineering functions, etc.

Learn how to use Excel functions by going to a blank cell and click the Paste Function icon f_∞. Explore the Paste Function dialog box using simple test data. Build complex formulas by first testing individual components and then pasting together the final expression.

Many common mathematical, statistical, and financial functions have already been programmed into Excel. Other functions are available from third-party vendors. Vendors of these specialized Excel functions can be found using Web search tools.

Conditional Formatting

Excel offers the user a great number of options in terms of the cell's font, font size, text color, background color, or other characteristics. Some care should be taken to limit the number of colors and fonts in each worksheet; however, a carefully selected color combination may make using the worksheet easy to use. Use caution: Some printers and display units do a poor job with certain colors. It pays to check out both printing and display options before selecting a standardized color pattern for Excel workbooks.

Sometimes it is useful to have Excel automatically change the format when the value or contents of a cell meet certain conditions. Conditional Formatting is the tool for this task. Menu Command **Format > Con̲ditional Formatting** . . . generates the dialog box illustrated in Exhibit 4–11. In the case of column E, nonpositive Slack Days are displayed with a red background. Conditional Formatting is also used for column M to highlight outstanding shipments with a red background.

Entering Data

The worksheet Order Book, illustrated in Exhibit 4–1, was designed to allow the user to enter data in all the cells with a white background. These ranges have also been unprotected using **Format > Cells > Protection**, uncheck **Locked**. The dates in columns B and C are typically best edited by pressing the **F2** (edit) key and then making the desired changes or using the formula bar. The customer and product names in columns F and G can be typed directly or selected from the existing list on current names by right-clicking and selecting **Pick From List** . . . .

An alternative method of entering data is to first select the Range Orders (press **F5** and select **Orders**) and then **D̲ata > F̲orm** . . . . The form dialog box illustrated in Exhibit 4–12 is a very convenient method for entering data. Only the unprotected cells are available for user data input. An entire row (orders) can be deleted directly from the form dialog box. New

EXHIBIT 4–11
Conditional Formatting Dialog Box

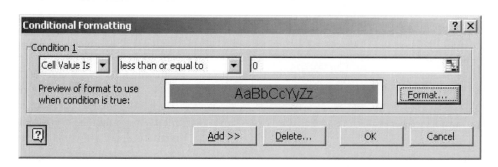

EXHIBIT 4–12   **Order Book Data Form Dialog Box**

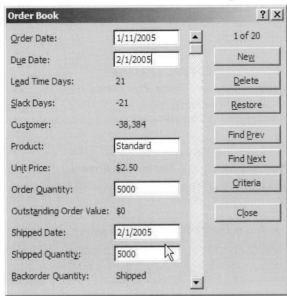

orders can be added but they won't necessarily contain the desired formulas and formatting.

Adding Row (Orders)

In normal operation, new worksheet Order Book rows are added as orders enter the system. Some of the special features used in this worksheet function are better accommodated by adding a new row just prior to the last row in Range Orders or between rows 22 and 23. This can be done by

1. Selecting row 23, and by clicking the number **23** in the left margin.
2. Copying row 23, **Ctrl-C** or **Edit > Copy**.
3. Adding new row 23, **Ctrl-+** or **Insert > Rows**.
4. Changing value of cell A24 to 21.
5. Entering new data in row 24.

This rather involved process assures that all formatting and ranges remain valid.

When a worksheet contains extensive sets of formula cells, it becomes difficult to determine just how each cell value has been calculated. When cells are moved by dragging, Excel normally automatically updates all dependent formulas. Occasionally, when cells with formulas are dragged or copied, Excel will display a message indicating a circular reference (see Exhibit 4–13). This means the current cell value has somehow been calculated based on itself. This is an error, which should be immediately located and corrected.

After many extensive changes to a worksheet, it is important to check that all calculations are still being made correctly. This is particularly true when the worksheet results are going to be used to make critical decisions.

A quick audit of a cell formula can be obtained by pressing the **F2** (edit) key. Exhibit 4–14 illustrates what happens when cell J4 is selected and the **F2** key is pressed to permit editing. The full formula is displayed both in the formula bar near the top of the window and immediately over the original cell. The formula is color-coded with each range reference having a different color. Those ranges, I4 (green), H4 (light blue), and L4 (blue), are

EXHIBIT 4–13
Circular Reference Message Box

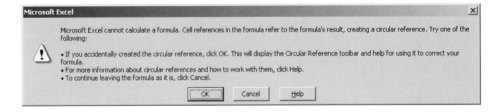

EXHIBIT 4–14
Order Book Cell J4 Formula Editing
Sheet order book |
Chapter 4
Worksheets.xls

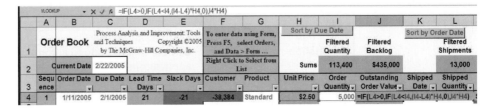

EXHIBIT 4–15
Auditing Drop-down Menu

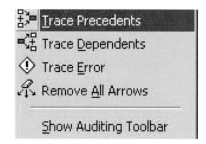

also color-coded. At this point the formula can be edited by typing or by dragging the colored ranges.

Auditing

A more graphical audit tool is available in Excel by selecting the **Tools > Auditing** menu command and then selecting **Trace Precedents** from the drop-down menu illustrated in Exhibit 4–15. This draws a blue arrow for all cells used in calculating the selected cell value. Exhibit 4–16 illustrates the precedents and dependents of cell J5.

EXHIBIT 4–16
Order Book Auditing of Cell J5
Sheet order book |
Chapter 4
Worksheets.xls

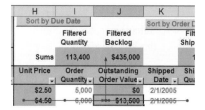

Selecting the **Remove All Arrows** option from the drop-down menu removes the auditing arrows from the worksheet.

Excel Worksheet Samples

Previous versions of Microsoft Excel included in the workbook **Sample.xls** that illustrates many advanced Excel features. We have included that workbook on the textbook CD and have listed its contents in Exhibit 4–17.

Visual Data Analysis

Decision makers need to understand the significance of data in as concise and meaningful a way as possible. Visual data analysis not only can provide excellent communication vehicles but can also reveal previously observed patterns and relationships. Through the use of multiple axes and color, high-dimensional data can be simplified for easier interpretation.

Visual data analysis facilitates expressing relationships between various variables in a simple way. Excel provides a variety of tools for effective visual data analysis, such as charts and geographic data maps.

EXHIBIT 4–17
Excel Worksheet Samples: Workbook Samples.xls
Sheet samples |
Chapter 4
Worksheets.xls

Worksheet	Application
Table of Contents	Table of Contents
Worksheet Functions	Sample formulas to complete common worksheet
Conditional Formatting	Demonstrates how to change the formatting applied to a cell depending on the current value of the cell
Data Validation	Shows how to set up restrictions for the values that can be entered into a cell
Chart Labeling	A macro (VBA) to automate the labeling of an XY-Scatter chart
Repeating Tasks	Sample looping macro code and an explanation of how to modify recorded code to repeat tasks on a range of cells or a selected range
Arrays	Macro code to demonstrate how to transfer array contents to a worksheet
API Examples	How to implement the use of API (Application Programming Interface) calls from within VBA
Events	Examples to demonstrate how some events can trigger macro code to run
Automation	Sample macro code to automate other Microsoft Office applications
ActiveX Data Objects	Examples that illustrate common database tasks via VBA code

EXHIBIT 4–18
Simple Data Set
Sheet simple data set |
Chapter 4
Worksheets.xls

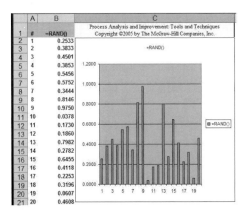

Charts (graphs and plots) are the most basic way of representing data. A variety of charts are available in Excel. These include vertical and horizontal bar charts, line charts, pie charts, area charts, scatter plots, three-dimensional surface charts, bubble charts, radar charts, and many other types of special charts.

Automatic Charts, F11

The Excel Chart Wizard, F11, provides an easy way to create charts from worksheet data. This can be illustrated by creating the simple data set illustrated in Exhibit 4–18, the worksheet **Simple Data Set**. The data in column A is a simple **Edit > Fill > Series** . . . . The data in column B were generated using the Excel random number generator

$$B2: = RAND().$$

The Excel function, RAND, generates a uniformly distributed random number from the range 0 to 1. Notice the values in column B will be changed each time the Excel recalculate key, **F9**, is pressed.

EXHIBIT 4–19   **Chart Location Dialog Box**

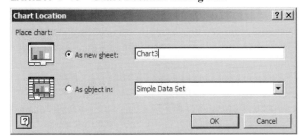

When cell range **B1:B21** is selected and the **F11** key is pressed, the default chart illustrated in the right part of Exhibit 4–18 is generated. This default chart is of the Column type. The Chart menu commands can be used to change the chart type, data sources, labeling, formatting, and chart location. By default, the Excel Automatic Chart is generated on a new worksheet with a name starting with **Chart**. We have changed the location to the worksheet Simple Data Set using the **Chart > Location** . . . **Dialog Box**, shown in Exhibit 4–19.

Worksheet Order Book Chart

The lower part of the worksheet Order Book contains a column type of chart based on the data in Range Orders. Exhibit 4–20 illustrates this chart when the data are sorted by Order Date. The reader should sort the order data by Due Date and observe how the chart changes.

EXHIBIT 4–20
Order Book Column Chart
Sheet order book |
Chapter 4
Worksheets.xls

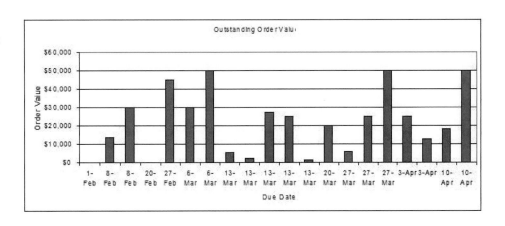

EXHIBIT 4–21
Chart Drop-down Menu

When an Excel chart object is selected, the **Chart** command appears on the Excel menu bar. Selecting the **Chart** menu option generates the drop-down menu illustrated in Exhibit 4–21. Its major functions are outlined next.

Chart Type Dialog Box   Exhibit 4–22 illustrates the Chart Type dialog box used to generate the chart in Exhibit 4–20. The Chart type is Column, while the sub-type is the simplest. The reader is encouraged to test impact of alternative chart types.

Column, Bar, Line, and Pie charts are a typical way to present business data such as sales, marketing, and financial data. By reducing information in a visual format to lower dimensions, it is easier to understand and put data together. Special charts such as bubble and radar charts prove useful to present these data. Select a new chart type and then press the button labeled **Press and Hold to View Sample** to view the chart change before making it on the worksheet. Try several chart types to find the one that best conveys the information to the intended audience.

Chart Source Data Series Dialog Box   Exhibit 4–23 illustrates the Chart Source Data Series dialog box used to generate the chart in Exhibit 4–20. The chart name is found in cell J3, the values in range J4: J23, and X-axis labels in range C4: C23. Note that when Excel includes $ signs in the range definitions, they are referred to as *absolute addresses*. The Data Range tab of the Source Data dialog box is used to specify the overall data range for the chart and can be used to swap rows and columns in the basic data structure for the chart.

EXHIBIT 4–22   **Chart Type Dialog Box**

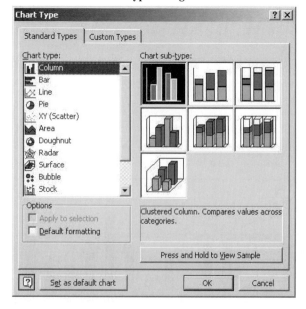

EXHIBIT 4–23   **Chart Source Data Series Dialog Box**

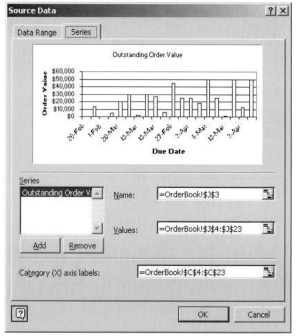

EXHIBIT 4–24   **Chart Options Dialog Box**

Excel chart samples

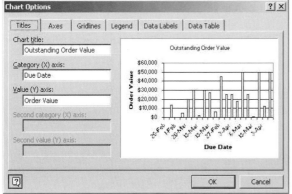

Chart Options Dialog Box   Exhibit 4–24 illustrates the Chart Options dialog box used in generating the chart in Exhibit 4–20. The chart title is **Outstanding Order Value**, the chart axes are labeled **Due Date** and **Order Value**. The Axes tab of the Options dialog box is used to control the chart axes. The Gridlines tab of the Options dialog box is used to add or remove horizontal or vertical gridlines. The Legend tab can be used to place color-coded data legends at standard locations on the chart. The user can then drag those legends to a new location. The Data Labels tab can be used to show values and/or labels for each data point. The Chart Options dialog box shown in Exhibit 4–24 can also be used to show values and/or labels for each data point.

The Excel user should be careful not to include too much data or too many labels on a single chart. The small chart in the dialog box shows the general form of the chart with the new option. If it looks too busy, omit the option.

Previous versions of Microsoft Excel contained a workbook **xl8Galry.xls** that illustrates many types of Excel charts. We have included that workbook on the textbook CD and have listed its contents in Exhibit 4–25.

Data Sorting and Filtering

Sorting is the most common data manipulation task. Sorting is often needed to rank alternatives, particularly when multiple criteria are involved. Excel provides many ways to sort lists—by rows or columns, in descending or ascending order, and using custom sorting schemes. For large datasets, finding a particular subset of records by sorting can be tedious. A more effective way is to retrieve only the subsets of the data having certain characteristics.

EXHIBIT 4–25

Excel Chart Samples: Workbook xl8Galry.xls

Sheet xl8Galry |
Chapter 4
Worksheets.xls

Worksheet	Application
Logarithmic	Horizontal bar chart
Worksheet Functions	Logarithmic line chart
Column - Area	Column chart
Lines on 2 Axes	Line chart
Line - Column on 2 Axes	Combined line and column chart
Line - Column	Combined line and column chart
Smooth Lines	Line chart
Cones	Special chart
Area Blocks	Area chart
Tubes	Stacked bar chart
Pie Explosion	Exploded pie chart
Stack of Colors	Stacked column chart
Columns with Depth	3-D column chart
Blue Pie	Pie chart
Floating Bars	Bar chart
Colored Lines	Line chart
B&W Column	Column chart
B&W Line - Timescale	Line chart
B&W Area	Area chart
B&W Pie	Pie chart

EXHIBIT 4–26
Go To Orders
Dialog Box

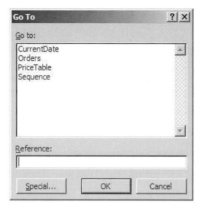

Sorts

As illustrated in Exhibit 4–1, order data is sorted by ascending Order Date. It is often useful to view this same data sorted by Due Date. To do this, first highlight the range of data to be sorted, **F5 > Orders**, as shown in Exhibit 4–26.

Then select the Sort option in the Data dialog box, **Data > Sort** (see Exhibit 4–27), and identify the row or column on which to sort and in what order. Select the field **Due Date** as the first sort key and the field **Sequence** as the second sort key using the arrow at the right. Click the **OK** button to sort the data.

EXHIBIT 4–27 Sort Dialog Box

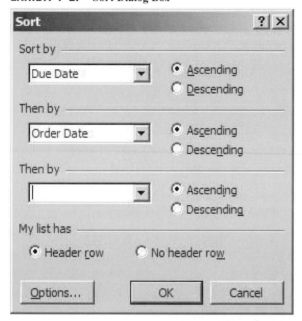

Return to the original data sequence by sorting on either the Order Date or Sequence fields. Notice in Exhibit 4–27 that the **"My list has" Header Row** option has been selected. This means that row 3 is included in the sort range as a descriptive header or field name, but row 3 is not sorted into the data.

Sorting is a very powerful tool for quickly organizing limited data sets and checking for proper data entry and/or duplicate entries. It is important to select the entire data range to be sorted. Data in columns not selected will not be sorted and could possibly become mixed in with the sorted data. A first-time user of the Sort feature will often find the Undo feature extremely helpful. It is also helpful to make a backup copy of the workbook before attempting new techniques such as sorting.

Data AutoFilter

The Excel Data AutoFilter is used to filter a list, that is, to extract all rows that meet specified criteria. Excel provides two filtering tools: AutoFilter for simple criteria and Advanced Filter for more complex criteria. Only AutoFilter is demonstrated in this text. The AutoFilter can be used sequentially to select data. In Exhibit 4–1, cells F3 and G3 have a small selection arrow in the lower right corner. These arrows are the AutoFilter selectors. AutoFilter selectors can be removed or added using the menu command sequence **Data > Filter > AutoFilter**, demonstrated in Exhibit 4–28.

EXHIBIT 4–28
AutoFilter Menu
Selection

EXHIBIT 4–29
AutoFilter
Dialog Box

Pressing the selection arrow in cell F3 of worksheet Order Book generates the dialog box illustrated in Exhibit 4–29. At this point any of the listed customers can be selected. **The All, Top 10 . . .** , and **Custom** options can also be selected.

Two columns, F and G, have been selected for AutoFiltering in the worksheet Order Book. Exhibit 4–30 illustrates the resulting display when customer **Ajax** has been selected. Three data rows of orders for customer Ajax only are displayed. Also note the values in range I2:M2 indicate only the sums for the

EXHIBIT 4–30
Order Book Filter
Sheet order book |
Chapter 4
Worksheets.xls

	A	B	C	D	E	F	G	H	I	J	K	L	M
1		Order Book	Process Analysis and Improvement: Tools and Techniques Copyright ©2005 by The McGraw-Hill Companies, Inc.			To enter data using Form, Press F5, select Orders, and Data > Form …		Sort by Due Date	Filtered Quantity	Filtered Backlog	Sort by Order Date	Filtered Shipments	Filtered Backorders
2		Current Date	2/22/2005			Right Click to Select from List		Sums	36,000	$125,000		10,000	0
3	Sequ ence	Order Date	Due Date	Lead Time Days	Slack Days	Customer	Product	Unit Price	Order Quantity	Outstanding Order Value	Shipped Date	Shipped Quantity	Backorder Quantity
4	1	1/11/2005	2/1/2005	21	-21	Ajax	Standard	$2.50	5,000	$0	2/1/2005	5,000	Shipped
7	4	1/7/2005	2/20/2005	44	-2	Ajax	Widget	$5.00	5,000	$0	2/22/2005	5,000	Shipped
8	5	1/30/2005	2/27/2005	28	5	Ajax	Improved	$4.50	10,000	$45,000			Active
9	6	1/23/2005	3/6/2005	42	12	Ajax	Widget	$5.00	6,000	$30,000			Active
23	20	2/20/2005	4/10/2005	49	47	Ajax	Widget	$5.00	10,000	$50,000			Active

displayed rows. Notice that when a column or field has been filtered, the displayed selection arrow color changes from black to blue.

Selecting the All AutoFilter option returns the full display. The Top 10 option has meaning with large sets of numerical data. The AutoFilter Custom option allows specifying two criteria for the chosen column. The criteria options include equals, does not equal, greater than, greater than or equal to, less than, less than or equal to, begins with, does not begin with, ends with, does not end with, contains, and does not contain. The two criteria may be connected by logical operators *and* or *or*. *And* implies that only records meeting both criteria will be listed, whereas *or* lists those records that satisfy either or both of the criteria. The Custom option can be used with either numerical or character data. Exhibit 4–31 illustrates the dialog box for selecting the products **Beta** and **Standard**.

The AutoFilter listing of entries in a given column is a quick approach to checking for data errors. By invoking the AutoFilter and selecting the drop-down menu for a column, a list of the values of that column appears. Incorrect values should be quickly evident when the list is displayed alphabetically in the AutoFilter dialog box (see Exhibit 4–29).

EXHIBIT 4–31   **Custom AutoFilter Dialog Box**

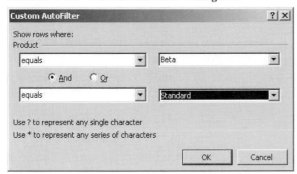

Excel Subtotal

The Filtered sums for Order Quantity, Outstanding Order Value (Backlog), Shipments, and Backorders are calculated as follows:

$$\text{I2: } = \text{Subtotal } (9, \text{I4:I23})$$

$$\text{J2: } = \text{Subtotal } (9, \text{J4:J23})$$

$$\text{K2: } = \text{Subtotal } (9, \text{K4:K23})$$

$$\text{M2: } = \text{Subtotal } (9, \text{M4:M23})$$

The Excel Subtotal (9, range) function calculates the sum of the filtered rows. Try different filtering options and see how the values in row 2 change. Exhibit 4–32 lists the Excel Subtotal functions.

EXHIBIT 4–32   **Excel Subtotal Functions**
Sheet subtotal functions | Chapter 4 Worksheets.xls

Value	Function	Function Definition
1	AVERAGE	Average or mean
2	COUNT	Cells with numeric values
3	COUNTA	Cells with data
4	MAX	Maximum value
5	MIN	Minimum value
6	PRODUCT	Product of values
7	STDEV	Sample standard deviation
8	STDEVP	Population standard deviation
9	SUM	Sum of values
10	VAR	Sample variance
11	VARP	Population variance

Challenge	**Advanced Filter**
	The Advanced Filter dialog box, depicted in Exhibit 4–33, is a more complicated version of the AutoFilter. It allows specifying criteria for filtering two or more columns simultaneously and specifying three or more restrictions for a given column. The filtering criteria are entered in a separate

EXHIBIT 4–33
Advanced Filter
Dialog Box

section of a worksheet, and the range of these criteria is an input in the Advanced Filter dialog box. The location of the list under consideration (including headers) is placed in the List range section. The range of the criteria for filtering (including headers) is placed in the Criteria range section. The Criteria range must have at least two rows (column headings that match the list and filtering criteria). If the **Copy to another location** option is selected (instead of **Filter the list, in place**), the desired location for filtered data is placed in the **Copy to section**.

Advanced-Level Excel Concepts

Analyzing Data with PivotTables

Excel provides many data analysis tools, but the PivotTable feature may be the most useful tool overall. PivotTables are valuable for summarizing information that is contained in a database, and which can be stored in a worksheet or in an external file. A PivotTable enables the creation of frequency distributions and cross-tabulations of several different data dimensions. A PivotTable is a powerful tool for summarizing statistical information for selected data contained in lists or tables within an Excel worksheet. PivotTables extend the AutoFilter capability by incorporating statistical summaries. Excel supports one-way, two-way, or three-way PivotTables.

One-way PivotTable summarize information for one factor. In this case, we place the field or factor in the row section and data in the body of the table. Placing headers in the column and page section of the PivotTable dialog box can generate two- and three-way PivotTables to summarize information for two or three factors.

A PivotTable report is an interactive table that can quickly summarize a large amount of data. Rows and columns can be rotated to see different summaries of the source data, to filter data by displaying different pages, or to display details for areas of interest. A PivotTable report can be used to compare related totals, especially when a data set is to be summarized and compared using several facts about each data element. The Excel PivotTable reports can be used for sorting, subtotaling, and totaling. A PivotTable report can be displayed in indented format, to view all the summary figures of the same type in one column, or can display the data graphically.

PivotTable Example

Exhibit 4–34 illustrates the top portion of worksheet **February | Chapter 4 Worksheets.xls**, which is used to create a PivotTable. Notice that each column contains an AutoFiltering selection arrow. Column A indicates when the account was opened. Column B indicates the opening account amount. Column C indicates the account type (Checking, CD, IRA, or Savings). Column D indicates who initially serviced the account (Manager, New Accounts, or Teller). Column E indicates the branch (Minneapolis, Richfield, Saint Paul, or Woodbury). Column F indicates the type of customer: existing or new.

EXHIBIT 4–34   PivotTable Data
Sheet February | Chapter 4 Worksheets.xls

	A	B	C	D	E	F
1	Date	Amount	AcctType	Serviced	Branch	Customer
2	2/1/2005	$15,270	CD	New Accounts	Minneapolis	Existing
3	2/1/2005	$340	Checking	New Accounts	Minneapolis	Existing
4	2/1/2005	$124	Checking	Teller	Minneapolis	Existing
5	2/1/2005	$5,879	Checking	New Accounts	Minneapolis	Existing
6	2/1/2005	$5,000	Checking	New Accounts	Minneapolis	Existing
7	2/1/2005	$50,000	Savings	New Accounts	Minneapolis	Existing
8	2/1/2005	$15,750	CD	Teller	Richfield	Existing
9	2/1/2005	$12,000	CD	New Accounts	Richfield	Existing
10	2/1/2005	$14,644	CD	Manager	Richfield	New
11	2/1/2005	$3,171	Checking	New Accounts	Richfield	Existing
12	2/1/2005	$5,000	Savings	New Accounts	Richfield	Existing
13	2/1/2005	$90,000	CD	Manager	Saint Paul	Existing
14	2/1/2005	$16,000	CD	Manager	Saint Paul	New

Creating a PivotTable is a three-step process. These steps are to

1. Identify the data source.
2. Specify the data, including headers.
3. Specify the location for the PivotTable and layout the output table. Statistics such as max, min, sum, count, average, and so on can be obtained by double-clicking on the table entry and selecting from the PivotTable dialog box.

This process is controlled by the Excel PivotTable Wizard.

PivotTable Wizard

The Excel PivotTable Wizard is launched using the **Data > PivotTable . . .** menu command. This invokes a series of three wizard dialog boxes illustrated in Exhibits 4–35 to 4–37.

Exhibit 4–35 illustrates wizard step 1 that is used to identify the data source for the PivotTable and the type of report to be generated. The data source does not need to be in Excel; however, this text will only cover the Excel option. A PivotTable can also be generated from a prior PivotTable. The PivotTable report may include a PivotChart if it contains a column chart type default.

Exhibit 4–36 illustrates wizard step 2 of 3 that is used to identify the specific data source for the PivotTable. In this example, we will use the entire worksheet February. We also could have selected only a portion of a worksheet.

Exhibit 4–37 illustrates the final wizard step, which is used to indicate the location of the PivotTable report. In this example, we have selected a new worksheet in the same workbook. Typically, at this point it is useful to click the **Layout** button to format the PivotTable report using the dialog box illustrated in Exhibit 4–38.

Exhibit 4–38 illustrates the PivotTable wizard layout dialog box. This dialog box is used to drag the PivotTable fields (worksheet column headers) to their desired location in the

EXHIBIT 4–35
PivotTable Wizard
Step 1 of 3

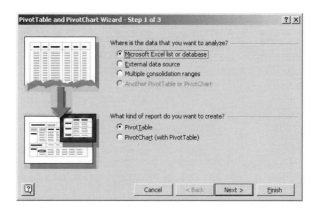

EXHIBIT 4–36 **PivotTable Wizard Step 2 of 3**

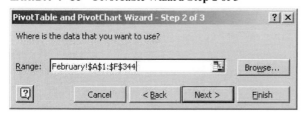

EXHIBIT 4–37 **PivotTable Wizard Step 3 of 3**

EXHIBIT 4–38
PivotTable Wizard
Layout Dialog Box

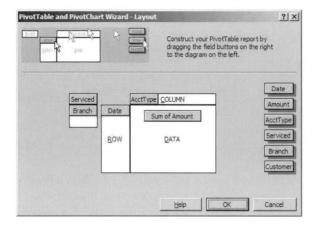

EXHIBIT 4–39
PivotTable Field
Dialog Box

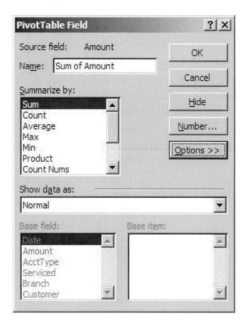

PivotTable report. The field locations are Page, Row, Column, and Data. In Exhibit 4–38, the **Serviced** and **Branch** fields were placed in the page area. **Acct Type** is used for column and **Date** for row. The data will be the **Sum of Amount** field. Double-click this box to make another selection, that is, average, count, minimum, and so forth. (See Exhibit 4–39.)

PivotTable Report

Exhibit 4–40 illustrates the PivotTable generated from the dialog boxes illustrated in Exhibits 4–35 through 4–38. The newly generated PivotTable is typically named **worksheet Sheet 1**, but was renamed for this text as worksheet **FebPivotTable**. Compare the layout of Exhibit 4–40 with the PivotTable Wizard Layout dialog box in Exhibit 4–38.

EXHIBIT 4–40
PivotTable Result
Sheet February
PivotTable | Chapter 4
Worksheets.xls

	A	B	C	D	E	F
1	Serviced	(All)				
2	Branch	(All)				
3						
4	Sum of Amount	AcctType				
5	Date	CD	Checking	IRA	Savings	Grand Total
6	2/1/2005	169357	15014		70623	254994
7	2/4/2005	182067	19565	4000	80185	285817
8	2/5/2005	114000	20100	3000	1000	138100
9	2/6/2005		15756			15756
10	2/7/2005	136852	11930	2000	19462	170244
11	2/8/2005	280443	36849	4000	33237	354529
12	2/11/2005	12505	23169	2000	10500	48174
13	2/12/2005	39019	17879	2000	76878	135776
14	2/13/2005		16000	2000	10623	28623
15	2/14/2005	54644	7291		7250	69185
16	2/15/2005	137500	31794	3000	38200	210494
17	2/18/2005	78208	11327	2000	6762	98297
18	2/19/2005			1000	840	1840
19	2/20/2005	18000	100		21000	39100
20	2/21/2005	23892	8200			32092
21	2/22/2005	407463	96397	13500	177512	694872
22	2/25/2005	90208	14090	3000	8852	116150
23	2/26/2005	13000	16979		2878	32857
24	2/27/2005	1500	6075	1000	2000	10575
25	2/28/2005	140163	21142	2000	30825	194130
26	Grand Total	1898821	389657	44500	598627	2931605

EXHIBIT 4–41
PivotTable Menu

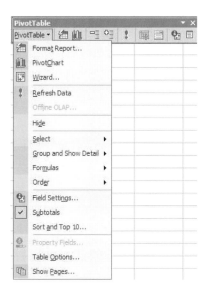

Modifying PivotTables

After a PivotTable is created, it can be modified as you like. Exhibit 4–41 illustrates the PivotTable menu that appears when the PivotTable report is selected by clicking anywhere in the PivotTable range. The PivotTable menu is used to control the following functions:

- Pivoting fields.
- Removing a field.
- Adding a new field.
- Customizing a PivotTable field.
- Formatting a PivotTable.
- Grouping PivotTable items.
- Seeing the details.
- Displaying a PivotTable on different worksheets.
- Inserting a calculated field into a PivotTable.
- Inserting a calculated item into a PivotTable.

EXHIBIT 4–42
Excel Toolbar Dialog Box

In some cases the PivotTable menu is not present or has been turned off. Right clicking on any icon and checking the PivotTable toolbar can turn it on. See Exhibit 4–42.

Notice the AutoFilter type of selection arrows on the PivotTable. These can be used to view a subset of the full data set. The individual data sets can also be separated into individual worksheets by selecting the **Show Pages** option on the PivotTable submenu, shown in Exhibit 4–42.

Fields can be dragged between the PivotTable report and the PivotTable dialog box. Use the right mouse button to find specific options for any cell in the PivotTable report. The best way to master the PivotTable feature of Excel is to experiment with some examples, until the reader understands how the feature works. Also check out Excel online, **F1**, **help**, and type **PivotTable**.

The detailed information behind any PivotTable cell can be displayed on a separate worksheet by double-clicking the cell of interest. For example, if cell B6 in Exhibit 4–40 is double-clicked, a detailed worksheet is generated for the entries that made up the $169,357 of CD deposits on 2/1/2005. Exhibit 4–43 illustrates that detailed information. Notice that the single cell in Exhibit 4–40 represents the sum of eight individual deposits.

EXHIBIT 4–43
PivotTable Detail Worksheet
Sheet February detail | Chapter 4 Worksheets.xls

	A	B	C	D	E	F
1	Date	Amount	AcctType	Serviced	Branch	Customer
2	38384	15270	CD	New Accounts	Minneapolis	Existing
3	38384	693	CD	Manager	Woodbury	Existing
4	38384	5000	CD	New Accounts	Woodbury	Existing
5	38384	16000	CD	Manager	Saint Paul	New
6	38384	90000	CD	Manager	Saint Paul	Existing
7	38384	14644	CD	Manager	Richfield	New
8	38384	15750	CD	Teller	Richfield	Existing
9	38384	12000	CD	New Accounts	Richfield	Existing

Exercises

1. Use the worksheet Order Book of workbook **Chapter 4 Worksheets.xls** to perform the following operations:

   a. Change the current date from **2/22/2005** to **3/22/2005** and note all changes in the worksheet.

   b. Indicate that all orders due in February have been shipped.

   c. Sort the data by Order Date.

   d. Add two more orders.

   e. Add a new product and include a few orders for that product.

   f. Add a new customer and include a few orders for that customer.

   g. Sort the data by Due Date.

   h. What cells are now assigned to range Orders?

2. Develop an Excel workbook to track your checking account balance. Use AutoFiltering to selectively view items. Chart your account balance over time.

3. Generate an Excel workbook that contains at least five types of charts. Use a data set of your choosing. *Hint:* Try to find the performance of a favorite stock over the past year.

4. Using data from the worksheet March of workbook **Chapter 4 Exercises.xls**, complete following tasks:

   a. Develop a PivotTable showing counts of Amount groups of $5,000 increments for various account types.

   b. Develop a PivotTable for various branches showing a data relationship between Customer and Account Opened By in terms of sum of amounts. Assume that management wants to increase deposits by 15 percent and wants to compare projected deposits to current deposits. Modify the table to reflect this change.

   c. Develop a PivotTable for various branches showing a data relationship between Account Type and Customer in terms of sum of amounts. Management wants to look at CD accounts combined with savings accounts. Include this additional item in the table just developed.

Challenge

5. Using data from workbook **Chapter 4 Exercises.xls** worksheets Store1, Store2, and Store3, which contains monthly sales data for three different stores in a music store chain. Consolidate this information into a single table for all three stores using a PivotTable.

Applications Using Excel

Summary and Learning Objectives

This chapter describes how to use advanced Excel add-in features for statistical analysis and optimization. It also demonstrates several business applications developed in Excel and explains the theory behind such applications, including Quality Function Deployment, Technology Function Deployment, Six Sigma, and Operating Repair Cycle.

The learning objectives for this chapter are to

1. Solve a linear optimization problem using Excel Solver.
2. Solve a transportation model using Excel Solver.
3. Develop technical specifications for a new product or process using Quality Function Deployment (QFD).
4. Develop a technology road map for a business operation using Technology Function Deployment (TFD).
5. Apply Six Sigma concepts and principles to improve a business process.
6. Develop an operating repair cycle for multiple machine processes.

Excel Add-In Tools

Other powerful data analysis tools are Excel add-ins. These add-ins are part of standard Excel but are not normally included in the typical software installation. Therefore, the add-ins may require separate installation by the Excel user. First, load the add-in software from the Microsoft Office or Excel CD-ROM using the menu commands **Tools > Add-Ins**; then check **Analysis ToolPak** and **Solver add-in** in the dialog box. See Exhibit 5–1.

EXHIBIT 5–1 **Excel Add-Ins Dialog Box**

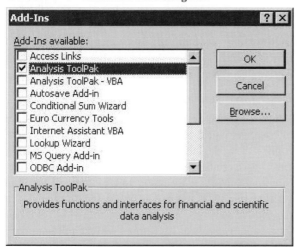

Data Analysis

The Analysis ToolPak is an add-in that provides analytical capability through various statistical analysis tools. For example, to generate Anova: Single Factor for a data set, use the following menu commands: **Tools > Data Analysis** and then select **Anova: Single Factor** from the dialog box, as illustrated in Exhibit 5–2.

After the Analysis ToolPak add-in has been installed, the statistical analysis tools listed in Exhibit 5–3 will be

EXHIBIT 5–2
Data Analysis
Dialog Box

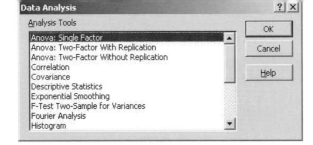

EXHIBIT 5–3
Excel Statistical
Analysis Tools
Sheet Statistical
Analysis Tools |
Chapter 5
Worksheets.xls

Tools	Major Options	Purpose
Analysis of variance	Single factor, two-factor with replication, and two-factor without replication	Determines whether two or more samples are drawn from same population or not
Correlation		Measure the degree to which two sets of data vary together
Covariance		Measure the degree to which two variables vary together
Descriptive statistics		Describes data with some standard statistics
Exponential smoothing		Predict data based on previous data point and previously predicted data point
Fourier analysis		Performs a fast Fourier transformation of a range of data
F-test		Statistical test to compare two population variances
Histogram		Produce data distributions and histogram charts
Moving average		Smooth out a data series that has a lot of variability
Random number generation	Uniform, normal, Bernoulli, binomial, Poisson, patterned, and discrete	Generate a wide variety of random numbers
Rank and percentile		Produces a table that contains the ordinal and percentage rank of each value in a data set. You can analyze the relative standing of values in a data set.
Regression	Simple linear	Determine the extent to which one range of data varies as a function of the values of one or more other ranges of data.
Sampling		Generate a random sample from a range of input values.
t-test	Paired two-sample for means, two-sample with equal variances, and two-sample with unequal variances	Determine whether a statistically significant differences exist between two small samples
z-test	Two-sample test for means	Determine whether a statistically significant differences exist between two small samples

EXHIBIT 5–4 Descriptive Statistics Dialog Box

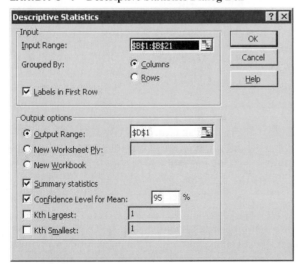

available. Two commonly used statistical analysis tools, Regression and ANOVA, are reviewed in this chapter. The Descriptive Statistics and Histograms statistical analysis tools were illustrated in Chapter 2 but are also reviewed in this section. As always, the online help key, F1, connects to available sources of information.

Descriptive Statistics

The Descriptive Statistics analysis tool performs a set of basic statistical calculations on a set of Excel data. Exhibit 5–4 illustrates the dialog box for generating descriptive statistics for the data set in worksheet Simple_DataSet. The input range was selected as B1:B21, which contains a label in the first row. The descriptive statistics will be stored starting in cell D2 of the current worksheet. The output will include summary statistics and a 95 percent confidence level for the mean.

EXHIBIT 5–5
Descriptive Statistics
Sheet Simple Data
Set | Chapter 5
Worksheets.xls

=RAND()

Mean	0.522
Standard Error	0.071
Median	0.543
Mode	#N/A
Standard Deviation	0.316
Sample Variance	0.1
Kurtosis	-1.239
Skewness	0.01
Range	0.945
Minimum	0.048
Maximum	0.994
Sum	10.43
Count	20
Confidence Level(95.0%)	0.148

Exhibit 5–5 illustrates the generated descriptive statistics. One item to note is that Excel calculates descriptive statistics only for the current data set. The descriptive statistics are not automatically updated if the data set changes. Because the values in range B2:B21 are random variables, they change every time the Recalculate key, F9, is pressed. The values in column E do not get updated.

Histogram

The Histogram analysis tool performs a set of basic statistical calculations on a set of Excel data. Exhibit 5–6 illustrates the dialog box for generating a histogram for the data set in worksheet Simple_DataSet. The input range was selected as B1:B21, which contains a label in the first row. The histogram will be stored starting in cell F2 of the current worksheet. The output will include Cumulative Percentage and Chart Output. The generation of a Histogram may involve the specification of bin or cell ranges. In this case, we used bin with the following five bin ranges: 0.0 to 0.2, 0.2 to 0.4, . . . , and 0.8 to 1.0. The selection of bin range has a great impact on the look and usefulness of the histogram. The reader should try some other bin ranges to see the impact. The resulting histogram is illustrated in Exhibit 5–7.

Like descriptive statistics, Excel histograms are not automatically updated if the data set should change. Because the values in range B2:B21 are random variables, they change every time the Recalculate key, F9, is pressed. The values in columns H and I and in the chart do not get updated. To update the histogram, recall the Histogram dialog, shown in Exhibit 5–6, and press OK to regenerate. The message shown in Exhibit 5–8 may be displayed. If so, press OK.

EXHIBIT 5–6 Histogram Dialog

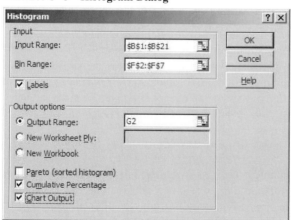

EXHIBIT 5–7 Histogram
Sheet Simple Data Set | Chapter 5 Worksheets.xls

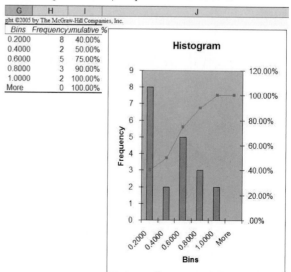

EXHIBIT 5–8
Histogram Error Message

Linear Regression

Linear regression analysis uses the "least squares" method to fit a line through a set of observations. Linear regression analysis allows the user to develop models that describe relationships between a dependent variable and one or more independent variables. These models can be used for estimation or prediction, as well as to test the significance of the relationship statistically.

The Excel user can analyze how a single dependent variable is affected by the values of one or more independent variables, for example, how an athlete's performance is affected by such factors as age, height, and weight. The Excel user can apportion shares in the performance measure to each of these three factors, based on a set of performance data, and then use the results to predict the performance of a beginning, untested athlete.

Regression models can be *linear* or *nonlinear.* Linear regression involves models for which the relationship between the dependent variable and independent variable is linear in the model parameters. Even models that appear nonlinear in the parameters often can be transformed into linear models. This text will only discuss simple linear models. *Simple linear regression* deals with a single independent variable, whereas multiple linear regressions involve several independent variables.

EXHIBIT 5–9 **Tractor Maintenance Cost Data**
Sheet Regression | Chapter 5 Worksheets.xls

Cost of Tractor Maintenance		
Observation Number	Age (years)	Annual Cost
1	4.5	$1,238
2	4.5	$2,098
3	4.5	$2,066
4	4.0	$990
5	4.0	$1,446
6	4.0	$1,362
7	5.0	$1,780
8	5.0	$3,044
9	5.5	$1,974
10	5.0	$2,388
11	0.5	$326
12	0.5	$364
13	6.0	$1,568
14	6.0	$2,746
15	1.0	$1,956
16	1.0	$932
17	1.0	$1,098

Simple Linear Regression A simple linear regression model has the following form:

$$\hat{y} = b_0 + b_1 x$$

where

b_0 is the estimated y-intercept,

b_1 is the estimated slope of the regression line, and

$\hat{y}$ is the estimated value of the dependent variable.

The values of b_0 and b_1 are calculated to provide the "best-fitting line" to the data points using the least squares measure of fit. That is, the values of b_0 and b_1 minimize the sum of squared errors, where the error for each of the data points is defined as the observed value of the dependent variable minus the fitted value of the dependent variable.

Tractor Maintenance Cost Example The tractor maintenance cost data in Exhibit 5–9 were created as worksheet Regression to demonstrate the application of regression analysis using Excel. The **Tools > Data Analysis** menu commands were followed by the selection of Regression from the dialog box illustrated in Exhibit 5–2. The Regression dialog box illustrated in Exhibit 5–10 is then displayed. The selected Regression dialog box options illustrated in Exhibit 5–10 provide the full linear regression analysis available in Excel.

EXHIBIT 5–10
Regression
Dialog Box

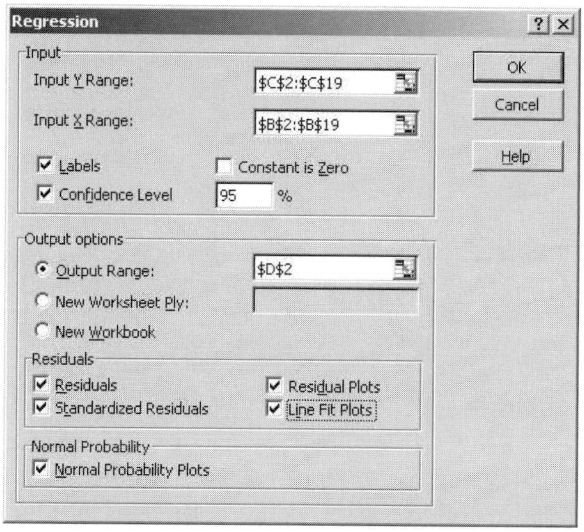

EXHIBIT 5–11
Regression Dialog Box Definitions
Sheet Regression Dialog | Chapter 5 Worksheets.xls

Label	Application
Input Y range	Enter the reference for the range of dependent data The range must consist of a single column of data
Input X range	Enter the reference for the range of independent data Microsoft Excel orders independent variables from this range in ascending order from left to right The maximum number of independent variables is 16
Labels	Select if the first row or column of your input range or ranges contains labels
Confidence level	Select to include an additional level in the summary output table In the box, enter the confidence level you want applied in addition to the default 95 percent level
Constant is zero	Select to force the regression line to pass through the origin
Output range	Enter the reference for the upper left cell of the output table Allow at least seven columns for the summary output table, which includes an ANOVA table, coefficients, standard error of y estimate, R2 values, number of observations, and standard error of coefficients
New worksheet	Click to insert a new worksheet in the current workbook and paste the results starting at cell A1 of the new worksheet To name the new worksheet, type a name in the box
New sorkbook	Click to create a new workbook and paste the results on a new worksheet in the new workbook
Residuals	Select to include residuals in the residuals output table
Standardized residuals	Select to include standardized residuals in the residuals output table
Residual plots	Select to generate a chart for each independent variable versus the residual
Line fit plots	Select to generate a chart for predicted values versus the observed values
Normal probability plots	Select to generate a chart that plots normal probability

Exhibit 5–11 defines the Excel Regression dialog box terminology.

Exhibit 5–12 illustrates the statistical summary output provided by Excel. The results listed in the table indicate that the "least squares" regression line for the data provided in Exhibit 5–9 is

$$\text{Annual cost} = \$644 + \$265 * \text{Tractor age}$$

where the value 644 is labeled as *Intercept Coefficient* and 270 is labeled as *Age (years) Coefficients* in Exhibit 5–12.

EXHIBIT 5–12

**Regression Summary
Output**

Sheet Regression |
Chapter 5
Worksheets.xls

SUMMARY OUTPUT

Regression Statistics	
Multiple R	0.695
R Square	0.483
Adjusted R Square	0.448
Standard Error	563.7
Observations	17

ANOVA

	df	SS	MS	F	Significance F
Regression	1	4,448,267	4,448,267	14.00	0.0020
Residual	15	4,767,007	317,800		
Total	16	9,215,274			

	Coefficients	Standard Error	t Stat	P-value	Lower 95%	Upper 95%
Intercept	644.18	292.21	2.20	0.044	21.35	1267.01
Age (years)	264.92	70.81	3.74	0.002	113.99	415.85

EXHIBIT 5–13

**Regression Line
Fit Plot**

Sheet Regression |
Chapter 5
Worksheets.xls

The information at the top of Exhibit 5–12 can be used to judge the quality of the data fit provided by the linear regression model. The term label *R square* is the standard statistical measure calculated by the ratio of the Regression Sum of Squares (SS) to the Total SS. In this example,

$$R^2 = 4,448,267 \div 9,215,274 = 0.483$$

The value R square represents the fraction of the total variability in the data explained or accounted for by the regression equation. Typically, it is desirable to have an R square value that is very close to one. Values greater than 0.80 are generally acceptable. Unfortunately, the data in this example are highly variable, indicated by an R square value of 0.483. This means that the regression line accounts for less than half of the observed data variability. This lack of fit is graphically illustrated in Exhibit 5–13, the Regression Line Fit Plot. The dots represent the observed data pairs, while the straight line is the regression line for the equation presented above.

Additional plots and analysis statistics are available on the worksheet Regression and are left for the reader to interpret.

Challenge

Multiple Linear Regression

Often a number of independent variables affect a single dependent variable. Regression models having several independent variables are called *multiple linear regression models.* A multiple linear regression model is of the form

$$\hat{y} = b_0 + b_1x_1 + b_2x_2 + \ldots + b_kx_k$$

where

b_0 is the estimated y-intercept,

b_j is the regression coefficient of x_j, $j = 1, 2, \ldots, k$,

x_j is the jth independent variable, $j = 1, 2, \ldots, k$, and

$\hat{y}$ is the estimated value of the dependent variable.

The same principles and concepts apply to multiple linear regressions as to simple linear regression. However, the interpretation of the coefficients of the independent variables is slightly different. In the multiple regression case, b_j is the rate of change of the dependent variable with respect to the independent variable x_j, with all other independent variables held at fixed values. In terms of its use as a predictive tool, multiple linear regression is a natural extension of the simple linear regression case. From the observed values of $x_1, x_2, \ldots, x_k$, we may estimate the value y using $\hat{y}$ from the estimated regression equation.

The goal of most regression applications is to determine which variables or factors are best predictors of the dependent variable, or have the most significant influence on the dependent variable. Thus, from perhaps a long list of possible independent variables, we seek the set of variables that gives us the "best model." One approach would be to run all possible models, that is, perform a separate regression for each possible subset of variables. The best model would be the one with the highest adjusted R^2.

If the number of possible independent variables is large, it might be too time-consuming to run regressions for all possible subsets (for n variables, there are $2^n - 1$ subsets). In these cases, good judgment must be used to decide which models to test. If two possible variables are known to be highly correlated, there is likely to be little benefit from including them both in the model, since they will correlate with the dependent variable in the same manner.

Exhibit 5–14 illustrates an expanded set of data for the tractor maintenance example. The initial linear regression analysis resulted in rather poor results, explaining only 58 percent of the total

EXHIBIT 5–14
Expanded Tractor Maintenance Cost Data
Sheet Regression Multiple | Chapter 5 Worksheets.xls

Cost of Tractor Maintenance			
Observation Number	Annual Cost	Age (years)	Hours Used
1	$1,238	4.5	900
2	$2,098	4.5	2,100
3	$2,066	4.5	1,800
4	$990	4.0	950
5	$1,446	4.0	1,200
6	$1,362	4.0	1,050
7	$1,780	5.0	1,250
8	$3,044	5.0	2,050
9	$1,974	5.5	800
10	$2,388	5.0	2,400
11	$326	0.5	250
12	$364	0.5	400
13	$1,568	6.0	1,250
14	$2,746	6.0	3,000
15	$1,956	1.0	800
16	$932	1.0	600
17	$1,098	1.0	500

EXHIBIT 5–15
Multiple Regression Summary Output
Sheet Regression Multiple | Chapter 5 Worksheets.xls

Regression Statistics	
Multiple R	0.860
R Square	0.739
Adjusted R Square	0.702
Standard Error	414.294
Observations	17

ANOVA

	df	SS	MS	F	Significance F
Regression	2	6,812,322	3,406,161	20	0.00008
Residual	14	2,402,952	171,639		
Total	16	9,215,274			

	Coefficients	Standard Error	t Stat	P-value	Lower 95%	Upper 95%
Intercept	462.77	220.24	2.10	0.05	-9.60	935.13
Age (years)	70.28	73.88	0.95	0.36	-88.18	228.74
Hours Used	0.71	0.19	3.71	0.00	0.30	1.12

variability. The additional data included total number of hours for which the tractors had been used. Exhibit 5–15 illustrates the results of the multiple regression analysis using Excel. The new equation for tractor maintenance cost is

Annual cost = $463 + $70 * Tractor age + 0.71 * Tractor hours

As illustrated in Exhibit 5–15, this new regression explains 74 percent of the data variability (R squared). This is better than the first equation, but it is still not in the 80 percent plus range typically hoped for in this type of analysis.

Analysis of Variance (ANOVA)

Process improvement requires comparing multiple population means. For example, we might wish to compare the mean sales obtained by using three different advertising campaigns in order to improve a company's marketing process. Or, we might wish to compare the mean production output obtained by using four different manufacturing processes in order to improve productivity. The Analysis of Variance (ANOVA) analysis tool performs simple tests of the hypothesis in which two or more samples are equal (drawn from populations with the same mean). The ANOVA technique expands on the tests for two means, such as the t-test.

The Excel Analysis ToolPak provides three analysis of variance tools. The tool to use depends on the number of factors and the number of samples available for testing. These factors include the following:

- **Single-factor** A single-factor ANOVA allows for the manipulation of only one factor or variable during the course of the experiment.

- **Two-factor with Replication** A two-way ANOVA with multiple samples or replication for each group of data allows for learning about both factors and their possible interrelationship.

- **Two-factor without Replication** A two-way ANOVA, with a single sample (or replication) for each group of data.

ANOVA Example To demonstrate the ANOVA procedure using Excel, a data set is presented in Exhibit 5–16. This data set was collected for the breaking strength of five fabric samples each from five different concentrations of cotton fiber. The menu commands **Tools > Data Analysis** were used followed by the selection of the appropriate ANOVA. The

EXHIBIT 5–16
ANOVA Data
Sheet ANOVA |
Chapter 5
Worksheets.xls

	A	B	C	D	E	F	G
1	**ANOVA Data Set**		Observations (Breaking Strength)				
2	**Cotton (%)**	**1**	**2**	**3**	**4**	**5**	**Average**
3	15	7	7	15	11	9	9.8
4	20	12	17	12	18	18	15.4
5	25	14	18	18	19	19	17.6
6	30	19	25	22	19	23	21.6
7	35	7	10	11	15	11	10.8
8	Source: *Applied Statistics and Probability for Engineers*, Montgomery and Runger, 2003, p. 485.						

EXHIBIT 5–17
ANOVA Dialog Box

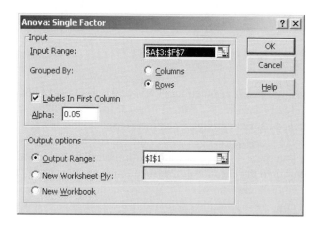

EXHIBIT 5–18
ANOVA Dialog Box Definitions
Sheet ANOVA Dialog |
Chapter 5
Worksheets.xls

Label	Application
Input range	Enter the cell reference for the range of data you want to analyze. The reference must consist of two or more adjacent ranges of data arranged in columns or rows.
Grouped by	To indicate whether the data in the input range is arranged in rows or in columns, click **Rows** or **Columns**.
Labels in first row / labels in first column	If the first row of your input range contains labels, select the **Labels in First Row** check box. If the labels are in the first column of your input range, select the **Labels in First Column** check box. This check box is clear if your input range has no labels; Microsoft Excel generates appropriate data labels for the output table.
Alpha	Enter the level at which you want to evaluate critical values for the F statistic. The alpha level is a significance level related to the probability of having a type I error (rejecting a true hypothesis).
Output range	Enter the reference for the upper left cell of the output table. Microsoft Excel automatically determines the size of the output area and displays a message if the output table will replace existing data or extend beyond the bounds of the worksheet.
New worksheet	Click to insert a new worksheet in the current workbook and paste the results starting at cell A1 of the new worksheet. To name the new worksheet, type a name in the box.
New workbook	Click to create a new workbook and paste the results on a new worksheet in the new workbook.
Rows per sample	Two-Factor with Replication dialog box: Enter the number of rows contained in each sample. Each sample must contain the same number of rows, because each row represents a replication of the data.

ANOVA dialog box illustrated in Exhibit 5–17 is then displayed. Exhibit 5–18 defines the labels or terms of the ANOVA dialog box.

Exhibit 5–19 presents the ANOVA results generated by Excel for the sample data set presented in Exhibit 5–16. For a chosen significance level $\alpha = 5$ percent (Type I error), $F_{.05,\ 4,\ 20} = 2.86608$. The F distribution can be found in most statistics textbooks or

EXHIBIT 5–19
ANOVA Results
Sheet ANOVA |
Chapter 5
Worksheets.xls

Anova: Single Factor		SUMMARY		
Groups	Count	Sum	Average	Variance
15	5	49	9.8	11.2
20	5	77	15.4	9.8
25	5	88	17.6	4.3
30	5	108	21.6	6.8
35	5	54	10.8	8.2

ANOVA						
Source of Variation	SS	df	MS	F	P-value	F crit
Between Groups	475.76	4	118.94	14.76	0.0009%	2.87
Within Groups	161.20	20	8.06			
Total	636.96	24				

generated using the Excel function, $FINV (0.05, 4, 20) = 2.86608$. Since the calculated value of F greatly exceeds the critical F test value, 2.86608, we reject the null hypothesis of no difference between groups. Therefore, based on this test we can conclude the groups, that is, cotton concentration does make a difference. Note also from the ANOVA table (Exhibit 5–19) that the P-value (associated with the calculated F-value) of 0.0009 percent is much smaller than the chosen significance level $\alpha = 5$ percent. So we reject the null hypothesis of no difference between the groups (cotton concentrates). While this analysis indicates that cotton concentration seems to make a difference, it does not provide an insight into what concentrations cause these apparent differences. Unfortunately, Excel does not automatically provide the tools needed to complete this more detailed analysis. More comprehensive statistical packages such as Minitab provide more robust ANOVA tools.

Optimization

Optimization is one of the oldest branches of science. As stated by F. C. Jelen (1970), "Optimization or the urge for efficiency has a psychological origin. The human mind can confront a task or problem and recognize more than one course of action. This recognition is followed by a second phase, the selection of what is considered the best action. The second phase is the decision step. The two steps taken together, recognition of alternatives and decision, constitute optimization."

Optimization can be *qualitative,* judged by human preference, or *quantitative,* determined by exact mathematical means. As technology advances and the industrial world becomes more competitive, methods for optimizing become more exact and the potential rewards greater. Optimization in a general sense involves the determination of a highest or lowest value over some range. Thus, a problem can be maximized for profit or minimized for loss.

In working on optimization problems, the analyst must formulate the problem in such a way as to optimize for the proper goal. This is elementary but frequently a source of error because the result depends on the goal sought. Having obtained a result, the analyst should answer the following questions:

- *Is the answer feasible or realizable?* The answer may not be feasible for several reasons. For one, physical barriers may exist. For instance, mathematical calculations may determine that for optimum conditions, water at −30 degrees F should be pumped into the tubes of a heat exchanger, but water at −30 degrees F is solid.

- *Is the answer optimal?* For instance, the apparent solution may be minimum instead of the desired maximum, or the solution may be only a local maximum.
- *How sensitive is the optimum value to the parameters and how responsive is it to a variation of the independent variables from their optimum values?* Knowledge of the sensitivity of the optimum value to the parameters is essential. The analyst should know which components are most important and require the most study, and which are insignificant and can be ignored.

Optimization Methods

Three powerful general methods are typically used for optimization: Analytical, Graphical or Tabular, and Incremental. We will briefly introduce these methods before turning to the Excel Solver.

Analytical Method for Optimization   Let the problem be to optimize Y, which is a continuously differentiable function of the single independent variable X. That is, $Y = F(X)$. Generally, an optimum value of Y will be a mathematical maximum or minimum. For this condition,

$$\frac{dY}{dX} = \frac{dF(X)}{dX} = 0$$

Graphical Method for Optimization   If $Y = F(X)$, then a tabulation and plot of Y against X over the feasible range of X will yield all the information for the optimization of Y. A plot or tabulation has the advantage of distinguishing among mathematical maxima and minima, inflexion points, and highest and lowest values. The graphical method is widely applicable and is useful when $F(x)$ is a function of single variable. In this case, the data can be analyzed in analytical, tabular, or graphical forms.

Incremental Method for Optimization   This method amounts to operating at one value of the independent variable, changing the variable somewhat, and determining by calculation or observation whether the change is advantageous. It is suitable for trial by experiment, including uncertainty in individual observations. With uncertainty, trials are repeated to establish probable values by means of statistical analysis. The incremental method is applicable to analytical or tabular data and can be used for continuous or discrete variables.

Excel Solver

The Excel Solver is another add-in that facilitates the solution of Linear and Integer Programming problems. In these problems, Excel determines values that need to be entered in multiple input cells to produce a result that is desired. Solver enables

- Specifying multiple adjustable cells.
- Specifying constraints on values that adjustable cells can have.
- Generating a solution that maximizes or minimizes a particular worksheet cell.
- Generating multiple solutions to a problem.

Problems that are suitable for Solver involve situations that meet the following criteria:

- A target cell depends on other cells and formulas.
- Typically, one wants to maximize or minimize this target cell or set it equal to some value.
- The target cell depends on a group of cells (called changing cells) that Solver can adjust to affect the target cell.
- The solution must adhere to certain limitations, or constraints.

EXHIBIT 5–20

Excel Solver Samples
Sheet SolvSamp |
Chapter 5
Worksheets.xls

Worksheet	Application
Quick tour	Solves a basic advertising/sales optimization problem
Product mix	Product mix problem with diminishing profit margin
Shipping routes	Transportation problem (3 plants and 5 regional warehouses)
Staff scheduling	Personnel scheduling for an amusement park
Maximizing income	Working capital management using 1, 3, or 6 month CDs
Portfolio of securities	Efficient stock portfolio: Sharpe single-index model
Engineering design	Value of a resistor in an electrical circuit

After the worksheet is set up appropriately, one can use Solver to adjust changing cells and produce the result that one wants in the target cell, and at the same time meet all constraints that one has defined.

Microsoft Example Workbook Previous versions of Microsoft Excel included workbook **Solvsamp.xls** that illustrates Excel Solver application. We have included that workbook on the textbook CD and have listed its contents in Exhibit 5–20. The reader is encouraged to study those Solver samples on his or her own. The next section covers two simple linear programming examples, solved using the Excel Solver.

Linear Programming Example The simple integer linear programming example solved in this section using the Excel Solver involves determining the optimal number of two products (A and B) for production, subject to a set of constraints.

Problem Definition The objective of this sample problem is to find the optimal values of X_1, the number of product A to produce and X_2, the number of product B to produce. The measure of performance in this example is total profit. Each unit of product A generates a profit of $3, while each unit of product B generates a profit of $1. The problem objective is to maximize total profit or *Z*, which is calculated with the following expression:

$$Z = \$3 * \text{NumbertoMakeA} + \$1 * \text{NumbertoMakeB}$$

The objective is to maximize the total profit or the value in cell D5. This example problem has three types of constraints:

1. The number of products A and B produced must be nonnegative.
2. Two maximum demand constraints must be met.
   a. The maximum demand for product A has a limit of 25.
   b. The maximum demand for product B has a limit of 28.
3. Two resource constraints must be met.
   a. Resource 1 has a capacity limit of 60, each unit of product A requires 2 units of resource 1 and each unit of product B requires 1 unit of resource 1.
   b. Resource 2 has a limit of 90, each unit of product A requires 1 unit of resource 1 and each unit of product B requires 3 units of resource 2.

Graphical Solution We use Visio to illustrate the feasible regions defined by the constraint set outlined in the previous problem. This Visio drawing page includes several layers, which can be selectively viewed to illustrate how the Solver example can be displayed and solved graphically. The horizontal axis represents the number of Product A, X_1, to be produced. The vertical axis represents the number of Product B, X_2, to be produced. Exhibit 5–21 illustrates constraint 1 (nonnegative) and constraint 2 (maximum) demand. Exhibit 5–22 illustrates constraint 1 (nonnegative) and constraint 3 (resource capacity) demand. These constraints are combined in Exhibit 5–23 to illustrate the combined feasible

EXHIBIT 5–21   **Solver Example Demand Constraints**
Page Solver Graph | Chapter 5 Drawings.vsd

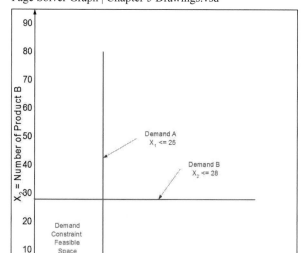

EXHIBIT 5–22   **Solver Example Resource Constraints**
Page Solver Graph | Chapter 5 Drawings.vsd

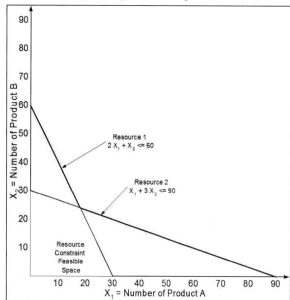

EXHIBIT 5–23   **Solver Example Combined Constraints**
Page Solver Graph | Chapter 5 Drawings.vsd

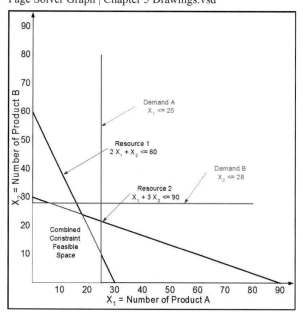

solution space. The final solution must have integer values for X_1 and X_2.

The optimal feasible solution must lie somewhere in the combined feasible space illustrated in Exhibit 5–23. One method to find the optimal solution would be to simply evaluate the total profit equation for every combination of X_1 and X_2 values in the combined feasible space. Although this may be a practical way to solve this limited example problem, it would quickly become impractical for large problems. Without going into too many details, we will illustrate the general approach taken by the Excel Solver and other Linear and Integer Program algorithms.

In Exhibit 5–24 we have superimposed three lines over the combined feasible space illustrated in Exhibit 5–23. These lines represent combinations of product mixes that would produce identical profit. These lines can be called iso-profit lines. The lower left iso-profit line represents a combination that would produce a profit of $30. This iso-profit line passes through a point representing 10 units of product A and 0 units of product B and another point representing 0 units of product A and 30 units of product B. Similar iso-profit lines are illustrated for a total profit of $60 and $90. Notice that the $90 iso-profit line is not within the combined feasible space and is, therefore, infeasible. Notice that the profit increases as we move away from the origin. Thus, the maximum or optimal profit will occur at the last point of intersection of an iso-profit line and the combined feasible space. We'll now explore how the Excel Solver finds the optimal solution.

EXHIBIT 5–24
Solver Example Combined Constraints with Objective Functions
Page Solver Graph | Chapter 5 Drawings.vsd

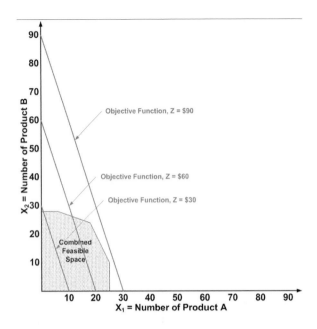

EXHIBIT 5–25
Solver Initial Model
Sheet Solver | Chapter 5 Worksheets.xls

	A	B	C	D	E	F	G
1	**Simple Linear Programming**					Process Analysis and Improvement: Tools and Techniques Companies, Inc.	Copyright ©2005 by The McGraw-Hill
2		**Product A**	**Product B**				
3	**Number to Make**	0	0	Totals			**Excel Expressions**
4	**Profit**	3	1	0	Z	Maximize	D4 = B4 * NumbertoMakeA + C4 * NumbertoMakeB
5	**Constraints**			Used		Capacity	
6	**Demand Product A**	1	0	0	<=	25	D6 = B6 * NumbertoMakeA + C6 * NumbertoMakeB
7	**Demand Product B**	0	1	0	<=	28	D7 = B7 * NumbertoMakeA + C7 * NumbertoMakeB
8	**Resource 1**	2	1	0	<=	60	D8 = B8 * NumbertoMakeA + C8 * NumbertoMakeB
9	**Resource 2**	1	3	0	<=	90	D9 = B9 * NumbertoMakeA + C9 * NumbertoMakeB

EXHIBIT 5–26 Solver Parameters Dialog

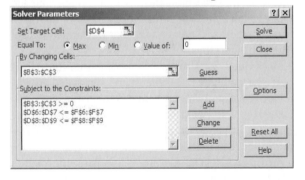

Excel Solver Solution Exhibit 5–25 illustrates the standard format for the Excel Solver. Exhibit 5–26 illustrates the Solver Parameters dialog used to set up the solution of this example.

The objective is to maximize the total profit or the value in cell D4 or Set Target cell. The Objective is selected to be Maximization. The decision variables for this problem are defined as

- X_1 = cell B3 = Label: NumbertoMakeA.
- X_2 = cell C3 = Label: NumbertoMakeB.

This example has three types of constraints:

1. The nonnegative constraints are specified as **B3:C3 >= 0**.
2. Two maximum demand constraints are specified as **D6:D7 <= F6:F7**.
3. Two resource constraints are specified as **D8:D9 <= F8:F9**.

If the Options button is clicked, the Solver Options dialog box illustrated in Exhibit 5–27 is generated. The Solver Options dialog box would be used to set up nonlinear programming problems. Exhibit 5–28 defines the labels or terms associated with the Excel Solver dialog box.

EXHIBIT 5–27
Solver Options
Dialog Box

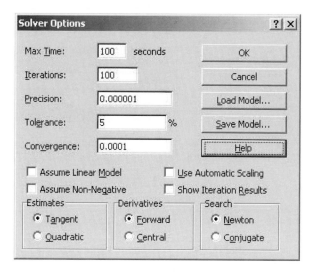

EXHIBIT 5–28   **Solver Dialog Box Definitions**   Sheet Solver Dialog | Chapter 5 Worksheets.xls

Label	Application
Set target cell	Specifies the target cell that you want to set to a certain value or that you want to maximize or minimize This cell must contain a formula
Equal to	Specifies whether you want the target cell to be maximized, minimized, or set to a specific value If you want a specific value, type it in the box
By changing cells	Specifies the cells that can be adjusted until the constraints in the problem are satisfied and the cell in the **Set Target Cell** box reaches its target The adjustable cells must be related directly or indirectly to the target cell
Guess	Guesses all nonformula cells referred to by the formula in the **Set Target Cell** box, and places their references in the By Changing Cells box
Subject to the constraints	Lists the current restrictions on the problem
Add	Displays the Add Constraint dialog box
Change	Displays the Change Constraint dialog box
Delete	Removes the selected constraint
Solve	Starts the solution process for the defined problem
Close	Closes the dialog box without solving the problem Retains any changes you made by using the Options, Add, Change, or Delete buttons
Options	See the online help, F1, for more details
Answer	Lists the target cell and the adjustable cells with their original and final values, constraints, and information about the constraints
Keep solver solution	Click to accept the solution and place the resulting values in the adjustable cells
Limits	Lists the target cell and the adjustable cells with their respective values, lower and upper limits, and target values This report is not generated for models that have integer constraints The lower limit is the smallest value that the adjustable cell can take while holding all other adjustable cells fixed and still satisfying the constraints The upper limit is the greatest value
Load model	Displays the Load Model dialog box, where you can specify the reference for the model you want to load
Reports	Creates the type of report you specify, and places each report on a separate sheet in the workbook
Reset all	Clears the current problem settings, and resets all settings to their original values
Restore original values	Click to restore the original values in the adjustable cells
Save model	Displays the Save Model dialog box, where you can specify where to save the model Click only when you want to save more than one model with a worksheet — the first model is automatically saved
Save scenario	Opens the **Save Scenario** dialog box, where you can save cell values for use with the Microsoft Excel Scenario Manager
Sensitivity	Provides information about how sensitive the solution is to small changes in the formula in the **Set Target Cell** box in the **Solver Parameters** dialog box or the constraints This report is not generated for models that have integer constraints For nonlinear models, the report provides values for reduced gradients and Lagrange multipliers For linear models, the report includes reduced costs, shadow prices, objective coefficient (with allowable increase and decrease), and constraint right-hand side ranges

EXHIBIT 5–29 **Solver Results Dialog Box**

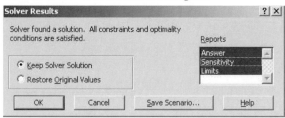

EXHIBIT 5–30 **Solver Final Solution**

Sheet Solver | Chapter 5 Worksheets.xls

	Product A	Product B			
Number to Make	25	10	Totals		
Profit	3	1	85	Z Maximize	
Constraints			Used		Capacity
Demand Product A	1	0	25	<=	25
Demand Product B	0	1	10	<=	28
Resource 1	2	1	60	<=	60
Resource 2	1	3	55	<=	90

EXHIBIT 5–31

Solver Answer Report

Sheet Answer Report | Chapter 5 Worksheets.xls

Answer Report

Target Cell (Max)

Cell	Name	Original Value	Final Value
$D$5	Profit Total	0	85

Adjustable Cells

Cell	Name	Original Value	Final Value
$B$4	NumbertoMakeA	0	25
$C$4	NumbertoMakeB	0	10

Constraints

Cell	Name	Cell Value	Formula	Status	Slack
$D$7	Demand Product A Used	25	$D$7<=$F$7	Binding	0
$D$8	Demand Product B Used	10	$D$8<=$F$8	Not Binding	18
$D$9	Resource 1 Used	60	$D$9<=$F$9	Binding	0
$D$10	Resource 2 Used	55	$D$10<=$F$10	Not Binding	35
$B$4	NumbertoMakeA	25	$B$4>=0	Not Binding	25
$C$4	NumbertoMakeB	10	$C$4>=0	Not Binding	10

When the Solve button is clicked on the Solver Parameters dialog box, the Solver Results dialog box, Exhibit 5–29, is generated. Three types of reports are available: Answer, Sensitivity, and Limits.

Exhibit 5–30 illustrates the optimal solution for the example problem. This solution generates a profit of 85 by producing 25 units of product A and 10 units of product B. The maximum demand of 25 units of product A has been satisfied. Only 10 units of the maximum demand of 28 units of product B have been satisfied. All 60 units of resource 1 have been consumed, while only 55 of the 90 units of resource 2 have been consumed.

Solver Reports The three selected reports are illustrated in Exhibits 5–31 through 5–33. These reports would normally be saved as separate worksheets: Answer Report 1, Sensitivity Report 1, and Limits Report 1.

1. **Answer Report**, shown in Exhibit 5–31 Lists target cell and adjustable cells with their original and final values, constraints, and information about constraints. The binding (slack = 0) and not binding (slack > 0) constraints are identified. The Slack indicates the amount of the constraint unused by the final solution. The capacity of resource 1 and the demand for product A are the binding constraints. Increasing the values in cells F6 or F8 will increase total profit, cell D4. The next report indicates the amount of potential profit increase.

2. **Sensitivity Report**, shown in Exhibit 5–32 Provides sensitivity of the solution to small changes in the formula in the Set Target Cell box or the constraints. For linear models, the

EXHIBIT 5–32
Solver Sensitivity Report
Sheet Sensitivity Report | Chapter 5 Worksheets.xls

Sensitivity Report

Adjustable Cells

Cell	Name	Final Value	Reduced Gradient
$B$4	NumbertoMakeA	25	0
$C$4	NumbertoMakeB	10	0

Constraints

Cell	Name	Final Value	Lagrange Multiplier
$D$7	Demand Product A Used	25	1
$D$8	Demand Product B Used	10	0
$D$9	Resource 1 Used	60	1
$D$10	Resource 2 Used	55	0

EXHIBIT 5–33
Solver Limits Report
Sheet Limits Report | Chapter 5 Worksheets.xls

Limits Report

Cell	Target Name	Value
$D$5	Profit Total	85

Cell	Adjustable Name	Value	Lower Limit	Target Result	Upper Limit	Target Result
$B$4	NumbertoMakeA	25	0	10	25	85
$C$4	NumbertoMakeB	10	0	75	10	85

report includes reduced costs, shadow prices, objective coefficient (with allowable increase and decrease), and constraint right-hand side ranges. The cells labeled *Lagrange Multiplier* indicate the potential for increased profit for each additional unit of the constraining factor. The Lagrange multipliers have a value of one for both the Demand Product A Used and Resource 1 Used. This indicates that either increase in the value in cell F6 from 25 to 26 or the value cell F8 from 60 to 61 should increase total profit from 85 to 86. The reader is encouraged to test this observation. Take note of how the values in cells B3:C3 change.

3. **Limits Report**, shown in Exhibit 5–33 Lists target cell and adjustable cells with their respective values, lower and upper limits, and target values. Lower limit is the smallest value that the adjustable cell can take while holding all other adjustable cells fixed and still satisfying the constraints. The upper limit is the greatest value.

Solver—Graphical Solution Using Visio Exhibit 5–34 illustrates a Visio drawing for the optimal solution. The last point where Objective 85 intersects the Feasible-Space represents the optimal solution: $Z = \$85, X_1 = 25$ and $X_2 = 10$.

Several observations can be made from Exhibit 5–34. Relaxing the maximum demand constraint for product A will increase profits up to a maximum of 30 units.

EXHIBIT 5–34 **Solver Graphical Solution**
Page Solver Graph | Chapter 5 Drawing.vsd

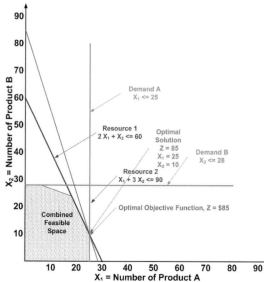

EXHIBIT 5–35
Transportation Model Supply and Demand
Sheet Supply and Demand Model | Chapter 5 Worksheets.xls

Plants	Supply Available
Georgia	310
Tennessee	260
Arizona	280
Total Supply	850

Warehouses	Demand Requirements
San Francisco	180
Denver	80
Chicago	200
Dallas	160
New York	220
Total Demand	840

Relaxing the resource 1 constraint will increase profits up to the point where resource 2 becomes binding, $Z = \$96.67$, $X_1 = 25$ and $X_2 = 21.67$ using 71.67 units of resource 1 and 90 units of resource 2. Notice that this solution does not yield an integer result.

Transportation Model Example   Logistics of transporting goods provides a vital physical link in any supply chain. The problem presented involves shipment of goods from three plants to five regional warehouses. Goods can be shipped from any plant to any wholesaler, but it obviously costs more to ship goods over long distances than over short distances. The problem is to determine the quantities to ship from each plant to each wholesaler at a minimum shipping cost in order to meet the regional demand, while not exceeding the plant supplies.

Mathematical programming has been successfully applied to a variety of important problems in supply chain management. These problems address the movement of products across various links of the supply chain, including suppliers, manufacturers, and customers. In this section, we will focus on an important subset of supply chain problems, namely, transportation. Logistics of transporting goods provides a vital physical link in any supply chain. The reason that we consider transportation separately is that these problems belong to a special class of mathematical programming problems called *network flow problems*.

Problem Definition   The transportation problem has found many practical applications because it addresses the movement of goods between two links in the supply chain, such as the manufacturer and the customer. Usually, the quantities of goods available at the supply and demand locations are known and limited. The objective is often to minimize the total cost of shipping goods from the supply to the demand locations, yet still meeting demand and not exceeding supply. We begin by formulating the fundamental version of this problem.

The problem presented involves the shipment of microwave oven units from three manufacturing plants (origins) to five regional warehouses (destinations) each week. Microwave oven units can be shipped from any manufacturing plant to any regional warehouse, but it obviously costs more to ship goods over long distances than over short distances. The problem is to determine quantities to ship from each plant to each warehouse at minimum shipping cost in order to meet regional demand, while not exceeding the plant supplies.

Plant capacities and demand at the warehouses are illustrated in Exhibit 5–35. Notice that in this case the total supply of 850 units exceeds the total demand by 10 units. A

EXHIBIT 5–36
Transportation Model Supply and Demand Map
Page Supply and Demand Map | Chapter 5 Drawings.vsd

EXHIBIT 5–37   **Shipping Costs: Plants to Warehouses**
Sheet Shipping Costs | Chapter 5 Worksheets.xls

Shipping costs from plant to warehouse	Warehouse				
Plants	San Francisco	Denver	Chicago	Dallas	New York
Georgia	$10	$8	$6	$5	$4
Tennessee	$6	$5	$4	$3	$6
Arizona	$3	$4	$5	$5	$9

feasible solution is possible. Exhibit 5–36 illustrates a map of the United States drawn in Visio with the sources (plants) and sink (warehouses) identified.

The cost of shipping microwaves by truck from each plant to each warehouse differs according to distance. The shipping cost per microwave unit for each route is given in Exhibit 5–37. For example, shipping from the Georgia plant to the San Francisco warehouse has a cost of $10 per microwave, whereas that same warehouse could be supplied from the Arizona plant for $3.

The objective is to determine the amount of microwave units that should be shipped from each plant to each warehouse. The network for this problem is given in Exhibit 5–38. The circles are referred to as *nodes* and the directed line segments connecting the nodes are called *arcs*. Each plant and warehouse is represented as a node, while each possible shipping route (origin–destination pair) is represented by an arc. Supplies and demands are

EXHIBIT 5–38
Transportation Model Network
Page Supply and Demand Map | Chapter 5 Drawings.vsd

placed next to their respective nodes. The number of microwave units shipped from the plants to the stores represents the flow in the network.

Problem Formulation and Solution Using the information given about this problem in Exhibits 5–35 and 5–37, we are now ready to formulate the transportation problem using Excel Solver. From the previous Excel Solver example we know that developing a mathematical programming problem requires first identifying the decision variables and then formulating the objective function and the constraints. Each of these three steps is described as follows.

• **Identify and Define the Decision Variables** The decision variables in this problem represent microwave oven units that are shipped from each of the plants to each of the warehouses. Since there are three plants and five regional warehouses, there are 15 possible shipping routes, and therefore, 15 decision variables.

• **Formulate the Objective Function** The objective for this problem is to minimize the total shipping cost, which is obtained by multiplying the shipping cost by the amount of microwave units shipped over a given route and then summing over all routes.

• **Formulate the Constraints** This problem is called an *unbalanced transportation problem* since the total plant supply (850 units) exceeds the total warehouse demand (840 units). This implies that all demands will be met and a portion of supplies will not be utilized. Therefore, supply constraints are needed to ensure that almost all of the microwave units that are available at each plant are shipped. Demand constraints are needed to guarantee that each warehouse receives the exact amount of microwave units needed.

The supply constraints can be stated: For each plant, the quantity of microwave units shipped to all warehouses must be less than or equal to the supply of the plant. For example, from Exhibit 5–38 we see that there are five arcs leaving each plant. The sum of the amount of microwave units shipped over these five arcs or routes must be less than or equal to the plant's supply.

The demand constraints are expressed as follows. For each warehouse, the quantity of microwave units shipped from all plants must equal the demand of the warehouse. For example, from Exhibit 5–38 we see that there are three arcs entering each warehouse. The sum of the quantity of microwave units shipped over these three arcs or routes must equal the warehouse's demand.

We assume that this company cannot make fractional microwave unit shipments. This means that the decision variables must be integer valued. One extension of this transportation problem is when faced with a restricted route(s). For example, suppose there is a strike by the shipping company such that the route from plant 2 to warehouse 3 cannot be used. The original model can be modified to address this situation by simply adding a constraint that guarantees that zero units of microwave will be shipped from plant 2 to warehouse 3.

The Excel Solver was introduced here in Chapter 5; we will now apply that tool to find an optimal solution to the Transportation Problem.

Transportation Model Specifications The objective of this transportation model is to minimize the costs of shipping goods from production plants to warehouses near metropolitan demand centers, while not exceeding the supply available from each plant but still meeting the demand from each metropolitan area. These problem specifications are summarized in Exhibit 5–39 along with their link to the worksheet Cell Ranges.

Excel Solver Solution A problem of this type has an optimum solution only if the quantities to ship are integers, and all of the supply and demand constraints are integers. Exhibit 5–40 illustrates the Excel Solver worksheet for the transportation problem.

EXHIBIT 5–39
**Transportation
Model Specifications**
Sheet Transportation
Specifications |
Chapter 5
Worksheets.xls

Component	Cell Range	Operator	Limit	Comment
Target cell (objective)	B19			Goal is to minimize total shipping cost
Changing cells (decision variables)	C7:G7			Amount to ship from each Plant to each Warehouse
Constraint 1	B7:B9	<=	B15:B17	Total shipped must be less than or equal to supply at plant
Constraint 2	C11:G11	>=	C13:G13	Totals shipped to warehouses must be greater than or equal to the demand at warehouses
Constraint 3	C7:G9	>=	0	Number to ship must be greater than or equal to 0

EXHIBIT 5–40   **Excel Solver Transportation Model**
Sheet Transportation Model | Chapter 5 Worksheets.xls

		Total	San Fran	Denver	Chicago	Dallas	New York
3	Color Coding Changing cells		Constraints		Target cell		
5		Number to ship from plant x to warehouse y (at intersection):					
6	Plants:	Total	San Fran	Denver	Chicago	Dallas	New York
7	Georgia	0	0	0	0	0	0
8	Tennessee	0	0	0	0	0	0
9	Arizona	0	0	0	0	0	0
11	Totals:		0	0	0	0	0
13	Demands by Warehouse -->		180	80	200	160	220
14	Plants:	Supply	Shipping costs from plant x to warehouse y (at intersection):				
15	Georgia	310	10	8	6	5	4
16	Tennessee	260	6	5	4	3	6
17	Arizona	280	3	4	5	5	9
19	Totals:	$0	$0	$0	$0	$0	$0

EXHIBIT 5–41
Excel Solver Dialog

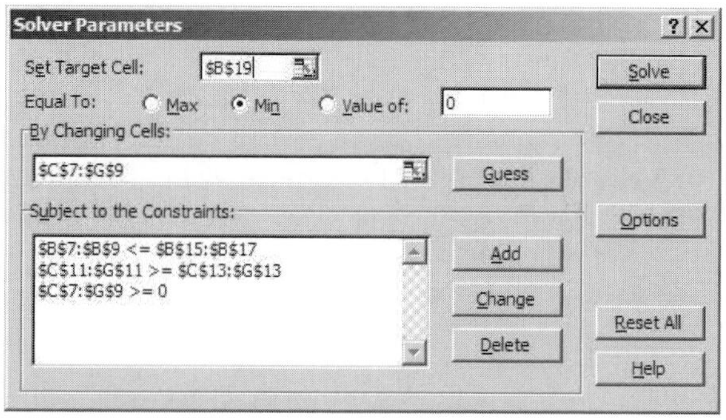

Solver Parameters

Set Target Cell: $B$19

Equal To: ○ Max ● Min ○ Value of: 0

By Changing Cells:
$C$7:$G$9

Subject to the Constraints:
$B$7:$B$9 <= $B$15:$B$17
$C$11:$G$11 >= $C$13:$G$13
$C$7:$G$9 >= 0

[Solve] [Close] [Guess] [Options] [Add] [Change] [Delete] [Reset All] [Help]

You can solve this problem faster by selecting the **Assume linear model** check box in the Solver Options dialog box before clicking **Solve**. Exhibit 5–41 illustrates the Excel Solver dialog for the transportation problem.

Exhibit 5–42 illustrates the optimal Excel Solver solution for the transportation problem.

This optimal solution has a total cost of $3,200. It ships 300 units from the Georgia plant to the warehouses in Dallas (80) and New York (220). The 260 units from the Tennessee plant are shipped to the warehouses in Dallas (80) and Chicago (180). The 280 units from the Arizona plant are shipped to the warehouses in San Francisco (180), Denver (80), and Chicago (20). Notice that 10 units at the Georgia plant are not shipped. Exhibit 5–43

EXHIBIT 5–42
Transportation Model Solution
Sheet Transportation Model | Chapter 5 Worksheets.xls

Color Coding	Changing cells		Constraints		Target cell	
		Number to ship from plant x to warehouse y (at intersection):				
Plants:	**Total**	**San Fran**	**Denver**	**Chicago**	**Dallas**	**New York**
Georgia	300	0	0	80	0	220
Tennessee	260	0	0	100	160	0
Arizona	280	180	80	20	0	0
Totals:		180	80	200	160	220
Demands by Warehouse -->		180	80	200	160	220
Plants:	**Supply**	**Shipping costs from plant x to warehouse y (at intersection):**				
Georgia	310	10	8	6	5	4
Tennessee	260	6	5	4	3	6
Arizona	280	3	4	5	5	9
Totals:	$3,200	$540	$320	$980	$480	$880

EXHIBIT 5–43
Transportation Model Solution
Page Supply and Demand Map | Chapter 5 Drawings.vsd

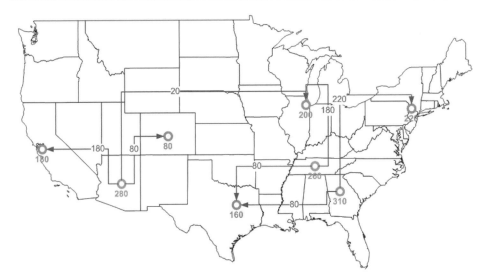

provides a visual representation of the optimal shipping routes solution to the example transportation problem drawn using Visio.

Quality Function Deployment (QFD)

Quality Function Deployment (QFD) was developed in Japan in 1972. It is a highly structured format used to translate customer value requirements into specific product and service characteristics, and ultimately into the processes and systems that provide the valued products and services. The aim of QFD is to translate customer needs or wants into detailed technical requirements, and to set priorities using competitive data. QFD should help organizational processing activities and outputs match customer wants (Cole, 1989).

QFD calls for a structured process of converting customer requirements into product design and manufacturing needs. It is a management planning technique wherein group discussions among concerned personnel are held and a clear consensus on how the customer needs are to be achieved is reached. QFD can be used in any phase of production. For example, for the entire facility, the customer may be the ultimate consumer of the product, whereas within the plant, the consumer may be the next sequential department to process the part. QFD is also used to compare a product against its competitors in the market.

EXHIBIT 5–44 **Structure of House of Quality**
Page House of Quality | Chapter 5 Drawing.vsd

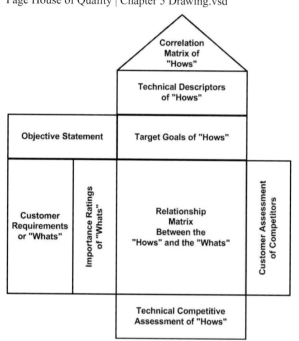

Development of QFD may start with identifying the customer (internal or external to the organization) and his or her wants. Questions such as *what, when, where, why,* and *how* the customer will use the product should help in identifying his or her needs. Exhibit 4–20 illustrated a cause and effect diagram indicating the what, when, where, why, and how concerns related to the development of a coffeemaker.

Exhibit 5–44 illustrates the components of the "house of quality" on which the QFD matrix is built.

A typical QFD matrix is shown in Exhibit 5–44. On the left side of Exhibit 5–44 are the customer requirements: what the customer wants in the product or service. The top of the QFD matrix shows the manufacturer's or service provider's requirements, what the manufacturer or service provider does to ensure the consistency of the product or service. These can be items that are measured by the manufacturer or service provider and are specified by suppliers.

The right side of the QFD matrix indicates the planning matrix. This matrix specifies the level of services or product to be provided or produced after evaluating the customers' priorities and the competition. The QFD team selects the services or product attributes which have the greatest potential for success in the marketplace. This is achieved by assigning weights to product or service characteristics or attributes. The peak of the QFD matrix represents the manufacturer's or service provider's requirements. This is where viable product or service attributes trade-offs are identified. By identifying viable trade-offs at an early stage, product or service designers can narrow their development efforts, thereby speeding up the development cycle.

The body of the QFD matrix translates customers' requirements into manufacturer's or service provider's terms. It is also where interactions among several interest groups are identified so that the synergistic effect can be seen. The bottom of the QFD matrix is the prioritized manufacturer's or service provider's requirements. This identifies the requirements that are most critical for the success of the product or service. The degree of technical difficulty to achieve goals is also indicated in this matrix.

As shown in Exhibit 5–44, QFD employs a "what-how" matrix listing of customer wants (the "what"), technical requirements (the "how"), and competitive assessments using customers' subjective perceptions and the organization's own objective engineering measurements (King, 1989). Thus, QFD provides a way to integrate and subordinate specialized functions and departments into coordinated, collaborative activity that provides customer value. While many organizations will choose not to use such a structured technique, they will have to write operational definitions that clearly articulate the means of providing value to customers. These definitions will have to be translated into processes and operations to produce products and services. QFD simply provides the structured methodology that promotes communication among specialized experts who must do this work. There is more to QFD than simply filling out a "house of quality" matrix. It involves implementing a customer-oriented philosophy (Hauser and Clausing, 1988).

The principal advantage of the QFD approach over other mechanisms is that it integrates, at a system level, different departmental activities through common task requirements. This minimizes deviation from customer wants throughout the product design and production cycle (Cole, 1989). Companies that use QFD can achieve a competitive advantage by delivering products and services that customers want. These outputs will be efficiently and effectively designed and delivered more quickly than those of competitors.

Implementing the QFD Process

The house of quality is the first step in negotiating what suppliers agree the product design will achieve for customers. It defines those cost-effective design attributes that can be delivered to achieve customer's perceptions of value. QFD has stages similar to the traditional U.S. phase-review development process (Anderson, 1997). However, with the simultaneous consideration of customer needs, engineering capabilities, and process analysis, QFD can contribute to continuous cross-functional participation from start to finish and can generate consensus decisions about trade-off (Griffin, 1992). The QFD process helps team members from each department to understand external customer values and their contribution to the systems and processes that provide the value. This understanding provides a basis for cross-functional teamwork and collaboration. The worksheet QFD Template is provided as a blank template that can be utilized to implement the QFD process.

Coffeemaker Example

In this example, we will translate customers' comments into product design attributes and develop a QFD chart, Exhibit 5–45. This is a cross-matrix chart that shows a correlation between customer needs and how these needs can be achieved by proposed design features. Before entering the needs into the chart, however, the customer's raw statements should be evaluated and identical needs that are worded differently should be consolidated into one logical statement. This prevents one demand feature from being repeated several times in the chart.

The design attributes are listed after considerable discussion between the team members. Typically, such a group may consist of the design engineer, a manufacturing engineer, a marketing person, and other administrative personnel. For example, good taste is a function of the rate of steam flow through the coffee grounds. Flow, in turn, is a function of the number of cups of coffee to be made. A variable heater setting that controls the wattage would

EXHIBIT 5–45
Quality Function Deployment Coffee Maker Example
Sheet QFD Coffee Maker | Chapter 5 Worksheets.xls

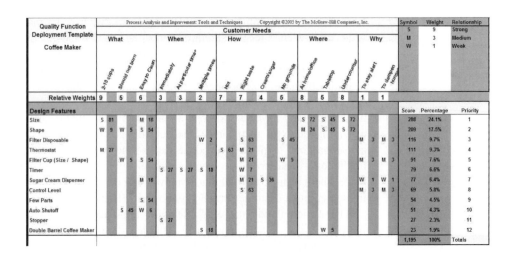

ensure uniform steam generation and assure a consistent taste. Thus, the design of the control level is included in the QFD. The QFD chart not only lists the positive relations between the needs and proposed design features but also notes any negative effects. For example, a double-barrel coffeemaker (a two-filter system, with one used to make the first pot and another used to make the second pot without refilling the coffee) would not be easy to clean, and may be indicated by an X.

The stage is now set to determine which design features should be included in the product. Again, a group discussion can lead to a subjective assignment of weights for each consumer statement. Factors that may influence the weight include possible sales potential, features of a competing product, production feasibility, reliability, and quality. The row labeled Relative Weights indicates the importance of each customer need. For instance, under the "what" criteria, "capacity of 2 to 10 cups" carries a relative weight of 9, whereas another attribute, "It should be easy to clean," carries a relative weight of 6, thus is only two-thirds as important. These may be high weights compared to some other categories such as, "when" or "why" categories, probably because of the designers' subjective opinions as to what may sell. There will also be relationship symbols, which also carry a weight (relationships could be Strong, Medium, or Weak carrying weights of say 9, 3, and 1 respectively). The product of relationship weight and relative weight is noted for each entry in the matrix itself. The sum of all products for each column determines the score for that design feature. The relative importance of a design feature is obtained by dividing the score for the feature by the sum of the scores for all design features.

Technology Function Deployment (TFD)

In a rapidly changing marketplace, enterprises must have a very clear understanding of the company's technological needs and opportunities. The enterprises' plans must be sufficiently detailed so that they identify what technology is needed, when the technology is expected to be used, and who will be involved in developing it. Resources must be committed to assure that plans are met. The enterprise that expects to use technology as a potential tool to compete must assure that its technology plans are fully supportive of the overall business plan. The product cycle plan, which is part of an overall business plan, shows detailed plans of new product launches, upgrades of existing products, and obsolete products that have completed their useful life. The final result of this planning process should be a road map of the enterprise's technological needs that involve a consensus understanding of the risks associated with this plan in terms of timing, costs, and capabilities of the organization.

The approach to accomplishing this road map will involve asking numerous questions concerning the needs for technology as well as exploring opportunities that technology may offer to the enterprise. To formalize answers to these questions, we use a number of matrices that encourage the exploration of the important questions by involving all segments of the enterprise. These matrices are tools to assist the enterprise and their principal value is not in their completion, but in the assistance they offer in assuring that questions are not omitted inadvertently. These matrices are part of the Technology Function Deployment process, which is intended to provide managers of technology with a procedure that will help them to support the proper technology at the proper time with the proper level of resources.

The Technology Function Deployment process is implemented by constructing a set of four matrices and a technology road map:

1. Matrix I, Technology Needs as Determined by Plans for Products, Processes, and Services

2. Matrix II, Consolidated Technological Needs Determined by Plans for Products, Processes, and Services

3. Matrix III, Assessment of Opportunities Presented by Technology

4. Matrix IV, Need for New Engineering and Systems Tools

5. Technology Road map

Let us go over how you would complete various matrix templates. We provide here a real-life industry example where the TFD process is applied. It pertains to enhancing the cleaning capability of the Advanced Technology Vacuum Cleaner. After each template is introduced, the corresponding example matrix is illustrated for an Advanced Technology Vacuum Cleaner.

Matrix I, Technology Needs

The Technology Function Deployment Matrix I Template is used to specify technology needs as determined by plans for products, processes, and services. Matrix I identifies and prioritizes technologies needed in support of the attribute to be incorporated in a given product.

We start by listing the following product cycle plan information:

1. Product description.
2. Expected date of introduction.
3. Estimated sales by year for first three years.
4. Customer.
5. Competitors.
6. Competitor product.
7. Best-in-class product.

We next use the following steps to facilitate the completion of matrix I:

- Consider an important attribute, which was introduced with this product.
- List the associated developments needed to introduce this attribute in the proposed product.
- Identify the supporting technology or technologies needed for each development initiative.
- Classify each technology as B for base; CA for competitive advancement; or R for revolutionary.
- Assign a number based on a scale of 1 to 10 (1 is low, 10 is high) to rate the availability of each technology.
- Assign a number based on a scale of 1 to 10 (1 is low, 10 is high) to rate the capability of the firm to develop this technology.
- Assign a number based on a scale of 1 to 10 (1 is low, 10 is high) to rate the likelihood of success in utilizing such technology.
- Add the rankings of each technology relative to its availability, capability of the firm to develop the technology, and its likelihood of success in utilizing such technology.
- Provide a preliminary assessment of the technology. Should it be pursued aggressively (A)? Considered further (F) for evaluation? Or should its implementation be delayed?

The matrix I template is found as worksheet **TFD Matrix I** of Chapter 5 Worksheets.xls. Template rows should be added or removed as required to define the product. Exhibit 5–46 illustrates a completed matrix I for an Advanced Technology Vacuum Cleaner.

EXHIBIT 5–46
Technology Function Deployment Matrix I Vacuum Example
Sheet TFD Matrix I Vacuum | Chapter 5 Worksheets.xls

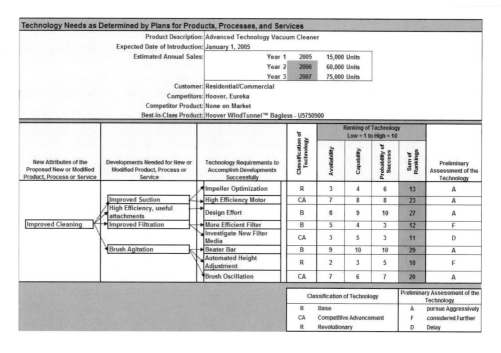

EXHIBIT 5–47
Technology Function Deployment Matrix II Vacuum Example
Sheet TFD Matrix II Vacuum | Chapter 5 Worksheets.xls

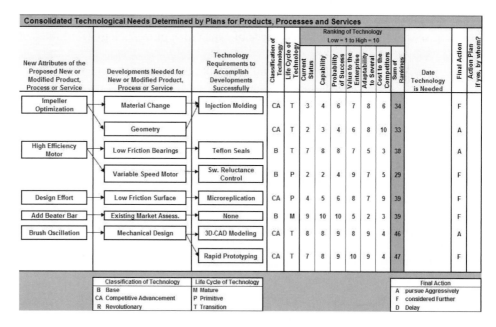

Matrix II, Consolidated Technological Needs

The Technology Function Deployment Matrix II Template is used to specify the consolidated technological needs determined by plans for products, processes, and services. This matrix consolidates the technological needs consisting of various products (new or enhanced) planned for development and introduction to market. Worksheet template rows should be added or removed as required to define the product. Exhibit 5–47 illustrates a completed matrix II for an Advanced Technology Vacuum Cleaner.

Matrix III, Assessment of Opportunities

The Technology Function Deployment Matrix III Template is used to specify the assessment of opportunities presented by technology. The matrix III template is found as worksheet **TFD Matrix III** of Chapter 5 Worksheets.xls. Worksheet template rows should be added or removed as required to define the assessment of opportunities presented by the technology. This matrix provides an assessment of opportunities presented by various technologies (other than those identified in matrices I and II), which are of interest to the enterprise.

The following steps facilitate the completion of matrix III:

- List the technologies of interest to a given enterprise. Do not list technologies identified in Matrix I and Matrix II.
- Indicate which product attribute the identified technology will support.
- Indicate what level of knowledge of the technology the firm has (high, medium, or low).
- Indicate the probability of successful technology development (high, medium, or low).
- Identify the level of maturity of the technology that will be challenged by this new technology (P for primitive, T for in transition, or M for mature).
- List key problems to be addressed prior to implementation of the new identified technology.
- List how you will have to respond to the competitor for the new technology (urgent, moderate, or no response).
- Indicate the desirability of the technology for further consideration (yes or no).
- Indicate who will be responsible for the detailed assessment of technology.
- Indicate the mode of exploration of technology (I for internal, E for external, or J for joint).
- Indicate who will be responsible for the action plan.
- Indicate who will have final responsibility for the program.
- Indicate the reviewing authority for the program (may be some committee).

Exhibit 5–48 illustrates a completed Matrix III for an Advanced Technology Vacuum Cleaner.

EXHIBIT 5–48

Technology Function Deployment Matrix III Vacuum Example
Sheet TFD Matrix III Vacuum | Chapter 5 Worksheets.xls

Proposed Technological Opportunities	New or Modified Products, Processes, or Services that Technology May Allow	Level of Knowledge	Probability of Success	Life Cycle of Competing Technology	Key Problems that must be Solved Before Technology Can Be Used Successfully	Assessment of Competitors Response	Desirability Further Consideration	Detailed Assessment (if yes, by whom)	Mode of Exploration	Action Plan (if yes, by whom)	Final Responsibility for Program	Review Authority
Variable Speed, Higher Efficiency Motor	Better Suction, Lower Power Required, Easier Vacuuming of Loose Rugs	High	High	M	Cost, MTBF	Protect Existing Technology	High	Yes-Engineering, Marketing	Internal	Yes-Engineering, Marketing	Electrical Engineering	V.P. Engineering
Low Friction Bearings	Better Suction, Longer Life	Medium	Medium	T	Cost	Protect Existing Technology	Low	No		n/a	n/a	n/a
High Strength Plastic Impeller	Lighter Weight, Better Suction	Medium	Medium	T	Strength, Materials Aging	Investigate New Technologies	Medium	Yes-Engineering	Joint	Yes-Engineering	Mechanical Engineering	V.P. Engineering
Use of Recycled Plastics	Better for the Environment	Low	High	T	Availability, Strength, Materials Aging	Investigate New Technologies	Medium	Yes-Engineering, Marketing	External	Yes-Engineering	Mechanical Engineering	V.P. Marketing
Bio-Degradable Bag Material	Better for the Environment	Low	Low	P	Availability, Durability, Shelf Life	Protect Existing Technology	Low	No		n/a	n/a	n/a
Dirt Sensing Technology	Better User Knowledge of Cleanliness	High	High	M	Cost, MTBF	Protect - Technology Already Deployed	High	Yes-Engineering, Marketing	Internal	Yes-Engineering, Marketing	Electrical Engineering	V.P. Engineering
Optimized Impeller Design	Better Suction	Low	Low	T	ROI, Amount of Improved Airflow	Protect Existing Technology	Low	No		n/a	n/a	n/a

Level		Life Cycle of Technology		Mode	
High		M	Mature	Internal	
Low		P	Primitive	External	
Medium		T	Transition	Joint	

Assessment of Opportunities Presented By Technology

Matrix IV, Need for New Engineering and Systems Tools

The Technology Function Deployment Matrix IV Template is used to specify the need for new engineering and systems tools. This matrix lists various technologies that are needed for the development of the identified engineering and system tools.

The following steps facilitate the completion of matrix IV:

- List the engineering and system needs for a given enterprise.
- Indicate the new tools needed to satisfy engineering and system needs of the enterprise.
- List the tasks required to provide the new tools for the enterprise.
- In the next three columns, provide a ranking on the basis of 1 to 10, with the highest being 10, of three items that will strongly influence whether the enterprise will choose to give further consideration to the exploration of technology.
    - *The adequacy of the technology* applies to whether the current level of development of the technology is adequate for the new tool.
    - *The availability of technology* applies to whether the person in charge of the technology will refuse to provide it or will demand an unreasonable price. It gauges whether the technology can readily be available for your use.
    - *The expected lifetime of the tool* refers to the probable period of time that the tool will be useful to the organization. A tool that can be expected to be used over a long period of time will have a high ranking.
- Add the rankings of each technology relative to its adequacy, availability, and expected lifetime. A high value suggests that the technology and the expected value of the tools over a long period of time are good.
- Next, make a preliminary conclusion as to the desirability of proceeding further. This decision is based on perceived needs, the fact that new tools are appropriate, that the tasks that are required to provide the tools are not excessive, and the sum of the rankings for the technology.
- Try to ascertain whether a detailed technology assessment is needed.
- Establish a realistic date for completion of the tool.
- We then decide on the mode of exploration of the tool, which could be internal, external, or joint based on such factors as the availability of the proper internal technical capability, an understanding of the system by a group outside the company, the desirability and capability of controlling the dissemination of results, and probable costs of each mode.
- Based on the previous information, make a decision about the desirability of pursuing the development of the tool or delaying further consideration.
- If it is the conclusion that further action is warranted, indicate the need for a plan that will provide preliminary details concerning timing and costs.
- Identify who will be responsible for carrying out the final program.
- Identify the person or committee who will have continual purview over the progress of the program, recognizing that the development of some tools requires a long-term commitment.

The matrix IV template is found as worksheet **TFD Matrix IV** of Chapter 5 Worksheets.xls. Worksheet template rows should be added or removed as required to define the need for new engineering and systems tools. Exhibit 5–49 illustrates a completed Matrix IV for an Advanced Technology Vacuum Cleaner.

EXHIBIT 5–49
Technology Function Deployment Matrix IV Vacuum Example
Sheet TFD Matrix IV Vacuum | Chapter 5 Worksheets.xls

Need for New Engineering and Systems Tools

Engineering and System Needs	New Tools Needed to Satisfy Needs	Tasks Required to Provide the New Tools	Ranking of Technology Low = 1 to High = 10				Desirability Further Consideration	Detailed Assessment (if yes, by whom)	Expected Completion Date	Mode of Exploration	Recommended Action	Action Plan (if yes, by whom)	Final Responsibility for Program	Review Authority
			Adequacy	Availability	Expected Lifetime of Tool	Sum of Rankings								
Noise Modeling	Noise Simulation Software	Product Evaluation, Vendor Evaluation, Training and Procurement	8	10	8	26	High	No	10/1/2002	Joint	Consider Further	Yes Mech. Eng.	Mech. Eng.	V.P. Eng.
Air Flow Modeling	Air Flow Simulation Software	Product Evaluation, Vendor Evaluation, Training and Procurement	9	10	8	27	High	Yes Mech. Eng.	9/1/2002	Joint	Aggressive	Yes Mech. Eng.	Mech. Eng.	V.P. Eng.
Calibrated Particulate Measurement System	Particulant Measurement Apparatus	Product Evaluation, Vendor Evaluation., Training and Procurement	5	2	7	14	High	Yes Mech. Eng.	2/1/2002	Joint	Consider Further	Yes Elect. Eng.	Elect. Eng.	V.P. Eng.
Accelerated Plastics Life Testing	Oven, Chemical Bath	Define Tests, Evaluation Oven, Evaluation needed chemicals, Training and Procurement	10	10	7	27	High	Yes Mech. Eng.	1/1/2002	Internal	Aggressive	Yes Mech. Eng.	Mech. Eng.	V.P. Eng.
Plastics Durability Testing	Oven, Test Fixture	Define Tests, Training and Procurement	5	10	6	21	High	Yes Mech. Eng.	10/1/2002	Joint	Aggressive	Yes Mech. Eng.	Mech. Eng.	V.P. Eng.
Accelerated Motor Life Testing	Load Simulator	Define Tests, Evaluation System and Procurement	10	10	8	28	High	No	12/15/2002	Internal	Aggressive	No	Elect. Eng.	V.P. Eng.
Noise Measurement	Calibrated Sound Measurement System	Competitive Evaluation, Procurement	10	10	10	30	High	No	11/1/2002	External	Aggressive	No	Mech. Eng.	V.P. Eng.

High
Low
Meduim

Mode	Recommended Action
Internal	Aggressive
External	Consider Further
Joint	Delay

EXHIBIT 5–50
Technology Road Map
Sheet Technology Roadmap Vacuum | Chapter 5 Worksheets.xls

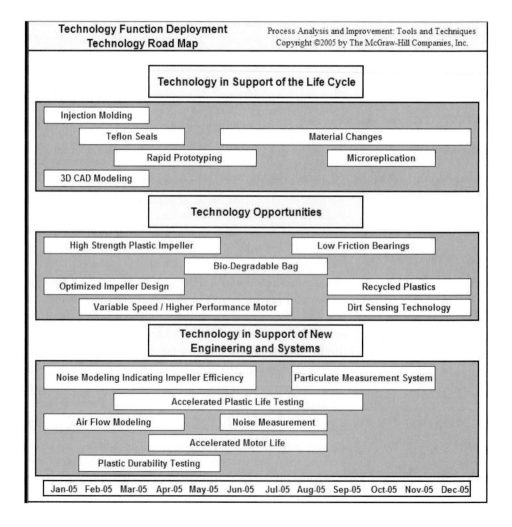

Technology Road Map

The Technology Road Map Template presents the technology plan or road map that the enterprise will follow in the years ahead. It provides a description of all technologies that will be under study by the enterprise in the time frame extending to at least the end of the cycle plan for the new products and perhaps longer for the exploration of new technological opportunities and for the development of new engineering tools and technologies. This technology road map is what is illustrated in Exhibit 5–50 on the previous page. The technology road map indicates the time period during which each activity should be accomplished. It is at this point that final budgets and plans for each technology must be finalized.

The technology road map template is found as worksheet **Technology Road map** of Chapter 5 Worksheets.xls. Worksheet template columns and rows can be added or removed as required to define the technology road map. Due to its graphical nature, Visio might be considered as the tool for developing the technology road map.

The authors strongly believe TFD is an important tool for companies in formulating a strategic product plan for identifying and planning for technologies to support products and processes.

Six Sigma Calculations Using Excel

Motorola started the Six Sigma Quality Program in January 1987. It was a corporate program that established Six Sigma as the required capability level to approach the standard of zero defects in products, process, services and administration. The Six Sigma Quality Program was defined at two levels. The first is the managerial level in which every individual belonging to the organization is responsible for his or her process, product, and service by improving its quality to six sigma performance levels to attain total customer satisfaction. The second is the operational level, which requires the use of statistical metrics such as process potential (C_p), process capability (C_{pk}), Sigma, parts-per-million (ppm), and defects-per-unit (dpu) to characterize both manufacturing processes and non-manufacturing processes such as administrative, service, or transactional operations. The following Six Sigma calculations are based on the assumption that the underlying process follows the normal probability distribution. Proof of this assumption is beyond the scope of this text.

The approach used was to continuously improve the process from a system's standpoint. That is, products and processes had to be designed to be Six Sigma. The results of such design efforts were to reduce variation, improve quality, enhance productivity, and provide greater ease and efficiency in the operation of the process and building the product. This could be done only by characterizing, optimizing, and controlling the total process, not just parts of the total process. It was equally important to reduce or eliminate errors and mistakes in all administrative, service, and transactional processes in order to provide total customer satisfaction. Motorola applied the same concepts of quality to all aspects of their business.

EXHIBIT 5–51
Six Sigma Chart
Sheet 6 Sigma
Calculations |
Chapter 5
Worksheets.xls

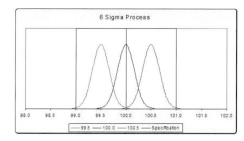

Motorola defined Six Sigma as having plus or minus six sigma ($\pm 6\sigma$), or process standard deviations, within specification limits. Exhibit 5–51 illustrates the basic Six Sigma process concepts. That is, given a particular product characteristic, which has a design specification, that design specification has both an upper specification limit (USL) and a lower specification limit

(LSL). These two limits demarcate a design tolerance. In this example, we have a process with a requirement to produce parts with a critical dimension or design specification of 100 ± 1 mm. The actual distribution of part sizes assuming a centered–six sigma process is illustrated by the bell-shaped normal distribution curve.

Motorola held that the design tolerance should be such that it should fit within 12 standard deviations or $\pm$ six sigma. In their explanation of "Why Six Sigma?" Motorola asserted that if a process were made to be six sigma by having the design specifications twice the process width, the process would be extremely robust. Even if the process encountered a significant or detrimental shift in average, as high as $+1.5$ sigma, the customers would not perceive degradation in quality. At the worst case, a shift of 1.5 sigma would make a zero-defects product to be 3.45 ppm, and the customer would only perceive an increase of from zero to three products defective, assuming a production run of 1 million.

For an organization to implement a Six Sigma Quality Program means delivering top-quality service and products, while at the same time eliminating all internal inefficiencies. In manufacturing processes, implementing a six sigma program means not just delivering a defect-free product after its final test or inspection because that can easily be accomplished while sustaining high levels of defects, rework, scrap, and overall process inefficiencies. It means delivering a top-quality product while concurrently maintaining in-process yields around 99.9999998 percent, defective rates below 0.002 parts-per-million and basically no defects, rework, and scrap.

Additional characteristics required to maintain six sigma would be to run processes under statistical control, to control the input process variables, to maximize equipment uptime, and to optimize cycle time.

Process Potential (C_p)

The process potential (C_p), measures a process's potential capability, which is defined as the ratio of the allowable spread over the actual spread. The allowable spread is the difference between the upper specification limit (USL) and the lower specification limit (LSL). The actual spread is determined from the process data collected and is calculated by multiplying six times the process standard deviation, σ, i.e., six sigma.

$$C_p = \frac{USL - LSL}{6\sigma}$$

The standard deviation quantifies a process's variability. As the standard deviation increases in a process, the C_p decreases in value. As the standard deviation decreases, that is, as the process becomes less variable, the C_p increases in value. By convention, when a process has a C_p value less than 1, it is considered potentially incapable of meeting specification requirements. Conversely, when a process C_p is greater than or equal to 1, the process has the potential of being capable.

Ideally, the C_p should be as high as possible. The higher the C_p, the lower the variability with respect to the specification limits. In a process qualified as a Six Sigma Quality Program, that is, one that allows plus or minus six standard deviations within the specifications limits, the C_p is greater than or equal to 2.

However, a high C_p value does not guarantee that a production process falls within specification limits because the C_p value does not imply the actual spread coincides with the allowable spread or the specification limits. This is why the C_p is called the *process potential*.

Process Capability (C_{pk})

The process capability (C_{pk}), measures a process's ability to create product within specification limits. The C_{pk} represents the difference between the actual process average and the closest specification limit of plus or minus three standard deviations.

$$C_{pk} = Min\left\{\frac{\overline{X} - LSL}{3\sigma}, \frac{USL - \overline{X}}{3\sigma}\right\}$$

By convention, when the C_{pk} is less than one, the process is said to be incapable. But when the C_{pk} is greater than or equal to one, the process is considered to be capable of producing a product within specification limits. In a six sigma process, the C_{pk} equals 2.

The C_{pk} is inversely proportional to the standard deviation, or variability of a process. The higher the C_{pk}, the narrower the process distribution as compared with the specification limits, and the more uniform the product. As the standard deviation increases, the C_{pk} index decreases. At the same time, the potential to create a product outside the specification limits increases.

C_{pk} can have only positive values. It will equal zero when the actual process average matches or falls outside one of the specification limits. The C_{pk} index can never be greater than the C_p, only equal to it. This happens when the actual process average falls in the middle of the specification limits.

The worksheet **Six Sigma Calculations** of Chapter 5 Worksheets.xls provides a template for calculating the process potential and process capability as a function for the process specification and the process parameters; mean, standard deviation, and shift. Exhibit 5–52 illustrates those results.

The process potential is a straightforward calculation based on the specification limits (100 ± 1 or 99 to 101 mm) and the process standard deviation. The process standard deviation is equal to the specification half-width divided by the process sigma level:

$$\sigma = \text{Specification ½ width/Process sigma}$$

The specification limits are input by providing the mean in cell C2 [Mean] and the specification half-width in cell C3 [width]. From these values the lower specification limit is calculated by

$$C4 \text{ [LSL]} = C2 \text{ [Mean]} - C3 \text{ [Width]} = 99.0$$
$$C5 \text{ [USL]} = C2 \text{ [Mean]} + C3 \text{ [Width]} = 101.0$$

Labels in square brackets [] represent the Excel cell ranges assigned by authors. The reader should change the specification values in cell range C2:C3 and observe the impact on the entire worksheet.

In this example, we varied the process standard deviation, cell range B7:B12, from 1 to 0.167 mm corresponding to a sigma range of 1 to 6, cell range A7:A12. The process potential ranged from 0.33 to 2.00, cell range C7:C12 and was calculated using the following Excel expression:

$$C12 = (C5 \text{ [USL]} - C4 \text{ [LSL]}) / (6 * B12) = 2.0$$

EXHIBIT 5–52
Process Potential and Process Capability Calculations
Sheet 6 Sigma Calculations | Chapter 5 Worksheets.xls

	A	B	C	D	E	F	G	H	I	J	K	L	M	N	O
2	Specification Mean		100.0	mm						Process Shift					
3	Specification 1/2 Width		1.0	mm	-0.5	-0.4	-0.3	-0.2	-0.1	0.0	0.1	0.2	0.3	0.4	0.5
4	Lower, LSL		99.0	mm						Process Mean					
5	Upper, USL		101.0	mm	99.5	99.6	99.7	99.8	99.9	100.0	100.1	100.2	100.3	100.4	100.5
6	Process Sigma	Standard Deviation = Half Width / Sigma	Process Potential, C_p $C_p = \frac{USL - LSL}{6\sigma}$		Process Capability, C_{pk} $C_{pk} = Min\left\{\frac{\overline{X} - LSL}{3\sigma}, \frac{USL - \overline{X}}{3\sigma}\right\}$										
7	1	1.000	0.33		0.17	0.20	0.23	0.27	0.30	0.33	0.30	0.27	0.23	0.20	0.17
8	2	0.500	0.67		0.33	0.40	0.47	0.53	0.60	0.67	0.60	0.53	0.47	0.40	0.33
9	3	0.333	1.00		0.50	0.60	0.70	0.80	0.90	1.00	0.90	0.80	0.70	0.60	0.50
10	4	0.250	1.33		0.67	0.80	0.93	1.07	1.20	1.33	1.20	1.07	0.93	0.80	0.67
11	5	0.200	1.67		0.83	1.00	1.17	1.33	1.50	1.67	1.50	1.33	1.17	1.00	0.83
12	6	0.167	2.00		1.00	1.20	1.40	1.60	1.80	2.00	1.80	1.60	1.40	1.20	1.00

EXHIBIT 5–53
Three Sigma Process
Sheet 6 Sigma
Calculations |
Chapter 5
Worksheets.xls

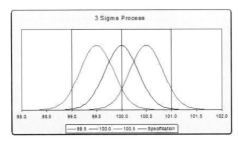

The process capability must also take into account the process mean. When the process mean exactly matches the specification mean, 100 mm, the process potential and the process capability are equivalent. However if the process mean shifts either above or below the specification mean the process capability will be less than the process potential. For example, should the process mean shift upward to 100.3 mm, the process capability has a maximum of 1.40 for the six sigma process as calculated using the following Excel expression:

$$M12 = Min\ ((M5 - C4\ [LSL])/(3 * B12),\ (C5\ [USL] - M5)/(3 * B12)) = 1.4$$

Notice from Exhibit 5–52 that a six sigma process can experience a shift of 0.5 mm and still retain a process capability of at least 1.0. This same shift would reduce the process capability of a three sigma process to 0.5.

This impact is illustrated graphically in Exhibits 5–51 and 5–53. Notice that the three curves plotted in Exhibit 5–51 for a six sigma process lie almost exclusively within the specification limits. The same finding does not hold for Exhibit 5–53, where the left-most curve (process mean = 99.5 mm) has a significant portion below the LSL = 99.0, while the right-most curve (process mean = 100.5 mm) has a significant portion above the USL = 101.0. We demonstrate the calculation of the number of defects in the next section. The value in worksheet cell C20 sets the Sigma level.

Parts-per-Million (ppm)

The metric parts-per-million applies to defective products, or parts, as well as to defects, errors, and mistakes. In six sigma language, we talk about defects-per-million, errors-per-million, mistakes-per-million, and defectives-per-million, which is also called parts-per-million, ppm, defective. The ppm estimates the number of units, piece-parts, or products that are defective when a million is produced.

Exhibit 5–54 illustrates the parts-per-million calculations. The selected value for a three sigma process with the process mean equal to the specification mean is calculated by the following Excel expression:

$$J16 = 1000000 * (NORMDIST\ (LSL, J5, B16, 1) + 1 - NORMDIST\ (USL, J5, B16, 1))$$
$$= 2,700$$

Excel function NORMDIST (LSL, J5, B16, 1) returns the fraction area under the normal curve to the left of LSL = 99.0 mm with a mean of J5 = 10 mm and standard deviation of B16 = 0.333. This value is also referred to as the *fraction defective not meeting the lower specification limit.* Excel function 1 − NORMDIST (USL, J5, B16, 1) returns the fraction area under the normal curve to the right of USL = 101.0 mm with the same process parameters. This value is also referred to as the *fraction defective not meeting the upper specification limit.* Multiplying the total fraction defective by 1 million results in the ppm level or parts-per-million defective of 2,700. Exhibit 5–54 contains the ppm values for all sigma levels and the various process shift values. We have used

EXHIBIT 5–54   Six Sigma Parts Per Million, ppm

Sheet 6 Sigma Calculations | Chapter 5 Worksheets.xls

	A	B	C	D	E	F	G	H	I	J	K	L	M	N	O
2	Specification Mean	100.0	mm							Process Shift					
3	Specification 1/2 Width	1.0	mm		-0.5	-0.4	-0.3	-0.2	-0.1	0.0	0.1	0.2	0.3	0.4	0.5
4	Lower, LSL	99.0	mm							Process Mean					
5	Upper, USL	101.0	mm		99.5	99.6	99.7	99.8	99.9	100.0	100.1	100.2	100.3	100.4	100.5
13	Process Sigma	Standard Deviation = Half Width / Sigma							Defective parts per million, ppm						
14	1	1.000			375,345	355,010	338,764	326,925	319,726	317,311	319,726	326,925	338,764	355,010	375,345
15	2	0.500			160,005	117,625	85,418	62,997	49,834	45,500	49,834	62,997	85,418	117,625	160,005
16	3	0.333			66,811	35,944	17,912	8,357	3,951	2,700	3,951	8,357	17,912	35,944	66,811
17	4	0.250			22,750	8,198	2,555	688	165	63	165	688	2,555	8,198	22,750
18	5	0.200			6,210	1,350	233	32	3	1	3	32	233	1,350	6,210
19	6	0.167			1,350	159	13	1	0	0	0	1	13	159	1,350

EXHIBIT 5–55
Original Process
Calculations
and Chart
Sheet Process
Original | Chapter 5
Worksheets.xls

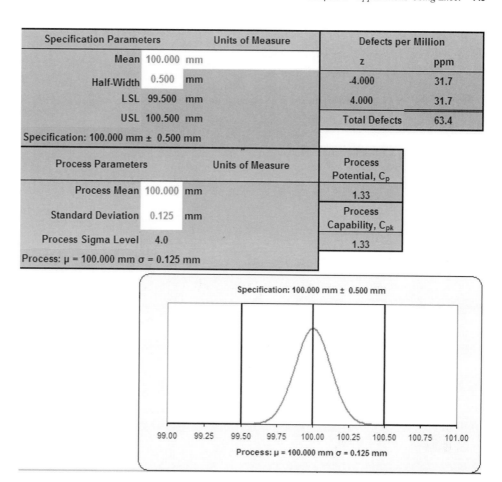

conditional formatting in this worksheet to change the background color as function of the ppm value.

Meeting Customer Requirements Calculations

Let us illustrate how to calculate the fraction defective and parts-per-million defective and the application of the normal distribution. Exhibit 5–55 illustrates the chart calculations for a component of a product made from silicon wafer whose in-process specification for thickness is 100.0 ± 0.5 mm. The performance capability of the micro-machining process used to make this component is at $\pm$ four sigma, and at a 63.4 ppm level.

The complete production line for this product was moved to a new facility. Upon arrival and setup of operations, various lots of production exhibited a significant variability in the component in focus. Upon collecting data from various lots, the component thickness averaged 100.35 mm and the standard deviation 0.125 mm. Exhibit 5–56 illustrates the process after its move.

Apparently, the operation does not perform at the same level in the new facility that it did prior to the move. Now we are interested in determining, first, what is the current fraction defective and ppm level, as well as the new sigma level of performance, and second, what is the cost and profit impact.

To compute the fraction defective, we first compute the standard normal or z score for the lower specification limit, z_{LSL}, and then the z score for the upper specification limit, z_{USL}.

EXHIBIT 5–56
Process After Move Calculations and Chart
Sheet Process After Move | Chapter 5 Worksheets.xls

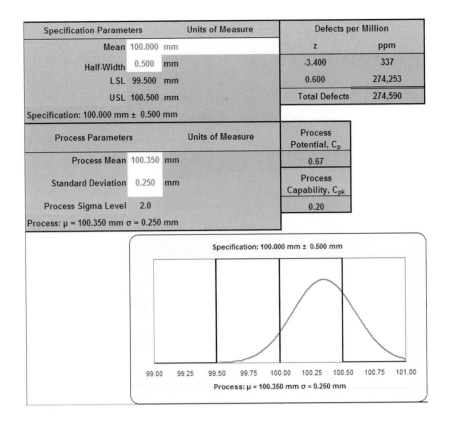

Specification Parameters		Units of Measure	Defects per Million	
Mean	100.000	mm	z	ppm
Half-Width	0.500	mm	-3.400	337
LSL	99.500	mm	0.600	274,253
USL	100.500	mm	**Total Defects**	**274,590**
Specification: 100.000 mm ± 0.500 mm				

Process Parameters		Units of Measure	Process Potential, C_p
Process Mean	100.350	mm	0.67
Standard Deviation	0.250	mm	Process Capability, C_{pk}
Process Sigma Level	2.0		0.20
Process: μ = 100.350 mm σ = 0.250 mm			

Specification: 100.000 mm ± 0.500 mm

Process: μ = 100.350 mm σ = 0.250 mm

$$D5 = z_{LSL} = (99.5 - 100.35)/0.25 = -3.40$$
$$D6 = Z_{USL} = (101.5 - 100.35)/0.25 = 0.60$$

We look for this z score in a normal distribution table found in most statistical textbooks. However, the commonly tabulated values do not provide the level of precision required for six sigma calculation so we turn to Excel for a solution. We use the Excel NORMSDIST function "lookup" to actually calculate the appropriate probability values:

$$E5 = 1,000,000 * NORMSDIST (-3.40)) = 337$$
$$E6 = 1,000,000 * (1 - NORMSDIST (0.6)) = 274,253$$

We multiplied by 1 million in the expressions above to calculate ppm. Both these ppm levels are added together to obtain a total parts-per-million defective of 274,590 ppm.

Supposing the cost of processing this component is $400 per 4-inch wafer. The output of a 4-inch wafer is up to 16,000 components per wafer. At the commodity price of 5 cents per component, the profit is at $400 per 4-inch wafer. At the current ppm level of performance in this new facility, the yield per wafer would be reduced to an average of

$$16,000 * (1 - 0.274590) = 11,607 \text{ components/wafer}$$

reducing the profit per wafer to about:

$$\$400 - 11,607 \text{ components/wafer} * \$0.05 = \$180.35 \text{ per wafer}$$

Defects-per-Million Opportunities (DPMO)

The number of defects per million opportunities, or DPMO, is a metric for quantifying the total number of defects should a million be produced and dividing it by the total number of opportunities for defects.

In the DPMO formula, the numerator is the defects-per-million (dpm) level of performance or operation and the denominator is a weighting factor representing the difficulty of the process or operation. This weighting factor, which represents the total number of opportunities for defects, allows the DPMO to be used for comparing processes with different levels of complexity against each other.

$$DPMO = \frac{dpm}{TOFD}$$

where

$$dpm = dpu * 1,000,000$$

$$dpu = defects\ per\ unit = d \div n$$

$$d = sample\ defects$$

$$n = sample\ size$$

$$TOFD = total\ opportunities\ for\ defects$$

For instance, let us compare two production processes of different complexities generating defects. In the first process, an operator takes two parts, aligns them, and assembles them, producing a final assembly. In the second process, the operator takes seven parts and inserts them into a housing. The operator then takes four distinct subassemblies and puts them all together in the appropriate sequence onto the housing. The operator proceeds by taking eight identical screws and drives them into the subassemblies to secure them to the housing. Finally, the operator attaches a bar code label to the housing and a product label in front of the housing. Exhibit 5–57 calculates the total opportunities for defects for the two processes. The second process involves more steps and thus opportunities for defects.

By computing the DPMO, we can compare the two processes by their incidence for defects weighed by their complexity. Let us quantify the current performance of the two processes according to their incidence for defects. We collect data for a predetermined time and size of sample and compute the total number of defects found. For the first process, let us say that the total number of opportunities for defects is equal to 2. On the second process, we have 23 opportunities for defects, as illustrated in Exhibit 5–57.

We then compute the defects-per-unit (dpu), (row 15), by taking the total number of defects found, *d,* row 14, and dividing it by the sample size, *n,* (row 13). After that, we compute the defects-per-million (dpm), (row 16), by multiplying the dpu times 1 million, and finally the dpm is divided by the total number of defect opportunities (TOFD), (row 12), to produce the defects per million opportunities (DPMO), (row 17).

Row 18 indicates the sigma performance for the two processes using the Excel expression:

$$Sigma = -NORMSINV\ (DPMO \div 2,000,000)$$

Row 19 indicates the first pass yield (FPY), which represents the number of good units produced by the process without rework. The formula for calculation of first pass yield is

$$FPY = 1 - dpu$$

From these DPMOs we can determine whether the complex process is performing much better in comparison to the simple process. The DPMO applies a weight for the complexity of the process to allow their comparison. The DPMO is a metric for the purpose of comparing the performances of different processes, products, facilities,

EXHIBIT 5–57 **DPMO Calculations Using Excel**

Sheet DPMO | Chapter 5 Worksheets.xls

	A	B	C	D
1	**DPMO Calculations**		Process Analysis and Improvement: Tools and Techniques Copyright ©2005 by The McGraw-Hill Companies, Inc.	
2			Process	
3		Simple	Complex	
4	Product Components	Opportunities for defects		Excel Expressions
5	Parts	2	7	
6	Housing		1	
7	Sub-assemblies		4	
8	Sequence		1	
9	Screws		8	
10	Bar Code		1	
11	Product Label		1	
12	Total Opportunities For Defects, TOFD	2	23	= SUM (D5 : D11)
13	Sample Size, n	2,500	3,750	
14	Number of Defects, d	95	150	
15	Defects per Unit, dpu	0.038	0.040	= D14 / D13
16	Defects per Million, dpm	38,000	40,000	= D15 * 1000000
17	Defects per Million Opportunities, DPMO	19,000	1,739	= D16 / D12
18	Sigma Performance	2.35	3.13	= - NORMSINV (D17 / 2000000)
19	First Pass Yield, FPY	96.2%	96.0%	= 1 - D15

equipment, and processes given their complexity and inherent differences. In some cases, the DPMO could be further converted into a sigma performance level.

On the other hand, if the presence of a defect makes the output of each process a defective product, then both of them are equally bad. Their first-pass yield would be 96.2 percent for the simple process and 96.0 percent for the complex process.

Errors-per-Million Opportunities (EPMO)

EPMO is a metric for measuring and comparing the performances of distinct administrative, service, or transactional processes. The EPMO quantifies the total number of errors or mistakes produced by a process per million iterations of the process. It takes into account the opportunities for that process to have errors or mistakes. The premise is true if an administrative, service, or transactional process is simple; it should not present too many chances for committing errors or making mistakes. On the other hand, if the process is complicated, cumbersome, difficult, or not well-defined, it may present many chances for errors and mistakes.

$$EPMO = \frac{epm}{TOFE}$$

where

$epm = epu * 1,000,000$

$epu = $ errors per unit $ = e \div n$

$e = $ sample errors

$n = $ sample size

TOFE $ = $ Total opportunities for errors

To derive the EPMO, we first compute the errors-per-unit (epu). The epu is equal to the total number of errors found in a sample, *e,* divided by the sample size, *n.* We then compute the errors-per-million by multiplying the epu times a million. Then we divide the epm by the total number of opportunities for errors presented by the process. EPMO takes into consideration the complexity of the process and the metric lends itself to comparing the performance of different administrative, service, or transactional processes regarding their level of difficulty.

Let us consider two distinct administrative processes, and one is significantly more difficult than the other, and we would like to use a metric to compare them. One administrative process is the generation of invoices by the billing department, and the other is the generation of payroll checks by the payroll department. One administrative process is more complex than the other and their difficulty correlates to a high incidence of errors.

A simple process, such as the generation of payroll checks, may have about 10 opportunities for errors in such areas as work hours, overtime hours, amount withheld, social security number, name, address, check amount, date, medical insurance, and life insurance. The process for generating invoices may have about 20 opportunities for errors. How can we compare these two distinct processes when one is more complex than the other and has more opportunities for the generation of errors? The EPMO uses a weighting factor for opportunities for making errors or mistakes to account for the complexity of the process. These data and the associated calculations are illustrated in Exhibit 5–58.

The audit of the process was done over a period of one month, encompassing a sample of 1,500 checks and 1,800 invoices respectively (row 6). The audit found 84 errors in the Payroll Check process (row 7), and the errors-per-million were computed as 56,000 epm (row 9). In the case of the Invoicing process, 550 errors were found and the errors-per-

EXHIBIT 5–58   **EPMO Calculations Using Excel**

Sheet EPMO | Chapter 5 Worksheets.xls

	A	B	C	D
1	EPMO Calculations	Process Analysis and Improvement: Tools and Techniques Copyright ©2005 by The McGraw-Hill Companies, Inc.		
2		Administrative Process		
3		Simple Payroll	Complex Invoices	Excel Expressions
4	**Product Components**			
5	Total Opportunities For Errors, TOFE	10	20	
6	Sample Size, n	1,500	1,800	
7	Number of Errors, e	84	550	
8	Errors per Unit, epu	0.056	0.306	= D7 / D6
9	Errors per Million, epm	56,000	305,556	= D8 * 1000000
10	Errors per Million Opportunities, EPMO	5,600	15,278	= D9 / D5
11	Sigma Performance	2.77	2.43	= - NORMSINV (D10 / 2000000)
12	First Pass Yield, FPY	94.4%	69.4%	= 1 - D8

million was computed as 305,556 epm. Since this epm takes into consideration the process difficulty, we divide the number by the total number of opportunities for errors, so the EPMOs were equal to 5,600 and 15,278 respectively for the two administrative processes (row 10).

Row 11 indicates the sigma performance for the two processes using the Excel expression:

$$\text{Sigma} = -\text{NORMSINV (EPMO/2000000)}$$

Row 12 indicates the first pass yield, FPY. The formula for the calculation of first pass yield is

$$\text{FPY} = 1 - \text{epu}$$

Challenge

Operating/Repair Cycle

One common part of developing process simulation models that represent manufacturing systems is modeling the equipment operating/repair cycle. Because of its common occurrences, many simulation languages have built-in functions to model equipment operating/repair cycles. The key input data required of the model developer is the statistical distribution of the equipment operating and repair times with their appropriate parameters. Based on the authors' experiences in developing simulation models of manufacturing processes, very few companies maintain sufficiently accurate data to be able to conduct the statistical analysis required to develop the distributions and parameters.

Based on extensive data analysis, Law (1990) found that the operating period of typical manufacturing equipment can be modeled using the Gamma probability density function with a shape parameter of 0.7. The repair period can be modeled using the Gamma probability density function with a shape parameter of 1.4. Using these findings, the simulation model developer need know only the mean or average operating and repair times to build a functional equipment operating or repair cycle model.

Unfortunately, even the average operating and repair data is not widely available for most manufacturing equipment. The worksheet illustrated in Exhibit 5–59 has been developed to assist the simulation model developer to construct reasonable models for equipment operating and repair cycles.

Columns J and K of Exhibit 5–59 indicate the average operating and repair periods in units of minutes. These values can be directly input by the worksheet user or can be automatically generated using built-in Excel formulas that will be outlined later. Columns L and M of Exhibit 5–59 indicate the Gamma distribution shape parameters as suggested by Law.

Selecting an equipment type in the Failures worksheet and pressing the button labeled **Display DensityFunctions Worksheet** generates the plots illustrated in Exhibit 5–60. This operation utilizes VBA code that will be discussed in Chapter 8.

The Excel charts illustrated in Exhibit 5–60 are generated based on the values at the top of the worksheet:

Cell	Contents	Value
H2	Average Operating Minutes	55.0
H3	Average Repair Minutes	5.0
J2	Operating Period Gamma Distribution Shape Parameter	0.70
J3	Repair Period Gamma Distribution Shape Parameter	1.40

These distribution parameters can be changed directly on worksheet DensityFunctions to enable the user to

EXHIBIT 5–59   **Operating/Repair Cycle Calculations**

Sheet Failures | Chapter 5 Worksheets.xls

	A	B	C D	E	F	G	H	I	J	K	L	M
1	Failures Worksheet		Data Input Option B				Data Input Option A		Process Analysis and Improvement: Tools and Techniques Copyright ©2005 by The McGraw-Hill Companies, Inc.			
2	Data in Red May Be Changed				Period Length in Hours	Average Repair Minutes	Average Operating Failures /		Display DensityFunctions Worksheet		Gamma Distribution Shape Parameter	
			Failures per Period				Average Minutes					
3	# Equipment Label		Failures per Period		Period Length in Hours	Average Repair Minutes	Percent	Hour	Operating MTBF	Repair MTTR	Operating	Repair
4	1 Cartoner	8 / Shift		8	5.0	91.67%	1.000	55.0	5.0	0.7	1.4	
5	2 Case Packer	4 / Day		24	5.0	98.61%	0.167	355.0	5.0	0.7	1.4	
6	3 Filler	8 / Week		168	30.0	97.62%	0.048	1,230.0	30.0	0.7	1.4	
7	4 Mixer	5 / Week		168	10.0	99.50%	0.030	2,006.0	10.0	0.7	1.4	
8	5 Palletizer	2 / Month		672	480.0	97.62%	0.003	19,680.0	480.0	0.7	1.4	

		Periods	Hours / Period	Period Multiplier
10		Periods	Hours / Period	Period Multiplier
11		Shift	8	1
12		Day	24	3
13		Week	168	7
14		Month	672	4
15		Year	8,064	12

EXHIBIT 5–60
Operating/Repair Cycle Density Functions
Sheet
DensityFunctions |
Chapter 5
Worksheets.xls

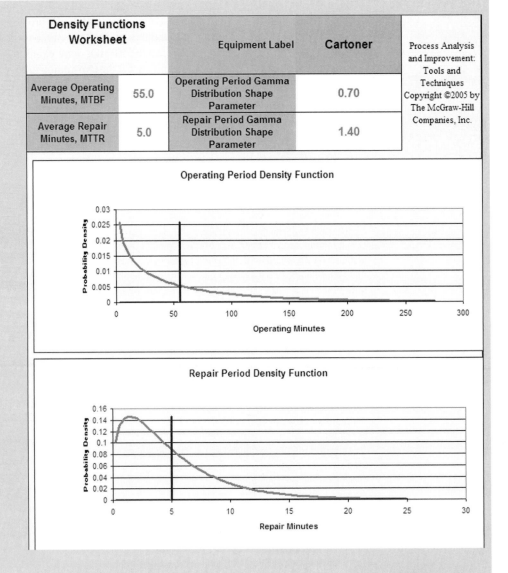

Density Functions Worksheet		Equipment Label	Cartoner	Process Analysis and Improvement: Tools and Techniques Copyright ©2005 by The McGraw-Hill Companies, Inc.
Average Operating Minutes, MTBF	55.0	Operating Period Gamma Distribution Shape Parameter	0.70	
Average Repair Minutes, MTTR	5.0	Repair Period Gamma Distribution Shape Parameter	1.40	

instantly view the impact of changing the distribution parameters. Note that a Gamma distribution with a shape parameter of 1 is identical to the negative exponential distribution. Also, note that as the shape parameter grows, if the user tries a value of 50, the density function approaches the normal distribution in general shape. Notice that changes on worksheet DensityFunctions do not shift the plot of the distribution mean or average value. These values on the DensityFunctions worksheet also do not automatically transfer back to the Failures worksheet.

Rather than making changes on worksheet DensityFunctions, the VBA link between it and worksheet Failures should be explored. Both worksheets include a command button that transfers control to the opposite worksheet. In the case of the Failures worksheet, the command button labeled *Display DensityFunction Worksheet* executes VBA subroutine **psSubGenerateCharts**. This subroutine determines the current row of the Failures worksheet and then transfers the values in columns J through M to the corresponding cells in the DensityFunctions worksheet. The corresponding Excel chart is then generated with appropriate X axis limits for the current average values. In the case of the DensityFunction worksheet, the command button labeled *Display Failures Worksheet* executes VBA routine **psSubSheetFailures**, which simply returns to the Failures worksheet.

As stated earlier, a major problem in developing the data required to model the equipment operating/repair cycle is the lack of specific information based on actual operating experience. Sometimes when new equipment is involved, no such data is available and can only be estimated based on past experience. Worksheet Failures has two options for estimating the equipment operating and repair average values.

Columns H and I are labeled *Data Input Option A.* The worksheet user enters the average equipment operating percent in column H and the corresponding average number of repairs per hour in column I. From these two values the average operating and repair minutes are calculated using the following Excel formulas:

J4: = IF(I4 > 0, 60 * H4 / I4, 99999)

K4: = IF(I4 > 0, 60 * (1 − H4) / I4, 0.001)

The IF functions are used to assure that the average repairs per hour is not zero. The calculation can be stated as follows:

Average Operating Minutes = 60 * Average operating percent / Average repairs per hour

Average Repair Minutes = 60 * (1 − Average operating percent) / Average repairs per hour

A second input data alternative labeled *Data Input Option B* is available in columns C through G. The worksheet user selects the appropriate time period in column E. The available or valid time periods are defined in range E11:E15. In the case of equipment type Filler, the period type Week was selected. The worksheet user then indicates the number of failures per period in column C. A value of 8 is indicated for the Filler equipment. Column F is automatically generated based on the period selected in Column E. The value of 168 in cell F6 is the number of hours per week. That value is calculated in Range E11:G15 where the number of working hours per shift (cell F11) and the number of shifts per day (cell G12), days per week (cell G13), weeks per month (cell G14), and months per year (cell G15) are indicated.

The final data element, average repair minutes, is indicated in column G. From these values the Average Operating Percent and the Average Failures per Hour are calculated using the following Excel formulas:

H4: = 1 − C4 * G4 / F4 / 60

I4: = C4 / F4

The calculation can be stated as follows:

Average operating percent = 1 − Failure per period * Average repair minutes
/ Period length in hours / 60 average repairs per hour
= Failure per period / Period length in hours

The values in columns H and I are then used to calculate the values in columns J and K. Those values, in turn, must be transferred to an Arena simulation model.

Exercises

1. Use Excel to conduct a linear regression analysis on the data illustrated in Exhibit 5–61. What is the R^2 value? Is this a reasonable linear model?

2. Student Rentals Incorporated is a low-priced apartment rental company that focuses in and around university campuses and would like to construct a model to help assess new locations under consideration. Data of interest, collected from its current locations, are shown in Exhibit 5–62. The company would like to develop a predictive model to estimate the profitability of new sites under consideration.

   a. Draw the scatter plots of Profit as a function of Students and Profit as a function of Population per apartment complex.

   b. After completing step *a.,* observe that both relationships appear relatively linear indicating a multiple linear regression is appropriate.

EXHIBIT 5–61
Rainfall Data
Sheet Rainfall Data |
Chapter 5
Exercises.xls

Rainfall volume (m^3)	Runoff volume (m^3)
5	4
12	10
14	13
17	15
23	15
30	25
40	27
47	46
55	38
67	46
72	53
81	70
96	82
112	99
127	100

Source: *J. of Envir. Engr.*, 1998, pp. 131-137.

EXHIBIT 5–62 **Student Rentals**
Sheet Rental Data | Chapter 5 Exercises.xls

Profit	Students	Population / Apartment Complex
$36,000	8,000	8,000
$38,000	10,000	7,000
$40,000	10,000	3,800
$45,000	13,000	2,000
$50,000	13,000	3,200
$52,000	15,000	5,000
$55,000	17,000	4,200
$53,000	20,000	3,400
$52,000	23,000	6,000
$58,000	24,000	1,200

EXHIBIT 5–63 **Sandwich Calories per Dollar**
Sheet Calories per Dollar| Chapter 5 Exercises.xls

Sandwiches	Calories	Price
Hamburger	280	$0.89
Cheeseburger	330	$0.99
Filet-O-Fish	470	$1.99
Crispy Chicken	550	$2.79
Quarter Pounder	430	$2.29
Big N' Tasty	540	$2.29
Big Mac	590	$2.39
Chicken McGrill	450	$2.89
Double Quarter Pounder	760	$2.99

Source: *Nutrition Action Health Letter*, April 2004, p. 2.

c. Using the Regression tool in Excel, develop the estimated regression equation for the data in the table. Review the regression output and look at adjusted R^2 value as to how good a fit the regression model is to the above data.

d. Draw the normal probability plot for the Profit and residual plots for Population per apartment complex and Students and review the plots to determine whether they are linear in support of the regression model determined in step *c.*

3. Exhibit 5–63 illustrates the prices and calorie contents of several fast-food sandwiches. Use Excel to investigate the relationship between price and calorie contents. Develop an equation for predicting the calorie contents of sandwiches based on price.

4. No Tickets Incorporated manufactures high-tech radar detectors, and assembles two models: Laser-Stop and SpeedBuster. Both models use many of the same electronic components. Two of these components, which have very high quality and reliability requirements, can only be obtained from a single overseas manufacturer. For the next month, the supply of these components is limited to 6,000 of component A and 3,500 of component B. How many of each product should be assembled during the next month to maximize No Tickets Incorporated's profit? Assume that the firm can sell all it produces. Comment on Shadow Prices and Reduced Cost. Use the worksheet **Solver** of workbook Chapter 5 Worksheet.xls as a starting point.

5. Custom Vehicles is small company that produces many specialized cars and trucks. Each vehicle must be processed in the body assembly shop and then the paint shop. If the body shop were producing only cars, it could process 50 per day. If the body shop were producing only trucks, it could process 50 per day. If the paint shop were painting only trucks, 50 per day could be painted. If the paint shop were painting only cars, 60 per day could be painted. Each truck contributes $3,000 to profit, and each car contributes $2,000 to Custom Vehicles profit.

a. Use an Excel Solver linear programming model to determine a daily production schedule that will maximize Custom Vehicles' profits. Also, comment on reduced cost and dual price.

b. Suppose that auto dealers require that Custom Vehicles produce at least 30 trucks and 20 cars. Find the optimal solution to the new problem. Also, comment on reduced cost and dual price.

6. The Midwest Meats Company is a producer of canned foods. The company's food production plants are located in Minneapolis and Chicago. Distribution centers are located in Cleveland, Des Moines, St. Louis, and Omaha. The company's logistics

EXHIBIT 5–64
Midwest Meats
Supply, Demand, and
Cost Data
Sheet Midwest Meats |
Chapter 5
Exercises.xls

Production Facilities	Production Capacity
Minneapolis	3,500
Chicago	4,500
Totals	8,000

Distribution Centers	Demand Quantities
Cleveland	1,500
Des Moines	2,000
St. Louis	2,500
Omaha	1,500
Totals	7,500

Shipment Costs ($) Production Facilities	Distribution Centers			
	Cleveland	Des Moines	St. Louis	Omaha
Minneapolis	$6.50	$1.50	$6.10	$3.50
Chicago	$4.00	$3.20	$2.75	$4.50

department wants to minimize the cost of shipping the goods from the processing plants to the distribution centers. The cost of shipping a case of canned food from each processing center to each distribution center is given in the table in Exhibit 5–64. The weekly capacity at the two processing centers as well as the weekly requirements at the distribution centers are also illustrated in Exhibit 5–64.

a. Develop a transportation model to minimize the cost of shipping while meeting capacity and demand requirements.

b. Implement the model on a spreadsheet and find an optimal solution using the Excel Solver.

7. Midwest Meats is trying to determine how sales are related to advertising for a product. Data are available for the past 20 months. The amount of money spent on advertising and the resulting sales revenues are shown in Exhibit 5–65.

a. Generate an Excel scatter chart.

b. Using the Excel Tools Data Analysis functions, find sample covariance and sample correlation.

c. What can you conclude about the relationship between advertising and sales revenues based on your answers to steps a. and b.

d. Using the Regression tool in the Excel Tools Data Analysis functions, perform a regression analysis on the data given in the table.

EXHIBIT 5–65
Midwest Meats
Advertising Data
Sheet Advertising
Data | Chapter 5
Exercises.xls

Advertising Expense	Sales Revenues
$200	$52,200
$500	$51,070
$800	$54,580
$1,000	$55,890
$1,100	$52,860
$1,300	$56,120
$1,700	$58,100
$1,700	$56,400
$2,000	$58,080
$2,200	$58,380
$2,300	$57,490
$2,500	$62,400
$2,700	$60,470
$2,900	$63,850
$3,100	$63,750
$3,300	$64,720
$3,400	$65,600
$3,800	$69,100
$3,900	$67,710
$4,000	$69,500

The transshipment problem is an extension of the transportation problem in which intermediate nodes, referred to as *transshipment nodes,* are added to account

EXHIBIT 5–66 **Health Foods Supply, Demand, and Cost Data**

Sheet Health Foods | Chapter 5 Exercises.xls

Production Facilities	Production Quantities
Detroit	600
Memphis	400
Totals	1,000

Retail Outlets	Demand Quantities
Chicago	200
Miami	150
Dallas	350
Los Angeles	300
Totals	1,000

Shipment Costs ($) Production Facilities	Warehouse	
	Denver	Cincinnati
Detroit	$3.00	$1.50
Memphis	$2.00	$3.00

Shipment Costs Retail Outlets	Warehouse	
	Denver	Cincinnati
Chicago	$4.00	$2.00
Miami	$6.00	$4.00
Dallas	$3.00	$5.00
Los Angeles	$5.00	$8.00

for locations such as warehouses. In this more general type of distribution problem, shipments are permitted to occur between any pair of the three general types of nodes: origin nodes, transshipment nodes, and destination nodes. For example, the transshipment problem permits the shipments of goods from one supply location (origin) to another supply location, from one transshipment location to another, from one destination location to another, and directly from origins to destinations. As is true for the transportation problem, the supply available at each origin is limited, and the demand at each destination is known. The objective in the transshipment problem is to determine how many units should be shipped over each arc in the network so that all destination demands are satisfied with the minimum possible total transportation cost.

8. The Health Foods Company is a consumer products manufacturer with production facilities located in Omaha and Kansas City. Products produced in either facility may be shipped to either of the firm's regional warehouses, which are located in Denver and Cincinnati. From the regional warehouses, the firm supplies retail outlets in Chicago, Miami, Dallas, and Los Angeles. The supplies and demands and also transportation cost per unit for each distribution route are illustrated in Exhibit 5–66.

Set up the problem by first defining the variables, objective function, origin node constraints, transshipment node constraints, and destination constraints. Determine the optimal solution to the transshipment problem faced by the Samuel consumer products company by identifying routes (from and to locations), units shipped using these routes, cost per-unit for these routes, total cost for each route, and also total transportation cost for all the routes combined.

9. As we described in the chapter, TFD is an important tool for companies to generate the technology road map (for identifying and planning for technologies to support products or processes). An example of a developing technology road map was also presented for a product chosen to be vacuum cleaner. Using this example as the basis of your understanding of the TFD process, select a product or two (it can be an obsolete one) for a company, identify one or two important attributes that were introduced in the product(s), and develop a technology road map for the product(s) by completing the templates provided for the five TFD matrices.

10. Carry out the four-step Quality Function Deployment (QFD) process for developing a quality textbook for a student.

   a. Complete a QFD template identifying the set of customer requirements believed to be critical to the customer. The customer is a student.

   b. Complete a QFD template creating a relationship matrix between customer requirements and product characteristics. The product is a textbook.

   c. Complete a QFD template identifying the critical determinants of product characteristics.

   d. Complete a QFD template creating an action list for implementing critical determinants of product characteristics.

11. Consider the airline transportation industry. Develop a house of quality to show customer requirements and technical descriptors. Use the **Page House of Quality** of Chapter 5 Drawing.vsd, Exhibit 5–44, as a template.

12. Develop a technology road map of the semiconductor industry using TFD approach.

13. What are the advantages of using quality function deployment? Name some key ingredients that are necessary for its success.

14. Describe Motorola's concept of six sigma quality and explain the level of nonconforming product that could be expected from such a process.

15. Precision Machining Incorporated produces connecting rods with an outer diameter that has a $1 \pm .01$ inch specification. An operator takes several sample measurements over time and determines the sample mean outer diameter to be 1.002 inches with a standard deviation of .0029 inch.

    a. Calculate the process capability index.

    b. What does this calculation tell you about the process?

16. Precision Machining Incorporated is attempting to determine whether an existing unit of equipment is capable of machining a part that has a key specification of $4 \pm .003$ inches. After a test run on this machine, Precision Machining has determined that the machine has a sample mean of 4.001 inches with a standard deviation of .002 inch.

    a. Calculate the C_{pk} for this equipment.

    b. Should Precision Machining use this equipment to make this part? Why or why not?

17. Product design specifications require that a key dimension should measure 100 ± 8 units. A process being chosen for making this product has a standard deviation of 3 units.

    a. What can you say quantitatively regarding the process capability?

    b. Suppose the process average shifts to 93. Calculate the new process capability.

    c. What can you determine about the process after the shift? Approximately what percentage of the items produced will be defective?

18. Use the six sigma approach described in this chapter to analyze a process you are familiar with—either a service process or a manufacturing process or a combination of the two, clearly identifying inputs, the process itself, and the outputs. Using the templates identified in this chapter and used in the two examples pertaining to manufacturing and service processes, study the process selected by fitting a normal distribution, establishing lower and upper specification limits, computing ppm, C_p, C_{pk}, dpu, dpm, TOFD, DPMO, and so on.

19. The emergency service unit of a hospital has a goal of 3.5 minutes for the waiting time of patients before being treated. A random sample of 20 patients is chosen and the sample average waiting time is found to be 2.3 minutes with a sample standard deviation of 0.5 minutes. Find an appropriate process capability index. Comment on the ability of the emergency service unit to meet the desirable goal. What are some possible actions to consider?

Challenge

20. Develop an operating and repair cycle worksheet for a computer network. Include elements such as printers, personal computers, and a server.

21. Collect time to failure and time to repair data from an automated system. Use the Goodness-of-Fit, Input Process from Arena to test the appropriateness of the Gamma distributions found by Law. Typical data for several hundred cycles must be collected in order to conduct a meaningful Goodness-of-Fit test. Comment on the suitability of your data and problems associated with collecting this type of information. Could such information be automatically collected by the equipment's electronic control system?

Process Simulation Using Arena

Summary and Learning Objectives

This chapter introduces the reader to analysis of queuing processes using Excel spreadsheet analysis and Arena simulation. It describes the Arena simulation environment and how the Arena simulation model can be applied to a simple queuing process. It shows a comparison of alternative queuing processes using Arena. A number of Arena modeling techniques are described using Arena examples and Smart models.

The learning objectives for this chapter are to

1. Analyze queuing processes using Excel and Arena.
2. Develop and utilize Arena simulation models for a simple queuing process.
3. Use Arena to compare alternative queuing processes.
4. Develop new Arena modeling techniques using Arena Example and Smart models.

Analysis and Simulation of Queuing Processes

Process simulation is an easy-to-use tool that allows the process analyst to create models and run experiments of processes involving queues or waiting lines. By testing out ideas in a computer "laboratory," the process analyst can predict the future with confidence, without disrupting the current operation.

Arena and its underlying simulation language SIMAN are based on the process flow simulation modeling concept originally introduced in 1961 by Jeffery Gordon of IBM with the GPSS simulation language. This simulation modeling concept tracks the flow of material or information (entities) through a process of limited capacity resources. The flow of entities is delayed in time when specific processing takes place or when the entity must wait in a queue to gain control of a limited capacity resource. Let us begin with a brief review of queuing process analysis using Excel and then learn about Arena's history.

Queuing Process Analysis Using Excel

The discrete event or process flow type of simulation modeling supported by Arena is typically applied to the modeling and analysis of queuing processes. Exhibit 6–1 illustrates a simple single server queue process. This Visio drawing was developed using a custom Visio stencil file **Queue Stencil.vss** that has been supplied on the text CD-ROM. This queuing process comprises four major components:

1.	**Process Boundary**	Defines process limits.
2.	**Arrival Source**	Supplies process customers.
3.	**Queue**	Allows customers to wait for service.
4.	**Server**	Provides customer service.

EXHIBIT 6–1
M/M/1 Queuing
Process Diagram
Page MM1 | Chapter 6
Drawing.vsd

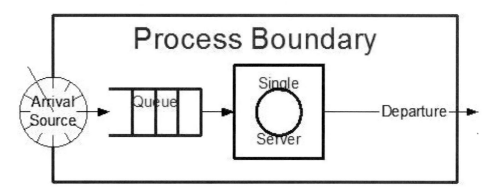

Customers arrive at the process from an external source following some pattern or statistical distribution with its associated parameters. If the arriving customer finds the server busy he or she must wait in the queue. When the server is available and a customer is present, service starts following some pattern or statistical distribution with its associated parameters. In most queuing processes and simulation models, the queue is assumed to be limited in capacity and customers are served in the order they arrive, the First In First Out (FIFO) queuing rule. These assumptions can be changed to more accurately model real-life processes.

Process analysts are faced with two conflicting objectives that must be balanced to meet the overall process goals. The number of customers forced to wait in the queues and the time the server is idle should both be minimized. However, the two measures of process performance are interdependent and cannot in general be simultaneously minimized. Thus, the process analyst must attempt to find a reasonable balance between these two objectives. In general, when the expected server utilization is greater than 90 percent, the number of customers forced to wait in the queue and their waiting time becomes significant.

M/M/1 Queue

The queuing process illustrated in Exhibit 6–1 is classified as M/M/1 for the following reasons:

•	**M**	The time between arrivals follows the exponential distribution.
•	**M**	The time for service follows the exponential distribution.
•	**1**	The process has one server.

The basic M/M/1 queuing process has been widely studied, with analytical results available for the typical queuing process measures of performance.

The exponential distribution is defined by the following:

$$f(x) = \lambda e^{-\lambda x}, \text{ for } 0 \leq x < \infty$$

$$E(X) = 1/\lambda \text{ and } V(X) = 1/\lambda^2$$

$$F(x) = 1 - e^{-\lambda x}, \text{ for } 0 \leq x < \infty$$

Exhibit 6–2 illustrates the exponential distribution density function for λ values of 1.0, 1.5, and 2.0 corresponding to mean values of 1, 0.667, and 0.5. Notice that the exponential distribution is highly skewed to the right and may not accurately model many real process arrival and service patterns. It is widely used because the associated queuing process measures of performance can be directly calculated.

The typical queuing theory calculations for an M/M/1 queuing process are illustrated in Exhibit 6–3. In this case, the customer arrival process has an average of one arrival per minute or

EXHIBIT 6–2 **Exponential Probability Density Functions**

Sheet exponential | Chapter 6 Worksheets.xls

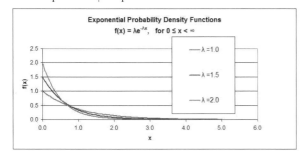

EXHIBIT 6–3 **M/M/1 Queue Calculations**

Sheet MM1 | Chapter 6 Worksheets.xls

	A	B	C	D	E	F	G	H	I	J
2	Label	Mean Inter-Arrival Time	Mean Arrival Rate	Mean Service Time	Mean Service Rate	Traffic Intensity	Expected Number in Process, Lp	Expected Number in Queue, Lq	Expected Time in Process, Wp	Expected Time in Queue, Wq
3	Formula	1/λ	λ	1/μ	μ	ρ = λ/μ	ρ/(1-ρ)	Lp = ρ²/(1-ρ)	Lp = 1/(μ-λ)	Lq = ρ/(μ-λ)
4	Units	Seconds	Customers /Minute	Seconds	Customers /Minute		Customers	Customers	Minutes	Minutes
5		60.0	1.0	10.0	6.00	0.167	0.20	0.03	0.20	0.03
6		60.0	1.0	20.0	3.00	0.333	0.50	0.17	0.50	0.17
7		60.0	1.0	30.0	2.00	0.500	1.00	0.50	1.00	0.50
8		60.0	1.0	35.0	1.71	0.583	1.40	0.82	1.40	0.82
9		60.0	1.0	40.0	1.50	0.667	2.00	1.33	2.00	1.33
10		60.0	1.0	45.0	1.33	0.750	3.00	2.25	3.00	2.25
11		60.0	1.0	50.0	1.20	0.833	5.00	4.17	5.00	4.17
12		60.0	1.0	55.0	1.09	0.917	11.00	10.08	11.00	10.08
13		60.0	1.0	56.0	1.07	0.933	14.00	13.07	14.00	13.07
14		60.0	1.0	57.0	1.05	0.950	19.00	18.05	19.00	18.05
15		60.0	1.0	58.0	1.03	0.967	29.00	28.03	29.00	28.03
16		60.0	1.0	59.0	1.02	0.983	59.00	58.02	59.00	58.02
17	Excel Expressions	60 / B5		60 / D5	C5 / E5	F5 / (1 - F5)	G5 - F5	G5 / C5	H5 / C5	

an average time between arrivals of 60 seconds. The time between arrivals follows the exponential distribution. The exponential distribution is commonly used in queuing theory; however, it is seldom observed in actual practice. The average service time is varied from 10 to 59 seconds, also with an exponential distribution.

The appropriate M/M/1 calculations for the standard queuing process measures of performance are illustrated in Exhibit 6–4.

The Excel chart illustrated Exhibit 6–5 plots the Expected Number in Process and the Expected Number in Queue versus the Traffic Intensity, where the Traffic Intensity is calculated by

$$\rho = \text{Traffic intensity} = \frac{\text{Mean arrival rate}}{\text{Mean service rate}}$$

$$= \frac{\text{Mean service time}}{\text{Mean inter-arrival time}}$$

For example, when the Mean Inter-Arrival time is 60 seconds and the Mean Service Time is 55 seconds, the corresponding Mean Arrival Rate is

$$\lambda = 1 \div 60 = 0.0167 \text{ Customers per seconds} = 0.0167 * 60 = 1.00 \text{ Customers per minute}$$

and the Mean Service Rate is

$$\mu = 1 \div 55 = 0.0182 \text{ Customers per seconds} = 0.0182 * 60 = 1.09 \text{ Customers per minute}$$

and the corresponding Traffic Intensity is

$$\rho = 1.00 \div 1.09 = 0.917$$

It should be noted that the number of customers waiting and the waiting time greatly increases when the Traffic Intensity increases above 0.90.

The two curves plotted in Exhibit 6–5 differ by ρ, the traffic intensity or the fraction of time the server is expected to be busy.

$$\text{Expected number in process} = L_p = \frac{\rho}{1 - \rho}$$

$$\text{Expected number in queue} = L_q = L_p - \rho = \frac{\rho^2}{1 - \rho}$$

$$L_p - L_q = \rho$$

EXHIBIT 6–4

M/M/1 Queue Calculations

Sheet MM1 Calculations | Chapter 6 Worksheets.xls

Column	Customers / Minute	Formula	Units	Source
B	Mean Inter-Arrival Time	$1 / \lambda$	Seconds	Input
C	Mean Arrival Rate	λ	Customers / Minute	60 / Column B
D	Mean Service Time	$1 / \mu$	Seconds	Input
E	Mean Service Rate	μ	Customers / Minute	60 / Column D
F	Traffic Intensity	$\rho = \lambda / \mu$	Dimensionless	Column C / Column E
G	Expected Number in Process	$L_p = \rho / (1 - \rho)$	Customers	Column F / (1 - Column E)
H	Expected Number in Queue	$L_q = L_p - \rho = \rho^2 / (1 - \rho)$	Customers	Column G - Column F
I	Expected Time in Process	$W_p = L_p / \lambda = 1 / (\mu - \lambda)$	Minutes	Column G / Column C
J	Expected Time in Queue	$W_q = L_q / \lambda = \rho / (\mu - \lambda)$	Minutes	Column H / Column C

EXHIBIT 6–5   **M/M/1 Queue Measures of Performance versus Traffic Intensity**

Sheet MM1 | Chapter 6 Worksheets.xls

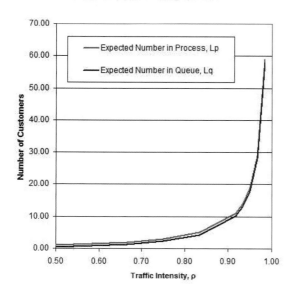

M/M/3 Queue

Exhibit 6–6 illustrates a queuing process diagram for an M/M/3 queue. This process has three servers operating in parallel with a single or pooled queue. If any of the three servers are idle at the time an incoming customer arrives, service starts immediately; otherwise, the customer must wait in the queue. All three servers share a common queue. We will compare this process design to the case with individual queues for each server using an Arena simulation model later in this chapter. In general, a single or pooled queue reduces the expected customer waiting time compared to individual queues for each server.

The problem becomes more complex as the number of servers increases. The calculation of the number of customers in the queue and the customer waiting times for multiple server processes is beyond the scope of this textbook. Process simulation rapidly becomes a viable tool for improving complex processes. Before introducing the Arena simulation tool, we will develop an Excel-based simulation model for a single server process.

Manual Simulation Using Excel

Excel includes a random number generator that can be used to generate the time between arrivals and the service times for an M/M/1 queue. Exhibits 6–7 through 6–12 illustrate a worksheet that we have developed to manually carry out such simulations. The user provides four operating parameters to use the worksheet.

1. Mean Inter-Arrival Time in seconds, 60
2. Mean Service Time in seconds, 50
3. Arrival Option, 0 = Fixed or 1 = Exponential
4. Service Option, 0 = Fixed or 1 = Exponential

Exhibits 6–7 and 6–8 illustrate the simulation of F/F/1 queue or a deterministic process. The first customer arrives at time zero (cell D10). Because the server is not busy, service begins immediately at time zero (cell G10). Because all services take a fixed 50 seconds (cell F10), service is complete at time 50 (cell H10). Neither the customer (cell I10) nor the

EXHIBIT 6–6
M/M/3 Queuing Process Diagram
Page MM3 | Chapter 6 Drawing.vsd

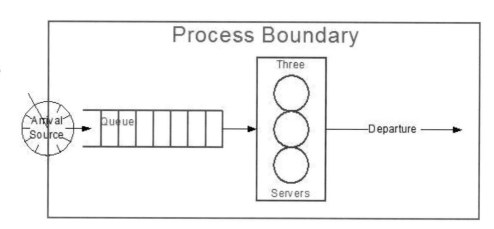

EXHIBIT 6–7 **F/F/1 Queue Simulation Calculations**

Sheet manual simulation | Chapter 6 Worksheets.xls

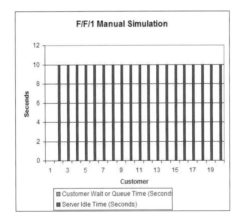

	A	B	C	D	E	F	G	H	I	J
1	Manual Simulation						Process Analysis and Improvement: Tools and Techniques Copyright ©2005 by The McGraw-Hill Companies, Inc.			
2	Mean Inter Arrival Time	1 / λ	60		Seconds					
3	Mean Arrival Rate	λ	1.00		Customers / Minute					
4	Mean Service Time	1 / μ	50		Seconds					
5	Mean Service Rate	μ	1.20		Customers / Minute					
6	Traffic Intensity	ρ = λ / μ	83%		Dimensionless					
7		Arrival Option	0	F	Service Option	0	F		Server Utilization	84%
8		Mean	60		Mean	50			Totals	0	190
9	Customer Number	Random Variable	Arrival Seconds	Time (Seconds)	Random Variable	Service Seconds	Service Start Time (Seconds)	Finish Time (Seconds)	Wait or Queue	Idle Time (Seconds)
10	1	0.1466		0	0.2110	50	0	50	0	0
11	2	0.7516	60	60	0.8483	50	60	110	0	10
12	3	0.0098	60	120	0.3808	50	120	170	0	10
13	4	0.1008	60	180	0.4217	50	180	230	0	10
14	5	0.3952	60	240	0.3794	50	240	290	0	10
15	6	0.9277	60	300	0.5226	50	300	350	0	10
16	7	0.8836	60	360	0.0161	50	360	410	0	10
17	8	0.8237	60	420	0.1966	50	420	470	0	10
18	9	0.6407	60	480	0.3172	50	480	530	0	10
19	10	0.9888	60	540	0.0597	50	540	590	0	10
20	11	0.4788	60	600	0.8805	50	600	650	0	10
21	12	0.2547	60	660	0.5091	50	660	710	0	10
22	13	0.8078	60	720	0.2868	50	720	770	0	10
23	14	0.5777	60	780	0.9351	50	780	830	0	10
24	15	0.7343	60	840	0.5246	50	840	890	0	10
25	16	0.9854	60	900	0.1708	50	900	950	0	10
26	17	0.0244	60	960	0.6334	50	960	1,010	0	10
27	18	0.9689	60	1,020	0.8819	50	1,020	1,070	0	10
28	19	0.4823	60	1,080	0.2996	50	1,080	1,130	0	10
29	20	0.0901	60	1,140	0.5757	50	1,140	1,190	0	10

EXHIBIT 6–8

F/F/1 Queue Simulation Chart

Sheet manual simulation | Chapter 6 Worksheets.xls

F/F/1 Manual Simulation

(chart with y-axis "Seconds" ranging 0 to 12, x-axis "Customer" 1 through 19)

Legend:
■ Customer Wait or Queue Time (Seconds)
■ Server Idle Time (Seconds)

server (cell J10) is forced to wait. The second customer arrives at fixed 60 seconds (cell C11) after the first or at time 60 (cell D11). The service start and end times are calculated by Excel in a manner similar to the first customer. This pattern is repeated for an additional 18 customers. The column chart at the right indicates the waiting time in seconds for both customers and the server. In this case, no customer was forced to wait, but the server waited 10 seconds between each customer. The overall server utilization for handling the first 20 customers can be calculated using

$$\text{Server utilization} = 1 - 190 \div 1{,}190 = 84\%$$

where 190 is the total server idle time and 1,190 is the time the service of the last customer was completed.

The manual simulation becomes more interesting as we add variability to the inter-arrival and service times. First, we make the inter-arrival variable by setting the Arrival Option to 1, which results in the worksheet illustrated in Exhibit 6–9. The time between customer arrivals is no longer a fixed time of 60 seconds. Rather, the inter-arrival time is randomly generated from a population with an exponential distribution with a mean of 60 seconds. This is accomplished using the values in column B, each of which has the following expression:

$$B11 = \text{RAND}() = 0.4507$$

This function returns a random variable in the range of 0 to 1. Each time the worksheet is recalculated by pressing the F9 key, all of the values in columns B and F are regenerated. The desired random variables with an exponential distribution having a mean of 60 are generated using the expression

$$C11 = -\text{LN}(B11) * D\$2 = -\text{LN}(0.4507) * 60 = 48$$

where LN is the natural logarithm function, B11 is the current [0, 1] random variable, and D$2 is the mean inter-arrival time, 60 seconds.

Notice from the chart shown in Exhibit 6–10 that both customers and the server are forced to wait at times during the handling of the first 20 customers. In this case, the 20 customers waited a total of 815 seconds while the server was idle 402 seconds for a utilization rate of 71 percent. The worksheet uses several special calculations to assure the proper accumulation of information.

The customer Arrival Time is calculated by

$$D11 = D10 + C11 = 0 + 48 = 48$$

where D10 is prior customer arrival time and C11 is the inter-arrival time between the first and second customers.

The Service Start Time is calculated by

EXHIBIT 6–9   M/F/1 Queue Simulation Calculations

Sheet manual simulation | Chapter 6 Worksheets.xls

Manual Simulation — Process Analysis and Improvement: Tools and Techniques, Copyright ©2005 by The McGraw-Hill Companies, Inc.

Mean Inter Arrival Time	1 / λ	60	Seconds			
Mean Arrival Rate	λ	1.00	Customers / Minute			
Mean Service Time	1 / μ	50	Seconds			
Mean Service Rate	μ	1.20	Customers / Minute			
Traffic Intensity	ρ = λ / μ	83%	Dimensionless			

Arrival Option	1	M	Service Option	0	F	Server Utilization	83%
Mean	59		Mean	50		Totals	801	210

Customer Number	Random Variable	Arrival Seconds	Time (Seconds)	Random Variable	Service Seconds	Service Start Time (Seconds)	Finish Time (Seconds)	Wait or Queue	Idle Time (Seconds)
1	0.0229		0	0.8647	50	0	50	0	0
2	0.8416	10	10	0.2635	50	50	100	40	0
3	0.6151	29	40	0.3429	50	100	150	60	0
4	0.1476	115	154	0.4364	50	154	204	0	4
5	0.1899	100	254	0.1901	50	254	304	0	50
6	0.9309	4	258	0.5066	50	304	354	46	0
7	0.1210	127	385	0.5533	50	385	435	0	31
8	0.9874	1	386	0.9514	50	435	485	49	0
9	0.6950	22	407	0.8348	50	485	535	77	0
10	0.2135	93	500	0.0071	50	535	585	35	0
11	0.9902	1	501	0.6115	50	585	635	84	0
12	0.7102	21	521	0.2310	50	635	685	114	0
13	0.0971	140	661	0.8440	50	685	735	24	0
14	0.0364	199	860	0.2262	50	860	910	0	125
15	0.7219	20	879	0.7713	50	910	960	30	0
16	0.8242	12	891	0.6242	50	960	1,010	69	0
17	0.5777	33	924	0.7567	50	1,010	1,060	86	0
18	0.1742	105	1,029	0.3876	50	1,060	1,110	31	0
19	0.3774	58	1,087	0.3627	50	1,110	1,160	23	0
20	0.5168	40	1,127	0.5029	50	1,160	1,210	33	0

$$G11 = MAX(D11,H10) = MAX (48, 50) = 50$$

where D11 is the customer arrival time and H10 is the Service Finish Time for the prior customer. Notice that this expression prevents service from starting before the customer has arrived and the prior service has been completed. In this case, the customer was required to wait 2 seconds, which is calculated in cell I11. The server had no wait, cell H11.

The Service Finish Time is calculated by

$$H11 = F11 + G11 = 50 + 50 = 100$$

where F11 is the service time and G11 is the Service Start Time. Similar calculations are performed for the remaining 18 customers.

Exhibits 6–11 and 6–12 illustrate the impact of making both the inter-arrival and service time follow the exponential distribution. It should be noted that both Exhibits 6–9 and 6–11 illustrate only a single random sample of the infinite variety of simulation results available from this Excel-based model. Each time the Recalculation key (F9) is pressed, a new result will be displayed. Test the wide variation in the graphical results each time the F9 key is pressed. Recall that this variation occurred with a traffic intensity of 83 percent. The results will be more dramatic as the traffic intensity approaches 100 percent.

The manual simulation model developed on the worksheet Manual Simulation could be modified to handle other types of statistical distribution for both the inter-arrival and service time. However, this Excel-based approach becomes much more difficult to implement for a multiple service process as illustrated in Exhibit 6–6. The expression column G would have to take into account the specific server as to a particular customer. While such a model using Excel might be feasible, it is beyond the scope of this textbook and better left to tools such as as Arena. Before introducing Arena, we first review the five tasks generally associated with any process simulation activity.

Process Simulation Tasks

Any business environment, from customer service to manufacturing to health care, can benefit from process simulation. And whether an existing supply chain or a new emergency-room layout is being analyzed, the same five easy tasks are used to develop a simulation model and to experiment with the model to improve a business process

1. **Create a simple process model.** Arena provides an intuitive, flowchart-style environment for building an "as-is" model of your process. Simply drag Arena's modules—the shapes in the flowchart—into the model window and connect them to define process flow.

2. **Refine the model.** Add real-world data (e.g., process times, resource requirements, staffing levels) to your model by double-clicking on modules and adding information

EXHIBIT 6–10

M/F/1 Queue Simulation Chart
Sheet manual simulation | Chapter 6 Worksheets.xls

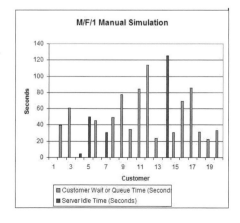

M/F/1 Manual Simulation

Seconds (y-axis) vs Customer (x-axis)

■ Customer Wait or Queue Time (Seconds)
■ Server Idle Time (Seconds)

EXHIBIT 6–11 **M/M/1 Queue Simulation Calculations**
Sheet manual simulation | Chapter 6 Worksheets.xls

Mean Inter Arrival Time	1/λ	60	Seconds						
Mean Arrival Rate	λ	1.00	Customers / Minute						
Mean Service Time	1/μ	50	Seconds						
Mean Service Rate	μ	1.20	Customers / Minute						
Traffic Intensity	p = λ/μ	83%	Dimensionless						
	Arrival Option	1	M	Service Option	1	M	Server Utilization		81%
	Mean	64		Mean	59		Totals	1,488	260
Customer Number	Random Variable	Arrival Seconds	Time (Seconds)	Random Variable	Service Seconds	Service Start Time (Seconds)	Finish Time (Seconds)	Wait or Queue	Idle Time (Seconds)
1	0.8677		0	0.3674	50	0	50	0	0
2	0.4554	47	47	0.7770	13	50	63	3	0
3	0.4719	45	92	0.2087	78	92	171	0	30
4	0.0290	212	305	0.4446	41	305	345	0	134
5	0.1645	108	413	0.7248	16	413	429	0	68
6	0.4017	55	468	0.0661	136	468	604	0	39
7	0.9731	2	469	0.9804	1	604	605	134	0
8	0.2959	73	542	0.1989	81	605	685	62	0
9	0.4156	53	595	0.7847	12	685	697	90	0
10	0.1548	112	707	0.0234	188	707	895	0	10
11	0.7737	15	722	0.5510	30	895	925	172	0
12	0.4767	44	767	0.7851	12	925	937	158	0
13	0.2546	82	849	0.6638	20	937	957	88	0
14	0.9076	6	855	0.1423	97	957	1,055	103	0
15	0.0438	188	1,042	0.0259	183	1,055	1,237	12	0
16	0.2726	78	1,120	0.4950	35	1,237	1,273	117	0
17	0.8923	7	1,127	0.6052	25	1,273	1,298	145	0
18	0.5980	31	1,158	0.8082	11	1,298	1,308	140	0
19	0.5608	35	1,193	0.3876	47	1,308	1,356	116	0
20	0.7879	14	1,207	0.1477	96	1,356	1,451	149	0

EXHIBIT 6–12
M/M/1 Queue Simulation Chart
Sheet manual simulation | Chapter 6 Worksheets.xls

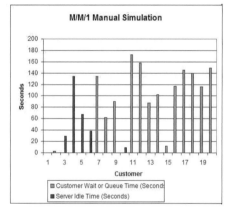

EXHIBIT 6–13
Process Simulation Tasks
Page simulation tasks | Chapter 6 Drawings.vsd

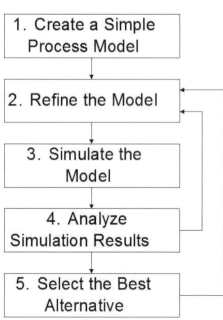

to Arena's data forms. To create a more realistic picture of your process, replace the animation icons that Arena automatically supplies with graphics of your own (e.g., from ClipArt or other drawing packages).

3. **Simulate the model.** Run the simulation to verify that the model properly reflects the actual process. Identify bottlenecks and communicate with others through the dynamics of Arena's graphical animation.

4. **Analyze simulation results.** Arena provides automatic reports on common decision criteria, such as resource utilization and waiting times. Augment the built-in statistics with your own so that Arena reports what is important for your decision-making needs.

5. **Select the best alternative.** Make changes to the model to capture the possible scenarios you want to investigate and then compare the results to find the best "to-be" solution.

Exhibit 6–13 illustrates the simulation tasks drawn using Visio. This process map indicates the possible need for repeating some of the simulation tasks when analyzing or improving a business process. A key feature of a simulation tool such as Arena is the ease with which details can be added to an existing model. It is typically best to start with a simple model and to add detail as the model is used to explain the process operation.

Why Use Arena for Process Analysis and Improvement?

The history of Arena dates to 1982, when Dr. Dennis Pegden developed a simulation tool named SIMAN while teaching Industrial Engineering at Pennsylvania State University. Since that time, SIMAN has been updated numerous times to incorporate new capabilities to meet user needs and to take advantage of improvements in personal computer hardware and software. Amazingly, SIMAN models developed in 1982 can still be executed on the current Arena software version. SIMAN was designed to split the simulation model development effort into two parts: flow logic and control data. This division of modeling information was originally done in part to permit SIMAN to be executed on the original IBM personal computers. This division of simulation modeling information is roughly equivalent to data structures of Visio (flow logic) and Excel (control data).

EXHIBIT 6–14
Model MM1.doe in
Arena Modeling
Environment

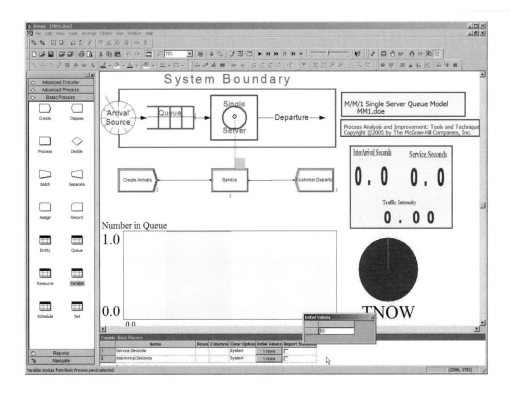

Arena is not the only process simulation tool. Other simulation software packages such as ProModel, Witness, AutoMod, and Flexsim all have similar capabilities. We have focused on Arena because of its long history of continued improvement and widespread application in many types of business processes. Arena is a market-leading simulation software tool. It was the first simulation software to incorporate VBA and to provide links to Visio for direct model logic transfer. A division of Allen-Bradley Automation, Rockwell Software markets Arena and annually increases the capabilities of the software. Arena 6.0, introduced in 2002, includes a Factory Analyzer edition that links directly to other Rockwell Software manufacturing data processes. Future versions of Arena are planned to include more seamless integration to supply chain and enterprise software tools such as SAP. See Chapter 12 to learn more about the future of software tools.

Arena Simulation Environment

The typical Arena window or modeling environment is illustrated in Exhibit 6–14. The Arena model file **MM1.doe** is illustrated and should be loaded into Arena from the text CD-ROM to gain an understanding of the material presented through the balance of this chapter.

In addition to the normal Windows toolbars at the top of the screen, Arena divides the work area into four windows: Project Bar (at left), Flowchart Window (upper right), Spreadsheet Window (lower right), and Status Bar (at the very bottom of the screen). The Project Bar can be activated and deactivated using the **View > Project Bar** menu command. The Spreadsheet Window can be activated and deactivated using the **View > Split Screen** menu command. The Status Bar can be activated and deactivated using the **View > Status Bar** menu command. The Flowchart Window is always active, but the user can select the specific area or submodel to be viewed.

The Arena simulation software includes five major components:

1.	**Modeling Environment**	Exhibit 6–14
2.	**Template Panel Modules**	Exhibit 6–21
3.	**Simulation Engine**	Exhibit 6–33
4.	**VBA Interface**	Chapter 8
5.	**Stand-Alone Programs**	Exhibit 6-56

These components are summarized in Exhibit 6–15. Like other windows-based tools, Arena permits the user to customize the Modeling Environment toolbar. The major toolbar options are illustrated in Exhibit 6–15.

The five Arena simulation software components are outlined in the next sections.

Arena Modeling Environment

The Arena modeling environment provides a basic structure for developing, executing, and viewing the Arena simulation model and its results. All model development work is done in the flowchart and spreadsheet windows. Exhibit 6–16 illustrates the flow of information between the files that make up the Arena application.

Arena model files have an extension of .doe. Exhibit 6–16 illustrates the file structure for an arbitrary Arena model, FileName.doe. The Arena model file contains all model logic and data collected and constructed by the model developer. The model file may also contain graphic or text objects used to animate or illustrate the model's operation.

Arena models are developed using the template panel illustrated in Exhibit 6–16: **BasicProcess.TPO**. The structure and use of these Standard Arena edition template panels are developed in the next section. Files BasicProcess.PLB is one of many icon or picture libraries available to the Arena user for animating the Arena model.

When the model logic and data structure have been loaded into Arena and saved as a model file, FileName.doe shown in Exhibit 6–16, the model is ready for initial testing and execution. This process is controlled by toolbar icons or function keys. The general soundness or surface validity of the model can be checked by pressing the **F4** key, selecting the **Run > Check Model** menu command, or clicking on the check mark button ✓ . Assuming that no errors have been detected, the Arena model can now be run or executed by pressing the **F5** key, selecting the **Run > Go** menu command, or clicking on the VCR-type play button ▶ .

When the model execution is initialized, a series of data files are generated. These files have legacy in Arena's origin as a text basic simulation language called *SIMAN*. As illustrated in Exhibit 6–16, the files **FileName.MOD** and **FileName.EXP** are generated containing

EXHIBIT 6–15
Arena Simulation Model Development Environment Components
Sheet arena components | Chapter 6 Worksheets.xls

Components	Elements	Applications
Model Development Environment		
Toolbar	Standard	File handling, undo, views, layers, run control
	Draw	Drawing shapes, text, colors, & fills
	Animate	Basic Animation elements: clock, calendar, values, bars, plots, histogram, queues, resources, global
	Integration	Module Data Transfer & VBA
	View	Main Screen control
	Arrange	Shape alignment, grouping, front/back
	Run interaction	Advanced run control
	Animate transfer	Transfer element animation
	Profession	Professional Edition template tools
Project Bar	Template panels	Used for model-building
	Reports	Select Report Categories
	Navigate	Move between Named Views and Submodel
Status Bar		Horizontal bar on the bottom edge of the screen
		Brief description of the current function
Flowchart Window		Model logic development & animation area
Spreadsheet Window		Model data area (Not visible during model execution)

the model logic and data in the original SIMAN file format. These files are automatically translated to an intermediate form, FileName.M and FileName.E, and combined into the final program run format or file FileName.P. Most beginning Arena users will have little need to examine any of these files; however, they can be a valuable aid in model debugging. The program run file, FileName.P, is used to execute the Arena model and is also used by the Arena Process Analyzer or PAN program and OptQuest for Arena, an optimizer program.

As the Arena simulation model is executed, an on-screen display is generated as illustrated in Exhibit 6–17. When the model is being executed, the spreadsheet view is automatically removed as are selected parts of the model structure. Other parts of the display illustrate the dynamic nature of the simulation model. As demonstrated in Exhibit 6–17,

EXHIBIT 6–16
Arena File Structure
Page Arena file
structure | Chapter 6
Drawings.vsd

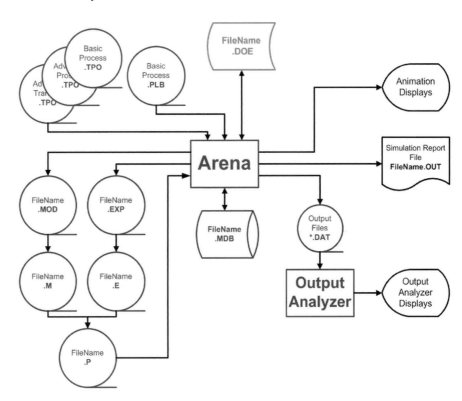

EXHIBIT 6–17
Model MM1.doe at
TNOW = 60 Minutes

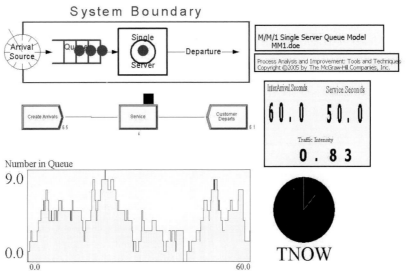

EXHIBIT 6–18 Model MM1.doe Run Setup Dialog

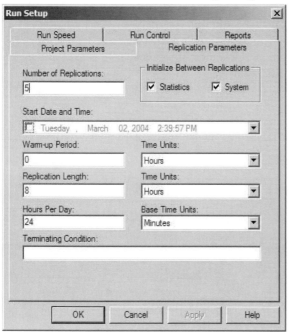

this display can include the simulation clock, the circle in the lower right corner. The current simulation time is also shown in the Status Bar near the bottom right corner. The simulation time in Exhibit 6–17 is 60.0, the end of the first hour. The replication parameters for this model were set using the **Run > Setup** dialog box illustrated in Exhibit 6–18. In this case, five replications of 480 minutes or 8 hours each were selected. The simulation clock started at the default 12:00 and now reads about 1:00.

The most significant element of Exhibit 6–17 is the plot illustrating the number of entities (customers or clients) waiting for service in the queue. During the illustrated period of simulation time, 0 to 60 minutes or during the first simulated hour, the number waiting was typically in the range of 0 to 4 entities or customers with a maximum of 9. The number 4 just below the process module labeled "Service" indicates the number of entities currently at the Service module. The string of icons or pictures at the center top of the screen illustrates the entities (customers) currently waiting for service. The numbers at the lower right corner of the Create Arrivals and Customer Departs modules indicate the number of entities processed by those modules during this simulation run. Notice that $65 - 61 = 4$, the number currently in process.

The simulation reports being collected by the Crystal Reports software and stored in file **FileName.MDB** can be viewed both during the simulation model's execution and after the entire run has been completed. Exhibit 6–19 illustrates part of the Crystal Reports along with the associated support windows designed to navigate through the report structure. The Queue report is illustrated in Exhibit 6–19. The first report line indicates that the average customer spent 4.42 minutes waiting in the queue for service, with an overall range of 0.0 to 19.16 minutes. Of the five replications, the average minimum time in the queue was 2.89 minutes, while the average maximum time in the queue was 6.39 minutes. The second report line indicates that an average of 4.51 customers were waiting in the queue for service, with an overall range of 0 to 21 customers waiting. Of the five replications, the average minimum number in the queue was 3.04, while the average maximum number in the queue was 6.55 customers.

EXHIBIT 6–19 Model MM1.doe Category Overview Report (Queue)

Preview						
⊟·MM1 Single Server Queue	2:41:12PM	**Category Overview**				March 2, 2004
⊞·Entity		*Values Across All Replications*				
⊞·Process	**MM1 Single Server Queue**					
⊞·Queue						
⊞·Resource	Replications:　5　　Time Units:　Minutes					
	Queue					
	Time					

Waiting Time	Average	Half Width	Minimum Average	Maximum Average	Minimum Value	Maximum Value
Service.Queue	4.4163	1.71	2.8923	6.3899	0.00	19.1586

Other

Number Waiting	Average	Half Width	Minimum Average	Maximum Average	Minimum Value	Maximum Value
Service.Queue	4.5141	1.74	3.0394	6.5524	0.00	21.0000

EXHIBIT 6–20
M/M/1 Queue Comparison: Theoretical versus Simulated
Sheet MM1 comparison | Chapter 6 Worksheets.xls

Label	Formula	Units	Theoretical Calculations	MM1.doe Results			
Mean Inter Arrival Time	$1/\lambda$	Seconds	60.0	5 480-minute replications			
Mean Arrival Rate	λ	Customers / Minute	1.0				
Mean Service Time	$1/\mu$	Seconds	50.0		95% Confidence Interval		
Mean Service Rate	μ	Customers / Minute	1.20	Mean	Width	Lower	Upper
Traffic Intensity	$\rho = \lambda/\mu$		0.83	0.87	0.03	0.84	0.90
Expected Number in Process, Lp	$\rho/(1-\rho)$	Customers	5.00	5.29	1.74	3.55	7.03
Expected Number in Queue, Lq	$L_s - \rho = \rho^2/(1-\rho)$	Customers	4.17	4.42	1.71	2.71	6.13
Expected Time in Process, Wp	$L_s/\lambda = 1/(\mu-\lambda)$	Minutes	5.00	5.38	1.77	3.61	7.15
Expected Time in Queue, Wq	$Lq/\lambda = \rho/(\mu-\lambda)$	Minutes	4.17	4.51	1.74	2.77	6.25

EXHIBIT 6–21
Arena Template Panel Modules
Sheet arena components | Chapter 6 Worksheets.xls

▾ |Components	▾ |Elements	▾ |Applications
Template Panel Modules	Template Files	
Basic Edition	BasicProcess.tpo	Basic modeling modules
Standard Edition	AdvancedProcess.tpo	Advanced modeling modules
Standard Edition	AdvancedTransfer.tpo	Material handling system modeling modules
SIMAN	Blocks.tpo	Original SIMAN logic modules or blocks
SIMAN	Elements.tpo	Original SIMAN data/definition modules or elements
Contact Center Edition	ContactData.tpo	Contact Center Edition Template
Contact Center Edition	Script.tpo	Contact Center Edition Template
Contact Center Edition	CSUtil.tpo	Custom Template building capabilities
Packaging Edition	Packaging.tpo	Arena Packaging Edition Template
Factory Analyzer Edition	Factory.tpo	Factory Analyzer Modules
Factory Analyzer Edition	FactoryBlocks.tpo	Factory Analyzer Blocks Panel
Factory Analyzer Edition	FactoryElements.tpo	Factory Analyzer Elements Panel
Professional Edition	UtlArena.tpo	Custom Template building capabilities

The simulation statistics presented in Exhibit 6–19 should be compared to theoretical calculations presented in Exhibit 6–5. Based on Exhibit 6–5, the calculated values for an average service time of 50 seconds are summarized in Exhibit 6–20. Notice the very close agreement between the theoretical calculations and the simulation results.

The Arena user can use the Project Bar or tree structure at the left side of the report window to navigate through the available reports. A search engine is also available to find a particular Entity, Resource, or Transporter name. Selected report elements can also be exported to an Excel workbook or a database program format.

Arena also generates a text-based simulation report at the end of each replication that is available as **FileName.OUT**. This text file can be viewed and edited with any text editor, such as WordPad. Optionally Arena can also selectively generate files with an extension of DAT that can be read, graphed, and analyzed using the Arena Output Analyzer.

Arena Template Panel Modules

The Arena Modeling environment provides access from its project bar to its template panels. The number and type of templates available to the Arena user depends on the edition of Arena licensed for the particular computer. Exhibit 6–21 lists the various Arena template panels. The academic or demonstration version of Arena provides limited access to all Arena templates for an application demonstration or for a limited size trial use.

Arena models are developed by first constructing a logical flowchart model of the process and then detailing the appropriate data elements. The difference between a Visio-based flowchart and an Arena flowchart is the ability of Arena to dynamically move entities through the Arena flowchart. These Arena entities may represent process elements such as work orders, messages, container or pallets, or operators. All Arena models must have at least one point or Create module where entities enter the flow and may have one or more exit points or Dispose modules. At any point in time only one entity is active moving through the Arena flow. When a particular entity is in control, it attempts to move as far as possible through the flowchart. This flow is stopped when an entity is delayed for a period of time, requests an unavailable resource or transporter, or must wait for some condition or signal to occur. When an entity reaches such a delay point, control is transferred to another entity that is now able to continue to move through the Arena flowchart. At any point in time, Arena may have many active entities. The academic version of Arena is limited to approximately 100 entities at any one time. The commercial version of Arena is not limited in terms of the total number entities that can be simultaneously active in the model.

EXHIBIT 6–22   **Arena Basic Process Panel Modules**

Sheet arena modules | Chapter 6 Worksheets.xls

Panel	Module Type	Module	Reference
Basic Process	Data	Entity	Entity
Basic Process	Data	Queue	Queue
Basic Process	Data	Resource	Resource
Basic Process	Data	Schedule	Resource
Basic Process	Data	Set	System
Basic Process	Data	Variable	System
Basic Process	Flowchart	Assign	Entity
Basic Process	Flowchart	Batch	Entity
Basic Process	Flowchart	Create	Entity
Basic Process	Flowchart	Decide	Entity
Basic Process	Flowchart	Dispose	Entity
Basic Process	Flowchart	Process	Resource
Basic Process	Flowchart	Record	Entity
Basic Process	Flowchart	Separate	Entity

EXHIBIT 6–23   **Arena Basic Process Panel Module Icons**

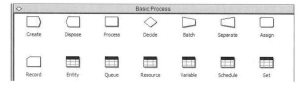

EXHIBIT 6–24   **Model MM1.doe Create Module Dialog Box**

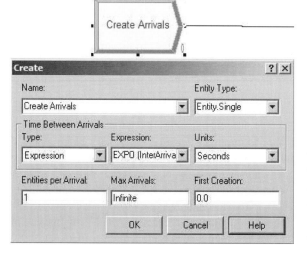

Exhibit 6–22 lists the modules available in the Arena basic process panel. More detailed information on each Arena module can be found using the online Help by pressing the **F1** key or in worksheets **Modules-BasicProcessPanel**, **ModulesAdvancedProcessPanel**, and **ModulesAdvancedTransferPanel** of Chapter 6 Worksheets.xls. Exhibit 6–23 illustrates these same basic process panel modules in the icon format of the Arena project bar. Dragging the appropriate icons from the template panel develops arena flowchart models.

The MM1.doe model illustrated in Exhibits 6–1 and 6–17 illustrates the most basic model flowchart. Four modules have been selected or dragged from the Basic Process panel. The Create module generates a stream of entities or customers into this simple model of an M/M/1 (Exponential Arrivals and Service with one server) queuing process. The Assign module performs mathematical calculations or assignments. The Process module simulates the server resource and its associated queue or waiting line. The Dispose module removes customers from the process and collects entity or customer statistics.

Flow lines connect the modules and specify the path that entities follow through the process model. Arena modules generally flow from left to right and have a limited number of connect points, related to their relative position in the model flowchart. For example, one outbound flow line must connect the right side of the Create module to its next logical module. Any positive number of inbound flow lines may connect to the left side of the Process and Dispose modules. Like the Create module, exactly one outbound flow line must leave the right side of the Process module.

Detailed information must be provided for each module in order to define how that module handles entities.

Create Module

Double-clicking on the Create module in the MM1.doe model generates the dialog box illustrated in Exhibit 6–24. The Create module is used to control the entry of entities into the Arena model. Almost all Arena models must have at least one Create module. Multiple Create modules can be used to generate the arrival of several different types of Arena entities.

The Create module illustrated in Exhibit 6–24 is labeled *Create Arrivals.* The default name would have been *Create 1.* While this default is not very descriptive, the module can be duplicated and automatically renamed to avoid a naming conflict. Arena does not permit the duplication of module names. The entities generated by this Create Module will be of type Entity.Single. Every

EXHIBIT 6–25
Model MM1.doe
Process Module
Dialog Box

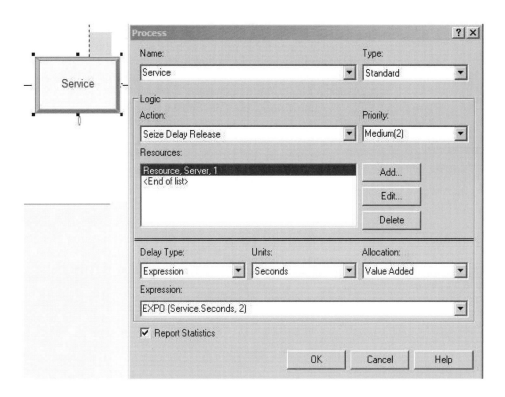

Arena entity carries with it a type, which can be changed at an Assign Module and is used for gathering Entity statistics.

Entities generated by module Create Arrivals will have a time between arrivals drawn from an Exponential distribution with a mean of InterArrival.Seconds. This was accomplished using the expression EXPO (InterArrival.Seconds, 1), where *EXPO* is the Arena Exponential distribution random number generator function; *InterArrival.Seconds* is a user-defined Arena Variable with a value of 60; and the numeric *1* specifies the random number generate stream.

Each arrival will introduce one entity into the model flow. The total number of arrivals to this model is not limited. The arrival will occur at the beginning of the simulation run, TNOW = 0.

The dialog box illustrated in Exhibit 6–24 is a typical application for the Create module. It creates a random stream of arrivals over the entire duration of the simulation run. Other Create module applications may include entities that arrive at the end of the hour to control collection of production statistics or an entity that only arrives at the beginning of the simulation run to initiate some model procedure.

Process Module

Double-clicking on the Process module in the MM1.doe model generates the dialog box illustrated in Exhibit 6–25. The Process module is used to model service or the time delay of an entity while some type of process takes place. The Process module illustrated in Exhibit 6–25 requires the use of a resource. This requirement is specified by the Logic Action option of Seize Delay Release. The resource required for this process is specified in the Resources dialog illustrated in Exhibit 6–26. In this case, a single resource named *Server* is required to perform the process. If the resource is not currently available when the entity enters the Process module, the entity must wait in a queue until the resource becomes available. By default, the queue is named *Service.Queue,* where *Service* is the Process module name. Also, by default this is a FIFO or First In First Out queue.

A Medium level or level 2 is assigned to this Process module. In this simple example, only one Process module is seeking to use a Resource Server. If multiple Process modules were simultaneously attempting to seize a Resource server, the Process module with the highest priority would gain control of the resource first. If several Process modules each have the same priority, control of the resource is given to entity, which has waited the longest time. Priority level one is the highest in Arena.

The process time for the entity after it has gained control of the Resource server is a random variable generated from an Exponential distribution mean value Service.Seconds using the expression EXPO (Service.Seconds, 2). *Service.Seconds* is an Arena variable, which must be defined elsewhere in the model.

This process is declared to be of the value added type for the cost accumulation functions of Arena. The rectangle in Exhibit 6–25 is the icon used to represent the status of the Resource server. Double-clicking on the icon opens the Resource Picture Placement window illustrated in Exhibit 6–27. This window defines how the Resource server will be displayed as a function of its status or state (Idle, Busy, Inactive, or Failed). The Arena model builder can use much more detailed resource icons, but simple colors provide a reasonable display of process status.

EXHIBIT 6–26
Model MM1.doe
Process Module
Resource Detail
Dialog Box

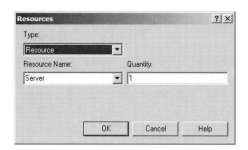

Dispose Module

Double-clicking on the Dispose module in the MM1.doe model generates the dialog box illustrated in Exhibit 6–28. The Dispose module is used to remove entities from the Arena model. Most Arena models must have at lease one Dispose module. The check mark indicates that entity statistics will be gathered for all entities leaving the model via this Dispose module. Some Arena models do not have a Dispose module; rather entities are recycled for the duration of simulation run. This form of model development might be applied when modeling a closed machine cycle.

The three flowchart modules outlined above define the logical component of the MM1.doe model. The other screen display

EXHIBIT 6–27
Arena Resource
Picture Placement
Window

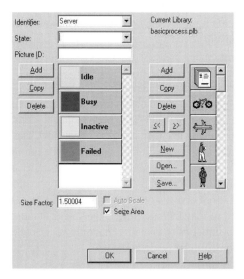

EXHIBIT 6–28
Model MM1.doe
Dispose Module
Dialog Box

objects illustrated in Exhibit 6–1 are used to animate or illustrate the model during its execution. When the flowchart modules were added to the model and their functions defined using the dialog boxes previously illustrated, certain other data elements were also automatically added to the model. Those model elements can be edited in the Spreadsheet Window by clicking on the appropriate panel icon.

Entity Spreadsheet

Exhibit 6–29 illustrates the Entity spreadsheet for the MM1.doe model. The entity Entity.Single was defined in the Create module. No additional data were added in the illustrated spreadsheet. It is possible to define cost components for each model entity.

Queue Spreadsheet

Exhibit 6–30 illustrates the Queue spreadsheet for the MM1.doe model. The queue Service.Queue was defined in the Process module. No additional data were added in the illustrated spreadsheet.

Resource Spreadsheet

Exhibit 6–31 illustrates the Resource spreadsheet for the MM1.doe model. The Resource server was defined in the Process module. No additional data were added in the illustrated spreadsheet. This spreadsheet can be used to define a resource with a fixed capacity greater than one or a capacity that varies over time according to schedule. This spreadsheet can also be used to define a failure pattern for the resource.

Variable Spreadsheet

Exhibit 6–32 illustrates the Variable spreadsheet for the MM1.doe model. The variable InterArrival.Seconds is used in the Create module but must be defined in the spreadsheet. Its initial value is set to 60. That value is also displayed on the Arena screen, Exhibit 6–17, when the model is being run.

EXHIBIT 6–29
Model MM1.doe
Entity Spreadsheet

	Entity Type	Initial Picture	Holding Cost / Hour	Initial VA Cost	Initial NVA Cost	Initial Waiting Cost	Initial Tran Cost	Initial Other Cost	Report Statistics
1	Entity.Single	Picture.Red Ball	0.0	0.0	0.0	0.0	0.0	0.0	☑

Double-click here to add a new row.

EXHIBIT 6–30
Model MM1.doe
Queue Spreadsheet

	Name	Type	Shared	Report Statistics
1	Service.Queue	First In First Out	☐	☑

Double-click here to add a new row.

EXHIBIT 6–31
Model MM1.doe
Resource Spreadsheet

	Name	Type	Capacity	Busy / Hour	Idle / Hour	Per Use	StateSet Name	Failures	Report Statistics
1	Server	Fixed Capacity	1	0.0	0.0	0.0		0 rows	☑

Double-click here to add a new row.

EXHIBIT 6–32
Model MM1.doe
Variable Spreadsheet

	Name	Rows	Columns	Clear Option	Initial Values	Report Statistics
1	Service.Seconds			System	1 rows	☐
2	InterArrival.Seconds			System	1 rows	☐

Double-click here to add a new row.

Initial Values
60.0

Challenge

Arena Simulation Engine

In addition to the Arena Modeling environment, Arena provides the simulation engine required to execute and collect statistics from the model. Exhibit 6–33 lists some of features of the Arena simulation engine.

Entity

The dynamic elements in the Arena model are the entities. Entities enter the model via a Create module and exit via a Dispose module. Although a large Arena model may contain thousands of entities at any one time, only one entity is currently active. The active entity attempts to move as far as possible through the logic modules of the model. In model MM1.doe, the only point at which an entity can be delayed is the Process module. When an entity enters the Service Process module, either the service function is started immediately or the entity is held in the Service.Queue. If the Resource server is available, the duration of the service is determined based on the random expression. The Arena simulation engine schedules an End-Of-Service event on the Event Calendar to take place at a future point in time.

If the Resource server is not available, the duration of the time in queue cannot be determined. The entity will be released from the queue only after the server has processed all previously waiting entities.

EXHIBIT 6–33   Arena Simulation Engine

Sheet Arena Components | Chapter 6 Worksheets.xls

Components	Elements	Applications
Simulation Engine		
Entity	Dynamic element that flows through the model logic structure	
Simulation Clock	Tnow is the current simulation time	
Event Calendar	Controls time advance & sequence of events	
Random Number Generator	BETA (Alpha1, Alpha2)	Beta distribution (continuous)
	CONTinuous (Prob1, Value1, Prob2, Value2, ...)	Empirical (user defined) distribution (continuous)
	DISCrete (Prob1, Value1, Prob2, Value2, ...)	Empirical (user defined) distribution (discrete)
	EXPOnential (Mean)	Exponential distribution (continuous)
	GAMMa (Beta, Alpha)	Gamma distribution (continuous)
	JOHNson (gamma, delta, lambda, xi)	Johnson distribution (continuous)
	ERLAng (Mean, k)	k-Erlang distribution (continuous)
	LOGNormal (LogMean, LogStd)	Lognormal distribution (continuous)
	NORMal (Mean, SD)	Normal distribution (continuous)
	POISson (Mean)	Poisson distribution (discrete)
	TRIAngular (Min, Mode, Max)	Triangular distribution (continuous)
	UNIForm (Min, Max)	Uniform distribution (continuous)
	WEIBull (Beta, Alpha)	Weibull distribution (continuous)
Statistic Collection Tools	Counters	Count Block collected statistic
	Cstats	Continuous Variable Time-Persistent statistics
	Dstats	Discrete Variable Time-Persistent statistics
	Frequency	Resource state or Expression Value statistics
	Outputs	Value of Arena expression at end of replication
	Tallies	Dispose Module & Tally Block collected statistic
Report Generation, Text File	Model.out	Can be viewed or printed using any text editor
Crystal Reports, Model.mdb	Category Overview	System summary, conveyor, entity, process, queue, resource, transporter, and user-specified statistic information summarized across all replications
	Category by Replication	Same as Category Overview except by replication
	Entities	Cost, Time, and Number In/Out statistics by Entity type
	Frequencies	Resource State or Expression Value statistics
	Processes	Cost and Time statistics by Process
	Queues	Time and Number Waiting statistics by Queue
	Transfers	As specified in the Advanced Transfer panel
	User Specified	As specified in the Advanced Process panel Statistics Module

Simulation Clock and Event Calendar

The principal function of the Arena Simulation Engine is to control the flow of entities through the logic flow chart. When one entity has moved as far as it can, the Arena Simulation Engine must select the next entity to attempt to move. If no entity can be moved at the current simulation time, the Arena Simulation Engine advances the Simulation Clock to the next scheduled event. Entities that are delayed for a specific period of time are entered into the Simulation Event Calendar. The Simulation Event Calendar manages the advance of the Simulation Clock.

To gain a better understanding of how the Simulation Clock and the Simulation Event Calendar work, see Exhibit 6–34 for an extract of the trace file that Arena can generate as the simulation is executed. The trace follows in exact detail the steps taken by the entities as they move through the model flowchart modules.

At simulation time, TNOW = 0.0 minutes, entity number 2 enters the model and moves forward to the point of starting service by the Resource server. The length of that service is generated from an Exponential distribution mean of 50 seconds. The simulated service time for entity number 2 is 1.187813 minutes.

At simulation time, TNOW = 0.13583246 minutes, entity number 3 enters the model and moves forward to the point of starting service by the Resource server where it starts its wait in queue Service.Queue.

The two steps illustrated in Exhibit 6-34 are repeated for the approximately 480 entities, which are processed during each 480-minute simulation replication. Clearly, this trace report is too lengthy

EXHIBIT 6–34
Model MM1.doe
Trace Report
Extract

```
SIMAN System Trace Beginning at Time: 0.0
Seq#  Label          Block      System Status Change
____  _____    _____    _____

Time:  0  Entity: 2
   1 2$              CREATE
                                Entity Type set to Entity.Expo
                                Next creation scheduled at time 0.13583246
                                Batch of 1 Entity.Expo entities created
   2 3$              ASSIGN
                                Create Arrivals.NumberOut set to 1.0
   3 1$              ASSIGN
                                Service.NumberIn set to 1.0
                                Service.WIP set to 1.0
   4 35$             STACK
                                Saving 1 copies of internal attributes
   5 9$              QUEUE
                                Entity 2 sent to next block
   6 8$              SEIZE
                                Tally Service.Queue.WaitingTime recorded 0.0
                                Seized 1.0 unit(s) of resource Server.1
   7 7$              DELAY
                                Delayed by 1.187813 until time 1.187813
Time: 0.13583246  Entity: 3
   1 2$              CREATE
                                Entity Type set to Entity.Expo
                                Next creation scheduled at time 0.51933194
                                Batch of 1 Entity.Expo entities created
   2 3$              ASSIGN
                                Create Arrivals.NumberOut set to 2.0
   3 1$              ASSIGN
                                Service.NumberIn set to 2.0
                                Service.WIP set to 2.0
   4 35$             STACK
                                Saving 1 copies of internal attributes
   5 9$              QUEUE
                                Entity 3 sent to next block
   6 8$              SEIZE
                                Could not seize resource Server.1
                                Entity 3 added to queue Service.Queue at rank 1
```

for casual reading, but it can be invaluable when attempting to learn how Arena handles particular simulation functions.

Random Number Generator

Exhibit 6-33 illustrates the random number generators provided by Arena. These generators correspond to the widely used statistical distributions.

BETA (Alpha1, Alpha2)
EXPOnential (Mean)
GAMMa (Beta, Alpha)
JOHNson (gamma, delta, lambda, xi)
ERLAng (Mean, k)
LOGNormal (LogMean, LogStd)
NORMal (Mean, SD)
POISson (Mean)
TRIAngular (Min, Mode, Max)
UNIForm (Min, Max)
WEIBull (Beta, Alpha)

Notice that the first four letters of the distribution names are capitalized and that the model builder may use the shortened (four-letter) form of the distribution names. The optional parameter Stream can be used to control how the specific random variables are generated by Arena. Advanced model builders should consult the Arena documentation for specifics related to control of random number streams.

Arena also provides two means to model user or empirical data:

CONTinuous(Prob1,Value1,Prob2, Value2, . . .)
DISCrete(Prob1,Value1,Prob2, Value2, . . .

The CONTinuous function returns a sample from the continuous probability function while the DISCrete function returns a sample from the discrete probability function. Operands Prob1,Value1, Prob2, Value2, ... contains pairs of probability and value pairs in order of increasing cumulative probability. We used the DISCrete function in Chapter 1 for the D&E.doe model Disc (0.11, 1, 0.28, 2, 0.46, 3, 0.69, 4, 0.90, 5, 1, 6).

Exhibit 6–35 illustrates the input data for this example. With this flexibility, the Arena model builder can model almost any type of random phenomena.

EXHIBIT 6–35
Items Ordered Data
Sheet D and E order size | Chapter 6 Worksheets.xls

Items Ordered	Frequency	Cumulative Frequency
1	11	11
2	17	28
3	18	46
4	23	69
5	21	90
6	10	100

Statistic Collection Tools

By default, Arena collects the commonly used statistics related to queuing processes: utilization, number wait, time waiting, and more. Some of these default statistics for model MM1.doe were illustrated in Exhibit 6–9. In order to demonstrate the variety of statistic output available from Arena, we have modified the original model to form model MM1 Statistics.doe. We now review how these new statistics are collected and then illustrate their output in Crystal Reports.

Counter   An Arena Counter is typically used to count the number of entities passing a particular point in the model network logic. Some counters come with the module, such as the Decide and Dispose modules. It is, however, a good practice to include a few counters in a model to assure that the entities flow in the manner expected by the model builder. Exhibit 6–36 illustrates the Record module used to count the number of customers or entities completing service. Notice that this information would also be available from the Dispose module. The Record type of Count was selected. We'll demonstrate another record option in the next section. We provided a Counter name "Number served." In order to view the results of this counter, it is necessary to use the Statistic module from the Advanced Process Panel. Exhibit 6–37 illustrates that module for five different types of statistics. The Number Served is defined in row 1 of Exhibit 6–37. Notice that we have elected to initialize this counter for each replication. Therefore, the reported counter will apply only to a single replication. We display the counter results later in the section on "Output."

Tally   Arena Tallies are used record statistics, such as the time between entity passage or the throughput time of an entity from its creation to a particular point in the model. In the case illustrated in Exhibit 6–38, we are recording or tallying the time between entities

EXHIBIT 6–36
Model MM1.doe
Record Number Served

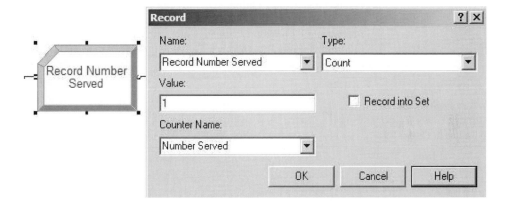

EXHIBIT 6–37
Model MM1.doe
Advanced Process Statistics Module

	Name	Type	Tally Name	Counter Name	Initialization Option	Expression	Report Label	Frequency Type	Resource Name	Report Label	Categories
1	Number Served	Counter	Tally 1	Number Served	Replicate		Number Served	Value		Number Served	0 rows
2	Time Between	Tally	Record Time Between	Counter 2	Replicate			Value		Time Between	0 rows
3	Number Waiting	Time-Persistent	Tally 3	Counter 3	Replicate	NQ (Service Queue)	Number Waiting	Value		Number Waiting	0 rows
4	Number Arriving	Output	Tally 4	Counter 4	Replicate	EntitiesIn(Entity.Single)	Number Arriving	Value		Number Arriving	0 rows
5	Server Frequency	Frequency	Tally 5	Counter 5	Replicate		Server Frequency	State	Server	Server Frequency	0 rows

Double-click here to add a new row.

EXHIBIT 6–38
Model MM1.doe
Record Time Between

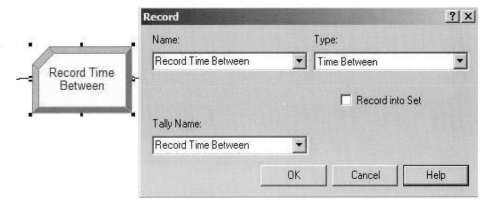

leaving the Service module. The user-specified statistic for this tally is illustrated in the second row of Exhibit 6–37. It is possible to record each Tally on an Arena data file for additional analysis using the Arena Output Processor.

Time Persistent Time Persistent statistics track the value of an Arena variable or expression over the course of the simulation run. The third row of Exhibit 6–37 defines a Time Persistent statistic named "Number Waiting" using the expression **NQ (Service.Queue)** or the number of entities or customers waiting in the Service.Queue. This expression could be generated using the Arena Expression Builder as illustrated in Exhibit 6–39. The Arena Expression Builder is invoked by right-clicking whenever the Arena dialog requests an expression and selects the **Build Expression . . .** option. Like the Tallies, Time Persistent statistics can be saved on Arena data files for analysis using the Arena Output processor.

Output Output statistics record the value of an Arena variable or expression at the end of the simulation run. The fourth row of Exhibit 6–37 defines an Output statistic named "Number Arriving" using the expression **EntitiesIn(Entity.Single)** or the number of entities of type Entity.Single created by the Create module. This expression could be generated using the Arena Expression Builder as illustrated in Exhibit 6–40. Like the Tallies and Time Persistent statistics, Output statistics can be saved on Arena data files.

Frequency Frequency statistics can track the use of Arena resource overtime. The fifth row of Exhibit 6–37 defines a Frequency statistic named "Server Frequency" to track the state of the Resource Server. Frequency statistics can be saved on Arena data files. One or more categories may be excluded from the Frequency calculations in order to gather statistics on a restricted subset. This is indicated by specifying Exclude for the Category Option field for Frequency type statistics. The summary report displays statistics for both standard and restricted categories for all frequencies specified.

Crystal Reports Statistic Output

We will now review the Crystal Reports Statistic Output resulting from the five statistics requested in Exhibit 6–37. Exhibit 6–41 illustrates the User Specified report for the first simulation replication or 480-minute period. This report is divided by statistic type: Tally, Counter, Time Persistent, and Output.

Tally The time between tally indicates the period of time in minutes between consecutive completions of service. When the server is continuously busy, this statistic should represent the service times, which in this case should average 50 seconds. When the server is not continuously busy, the statistic also includes the server idle gap. The average time between service completions

EXHIBIT 6–39
Arena Expression Builder, Current Number in Queue

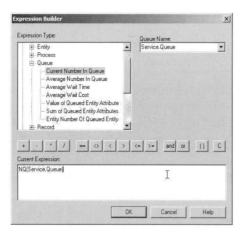

EXHIBIT 6–40
Arena Expression Builder, Number In Entity

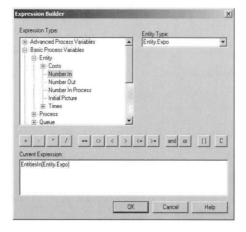

was 0.999 minutes with a range of 0.001 to 8.3379 minutes. The 95 percent confidence Half Width is 0.096 for a confidence interval of 0.999 ± 0.096 or (0.903 to 1.095 minutes).

Counter   The counter indicates the number of customers served during the first simulation replication was 485.

Time Persistent   The number of customers waiting in queue varied from 0 to 21 with a mean of 6.55. Arena was not able to provide an estimate of Half Width due to a strong level of correlation in the individual values of NQ (Service.Queue).

Output   Output shows the number of arriving customers during the first simulation replication was 494. Comparing that value to the Counter above, 494 − 485 = 9, customers must have been in the process at time 480 minutes.

Frequency   Exhibit 6–42 illustrates the Frequencies report for all five simulation replications. The Server Resource has only two states: Busy and Idle. Over the five simulation replications, the percent of time the Server Resource was busy ranged from 83.5 percent to 89.8 percent. The percent of time the Server Resource was idle is, of course, the complement of these values. The Average busy period ranged from 4.5 to 10.0 minutes. Because each service was expected to take 50 seconds, the number of customers serviced per busy period can be calculated by the following expressions:

$$4.5 \text{ minutes} * 60 \text{ (seconds per minute)} \div 50 \text{ seconds} = 5.4 \text{ customers}$$

$$10.0 \text{ minutes} * 60 \text{ (seconds per minute)} \div 50 \text{ seconds} = 12 \text{ customers}$$

The server idle periods ranged from 0.81 to 1.17 minutes.

Other Queuing Process Models

So far in this chapter, we have reviewed two Arena models of an M/M/1 queuing process. These models—MM1.doe and MM1 Statistics.doe—introduced a few of the basic Arena modules. We will now introduce three additional queuing process–related Arena models to both introduce some new Arena modules and to provide more insight on the behavior of queues.

EXHIBIT 6–41
Model MM1.doe
User Specified
Report

- User Specified.rpt
  - MM1 Single Server Que
    - Replication 1
    - Replication 2
    - Replication 3
    - Replication 4
    - Replication 5

Replication 1	Start Time:	0.00	Stop Time:	480.00	Time Units:	Minutes

Tally

Between	Average	Half Width	Minimum	Maximum
Record Time Between	0.9892	0.096116313	0.00177476	8.3793

Counter

Count	Value
Number Served	485.00

Time Persistent

Time Persistent	Average	Half Width	Minimum	Maximum
Number Waiting	6.5524	(Correlated)	0	21.0000

Output

Output	Value
Number Arriving	494.00

Model MM3.doe

Exhibit 6–6 shows the M/M/3 Queuing Process diagram where three servers work in parallel from a common queue. Model MM3.doe illustrated in Exhibit 6–43, is a very simple set of modifications of model MM1.doe. First, the capacity of the Resource Server was increased from 1 to 3. Secondly, the value of the Variable InterArrival.Seconds was reduced from 60 to 20 seconds. The background picture of the queuing process copied from a Visio drawing was also modified.

Exhibit 6–44 illustrates model MM3.doe at simulation time, TNOW = 60 minutes. Up to this point, 182 customers have arrived, 179 have completed service, and the difference of 3 customers is currently being served. Because this model included a total of three servers, all are busy at this point in time, and no customers are waiting in the queue. The plot at the bottom of Exhibit 6–44 indicates that the number of customers waiting in the queue over the first hour varied as high as 10 while the average number was 1 or 2.

Exhibit 6–45 illustrates the Category Overview report of queue statistics for the five 480-minute replications. The number of customers in the queue averaged 3.42 with a half width of 0.31. Thus, the 95 percent confidence interval for the mean number of customers in the queue is 3.11 to 3.73. The actual number of customers in the queue varied from 0 to 21. The minimum average was 3.15, which indicates that on one of the five replications, the mean number of customers in the queue was as low as 3.15. In another replication, the mean was as high as 3.81. The waiting time for customers in the queue averaged 1.12 minutes with a half width of 0.09. Thus, the 95 percent confidence interval for the mean waiting time for customers in the queue is 1.03 to 1.21. The actual waiting time for customers in the queue varied from 0 to 6.01 minutes. The minimum average was 1.04, which indicates that on one of the five replications the mean waiting time for customers in the queue was as low as 1.04 minutes. In another replication the mean was as high as 1.23 minutes.

Model Comparison.doe

It can be shown theoretically that service provided by a group of servers will have a lower average number of waiting customers and customer waiting time if a pooled queue is used rather than a separate queue for each server. In the United States, most post offices and air-

EXHIBIT 6–42

Model MM1.doe Frequencies Report

Frequencies.rpt				
MM1 Single Server Queue				Replications: 5

Replication 1   Start Time: 0.00   Stop Time: 480.00   Time Units: Minutes

Server Frequency	Number Obs	Average Time	Standard Percent	Restricted Percent
BUSY	43	10.0193	89.76	89.76
IDLE	42	1.1707	10.24	10.24

Replication 2   Start Time: 0.00   Stop Time: 480.00   Time Units: Minutes

Server Frequency	Number Obs	Average Time	Standard Percent	Restricted Percent
BUSY	90	4.5355	85.04	85.04
IDLE	89	0.8068	14.96	14.96

Replication 3   Start Time: 0.00   Stop Time: 480.00   Time Units: Minutes

Server Frequency	Number Obs	Average Time	Standard Percent	Restricted Percent
BUSY	79	5.0730	83.49	83.49
IDLE	79	1.0030	16.51	16.51

Replication 4   Start Time: 0.00   Stop Time: 480.00   Time Units: Minutes

Server Frequency	Number Obs	Average Time	Standard Percent	Restricted Percent
BUSY	69	6.1066	87.78	87.78
IDLE	68	0.8624	12.22	12.22

Replication 5   Start Time: 0.00   Stop Time: 480.00   Time Units: Minutes

Server Frequency	Number Obs	Average Time	Standard Percent	Restricted Percent
BUSY	54	7.9424	89.35	89.35
IDLE	53	0.9643	10.65	10.65

EXHIBIT 6–43 **Model MM3.doe Network Logic Flow**

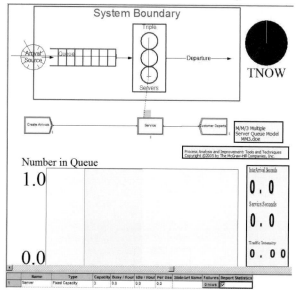

EXHIBIT 6–44 **Model MM3.doe at TNOW = 60 Minutes**

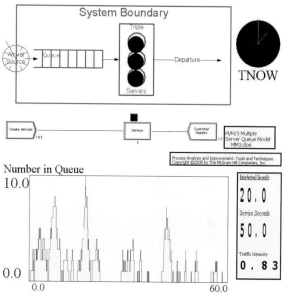

ports use pooled queues. However, U.S. supermarkets have yet to find a suitable means to pool customers into a single queue feeding multiple servers or checkout clerks. We have developed an Arena simulation model to demonstrate the advantage of using a pooled queue. Exhibit 6–46 illustrates the general structure of the model.

The top half of Exhibit 6–46 shows three servers operating independently in parallel. Each server has its own customer generation process. The bottom half of the exhibit has three servers operating jointly being fed by a single queue. As each customer enters the independent server process, a duplicate or clone is sent to the pooled queue process. Thus, an identical stream of customers presents themselves to both processes. Exhibit 6–47 illustrates Arena model Comparison.doe that we have developed to test the impact of pooled versus independent queuing processes.

Separate Module

The Model Comparison.doe uses three separate Create modules to generate independent customer arrival streams. Each arriving customer entity enters a separate module, which is used to split or clone the original customer entity. Exhibit 6–48 illustrates module Separate 1, which duplicates the original entry and sends both entities to a different module. The original entity goes directly to Service 1. The duplicate entity goes to Assign module, Assign as Parallel. Exhibit 6–49 illustrates module Assign as Parallel.

EXHIBIT 6–45
Model MM3.doe Category Overview Report (Queue)

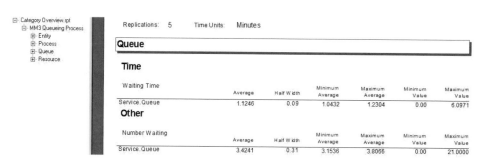

EXHIBIT 6–46
Two Queuing Process Analysis Diagram
Page comparison |
Chapter 6 Drawing.vsd

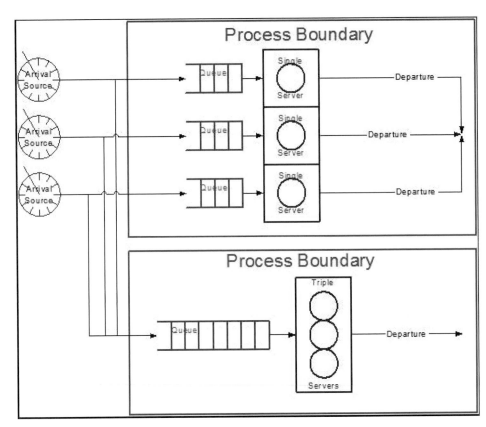

EXHIBIT 6–47 **Model Comparison.doe Network Logic Flow**

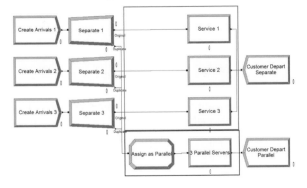

Assign Module

Module Assign as Parallel makes two assignments. First, the Entity Type is changed from **Entity.Single** set in the Create module to **Entity.Parallel**. Next, Entity Picture Icon is changed from **Picture.Red Ball** (the default set in the Entity spreadsheet, see Exhibit 6–21) to **Picture.Blue Ball**. Every Arena entity can have a picture or icon associated with it for animation.

The Assign module illustrated in Exhibit 6–49 only illustrates part of the Arena Assign module capability. Exhibit 6–50 illustrates the Assignments dialog box that is displayed when the Add button is pressed on the Assign module. Arena permits five types of assignment using the Assign module. We will discuss each of these in detail.

Variables Arena Variables are global names associated with a numeric value. Arena Variables may be singular or may have one (list) or two (table) dimensions. Singular Variables can be defined directly in an Assign module. Dimensioned Variables must be defined in the Variable spreadsheet (see Exhibit 6–32). The values contained by an Arena Variable can be referenced or changed anywhere in the Arena model. Arena Variable values can also be displayed on the Arena animation screen. All models in this chapter use two Arena Variables: InterArrival.Seconds and Service.Seconds. Their values are initially set in the Variable spreadsheet, Exhibit 6–32, and not changed during the course of the simulation. Their val-

EXHIBIT 6–48
Model
Comparison.doe
Module Separate 1

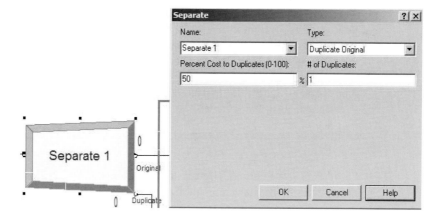

EXHIBIT 6–49
Model
Comparison.doe
Module Assign as
Parallel

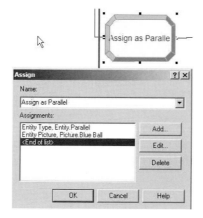

EXHIBIT 6–50   Model Comparison.doe Assignments
Dialog

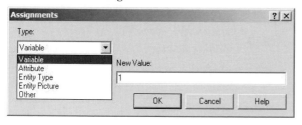

ues are displayed on the simulation animation (see Exhibits 6–7, 6–44, 6–53, and 6–57). If the model user wishes to change either of these two Variable values, it must be done in the Variable spreadsheet.

In addition to the user-defined Variables such as InterArrival.Seconds and Service.Seconds, Arena automatically generates many variables that can be referenced through the model. For the most part, these automatic variables cannot be changed in value by the user, but their current values can be used to make a model decision or to generate statistic results. Some of these automatic variable values are displayed on the Arena animation during the simulation. For example, each Create module displays the current value of the name.NumberOut or specifically of all models of this chapter except Comparison.doe and Create Arrivals.NumberOut.

Attributes   Arena Attributes appear and are used similar to Arena Variables, however, they are associated only with Arena Entities. Each Arena Entity carries with it a set of numeric Attribute values. A given Arena Entity in general knows the value only of its Attributes. Attributes are used to carry with the Entity information such as the Work Order Number, Order Quantity, and Order Due Date. Thus, Arena Attributes act like a Job Ticket or Routing Slip. Attributes are used to differentiate between entities. All Arena Entities automatically have six attributes:

1. Entity.HoldCostRate
2. Entity.JobStep
3. Entity.Picture
4. Entity.Sequence
5. Entity.Station
6. Entity.Type

For example, the Module Assign as Parallel in model Comparison.doe is used to reclassify the Entity Type and Entity Picture. Thus, unlike automatic Variables, automatic Attributes can be changed by model code in Assign modules. The models in this chapter have not used any user-specified Attributes.

Arena Attributes may be singular or may have one (list) or two (table) dimensions. Singular Attributes can be defined directly in an Assign module. Dimensioned Attributes must be defined the Attributes element of the SIMAN Elements template.

Entity Type   Entity Type is a special automatic Attribute, Entity.Type, used to statistically track Entities.

Entity Picture   Entity Picture is a special automatic Attribute, Entity.Picture, used to display Entities in the Arena animation.

Other   The Other type of assignment type is used to make assignments to dimensions Attributes and Variables and other special variables. The default special variable is *J*, the only integer-valued Arena variable.

EXHIBIT 6–51
Entity Pictures
Dialog Window

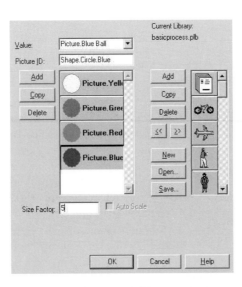

Entity Icon

While Arena provides a large number of default icons, the user can select and edit the pictures to be displayed using the **Edit > Entity Pictures . . .** menu command. Exhibit 6–51 shows the resulting dialog for model Comparison.doe. From this dialog, the Arena model builder can select appropriate pictures from a variable of library files. In this case, we are using file **basicprocess.plb**. Double-clicking on an icon opens a picture-editing window as illustrated in Exhibit 6–52. Simple drawing command can be used to modify the picture. Pictures can also be copied from more advanced drawing software, such as Visio.

EXHIBIT 6–52
Arena Picture Editor

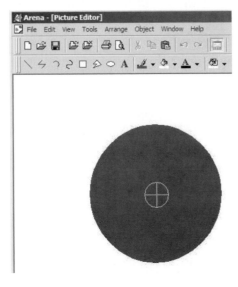

Simulation Results

Exhibit 6–53 illustrates model Comparison.doe at simulation time, TNOW = 60 minutes. Up to this point 65, 49, and 40 customers have entered the service streams for Server.1, Server.2, and Server.3, respectively. A total of 154 customers have entered the process, while 149 have left the independent queue process and 150 have left the pooled queue process. This indicates a slight advantage for the pooled queue, but we will address this later in more detail. At simulation time 60 minutes, all servers were busy with two customers waiting for Server.1 and one waiting for the pooled servers. The plot at the bottom of Exhibit 6–53 illustrates the number of customers in

EXHIBIT 6–53   Model Comparison.doe at TNOW = 60 Minutes

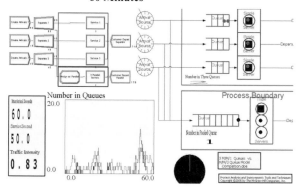

the two queuing processes of the first 60-minute simulation period. In general, the independent queues have more customers waiting than the pooled queue. We will next review the Crystal Reports for this model to verify this conclusion.

Exhibit 6–54 illustrates the Category Overview report for Time Persistent statistics for the five 480-minute replications. The advantage of the pooled queue is very clear. The average number of customers waiting for the independent queuing process was 12.13 with a maximum of 49, while the average number of customers waiting for the pooled queuing process was 2.78 with a maximum of 29. Thus, the pooled queue process enjoys about a fourfold advantage over the independent queuing process.

Similar differences in the average wait time can be found in the Crystal Reports of the Comparison.doe model. The reason that the pooled queue process appears to have such a large advantage is the fact that our model did not permit queue jumping. In the United States, many customers caught in a slow-moving queue will leave that queue and enter another shorter queue. This is particularly true when one or more servers are idle with several customers waiting for the currently busy server. The reader is encouraged to modify model Comparison.doe to permit customers to switch between queues. What type of decision rules would be required to implement such a policy?

Model MV1.doe

We have developed one additional Arena model to investigate the impact of the M/M/1 queuing process assumptions. As we stated previously, few real processes might actually operate with an exponential service time. Exhibit 6–55 illustrates model MV1.doe that directs a single stream of arriving customers into three single server queuing processes. Service Fixed operates with a fixed service time of 50 seconds. Because the arrival process is exponential, this is equivalent to the M/F/1 queuing process illustrated in Exhibit 6–9. Service Expo operates with an exponential service time and a mean of 50 seconds. This is identical to our model MM1.doe presented earlier. Service Normal operates with a normal distribution service time of mean 50 seconds and standard deviation 12.5 seconds.

Again, this model introduces a new model module. In this case, it is the Branch block from the Blocks template. Notice that this module is not colored and represents one of the original SIMAN Blocks that predate Arena. Because the Standard Edition of Arena includes both the Blocks and Elements Templates, Arena model could be composed of basic

EXHIBIT 6–54
Model Comparison.doe Number in Queues Report

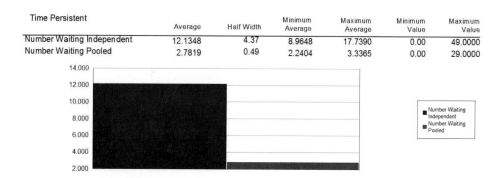

Time Persistent	Average	Half Width	Minimum Average	Maximum Average	Minimum Value	Maximum Value
Number Waiting Independent	12.1348	4.37	8.9648	17.7390	0.00	49.0000
Number Waiting Pooled	2.7819	0.49	2.2404	3.3365	0.00	29.0000

EXHIBIT 6–55
Model MV1.doe
Network Logic Flow

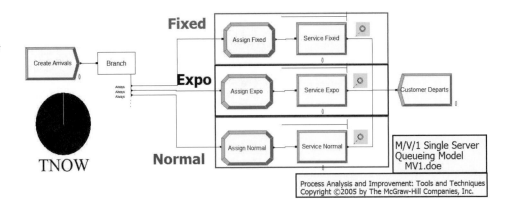

SIMAN code. In general, we do not recommend developing models at this basic level but in some cases steps can be saved by using these primitive blocks and elements. Exhibit 6–56 illustrates the Branch block. The Branch block can be used in a fashion similar to the Separate module illustrated in Exhibit 5–50. In this case we are using a single Branch block to create two new entities or clones and to send the three entities to the Assign modules named *Assign Fixed, Assign Expo,* and *Assign.Normal.* The Branch block can also be used in place of the Decide module, which will be introduced in Chapter 7. SIMAN level blocks also can include a label that can be used to control entity flow similar to Go To statements in FORTRAN or Basic.

Exhibit 6–57 illustrates model MV1.doe at simulation time, TNOW = 60 minutes. At this point, all three servers are busy with three customers waiting in the Service Expo queue.

Exhibit 6–58 illustrates the number of customers waiting in queue for the three different service processes. Notice that the average queue lengths are nearly identical for the Fixed and Normal service time distributions. However, the queue length was about twice as long for the Exponential service time process.

The Arena models presented in this chapter illustrate how simple queuing processes can be modeled. We have introduced a few of the many available Arena modules. A more com-

EXHIBIT 6–56   Model MV1.doe Branch Block

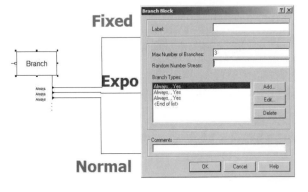

EXHIBIT 6–57   Model MV1.doe at TNOW = 60 Minutes

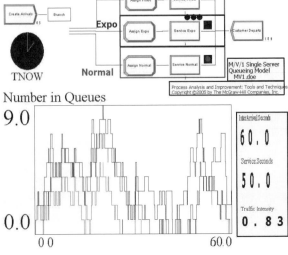

EXHIBIT 6–58
Model MV1.doe
Number in Queues
Report

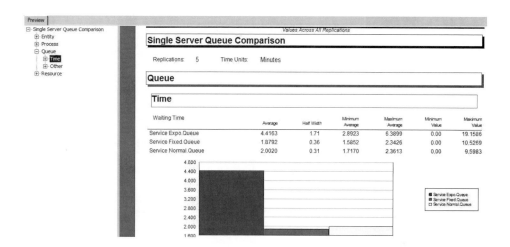

prehensive review of Arena modules is covered in the next chapter. The queuing models that we have developed in this chapter were designed to be part of more complex models. The queuing model in Chapter 7 will link several queuing processes together in order to model manufacturing processes. We next introduce the stand-alone programs provided with the Arena software and the example models that can be used as an instruction guide.

Other Arena Programs

Arena includes several stand-alone programs that can be executed independently or from the Arena toolbar. Exhibit 6–59 lists several stand-alone programs included in Arena. Application of these stand-alone programs is demonstrated in Chapter 9.

EXHIBIT 6–59 **Arena Stand-Alone Programs**

Sheet Arena components | Chapter 6 Worksheets.xls

Components	Elements	Applications
Stand Alone Programs		
Input	Input data analyzer	Goodness-of-fit testing program
OptQuest for Arena	Arena Optimizer program	Heuristic search for best "Optimal" model solution
Output	Graphical analyzer program	Read & displays Arena output file (FileName.dat)
Pan	Process ANalyzer program	User defined search for best model solution

Arena Examples

The best way to develop an Arena model is to start with a well-written example. Rockwell Software has provided two types of Arena examples on its distribution CD-ROM. First, a set of complete examples are documented and illustrated in Exhibit 6–60. These example model files are typically stored in the folder **..\Program Files\Rockwell Software\Arena\Examples**. Some of these example model files are too large to be modified using the academic version of Arena; however, all the example model files can be directly executed.

The beginning Arena user may find the example model files too complex for learning how to model a specific application. To assist in this process, Rockwell Software has developed a set of Smarts model files for each Arena version. Exhibit 6–61 illustrates the Smarts files of Arena Standard Edition. A complete list of those files with filtering is available on the worksheet Smarts. The Smarts model files are typically stored in folder **..\Program Files\Rockwell Software\Arena\Smarts**. Worksheets **FSmart** and **HSmart** list the Smarts files for the Arena Factory Analyzer and Packaging Editions but are not illustrated in this text.

EXHIBIT 6–60

Arena Examples
Sheet Examples |
Chapter 6
Worksheets.xls

..\Program Files\Rockwell Software\Arena\Examples	
Model Name (*.doe) ▾	Description ▾
ACME Medical Equipment	Example of how Arena can be used to model a complete business process Concepts illustrated: Process module, Decide module, animation of several different resources, changing entity picture in mid-model to represent current status, generating a job number automatically in Arena, attaching the job number to an entity (Assign module), and permanent batching
Bank Kiosk Analysis	This study examines alternatives for utilizing automatic ("self-serve") kiosks in a bank lobby The optimization problem is to minimize the total resource cost (of tellers and kiosks), while providing acceptable customer service Options include how many tellers to assign to customer transactions, how many kiosks to place in the bank, and what proportion of customers will use tellers
Banking Transactions	Demonstrates the various transactions and activities at a bank, including ATM, teller, and drive-thru transactions
Billing Department	Complex model of a standard billing center Concepts illustrated: Process module, assigning an attribute (Assign module), different processing by attribute (Decide module by condition), resource animation, modeling an error checking scenario, entity duplication for parallel processing, and modeling resource cost

EXHIBIT 6–61

Arena Smarts Files
Sheet Smarts | Chapter
6 Worksheets.xls

Arena Smarts files, a collection of small example models that demonstrate a variety of modeling techniques and situations commonly encountered
Smarts files have been specifically designed for use as a training or reference tool.
Each Smarts File is listed in one or more of the categories below.

\Program Files\Rockwell Software\Arena\Smarts	258	Number of Smart models

Category ▾	Model Name Smarts*.doe ▾	Application ▾
VBA and Visual Basic	001	VBA—VariableArray Value
Modules	002	Batch and Separate Modules
Batching	002	Batch and Separate Modules
Modules	003	Assign Module Example
Resources	004	Defining a Resource Capacity
Decision Logic	005	Decide Module Example
Modules	005	Decide Module Example
Named Views	006	Using Named Views
Basic Concepts	007	Basic Modeling
Hierarchical Submodels	008	Hierarchical Modeling
Hierarchical Submodels	009	Nested Submodel Example

Exercises

The Arena model files provided with this chapter, MM1.doe, MM3.doe, and Comparison.doe all used a mean inter-arrival time of 60 seconds and a mean service time of 50 seconds. Worksheet MM1 Comparison (Exhibit 6-20) compared the theoretical versus simulated results for a M/M/1 Queue Comparison. *Hint:* When making changes to an Arena model provided on the textbook CD, first save the modified model with a new name on your hard drive before making any changes.

1. Compare the simulation results with those presented above based on queuing theory. Discuss any apparent difference. Use an Excel worksheet to compare the results from different models.

2. Increase the traffic intensity to 95 percent by increasing the mean service time. Rerun both simulation models and compare it to the queuing theory predictions. Estimate the maximum queue lengths. *Hint:* Arena model file Comparison.doe simultaneously simulates both the single server and parallel server processes.

3. Increase the traffic intensity to 98 percent by increasing the mean service time. Rerun both simulation models and compare it to the queuing theory predictions. Estimate the maximum queue lengths.

4. Develop an Arena model for a set of three servers with queues in series. The first has a traffic intensity of 90 percent, the second 95 percent, and the third 80 percent. What is the bottleneck? Using an Arena resource set to allow servers 2 and 3 to share the work. How much does this work sharing improve the process capacity?

5. Arena model file MV1.doe compares three single-server queuing processes operating from a common source. The three servers differ by the statistic distribution used to model their service times: Fixed, Exponential, and Normal. Compare how the queue lengths differ as a function of the service time distribution. The Coefficient of Variation is equal to the Standard Deviation divided by the Mean. By default, Arena model file MV1.doe uses a coefficient of variation of 25 percent. Test the impact of changing the coefficient of variation to 10 percent, 5 percent, and 0 percent.

6. Repeat problem 5 by changing the traffic intensity to 95 percent, 98 percent, and 99 percent. *Hint:* Only the value of variable Service.Seconds needs to be changed. Does traffic intensity seem to change the relationship between the three service time distributions?

7. Modify model Comparison.doe to permit customers to switch between queues. What type of decision rules are required to implement such a policy? Experiment with different switching decision rules to balance the number of switches and the total customer waiting time.

Applications Using Arena

Summary and Learning Objectives

This chapter offers a review of the primary concepts to model manufacturing systems through Arena simulation models using a number of manufacturing cell–related examples. The chapter also introduces readers to simulation models built around a manufacturing cell to illustrate the inspection, rejection, and rework taking place after the final processing operation. In addition, simulation models are developed to model material handling operations using Arena's advanced transfer template panel function. Finally, the chapter presents a checklist for simulation model design decisions.

The learning objectives for this chapter are the

1. Ability to model manufacturing cells using Arena.
2. Ability to incorporate inspection and rework into manufacturing cells models.
3. Ability to use Arena's advanced transfer template panel to model material handling processes.
4. Ability to develop a preliminary simulation model design using a design checklist.

Manufacturing Simulation Models

We have developed a set of manufacturing cell-related examples to illustrate some of the primary concepts used to model manufacturing systems. Typically, we model this type of manufacturing cell to gain an understanding of the cell's capacity under a variety of conditions. This chapter demonstrates how a basic simulation model can be expanded to include additional detail to improve the model's ability to predict the performance of the manufacturing cell. These models have been designed and are presented in the manner most simulation models are developed—start simple and add complexity, as it is needed. Exhibit 7–1 illustrates the general flow or outline of various manufacturing cell models.

Models Manufacturing Cell 1.doe through Manufacturing Cell 6.doe build progressively. Model Manufacturing Cell 2.doe is used as the basis for the development of two series of additional example models. Models Reject Batch.doe, Reject Single.doe, Rework Batch.doe, and Rework Single.doe illustrate the inspection and possible rework of completed batches.

EXHIBIT 7–1 Manufacturing Cell Models

Page manufacturing cell models | Chapter 7 Drawings.vsd

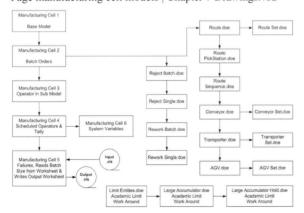

EXHIBIT 7–2 **Manufacturing Cell Flow Chart**

Page manufacturing cell flow | Chapter 7 Drawings.vsd

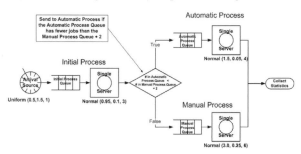

Models Route.doe, Route Set.doe, Route PickStation.doe, Route Sequence.doe, Conveyor.doe, Conveyor Set.doe, Transporter.doe, Transporter Set.doe, AGV.doe, and AGV Set.doe illustrate some of the modeling options available when using the Advanced Transfer template panel modules. Models Products Separate.doe, Products Combined.doe, and Products Sequence.doe illustrate the modeling of two products moving through a set of shared processes.

Exhibit 7–2 illustrates the flow of work orders through the manufacturing cell. In the basic Manufacturing Cell model, work orders enter the system on an average of one every minute. These are Uniform (0.5, 1.5) minutes. All work orders are first processed by the Initial Process with a service time from the normal distribution, Normal (0.95, 0.1) minutes. After leaving the Initial Process, work orders are selectively dispatched to either Automatic Process or Manual Process. The Automatic Process is the preferred choice with a service time of Normal (1.5, 0.05) minutes. The service time for the Manual Process is Normal (3.0, 0.25) minutes. The choice between Automatic Process and Manual Process is based on the number of jobs waiting to be processed by the two operations. Automatic Process is selected if its queue has less than two more jobs than Manual Process. After the second processing step, entity statistics are collected and the WorkOrder entity is removed from the manufacturing cell.

Our objective in modeling the manufacturing cell illustrated in Exhibit 7–2 is to determine the throughput rate or capacity of the cell. Exhibit 7–3 illustrates a static capacity analysis of this manufacturing cell, developed using Excel. This static analysis is based strictly on expected or average values. It does consider the impact of process variability. As we saw in Chapter 6, queueing processes can be adversely impacted due to the variability in either the arrival or service processes. The expected time per unit is simply the mean value of the associated process statistical distribution. The expected units per hour is calculated using this expression:

$$\text{Expected units per hour} = 60 \div \text{Expected time per unit}$$

The calculation of the planned units per hour is slightly more complex because it is dependent on the flow of the work order through the manufacturing cell. The planned units per hour is constrained by the capacity of the upstream processes. All work orders pass through Arrival and Initial processes. Therefore, Initial process cannot process more than its incoming supply. See the following calculation.

$$\text{Planned units per hour (Initial)} = \text{MIN (Expected units per hour (Arrival)},$$
$$\text{Expected units per hour (Initial))} = \text{MIN (60.0, 63.2)} = 60.0$$

Likewise the Automatic process is restricted:

$$\text{Planned units per hour (Automatic)} = \text{MIN (Expected units per hour (Initial)},$$
$$\text{Expected units per hour (Automatic))} = \text{MIN (60.0, 40.0)} = 40.0$$

EXHIBIT 7–3

Manufacturing Cell Static Analysis

Sheet static analysis | Chapter 7 Worksheets.xls

Process	Distribution	Expected Time / Unit (Minutes)	Expected Units / Hour	Planned Units / Hour	Expected Utilization
Arrival	Uniform (0.5, 1.5)	1.00	60.0	60.0	
Initial	Normal (0.95, 0.10)	0.95	63.2	60.0	95.0%
Automatic	Normal (1.50, 0.05)	1.50	40.0	40.0	100.0%
Manual	Normal (2.00, 0.10)	2.00	30.0	20.0	66.7%

The Manual process serves as the overflow from the Automatic process. Therefore, planned units per hour is simply the difference between the capacity of the Initial and Automatic processes subject to its own capacity constraint:

$$\text{Planned units per hour (Manual)} = \text{MIN (Expected units per hour (Manual),}$$
$$\text{Expected units per hour (Initial)} - \text{Expected units per hour (Automatic))} =$$
$$\text{MIN (30.0, 60.0} - \text{40.0)} = 20.0$$

The Expected Utilization is calculated using

$$\text{Expected utilization} = \text{Planned units per hour} \div \text{Expected units per hour}$$

The Expected Utilization of the Initial process is calculated by

$$\text{Expected utilization} = 60.0 \div 63.2 = 95.0\%$$

In addition to the impact variability, these static calculations do not take into account the impact of operator availability or process equipment downtime. We'll use Arena process simulation to introduce and evaluate these features.

After we present the six manufacturing cell models, we present Exhibit 7–38 on page 199, which tabulates the simulation results, comparable to the static analysis presented in Exhibit 7–3.

Four additional Arena models have been developed using model Manufacturing Cell 2.doe as a starting point. View Exhibit 7–1 on page 186 (Manufacturing Cell Models) to identify the model names. Exhibits 7–4 and 7–5 detail the additional features introduced in each of these models.

1. Manufacturing Cell 1 processes individual jobs as separate work orders.
2. Manufacturing Cell 2 processes batches averaging 10 jobs each.
3. Manufacturing Cell 3 adds operators to service the Automatic and Manual Processes. The Automatic Process is divided into five processing steps in an Arena Submodel.
4. Manufacturing Cell 4 schedules operators and adds a Tally of the batch order size Batch.Size.
5. Manufacturing Cell 5 adds resource failures, reads batch order size Batch.Size from a worksheet, and writes an output worksheet.
6. Manufacturing Cell 6 adds Arena Variables.

Next, we consider the models Manufacturing Cell 3 through Manufacturing Cell 6.

Exhibit 7–6 lists the Arena resources used by this model set and the cost per hour associated with each resource.

Single Item Base Model Manufacturing Cell 1.doe

The Visio flow model illustrated in Exhibit 7–2 has been modeled as Arena model Manufacturing Cell 1.doe. Its screen display is illustrated in Exhibit 7–7. Notice the icon or

EXHIBIT 7–4 Manufacturing Cell Models Part A
Sheet manufacturing cell models | Chapter 7 Worksheets.xls

Manufacturing Cell #.doe											
#	Model Description	Time Between Order Arrivals	Batch Size	Tally Batch Sizes	Sub Model	Operator Resource	Automatic Process Operator	Manual Process Operator	Operator Schedules	Process Failures	Arena Variables
1	Basic Model	UNIF (0.5, 1.5, 1)	1								
2	Batching of Orders	UNIF (5, 15, 1)	Normal (10, 3, 2)								
3	Operators and SubModel				Yes	Yes	Operator.Level.1 or Operator.Level.2 for Load and Unload	Operator.Level.2			
4	Scheduled Operators, Operator Set, and Tally			Yes	Yes	Yes			Yes		
5	Resource Failures, Reads Batch.Size from Worksheet, and Writes Output Worksheet	Gap	Read from Input.xls		Yes	Yes			Yes	Yes	
6	Arena Variables	UNIF (Batch.Mean, Batch.Stdev, 1)	Normal (Batch.Mean, Batch.Stedev, 2)		Yes	Yes	Operator.Level.1 for Load and Unload		Yes	Yes	Yes

EXHIBIT 7–5 Manufacturing Cell Models Part B
Sheet manufacturing cell models | Chapter 7 Worksheets.xls

Manufacturing Cell #.doe		Process Times in Minutes			Worksheet Input / Output			Times in Minutes		
#	Model Description	Initial Process Time	Automatic Process Time	Manual Process Time	Reads from	Write to	Initial Process Up Time (Failure Count)	Initial Process Down Time (Failure Count)	Automatic Process Up Time (Failure Time)	Automatic Process Down Time (Failure Time)
1	Basic Model	Normal (0.95, 0.1, 3)	Normal (1.5, 0.01, 4)	Normal (2.0, 0.2, 6)						
2	Batching of Orders	BatchSize * Normal (0.95, 0.1, 3)	BatchSize * Normal (1.5, 0.01, 4)	BatchSize * Normal (2.0, 0.2, 6)						
3	Operators and SubModel		Normal (1.0, 0.2, 4) + BatchSize * 1.5 + Normal (1.0, 0.2, 5)							
4	Scheduled Operators, Operator Set, and Tally									
5	Resource Failures, Reads Batch.Size from Worksheet, and Writes Output Worksheet				Input. xls	Output. xls	Count = 20	Normal (15 , 3, 9)	GAMM (81.429, 0.7, 10)	GAMM (2.143, 1.4, 10)
6	Arena Variables	Batch.Size * Normal (Initial.Mean, Initial.Stdev, 3)	Normal (Load.Mean, Load.Stdev, 4) + Batch.Size * Automatic.Mean + Normal (Unload.Mean, Unload.Stdev, 5)	Batch.Size * Normal (Manual.Mean, Manual.Stdev, 6)			Count = Failure.Count	Normal (Failure.Count.Mean , Failure.Count.Stdev, 9)	GAMM (Failure.UpTime.Mean, 0.7, 10)	GAMM (Failure.DownTime.Mean, 1.4, 10)

EXHIBIT 7–6 **Resource Definitions for Manufacturing Cell Models**

Sheet resources | Chapter 7 Worksheets.xls

Arena Resource Name	Capacity / Schedule	Busy Cost / Hour	Idle Cost / Hour	Cost / Use	Used in Models	Failures Used in Models 5 - 6
R.Initial	1	$25.00	$25.00	$0.00	1 - 6	Failure Count
R.Automatic	1	$50.00	$25.00	$0.00	1 - 6	Failure Time
R.Manual	1	$35.00	$25.00	$0.00	1 - 6	
Operator.Level.1	Schedule.1	$10.00	$10.00	$0.00	3 - 6	
Operator.Level.2	Schedule.2	$20.00	$20.00	$0.00	3 - 6	

EXHIBIT 7–7 **Model Manufacturing Cell 1.doe Screen Display at TNOW = 8 Hours**

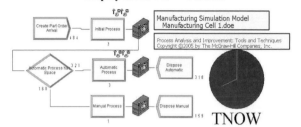

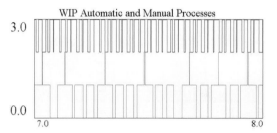

picture nut and bolts (widgets) represent the entity WorkOrder as it moves through the model. At the time this simulation snap shot was taken (TNOW = 8 hours), a total of 484 work orders had entered the system. The Initial Process is holding three work orders: one is being processed and two are waiting in the Initial Process.Queue. The Automatic Process indicates that the Space Decide module has cleared 321 work orders to Automatic Process and 160 to Manual Process. Note that

$$321 + 160 + 3 = 484$$

The Automatic Process holds three work orders while the Manual Process has one work order. The Automatic Process has completed 318 work orders while the Manual Process has completed 159 work orders. Note that

$$318 + 3 = 321$$
$$159 + 1 = 160$$

The Arena Plot at the bottom of Exhibit 7–7 illustrates the number of work orders at both the Automatic and Manual Processes. Notice that the black plot (Automatic Process) is typically one or two work orders above the plot for Manual Process. At no time was the number in the Automatic Process queue greater than three.

The icons at the right of the Process modules indicate the status of the three model resources: R.Initial, R.Automatic, and R.Manual. Each of these resources has a capacity of one.

EXHIBIT 7–8 **Automatic Process has Space Decide Module Dialog**

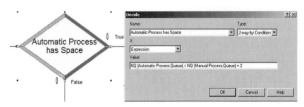

Exhibit 7–8 illustrates that the Automatic Process has a Space Decide module dialog that is used to implement the decision logic required for model Manufacturing Cell 1.doe. The expression value **NQ (Automatic Process.Queue) < NQ (Manual Process.Queue) + 2** could be generated with the use of the Arena expression editor by right-clicking in the expression value window.

Model Manufacturing Cell 1.doe includes Arena costing parameters. Exhibit 7–9 illustrates the summary costs displayed by Crystal Reports after five replications each of 24 hours. The cost statistics are displayed for

EXHIBIT 7–9 **Model Manufacturing Cell 1.doe**
 Crystal Reports Cost Summary

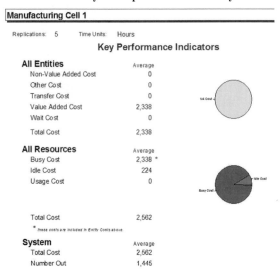

both entities and resources with the cost values representing the averages over five replications. Costs for this model were calculated based on the input data summarized in Exhibits 7–10 and 7–11. Resource R.Initial accumulated cost at a rate of $25.00 per hour while either working or idle. Resource R.Automatic accumulated cost while working at a rate of $50.00 per hour and $25.00 per hour while idle. Resource R.Manual accumulated cost while working at a rate of $35.00 per hour and $25.00 per hour while idle. The entity VA (Value Add) Average Cost is $2,338, which equals the resource busy cost. Idle resources also accumulated a cost of $224 for total average cost per replication of $2,562.

Model Manufacturing Cell 1.doe processed each work order or entity WorkOrder as single item. While this is a goal in many manufacturing organizations, the more typical approach is to group orders into batches for processing. The remaining examples in this chapter assume that batches of similar items are processed together. Model Manufacturing Cell 2.doe introduces the concept of batch processing and will be used as the starting point for subsequent manufacturing models.

Batch Mode Base Model Manufacturing Cell 2.doe

The model illustrated in Exhibit 7–12 is the batch process base model or Manufacturing Cell 2.doe. Exhibit 7–12 is quite similar to Exhibit 7–7 except for the Assign module labeled *Assign Batch Size*. Exhibit 7–13 illustrates the dialog for that module. In fact, more model changes have been made than are apparent at first glance. The time between work order arrivals has been increased from UNIForm (0.5, 1.5) to UNIForm (5, 15) minutes. This reduces the flow into the model by a factor of 10. To maintain a similar work level, model Manufacturing Cell 2.doe incorporates a batch size of approximately 10 items each. The Assign Batch Size workbook illustrated in Exhibit 7–13 randomly generates a value for the new entity attribute **Batch.Size** using the following expression:

$$\text{Batch.Size} = \text{MAX (ANINT (Normal (10, 3, 2)), 1)}$$

This expression first generates a random variable from a normal distribution with a mean of 10 and standard deviation of 3, then uses function **ANINT** to round that value to the nearest integer value, and finally uses function **MAX** to assure a positive value.

EXHIBIT 7–10

Model Manufacturing Cell 1.doe Entity Spreadsheet

	Entity Type	Initial Picture	Holding Cost / Hour	Initial VA Cost	Initial NVA Cost	Initial Waiting Cost	Initial Tran Cost	Initial Other Cost	Report Statistics
1	WorkOrder	Picture.Widgets	0	0.0	0.0	0.0	0.0	0.0	☑

Double-click here to add a new row.

EXHIBIT 7–11

Model Manufacturing Cell 1.doe Resource Spreadsheet

	Name	Type	Capacity	Busy / Hour	Idle / Hour	Per Use	StateSet Name	Failures	Report Statistics
1	R.Initial	Fixed Capacity	1	25	25	0.0		0 rows	☑
2	R.Automatic	Fixed Capacity	1	50	25	0.0		0 rows	☑
3	R.Manual	Fixed Capacity	1	35	25	0.0		0 rows	☑

EXHIBIT 7–12 **Model Manufacturing Cell 2.doe Screen Display at TNOW = 8 Hours**

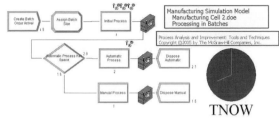

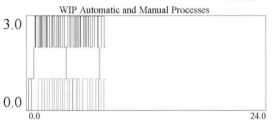

To further facilitate the processing of jobs in batches, the Process model times had to be modified to function properly with a variable batch size stored as attribute Batch.Size. Exhibit 7–14 illustrates the workbook view for the three modified Process modules. Notice that the individual item processing times expression has been multiplied by the value of Batch.Size.

$$\text{Batch.Size} * \text{Normal} (0.95, 0.10, 3)$$
$$\text{Batch.Size} * \text{Normal} (1.50, 0.05, 4)$$
$$\text{Batch.Size} * \text{Normal} (2.00, 0.10, 6)$$

The parameters of the Arena Normal distribution are mean, standard deviation, and random number stream. We have designed the models in this chapter to generate each random variable using a different random number stream. By default, Arena supports 10 unique random number streams.

Comparing the Arena displays illustrated in Exhibits 7–7 and 7–12, few entities (Batch.Order verses Work.Order) significantly changed the plot characteristics. The reduced number of entities made the plot in Exhibit 7–12 more readable. Again notice the relationship between the plotted expressions. The Manual Process WIP plot is never greater than the Automatic Process WIP plot. The reader should consider under what conditions the Manual plot might actually be higher than the Automatic plot.

Manufacturing Cell 3.doe Operator in Submodel

Arena model Manufacturing Cell 3.doe introduces the concept of an operator to tend the Automatic and Manual Processes. A Resource Operator.Level.2 must be present in order to operate resource R.Manual. Resource Operator.Level.1 must be present to load and to unload resource R.Automatic; however, the process operates automatically without operator assistance. In order to model this additional level of detail without making the overall model appearance too complex, a submodel was substituted for Automatic Process. That submodel is illustrated in Exhibit 7–15. The submodel can be viewed from the navigate tab of the Arena Project Bar or by right-clicking on the Process module. Process modules that contain submodels are indicated with a curved arrow in the upper right corner. Note that submodels may also contain submodels.

In Exhibit 7–15 the Automatic Process module has been replaced by three process modules, one Seize module, and one Release module in the form of a submodel. These additional

EXHIBIT 7–13
Model Manufacturing Cell 2.doe Assign Batch Size Dialog

EXHIBIT 7–14
Model Manufacturing Cell 2.doe Process Spreadsheet View

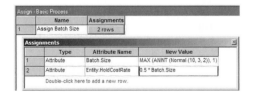

EXHIBIT 7–15
Model
Manufacturing Cell
3.doe Automatic
Process Submodel

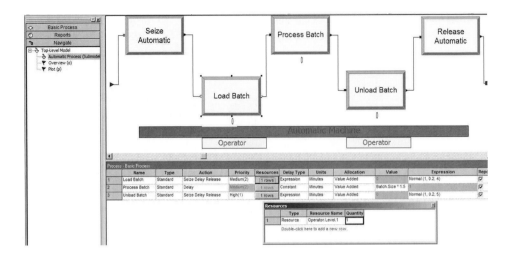

modules are required to accurately model the need for the operator to be present only during part of the process cycle. Exhibit 7–15 also illustrates the associated Process module workbook that further demonstrates the operator's interaction.

The Seize Automatic module gains control of the primary resource R.Automatic. The Load Batch process module is entered by an entity WorkOrder that already controls resource R.Automatic. This process seizes the resource Operator.Level.1, performs the load operation a Normal (1.0, 0.2, 4) minute delay, and then releases resource Operator.Level.1. Process Batch only functions to delay the entity WorkOrder for the processing time Batch.Size * 1.5 minutes. The Unload Batch process seizes the resource Operator.Level.1, performs the unload operation a Normal (1.0, 0.2, 5) minute delay, and then releases resource Operator.Level.1. The Release Automatic module releases control of the primary resource R.Automatic.

The combinations of Seize-Delay-Release actions illustrated in this model are very typical of those required in many manufacturing applications. Because the resource Operator.Level.1 is used twice in this submodel, a higher priority is given to the Unload Batch process to assure that it occurs before the work order is loaded on to resource R.Automatic. In this case, the fact that resource R.Automatic is continuously held by the entity WorkOrder assures that potential deadlocking cannot happen.

There are five queues associated with model Manufacturing Cell 3. These queues are illustrated in Exhibit 7–16. Seize Automatic.Queue, Load Batch.Queue, and Unload Batch.Queue are associated with the submodel illustrated in Exhibit 7–15. The animation of those queues has been moved from the submodel to the Top-Level model to be visible during the normal running of the model.

Manufacturing Cell 4.doe

Unlike machines, human operators require occasional breaks. Sometimes breaks are ignored in the simulation model and, as long the overall operator utilization is not too great, say 75 percent, it is assumed that an operator can take a break during these unassigned periods. However, in many manufacturing systems these unassigned periods may be relatively short in duration, one minute or less. Such a short period may be of little benefit to the operator in terms of getting to the restroom or going to lunch. Arena contains a Schedule module in the Basic Process template panel.

EXHIBIT 7–16
Model
Manufacturing Cell
3.doe Queue
Spreadsheet

	Name	Type	Shared	Report Statistics
1	Manual Process.Queue	First In First Out	☐	☑
2	Initial Process.Queue	First In First Out	☐	☑
3	Seize Automatic.Queue	First In First Out	☐	☑
4	Unload Batch.Queue	First In First Out	☐	☑
5	Load Batch.Queue	First In First Out	☐	☑

EXHIBIT 7–17
Model
Manufacturing Cell
4.doe Schedule.1

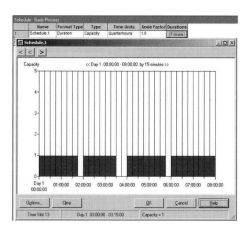

Scheduled Operators

Arena model Manufacturing Cell 4.doe incorporates schedules for both operator resources. Exhibit 7–17 illustrates the schedule developed for resource Operator.Level.1. Schedule 1 has one operator except during breaks between 1:45–2:00, 3:30–4:00, and 5:45–6:00. This eight-hour schedule is repeated three times for each 24-hour simulation replication. Schedule 2 is similar with the breaks directly following those of Schedule 1.

Instead of assigning a fixed capacity of one to resource Operator.Level.1 and Resource Operator.Level.2, Schedule.1 and Schedule.2 are assigned in the Resource Spreadsheet illustrated in Exhibit 7–18.

EXHIBIT 7–18   Model Manufacturing Cell 4.doe
Resource Spreadsheet

	Name	Type	Capacity	Schedule Name	Schedule Rule	Busy / Hour	Idle / Hour	Per Use
1	R.Automatic	Fixed Capacity	1		Wait	50	25	0.0
2	R.Initial	Fixed Capacity	1		Wait	35	25	0.0
3	R.Manual	Fixed Capacity	1		Wait	25	25	0.0
4	Operator.Level.1	Based on Schedule	Schedule.1	Schedule.1	Wait	10	10	0.0
5	Operator.Level.2	Based on Schedule	Schedule.2	Schedule.2	Wait	20	20	0.0

Double-click here to add a new row.

Notice in Exhibit 7–18 that to schedule two types of operators, the "Wait" Schedule rule has been used. Clicking on this cell indicates three Schedule Rule options: Wait, Ignore, and Preempt. These rules come into play when the resource is being used at the time its capacity is scheduled to be reduced. The default Wait option allows the resource to continue to be used. At the time of release, the value of the resource's capacity is reduced for the duration of the scheduled period. This ensures a full duration (but possibly postponed) scheduled period. The Ignore option delays the start of the scheduled period but assures the desired end of the scheduled period. The Preempt option assures exact control of the scheduled period.

Operator Set

Because operators are required to operate resource R.Manual and to load and unload resource R.Automatic, the breaks permitted in Schedule.1 and Schedule.2 would mean that at times work order entities can be delayed when the required operator is on break. The Resource Operator.Level.2 that normally operates Resource R.Manual has more experience than the Resource Operator.Level.1 and can do those tasks. Thus, when the Resource Operator.Level.1 is not available (the operator is on break) and the Resource Operator.Level.2 is available, the Resource Operator.Level.2 should be allowed to either load or unload resource R.Automatic. This interchangeability of operators can be modeled in Arena using the Set module of the Basic Process template panel.

Exhibit 7–19 illustrates the Set module spreadsheet with the associated list detail. The set is named *Operator* and functions as an index:

Operator (1) → Resource Operator.Level.1.
Operator (2) → Resource Operator.Level.2.

Process Modules Load Batch and Unload Batch are modified to select from the Operator set as illustrated in Exhibit 7–20.

In Exhibit 7–20 the Resource type is changed from Resource to Set and the Set Name is specified as Operator. Since a set

EXHIBIT 7–19
Model
Manufacturing Cell
4.doe Set Spreadsheet

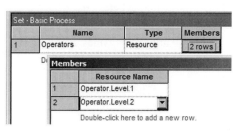

EXHIBIT 7–20 Model Manufacturing Cell 4.doe Load Batch Process Module Dialog

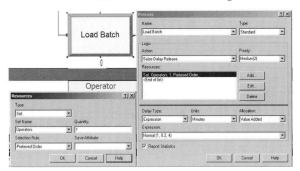

EXHIBIT 7–21 Model Manufacturing Cell 4.doe Record Module Dialog

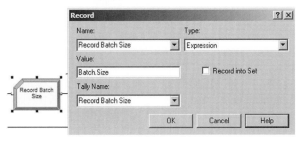

contains more than one element, in this case resource, the particular resource must be specified and recorded. In this case the resources were selected in the Preferred Order, i.e., Resource Operator.Level.1 and then Resource Operator.Level.2. Other available Selection Rules are Cyclical, Random, Specific Member, Largest Remaining Capacity, and Smallest Number Busy. See Arena Help for more details.

Tally

Arena Tallies are created in the Record module from the Basic Process template panel. Exhibit 7–21 illustrates the Record module and the associated dialog. This Record module records or tallies the Batch.Size. Exhibit 7–22 illustrates the Crystal Report User Specified for this Tally Set. Notice that the Batch Size Tally has an average of 10.1 or slightly more than the expected mean value of 10. The value of Batch.Size ranged from 1 to 19 or approximately ± standard deviations.

The Record module can also be used to record or tally Time Interval Statistics and Time Between Statistics. Time Interval Statistics record the difference between the current simulation time (TNOW) and the value of the entity's attribute, perhaps Time Stamp. Time between Statistics records the time between entity arrivals at the Record module.

Manufacturing Cell 5.doe Input/Output

Arena model Manufacturing Cell 5.doe expands the current model example set by adding resource failures and Input/Output from or to Excel workbooks.

Resource Failures

Failures are used to remove Arena resources from service much like the Schedule module used in the prior example. Exhibit 7–23 illustrates a Failure module workbook from the Advanced Process template panel. Failure Count will occur after each time an entity Work-Order seizes the associated resource 20 times. The resource is then held in the failed state for a period of time generated from the NORM (15, 3, 9) distribution. Failure Time uses random variables to define both the Up and Down Times. The Up Time passage is only counted when the associated resource is in the Busy (nonidle) state. The parameters for the Failure Time Up and Down Times were generated on worksheets Failures and DensityFunctions. These worksheets are illustrated in Exhibits 7–24 and 7–25.

The resource R.Automatic using Failure Time will be up or available for service 95 percent of the time. It will fail on average once per hour. The worksheet converts

EXHIBIT 7–22 Model Manufacturing Cell 4.doe User Specified Crystal Report

User Specified						
Tally						
Expression	Average	Half Width	Minimum Average	Maximum Average	Minimum Value	Maximum Value
Record Batch Size	10.1078	0.38	9.8531	10.6301	1.0000	19.0000

EXHIBIT 7–23
Model
Manufacturing Cell
5.doe Failure
Spreadsheet

	Name	Type	Up Time	Up Time Units	Count	Down Time	Down Time Units	Uptime in this State only
1	Failure Count	Count	0	Hours	20	NORM(15 , 3, 9)	Minutes	
2	Failure Time	Time	GAMM (81.429, 0.7, 10)	Minutes	Min	GAMM (2.143, 1.4, 10)	Minutes	Busy

EXHIBIT 7–24   **Failure/Repair Cycle Calculations**

Sheet failures | Chapter 7 Worksheets.xls

Use Ctrl-Shift-R to return to the Exhibits Worksheet			Display DensityFunctions Worksheet		Gamma Distribution Shape Parameter		Arena Expressions in Minutes	
	Average Operating Percent	Failures / Hour	Average Minutes Operating MTBF	Repair MTTR	Operating	Repair	Operating (Up Time)	Repair (Down Time)
# Equipment Label								
1 Failure Time	95.00%	1.000	57.0	3.0	0.7	1.4	Gamma (81.429, 0.7, 10)	Gamma (2.143, 1.4, 10)

EXHIBIT 7–25
Failure/Repair Cycle Density Functions

Sheet DensityFunctions | Chapter 7 Worksheets.xls

Density Functions Worksheet		Equipment Label	**Failure Time**	Process Analysis and Improvement: Tools and Techniques Copyright ©2005 by The McGraw-Hill Companies, Inc.
Average Operating Minutes, MTBF	57.0	Operating Period Gamma Distribution Shape Parameter	0.7	
Average Repair Minutes, MTTR	3.0	Repair Period Gamma Distribution Shape Parameter	1.4	

EXHIBIT 7–26   **Model Manufacturing Cell 5.doe**
                   Statistic Spreadsheet

	Name	Type	Frequency Type	Resource Name	Report Label	Output File	Categories
1	State Operator Level 1	Frequency	State	Operator.Level.1	State Operator Level 1		0 rows
2	State Operator Level 2	Frequency	State	Operator.Level.2	State Operator Level 2		0 rows
3	State R.Automatic	Frequency	State	R.Automatic	State R.Automatic		0 rows
4	State R.Initial	Frequency	State	R.Initial	State R.Initial		0 rows
5	State R.Manual	Frequency	State	R.Manual	State R.Manual		0 rows

Double-click here to add a new row

these basic parameters into a Mean Time Before Failure (MTBF) of 57 minutes and Mean Time to Repair (MTTR) of 3 minutes. Notice that

$$1 - 3 \div (57 + 3) = 95\%$$

These average values convert into the following Gamma distribution expressions in the Arena model:

$$\text{GAMM (81.429, 0.7, 10)}$$
$$\text{GAMM (2.143, 1.4, 10)}$$

The defined Failures must be linked to Resources in the Resource Spreadsheet. In model Manufacturing Cell 5.doe, Failure Count → Resource R.Initial and Failure Time → Resource R.Automatic. Multiple Arena resources can independently share one Arena Failure definition.

Frequency Statistics

In order to validate the occurrence of resource downtimes, the Advance Process template panel Statistic workbook was used to collect Frequency data on the model resources. Exhibit 7–26 illustrates the Statistic workbook for model Manufacturing Cell 5.doe.

Exhibit 7–27 illustrates the resulting Frequency data for the first replication of model Manufacturing Cell 5.doe. Resource R.Initial failed a total of six times during the first replication and was down for an average of 0.226 hours or 13.6 minutes. Resource R.Automatic failed twice during the first replication and was down for an average of 0.014 hours or 0.86 minutes. These values compare to the expected values of 3.0 minutes and 5 percent downtime.

Exhibit 7–27 also illustrates the impact of schedule on the operators. Each operator was inactive nine times for an average of 12.5 percent of the 24-hour replication. The nine inactive periods correspond to three inactive periods during each eight-hour shift.

Worksheet Input and Output

A second feature added to model Manufacturing Cell 5.doe is input and output from external files. The input and output is conducted in the model flow using the ReadWrite module of the Advanced Process template panel. This module also requires the definition of the source file using the File module workbook.

Exhibit 7–28 illustrates a model segment that can be used to read input information from a worksheet. In this model, the Create module generates only a single WorkOrder entity.

EXHIBIT 7–27 Model Manufacturing Cell 5.doe
Frequency Statistics Replication 1

Manufacturing Cell 5				Replications: 5
Replication 1	Start Time: 0.00	Stop Time: 24.00	Time Units: Hours	

State Operator Level 1	Number Obs	Average Time	Standard Percent	Restricted Percent
BUSY	78	0.03176175	10.32	11.80
IDLE	78	0.2375	77.18	88.20
INACTIVE	9	0.3333	12.50	--

State Operator Level 2	Number Obs	Average Time	Standard Percent	Restricted Percent
BUSY	18	0.8963	67.23	76.83
IDLE	12	0.4055	20.27	23.17
INACTIVE	9	0.3333	12.50	--

State R.Automatic	Number Obs	Average Time	Standard Percent	Restricted Percent
BUSY	4	5.8119	96.86	96.86
FAILED	2	0.01401658	0.12	0.12
IDLE	2	0.3623	3.02	3.02

State R.Initial	Number Obs	Average Time	Standard Percent	Restricted Percent
BUSY	17	1.2502	88.56	88.56
FAILED	6	0.2264	5.66	5.66
IDLE	10	0.1388	5.78	5.78

State R.Manual	Number Obs	Average Time	Standard Percent	Restricted Percent
BUSY	21	0.7641	66.85	66.85
IDLE	21	0.3788	33.15	33.15

EXHIBIT 7–28 Model Manufacturing Cell 5.doe Input
Cycle

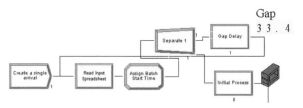

EXHIBIT 7–29 Model Manufacturing Cell 5.doe Read
Input File Module Dialog

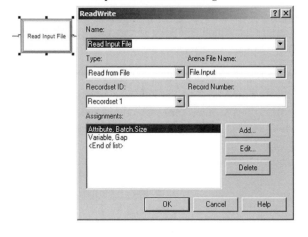

That entity enters the Read Input File module whose contents are illustrated in Exhibit 7–29.

Exhibit 7–29, the Read Input File Module, indicates that two values, attribute Batch.Size and variable Gap, are read respectively from columns A and B of workbook Input.xls. The ReadWrite module generates an entry in the File module workbook, which is illustrated in Exhibit 7–30. Arena filename **File.Input** is linked to the external or operating system filename, Input.xls. Column A will be read as the attribute **Batch.Size** and column B as the variable **Gap.** The first entity WorkOrder arrives at **TNOW = 0.0** and reads **Batch.Size = 1** and **Gap = 33.4.** This same entity returns after waiting the Gap time at **TNOW = 33.4** and reads **Batch.Size = 12** and **Gap = 9.8.** This same entity returns after waiting the Gap time at **TNOW = 33.4 + 9.8 = 43.2** and reads **Batch.Size = 13** and **Gap = 5.2.** The current value of the variable Gap is displayed on the Arena animation. Exhibit 7–31 illustrates a Gap value of 33.4 just after the first workbook record has been read.

EXHIBIT 7–30
Model
Manufacturing Cell
5.doe File
Spreadsheet

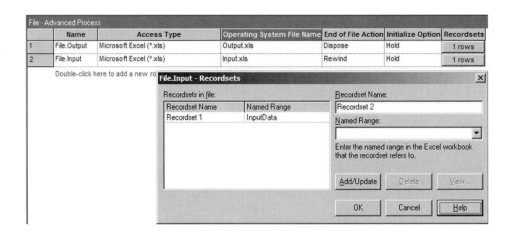

EXHIBIT 7–31
Workbook Input.xls

	A	B
1	**Batch Size**	**Gap**
2	1	33.4
3	12	9.8
4	13	5.2
5	9	13.8
6	11	2.1
7	8	4.5
8	3	34.1
9	13	15.8
10	15	4.4

If the entire workbook is read, the sequence is started over again at row 2. Each read starts a new workbook row. Columns cannot be skipped without reading a value into a dummy variable. Arena is numeric based, and there will be skipped cells with no numeric values. The ReadWrite module provides for a very rigorous form of data error check that is normally required when reading user-generated input data.

After the Read Input File module, the entity enters the Assign Batch Start Time module, which is illustrated in Exhibit 7–32. This module makes three assignments. First, the current simulation time, TNOW, is saved in Attribute Batch.Start.Time. Next, a new Arena Variable Batch.Number is incremented by one to generate a sequential number for each batch. Finally, the current value of Variable Batch.Number is saved in Attribute Batch.Number.

The next module entered by the entity duplicates or clones the original entity. The original entity WorkOrder continues to the Gap Delay process module, while a duplicate entity enters the normal model flow, Initial Process module. The Gap Delay process module delays the entity for Gap minutes. Following this time gap, the next workbook row is read and the cycle continues.

Arena model Manufacturing Cell 5.doe also generates an output workbook. Exhibit 7–33 illustrates the Write Output File module dialog with a new row added each time an entity enters the module. This module writes the following four values into consecutive rows of workbook Output.xls:

1. Workbook column A, Current Simulation Time, TNOW.
2. Workbook column B, Batch Throughput Time, TNOW—Batch.Start.Time.
3. Workbook column C, Batch Number, Batch.
4. Workbook column D, Batch Size, Batch.Size.

Exhibit 7–34 illustrates part of workbook Output.xls. The values in row 2 indicate that the first batch was completed at time 0.075 hours. Having arrived at time zero, its Make Span or Batch Throughput Time is also 0.075 hours or 4.5 minutes.

EXHIBIT 7–32 **Assign Batch Start Time Module**

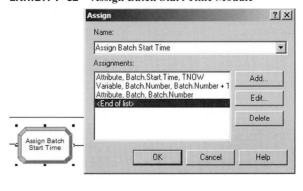

EXHIBIT 7–33 **Model Manufacturing Cell 5.doe Write Output File Module Dialog**

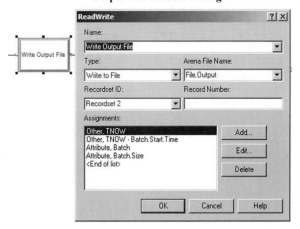

EXHIBIT 7–34 **Workbook Output.xls**

	A	B	C	D	E	F
1	TNOW	Make Span	Batch	Batch.Size	Minutes	
2	0.075	0.075	1	1	4.5	4.5
3	1.116	0.560	2	12	67.0	33.6
4	1.474	0.755	3	13	88.5	45.3
5	1.683	0.537	7	3	101.0	32.2
6	1.732	0.926	4	9	103.9	55.5
7	2.037	1.001	5	11	122.2	60.1
8	2.275	1.205	6	8	136.5	72.3
9	2.636	0.922	8	13	158.1	55.3
10	2.976	0.662	11	12	178.6	39.7
11	3.037	1.060	9	15	182.2	63.6
12	3.181	0.661	13	6	190.8	39.6

EXHIBIT 7–35
Entity Attributes for Manufacturing Cell Models
Sheet attributes | Chapter 7 Worksheets.xls

Arena Attribute	Initial Value	Models where used
Entity.Picture	Picture.Envelope	All
Entity.Type	JobOrder	All
BatchSize		2 - 6
Batch.Start.Time		5
Entity.Index		4 - 5
Gap		5
OperatorNumber		4 - 6

The models developed to this point have involved an increasing number of entity attributes. Exhibit 7–35 lists the Arena Entity Attributes used for the collection of Manufacturing Cell Models. Arena Standard Edition does not provide a direct means to define Entity Attributes; rather they are automatically generated when defined in an Assign or similar modules.

Manufacturing Cell 6.doe Variables

To this point all input data to the Manufacturing Cell models have directly input all model data into expressions. In general it is *not* a good modeling practice to embed all data directly into the model. Most models have to be changed several times over the course of their application; it is far too easy to miss changing those embedded data elements. Also it is nearly impossible to generate a report file that clearly indicates which data were used to execute the model. The answer to this shortcoming is **Arena Variables,** in particular, Arena Variables that can be changed directly from an Excel workbook and those changes can be documented in a report file. The Arena model **Manufacturing Cell 6.doe** demonstrates this procedure.

Exhibit 7–36 illustrates the Variable module spreadsheet for model Manufacturing Cell 6. The applications of these variables should be apparent from their names. The initial values for these variables can be changed by clicking in the Initial Values column of the workbook. This, however, is not the most user-friendly interface, and it does not provide a visual display of the current values. Chapter 8 covers model Manufacturing Cell VBA.doe that uses VBA code to update the Variable value from an Excel workbook.

Exhibit 7–37 illustrates the application of the Arena variables to the Failure Spreadsheet. Exhibit 7–37 should be compared to Exhibit 7–23. The former hard-coded each data value, whereas the latter uses a total of four Arena variables.

EXHIBIT 7–36 **Model Manufacturing Cell 6.doe**
Variable Spreadsheet

	Name	Rows	Columns	Clear Option	Initial Values	Report Statistics
	Variable - Basic Process					
1	Batch.Mean			None	1 rows	☐
2	Batch.Stdev			None	1 rows	☐
3	Initial.Mean			None	1 rows	☐
4	Initial.Stdev			None	1 rows	☐
5	Manual.Mean			None	1 rows	☐
6	Manual.Stdev			None	1 rows	☐
7	Load.Mean			None	1 rows	☐
8	Load.Stdev			None	1 rows	☐
9	Unload.Mean			None	1 rows	☐
10	Unload.Stdev			None	1 rows	☐
11	Automatic.Mean			None	1 rows	☐
12	Inter.Arrival.Max			None	1 rows	☐
13	Inter.Arrival.Min			None	1 rows	☐
14	Queue.Difference			None	1 rows	☐
15	Failure.Count			None	1 rows	☐
16	Failure.Count.Mean			None	1 rows	☐
17	Failure.Count.Stdev			None	1 rows	☐
18	Failure.UpTime.Mean			None	1 rows	☐
19	Failure.DownTime.Mean			None	1 rows	☐
	Double-click here to add a new row.					

Comparison of Expected Versus Simulated Results

We used the Crystal Reports feature of Arena to check a few basic performance measures for model Manufacturing Cell 1.doe through Manufacturing Cell 5.doe. Those results are illustrated in Exhibit 7–38. We did not tabulate results for Manufacturing Cell 6.doe because it is identical to Manufacturing Cell 4.doe.

We observed the average daily (24-hour replication) output from each of the Process modules and in the Create module. Notice that with the exception of Manufacturing Cell 5.doe, the Arrival and Initial process generated nearly the expected performance. Manufacturing

EXHIBIT 7–37
Model
Manufacturing Cell
6.doe Failure
Spreadsheet

	Name	Type	Up Time	Up Time Units	Count	Down Time	Down Time Units	Uptime in this State only
								Failure - Advanced Process
1	Failure Count	Count	0	Hours	Failure.Count	NORM (Failure.Count.Mean, Failure.Count.Stdev, 9)	Minutes	
2	Failure Time	Time	GAMM (Failure.UpTime.Mean, 0.7, 10)	Minutes	MinutesToBas	GAMM (Failure.DownTime.Mean, 1.4, 10)	Minutes	Busy

Double-click here to add a new row.

EXHIBIT 7–38 **Manufacturing Cell Simulation Analysis Results**

Sheet simulation analysis | Chapter 7 Worksheets.xls

Process	Planned Units / Day	Manufacturing Cell 1 Simulated Units / 24 Hour Replication	Manufacturing Cell 2 Simulated Units / 24 Hour Replication	Manufacturing Cell 3 Simulated Units / 24 Hour Replication Automatic Process includes additional time to Load and Unload batches	Manufacturing Cell 4 Simulated Units / 24 Hour Replication	Manufacturing Cell 5 Simulated Units / 24 Hour Replication
Arrival	1,440	1,446.2	1,440.0	1,440	1,440	1,412
Initial	1,440	1,446.6	1,434.0	1,434	1,434	1,380
Automatic	960	969.8	882.0	806	760	762
Manual	480	485.2	544.0	620	626	604

Process	Planned Units / Hour	Simulated Units / Hour	Simulated Units / Hour	Simulated Units / Hour	Simulated Units / Hour	Simulated Units / Hour
Arrival	60	60.3	60.0	60.0	60.0	58.8
Initial	60	60.2	59.8	59.8	59.8	57.6
Automatic	40	40.0	36.8	33.6	31.7	31.8
Manual	20	20.2	22.7	25.8	26.1	25.2

Process	Expected Utilization	Simulated Process Utilization	Simulated Process Utilization	Simulated Process Utilization	Simulated Process Utilization	Simulated Process Utilization
Initial	95%	95.2%	95.8%	95.9%	95.9%	92.0%
Automatic	100%	100.0%	99.8%	99.8%	99.8%	98.8%
Manual	67%	67.5%	67.7%	82.7%	86.6%	82.6%
Expected		Manufacturing Cell 1	Manufacturing Cell 2	Manufacturing Cell 3	Manufacturing Cell 4	Manufacturing Cell 5

EXHIBIT 7–39 **Manufacturing Cell Simulated Daily Production**

Sheet simulation analysis | Chapter 7 Worksheets.xls

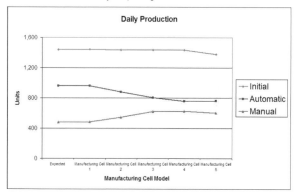

EXHIBIT 7–40 **Manufacturing Cell Simulated Process Utilization**

Sheet simulation analysis | Chapter 7 Worksheets.xls

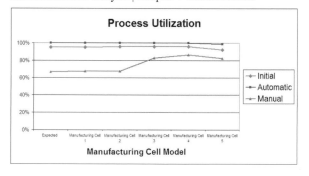

Cell 5.doe differed because its arrival was driven by the values in workbook Manufacturing Cell 5.xls and, therefore, is strictly dependent on that data set. Models Manufacturing Cell 2.doe through Manufacturing Cell 5.doe did not actually count the number of individual units arriving or being processed. To arrive at a total, we simply multiplied the number of batches by 10, the expected batch size.

The number of units processed by the Automatic Process declined from the expected value as the model number is increased. Correspondingly, the number of units processed by the Manual Process increased. This change was caused by the limits on the availability on the Automatic Process imposed by the models. First, Manufacturing Cell 3.doe increased the total batch processing time for the Automatic Process by incorporating a load-and-unload process step. In addition, Manufacturing Cell 4.doe included downtime or failures for the Automatic Process, further limiting its availability.

Exhibit 7–39 graphically illustrates the daily product simulated by the five models. The change in the Automatic and Manual Processes is very evident.

The next section of Exhibit 7–38 simply converts the daily production values to hourly values.

The last section of Exhibit 7–38 and Exhibit 7–40 illustrates the utilization of the process resources or machines associated with the three Process modules. The Initial Process resource was fully utilized in all models, except Manufacturing Cell 5.doe, where the arrival of work orders was dependent on the workbook data. The utilization of the Automatic Process resource was fairly constant again with the exception of the workbook-driven model. The utilization of the Manual Process resource increased as it was forced to take on additional work from the Automatic Process.

EXHIBIT 7–41
Model Reject
Batch.doe Special
Model Logic

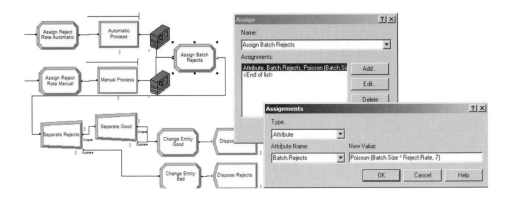

Modeling Inspection—Rejection—Rework

Most manufacturing systems, even those with ISO 9000 certification, incorporate some means to determine the quality of products being produced and to take corrective action, if defective products are found. A series of four models have been developed based on Manufacturing Cell 2.doe to model an inspection station after the final processing operation. The four models—Reject Batch.doe, Reject Single.doe, Rework Batch.doe, and Rework Single.doe—differ in the way defective products are handled.

Model Reject Batch.doe

Arena model Reject Batch.doe tests the quality of the entire batch of product and then separates the good and bad items. The bad items are rejected. Exhibit 7–41 illustrates the new model logic developed to handle the inspection and rejection processing.

Exhibit 7–41 also illustrates the Assign module dialog used to determine the number of defective products in the batch. The number of defects in the batch is calculated using the following expression:

$$\text{Batch.Rejects} = \text{Poisson (Batch.Size * Reject.Rate, 7)}$$

where Batch.Rejects is a new Attribute and Reject.Rate is an Attribute defined as 5 percent in the Assign Reject Rate Automatic module and 10 percent in the Assign Reject Rate Manual module. The Arena function Poisson, generates values from a Poisson distribution with mean, **Batch.Size * Reject.Rate,** and using random number stream 7. Attribute Batch.Rejects can take on the values 0, 1, 2, and so on.

The Separate Rejects module, shown in Exhibit 7–42, sends Batch.Rejects new entities to the Change Entity Bad Assign module and the original entity to the Separate Good module. Note that attribute Batch.Rejects may have a value of zero.

The Separate Good module, depicted in Exhibit 7–43, sends (Batch.Size − Batch.Rejects − 1) new entities to the Change Entity Good Assign module. The original entity is

EXHIBIT 7–42
Model Reject
Batch.doe Separate
Rejects

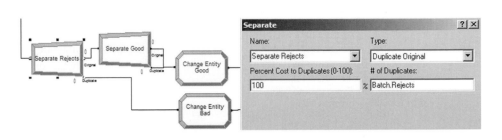

EXHIBIT 7–43   Model Reject Batch.doe Separate Good

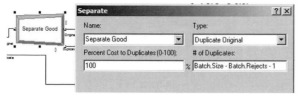

also sent to the Change Entity Good Assign module. Note that if **Batch.Rejects = Batch.Size,** this model will output one ItemGood type entity even though no good items were produced. This condition will automatically generate an incorrect good item count. The reader should attempt to construct a model modification to prevent this error from occurring.

Model Reject Single.doe

Arena model Reject Single.doe separates batches into individual entities and then tests the quality of individual entities or parts. Bad items are rejected and good items sent to Dispose Good. Exhibit 7–44 illustrates the new model logic developed to handle this processing.

Exhibit 7–45 illustrates the Decide module dialog used to determine whether an entity represents a defective product. The expression **Uniform (0, 1, 7) > Reject.Rate** generates a random variable between 0 and 1 and accepts (Good) the entity, if the random variable is greater than the value of the attribute Reject.Rate. If the random variable is less than or equal to the Reject.Rate, the entity is rejected and sent to the Change Entity Bad Assign module.

Model Rework Batch.doe

Arena model Rework Batch.doe, model Reject Batch.doe, tests the quality of the entire batch of product and then separates the good and bad items. The bad items are reworked using the Manual process. Exhibit 7–46 illustrates the model logic developed to handle this processing. Notice that if the batch contains no defects, the newly generated entity is disposed of rather than rerouted to Manual Process.

Exhibit 7–46 illustrates the Assign as Rework module dialog that is used to set the rework Batch.Size to the number of defective products in the batch. The total number of units sent to rework is accumulated in a new variable *Reworked.* The value of variable Reworked is displayed on the animation.

EXHIBIT 7–44
Model Reject Single.doe Special Model Logic

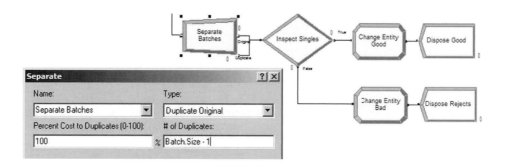

EXHIBIT 7–45   Model Reject Single.doe Decide Module Dialog

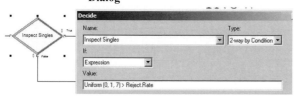

EXHIBIT 7–46
Model Rework
Batch.doe Special
Model Logic

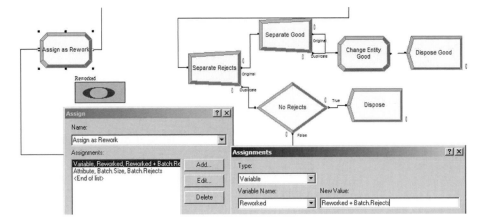

Model Rework Single.doe

Arena model Rework Single.doe tests the quality of each individual unit and then separates the good and the bad units. The bad units are reworked using the Manual process in a batch of size one. Exhibit 7–47 illustrates the new model logic developed to handle this processing. Notice that all entities eventually leave the system as a good item.

Exhibit 7–47 illustrates the Assign as Rework module dialog used to set the rework Batch.Size to one. The total number of units sent to rework is accumulated in a new variable Reworked. The value of variable *Reworked* is displayed on the animation.

The inspection and rework models illustrated in this section apply to many manufacturing system models. Care must be taken to assure that all entities eventually exit from the model and that all possible batch sizes are properly accounted for. A good first check is to assure that the number of units or work orders entering the system equals the number leaving, either as good units or rejected units.

EXHIBIT 7–47
Model Rework
Single.doe Special
Model Logic

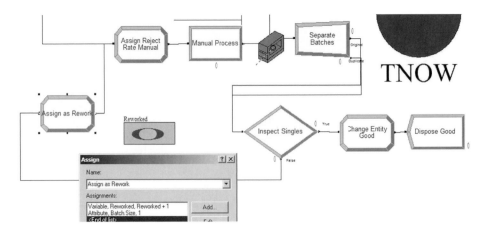

Challenge

Modeling Material Handling Equipment

Most manufacturing systems incorporate some means to move their product from one workstation to the next. A series of six models have been developed based on Arena model Manufacturing Cell 2.doe to demonstrate the modeling of material handling equipment using the Arena Advanced Transfer template panel. For more information about the Arena Advanced Transfer template panel, see the online Arena Help or sheet Modules Advanced Transfer Panel of workbook Chapter 7 Worksheets.xls.

The six Arena models—Route.doe, Route PickStation.doe, Route Sequence.doe, Conveyor.doe, Transporter.doe, and AGV.doe—differ in the way products are moved or the method used to determine the next workstation to visit. Each of these techniques requires that operations be defined as Arena Stations. Either the Station or the Enter modules can be used to define an Arena station. The models in this section route or move WorkOrder entities from Station Initial to either Station Automatic or Station Manual. This powerful concept allows the flow to be animated using icons from the Animate Transfer toolbar. Arena Stations are animated with the ⊂⊃ symbol. Station symbols are connected with Route, Segment, Network, or Distance animation constructs depending on the material handling equipment (route, conveyor, transporter, or AGV) being modeled. We also use the Arena Set construct to simplify the flow logic of several models.

The movement of entities or the material they represent takes time. For the Arena models introduced in this section, we have used five minutes for each movement. In the case of physical transporters such as forklift trucks and AGVs, a round trip is typically required. It takes five minutes to move the work order batch and another five minutes to return to obtain the next batch. This movement time could become a constraint on the manufacturing process.

Model Route.doe

Arena model Route.doe demonstrates a generic method to account for the time it takes to move batches of products between workstations. Exhibit 7–48 illustrates the model logic developed to handle the movement of entities using the Arena routing concept. The first requirement is to define an Arena Station for each workstation. The Station Initial module is illustrated in Exhibit 7–48. The Station Automatic and Station Manual are defined in the Enter modules illustrated in Exhibit 7–49. The Enter modules serve as the entity routine termination points.

The Leave for Station Automatic and Leave for Station Manual modules define the starting points for movement between Arena stations. Exhibit 7–50 illustrates the Leave module workbook used to model product batches flow from Station Initial to Station Automatic. Each movement takes five minutes and follows the path illustrated in Exhibit 7–48. The boxes define the Arena stations for animation purposes and the lines define the routing path.

EXHIBIT 7–48
Model Route.doe
Special Model Logic

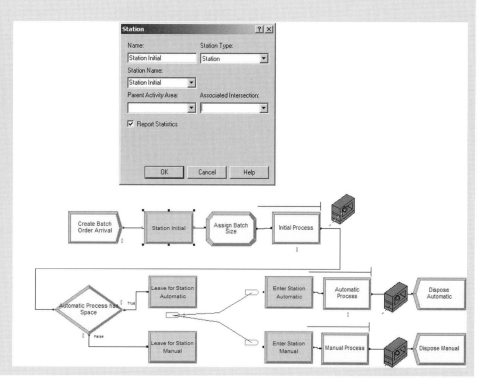

EXHIBIT 7–49

Model Route.doe

Enter Spreadsheet

Enter - Advanced Transfer

	Name	Station Type	Station Name	Report Statistics	Delay	Allocation	Units	Transfer In
1	Enter Station Automatic	Station	Station Automatic	☑	0.	Transfer	Minutes	None
2	Enter Station Manual	Station	Station Manual	☑	0.	Transfer	Minutes	None

EXHIBIT 7–50

Model Route.doe

Leave Spreadsheet

	Name	Allocation	Delay	Units	Transfer Out	Connect Type	Move Tme	Move Units	Station Type	Station Name
1	Leave for Station Automatic	Transfer	0.	Minutes	None	Route	5	Minutes	Station	Station Automatic
2	Leave for Station Manual	Transfer	0.	Minutes	None	Route	5	Minutes	Station	Station Manual

Model Route Set.doe modifies model Route.doe as illustrated in Exhibit 7–51. The Decide module and the two Leave modules have been replaced with the Leave module labeled *Leave for Final Processing Station*. This module selects the next station based on the following expression:

$$\text{Final Processing Stations } (2 - (\text{NQ (Automatic Process.Queue)} < \text{NQ} \\ (\text{Manual Process.Queue}) + 2))$$

An Arena set named *Final Processing Stations* is defined using the Advanced Set module illustrated in Exhibit 7–52. This workbook maps the following relationships:

$$\text{Final Processing Stations (1)} = \text{Station Automatic}$$
$$\text{Final Processing Stations (2)} = \text{Station Manual}$$

The logical expression

$$(\text{NQ (Automatic Process.Queue)} < \text{NQ (Manual Process.Queue)} + 2)$$

yields either a value of 0 or 1, depending on the relative number of entities in the two queues: Automatic Process.Queue and Manual Process.Queue. When this value is subtracted from two, the result properly selects the appropriate next station, Station Automatic, if it has fewer entities waiting than Station Manual.

Both models Route.doe and Route Set.doe as well as other models described in this section differ slightly from the original Manufacturing Cell 2.doe model. Model Manufacturing Cell 2.doe made the selection decision and instantaneously transferred the batch to the appropriate process. All of the models in this section have transfer delay associated with moving the batch to its next process. Thus, the decision is made based on current information at the Decide or Leave module while that process status is likely to change by the time the entity actually arrives at its next processing station. The impact of this delay is most likely slight but should be considered when formulating the decision rule.

Model Route PickStation.doe

Arena model Route PickStation.doe is functionally identical to model Route.doe. Exhibit 7–53 illustrates the new model logic developed to replace the Decide module and two Leave modules with a single PickStation module.

Exhibit 7–53 also illustrates the PickStation module dialog used to select the Station with the smallest number of entities waiting in the queue. The PickStation module also handles the routing to the selected station.

EXHIBIT 7–51 **Model Route Set.doe Leave for Final Processing Station**

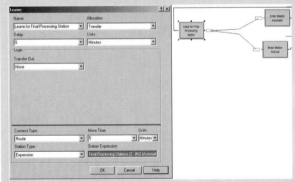

EXHIBIT 7–52

Model Route Set.doe Leave for Final Processing Station Detail

EXHIBIT 7–53
Model Route
PickStation.doe
PickStation Dialog

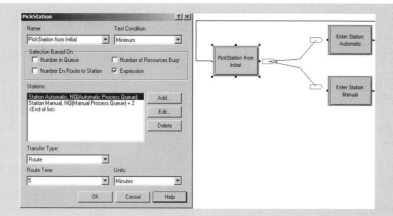

Model Route Sequence.doe

Arena model Route Sequence.doe uses the Arena Sequence approach to control the movement of entities between stations. Exhibit 7–54 illustrates the new model logic developed to handle this flow. Notice that the Station Type in the Leave from Station Initial module was changed to **By Sequence.**

This model uses Arena Sequence construct to control the flow between stations. Exhibit 7–55 illustrates the Sequence module workbook used to define the routing or sequence of flow between stations. Entities typically flow on a line-by-line basis through the set of stations listed in the sequence module workbook. The Sequence labeled *Sequence Manual* routes entities from Station Initial to Station Manual. The Sequence labeled *Sequence Automatic* routes entities from Station Initial to Station Automatic. These two sequences are linked as an Advanced Set named **Sequence Number,** which is illustrated in Exhibit 7–56.

EXHIBIT 7–54
Model Route
Sequence.doe Leave
Dialog

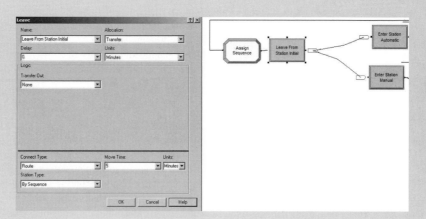

EXHIBIT 7–55   Model Route Sequence.doe Sequence Spreadsheet

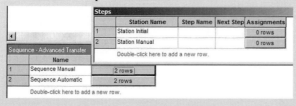

EXHIBIT 7–56
Model Route
Sequence.doe
Advanced Set
Spreadsheet

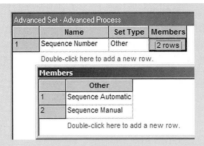

The method for the sequence branching is illustrated in Exhibit 7–57. The expression

$$\text{Entity.Sequence} = \text{Sequence number } (1+ (\text{NQ (Automatic Process.Queue)} >$$
$$\text{NQ (Manual Process.Queue)} + 2))$$

is used to select the proper sequence number. The logical evaluation yields a numeric value of either 1 or 2 depending on the relative conditions of the two queues. The term (NQ (Automatic Process.Queue) > NQ (Manual Process.Queue) + 2) is either true, value of 1 or false, value of 0. Entity.Sequence and Entity.JobStep are two automatically defined Arena entity attributes.

Model Conveyor.doe

Arena model Conveyor.doe demonstrates the use of Arena conveyors to move entities between workstations. Exhibit 7–58 illustrates the new model logic developed to handle movement by conveyors. The Access module is used to gain access to the conveyor. The Convey modules actually start movement on the conveyor while the Enter modules are used to remove the entity from the conveyor. Arena takes care of the details such as finding space on the conveyor and calculating the movement time to the desired location. Stop and Start modules can be used to stop and start the moving conveyor and its associated entities.

Exhibit 7–59 illustrates the Segment module spreadsheet used to define the segment or station pairs that make up the conveyor path. This conveyor travels from Station Initial to Station Automatic to Station Manual and then returns to Station Initial. The length of each conveyor segment is also defined. Exhibit 7–60 illustrates the Conveyor module workbook. This workbook links the conveyor to a segment, defines the conveyor type (Accumulating or Non-accumulating), the conveyor speed, and other characteristics. The timing and application of Arena conveyors are controlled by the cell size. The cell size is an arbitrary length that must be carefully selected by the model builder. Exact details are beyond the scope of this text.

Model Transporter.doe

Arena model Transporter.doe demonstrates the use of Arena transporters such as fork trucks to move entities between workstations. Exhibit 7–61 illustrates the new model logic developed to handle movement by transporters. The Request Transporter module is used to gain access to the Transporter material handling resource. The Transport to Station Automatic and Transport to Station Manual modules actually starts the movement of the transporter while the Enter modules are used to remove the entity from the transporter. Arena takes care of the details, such as finding the transporter, moving it to the required location, and calculating the movement time to the desired location.

EXHIBIT 7–57 **Model Route Sequence.doe Assign Spreadsheet**

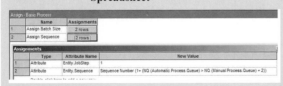

EXHIBIT 7–58 **Model Conveyor.doe Assign Spreadsheet**

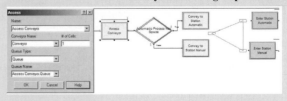

EXHIBIT 7–59
Model Conveyor.doe
Segment
Spreadsheet

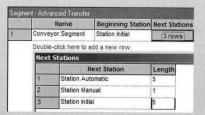

Segment - Advanced Transfer

	Name	Beginning Station	Next Stations
1	Conveyor.Segment	Station Initial	3 rows

Double-click here to add a new row.

Next Stations

	Next Station	Length
1	Station Automatic	5
2	Station Manual	1
3	Station Initial	5

EXHIBIT 7–60
Model Conveyor.doe
Conveyor
Spreadsheet

Conveyor - Advanced Transfer

	Name	Segment Name	Type	Velocity	Units	Cell Size	Max Cells Occupied	Accumulation Length	Initial Status	Report Statistics
1	Conveyor	Conveyor.Segment	Accumulating	1.	Per Minute	1	1	1	Active	☑

Double-click here to add a new row.

EXHIBIT 7–61
Model
Transporter.doe
Request Dialog

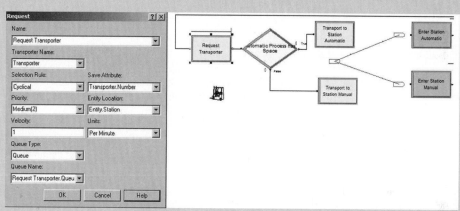

Exhibit 7–62 illustrates the Transporter module workbook that defines the Transporter and links it to the associated Distance Set. The workbook also defines the Transporter speed and Initial positions. Notice that multiple transporters (capacity > 1) of the same type can be defined. In that case, when a request for a transporter is received, Arena finds the idle transporter with the minimum time for the requesting station.

Exhibit 7–63 illustrates the Distance module workbook used to define the distance between Arena Stations serviced by the Transporter.

Model AGV.doe

Arena version 8.0 introduced a special type of transport to more accurately model the Automated Guide Vehicle (AGV) transporters. Arena model AGV.doe demonstrates the use of AGV transporters to move entities between workstations. Exhibit 7–64 illustrates the new model logic developed to handle movement by AGV transporters. The Request Transporter module is used to gain access to the AGV transporter material handling resource. The Transport to Station Automatic and Transport to Station Manual modules actually start the movement of the AGV transporter while the Enter modules are used to remove the entity from the AGV transporter. Arena takes care of the details such as finding the AGV transporter, moving it to the required location, and calculating the movement time to the desired location. AGV transporter travel time calculations can include the acceleration of the vehicle.

EXHIBIT 7–62 Model Transporter.doe Transporter
Spreadsheet

Transporter - Advanced Transfer

	Name	Number of Units	Type	Distance Set	Velocity	Units	Initial Position Status	Report Statistics
1	Transporter	1	Free Path	Transporter.Distance	1.	Per Minute	1 rows	☑

Double-click here to add a new row.

Initial Position Status

	Initial Position	Station Name	Initial Status
1	Station	Station Initial	Active

Double-click here to add a new row.

EXHIBIT 7–63
Model
Transporter.doe
Distance
Spreadsheet

Distance - Advanced Transfer

	Name	Stations
1	Transporter.Distance	2 rows

Double-click here to add a new row.

Stations

	Beginning Station	Ending Station	Distance
1	Station Initial	Station Automatic	5
2	Station Initial	Station Manual	5

Double-click here to add a new row.

EXHIBIT 7–64
Model AGV.doe
Request Dialog

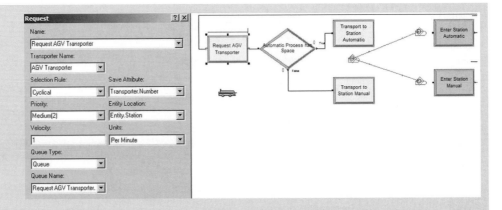

Exhibit 7–65 illustrates the Transporter module workbook that defines the AGV transporter and links it to the associated Network Set. The workbook also defines the AGV transporter speed and Initial positions. Notice that multiple AGV transporters (capacity > 1) of the same type can be defined. In that case, when a request for a transporter is received, Arena finds the idle AGV transporter with the minimum time to the requesting station.

Exhibit 7–66 illustrates the Network module workbook used to define the AGV transporter potential travel network in terms of Network Links. These Network Links are defined in the Network Link module workbook, shown in Exhibit 7–67. The Network Links define the travel time and direction of each link. Network Links begin and end at an intersection. These intersections are defined in the same modules that define stations. Exhibits 7–68 and 7–69 illustrate the Station Initial, Automatic, and Manual Intersection Definitions. The intersections are animated using the diamond-shaped symbol that can be seen in Exhibit 7–64.

EXHIBIT 7–65
Model AGV.doe
Transporter
Spreadsheet

	Name	Number of Units	Type	Network Name	Velocity	Units	Units	Turning Velocity Factor	Zone Control Rule	Initial Position S
1	AGV Transporter	1	Guided	AGV Transporter.Network	1.	Per Minute	Per Second Squared	1.0	Start	1 rows

Double-click here to add a new row.

Initial Position Status

	Initial Position	Station Name	Initial Status	Size Based On	Size Value
1	Station	Station Initial	Active	Length	1

EXHIBIT 7–66
Model AGV.doe
Network
Spreadsheet

Network - Advanced Transfer

	Name	Network Links
1	AGV Transporter.Network	4 rows

Network Links

	Network Link Name
1	Network Link 1
2	Network Link 2
3	Network Link 3
4	Network Link 4

EXHIBIT 7–67
Model AGV.doe
Network Link
Spreadsheet

Network Link - Advanced Transfer

	Name	Type	Beginning Intersection Name	Ending Intersection Name	Beginning Direction	Ending Direction	Number Of Zones	Zone Length	Velocity Change Facto
1	Network Link 1	Unidirectional	Intersection Initial	Intersection Automatic	0		5	1	1.0
2	Network Link 2	Unidirectional	Intersection Automatic	Intersection Initial	0		5	1	1.0
3	Network Link 3	Unidirectional	Intersection Manual	Intersection Initial	0		5	1	1.0
4	Network Link 4	Unidirectional	Intersection Initial	Intersection Manual	0		5	1	1.0

Double-click here to add a new row.

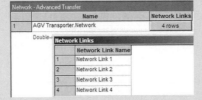

EXHIBIT 7–68

Model AGV.doe Station Initial Intersection Definition

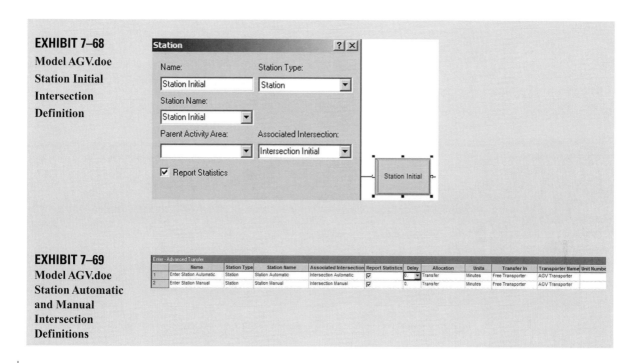

EXHIBIT 7–69

Model AGV.doe Station Automatic and Manual Intersection Definitions

	Name	Station Type	Station Name	Associated Intersection	Report Statistics	Delay	Allocation	Units	Transfer In	Transporter Name	Unit Number
1	Enter Station Automatic	Station	Station Automatic	Intersection Automatic	✓	0.	Transfer	Minutes	Free Transporter	AGV Transporter	
2	Enter Station Manual	Station	Station Manual	Intersection Manual	✓	0.	Transfer	Minutes	Free Transporter	AGV Transporter	

Modeling Multiple Product Flows

Most manufacturing processes involve the production of several different products in the same facility. Exhibit 7–70 illustrates the flow of two different products through a set of four processing cells. Cells A and C are used to produce both products. Cells B and D are used exclusively by product Types 1 and 2 respectively. A series of three models have been developed using the Arena Advanced Transfer template panel. The three Arena models—Products Separate.doe, Products Combined.doe, and Products Sequence.doe—differ in the method used to determine the next processing cell that the product must enter.

Model Products Separate.doe

Arena model Products Separate.doe, illustrated in Exhibit 7–71, uses an independent flow stream for each product type. Notice that two process modules are used to model cell A and another two to model cell C. Exhibit 7–72 illustrates the Process module spreadsheet for model Products Separate.doe. Arena takes care of managing the demand when more than one product uses a single cell or machine. For example, Type.1 entities wait in queue cell A Type 1.Queue for cell A, while Type.2 entities wait in queue cell A Type 2.Queue also for cell A. Since all Process modules operate on the same priority level, Medium (2), the entity in either queue waiting the longest will next seize Resource cell A.

This independent type of model building by product makes sense in simple models with only a few products and/or manufacturing cells. The model would become quite extensive if the number of products were large, for example, more than 10 products. In addition, extensive

EXHIBIT 7–70   **Two-Product Flowchart**

Page two-product flow | Chapter 7 Drawings.vsd

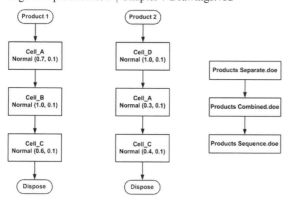

EXHIBIT 7–71
Model Products
Separate.doe Model
Logic

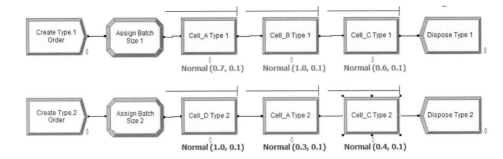

EXHIBIT 7–72
Model Products
Separate.doe Process
Spreadsheet

Process - Basic Process

	Name	Type	Action	Priority	Resources	Delay Type	Units	Allocation	Expression
1	Cell_A Type 1	Standard	Seize Delay Release	Medium(2)	1 rows	Expression	Minutes	Value Added	Batch.Size * Normal (0.7, 0.1, 5)
2	Cell_B Type 1	Standard	Seize Delay Release	Medium(2)	1 rows	Expression	Minutes	Value Added	Batch.Size * Normal (1.0, 0.1, 6)
3	Cell_C Type 1	Standard	Seize Delay Release	Medium(2)	1 rows	Expression	Minutes	Value Added	Batch.Size * Normal (0.6, 0.1, 7)
4	Cell_D Type 2	Standard	Seize Delay Release	Medium(2)	1 rows	Expression	Minutes	Value Added	Batch.Size * Normal (1.0, 0.1, 8)
5	Cell_A Type 2	Standard	Seize Delay Release	Medium(2)	1 rows	Expression	Minutes	Value Added	Batch.Size * Normal (0.3, 0.1, 5)
6	Cell_C Type 2	Standard	Seize Delay Release	Medium(2)	1 rows	Expression	Minutes	Value Added	Batch.Size * Normal (0.4, 0.1, 7)

model code would have to be added each time a new product is introduced to the manufacturing process.

Model Products Combined.doe

Arena model Products Combined.doe illustrated in Exhibit 7–73 uses only a single Process module for each of the four manufacturing cells. A Decide module is used to determine the path of the job through the manufacturing cells. Assign modules are used to set the Mean.Processing.Time attribute for the next Process cell.

Exhibit 7–73 also illustrates the Decide module dialog used to determine the Process cell to be visited next by entities leaving Process cell A. Type 1 products must next go to Process cell B, while Type 2 products must next go to Process cell C.

Exhibit 7–74 illustrates the Assign module dialog used to set the processing time mean, Mean.Processing.Time attribute, for Type 1 products entities about enter Process cell B. Exhibit 7–75 illustrates the Process module dialog that uses the Mean.Processing.Time attribute to calculate the Process delay time with the following expression:

$$Batch.Size * Normal (Mean.Processing.Time, 0.1)$$

EXHIBIT 7–73
Model Products
Combined.doe Model
Logic

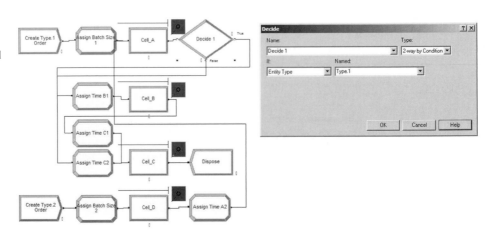

EXHIBIT 7–74

Model Products
Combined.doe Assign
Dialog

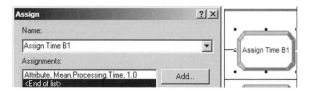

EXHIBIT 7–75

Model Products
Combined.doe
Process Spreadsheet

	Name	Type	Action	Priority	Resources	Delay Type	Units	Allocation	Expression	Report Statistics
1	Cell_A	Standard	Seize Delay Release	Medium(2)	1 rows	Expression	Minutes	Value Added	Batch.Size * Normal (Mean.Processing.Time, 0.1, 5)	☑
2	Cell_D	Standard	Seize Delay Release	Medium(2)	1 rows	Expression	Minutes	Value Added	Batch.Size * Normal (Mean.Processing.Time, 0.1, 8)	☑
3	Cell_B	Standard	Seize Delay Release	Medium(2)	1 rows	Expression	Minutes	Value Added	Batch.Size * Normal (Mean.Processing.Time, 0.1, 6)	☑
4	Cell_C	Standard	Seize Delay Release	Medium(2)	1 rows	Expression	Minutes	Value Added	Batch.Size * Normal (Mean.Processing.Time, 0.1, 7)	☑

EXHIBIT 7–76
Model Products
Sequence.doe Model
Logic

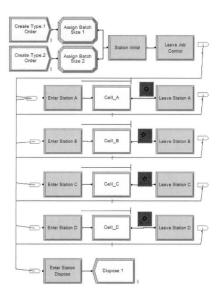

Model Products Sequence.doe

Arena model Products Sequence.doe uses the Arena Sequence concept to control the flow and provide the processing time for the two products moving through the four cells. Exhibit 7–76 illustrates the model logic developed to handle this processing. Each manufacturing process cell is modeled as an Arena station.

Exhibit 7–77 illustrates the Sequence module spreadsheet used to control the flow and provide the processing time. A separate sequence is used for each part type. Part Type.1 must visit Station A, Station B, Station C, and finally Station Dispose. Attributes Mean.Processing.Time and Travel.Time are assigned the processing and travel times for the next Process module.

Arena Academic Edition Limits

Exhibit 7–78 illustrates the academic edition limits imposed by Rockwell software on Arena version 8.0. The limit on the number of concurrent entities often requires jobs to be processed in batches rather than processed as single work orders. The limit on the number of module instances restricts the overall size of the Arena model. Note that each variable and expression definition is counted as a module instance. Thus, unfortunately, those modules must be used sparingly. There is no limit on the size of the VBA code that may be used with the academic edition of Arena.

Concurrent Entities

The academic edition of Arena 8.0 limits the number of concurrent entities to 150. This can restrict students who attempt to model real-life processes. An arrival rate slightly faster than the slowest processing module will very quickly cause the type of error illustrated in

EXHIBIT 7–77 Model Products Sequence.doe Sequence
Spreadsheet

	Name	Steps
1	Sequence Type.1	4 rows
2	Sequence Type.2	4 rows
	Double-click here to add a new row.	

	Station Name	Step Name	Next Step	Assignments
1	Station A			2 rows
2	Station B			2 rows
3	Station C			2 rows
4	Station Dispose			0 rows

	Assignment Type	Attribute Name	Value
1	Attribute	Mean.Processing.Time	0.7
2	Attribute	Travel.Time	5

EXHIBIT 7–78
Arena Academic
Edition Limits
Sheet academic limits |
Chapter 7
Worksheets.xls

Model Component	Academic Limit
Concurrent Entities	150
Siman Objects	300
Cinema Objects	150
Include Block/Elements	0

EXHIBIT 7–79

Arena Academic Edition 150 Entities Error Message

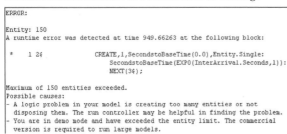

```
ERROR:

Entity: 150
A runtime error was detected at time 949.66263 at the following block:

*    1 2$             CREATE,1,SecondstoBaseTime(0.0),Entity.Single:
                      SecondstoBaseTime(EXPO(InterArrival.Seconds,1)):
                      NEXT(3$);

Maximum of 150 entities exceeded.
Possible causes:
- A logic problem in your model is creating too many entities or not
  disposing them. The run controller may be helpful in finding the problem.
- You are in demo mode and have exceeded the entity limit. The commercial
  version is required to run large models.
```

EXHIBIT 7–80 **Model Limit Entities.doe**

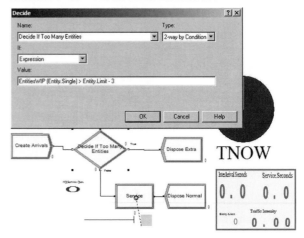

Exhibit 7–79. We present two Arena models, Limit Entities.doe and Large Accumulator.doe, which provide a reasonable solution to this Arena academic edition limit.

Limit Entities.doe

The Arena model Limit Entities.doe illustrated in Exhibit 7–80 provides one method to assure that the number of entities in the model does not exceed a specific limit. Exhibit 7–80 illustrates the dialog for the module Decide If Too Many Entities. This module is the key limit in this model design. The expression **EntitiesWIP (Entity.Single) > Entity.Limit − 3** diverts excess entities to the module Dispose Extra. That module simply removes the excess entities from the model. The normal processing is conducted on the lower part of Exhibit 7–80. The reader is encouraged to test the functioning of the model Limit Entities.doe. In this particular case, entities arrive on the average of one per minute. Process 1 requires an average of 1.5 minutes, thus in about 300 minutes, without the logic of module Decide If Too Many Entities, an error like that illustrated in Exhibit 7–79 would occur.

The logic demonstrated in the Arena model Limit Entities.doe also applies in many large-scale Arena simulation models where the arrival rate for entities must match the actual system capacity. The model should include a means to record the number of entities or fraction of total entities considered to be excess and removed by the module Dispose Extra.

Large Accumulator.doe

Arena model Large Accumulator.doe, which is illustrated in Exhibit 7–81, provides another method to model a large accumulator that would normally exceed the number of entities in the academic edition of Arena. The general strategy applied in developing the model Large Accumulator.doe is to count and then dispose of entities entering the accumulator and then

EXHIBIT 7–81
Model Large
Accumulator.doe

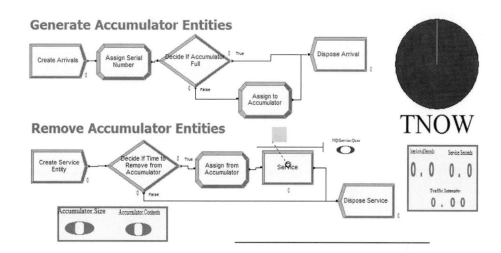

Generate Accumulator Entities

Remove Accumulator Entities

EXHIBIT 7–82
Model Large
Accumulator.doe
Assign 1 Detail

	Type	Variable Name	Attribute Name	New Value
1	Variable	Number.Serial	Attribute 1	Number.Serial + 1
2	Attribute	Variable 2	Serial.Number	Number.Serial

reversing this logic when entities are removed. The top portion of Exhibit 7–81 handles the entering entities, while the center portion handles those exiting the accumulator.

First, consider the arriving entities. Module Assign Serial Number prepares entities by assigning a serial number attribute using the logic displayed in Exhibit 7–82. Notice that this is a two-step process:

1. Variable Number.Serial is first incremented by one.
2. Attribute Serial.Number is then set to the current value of Variable Number.Serial.

The above two assignment steps have wide application wherever each entity must be assigned a consecutive serial number. Module Decide if Accumulator Full is used to control the contents of the accumulator. When the accumulator is full to its capacity of Accumulator.Size, this expression is true and the entity is dispose by module Dispose Arrival: **Accumulator.Contents > Accumulator.Size − 1.**

Whenever the accumulator has space, the previous expression is false; the logic in the module Assign to Accumulator is performed before the entity is disposed. Exhibit 7–83 illustrates the assignment steps.

1. The **Entity Type** is reset to facilitate statistic collection.

2. The variable **Accumulator.Contents** is increased by one to reflect the new entity being added to the accumulator.

3. The variable **Number.Stored** is increased by one to be used to generate a second entity attribute.

EXHIBIT 7–83
Model Large
Accumulator.doe
Assign to
Accumulator Detail

	Type	Variable Name	Attribute Name	Entity Type	Other	New Value
1	Entity Type	Variable 1	Attribute 1	Entity to Accumulator	J	1
2	Variable	Accumulator.Contents	Attribute 2	Entity 1	J	Accumulator.Contents + 1
3	Variable	Number.Stored	Attribute 3	Entity 1	J	Number.Stored + 1
4	Attribute	Variable 4	Stored.Number	Entity 1	J	Number.Stored
5	Variable	Pointer.Input	Attribute 5	Entity 1	J	MOD (Pointer.Input, Accumulator.Size) + 1
6	Other	Variable 6	Attribute 6	Entity 1	Attribute.Values (Pointer.Input, 1)	Serial.Number
7	Other	Variable 7	Attribute 7	Entity 1	Attribute.Values (Pointer.Input, 2)	Stored.Number
8	Other	Variable 8	Attribute 8	Entity 1	Attribute.Values (Pointer.Input, 3)	TNOW

4. The attribute **Stored.Number** is set equal to the current value of variable **Number.Stored.**

5. The variable **Pointer.Input** is increased by one using the expression **MOD (Pointer.Input, Accumulator.Size) + 1.** This expression uses the mathematical function MOD or remainder to assure that the value of variable **Pointer.Input** stays within the range of 1 to **Accumulator.Size.** The variable **Pointer.Input** is used in the following three assignments as an index to the variable array Attribute.Values.

6. The variable array **Attribute.Values (Pointer.Input, 1)** is used to store the **Serial.Number** of the current entity.

7. The variable array **Attribute.Values (Pointer.Input, 2)** is used to store the **Stored.Number** of the current entity.

8. The variable array **Attribute.Values (Pointer.Input, 3)** is used to store the value **TNOW,** which is current simulation time.

Next, consider the leaving entities. Module Create Service Entity generates removal entities at the maximum rate that entities may be removed from the accumulator. At module Decide if Time to Remove from Accumulator, the removal entity is tested using this expression to determine if the system can handle addition entities: **Accumulator.Contents > 0 .and. NQ (Process 1.Queue) < 2.**

If the expression is false, the entity is disposed. If the expression is true, the accumulator has at least one available entity and the system has room to handle its processing starting the module Assign from the accumulator. Exhibit 7–84 illustrates the following assignment steps.

1. The **Entity Type** is reset to facilitate statistic collection.

2. The variable **Accumulator.Contents** is decreased by one to reflect the entity being removed from the accumulator.

3. The variable **Pointer.Output** is increased by one using the expression **MOD (Pointer.Output, Accumulator.Size) + 1.** This expression uses the mathematical function MOD or remainder to assure that the value of variable **Pointer.Output** stays within the range of 1 to Accumulator.Size. The variable **Pointer.Output** is used in the following three assignments as an index to the variable array **Attribute.Values.**

4. The value of attribute **Serial.Number** for the current entity is set to the value stored variable array **Attribute.Values (Pointer.Output, 1).**

5. The value of attribute **Stored.Number** for the current entity is set to the value stored variable array **Attribute.Values (Pointer.Output, 2).**

6. The value of attribute **Arrival.Time** for the current entity is set to the value stored variable array **Attribute.Values (Pointer.Output, 3).**

The procedure illustrated in model Large Accumulator.doe could be duplicated several times in a relatively large model using the academic edition of Arena. This same logic could also be used to increase the execution speed of a full-scale Arena model with large accumulators.

EXHIBIT 7–84
Model Large Accumulator.doe Assign from Accumulator Detail

	Type	Variable Name	Attribute Name	Entity Type	New Value
1	Entity Type ▼	Variable 1	Attribute 1	Entity Process	1
2	Variable	Accumulator.Contents	Attribute 2	Entity 1	Accumulator.Contents - 1
3	Variable	Pointer.Output	Attribute 3	Entity 1	MOD (Pointer.Output, Accumulator.Size) + 1
4	Attribute	Variable 4	Serial.Number	Entity 1	Attribute.Values (1, Pointer.Output)
5	Attribute	Variable 5	Stored.Number	Entity 1	Attribute.Values (2, Pointer.Output)
6	Attribute	Variable 6	Arrival.Time	Entity 1	Attribute.Values (3, Pointer.Output)

Simulation Model Design Checklist

The models presented in this chapter have been designed to be expanded by the reader to model more complex processes. The experienced simulation model developer typically starts with a simple flow model and adds detail, as more detailed or specific answers are required. Exhibit 7–85 outlines the design decisions in a checklist format that should be considered when developing a process simulation model. This outline should be viewed as a starting point. Every process simulation requires a unique design that only experience can bring.

EXHIBIT 7–85
Simulation Model Design Checklist
Sheet model design checklist | Chapter 7 Worksheets.xls

Simulation Model Design Checklist
Process Description
What does this process do?
What are the process inputs?
What are the process outputs?
What causes the process not to operate at 100% efficiency?
What potential changes or features should be tested?
Simulation Model Objectives (Why build a simulation model)
Learn how Process Operates
Evaluate Potential Changes
Estimate Capacity
Types of Statistics Required
Queues (maximum length, waiting time)
Resource (utilization, frequencies)
Production per Period
Flow or Through Put Time
Cost
Entities
Attributes (time of arrival, picture or icon, color, size)
Grouping/Splitting (cases, pallets)
Maximum Number (150 academic version)
Arrival Process
When (Start time or 1st arrival and frequency)
Entity Type
Scheduled or read from Excel workbook
Limited Capacity Resources
How Many - (similar vs. different)
Cycle Time (Variability)
Operate/Repair Cycle (fixed verses random)
Schedules
Set Up or Changeovers
Why they don't always run at Maximum Speed
Experiment Plan
Validation & Verification
Model vs. Real World Process
Sensitivity Analysis
How will models be compared?
Base Case Model
Alternative Models
Process Analyzer (PAN)
Optimization (OptQuest)

Exercises

1. Consider model Manufacturing Cell 1.doe. The orders arrive on an average of one per minute. Decrease this average time between arrivals using decrements of 0.05 minutes until the process is not able to reliably handle the incoming stream of orders. What is the bottleneck in the process?

2. Consider model Manufacturing Cell 2.doe. The average batch size is 10 units. Increase this average batch size using increments of 0.5 units until the process is not able to reliably handle the incoming stream of orders. What is the bottleneck in the process?

3. Consider model Manufacturing Cell 4.doe. The average batch size was found to be near 9.75 rather than the desired 10.0. The problem lies in the expression used to generate the attribute Batch.Size and the shape of the Normal density function. Change the Assign Batch Size module to move the average batch size closer to the desired value.

4. Model Manufacturing Cell 5.doe includes machine failures. Add Failure2 to Resource R.Automatic and evaluate the impact on process performance. Also change the Failure2 Uptime and Downtime distributions from Gamma to Exponential and evaluate the impact on process performance.

5. It was determined that model Reject Batch.doe may allow the Batch.Rejects = Batch.Size. This is always true if the Batch.Size is zero. This will cause one ItemGood type entity to be disposed even though no good items were produced. This condition will automatically generate an incorrect good item count. Modify the model Reject Batch.doe to prevent this from occurring. Note that eliminating zero batch size will not completely eliminate this problem.

6. Modify model Rework Batch.doe to dispose and count any batches that have been reworked more than twice.

Challenge

7. Convert model Route Sequence.doe, so that the movement between operations is performed using transporter constructs.

8. Convert model Route Sequence.doe, so that the movement between operations is performed using conveyor constructs.

9. Using model Transporter.doe as a guide, develop an Arena model that links four workstations in series using transporter constructs.

10. Using model Conveyor.doe as a guide, develop an Arena model that links four workstations in series using conveyor constructs.

Visual Basic for Applications: Computer-Based Tools Integration

Summary and Learning Objectives

This chapter introduces some general concepts needed for the effective application of Visual Basic for Application (VBA) to integrate the software tools introduced in this textbook. We show how to record a macro in Excel and Arena and then review several VBA applications in Excel, Visio, and Arena.

The learning objectives for this chapter are to

1. Understand the structure of the VBA Integrated Development Environment.
2. Record VBA macros from Excel and Arena.
3. Understand the structure of Excel-based VBA code.
4. Develop Arena models that utilize the VBA block.
5. Develop Arena models using VBA that reads Variable values from an Excel workbook.
6. Develop Interactive Arena models using VBA OnKeystroke routine.

Introduction to Visual Basic for Applications

Microsoft Visual Basic for Applications is a powerful development technology for rapidly customizing software applications and integrating them with existing data and systems. VBA offers a sophisticated set of programming tools based on the Microsoft VBA development system, which developers can use to harness the power of packaged applications. VBA enables developers to buy off-the-shelf software and customize it to meet their specific business processes, rather than build solutions from scratch. This helps them save time and money, reduce risks, leverage their programming skills, and deliver precisely what users need.

VBA also includes support for Microsoft Forms, for creating custom dialog boxes, and ActiveX Controls, for rapidly building user interfaces.

The Integrated Development Environment (IDE) of VBA is available with Microsoft Visio, Excel, Word, and PowerPoint and in a wide variety of other software including Arena. VBA looks exactly the same no matter which of these applications you start it from. Each VBA application exposes its functionality as a set of programmable objects. Using VBA gives you access to these objects, making it possible for you to do anything in the application programmatically that you can do manually with the user interface or personal computer keyboard.

All VBA-enabled applications use a consistent syntax. This makes it much easier for you to apply the skills you acquire while learning to program one application to a wide range of other applications. This uniformity of language also makes it easier to create solutions that involve more than one application and to reuse code across applications.

Because VBA is being used by a wide variety of software applications beyond the Microsoft Office suite, it is well-documented in the popular literature. The reference book by Eric Wells (1995) is an excellent starting point for model developers familiar with Excel workbooks. The documentation and Smart examples supplied with the Arena software also provides a limited introduction to VBA concepts.

Use the following suggestions to get the most from the time you spend learning VBA.

Learn the Application First

We have introduced Microsoft Visio, Microsoft Excel, and Rockwell Software Arena in the text. All of these applications support VBA. With this background, the reader should be ready to start using VBA to automate function within and between these applications.

Most VBA procedures perform a sequence of actions, and most instructions in a procedure are equivalent to keyboard commands or actions. Consequently, working with VBA is a little like working with a software application without a user interface; instead of choosing commands and selecting options in dialog boxes, you write VBA instructions. The statements and functions you use to write instructions are much easier to understand if you're already familiar with the features they represent in Office.

Learn What You Need, When You Need It

Learn what you need for the task at hand. VBA can seem overwhelming at first, particularly if you don't have any experience with programming languages. A great way to begin learning VBA is to investigate how to accomplish a particular task programmatically. As you gain experience writing procedures that automate different types of tasks, you'll cover a lot of ground.

VBA Integrated Development Environment

Visio, Excel, and Arena come equipped with a full-featured Integrated Development Environment called the VBA Editor. The VBA Editor illustrated in Exhibit 8–1 provides a Project Window, a Properties Window, and debugging tools. The VBA Editor can be viewed from any VBA-enabled application by pressing the **Alt-F11** keys. The VBA Editor is a program designed to make writing and editing macrocode easy for beginners, and it provides plenty of online Help (**F1**). See Exhibit 8–2. The Excel and Arena user does not have to learn how to program or use the VBA language to make simple changes to VBA macros.

Properties Window

A property is a characteristic of an object, such as the object's color or caption. You set a property to specify a characteristic or behavior of an object. You can use the Properties window to set the properties of an object at design time. The Properties window is very useful when you're working with custom dialog boxes and ActiveX controls. If you don't think you'll be using the Properties window right now, you can close it to simplify your workspace a little. You can open it again at any time by clicking **Properties Window** on the View menu.

EXHIBIT 8–1
VBA Integrated
Development
Environment

EXHIBIT 8–2
VBA Integrated
Development
Environment Help
Window

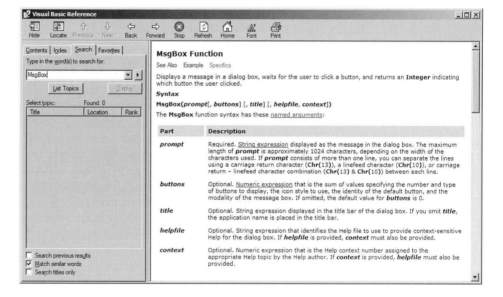

Project Explorer

All the code associated with a workbook, drawing, or model is stored in a *project* that is automatically stored and saved with the workbook, drawing, or model. In the Project Explorer of the VBA Editor, you can view, modify, and navigate the projects for every open or referenced workbook, drawing, or model. You can resize the Project Explorer and either dock it to or undock it from any of the sides of the VBA Editor window to make it easier to use.

Within a project, there can be application objects that have events associated with them, custom dialog boxes (called *forms* in the Project Explorer), standard modules, class modules, and references. Folders in the Project Explorer divide project elements into categories. If you don't see any folders, click the Toggle Folders button at the top of the Project Explorer.

In the Project Explorer, there is one project for each open or referenced workbook, drawing, or model. In each project, you may find objects (such as Drawing objects, Workbook objects, and Worksheet objects) that recognize events; forms (also called *UserForms*), which are custom dialog box interfaces and the code that controls how the user interacts with a particular dialog box; standard modules, which contain code that isn't associated with a particular object or form; class modules, which contain information about a custom object type; and references to other projects. To see the code in a module or the code associated with an object or form, click the element in the Project Explorer, and then click the **View Code** button at the top of the Project Explorer. To see the user interface for a particular object or form, click the object or form in the Project Explorer, and then click the **View Object** button at the top of the Project Explorer.

Code Window

To view the code in a project, go to the Project Explorer, click the element that contains the code, and then click the **View Code** button at the top of the Project Explorer. If you want to be able to see more than one procedure in the code window at a time, select the **Default to Full Module View** check box on the Editor tab in the Options dialog box (Tools menu). To view just one procedure at a time, clear this check box.

You can navigate the Code window by using the items listed in the Object and Procedure boxes at the top of the window. In the Object box, click **General**, and then click a procedure name in the Procedure box to see a procedure that isn't associated with a specific event. In the Object box, click an object, and then click an event in the Procedure box to see the code that runs when a specific event occurs.

VBA Help

Help, shown in Exhibit 8–2, is a powerful tool for learning VBA. For information about a particular window in the VBA Editor, click in the window and then press **F1** to open the appropriate Help topic. To see the Help topic for any other element of the VBA Editor, such as a particular toolbar button, search Help for the name of the element.

In a VBA module, you can type a keyword and, with the insertion point positioned somewhere in the keyword, press **F1** to immediately display the VBA Help topic for that keyword. Most VBA Help topics for keywords include examples that you can copy and paste into your macros. For more information, see the following section.

Microsoft provides an extensive Help system for the VBA language, the objects that Office supports, and the properties and methods of those objects. If you clicked **Typical** when you installed Office, you'll need to run Setup again to install Help for VBA for the applications you want to program in.

You can access VBA Help in any module in the VBA Editor in any of the following three ways:

1. Position the insertion point anywhere in an object name, property name, method name, event name, function name, or other keyword you've typed, and then press **F1** to get context-sensitive Help for that keyword.

2. Click **Microsoft VBA Help** (in the VBA Editor) or on the Help menu. You can then ask the Office Assistant a question, click **Search**, and click the topic you want to read in the "What would you like to do?"

3. Click **Object Browser** on the View menu, and then either press **F1** or click the **Help** button (the question mark button above the "Members of box") for information about the selected object, method, property, event, or function.

After you've displayed a Help topic, you can click the **Help Topics** button in the Help window to display the Help Topics dialog box, which contains three tabs: Contents, Index, and Find. You can then either look up a specific topic or VBA term on the Contents or Index tab or perform a full-text search from the Find tab.

Object Browser

When using the VBA Editor, pressing the **F2** key displays the object browser that permits searching for specific VBA objects and displaying their associated application context. Exhibit 8–3 illustrates results of a search for the VBA keyword **MsgBox.** We illustrate the use of a VBA MsgBox in Exhibit 8–28. Notice on the bottom of Exhibit 8–3 a full-context illustration for the **MsgBox** keyword. With the keyword **MsgBox** selected, pressing the Help key **(F1)** generates the context-sensitive Help illustrated in Exhibit 8–2.

Each Office application provides a file called an *object library,* or *type library,* that contains information about the objects, properties, methods, events, and built-in constants that the application exposes. You can use a tool called the *Object Browser* to look at the information in this file and to browse the object model it describes.

To open the Object Browser from the VBA Editor, click **Object Browser** on the View menu. In the Project/Library box, click the name of the object library whose objects you want to see, or click **All Libraries** to view a master list of all the objects in all the referenced object libraries. If the object library whose objects you want to view doesn't appear in the Project/Library box, you must create a reference to that object library by using the References dialog box (Tools menu).

The Classes box in the Object Browser displays the names of all objects and enumerated types in all the referenced object libraries. A class is a *type,* or description, of object. An object is an actual instance of a class. For example, the Workbook class contains all the information you need to create a workbook. A Workbook object only comes into existence when you use the information in the Workbook class to create an actual workbook (an instance of the Workbook class). Despite this technical distinction, these terms are often used interchangeably. The term *object* is used generically for both *class* and *object* in this chapter.

When you click the name of an object in the Classes box in the Object Browser, you see all the properties, methods, and events associated with that object in the "Members of box."

Click a property or method in the "Members of box." You can press **F1** to see the Help topic for the selected keyword, or you can look in the Details panel at the bottom of the Object Browser window to see the following: syntax information, a property's read-only or read/write status, the object library that the object belongs to, and the type of data or object that the property or method returns.

EXHIBIT 8–3
VBA Object Browser Window

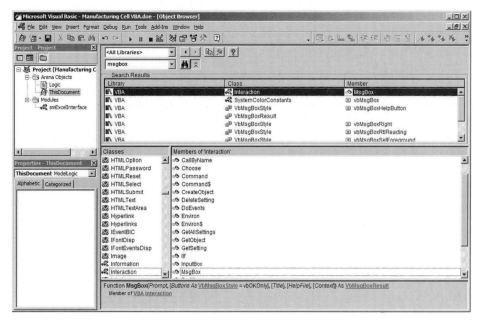

VBA Object Model Overview

Before you can programmatically gain access to an application's content and functionality, it's important to understand how the content and functionality of the application is partitioned into discrete objects and how these objects are arranged in a hierarchical model.

An application consists of two things: content and functionality. Content refers to the documents that the application contains and the words, numbers, or graphics included in the documents; it also refers to information about attributes of individual elements in the application, such as the size of a window, the color of a graphic, or the font size of a word. Functionality refers to all the ways you can work with the content in the application, for example, opening, closing, adding, deleting, copying, pasting, editing, or formatting elements in the application.

The content and functionality in an application are broken down into discrete units of related content and functionality called *objects.* You're already familiar with some of these objects, as elements of the user interface: Microsoft Excel workbooks, worksheets, and cell ranges; Visio drawings, pages, and shapes; and Arena models and modules.

The top-level object in an application is usually the Application object, which is the application itself. For instance, Microsoft Excel itself is the Application object in the Microsoft Excel object model. The Application object contains other objects that you have access to only when the Application object exists (that is, when the application is running). For example, the Microsoft Excel Application object contains Workbook objects. Because the Workbook object depends on the existence of the Excel Application object for its own existence, the Workbook object is said to be the child of the Application object; conversely, the Application object is said to be the parent of the Workbook object. Many objects that are children have children of their own. For example, the Microsoft Excel Workbook object contains, or is parent to, the collection of Worksheet objects that represent all the worksheets in the workbook. Exhibit 8–4 illustrates some parent-child relationships in Excel.

The way objects that make up an application are arranged relative to each other, together with the way the content and functionality are divided among the objects, is called the *object hierarchy* or the *object model.* To see a graphical representation of the object model for a particular application, see "Microsoft Excel Objects" in VBA Help for Excel. We have illustrated part of the Excel object model in Exhibit 8–5.

In addition to containing lower-level objects, each object in the hierarchy contains content and functionality that apply both to the object itself and to all objects below it in the hierarchy. The higher an object is in the hierarchy, the wider the scope of its content and functionality. For example, in Microsoft Excel, the Application object contains the size of the application window and the ability to quit the application; the Workbook object contains the filename and format of the workbook and the ability to save the workbook; and the Worksheet object contains the worksheet name and the ability to delete the worksheet.

You often don't get to what you think of as the contents of a file such as the values on a Microsoft Excel worksheet, until you've navigated through quite a few levels in the object hierarchy, because this specific information belongs to a very specific part of the application. In other words, the value in a cell on a worksheet

EXHIBIT 8–4   Excel Parent—Child Relationships
Page parent-child relationships | Chapter 8 Drawing.vsd

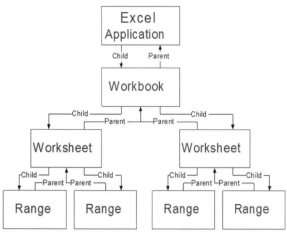

EXHIBIT 8–5
Excel Objects Model
Page Excel Objects
Model | Chapter 8
Drawing.vsd

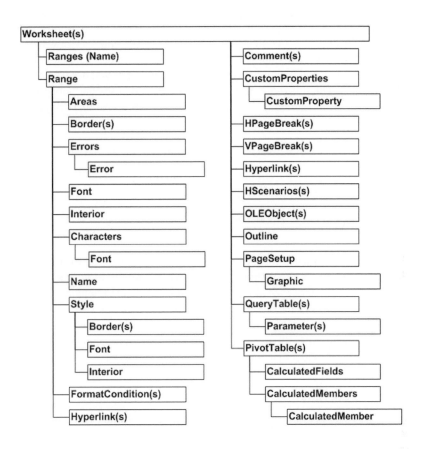

applies only to that cell, not to all cells on the worksheet, so you cannot store it directly in the Worksheet object. The content and functionality stored in an object are thus intrinsically appropriate to the scope of the object.

In summary, the content and functionality in an application are divided among the objects in the application's object model. Together, the objects in the hierarchy contain all the content and functionality in the application. Separately, the objects provide access to very specific areas of content and functionality.

Properties and Methods

There are two ways to interact with an application's objects: manually (using the user interface) or programmatically (using a programming language). In the user interface, you use the keyboard or the mouse, or both, to navigate to the part of the application that controls the data that you want to change or the commands you want to use. For example, in Microsoft Excel, to enter a value into cell B3 on the worksheet named "Sales" in the workbook named "Book1.xls," you open the Book1.xls workbook, click the tab for the Sheet1 worksheet, click in cell B3, and then type a value.

It's important to understand an object's place in the object model, because before you can work with an object, you have to navigate through the object model to get to it. This usually means that you have to step down through all the objects above it in the object hierarchy to get to it. For example, in Microsoft Excel, you cannot get to a particular cell on a worksheet without first going through the application, which contains the workbook that contains the worksheet that contains the cell.

In VBA statements, you navigate through the object model from the top-level object to the object that contains the content and functionality you want to work with, and you use properties and methods of that object to get to the content and functionality. To get to the content and functionality contained in an object, you use properties and methods of that object. The following Microsoft Excel example uses the Value property of the Range object to set the contents of cell B3 on the worksheet named "Sheet1" in the workbook named "Book1.xls."

Application.Workbooks("Book1.xls").Worksheets("Sheet1").Range("B3").Value = 3

The following example uses the Bold property of the Font object to apply bold formatting to cell B3 on the Sheet1 worksheet.

Application.Workbooks("Book1.xls").Worksheets("Sheet1").
Range("B3").Font.Bold = True

The following Word example uses the Close method of the Workbook object to close the file named "Book1.xls." The command is **Application.Workbooks("Book1.xls").Close.**

In general, you use properties to get to content, which can include the text contained in an object or the attribute settings for the object; and you use methods to get to functionality, which entails everything you can do to the content. Be aware, however, that this distinction doesn't always hold true; there are a number of properties and methods in every object model that constitute exceptions to this rule.

VBA References

The VBA Editor menu command sequence, **Tools > References,** generates the dialog illustrated in Exhibit 8–6. The dialog allows you to select another application's objects that you want available in your code by setting a reference to that application's object library. The object library is a file with the **.olb** extension that provides information to VBA about available objects. You can use the Object Browser, shown in Exhibit 8–3, to examine the contents of an object library to get information about the objects provided.

The References dialog section labeled "Available References" lists the references currently available to your project.

EXHIBIT 8–6
Excel-VBA References Dialog

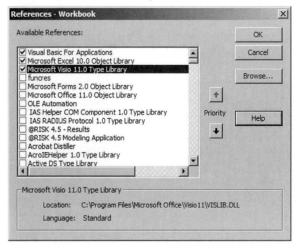

- After you set a reference to an object library by selecting the check box next to its name, you can find a specific object and its methods and properties in the Object Browser.

- If you are not using any objects in a referenced library, you should clear the check box for that reference to minimize the number of object references that Visual Basic must resolve, thus reducing the time it takes your project to compile. You can't remove a reference for an item that is used in your project.

- If you remove a reference to an object currently being used in your project, you will receive an error the next time you refer to that object.

- References not in use are listed alphabetically.

You can't remove the Visual Basic for Applications reference, because it is necessary for running VBA.

The Priority buttons move references up and down on the list. When you refer to an object in code, VBA searches each referenced library selected in the References dialog box in the order the libraries are displayed. If two referenced libraries contain objects with the same name, Visual Basic uses the definition provided by the library listed higher in the Available References box.

The box at the bottom of the References dialog displays the name and path of the reference selected in the Available References box, as well as the language version.

The Browse button displays the Add Reference dialog box, shown in Exhibit 8–7, so that you can search other directories for and add references to the Available References box for the following types:

- Type Libraries(*.olb, *.tlb, *.dll)
- Executable Files (*.exe, *.dll)
- ActiveX Controls (*.ocx)

The VBA Add References dialog illustrated in Exhibit 8–7 illustrates the potential references associated with Arena 8.0.

The VBA References dialog illustrated in Exhibit 8–6 indicates the references assumed by the workbooks associated with each chapter of this textbook: Chapter X Worksheets.xls, where X = 1, 2,…12. These are the proper references for a computer with Microsoft Office XP (version 10.0) and Microsoft Visio 2002. If your computer has some other version of these software programs installed you may need to change the VBA references. If any of the references cannot be found on your computer, the reference is marked as "Missing." Uncheck the reference box and scroll down to file the closest available reference. Check that box and then verify that all references have been satisfied by compiling the VBA using the **Debug > Compile** Workbook VBA menu command sequence.

Exhibit 8–8 illustrates the VBA References Dialog associated with the VBA-based Arena examples presented in this chapter: VBA Large Accumulator.doe, Manufacturing Cell VBA .doe, and VBA Output.doe.

Comparing Exhibits 8–6 and 8–8, notice that because the first case uses Visio, therefore, this reference is required: **Microsoft Visio 2003 Type Library.**

In the second case, because Visio has been replaced by Arena the reference above has been removed and these two references added: **Arena 7.0 Type Library** and **Microsoft Forms 2.0 Object Library.**

EXHIBIT 8–7   **VBA Add References Dialog Box**   **EXHIBIT 8–8**   **Arena-VBA References Dialog**

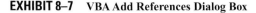

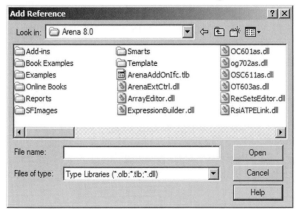

Recording VBA Macros

The quickest way to get started using VBA is to record a macro. Visio 2003, Excel, and Arena all support this feature. We provide examples using both Excel and Arena. After selecting a starting recording option from the menu, each user keystroke is converted into VBA code and stored. When completed, the VBA macro can be replayed, exactly duplicating the original keystrokes. Typically, the user will want to modify the VBA to produce a slightly different result.

Recording an Excel VBA Macro

EXHIBIT 8–9
Excel Recording Macro Selection Sequence
Sheet Variables |
Chapter 8
Worksheets.xls

Recording an Excel macro is the easiest way to generate VBA code. The code generated is pure VBA and with slight modification, could be executed from Arena or another application. Exhibit 8–9 illustrates the Excel menu path to initiate the recording of an Excel macro, **Tools > Macro > Record New Macro. . . .** We started this process from sheet **Variables** of workbook Chapter 8 Worksheets.xls.

Exhibit 8–10 illustrates the Excel Record Macro dialog. The default macro name of **Macro1** was not changed. We assigned a Shortcut Key of **Ctrl+Shift+C** to execute this macro from the original workbook. The macro will be stored in "This Workbook." A description is automatically added to the macro, which includes the recording data.

EXHIBIT 8–10   **Excel Recording Macro Dialog**

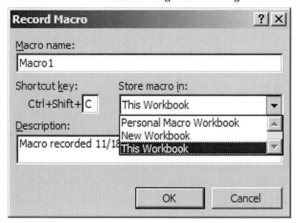

The macro is recorded by using normal Excel keystrokes and mouse movements. In this example, we wish to make a copy of the current worksheet and save it as new workbook named "Manufacturing Cell VBA.xls."

We started with the **Edit > Move** or **Copy Sheet .** **. .** command, which resulted in the dialog illustrated in Exhibit 8–11. At this dialog, we selected to put the worksheet in a new workbook and to create a copy. These options leave the original workbook unchanged.

The new workbook was saved on drive A: using the **File > Save As . . .** which leads to the dialog illustrated in Exhibit 8–12. We saved the workbook as **A:\Manufacturing Cell VBA.xls** on a diskette to supply to a colleague.

EXHIBIT 8–11
Excel Move or Copy Worksheet Dialog

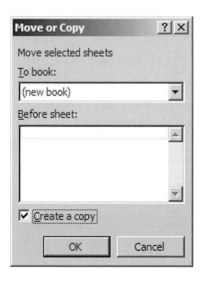

When you are done performing the tasks to be saved as the macro, click on the Stop button illustrated in Exhibit 8–13.

The VBA code we recorded can be viewed from the original workbook by pressing the **Alt-F11** keys. The VBA Editor is illustrated in Exhibit 8–14 with the macro we recorded. Notice as selected on the

EXHIBIT 8–12   **Save As Manufacturing Cell VBA.xls**

EXHIBIT 8–13   **Excel Recording Macro Stop Button**

EXHIBIT 8–14

Excel Macro Code in VBA Integrated Development Environment
Chapter 8 Worksheets.xls

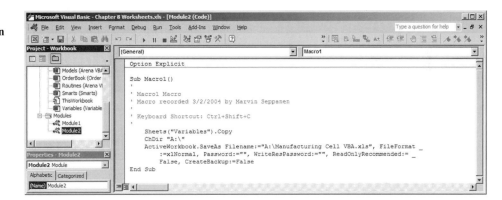

project bar (left side of the screen) that the macro is stored under **Module2.** We could now edit this very specific macro to make it more general in scope. We'll cover some of those features later.

We can execute our macro either by pressing the shortcut keys **Ctrl-Shift-C** or via the Execution dialog illustrated in Exhibit 8–15. We simply select the desired macro and press the **Run** button.

Recording an Arena VBA Macro

Arena supports VBA that can be used to automate tasks performed frequently and to con-

EXHIBIT 8–15   **Excel Macro Execution Dialog**

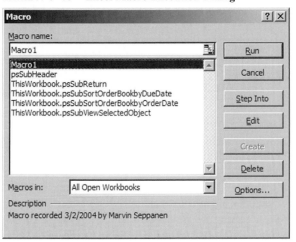

trol or exchange information with other tools such as Visio and Arena. Recording an Arena macro is the easiest way to generate VBA code. The code generated is pure VBA and with slight modification, could be executed from Arena or other application. Exhibit 8–16 illustrates the Arena menu path to initiate the recording of an Arena macro, **Tools > Macro > Record Macro.** We started this process with the default Arena model **Model1.doe.**

Exhibit 8–17 illustrates the Arena Recording Macro dialog. The default macro name of **Macro1** was not changed. We assigned a shortcut key of **Ctrl+Shift+M** to execute this macro from the resulting Arena model. A description is automatically added to the macro, which includes the recording data.

The macro is recorded by using normal Arena keystrokes and mouse movements. In this example, we

EXHIBIT 8–16   **Arena Recording Macro Selection Sequence**

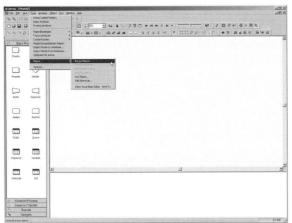

EXHIBIT 8–17   **Arena Recording Macro Dialog**

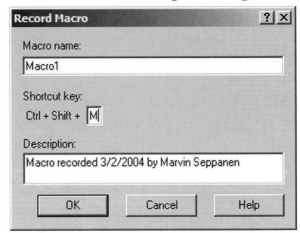

EXHIBIT 8–18   **Model VBA Generate.doe**

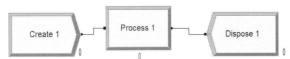

EXHIBIT 8–19   **Arena Recording Macro Stop Button**

generate a simple Create Process Dispose model and save that model as **A:\VBA Generate.doe.** Exhibit 8–18 illustrates the completed model.

When you are done performing the tasks to be saved as the macro, click on the right button, as illustrated in Exhibit 8–19.

The VBA code we recorded can be viewed from the original workbook by pressing the **Alt-F11** keys. The VBA Editor is illustrated in Exhibit 8–20 with the macro we recorded. Notice as selected on the project bar (left side of the screen) that the macro is stored under **Arena Objects—ThisDocument.**

We can execute our macro either by pressing the shortcut keys **Ctrl-Shift-M** or via the Execution dialog illustrated in Exhibit 8–21. We simply select the desired macro and press the **Run** button.

Excel Macros

Macro Security

Microsoft Excel provides safeguards against viruses that can be transmitted by macros. To share macros with others, certify them with a digital signature so that other users can verify that they are from a trustworthy source. Whenever opening a workbook that contains macros, their source can be verified before the macro is enabled. The Excel user can control access to the workbook, which contains VBA macros by one of two means. Select **Tools > Options** and then select the **Security** tab as illustrated in Exhibit 8–22.

A click on the Macro Security button generates the dialog illustrated in Exhibit 8–23. This same dialog can be reached by selecting **Tools > Options > Security.** From this dialog, the Excel user should select the desired macro security level. If the Excel user opens a

EXHIBIT 8–20
Arena Macro Code in VBA Integrated Development Environment

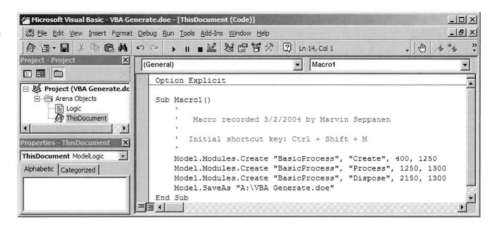

EXHIBIT 8–21 **Arena Macro Execution Dialog**

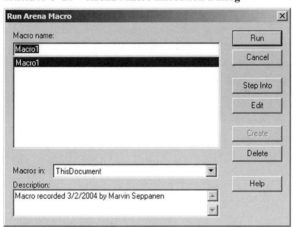

EXHIBIT 8–22 **Excel Options Dialog**

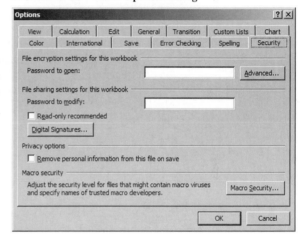

EXHIBIT 8–23 **Excel Security Options Dialog**

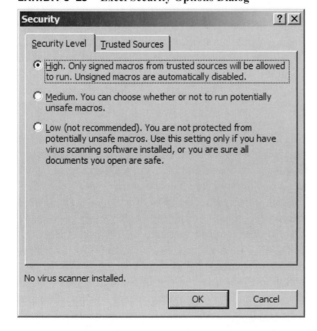

worksheet that contains a macro without security authorization a warning message such as the one in Exhibit 8–24 will be displayed. The workbook macros provided with this textbook are virus free and, therefore, the Enable macros button should be selected.

Preventing Macro Viruses

A macro virus is a type of computer virus that is stored in a macro within a workbook or add-in program. Viruses are programs that are written by individuals, usually with the intent to destroy or corrupt data. When an infected workbook opens or performs an action that triggers a macro virus, the virus can become active, be transmitted to computer, and be stored in **Personal.xls**, a hidden workbook, or some other undetectable location. From that point on, every workbook saved can be "infected" automatically with the virus. If other users open an infected workbook, the macro virus can also be transmitted to their computers.

EXHIBIT 8–24 Excel
Macro Dialog

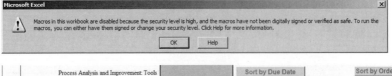

EXHIBIT 8–25
**Worksheet Order
Book**
Sheet order book |
Chapter 8
Worksheets.xls

Order Book	Process Analysis and Improvement: Tools and Techniques Copyright ©2005 by The McGraw-Hill Companies, Inc.		To enter data using Form, Press F5, select Orders, and Data > Form ...			Sort by Due Date			Sort by Order Date	
						Filtered Quantity	Filtered Backlog		Filtered Shipments	Filtered Backorders
Current Date	2/22/2004		Right Click to Select from List		Sums	113,400	$435,000		13,000	3,000
Sequence	Order Date	Due Date	Lead Time Days	Slack Days	Customer	Product	Unit Price	Order Quantity	Outstanding Order Value	Shipped Date	Shipped Quantity	Backorder Quantity
1	1/7/2004	2/20/2004	44	-2	Ajax	Widget	$5.00	5,000	$0	2/22/2004	5,000	Shipped
2	1/9/2004	2/8/2004	30	-14	Acme	Improved	$4.50	6,000	$13,500	2/1/2004	3,000	3,000
3	1/11/2004	2/1/2004	21	-21	Interstate	Standard	$2.50	5,000	$0	2/1/2004	5,000	Shipped

EXHIBIT 8–26
**Right Button Click
Menu**

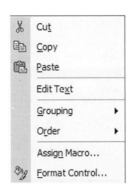

Microsoft Excel doesn't scan the floppy disk, hard disk, or network drive to find and remove macro viruses. That kind of antivirus software protection can be purchased and installed. However, Excel can display a warning message whenever a workbook is opened that contains macros. The Excel user can then decide whether to open the workbook with the macros enabled or whether to open the workbook with the macros disabled so that they can be examined and edited. A macro virus can be harmful only if it is allowed to run, so disabling the macros allows the Excel user to open the workbook safely.

Worksheet Order Book

Excel tasks that are frequently repeated are good candidates for automation using a VBA macro. Exhibit 8–25, the worksheet Order Book, contains two buttons in the range **H1:L1** linked to VBA macros for sorting the Orders data. Test those macros by clicking on each. Notice how the sort order of the data is automatically sorted.

Right-clicking on either of the buttons on worksheet Order Book generates the menu illustrated in Exhibit 8–26. These menu options can be used to control the button's text or location. The **Assign Macro ...** selection generates the menu illustrated in Exhibit 8–27. This menu listed all of the VBA macros already included in the current workbook. Selecting the macro named **psSubSortOrderBookbyOrderDate** with

EXHIBIT 8–27 **Macro Selection Menu**

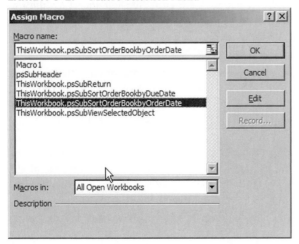

the Edit button opens the VBA Editor as illustrated in Exhibit 8–28 and assigns the macro to the selected button. When the selected button is next clicked, the corresponding VBA code is executed. That VBA code will be reviewed next.

The VBA Editor has been constructed to make the development and testing quite straightforward. All keywords are indicated in blue. Comments (text following the quote symbol) are colored green. When new information is entered, syntax errors are immediately flagged in red.

In order to introduce some of the basic VBA concepts, the individual code lines of Exhibit 8–28 are now reviewed in detail. The first statement, **Public Sub psSubSortOrderBookbyOrderDate(),** defines the subroutine name and makes it public so that it can be accessed

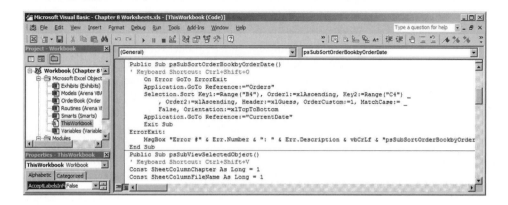

or executed from anywhere, whenever workbook Chapter 8 Worksheets.xls is loaded into Excel. The second statement that begins with single quote mark is a comment used to make the code easier to read.

The third statement, **On Error GoTo ErrorExit,** sets up error handling within the subroutine. If an error is encountered during the execution of the subroutine, control is transferred to the statement labeled **ErrorExit.**

The next statement, **Application.GoTo Reference:="Orders"** selects cell range orders to be used for sorting. This selected cell range is used by the next statement, which executes the desired sorting operation (column B is ascending and column C is ascending):

> Selection.Sort Key1:=Range("B4"), Order1:=xlAscending, Key2:=
> Range("C4"), Order2:=xlAscending, Header:=xlGuess, OrderCustom:=
> 1, MatchCase:= False, Orientation:=xlTopToBottom

Notice that the prior statement has been continued on several lines. The underscore symbol _ is used in VBA to continue a statement.

The next statement, **Application.GoTo Reference:="CurrentDate"** moves the cursor to cell range "CurrentDate."

The next statement ends execution of the subroutine: **Exit Sub.** The next statement is the label matching the On Error statement: **ErrorExit:.** Notice that VBA labels are terminated with a colon.

The next statement

> MsgBox "Error #" & Err.Number & ": " & Err.Description & vbCrLf &
> "psSubSortOrderBookbyOrderDate"

displays a message box like the one shown in Exhibit 8–29 if an error is encountered during the execution of the subroutine. The code **vbCrLf** represents a carriage return and line feed from typewriter terminology or a shift to a new message box line. The last statement terminates the subroutine: **End Sub.**

Workbook Chapter 8 Worksheets.xls

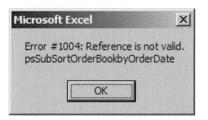

The workbooks associated with each chapter of this textbook, Chapter 8 Worksheets.xls for this chapter, contain a set of VBA subroutines executed by pressing buttons on the worksheet or by using the assigned keystrokes. One can quickly see the routines associated with a particular VBA module by clicking on the down arrow at the upper right of the

VBA Editor. Exhibit 8–30 illustrates the list of routines associated with the module This-Workbook. Notice the naming convention used with these routines. All routines were developed by a company named Productive System and, therefore, begin with the letters *ps* to indicate the source of the code. Subroutines are identified with text string *Sub,* while functions use *Fnt.* This naming schema has no direct meaning but has been found by the authors to easily identify the source of the VBA code.

Subroutine **psSubViewSelectedObject** as illustrated in Exhibit 8–31 is invoked from worksheet **Exhibit** by selecting a row and then clicking the button labeled **View Selected Worksheet or Drawing** or pressing the **Ctrl-Shift-V** keystrokes. The subroutine first determines the operating system path to the current workbook **FolderWorkbook,** the textbook chapter number **Chapter,** and the selected worksheet row **SheetRow** using the following four statements:

$$FolderWorkbook = ThisWorkbook.Path$$

$$Chapter = Trim(Cells(SheetRowChapter, SheetColumnChapter).Value)$$

$$SheetRow = Selection.Row$$

$$If\ SheetRow < SheetRowStart\ Then\ SheetRow = SheetRowStart$$

EXHIBIT 8–30
ThisWorkbook
Routines

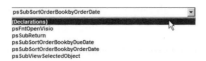

```
ps Sub SortOrderBookbyOrderDate                               ▼
(Declarations)
psFntOpenVisio
psSubReturn
ps Sub SortOrderBookbyDueDate
ps Sub SortOrderBookbyOrderDate
ps SubViewSelectedObject
```

EXHIBIT 8–31
Subroutine
psSubViewSelected
Object

```
Public Sub psSubViewSelectedObject()
' Keyboard Shortcut: Ctrl+Shift+V
Const SheetColumnChapter As Long = 1
Const SheetColumnFileName As Long = 1
Const SheetColumnSheetName As Long = 2
Const SheetRowChapter As Long = 1
Const SheetRowStart As Long = 3
Static Chapter As String
Static FolderWorkbook As String
Static First12 As String * 12
Static Name As String
Static SheetRow As Long
Static TestCharacter As String * 1
Static VisioApp As Visio.Application
Static VisioDocument As Visio.Document
    On Error GoTo ErrorExit0
    FolderWorkbook = ThisWorkbook.Path
    Call psSubReturn
    Chapter = Trim(Cells(SheetRowChapter, SheetColumnChapter).Value)
    SheetRow = Selection.Row
    If SheetRow < SheetRowStart Then SheetRow = SheetRowStart
    TestCharacter = Trim(Cells(SheetRow, SheetColumnFileName).Value)
    If TestCharacter Like "[W]" Then
' Here for a Workbook Sheet
        Name = Trim(Cells(SheetRow, SheetColumnSheetName).Value)
        First12 = Name
        If First12 Like "ThisWorkbook" Then
            MsgBox "Press Alt-F11 to enter the VBA Editor"
        ElseIf Len(Name) > 0 Then
            On Error GoTo ErrorExit1
            Sheets(Name).Select
        Else
            Beep
        End If
    ElseIf TestCharacter Like "[D]" Then
' Here for a Visio Drawing
        Name = Trim(Cells(SheetRow, SheetColumnSheetName).Value)
        Set VisioApp = psFntOpenVisio
        On Error GoTo ErrorExit2
        VisioApp.Documents.Open (FolderWorkbook & "\" & Chapter & " Drawings.vsd")
        On Error GoTo ErrorExit3
        VisioApp.ActiveWindow.Page = Name
    Else
        Beep
    End If
    Exit Sub
ErrorExit0:
    MsgBox "Error #" & Err.Number & ": " & Err.Description & vbCrLf & "psSubViewSelectedObject"
    Exit Sub
ErrorExit1:
    MsgBox "Workbook Sheet: " & Name & " not found"
    Exit Sub
ErrorExit2:
    MsgBox "Visio Drawing File: " & FolderWorkbook & "\" & Chapter & " Drawings.vsd" & " not found"
    Exit Sub
ErrorExit3:
    MsgBox "Visio Drawing Page: " & Name & " not found"
    Exit Sub
End Sub
```

The VBA function **Trim** removes any blank characters from the worksheet cell value. The selected worksheet row is checked against the first row containing valid data "SheetRowStart."

The first character of the filename is obtained from column A and the Visio page name, or the Excel sheet name is obtained from column B of the selected row using the following expressions:

TestCharacter = Trim(Cells(SheetRow, SheetColumnFileName).Value)

PageSheetName = Trim(Cells(SheetRow, SheetColumnSheetName).Value)

If the first letter of the filename is *W,* an Excel workbook is assumed. If the sheet name is greater than zero in length, this statement is executed to select the appropriate worksheet: **Sheets(PageSheetName).Select.**

If the first letter of the Filename is *D,* a Visio drawing is assumed. Because this VBA is running in an Excel application the processing is a bit more complex. The code must first open a Visio application and then load the appropriate drawing file and finally select the desired page. Of course, this presents several error possibilities, which we will cover later. The following statements are executed to accomplish the required tasks:

Set VisioApp = psFntOpenVisio

VisioApp.Documents.Open (FolderWorkbook & "\" & Chapter & " Drawings.vsd")

VisioApp.ActiveWindow.Page = PageSheetName).Select

The first statement in the preceding example calls a function we have written named **psFnt-OpenVisio** illustrated in Exhibit 8–32. This function performs the steps necessary to initiate a Visio application from another application. Function **psFntOpenVisio** could be used in Arena-related VBA to initiate a Visio application for use from Arena.

The remaining statements illustrated in the preceding example open file Chapter 8 Drawings.vsd and then make the desired page active.

Subroutine **psSubViewSelectedObject** includes four On Error statements and associated labels: **ErrorExit0, ErrorExit1, ErrorExit2,** and **ErrorExit4.** This code traps the error and generates an appropriate message box.

Subroutine **psSubReturn** illustrated in Exhibit 8–33 can be executed by pressing the **Ctrl-Shift-R** keystrokes or by clicking on the button labeled **Return to Exhibits Worksheet** found on most worksheets in the Chapter 8 Worksheet.xls workbooks.

EXHIBIT 8–32
Function
psFntOpenVisio

```
Public Function psFntOpenVisio() As Visio.Application
    On Error Resume Next
    Set psFntOpenVisio = GetObject("Visio.Application")
    If Err.Number <> 0 Then
        Set psFntOpenVisio = CreateObject("Visio.Application")
    End If
    Err.Clear
    psFntOpenVisio.Visible = True
End Function
```

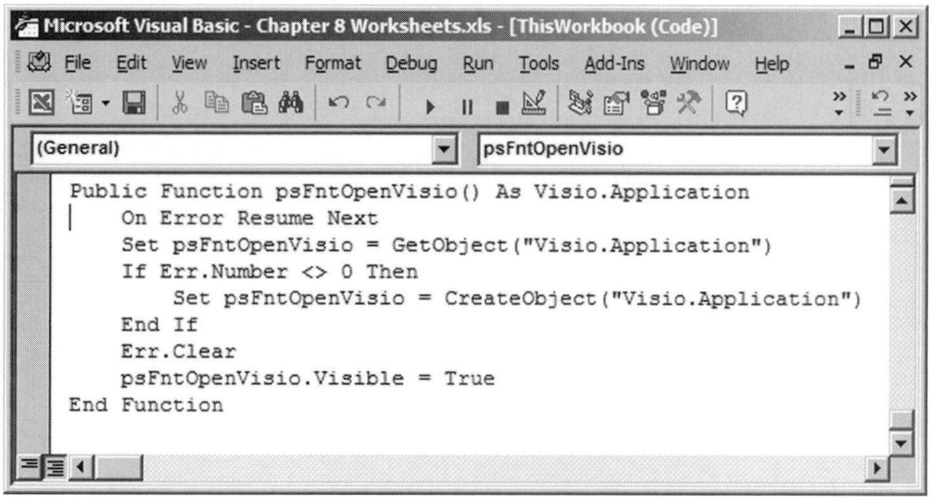

EXHIBIT 8–33
Subroutine
psSubReturn

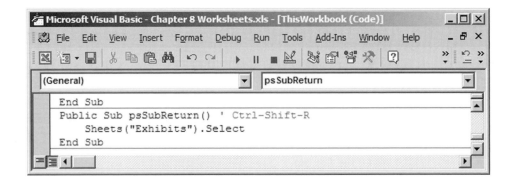

Arena Support of VBA

VBA is available to the Arena model builder through a number of modes. Exhibit 8–34 lists the VBA routines supported by Arena. These routines are invoked as the model file is loaded, executed, or terminated or as entities flow through the Arena model modules.

Arena Model Logic Routines

The first major type of interaction between Arena and VBA is via Model Logic routines that are automatically executed on the occurrence of specific events. Depending on their applications, these routines may exchange data with the Arena model. Of the 26 Model Logic routines listed in Exhibit 8–34, we have found four to be the most useful. Subroutine **RunBeginSimulation** is executed once when the simulation model is first executed. This routine can be used to read the input data, generate an input data report, initialize values of Arena Variables and Parameters, and set up the output Results Workbook. Subroutine **RunBeginReplication** is executed once at the beginning of each model replication. This routine can be used to reset replication counters, clear the system status, open replication specific data files, and schedule discrete events. Subroutine **RunEndReplication** is executed once at the end of each model replication. This routine can be used to report replication results, to clear the system status, and to close replication specific data files. Subroutine **RunEndSimulation** is executed once when the simulation model execution is terminated. This routine can be used to generate summary reports and to close active workbooks. Model Logic subroutines **UserFunction** and **UserRule** are called from the Arena code by referencing UF (J) or UR (J) respectively, where *J* is an integer value.

VBA-Based Arena Models

We use three Arena models to demonstrate the use of VBA in the process simulation environment. Exhibit 8–35 summarizes the VBA routines and modules used by these models. We'll also review some highlights of the Beer Game.doe model presented in Chapter 10.

Model VBA Large Accumulator.doe

First, to demonstrate a VBA application using VBA blocks, we have modified model **Large Accumulator.doe** from Chapter 7 and renamed it **VBA Large Accumulator.doe.** This model as illustrated in Exhibit 8–36 is designed to model very large accumulators by capturing the data from arriving entities and later releasing one entity at a time into the remainder of the network logic flow. Unlike the model presented in Chapter 7, this model stores the entity attributes in VBA code. VBA block 1 is used to store the incoming entity information, while VBA block 2 releases the information to the outgoing entity information.

EXHIBIT 8–34   **Arena's VBA Routines**

Sheet arena VBA routines | Chapter 8 Worksheets.xls

Arena VBA Routines	Process Analysis and Improvement: Tools and Techniques Copyright ©2005 by The McGraw-Hill Companies, Inc.		Parameters			
VBA ModelLogic Routine	**Description / Application**	**Routine Type**	**1**	**2**	**3**	**4**
DocumentOpen	Executed when DOE file is opened unless Shift Key is pressed	Subroutine				
DocumentSave	Executed when DOE file is saved	Subroutine				
OnClearStatistics	Executed when model Clears Statistics	Subroutine				
OnFileClose	Executed when Data File Closed	Subroutine	filesElementNumber	fileName		
OnFileRead	Executed when Data File Read	Subroutine	filesElementNumber	fileName	numberOfItems	readBuffer
OnFileWrite	Executed when Data File Write	Subroutine	filesElementNumber	fileName	numberOfItems	writeBuffer
OnKeystroke	Executed when User presses key	Subroutine	keyCode			
RealTimeInitialize	Initialize Real Time Process	Long Function	processName	remoteProcessName		
RealTimeReceive	Receive Real Time Message	Long Function	message			
RealTimeSend	Send Real Time Message	Long Function	message			
RealTimeTerminate	Terminate Real Time Process	Long Function				
RunBegin	Executed when Run started, F5 Key is pressed	Subroutine				
RunBeginReplication	Executes at the beginning of each Replication	Subroutine				
RunBeginSimulation	Executes at the beginning of the Simulation Run	Subroutine				
RunBreak	Executed when Esc Key is pressed	Subroutine				
RunEnd	Executes at the End of simulation Run	Subroutine				
RunEndReplication	Executes at the End of each Replication	Subroutine				
RunEndSimulation	Executes at the End of the Simulation Run	Subroutine				
RunFastForward	Executed when Run Fast Forward icon is clicked	Subroutine				
RunPause	Executed when Run Pause icon is clicked	Subroutine				
RunRestart	Executed when Run Restart icon is clicked	Subroutine				
RunResume	Executed when Run Resume icon is clicked	Subroutine				
RunStep	Executed when Run Step, F8 Key is pressed	Subroutine				
UserContinuousEquations	Executes at each continuous integrations step	Subroutine				
UserFunction	Executes whenever UF is found in a model code expression	Double Function	entityID	functionID		
UserRule	Executes whenever UR is found in a model code expression	Double Function	entityID	ruleID		
VBA Block Routine	**Description / Application**	**Routine Type**				
VBA_Block_n_Fire	Executes whenever VBA block number (n) is entered	Subroutine				

EXHIBIT 8–35

Arena Models Using VBA Routines

Sheet Arena VBA models | Chapter 8 Worksheets.xls

	VBA Routines Arena Object ThisDocument							Module smExcel Interface.bas
Model File Name	ModelLogic RunBegin Simulation	ModelLogic EndBegin Simulation	ModelLogic OnKeystroke	VBA Block 1 Fire	VBA Block 2 Fire	psSubVBA ArenaSetup	psSubSheet Variables Read	
VBA Large Accumulator.doe	X			X	X	X		
Manufacturing Cell VBA.doe	X					X	X	X
VBA Output.doe	X	X		X		X		X
Beer Game.doe (Chapter 10)	X		X			X	X	X

EXHIBIT 8–36
Model VBA Large Accumulator.doe Network Logic Flow

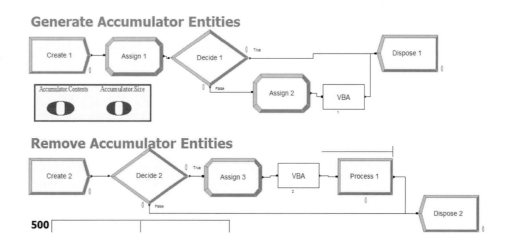

Generate Accumulator Entities

Remove Accumulator Entities

The VBA code in Arena model file VBA **Large Accumulator.doe** includes four subroutines and a declarations section, as shown in Exhibit 8–37:

ModelLogic_RunBeginSimulation (see Exhibit 8–38).
VBA_Block_1_Fire (see Exhibit 8–39).
VBA_Block_2_Fire (see Exhibit 8–40).

View these VBA subroutines by loading Arena model file VBA Large Accumulator.doe and pressing the **Alt-F11** keys. These subroutines are found in Arena Objects: "ThisDocument."

The VBA declarations illustrated in Exhibit 8–37 defines VBA variables used throughout the VBA project. By convention, we always include two options "Option Compare Text" and "Option Explicit." The former makes string comparisons more manageable, while the latter makes it necessary to define every variable used in the VBA project, thus making the code more robust. The global variables for this project are defined in Exhibit 8–37. The two following statements or their equivalent are required in VBA code using Arena:

Public ArenaModel As Arena.Model

Public Siman As Arena.Siman

These two variables are assigned in subroutine **ModelLogic_RunBeginSimulation,** illustrated in Exhibit 8–38.

Two VBA constants, AccumulatorSize and Attributes, are defined and assigned values of 500 and 2. These constants are used to define the size of array AttributesValues and used throughout the VBA code to assure that appropriate limits are maintained. Either of these two constant values could be changed if more entities or entity attributes need to be stored in the VBA code.

Variables **FileNameDoe, FolderArena,** and **FolderModel** are assigned in subroutine **ModelLogic_RunBeginSimulation** (see Exhibit 8–38). Variables **PointerInput** and **PointerOutput** are used to store and retrieve data from the array AttributeValues.

Subroutine **ModelLogic_RunBeginSimulation** (Exhibit 8–38) is executed when the **F5** key is pressed or the Run icon is clicked. Subroutine **ModelLogic_RunBeginSimulation** first assures that the value of variables **PointerInput** and **PointerOutput** are zero. Next this routine starts by setting variables ArenaModel and SIMAN defined in the declaring section (Exhibit 8–37) using the following two expressions:

Set ArenaModel = ThisDocument.Model

Set Siman = ArenaModel.Siman

The routine next finds the Arena application location **(FolderArena),** the Arena model name **(FileNameDoe)** and location **(FolderModel).** Lastly, the routine transfers the value of **AccumulatorSize** to Arena variable **Accumulator.Size** using the following expression:

Siman.VariableArrayValue(Siman.SymbolNumber("Accumulator.Size"))
= AccumulatorSize

EXHIBIT 8–37
Model VBA Large
Accumulator.doe
VBA Declarations

Property **Siman.VariableArrayValue** and function **Siman.SymbolNumber** are built into the Arena/VBA Object Model to enable the transfer of data between the VBA code and the Arena model.

When any entity in the model VBA Large Accumulator.doe (Exhibit 8–36) enters the VBA block 1, the code illustrated in Exhibit 8–39 is executed. First, the value of

EXHIBIT 8–38
Model VBA Large
Accumulator.doe
Subroutine
ModelLogic_Run
BeginSimulation

```
ModelLogic                                  ▼   RunBeginSimulation                    ▼
   Public Sub ModelLogic_RunBeginSimulation()
   Static ArenaView As view
   ' Subroutine executes when F5 is pressed
       On Error GoTo ErrorExit        ' Setups error recovery
       PointerInput = 0
       PointerOutput = 0
       Set SimanModel = ThisDocument.Model
       Set Siman = SimanModel.Siman
       With SimanModel
   ' Get the location of Arena and the current model
           ArenaFolder = Mid(.Application.FullName, 1, Len(.Application.FullName) - _
                 (Len(.Application.Name) + 4))
           ModelFolder = Mid(.FullName, 1, Len(.FullName) - Len(.Name))
           ModelFileName = Mid(.Name, 1, Len(.Name) - 4)
       End With
       Exit Sub
   ErrorExit: ' Jump here if an error occurs
       MsgBox "ModelLogic_RunBegin Error #" & Err.Number & ": " & Err.Description
   End Sub
```

EXHIBIT 8–39
Model VBA Large
Accumulator.doe
Subroutine
VBA_Block_1_Fire

```
VBA_Block_1                                 ▼   Fire                                  ▼
   Private Sub VBA_Block_1_Fire()
   Static AttributeNumber As Long
       On Error GoTo ErrorExit ' Setups error recovery
       PointerInput = (PointerInput Mod AccumulatorSize) + 1
       AttributeValues(PointerInput, 0) = Siman.RunCurrentTime
       For AttributeNumber = 1 To maxAttributes
           AttributeValues(PointerInput, AttributeNumber) = Siman.EntityAttribute(Siman.ActiveEntity, AttributeNumber)
       Next
       Exit Sub
   ErrorExit: ' Jump here if an error occurs
       MsgBox "Error #" & Err.Number & ": " & Err.Description & vbCrLf & "VBA_Block_1_Fire"
   End Sub
```

VBA variable **PointerInput** is incremented in round-robin fashion. After the value of VBA variable **PointerInput** reaches its maximum of 500, the value of VBA variable **Accumulator** starts over at one. Thus, array **AttributeValues** never overflows, but the Arena model code must assure that no more than 500 entities are concurrently stored. Two attribute values for the current entity (the one that invoked the VBA block) are retrieved and stored using the following expression:

$$\text{AttributeValues(PointerInput, AttributeNumber)} =$$
$$\text{Siman.EntityAttribute(Siman.ActiveEntity, AttributeNumber)}$$

Property **Siman.EntityAttribute** is built into the Arena/VBA Object Model to enable the transfer of data from the Arena model to the VBA code. VBA variable **AttributeNumber** is the index to facilitate the data transfer.

When any entity in the model VBA Large Accumulator.doe (Exhibit 8–36) enters the VBA block 2, the code illustrated in Exhibit 8–40 is executed. First, the value of VBA variable **PointerOutput** is incremented in a manner identical to **PointerInput.** Two attribute values from array **AttributeValues** are transferred to the attributes of the current entity using the following expression:

$$\text{Siman.EntityAttribute(Siman.ActiveEntity, AttributeNumber)} =$$
$$\text{AttributeValues(PointerOutput, AttributeNumber)}$$

Model VBA Large Accumulator.doe demonstrated the movement of data between the Arena model entity and the VBA code. The user of VBA from within Arena must remember that two independent data sets exist: one in Arena and another in VBA. Efficient transfer of these data is a requirement to make this type of modeling effective. Often VBA can be used to make complex decisions that could be difficult to model in the Arena network logic flow. When the decision has been made that information can be transferred back to

EXHIBIT 8–40
Model VBA Large
Accumulator.doe
Subroutine
VBA_Block_2_Fire

```
VBA_Block_2                                 ▼   Fire                                  ▼
   Private Sub VBA_Block_2_Fire()
   Static AttributeNumber As Long
       On Error GoTo ErrorExit ' Setups error recovery
       PointerOutput = (PointerOutput Mod AccumulatorSize) + 1
       For AttributeNumber = 1 To maxAttributes
           Siman.EntityAttribute(Siman.ActiveEntity, AttributeNumber) = AttributeValues(PointerOutput, AttributeNumber)
       Next
       Exit Sub
   ErrorExit: ' Jump here if an error occurs
       MsgBox "Error #" & Err.Number & ": " & Err.Description & vbCrLf & "VBA_Block_2_Fire"
   End Sub
```

Arena either by an attribute as demonstrated in subroutine **VBA_Block_2_Fire** (Exhibit 8–40) or a variable as demonstrated in subroutine **ModelLogic_RunBeginSimulation** (Exhibit 8–38). The next example model Manufacture Cell VBA.doe demonstrates the transfer of a large amount of data first from Excel to VBA and then to Arena.

Model Manufacturing Cell VBA.doe

Next, to demonstrate the reading of information from an Excel workbook we have added VBA code to model Manufacturing Cell 6.doe from Chapter 7 and renamed it **Manufacturing Cell VBA.doe.** This model reads worksheet "Variables" of workbook "Manufacturing Cell VBA.xls" to update the model variable values prior to executing the simulation model. Exhibit 8–41 illustrates the worksheet **Variables** of workbook **Manufacturing Cell VBA.xls.** The variable names are listed in cell range **A4:A24** and their associated values in cell range **B4:B24.** Cell range **C4:C24** indicates units associated with each Arena variable.

The VBA code in Arena model file Manufacturing Cell VBA.doe includes three subroutines and a declarations section (Exhibit 8–42):

ModelLogic_RunBeginSimulation (see Exhibit 8–43).

psSubSheetVariablesRead (see Exhibit 8–44).

View these VBA routines by loading Arena model file **Manufacturing Cell VBA.doe** and pressing the **Alt-F11** keys. These routines are found in Arena Objects: "ThisDocument." A separate module file **smExcelInterface.bas** created by Rockwell Software and provided on the textbook CD is also used to provide the link between Excel and VBA.

The VBA Declarations illustrated in Exhibit 8–42 are very similar to those in Exhibit 8–37 used by model VBA Large Accumulator.doe.

Three VBA constants, SheetName, SheetColumnStart, and SheetRowStart are defined and assigned values of variables, 1, and 4. These constants are used to define location of the data in the Excel workbook. **Variable FileNumberExcel** is used to access that workbook.

Subroutine **ModelLogic_RunBeginSimulation** (see Exhibit 8–43) is executed when the **F5** key is pressed or the **Run** icon is clicked. Subroutine **ModelLogic_RunBeginSimulation** first sets up the link between VBA and Arena. The routine next calls subroutine **smInitializeExcel** from module **smExcelInterface** to load the Excel application. The routine next calls function **smOpenExcelWorkbook** from module **smExcelInterface** to load the desired workbook and to return its number to VBA variable **FileNumberExcel.** Next, the subroutine **psSubSheetVariablesRead** (see Exhibit 8–44) is called to read the information from the workbook, find the corresponding Arena symbol location, and then, if necessary, transfer the changed value to Arena. When the entire workbook has been read, Excel is closed using the subroutine **smExitExcel** from module **smExcelInterface.**

The VBA code illustrated in Exhibit 8–44 was designed to work with singular (nondimensional) Arena variables. It could be modified to change the values for one-

EXHIBIT 8–41
Model Manufacturing Cell VBA.doe Input Data Worksheet
Sheet variables |
Chapter 8
Worksheets.xls

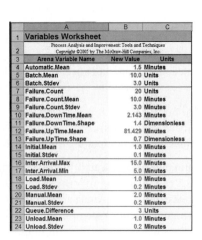

	A	B	C
1	Variables Worksheet		
2	Process Analysis and Improvement: Tools and Techniques Copyright ©2005 by The McGraw-Hill Companies, Inc.		
3	Arena Variable Name	New Value	Units
4	Automatic.Mean	1.5	Minutes
5	Batch.Mean	10.0	Units
6	Batch.Stdev	3.0	Units
7	Failure.Count	20	Units
8	Failure.Count.Mean	10.0	Minutes
9	Failure.Count.Stdev	3.0	Minutes
10	Failure.Down Time.Mean	2.143	Minutes
11	Failure.Down Time.Shape	1.4	Dimensionless
12	Failure.Up Time.Mean	81.429	Minutes
13	Failure.Up Time.Shape	0.7	Dimensionless
14	Initial.Mean	1.0	Minutes
15	Initial.Stdev	0.1	Minutes
16	Inter.Arrival.Max	15.0	Minutes
17	Inter.Arrival.Min	5.0	Minutes
18	Load.Mean	1.0	Minutes
19	Load.Stdev	0.2	Minutes
20	Manual.Mean	2.0	Minutes
21	Manual.Stdev	0.2	Minutes
22	Queue.Difference	3	Units
23	Unload.Mean	1.0	Minutes
24	Unload.Stdev	0.2	Minutes

EXHIBIT 8–42
Model Manufacturing Cell VBA.doe VBA Declarations

```
(General)                              (Declarations)

' Process Analysis and Improvement: Tools and Techniques
' Copyright ©2005 by The McGraw-Hill Companies, Inc.
Option Compare Text ' Upper & lower case are equivalent
Option Explicit     ' All variables must be defined
' Arena Variables available through entire project
Public SimanModel As Arena.Model
Public Siman As Arena.Siman
' User Constants & Variables available through entire project
Const SheetName As String = "Variables"
Const SheetColumnStart As Long = 1
Const SheetRowStart As Long = 4
Public ModelFileName As String
Public FileNumber As Long
Public ArenaFolder As String
Public ModelFolder As String
```

EXHIBIT 8–43 Model Manufacturing Cell VBA.doe Subroutine ModelLogic_RunBeginSimulation

```
ModelLogic                                RunBeginSimulation
Public Sub ModelLogic_RunBeginSimulation()
' Subroutine executes when F5 is pressed
   On Error GoTo ErrorExit          ' Setups error recovery
   Set SimanModel = ThisDocument.Model
   Set Siman = SimanModel.Siman
   With SimanModel
' Get the location of Arena and the current model
      ArenaFolder = Mid(.Application.FullName, 1, Len(.Application.FullName) - _
         (Len(.Application.Name) + 4))
      ModelFolder = Mid(.FullName, 1, Len(.FullName) - Len(.Name))
      ModelFileName = Mid(.Name, 1, Len(.Name) - 4)
   End With
   FileNumber = 0
   Call smInitializeExcel(False, 1) ' Setups the Excel interface
' Open and Read Excel Simulation Workbook
   If FileNumber = 0 Then
      FileNumber = smOpenExcelWorkbook(ModelFolder & "\" & ModelFileName & ".xls")
      Call psSubSheetVariablesRead
   End If
   Call smExitExcel                 ' Close Excel
   Exit Sub
ErrorExit: ' Jump here if an error occurs
   MsgBox "ModelLogic_RunBegin Error #" & Err.Number & ": " & Err.Description & vbCrLf & _
      "Error Reading Simulation Workbook " & ModelFileName
End Sub
```

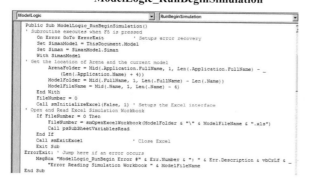

EXHIBIT 8–44 Model Manufacturing Cell VBA.doe Subroutine psSubSheetVariablesRead

```
(General)                                 psSubSheetVariablesRead
Public Sub psSubSheetVariablesRead()
Static SheetRow As Long
Static VBAChanges As Long
Static VariableName As String
Static VariableSymbolNumber As Long
Static VariableValueOriginal As Double
Static VariableValueWorkbook As Double
   On Error GoTo ErrorExit ' Setups error recovery
   VBAChanges = 0
   With smXL.Workbooks(FileNumber).Worksheets(SheetName)
      SheetRow = SheetRowStart
' Continue as long as Column 1 is not blank
      Do While Len(.Cells(SheetRow, SheetColumnStart).Value) > 0
' Get the Variable Name from Column 1
         VariableName = Trim(.Cells(SheetRow, SheetColumnStart).Value)
' Check if the Variable Name is known to this Arena model
         VariableSymbolNumber = Siman.SymbolNumber(VariableName)
         If VariableSymbolNumber > 0 Then
' Get the Variable Value from Column 2
            VariableValueWorkbook = .Cells(SheetRow, SheetColumnStart + 1).Value
            VariableValueOriginal = Siman.VariableArrayValue(VariableSymbolNumber)
            If VariableValueWorkbook <> VariableValueOriginal Then
' Change the Variable Value in the Arena model
               Siman.VariableArrayValue(VariableSymbolNumber) = VariableValueWorkbook
               If VBAChanges = 0 Then
                  Open ModelFolder & "\" & ModelFileName & ".TXT" For Output As #1
                  Print #1, "Workbook "; ModelFileName; Tab(40); "Changed Values"
                  Print #1, "Worksheet "; SheetName; Tab(40); "Initial"; Tab(50); "New"
               End If
               VBAChanges = VBAChanges + 1
               Print #1, VBAChanges; Tab(6); VariableName; _
                  Tab(40); VariableValueOriginal; Tab(50); VariableValueWorkbook
            End If
         Else
            MsgBox "Variable Name " & VariableName & " not found in Arena model " & ModelFileName
         End If
         SheetRow = SheetRow + 1
      Loop
   End With
   If VBAChanges > 0 Then
      Close #1
      Siman.VariableArrayValue(Siman.SymbolNumber("VBA.Changes")) = VBAChanges
      MsgBox VBAChanges & " VBA Variables Changed"
   Else
      MsgBox "No VBA Variables Changed"
   End If
   Exit Sub
ErrorExit: ' Jump here if an error occurs
   MsgBox "Error #" & Err.Number & ": " & Err.Description & vbCrLf & _
      "Error Reading Simulation Workbook " & ModelFileName & _
      vbCrLf & "Sheet Name: " & SheetName & " Sheet Row " & SheetRow
```

and two-dimensional Arena variables. **Subroutine psSubSheetVariablesRead** reads the variable name, **VariableName,** from worksheet column A and the variable value, **Variable-ValueWorkbook,** from column B using these expressions:

$$\text{VariableName} = \text{Trim(.Cells(SheetRow, SheetColumnStart).Value)}$$

$$\text{VariableValueWorkbook} = \text{.Cells(SheetRow, SheetColumnStart} + 1\text{).Value}$$

The variable name is checked against those available in the Arena model using this expression:

$$\text{VariableSymbolNumber} = \text{Siman.SymbolNumber(VariableName)}$$

If the VariableName is found, processing continues; otherwise a message box appears similar to the one shown in Exhibit 8–45. The value of the variable in the Arena model is obtained using the expression:

$$\text{VariableValueOriginal} = \text{Siman.VariableArrayValue(VariableSymbolNumber)}$$

If the workbook value differs from the current Arena value, the Arena value is changed and recorded in file **Manufacturing Cell VBA.txt.**

EXHIBIT 8–45 Model Manufacturing Cell VBA.doe Error Message Box

When the entire workbook has been read, that is, column A is blank, a message box similar to Exhibit 8–46 is displayed and control is returned to subroutine **ModelLogic_RunBeginSimulation,** which closes the Excel application and permits the simulation to start with the changed variable values. Model Manufacturing Cell **VBA.doe** displays the number of changed variables, **VBA.Changes,** on the right side of its animation.

The VBA code contained in model Manufacturing Cell VBA.doe can be used in any Arena model to read and change variable values from a workbook. The Excel

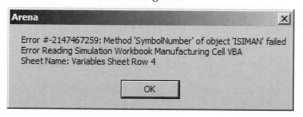

EXHIBIT 8–46
Model
Manufacturing Cell
VBA.doe Variable
Change Message Box

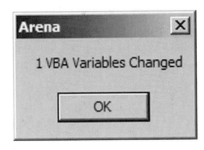

workbook name must be the same as the Arena model name. The worksheet name must be "Variables" unless the value of constant SheetName is changed in the declaration section of the VBA code (Exhibit 8–42).

Model VBA Output.doe

Next, to demonstrate the writing of information to an Excel workbook we have developed model VBA Output.doe. This model generates an Excel workbook named **VBA Output.xls.** The Arena network logic flow diagram for this model is illustrated in Exhibit 8–47.

This model involves a single entity generated at time one minute by the Create One Entity module. The entity enters the Update Variables 1 and 2 assign module. This module randomly adjusts the values of Variable.1 and Variable.2. Those values are displayed on the model animation. The entity next enters the VBA block from the SIMAN Blocks panel. This block invokes the VBA code illustrated in Exhibit 8–48. The Process Delay module delays the entity one minute before it returns to the Assign module and repeats the calculation and VBA steps.

VBA blocks are the standard technique by which an entity flowing through the Arena logic network interacts with VBA. In this case, as illustrated in Exhibit 8–48, VBA subroutine **VBA_Block_1_Fire** determines the current value of the two Arena variables Variable.1 and Variable.2 and writes those values along with current simulation time, TNOW, to both the Excel workbook and a text file.

The VBA expression

$$.Cells(SheetRow, KeyColumn).Value = Siman.RunCurrentTime$$

sets the value in the worksheet cell specified by row **SheetRow** and column **KeyColumn** to the current value of **Siman.RunCurrentTime,** an Arena VBA property that supplies the value of TNOW, the current simulation run time. The VBA expression

EXHIBIT 8–47 Model VBA Output.doe Network Logic Flow

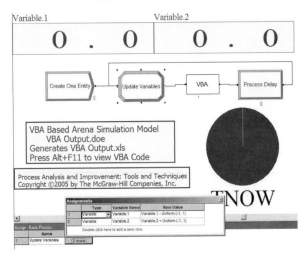

EXHIBIT 8–48 Model VBA Output.doe Subroutine VBA_Block_1_Fire

$$VariableValue = Siman.VariableArrayValue(VariableSymbolNumber(Index))$$

sets the value of VBA variable **VariableValue** to the value of **Variable.1** or **Variable.2** depending on the value of Index. We'll explain how the VBA variable **VariableSymbolNumber** gets set later. The VBA expression

$$.Cells(SheetRow, KeyColumn + Index).Value = VariableValue$$

sets the value in the worksheet cell specified by row **SheetRow** and column **KeyColumn + Index** to the current value of **VariableValue.**

While subroutine **VBA_Block_1_Fire** is executed each time an entity enters VBA block number 1, some additional coding is required to make this VBA interface work. First, we must declare global variables which are used throughout the VBA code. See Exhibit 8–49. Next subroutines **ModelLogic_RunBeginSimulation** (Exhibit 8–50) and **ModelLogic_RunEndSimulation** (Exhibit 8–51) are coded to provide VBA functionality.

Subroutine **ModelLogic_RunBeginSimulation** is provided in Arena by default in VBA Arena Objects "ThisDocument" and is executed each time the simulation model is started. Of course, the routine is skipped if the Arena model developer has not added any VBA code. As illustrated in Exhibit 8–50, subroutine **ModelLogic_RunBeginSimulation** first sets up the required interface between VBA and Arena. The location within Arena of Variable.1 and Variable.2 are stored in array **VariableSymbolNumber.**

Next subroutine **ModelLogic_RunBeginSimulation** opens the output text file and starts to write the first line of text. Then, two routines **smInitializeExcel** and **smNewExcelWorkbook** supplied with Arena in module **smExcelInterface.bas** were used to load Excel with a new workbook. The first row of the worksheet was generated and the worksheet was renamed as **VBA Output** using the VBA variable **SheetName.** The last executable statement in the routine increments the value of variable **SheetRow,** which is used to control the worksheet row for saving the output data.

Like subroutine **ModelLogic_RunBeginSimulation,** subroutine **ModelLogic_RunEndSimulation** (Exhibit 8–51) is provided in Arena by default in VBA Arena Objects "ThisDocument" to be executed when the simulation model is terminated. This routine saves the current worksheet and closes Excel.

The resulting worksheet is illustrated in Exhibit 8–52. It should be noted that the same results presented in this example could be accomplished using the Read/Write and File modules of the Advanced Process panel as introduced in model Manufacturing Cell 5.doe in Chapter 7. Model VBA Output.doe was developed to illustrate this point.

EXHIBIT 8–49 **Model VBA Output.doe Declaration Section**

```
(General)                                   (Declarations)
' Process Analysis and Improvement: Tools and Techniques
' Copyright ©2005 by The McGraw-Hill Companies, Inc.
Option Compare Text
Option Explicit
' Systems Modeling Variables
Public ArenaModel As Arena.Model
Public Siman As Arena.Siman
' Productive Systems Constants & Variables
Const KeyColumn As Long = 1
Const Variables As Long = 2
Const SheetName As String = "Output"
Dim FileNameDoe As String
Dim FileNumberSimulation As Long
Dim FolderArena As String
Dim FolderModel As String
Dim SheetRow As Long
Dim VariableSymbolNumber(Variables) As Long
```

EXHIBIT 8–50 **Model VBA Output.doe Subroutine ModelLogic_RunBeginSimulation**

```
ModelLogic                                  RunBeginSimulation
Private Sub ModelLogic_RunBeginSimulation()
Static ArenaView As view
Static Index As Long
    On Error GoTo ErrorExit
' Setup Interface to Arena
    Set ArenaModel = ThisDocument.Model
    Set Siman = ArenaModel.Siman
    With ArenaModel
        FolderArena = Mid(.Application.FullName, 1, Len(.Application.FullName) - _
            (Len(.Application.Name) + 4))
        FolderModel = Mid(.FullName, 1, Len(.FullName) - Len(.Name))
        FileNameDoe = Mid(.Name, 1, Len(.Name) - 4)
    End With
    VariableSymbolNumber(1) = Siman.SymbolNumber("Variable.1")
    VariableSymbolNumber(2) = Siman.SymbolNumber("Variable.2")
' Open a new Excel Workbook
    smInitializeExcel False, 1
    FileNumberSimulation = smNewExcelWorkbook
' Generate first row of Excel worksheet
    SheetRow = 1
    With smXL.Workbooks(FileNumberSimulation).Worksheets("Sheet1")
        .Cells(SheetRow, KeyColumn).Value = "Minutes"
        For Index = 1 To Variables
            .Cells(SheetRow, KeyColumn + Index).Value = "Variable." & Index
        Next
        Sheets("Sheet1").Name = SheetName
    End With
    SheetRow = SheetRow + 1
    Exit Sub
ErrorExit:
    MsgBox "ModelLogic_RunBegin Error #" & Err.Number & ": " & Err.Description
End Sub
```

EXHIBIT 8–51 **Model VBA Output.doe Subroutine ModelLogic_RunEndSimulation**

```
ModelLogic                                  RunEndSimulation
Private Sub ModelLogic_RunEndSimulation()
    On Error GoTo ErrorExit
    Call smSaveExcelWorkbook(1, FolderModel & FileNameDoe & ".xls")
    Call smExitExcel
    Exit Sub
ErrorExit:
    MsgBox "ModelLogic_RunBegin Error #" & Err.Number & ": " & Err.Description
End Sub
```

Model Beer Game.doe VBA Code

The Beer Game.doe and Two Units.doe models are presented in Chapter 10. Both contain VBA code very similar to that already covered in this chapter. Two important differences should be noted. First, subroutine **psSubSheetVariablesRead** reads data for dimensioned variables from columns B through E of the worksheet. This data must be matched to the dimensioned Arena variables using the following expression:

VariableSymbolNumber =
Siman.SymbolNumber(VariableName, Level, Unit)

where VBA variables Level and Unit represent the dimension indices.

Second, these models both include a feature which allows the model user to interact with VBA from the keyboard while the model is running. Exhibit 8–53 illustrates subroutine **ModelLogic_OnKeystroke.** Like the

EXHIBIT 8–52
Model VBA
Output.doe VBA
Output.xls

	A	B	C
1	Minutes	Variable.1	Variable.2
2	1	0.41481	-0.28137
3	2	0.941208	-1.16457
4	3	1.678747	-1.92976
5	4	0.793819	-1.83584
6	5	0.08717	-1.15261
7	6	0.823978	-0.51192
8	7	-0.08617	-1.28383
9	8	-0.02198	-1.21052
10	9	0.384284	-1.83373

EXHIBIT 8–53 **Model Beer Game.doe Subroutine ModelLogic_OnKeystroke**

other Arena ModelLogic routines listed in Exhibit 8–41, OnKeystroke automatically provides a link between Arena and VBA. In this case, the VBA is executed each time a key is pressed on the personal computer running the Arena model. The operating system passes the key identification via parameter keyCode. The VBA code illustrated in Exhibit 8–53 detects either an upper- or lowercase letter *d*. If the model user presses a lowercase letter *d* on the keyboard, the value of the VBA variable **DemandMean** is reduced by one and the new value is transferred to Arena variable **Demand.Mean.** This reduces the average daily retail demand by one keg. If the model user presses an uppercase letter *D* on the keyboard, the value of the VBA variable **DemandMean** is increased by one and the new value is transferred to Arena variable **Demand.Mean.** This increases the average daily retail demand by one keg.

The VBA coding illustrated in Exhibit 8–53 can be modified and incorporated in any Arena model to permit the user to actively interact with the simulation model.

Arena VBA Smarts Models

The Arena Smarts models are a good way to learn how to use particular features. Exhibit 8–54 lists the VBA-related Smarts models. Use these models to see how to perform a variety of tasks using VBA with Arena.

Exercises

1. Use the Excel Record Macro function to record a simple task, such as print the current page.
2. Use the Visio Record Macro function to record a simple task, such as print the current page.
3. Use the Arena Record Macro function to record a simple task, such as generate, check, save, and run a four-module model.

Challenge

4. Modify the VBA code of model VBA Output.doe to do the following additional functions:
   a. Change the worksheet name from **VBA Output.xls to Report.xls.**
   b. Limit the number of rows in each worksheet to 101. Name consecutive worksheets **Report1, Report2,....**

5. Modify the Arena model VBA Output.doe to do the following additional functions:
   a. Add a new variable to the Arena code called **Value.Squared** equal to Value ** 2.
   b. Include the current value of the variable **Value.Squared** in the Arena Plot.
   c. Save the value of the variable **Value.Squared** in column C of the Results.xls workbook.

6. Develop an Arena model using VBA code to do the following functions:
   a. Open the Results.xls workbook.
   b. Read and display the values from column B.
   c. Develop a means to determine when the last value has been read.

EXHIBIT 8–54
Arena VBA Smarts Models
Sheet Smarts | Chapter 8 Worksheets.xls

Arena Smarts files, a collection of small example models that demonstrate a variety of modeling techniques and situations commonly encountered using Arena.

Smarts files have been specifically designed for use as a training or reference tool.

Each Smarts File is listed in one or more of the categories below.

\Program Files\Rockwell Software\Arena\Smarts	29	Number of Smart models

Category	Model Name Smarts*.doe	Application
VBA and Visual Basic	001	VariableArray Value
VBA and Visual Basic	016	Displaying a UserForm
VBA and Visual Basic	017	Interacting with Variables
VBA and Visual Basic	024	Placing Modules and Filling in Data
VBA and Visual Basic	028	UserForm Interaction
VBA and Visual Basic	081	Using a Shape Object
VBA and Visual Basic	083	Ending a Model Run
VBA and Visual Basic	086	Creating and Editing Resource Pictures
VBA and Visual Basic	090	Manipulating a Module's Repeat Groups
VBA and Visual Basic	091	Creating Nested Submodels Via VBA
VBA and Visual Basic	098	Manipulating Named Views
VBA and Visual Basic	099	Populating a Module's Repeat Group
VBA and Visual Basic	100	Reading in Data from Excel
VBA and Visual Basic	109	Accessing Information
VBA and Visual Basic	121	Deleting a Module
VBA and Visual Basic	132	Executing Module Data Transfer
VBA and Visual Basic	142	Creating Nested Submodels in VBA
VBA and Visual Basic	143	Animation Status Variables
VBA and Visual Basic	155	Changing and Editing Global Pictures
VBA and Visual Basic	156	Grouping Objects
VBA and Visual Basic	159	Changing an Entity Attribute
VBA and Visual Basic	161	User Function
VBA and Visual Basic	166	Inserting Entities into a Queue
VBA and Visual Basic	167	Changing an Entity Picture
VBA and Visual Basic	174	Reading/Writing Excel Using VBA Module
VBA and Visual Basic	175	VBA Builds and Runs a Model
VBA and Visual Basic	176	Manipulating Arrays
VBA and Visual Basic	179	Playing Multimedia Files Within a Model
VBA and Visual Basic	182	Changing Model Data Interactively

Process Analysis and Improvement Application: Customer Service Center

Summary and Learning Objectives

In this chapter, we present a detailed case study to demonstrate the use of computer-based tools to analyze and improve business processes. It focuses on one particular business application, the customer service center or familiar 800 telephone number answering system. We also introduce the Arena Contact Center Edition specifically designed to simulate customer service center processes.

The learning objectives for this chapter are to

1. Prepare to analyze a business system in detail using the software tools presented in this text.
2. Use Visio to document and model process flow.
3. Use Excel to organize and analyze process data.
4. Use Arena to simulate dynamic process behavior.
5. Optimize process design parameters using OptQuest.
6. Understand the use of Arena Contact Center Edition to model a simple customer service center.

Exhibit 9–1 illustrates the flow of information between worksheets, models, and drawing pages presented in this chapter. Each symbol represents a specific sheet, model, or page with the linkage between various objects. Each of these objects will be reviewed in this chapter.

Customer Service Center

Description

Nearly every American has called an 800 telephone number. These "free" calls are typically routed to a customer service center staffed by a number of agents. These customer service centers are the lifeblood of many businesses. Many organizations rely almost exclusively on their 800 number for sales and/or customer support. To some extent, the Internet is supplanting some of this initial customer contact; however, when online problems arise, the human response from the customer service center may still be required and is perhaps even more critical.

As consumers, we all have sometimes found the 800 numbers to be busy (lost call) or the wait for the service agent to be too long (aborted call). Unhappy customers are likely to

EXHIBIT 9–1 **Chapter Exhibit Flowchart**

Page chapter flow | Chapter 9 Drawings.vsd

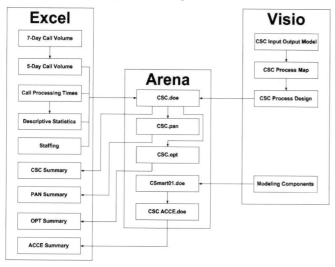

purchase less, find a new source for their purchase, or complain to others about the poor service obtained from a particular company. The customers would desire every call to be answered immediately by an experienced, knowledgeable customer service agent.

We know today's consumer is more demanding than ever. Being available to your customer quickly is expected. Companies are designing and implementing call center operations in view of sharper increases and decreases in demand. These organizations are learning to cope with these demand peaks, often in new and innovative ways, combining new technological solutions and new management practices. The term *call center* generally refers to reservations centers, help desks, information lines, or customer service centers, regardless of how they are organized or what types of transactions they handle. Technological developments have allowed the introduction of remote service delivery using telephone or Internet communication systems as a means of service delivery. One of the most distinctive features of these services is that the technology allows customers to access the process more immediately.

Examples of call centers in industry abound. A few significant ones are outlined here. The first prominent example relates to Dell Computer Corporation, which revolutionized its supply chain with its build-to-order concept. Now Dell is applying the same principle to its customer service and support business. It is an example of how the supply chain has grown beyond its roots in manufacturing to encompass intangibles such as service and support. Dell relies on SonicAir, a UPS Logistics Group Company, to manage its U.S. parts inventory and distribution for same-day and next-day service. Together, the two companies have achieved a 95 percent on time parts availability and delivery requirement.

SonicAir is just one element in a chain of events that starts as soon as a customer dials Dell's service line in Austin, Texas. The center fields an average of 60,000 calls a day. Dell's aim is to fix problems online without having to dispatch a technician. Call center staffers can get to the root of a caller's glitch through the phone line. Dell embeds diagnostic equipment into its products before they leave the factory, making it possible for call center staffers to run equipment checks and make fixes online. If the problem is not fixed within 15 minutes, the call center staffer will dispatch a technician or part. The clock starts running on its four-hour same-day and next-day services, the moment a call center staffer tells a customer that a technician is on the way.

An effective call center will reduce the need to dispatch a technician to a customer; it also will ensure that when a technician does get the call, the person will leave with the right part in hand. It is the reason Dell is confident enough to give customers a time frame for fixing the problem.

Dell maintains a centralized and distributed stocking strategy for its domestic business. Repairs are made at a facility in Austin, and then shipped to SonicAir's Louisville, Kentucky, site that handles all next-day orders.

Another prominent example is of a computer cataloger, PC Connection. The Merrimack, New Hampshire–based mailer is strictly a reseller; the more than 100,000 SKUs of computer hardware, software, and peripherals it carries are from outside manufacturers, including Apple, Compaq, Hewlett-Packard, IBM, and Microsoft. Since the company does not manufacture any of its own merchandise, the company has made quality service its unique selling proposition. Computer Telephony Integration (CTI) enables PC Connection to transfer buyer information from its customer database, such as buying history, to telephone representatives along with the actual phone call. To keep the computers and the telephones integrated, PC Connection relies on Symposium, a call center server application from Nortel Networks, and the IBM CallPath client/server from Call Pro/Cothern Computer Systems. Symposium tracks incoming orders, outgoing calls, and inventory, and ties together the company's four call centers and its Website.

Merrill Lynch, a renowned Wall Street financial and brokerage house has call centers to support its quality customer service. In its call centers in New Jersey and Florida, the company's Web and telephony portals support more than 50 million client contacts annually. The call centers provide the customer interactions that result from a broad range of product offerings to clients.

This chapter demonstrates how to use software tools to analyze a generalized version of the customer service center system.

Process Model

We start our analysis of the customer service center system by developing a process model to illustrate the major functional aspects of the system. Exhibit 9–2 illustrates the process model for the customer service center. Visio allows the user to selectively view drawing layers, which we illustrate in parts *a, b,* and *c* of Exhibit 9–2.

We illustrate in Exhibit 9–2a the primary customer service center input, incoming calls, and the resulting outputs, sales/orders, and revenues by displaying the Process, Input, and Output layers of the drawing. This basic diagram does not indicate the detailed internal relationship between inputs and outputs. Notice that the standard (Euro-American) flow is from left to right.

In Exhibit 9–2b the controls and measures layers are added to the basic process model. The staffing level or number of available customer service agents is the major customer service center control element. The number of customer service agents may be fixed for the

EXHIBIT 9–2A
Customer Service Center Process Model
Page CSC input output model | Chapter 9 Drawings.vsd

EXHIBIT 9–2B
Customer Service Center Process Model with Controls
Page CSC input output model | Chapter 9 Drawings.vsd

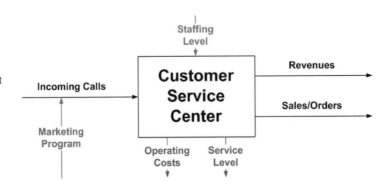

EXHIBIT 9–2C   **Customer Service Center Process Model**
with Controls and Feedback

Page CSC input output model | Chapter 9 Drawings.vsd

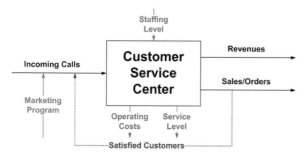

entire period of center operation (normally 24-hours and seven days per week) or more typically may be varying by the time of the day and day of the week. The cost of operating the customer service center and the resulting service levels are directly related to the staffing level. Too many agents result in a high cost but create the potential for a high level of customer service. Too few customer service agents have the opposite effect. Managing the staffing level is a key element in the profitability of the customer service center.

Another control factor that impacts the customer service center is the marketing program for products or service provided by the center. Many customer service centers deal with seasonal sales (i.e., Christmas) or find their call volume directly impacted by the delivery of catalogs or other promotional material to potential customers. The manager of the customer service center must be aware of significant changes in the overall marketing program. A small marketing change might greatly change the customer service center demand.

In Exhibit 9–2c we illustrate the potential feedback in the customer service center Process model (layer Feedback added). Satisfied customers are much more likely to generate repeat calls than those receiving incomplete or delayed service.

Process Analysis

We continue our analysis of the customer service center system by completing the Process Analysis Template introduced in Chapter1 and illustrated in Exhibit 9–3.

As with most commercial ventures, the goal of the customer service center is to maximize profit while maintaining a desired level of customer service. Those service factors are introduced into our Process Analysis using the Process Constraints and Criteria element. For the customer service center, the Process Constraints and Criteria can be divided into the following cost and service factors:

1. Cost Factors
   a. Hourly cost
      i. Agents = $10
      ii. Trunk lines = $1
   b. Call income = $5
   c. Lost call = $1
   d. Abandoned call = $2.50

2. Service Factors
   a. Fraction of calls serviced > 75 percent
   b. Fraction of calls serviced within 1 minute > 50 percent
   c. Average wait for service < 2 minutes

The Requirements elements defined for our customer service center process analysis are

1. Number of trunk lines.
2. Maximum customer wait for a service agent.
3. Service agent staffing pattern.
4. Level of marketing (demand level).

EXHIBIT 9–3
Customer Service Center Process Analysis
Page CSC process analysis | Chapter 9 Drawings.vsd

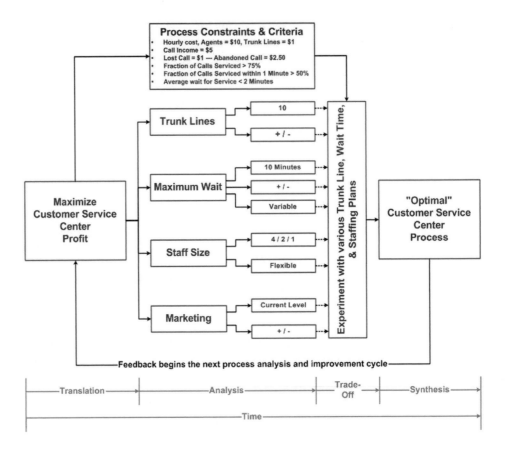

Each of these Requirement elements provides a number of alternatives that can be tested using process simulation to help find the optimal customer service center design.

Process Map

We continue our analysis of the system by developing a process map that follows an incoming call as it is processed through the customer service center. Exhibit 9–4 illustrates a process map for the customer service center. Details for developing process maps are more fully developed in Chapter 3 along with other applications for Visio.

An incoming call is immediately lost if the customer service center has too few telephone lines and the customer hears a busy signal. A customer with no choice is likely to attempt to reconnect by calling back within a few minutes. Customers seeking to make a purchase or reservation may immediately switch to an alternative source when encountering a busy signal. In the base case for the process simulation model, which we demonstrate later in this chapter, we have initially limited the number of incoming phone lines to 10. We will vary the number of incoming phone lines in an attempt to optimize the process design.

Customers able to connect with the service center are either directly assigned to a customer service agent or their call is placed in a waiting queue. Many customer service centers provide a voice message telling the customer that his or her call is important and to wait for the next available agent. Some customer service centers provide an estimate of the expected waiting time. Many customer service centers follow the message with music or advertisements for additional products or services. No customer likes to wait, and if the wait is sufficiently long, many potential customers will choose to hang up and try to find another service source. The simulation model demonstrated later in this chapter limits the

EXHIBIT 9–4   **Customer Service Center Process Map**

Page process map | Chapter 9 Drawings.vsd

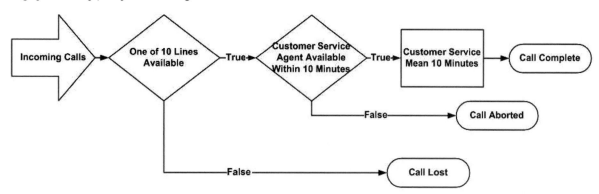

call waiting time to 10 minutes. In practice, not all customers will wait a full 10 minutes to receive service. As time passes, the number of waiting customers will gradually decline. We will use the simulation model to estimate how many customers will be served after a wait of one minute or less.

When a customer service agent is able to take the incoming call, the customer service is started. It is expected that each connected call will require 10 minutes to complete. The call processing time is a random variable drawn from a negative exponential population. In more complex cases, some incoming calls may be transferred to a second or supervisory agent. In other cases, an initial call may require a callback in order to complete the transactions.

In the next section, we examine how data might be collected and used to determine the customer service center staffing levels.

Data Analysis

Making sound design decisions for the customer service center requires effective data management and analysis. This section outlines some potential data management and analysis techniques using Excel and the Arena Input Processor.

The primary short-run determinant of customer service center profitability and the level of customer service is the agent staffing level plan. Too many agents are expensive. Too few agents result in poor customer service. The problem is complex because the optimal staffing level is likely to change throughout the day, week, month, season, and so forth. This is a very dynamic problem. For example, a short-term airfare reduction can greatly increase call volumes both when the initial advertisements appear and when the sale reaches its planned termination date. The customer service center must be prepared for this volume change or the impact of the marketing plan could be largely wasted.

Call Processing Times

We choose to start the task of determining the agent staffing level by estimating call processing time. These processing times can be collected by a stopwatch or by electronically monitoring the operation of the customer service center. Exhibit 9–5 illustrates the first 10 of 1,000 observations of call processing times that we collected and organized into an Excel worksheet format.

Exhibit 9–6 lists Excel Descriptive Statistics generated for the 1,000 call processing times from worksheet Call Processing Times. The Descriptive Statistics were generated using a standard add-in to Excel. New users of this Excel feature must first load the add-in software from the Microsoft Office CD-ROM using the menu commands **Tools > Add-Ins** and then checking **Analysis ToolPak** in the dialog. The Descriptive Statistics are generated

EXHIBIT 9–5
Call Processing Times
Sheet call processing times | Chapter 9 Worksheets.xls

Call Processing Times in Minutes
6.3
4.8
12.3
0.0
0.0
16.7
11.5
12.6
0.8
4.2

using the menu commands **Tools > Data Analysis** and then selecting **Descriptive Statistics** from the dialog. We include more detailed information on Excel add-ins in Chapter 5, "Applications Using Excel."

The Excel Descriptive Statistics, shown in Exhibit 9–6, indicate that the average call processing time is about 10 minutes. The standard deviation is also about 10 minutes. The Excel Descriptive Statistics do not indicate how the call processing times vary over time. The histogram illustrated in Exhibit 9–7 is based on the sample of 1,000 calls. We generated the histogram using the standard Excel add-in with the menu commands **Tools > Data Analysis** and then selecting **Histogram** from the dialog box.

Exhibit 9–7 clearly indicates that while the average call processing time was about 10 minutes, most calls were considerably shorter, although a few were quite long, over 60 minutes. The standard deviation of the call processing time is also very near 10 minutes, same as the average call processing time. These two observations are consistent with an assumption that the call processing times follow the negative exponential distribution.

Exhibit 9–8 lists the results obtained by using the Input Analyzer program of the Arena simulation software package. The Arena Input Analyzer can be used to test the Goodness of Fit (GOF) of a particular set of input data to a number of widely used statistical distributions. The Input Analyzer ranks the potential statistical distributions in terms of Square Error associated with each distribution's fit to the input data. In this case, the assumed negative exponential or its statistical equivalent, the Erlang distribution with parameter $k = 1$, provided the best overall fit. Exhibit 9–9 illustrates the histogram and best-fit distribution as generated by the Arena Input Analyzer for the call processing time data set.

EXHIBIT 9–6 **Call Processing Times Descriptive Statistics**
Sheet call processing times | Chapter 9 Worksheets.xls

Descriptive Statistics	Call Processing Times in Minutes
Mean	10.08
Standard Error	0.32
Median	7.05
Mode	1.50
Standard Deviation	10.03
Sample Variance	100.63
Kurtosis	4.16
Skewness	1.82
Range	65.4
Minimum	0.0
Maximum	65.4
Sum	10,085
Count	1000
Confidence Level(95.0%)	0.62

EXHIBIT 9–7 **Call Processing Times Histogram**
Sheet call processing times | Chapter 9 Worksheets.xls

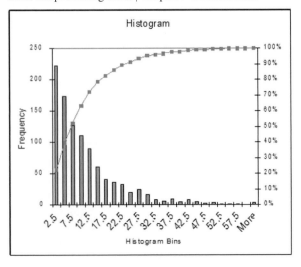

EXHIBIT 9–8
Call Processing Times GOF Test Results
Sheet goodness of fit | Chapter 9 Worksheets.xls

Arena Input Analyzer Results			
Distribution	Square Error	% of Best	Distribution (Parameters)
Erlang	0.000414	100%	ERLA (10.1, 1)
Exponential	0.000414	100%	EXPO (10.1)
Gamma	0.000432	104%	GAMM (10.5, 0.958)
Weibull	0.000594	143%	WEIB (9.81, 0.962)
Beta	0.000798	193%	66 * BETA (0.853, 4.62)
Lognormal	0.006040	1459%	LOGN (13.9, 32.3)
Normal	0.032400	7826%	NORM (10.1, 10)
Triangular	0.043500	10507%	TRIA (0.0, 1.06, 66)
Uniform	0.073400	17729%	UNIF (0.0, 66)

EXHIBIT 9–9
Arena Input Analyzer GOF Histogram

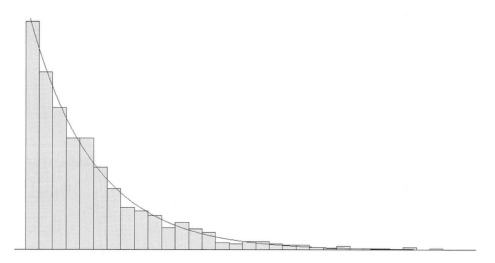

Call Volume

For the next step to determine the agent staffing level, we analyzed the call volumes based on a typical week. Exhibit 9–10 shows how these data might be organized on an hourly basis for a seven-day week. For a complete system analysis, similar data should be collected for several weeks or more. Care should be taken to account for special weeks, such as the last week in the quarter, weeks with holidays, and other special times. Excel charts are a quick way to gain an understanding of the incoming call process.

Exhibit 9–11 illustrates a bar chart of daily call volumes. This chart is generated from the bottom row of Exhibit 9–10. The bar chart illustrates an apparent lower call volume on the weekends. With sufficient data (at least one quarter, 13 weeks) a statistical test could be conducted to determine if there is a significant difference in the number of calls based on the day of the week. The number of calls on Wednesday and Thursday appears to be slightly lower than other weekdays.

The call volume differences among days might be caused by the type of customer (corporate versus consumer) and customer location (local versus domestic versus worldwide). Special days, such as holidays, can greatly impact daily call volume.

Similar charts and/or statistical analysis can be used to determine how the call volume varies by the time of day. Exhibit 9–12 illustrates the worksheet **Five-Day Call Volume** that includes only the data for the five workdays (Monday through Friday) found in the above analysis to be quite similar.

EXHIBIT 9–10
Daily Call Volume Worksheet
Sheet 7-day call volume | Chapter 9 Worksheets.xls

Customer Service Center 7-Day Call Volume									Period Length	60	Minutes
									Average Call Length	10	Minutes
Period		Observed Calls per Hour							Average Calls per Period	Required Agents	
Start	End	Monday	Tuesday	Wednesday	Thursday	Friday	Saturday	Sunday			
12:00 AM	1:00 AM	12	5	12	10	14	12	13	12.2	2.0	
1:00 AM	2:00 AM	9	6	2	4	6	3	6	5.1	0.9	
2:00 AM	3:00 AM	7	5	6	6	8	5	4	5.9	1.0	
3:00 AM	4:00 AM	4	6	6	2	1	4	2	3.6	0.6	
4:00 AM	5:00 AM	3	6	7	4	5	6	8	5.6	0.9	
5:00 AM	6:00 AM	4	6	3	4	9	9	7	6.0	1.0	
6:00 AM	7:00 AM	10	4	3	7	5	2	6	5.3	0.9	
7:00 AM	8:00 AM	4	10	9	7	8	11	7	8.0	1.3	
8:00 AM	9:00 AM	10	4	11	6	13	5	10	8.4	1.4	
9:00 AM	10:00 AM	24	35	22	29	18	24	10	23.1	3.9	
10:00 AM	11:00 AM	21	26	22	17	25	18	12	20.1	3.4	
11:00 AM	12:00 PM	31	33	25	21	24	17	15	23.7	4.0	
12:00 PM	1:00 PM	26	26	18	19	26	15	24	22.0	3.7	
1:00 PM	2:00 PM	9	24	21	20	23	14	8	17.0	2.8	
2:00 PM	3:00 PM	24	27	24	31	25	17	21	24.1	4.0	
3:00 PM	4:00 PM	34	16	24	28	19	17	21	22.7	3.8	
4:00 PM	5:00 PM	23	21	29	28	21	14	18	22.0	3.7	
5:00 PM	6:00 PM	18	9	13	17	13	5	10	12.1	2.0	
6:00 PM	7:00 PM	10	10	8	12	6	7	11	9.1	1.5	
7:00 PM	8:00 PM	8	17	10	10	10	6	7	9.7	1.6	
8:00 PM	9:00 PM	14	17	7	11	13	13	8	11.9	2.0	
9:00 PM	10:00 PM	12	12	11	7	9	8	6	9.3	1.5	
10:00 PM	11:00 PM	8	10	10	4	10	10	8	8.6	1.4	
11:00 PM	12:00 AM	5	5	10	7	7	16	7	8.1	1.4	
	Average	13.8	14.2	13.0	13.0	13.3	10.8	10.4	12.7	2.1	

Exhibit 9–13 illustrates the call volume bar chart by hour averaged over the five workdays (Monday through Friday) on the worksheet **5-DayCallVolume** of the workbook Chapter 9 Worksheets.xls. While Exhibit 9–13 illustrates considerable difference between the hours of the day, the biggest apparent difference is between the following three time blocks:

1. 9:00 AM to 5:00 PM
2. 5:00 PM to 1:00 AM
3. 1:00 AM to 9:00 AM

During those three time blocks, the average call volumes were 24.0, 10.3, and 6.0 calls per hour (see Exhibit 9–12).

EXHIBIT 9–11 **Daily Call Volume Bar Chart**
Sheet 7-Day Call Volume | Chapter 9 Worksheets.xls

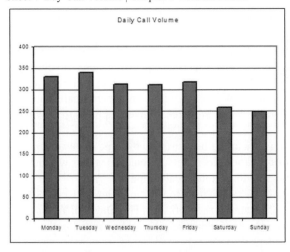

Required Staffing Level

We can use the average number of calls per hour and the average call processing time to make a rough-cut agent staffing level projection for the customer service center. The analysis we present in worksheet **Staffing,** shown in Exhibit 9–14, uses the average number of calls per hour originally presented in Exhibit 9–12. We multiplied the call volume per hour by the average call processing time, 10 minutes, to obtain the expected service minutes for each hour of the day.

Several methods might be used to actually assign the number of customer service agents to work during each of the 24 one-hour time slots. This assignment may take into account agent breaks, part-time agents, and so forth. To keep this initial case study relatively simple, we assume that each agent is continuously available for an eight-hour assignment and that all agents change shift at the same fixed intervals: 9:00 AM, 5:00 PM, and

EXHIBIT 9–12
Hourly Weekday Call
Volume Worksheet
Sheet 5-day call
volume | Chapter 9
Worksheets.xls

| Customer Service Center 5-Day Call Volume | | | | | | | Period Length | 60 | Minutes |
| | | | | | | | Average Call Length | 10 | Minutes |

| Period | | Observed Calls per Hour | | | | | Average Calls per Period | Shift Averages | Required Agents |
Start	End	Monday	Tuesday	Wednesday	Thursday	Friday			
12:00 AM	1:00 AM	12	5	12	10	14	10.6		1.8
1:00 AM	2:00 AM	9	6	2	4	6	5.4		0.9
2:00 AM	3:00 AM	7	5	6	6	8	6.4		1.1
3:00 AM	4:00 AM	4	6	6	2	1	3.8		0.6
4:00 AM	5:00 AM	3	6	7	4	5	5.0		0.8
5:00 AM	6:00 AM	4	6	3	4	9	5.2		0.9
6:00 AM	7:00 AM	10	4	3	7	5	5.8		1.0
7:00 AM	8:00 AM	4	10	9	7	8	7.6		1.3
8:00 AM	9:00 AM	10	4	11	6	13	8.8	6.0	1.5
9:00 AM	10:00 AM	24	35	22	29	18	25.6		4.3
10:00 AM	11:00 AM	21	26	22	17	25	22.2		3.7
11:00 AM	12:00 PM	31	33	25	21	24	26.8		4.5
12:00 PM	1:00 PM	26	26	18	19	26	23.0		3.8
1:00 PM	2:00 PM	9	24	21	20	23	19.4		3.2
2:00 PM	3:00 PM	24	27	24	31	25	26.2		4.4
3:00 PM	4:00 PM	34	16	24	28	19	24.2		4.0
4:00 PM	5:00 PM	23	21	29	28	21	24.4	24.0	4.1
5:00 PM	6:00 PM	18	9	13	17	13	14.0		2.3
6:00 PM	7:00 PM	10	10	8	12	6	9.2		1.5
7:00 PM	8:00 PM	8	17	10	10	10	11.0		1.8
8:00 PM	9:00 PM	14	17	7	11	13	12.4		2.1
9:00 PM	10:00 PM	12	12	11	7	9	10.2		1.7
10:00 PM	11:00 PM	8	10	10	4	10	8.4		1.4
11:00 PM	12:00 AM	5	5	10	7	7	6.8	10.3	1.1
	Average	13.8	14.2	13.0	13.0	13.3	13.4	13.4	2.2

EXHIBIT 9–13
Hourly Weekday Call
Volume Bar Chart
Sheet five-day call
volume | Chapter 9
Worksheets.xls

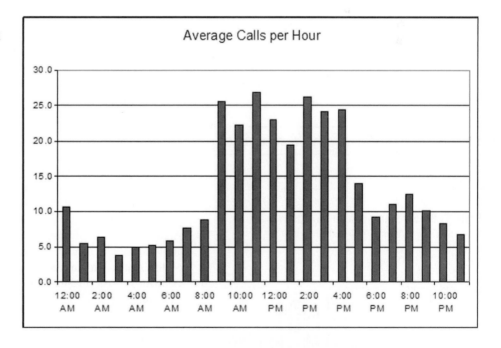

1:00 AM. In the analysis we present in Exhibit 9–14, four, two, and one customer service agents have been assigned to each of three daily eight-hour shifts. The Expected Agent Utilization column of Exhibit 9–14 indicates the fraction of the agent's time that is expected to be spent servicing incoming calls. Notice that this fraction is often greater than 1.0, indicating a potential for lost or aborted calls. The number of scheduled agents could be increased to assure that no hour would have an Expected Agent Utilization greater than 100

EXHIBIT 9–14
Staffing Level
Worksheet
Sheet staffing |
Chapter 9
Worksheets.xls

Customer Service Center Staffing			Period Length	60	Minutes		
			Average Call Length	10	Minutes		
Period Start	Period End	Call Volume / Period	Expected Service Minutes	Agents Scheduled	Available Agent Minutes	Expected Agent Utilization
12:00 AM	1:00 AM	10.6	106	2	120	88%
1:00 AM	2:00 AM	5.4	54	1	60	90%
2:00 AM	3:00 AM	6.4	64	1	60	107%
3:00 AM	4:00 AM	3.8	38	1	60	63%
4:00 AM	5:00 AM	5.0	50	1	60	83%
5:00 AM	6:00 AM	5.2	52	1	60	87%
6:00 AM	7:00 AM	5.8	58	1	60	97%
7:00 AM	8:00 AM	7.6	76	1	60	127%
8:00 AM	9:00 AM	8.8	88	1	60	147%
9:00 AM	10:00 AM	25.6	256	4	240	107%
10:00 AM	11:00 AM	22.2	222	4	240	93%
11:00 AM	12:00 PM	26.8	268	4	240	112%
12:00 PM	1:00 PM	23.0	230	4	240	96%
1:00 PM	2:00 PM	19.4	194	4	240	81%
2:00 PM	3:00 PM	26.2	262	4	240	109%
3:00 PM	4:00 PM	24.2	242	4	240	101%
4:00 PM	5:00 PM	24.4	244	4	240	102%
5:00 PM	6:00 PM	14.0	140	2	120	117%
6:00 PM	7:00 PM	9.2	92	2	120	77%
7:00 PM	8:00 PM	11.0	110	2	120	92%
8:00 PM	9:00 PM	12.4	124	2	120	103%
9:00 PM	10:00 PM	10.2	102	2	120	85%
10:00 PM	11:00 PM	8.4	84	2	120	70%
11:00 PM	12:00 AM	6.8	68	2	120	57%
	Totals	322.4	3,224	56	3,360	96%

percent. While this may be desirable from a customer service point of view, it could be cost-prohibitive and difficult to schedule without extremely flexible part-time agents. Exhibit 9–15 illustrates the relationship between the number of assigned agents and the expected call volume in the form of an Excel bar chart.

Dynamic Analysis Using Arena Process Simulation

EXHIBIT 9–15   **Staffing Level Bar Chart**
Sheet Staffing | Chapter 9 Worksheets.xls

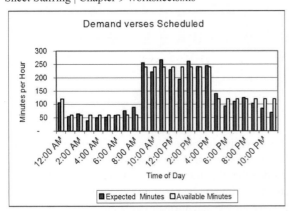

Because the actual arrival of incoming calls and the length of each call is a random variable, it is difficult to accurately analyze the customer service center taking into account this dynamic behavior of the system. The Arena simulation software is one such tool for modeling and analyzing dynamic or random systems. The details of the Arena simulation software were described in Chapter 6, "Process Simulation Using Arena." For this case study, we will briefly illustrate the use of the Arena simulation software.

The common steps for using the Arena simulation software are to

1. Develop a system process map.
2. Collect and organize the relevant system data.
3. Develop and validate the simulation model.
4. Use the simulation model to test alternative system configurations.

We have already completed steps 1 and 2 for the basic customer service center in the previous sections of this chapter. Arena offers two methods of developing the simulation model. The Visio Process Simulation stencil provided with Arena can be used for basic model development. A complete model development environment is also provided directly by Arena. In this chapter, we have developed our own Arena process simulation model. In addition, a second model has been developed using the Arena Contact Center Edition.

Arena Process Simulation Model Development

Exhibit 9–16 illustrates the Arena process simulation logic modules for the customer service center model. This logic flow is almost exactly identical to the process map illustrated in Exhibit 9–4. We will now review the major components of this model. The reader should load Arena file **CSC.doe** to track the model structure by locating the Arena concepts as we address them in the following sections.

Call Arrivals

The flow begins at the left with incoming customer calls. Based on the analysis presented above, the call arrival rate depends on the time of day (see Exhibits 9–12 through 9–14). Exhibit 9–17 illustrates the call arrival schedule we developed for the Arena CSC.doe model.

EXHIBIT 9–16
Model CSC.doe
Network Logic Flow

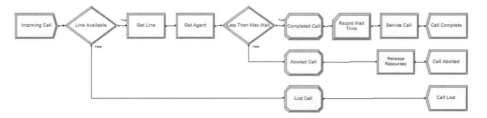

EXHIBIT 9–17
Model CSC.doe Call
Arrival Schedule
Chart

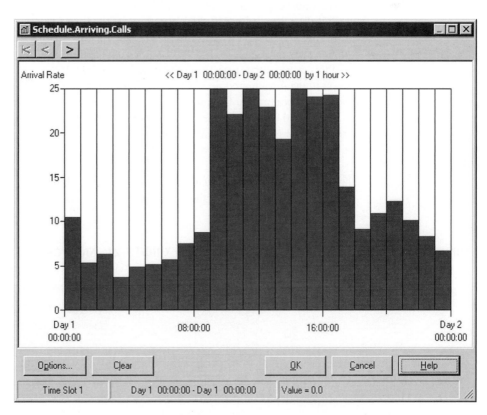

EXHIBIT 9–18

Model CSC.doe Call
Arrival Schedule
Spreadsheet

	Value	Duration
1	10.6	1
2	5.4	1
3	6.4	1
4	3.8	1
5	5	1
6	5.2	1
7	5.8	1
8	7.6	1
9	8.8	1
10	25.6	1
11	22.2	1
12	26.8	1
13	23	1
14	19.4	1
15	26.2	1
16	24.2	1
17	24.4	1
18	14	1
19	9.2	1
20	11	1
21	12.4	1
22	10.2	1
23	8.4	1
24	6.8	1

Exhibit 9–18 illustrates this same schedule information in the worksheet format for the Arena Schedule data module. The data in this worksheet was copied and pasted directly from cell range H5:H28 of worksheet Five-DayCallVolume (Exhibit 9–12).

If necessary, the scheduled number of arrivals per hour can be changed either numerically or using the cursor directly on the chart illustrated in Exhibit 9–17. The reader should save the Arena model with a name like **My CSC.doe** and attempt to make such changes.

Arena will randomly generate the simulation call arrivals using the exponential distribution and expected number of arrivals per hour. For example, in the first hour of the day, midnight to 1:00 AM, 10.6 calls are expected to arrive. This is equivalent to a mean time between call arrivals calculated by the following expression:

$$60 \div 10.6 = 5.66 \text{ minutes}$$

The mean time between call arrivals will automatically be varied by Arena to match the data illustrated in Exhibits 9–17 and 9–18.

Model Flows

The control of Arena customer entities in Arena CSC.doe model is accomplished by using Arena Decide modules and Resources. The Arena model illustrated in Exhibit 9–16 has two diamond-shaped Decide modules. These Decide modules determine the final disposition of each customer entity.

The first Decide module, Line Available, determines if an incoming customer call will reach a truck line or gets a busy signal. This decision is made based on the information provided in the Line Available Decide Module dialog, as illustrated in Exhibit 9–19.

The Arena expression **NR(Line) < MR(Line)** tests to determine if all the incoming 10 lines are full. This expression may look cryptic to a first-time Arena user, but it could be generated using the point-and-click-driven Arena Expression Builder. The expression can be interpreted as **if the number of busy lines is less than the total number of lines.**

If this expression is true, the entity proceeds to right. If the expression is false, the entity is sent to the Assign module labeled **Lost Call,** where it is classified as a lost call and then disposed of or removed from the model.

The second Decide module, **Less Than Max Wait,** determines if the incoming call reaches a truck line or gets a busy signal and hangs up. This decision is made based on the information provided in the Less Than Max Wait Decide Module Dialog, shown in Exhibit 9–20.

The Decide module Less Than Max Wait tests to determine if the current call has longer than Max.Wait.Minutes = 10 minutes. If the current call has waited 10 minutes or less, the call proceeds to the right. If the current call has waited more than 10 minutes, the call is

EXHIBIT 9–19   Model CSC.doe Line Available Decide
Module Dialog

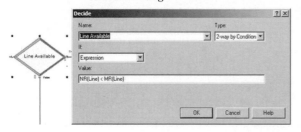

EXHIBIT 9–20   Model CSC.doe Less Than Max Wait
Decide Module Dialog

sent to the Assign module labeled **Aborted Call** where it is classified as an aborted call and then disposed of or removed from the model.

Model Resources

The time-related control of Arena entities is accomplished by using Arena Resources. Arena CSC.doe model uses two types of Arena Resource. These are

1. Resource **Line** with fixed capacity of 10.
2. Resource **Agent** with a variable capacity as generated in the worksheet Staffing, shown in Exhibits 9–14 and 9–15.

Exhibit 9–21 illustrates the **Agent** schedule that we developed for Arena CSC.doe model. Two agents are scheduled for the first period, midnight to 1:00 AM, one agent for the next eight periods, 1:00 AM to 9:00 AM, four agents for the next eight periods, 9:00 AM to 5:00 PM, and two agents for the last seven periods, 5:00 PM to midnight.

The two Arena Resources are used in the following manner:

1. Resource **Line** is seized or detained in the Process module Get Line and released in Process modules Service Call or Release Resources.
2. Resource **Agent** is seized or detained in the Process module Get Agent and released in Process module Service Call.

Because these Arena Resources are limited in capacity, the customer entity can only move forward when a unit of the resource is available to be seized. If no resource unit is available, the customer entity must wait in a queue until the required resource becomes available. Arena CSC.doe model has two such waiting areas or queues: Get Line.Queue and Get Agent.Queue. Because of the Decide model immediately before the Get Line Process module, the Get Line.Queue never holds any calls (the reader should verify this fact). The Get Agent.Queue may contain up to nine customer entities (the reader should verify this limit).

The actual call servicing or process is done in the Process module Service Call. At this point, the customer entity controls or owns both a Line and an Agent resource. The average call length was determined in the prior analysis to take 10 minutes and is subject to random variation using the exponential distribution as illustrated in Exhibit 9–9. Exhibit 9–22 illustrates the Service Call Process module dialog. The mean or average call service is stored in an Arena Variable named **Mean.Call.Processing.Minutes.** Having this or any other data

EXHIBIT 9–21   **Model CSC.doe Agent Schedule Chart**

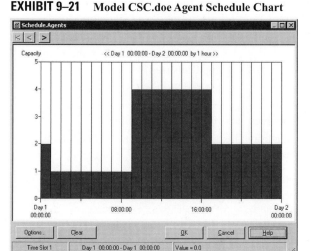

EXHIBIT 9–22   **Model CSC.doe Service Call Process Module Dialog**

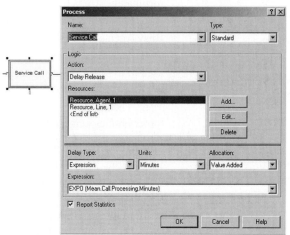

EXHIBIT 9–23
**Model CSC.doe Run
Setup Replication
Parameters Dialog**

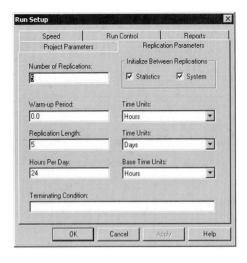

element defined as an Arena variable permits its value to be displayed when the model is being run or executed and to be systematically changed when model experimentation is being performed to find the "optimal" solution.

The remaining Arena modules perform the general housekeeping functions that were developed in more detail in Chapter 7. One additional item should be validated before testing the model using the **Run > Setup** dialog. Exhibit 9–23 illustrates the Run Setup Replication Parameters for the Arena CSC.doe model. This model has been set up to run five replications of five days each or a total of 25 days. Between each replication, all statistics are initialized or cleared, as are any in-process calls. In other words, the customer service center starts each week or replication empty at Sunday midnight. The replications differ from each other due to the random variations caused by the random numbers used to generate the call arrivals and call service times.

Model Extras

Exhibit 9–24 illustrates the complete CSC.doe model flowchart display. We added several features to make viewing of the operating CSC.doe model more informative. The colors referred to below should appear on your Arena display.

1. The blue text in the yellow box is simply descriptive.

2. The red text in the yellow boxes contains the value of variables or expressions while the model is being run.

    a. The value of Arena variable: Goal.Wait.Minutes = 1.

    b. The value of Arena variable: Max.Wait.Minutes = 10.

    c. The value of Arena expression: SchedValue (Schedule.Agents) = 1, 2, or 4 (Time dependent).

3. The blue circle and box at the lower right illustrate the current simulation time and date based on the indicated starting information. Note the calendar is not correct after the first week (replication). Each replication is five days in length and starts on Monday. Unfortunately, Arena has no easy means to only simulate weekdays.

4. The box in the lower left is an Arena plot that illustrates over time the number of Busy Agents (blue), Busy Lines (green), and Waiting Calls (red).

5. The small light blue boxes above the Get Agent and Service Call Process modules are used to indicate the Arena resource status. Unfortunately, Arena does a poor job of animating the status of multiple capacity resources, as is the case in this model.

6. The lines with small circles to the left of resource icons are storages that hold the customer entities being served by associated resources.

We are now ready to execute the model by pressing the Run key (**F5**) or clicking the VCR Play button. We will now review types of results generated by the model CSC.doe.

Arena Simulation Results

As the simulation is executed, a small number appears near the bottom of most Arena modules. That number indicates the number of customer entities that have entered or left each

EXHIBIT 9–24
Model CSC.doe
Display

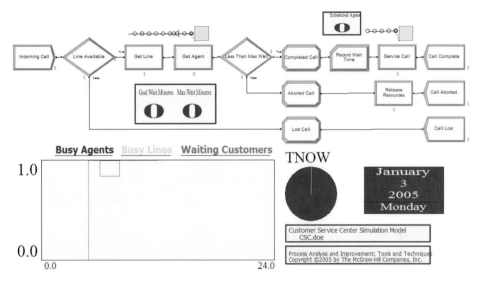

EXHIBIT 9–25
Model CSC.doe
Execution Display

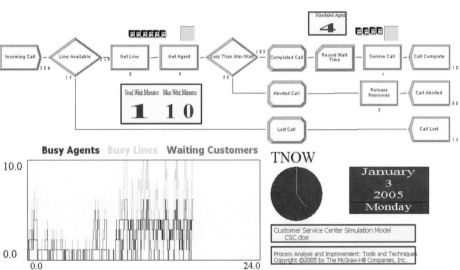

Create, Dispose, or Decision module. In the case of Process modules or shapes, the number indicates the number of calls currently being processed or waiting to be processed. The general flow of customer entities can be validated using the numeric values illustrated in Exhibit 9–25.

For example, at simulation time 17 hour or 5:00 PM as displayed in Exhibit 9–25, a total of 259 calls have entered the customer service center. Of these 259 calls, 13 calls found all 10 incoming telephone lines busy and were classified as Lost Calls. Of the remaining 246 calls, 6 are currently waiting for an agent and 4 are currently being served. A total of 181 calls were successfully completed while 55 were aborted after waiting 10 minutes for an agent. The plot at the lower left of Exhibit 9–25 illustrates how the number of Busy Agents, Busy Lines, and Waiting Calls has varied over the first 17 hours of this simulation run.

Although viewing the execution and checking the numeric values on the screen is useful when validating the structure of the Arena process simulation model, it does not give a long-range performance evaluation that the model was developed to provide. Rather, after the analyst has validated the simulation model, complete runs should be made and the resulting Crystal Reports carefully reviewed.

Crystal Report Displays

Arena's Crystal Report feature takes getting accustomed to, but with practice the feature can be a valuable source of information. Most of the data are also available from Arena in a text-based file format, CSC.out, that can be read using a text editor such as WordPad.exe. We have selected six Crystal Report displays to review the results for model CSC.doe. These are

1. Exhibit 9–26: Model CSC.doe Crystal Report, Cost Charts.
2. Exhibit 9–28: Model CSC.doe Crystal Report, Entities.
3. Exhibit 9–29: Model CSC.doe Crystal Report, Queues.
4. Exhibit 9–30: Model CSC.doe Crystal Report, Resources.
5. Exhibit 9–31: Model CSC.doe Crystal Report, Tallies and Time Persistent.
6. Exhibit 9–35: Model CSC.doe Crystal Report, Outputs.

All of the Crystal Reports illustrated in this section are summaries for the five model replications, each simulating five consecutive 24-hour days. Individual reports for each replication could be viewed to obtain insights on how the model results varied from replication to replication.

Cost Charts   Exhibit 9–26, Cost Charts, illustrates the first Crystal Report screen that is automatically displayed at the termination of the simulation run. The chart indicates total costs accumulated by customer entities and Arena resources.

Arena customer entities accumulate cost at a rate of $1.00, whenever a telephone line is being used and $10.00 whenever an agent is working to serve the customer. On average for the five replications, customer entities accumulated $2,397 while being serviced, and $125 while waiting online. In Exhibit 9–26, we will find that an average of 1,335 customers were successfully completed. The value of 1,632 represents all incoming calls processed by the customer service center, including those lost or aborted.

We can calculate the average cost per completed customer using the following expression:

$$(\$2,397 + \$125) \div 1,335 = \$1.89$$

The above calculation takes into account only the cost of active Arena Resources. The lower half of Exhibit 9–26 indicates a resource Idle Cost of $1,478. This accounts for idle Arena Resources, when all 10 lines or four agents are not servicing a customer. Including the idle cost, the average cost per completed customer is determined using the following expression:

EXHIBIT 9–26
Model CSC.doe
Crystal Report, Cost
Charts

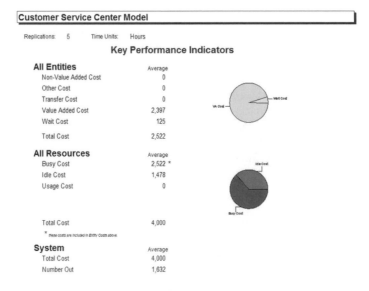

$$(\$2,522 + \$1,478) \div 1,335 = \$2.99$$

This later figure is very significant because the average revenue per completed call is only $5.00.

While the Crystal Report illustrated in Exhibit 9–26 is automatically displayed, additional reports can be selected using the Arena Crystal Report Tree Structure, which is illustrated in Exhibit 9–27. Each of these major report types is reviewed in the next sections.

Entity > Other > Number Out - WIP   Selecting the Entity report option from the Crystal Report tree structure (Exhibit 9–27) generates the report illustrated in Exhibit 9–28. The top half of Exhibit 9–28 indicates the statistics for the number of entities of each type leaving the simulation model. The column labeled *Average* is the overall average for the five replications. An average of 1,335 calls were successfully completed. The column labeled *Half Width* is the 95 percent confidence interval half width for the estimated population mean. The 95 percent confidence interval of the population mean can be calculated using the following expression:

$$1,335 \pm 22 = \{1,313 \text{ to } 1,357\}$$

Thus, we can say with 95 percent confidence that the expected number of successfully completed calls per one five-weekday period is in the range of 1,313 to 1,357.

The columns labeled *Minimum Average* and *Maximum Average* represent the corresponding minimum and maximum observed values over the five replications. For example, the Entity.Aborted.Call Number Out had values of 310, 259, 244, 262, and 193 for the five replications. Thus, the reported minimum is 193 and the maximum is 310 with a mean of 254 and a 95 percent confidence interval of 52. The number of incoming calls per week ranged from 1,569 to 1,707 with a mean of 1,633 and a confidence interval of 67. Similar statistics are reported for the number of lost calls.

The bottom half of Exhibit 9–28 indicates statistics for the Work in Process (WIP) for each type of simulation model entity. These statistics represent time-weighted averages of the entire simulation run.

The Entity.Aborted.Call type exists for zero time units as the Entity.Incoming.Call finally seizes an agent resource but has waited more than 10 minutes and is immediately disposed. The Entity.Lost.Call type exists for zero time units as the Entity.Incoming.Call finds all 10 lines busy and is immediately disposed. Therefore, the WIP

EXHIBIT 9–27
Model CSC.doe Crystal Report Tree Structure

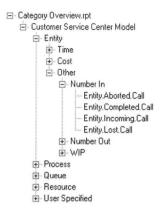

```
⊟ Category Overview.rpt
  ⊟ Customer Service Center Model
    ⊟ Entity
      ⊞ Time
      ⊞ Cost
      ⊟ Other
        ⊟ Number In
            Entity.Aborted.Call
            Entity.Completed.Call
            Entity.Incoming.Call
            Entity.Lost.Call
        ⊞ Number Out
        ⊞ WIP
    ⊞ Process
    ⊞ Queue
    ⊞ Resource
    ⊞ User Specified
```

EXHIBIT 9–28
Model CSC.doe Crystal Report, Entity > Other > Number Out, WIP

Number Out	Average	Half Width	Minimum Average	Maximum Average		
Entity.Aborted.Call	253.60	52.10	193.00	310.00		
Entity.Completed.Call	1334.60	21.67	1311.00	1359.00		
Entity.Incoming.Call	1633.40	67.20	1569.00	1707.00		
Entity.Lost.Call	43.4000	15.42	33.0000	64.0000		

WIP	Average	Half Width	Minimum Average	Maximum Average	Minimum Value	Maximum Value
Entity.Aborted.Call	0.00	0.00	0.00	0.00	0.00	1.0000
Entity.Completed.Call	1.8176	0.06	1.7613	1.8852	0.00	4.0000
Entity.Incoming.Call	1.0427	0.13	0.8937	1.1792	0.00	10.0000
Entity.Lost.Call	0.00	0.00	0.00	0.00	0.00	1.0000

statistics for Entity.Aborted.Call and Entity.Lost.Call are zero except for the maximum of 1, indicates the temporary existence of these entity types.

The Entity.Completed.Call type exists from the time an Entity.Incoming.Call type gains control of an agent resource until the service is completed. The WIP statistics for Entity.Aborted.Call are equivalent to the number of busy agent resources. The Entity.Completed.Call WIP averaged 1.82 ± 0.06. The columns labeled *Minimum Average* and *Maximum Average* represent the corresponding minimum and maximum average values over the five replications. The Entity.Completed.Call WIP had average values of 1.8852, 1.8473, 1.8028, 1.7913, and 1.7613 for the five replications. Thus, the reported minimum average is 1.7613 and the maximum average is 1.8852. The columns labeled *Minimum Value* and *Maximum Value* represent the corresponding minimum and maximum observed values over five replications, not surprisingly 0 and 4, respectively.

The Entity.Incoming.Call type exists from the time a customer call enters the customer service center until it is reclassified as one of three other entity types. Because of the limit on the number online, the Entity.Incoming.Call WIP is limited to 10 in number and represents that number of customers that control a line resource and are waiting for an agent resource. The Entity.Incoming.Call WIP averaged 1.04 ± 0.13. The columns labeled *Minimum Average* and *Maximum Average* represent the corresponding minimum and maximum average values over five replications. The Entity.Incoming.Call WIP had average values of 1.1792, 1.0491, 1.0121, 1.0795, and 0.8939 for five replications. Thus, the reported maximum average is 1.1792 and the minimum average is 0.8939. The columns labeled *Minimum Value* and *Maximum Value* represent the corresponding minimum and maximum observed values over five replications, 0 and 10, respectively.

Queue

Selecting the Queue report option from the Crystal Report tree structure (Exhibit 9–27) generates the Arena Queues statistics report illustrated in Exhibit 9–29. In this case, we have chosen to display the number of customer entities waiting in the two model queues: Get Line.Queue and Get Agent.Queue. Notice that while the Get Line.Queue exists, it never contains any entities because of the Decide module that precedes the Get Line Process module. The Get Agent.Queue had an average content of 1.04 ± 0.13 customers with minimum and maximum values of 0 and 9 respectively. The average contents of the Get Agent.Queue had values of 1.1792, 1.0491, 1.0121, 1.0795, and 0.8937 and therefore, the reported minimum and maximum averages of 0.8937 and 1.1792 respectively. The chart at the bottom of Exhibit 9–29 illustrates the average contents of all model queues. In this case, the chart adds little value but is useful when Arena models include many queues and the analyst is typically interested in finding queues with the large average contents. These queues typically precede the bottleneck processes.

Resource   Selecting the Resource report option from the Crystal Report tree structure (Exhibit 9–27) generates the report illustrated in Exhibit 9–30. Exhibit 9–30 illustrates the number of busy Arena Resources: Agent and Line. The top half of Exhibit 9–30 illustrates the number of busy resources while the bottom half illustrates the number of scheduled resources. Exhibit 9–21 illustrates the schedule for agents. The number of agent resources scheduled was 4, 2, and 1 each for 8 hours per day for an average of 2.33 agents. The number of line resources was a constant 10 for the entire simulation.

The number of busy agent resources averaged 1.81 ± 0.06 while the number of busy line resources averaged 2.86 ± 0.18. The difference 2.86 − 1.81 = 1.05

EXHIBIT 9–29   **Model CSC.doe Crystal Report, Queues**

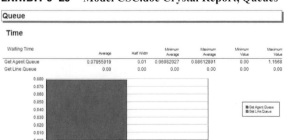

EXHIBIT 9–30
Model CSC.doe
Crystal Report,
Resources

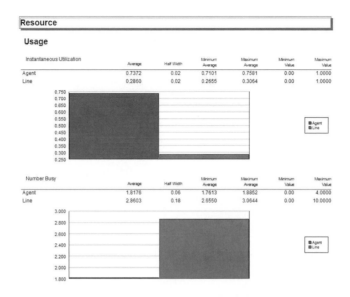

should equal the number of customers waiting for an agent resource (see Exhibit 9–29) where the average number waiting in the Get Agent.Queue was 1.0427. The out reported values are defined and calculated in a manner similar to those in the prior Crystal Report exhibits.

Notice the vertical scale of the graph in Exhibit 9–30. The lower value is 1.80 and, therefore, the relationship between the number of busy agents and lines is hard to judge graphically.

User Specified > Tally   Selecting the **User Specified > Tally** report option from the Crystal Report tree structure (Exhibit 9–27) generates the Tallies and Time Persistent report illustrated in Exhibit 9–31. The User Specific report options only exist if the Arena model contains Advanced Process Statistic module definitions for model CSC.doe, as illustrated in Exhibit 9–32.

The Tally labeled *Wait for Service* is defined in row 1 of Exhibit 9–32, the Statistic module. The tally data was collected on the Arena output file WaitforService.dat. The actual data collection takes place in the Record Wait Time module whose dialog is illustrated in Exhibit 9–33. An Arena tally functions like the standard manual tally we have all used to manually generate a histogram or count the number of occurrences within specific categories. In this case, each time a customer enters the Record Wait Time module the value of

EXHIBIT 9–31
Model CSC.doe
Crystal Report, User
Specified > Tally

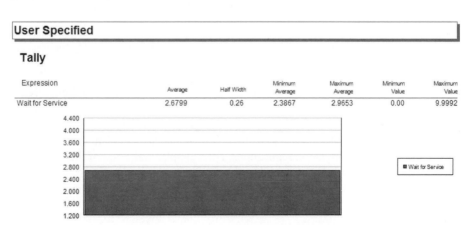

EXHIBIT 9–32
Model CSC.doe
Statistic Module
Spreadsheet

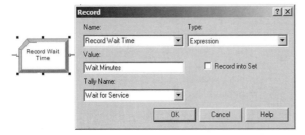

	Name	Type	Tally Name	Tally Output File	Expression	Report Label	Output File
1	Number of Customers Waiting	Time-Persistent	Tally 1		NQ (Get Agent.Queue)	Number of Customers Waiting	NumberCustomersWaiting.DAT
2	Number of Agents Idle	Time-Persistent	Tally 2		MR (Agent) − NR (Agent)	Number of Agents Idle	NumberAgentsIdle.DAT
3	Fraction Complete	Output	Tally 4		EntitiesOut(Entity.Completed.Call) / EntitiesIn(Entity.Incoming.Call)	Fraction Complete	
4	Fraction Aborted	Output	Tally 5		EntitiesOut(Entity.Aborted.Call) / EntitiesIn(Entity.Incoming.Call)	Fraction Aborted	
5	Fraction Within Goal	Output	Tally 10		Faction.Within.Goal	Fraction Within Goal	
6	Number Within Goal	Output	Tally 11		Number.Within.Goal	Number Within Goal	
7	Wait for Service	Tally	Wait for Service	WaitforService.DAT		Wait for Service	
8	Fraction Lost	Output	Tally 6		EntitiesOut(Entity.Lost.Call) / EntitiesIn(Entity.Incoming.Call)	Fraction Lost	
9	Profit	Output	Tally 8		Income - Total.ResourceCost - Losses	Profit	

EXHIBIT 9–33   **Model CSC.doe Record Module Dialog**

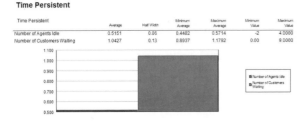

attribute Wait.Minutes is recorded in the tally name Wait for Service. The average of these Wait for Service tallies is 2.68 ± 0.26 minutes. The maximum value tallied was 9.9992 minutes, because the CSC.doe model considered all customers waiting longer than 10 minutes as aborted. One of the constraints for the customer service center was an average Wait for Service of two minutes or less. Clearly this model does not meet that constraint.

EXHIBIT 9–34   **Model CSC.doe Crystal Report, User Specified > Time Persistent**

Time Persistent

Time Persistent	Average	Half Width	Minimum Average	Maximum Average	Minimum Value	Maximum Value
Number of Agents Idle	0.5151	0.06	0.4482	0.5714	-2	4.0000
Number of Customers Waiting	1.0427	0.13	0.8937	1.1792	0.00	9.0000

Time Persistent   The Time Persistent statistics illustrated in Exhibit 9–34 were defined in rows 2 and 3 of the Statistic module worksheet (Exhibit 9–32). Arena Time Persistent statistics record each change of an expression's value and reports time waited statistics for the expression.

Exhibit 9–32 row 2 defines the Arena statistic Number of Customers Waiting using the expression **NQ (Get Agent.Queue)** or the number of customers waiting for an agent. The number of incoming calls waiting data is also collected on Arena output file NumberCustomersWaiting.dat. Exhibit 9–32 row 3 defines the statistic Number of Agents Idle using the expression **MR (Agent) − NR (Agent)** or the total number of scheduled agents minus the number of busy agents, hence the number of idle agents. The number of agents idle data is also collected on the Arena output file NumberAgentsIdle.dat.

Based on Exhibit 9–31, the number of idle agents has an average of 0.52 ± 0.06 with a minimum of -2 and a maximum of 4. It is easy to understand the maximum value, but the minimum value needs some explanation. At 5:00 PM each day, the number of scheduled agents changes from 4 to 2. If the number of busy agents at that time happened to be 4, the resulting expression value would be calculated as

$$\text{MR (Agent)} - \text{NR (Agent)} = 2 - 4 = -2$$

The number of calls (customers) waiting has an average of 1.04 ± 0.13 with minimum of 0 and maximum of 9. The reader should consider why the maximum value is 9 rather than 10, the number of incoming trunk lines.

User Specified > Output   Selecting the **User Specified > Output** report option from the Crystal Report tree structure (Exhibit 9–27) generates the Output report illustrated in Exhibit 9–35. The Output Statistics are defined in rows 4 through 9 of Exhibit 9–32 for CSC.doe. These statistics are collected as the final value of expressions at the end of the simulation replications. For example, at the end of the first replication, the following calculation was made:

$$\text{Fraction Lost} = \text{EntitiesOut(Entity.Lost.Call)} \div$$
$$\text{EntitiesIn(Entity.Incoming.Call)} = 310 \div 1{,}701 = 0.1816$$

EXHIBIT 9–35
Model CSC.doe
Crystal Report, User
Specified > Output

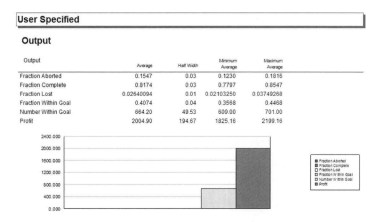

The fraction of calls lost calculated for the five replications were 0.1816, 0.1608, 0.1511, 0.1571, and 0.1230, thus the indicated average of 0.1547 with extremes 0.1230 and 0.1816.

The Fraction Complete is one of the constraints for the customer service center. The goal for the Fraction Complete was at least 0.8. Exhibit 9–35 indicates an average of 0.82 ± 0.03 with a range of 0.78 to 0.85. Thus, this constraint appears to be marginally met.

The Fraction within Goal is another of constraints for the customer service center. The goal for the Fraction within Goal was at least 0.50. Exhibit 9–35 indicates an average of 0.41 ± 0.04 with a range of 0.35 to 0.45. Thus, this constraint has not been met by the initial simulation configuration.

The CSC.doe model objective is profit maximization. Exhibit 9–35 indicates the following profit statistics: average of $2,007 ± $194 with a 95 percent confidence interval of $1,827 to $2,201.

Excel Simulation Results Summary   We developed the worksheet **CSC Summary** to analyze the CSC.doe simulation results on a weekly or replication basis. This worksheet is illustrated in Exhibit 9–36 and was developed using Crystal Reports by replication type Entities and User Specified. The number of incoming calls ranged from 1,569 to 1,707 per week with an average of 1,634. The number of completed calls had a very limited range of 1,312 to 1,361 per week with an average of 1,336. Because the number of incoming calls varied, the fraction of calls completed are calculated by the following expression:

$$\text{Calls complete} \div \text{Incoming calls} = 1,333 \div 1,707 = 78.1\%$$

The percentage of completed calls varied from 78.1 percent to 85.5 percent with an average of 81.8 percent.

Overall, for the five weeks the CSC.doe simulation was run, 15.5 percent of the calls were aborted after waiting 10 minutes for an agent. Only 2.7 percent were lost after initially receiving a busy signal. Slightly more than 40 percent were serviced within one minute. This was far less than the original constraint value of 50 percent. We now turn to the

EXHIBIT 9–36
Model CSC.doe
Simulation Results
Summary
Sheet CSC Summary |
Chapter 9
Worksheets.xls

CSC.doe Results	Week 1		Week 2		Week 3		Week 4		Week 5		5-Week Averages	
Incoming Calls	1,707		1,611		1,615		1,668		1,569		1,634	
Calls Complete	1,333	78.1%	1,312	81.4%	1,333	82.5%	1,361	81.6%	1,341	85.5%	1,336	81.8%
Calls Aborted	310	18.2%	259	16.1%	244	15.1%	262	15.7%	193	12.3%	254	15.5%
Calls Lost	64	3.7%	40	2.5%	35	2.2%	45	2.7%	33	2.1%	43	2.7%
Calls Answered < 1 min	609	35.7%	636	39.5%	681	42.2%	694	41.6%	701	44.7%	664	40.6%
Profit	$1,825		$1,870		$2,026		$2,103		$2,199		$2,005	

experimentation tools provided with the Arena software in an attempt to improve the overall customer service center performance.

Challenge

Arena Output Processor

One problem with the Crystal Reports provided by Arena is the fact that they represent only a summary of the simulated day's activities. Because the incoming call rate and the number of agents vary throughout the day, it is important to be able to see if one particular period should have a staffing level adjustment. The Advanced Process Statistic module illustrated in Exhibit 9–32 indicated that three data files were saved as the Arena CSC.doe model is executed. These data files can be viewed and analyzed using the Arena Output Processor.

Row 1 of the Advanced Process Statistic module (Exhibit 9–32) defined the Wait for Service tally and saved the results on Arena output filename **WaitforService.dat.** Exhibit 9–37 illustrates the Output Processor histogram for the Wait for Service tally. This histogram indicates most often no customers waiting for service. The Arena Output Processor also provides summary data for the histogram, shown in Exhibit 9–38, that can be viewed to reach additional conclusions. No customers were waiting 49.7 percent of the 25 simulated days. About 95 percent of the time, seven or fewer customers were waiting.

Exhibit 9–39 illustrates the Output Processor plot for the Number of Customers Waiting and the Number of Agents Idle for Day 1 (Monday) over the time period 9:00 AM to 5:00 PM (the day shift with four scheduled agent resources). This data collection was specified in rows 2 and 3 of the Advanced Process Statistic module (Exhibit 9–32). The solid plot on Exhibit 9–39 indicates the number of Customers Waiting while the dashed plot indicates the number of Idle Agents.

Several items should be noted from Exhibit 9–39. Never are both plots greater than zero, if customers are waiting, then agents cannot be idle. Only during three brief periods during this shift were all four agents idle. Quite frequently, one or two agents were idle. On about six occasions, six customers were waiting (all 10 lines busy). Some of these extremely busy periods seem to have lasted

EXHIBIT 9–37

**Model CSC.doe
Wait for Service
Tally Output
Processor
Histogram**

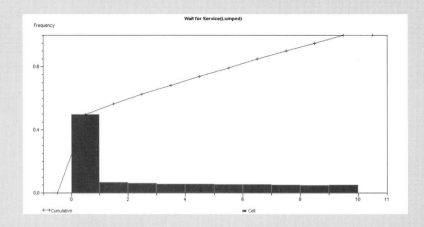

EXHIBIT 9–38

**Model CSC.doe

Wait for Service

Tally Output

Processor

Histogram

Summary**

Histogram Summary
Wait for Service(Lumped)

	Cell Limits		Abs. Freq.		Rel. Freq.	
Cell	From	To	Cell	Cumul.	Cell	Cumul.
1	-Infinity	0	0	0	0	0
2	0	1	3321	3321	0.497	0.497
3	1	2	458	3779	0.06854	0.5655
4	2	3	408	4187	0.06106	0.6266
5	3	4	371	4558	0.05552	0.6821
6	4	5	382	4940	0.05717	0.7393
7	5	6	367	5307	0.05492	0.7942
8	6	7	366	5673	0.05477	0.849
9	7	8	336	6009	0.05028	0.8993
10	8	9	332	6341	0.04969	0.949
11	9	10	341	6682	0.05103	1
12	10	+Infinity	0	6682	0	1

EXHIBIT 9–39
Model CSC.doe
Output Analyzer
Plots, Day 1—Shift
1 9:00 AM to 5:00 PM

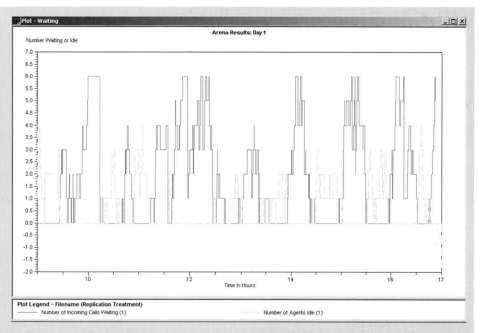

up to 30 minutes. Notice that shortly after 10:00 AM the number of waiting customers dropped from 6 to 0. Apparently all six customers had waited more than the maximum 10 minutes. They all were converted to the Entity.Aborted.Call type when the first agent became available. This is the shortcoming in the Arena CSC.doe model. The actual customer waiting time is not monitored on a continuous basis. The reader is encouraged to identify this shortcoming and attempt to develop an improved model.

Arena Experimentation Tools

The Arena simulation software provides two tools to assist the model user in seeking the best or optimal solution. The first is the Process Analyzer (PAN) that manually executes a set of user-specified model scenarios. The second is OptQuest that automatically seeks an optimal solution based on the objective and parameters specified by the model user.

Exhibit 9–40 illustrates the process required to use the Arena Process Analyzer.

Process Analyzer Results

We used the Arena Process Analyzer to conduct a series of simulation experiments by varying the number of lines and the maximum waiting time before abandoning the call. The number of lines was set to either 8 or 10. The maximum waiting time before abandoning the call was varied from 4 to 12 minutes in steps of 2 minutes. Exhibit 9–41 illustrates the PAN window setup to run the 10 scenarios with the appropriate Controls and Responses. A summary of the PAN results is illustrated in Exhibit 9–42.

Exhibit 9–42 indicates the profit and the values of the three design constraints:

1. Fraction Complete > 0.75.
2. Average Wait for Service < 2.00.
3. Fraction within Goal > 0.50.

The 10 scenarios are sorted by profit in descending order. The initial CSC.doe configuration (10 line and 10-minute wait) is highlighted on the worksheet. Infeasible values of the

EXHIBIT 9–40
Process Analyzer
Process Map
Page PAN tasks |
Chapter 9
Drawings.vsd

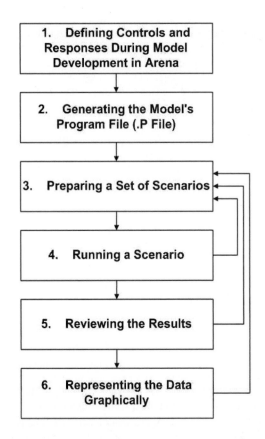

1. **Defining Controls and Responses During Model Development in Arena**

2. **Generating the Model's Program File (.P File)**

3. **Preparing a Set of Scenarios**

4. **Running a Scenario**

5. **Reviewing the Results**

6. **Representing the Data Graphically**

EXHIBIT 9–41
Model CSC.doe
Process Analyzer

	S	Scenario Properties			Controls		Responses			
		Name	Program File	Reps	Line	Max.Wait.Minutes	Profit	Fraction Complete	Fraction Within Goal	Wait for Service
1		Scenario 8 12	6 : CSC.p	5	8	12	2334.04	0.81	0.399	2.940
2		Scenario 8 10	6 : CSC.p	5	8	10	2094.34	0.79	0.409	2.440
3		Scenario 10 12	6 : CSC.p	5	10	12	2073.82	0.81	0.355	3.533
4		Scenario 10 10	6 : CSC.p	5	10	10	2004.90	0.82	0.407	2.680
5		Scenario 8 08	6 : CSC.p	5	8	8	1957.67	0.78	0.439	1.914
6		Scenario 10 08	6 : CSC.p	5	10	8	1703.11	0.79	0.421	2.106
7		Scenario 8 06	6 : CSC.p	5	8	6	1628.34	0.76	0.490	1.261
8		Scenario 10 06	6 : CSC.p	5	10	6	1424.40	0.77	0.480	1.355
9		Scenario 8 04	6 : CSC.p	5	8	4	1257.86	0.73	0.546	0.686
10		Scenario 10 04	6 : CSC.p	5	10	4	1032.55	0.74	0.536	0.728

constraint values are indicated in blue text. Unfortunately, all 10 test scenarios are infeasible because at least one of the system design constraints has been violated.

Exhibit 9–42 does provide some insight regarding this simulation model. The Fraction within the goal of service within one minute increases as the number of lines decreased. Service is started faster when more incoming calls are immediately lost for lack of a line. What does this finding do to your ideal for designing such a customer service center?

OptQuest Results

OptQuest is an add-in program to the Arena simulation software. OptQuest was developed by OptTek Systems and is incorporated into several different simulation software packages. The algorithms used by OptQuest are a trade secret but are designed to make multiple simulation runs and to select a search pattern to find the optimal solution.

The first step to use OptQuest is to develop, test, and validate your Arena model. Start with Arena model CSC.doe select OptQuest from the Tools menu. OptQuest checks the model to determine the parameters that may be included in the optimization search.

EXHIBIT 9–42
Model CSC.doe Process Analyzer Summary
Sheet PAN summary | Chapter 9 Worksheets.xls

Controls		Simulation Results 5-Week Averages			
Number of Lines	Maximum Wait Minutes	Goal Profit	Fraction Within Goal	Fraction Complete	Average Wait for Service
		Max	> 0.50	> 0.75	< 2.00
8	12	$2,334	0.40	0.81	2.94
8	10	$2,094	0.41	0.79	2.44
10	12	$2,074	0.36	0.81	3.53
10	10	$2,005	0.41	0.82	2.68
8	8	$1,958	0.44	0.78	1.91
10	8	$1,703	0.42	0.79	2.11
8	6	$1,628	0.49	0.76	1.26
10	6	$1,424	0.48	0.77	1.36
8	4	$1,258	0.55	0.73	0.69
10	4	$1,033	0.54	0.74	0.73

Next, specify the model controls and bounds to be varied when searching for the solution. Exhibit 9–43 illustrates the Controls selected for our search. We allowed the number of trunk lines to vary from 8 to 10 and the maximum wait time to vary from 4 to 12 minutes. We allowed only whole numbers for the maximum wait time to speed up the search process.

Next specify the optimization objective and the requirements for a feasible solution. Exhibit 9–44 illustrates the objective and requirements selected for our search. The objective is profit maximization. We have three requirements as illustrated in the process (Exhibit 9–44). OptQuest now has the information required to start its search.

Exhibits 9–45 and 9–46 indicate the general search path used by OptQuest. OptQuest attempts to immediately eliminate infeasible solutions. The best solution was found in the 11th simulation run. It appears from the performance graph that OptQuest tried several other potential solutions after the 11th simulation run but found none with a greater profit. We constructed Exhibit 9–47 using the OptQuest log file. This worksheet shows the optimization on

EXHIBIT 9–43
Model CSC.doe OptQuest Controls Window

Control Selection: Select controls and set bounds.

Select	Control	Lower Bound	Suggested Value	Upper Bound	Type	Category
☑	Line	8	10	10	Discrete (1)	Resource
☑	Max.Wait.Minutes	4	10	12	Discrete (1)	Variable
☐	Agent	1	2	3	Discrete (1)	Resource
☐	Faction.Within.Goal	0	0	0	Continuous	Variable

Reorder | OK | Cancel | Help

EXHIBIT 9–44
Model CSC.doe OptQuest Objective and Requirements Window

Objective and Requirement Selection: Select an objective and any requirements (reqs. must have a bound).

Select	Response	Lower Bound	Upper Bound	Value
Maximize Objective	Profit			Final
Requirement	Faction.Within.Goal	.5		Final
Requirement	Fraction Complete	.75		Final
Requirement	Wait for Service		2	Average
No	Agent.BusyCost			Final

Reorder | OK | Cancel | Help

EXHIBIT 9–45
Model CSC.doe
OptQuest Summary

			Optimization is Complete			
Simulatio	Maximize Profit	Requirement Faction.Within.Goal .5 <= Value	Requirement Fraction Complete .75 <= Value	Requirement Wait for Service Value <= 2	Line	Max.Wait.Minutes
1	2004.90	0.407371 - Infeasible	0.817418	2.67987 - Infeasible	10	10
2	1787.19	0.425151 - Infeasible	0.783215	2.01690 - Infeasible	9	8
3	1257.86	0.545617	0.731488 - Infeasible	0.686136	8	4
Best: 11	1241.62	0.514870	0.755686	0.984303	10	5

EXHIBIT 9–46
Model CSC.doe
OptQuest
Performance Graph

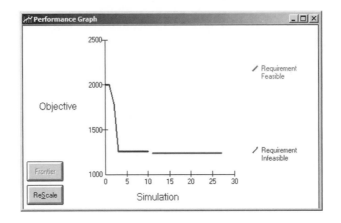

EXHIBIT 9–47
Model CSC.doe
OptQuest Log
Summary
Sheet OptQuest log
summary | Chapter 9
Worksheets.xls

	Controls		Simulation Results 5-Week Averages			
Simulation	Number of Lines	Maximum Wait Minutes	Goal Profit	Fraction Within Goal	Fraction Complete	Average Wait for Service
			Max	> 0.50	> 0.75	< 2.00
1	10	10	$2,005	0.41 - Infeasible	0.82	2.68 - Infeasible
2	9	8	$1,787	0.43 - Infeasible	0.78	2.02 - Infeasible
3	8	4	$1,258	0.55	0.73 - Infeasible	0.69
4	10	12	$2,074	0.36 - Infeasible	0.81	3.53 - Infeasible
5	10	4	$1,033	0.54	0.74 - Infeasible	0.73
6	8	11	$2,196	0.41 - Infeasible	0.79	2.67 - Infeasible
7	9	12	$2,284	0.39 - Infeasible	0.82	3.13 - Infeasible
8	9	4	$1,164	0.55	0.74 - Infeasible	0.69
9	10	7	$1,659	0.47 - Infeasible	0.79	1.61
10	8	8	$1,958	0.44 - Infeasible	0.78	1.91
11	10	5	$1,242	0.51	0.76	0.98
12	9	5	$1,313	0.51	0.75 - Infeasible	0.98
13	10	6	$1,424	0.48 - Infeasible	0.77	1.35
14	9	9	$1,950	0.42 - Infeasible	0.80	2.30 - Infeasible
15	10	8	$1,703	0.42 - Infeasible	0.79	2.11 - Infeasible
16	10	11	$2,120	0.40 - Infeasible	0.83	2.92 - Infeasible
17	10	9	$1,902	0.43 - Infeasible	0.81	2.34 - Infeasible
18	9	7	$1,687	0.45 - Infeasible	0.78	1.68
19	8	12	$2,334	0.40 - Infeasible	0.81	2.94 - Infeasible
20	8	5	$1,453	0.51	0.74 - Infeasible	0.96
21	8	7	$1,742	0.47 - Infeasible	0.77	1.57
22	8	10	$2,094	0.41 - Infeasible	0.79	2.44 - Infeasible
23	9	6	$1,629	0.50 - Infeasible	0.78	1.29
24	9	10	$2,131	0.40 - Infeasible	0.81	2.68 - Infeasible
25	8	9	$2,168	0.44 - Infeasible	0.81	2.13 - Infeasible
26	9	11	$2,218	0.39 - Infeasible	0.82	2.93 - Infeasible
27	8	6	$1,628	0.49 - Infeasible	0.76	1.26

a step-by-step basis. Notice that simulation run 11 was the only solution that satisfied all three requirements or constraints.

Experimentation Postscript

The control variables or experimentation parameters were the number of lines and maximum customer wait. From a practical sense, limiting the number of lines seems to have little impact because lines only cost $1.00 per hour compared to $10.00 per hour for agents. Secondly, how could the customer service center actually go about limiting the maximum customer wait time?

In actual practice, the experimentation presented above has used the wrong control variables or experimentation parameters because these were easy to do, but not those that really have an impact on the system performance. The staffing pattern illustrated in Exhibit 9–21 is the control factor that should be varied to find the best or optimal solution. Unfortunately, neither the Process Analyzer nor OptQuest has a means to vary directly an Arena Schedule as we used to model the staffing pattern.

Full experimentation would require the development of several models each with different staffing patterns. We leave that model development to the reader. In actual practice, the number of different staffing patterns can grow quickly, if we permit flexible work shifts. For example, we may want to have one of the day shift agents start work at 8:00 AM rather than the original 9:00 AM. This may also require an earlier schedule for one of the second shift agents.

A starting point for this detailed level of agent schedule development might be an analysis based on the number of waiting customers on an hourly basis. Arena CSC.doe model could be modified to provide that type of information.

Challenge

Arena Contact Center Edition

A demonstration version for the Arena Contact Center Edition is supplied with Arena 5.0. The Arena Contact Center Edition is designed as a special purpose simulator for modeling a customer service center system like that presented in this chapter. The Arena Contact Center Edition comprises two special-purpose template panels: Contact Data and Script, as well as a set of example models.

Smart File CSmart01.doe

A basic contact or call center model, Smart File CSmart01.doe, illustrates the basic structure of the Arena Contact Center Edition modeling environment. The Arena Contact Center Edition model CSmart01.doe screen display is illustrated in Exhibit 9-48.

The planning horizon for this model is one week. Calls enter the center and are queued for a customer service agent. If the caller has waited more than 10 minutes, the caller hangs up (is disconnected).

The user can navigate through the model by pressing the numeric keys; 1, 2, 3, and so forth, and read the following model descriptions.

1. The parameters for the basic calls are defined in the Call and Call Pattern modules. Calls utilize the trunk line. We expect the average talk time for a basic call to be 10 minutes (i.e., EXPO(10)).
2. The arrival stream for basic calls is assumed to be evenly distributed over the center's operational hours (Monday through Friday, 9 AM–5 PM).
3. There are 10 lines available for the trunk line. After a call successfully enters the call center, it is routed to the basic script.
4. The basic script specifies that a call queues up for a customer service agent. Calls wait 10 minutes and then hang up (disconnect) if they haven't been serviced.
5. There are four members in the customer service staff. Each member follows the basic schedule.
6. The customer service staff is available 9 AM to 5 PM, Monday through Friday.

EXHIBIT 9–48
Smart File Model
CSmart01.doe
Network Logic Flow

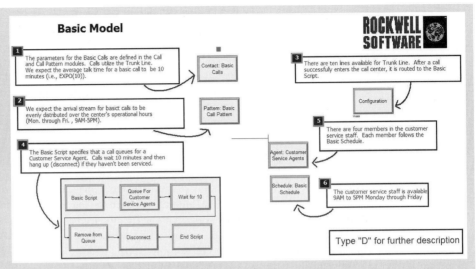

This model uses three Arena panels: Basic Process, Contact Data, and Script. The latter two are specific to the Arena Contact Center Edition software.

The Contact Data panel of the Arena Contact Center Edition include following modules: Agent, Animate, Call, Call Pattern, Configuration, Report, and Schedule. Except for Animate and Report modules, all Arena Contact Center Edition Data panel modules must be used to define an Arena Contact Center Edition model. The Call module defines the expected call processing time of 10 minutes with an exponential distribution. The Call Pattern module defines the expected call arrival pattern in terms of expected calls per hour for each hour of the week. The Configuration module defines the simulation run length and the number of trunk lines. The Agent module defines the number of agents and their scheduled work periods. The Schedule module defines the agent work schedules.

The Script panel of the Arena Contact Center Edition template includes following modules: Begin Script, Queue for Agent, Remove from Queue, Wait, Priority, Message, Disconnect, Overflow, Transfer to Script, Transfer to Agent, Conference, Branch, Assignment, and End Script. The Script panel modules are used to define the sequence of operations that each call passes through. For the CSmart01.doe model, this script included the following modules: Begin Script (names script), Queue for Agent (identifies agent), Wait (defines maximum wait time), Remove from Queue, Disconnect, and End Script.

EXHIBIT 9–49
Smart File Model
CSmart01.doe
Crystal Report
Display

Agent Group Summary

Usage

	Available	Busy	Est On Duty	Utilization
Customer Service	0.51	3.58	4.00	89.49

Cost

	Busy Cost	Idle Cost	Per Use Cost
Customer Service	0.00	0.00	0.00

Inbound and Outbound Utilization

	Inbound Util	Outbound Util
Customer Service Agents	89.49	0.00

Agent Utilization per Contact Type

	Call	Email	Fax	Other	Web Hit
Customer Service	89.49	0.00	0.00	0.00	0.00

Agent Utilization per Contact Name

	Util per Type
Customer Service Agents Basic Calls	89.49

Model CSmart01 simulates one week of Call Center operation. Exhibit 9–49 illustrates the simulation results as displayed by Arena's Crystal Reports database.

Two basic types of simulation results are available for this introductory model, Trunk Summary and Agent Group Summary.

The Trunk Summary indicates the utilization of the 10 trunk lines over the entire week (168 hours or 10,080 minutes). Because calls were only scheduled to arrive over a 40-hour period of the week (Monday through Friday, 9 AM–5 PM), the trunk line statistics are somewhat misleading. An average of 1.29 lines were in use, while 8.71 were idle for an overutilization of 12.88 percent. A more meaningful statistic could be obtained by weighting these statistics with 40 ÷ 168 = 23.8 percent, the scheduled operating time per week. The trunk line utilization during this period can be calculated as 1.29 ÷ 0.238 = 5.42 lines or 54.2 percent.

The Agent Group Summary indicates utilization of four agents' lines over their scheduled 40 hours. On an average, 3.58 agents were busy for an overall utilization of 89.5 percent. This basic model did not include costing information and only involved inbound calls.

Arena Contact Center Edition Model

We have modified model file CSmart01.doe to develop the CSC ACCE.doe model file. The major difference in the two models is the introduction of the call arrival rates developed previously in this chapter. Exhibit 9–50 illustrates the Daily Arrival Pattern dialog with the input data for Monday. This dialog is part of the Call Pattern module of the Contact Data panel. Notice that the Arena Contact Center Edition provides the tools to vary the call arrival rate on an hourly or a half-hourly basis for each day of the week. Model CSC ACCE.doe is available on the textbook's CD-ROM.

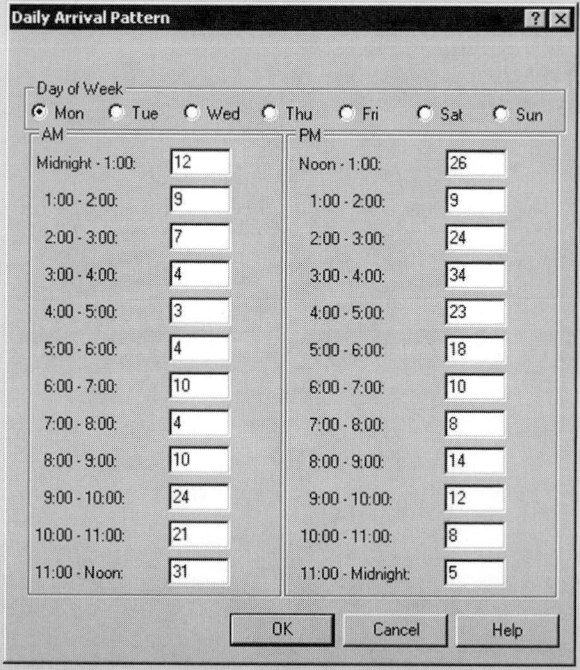

Exhibit 9–51 presents the Arena results for a five-week simulation using model file CSC ACCE.doe. The results presented in Exhibit 9–51 should be compared to those presented in Exhibit 9–32. One significant model difference should be noted. CSC.doe model only simulated the weekdays (Monday through Friday), while CSC ACCE.doe model simulated the entire seven-day week. The staffing was not reduced during the weekends in spite of an expected lower call volume.

Arena Contact Center Edition Concepts

The Arena Contact Center Edition, a special edition of Arena, focuses on contact or call center organizations. Rockwell Software sells the Arena Contact Center Edition as a separate product. However, limited-sized test models can be tested using the standard version of Arena.

Exhibit 9–52 lists the first few Arena Contact Center Edition Smart files. Notice that the user can selectively view this worksheet using the Excel filtering tool.

Exhibit 9–53 lists the first few Arena Contact Center Edition Example model files. Each of these Arena model files are too large to be modified and saved in the demonstration version of Arena. However, the Arena user can view the entire model structure.

EXHIBIT 9–50 **Model CSC ACCE.doe Daily Arrival Pattern Dialog**

EXHIBIT 9–51
Model CSC ACCE.doe Simulation Results Summary
Sheet ACCE summary | Chapter 9 Worksheets.xls

CSC ACCE.doe	Week 1		Week 2		Week 3		Week 4		Week 5		5-Week Averages	
Incoming Calls	2,084		2,106		2,158		2,129		2,139		2,123	
Calls Complete	1,690	81.1%	1,717	81.5%	1,770	82.0%	1,692	79.5%	1,680	78.5%	1,710	80.5%
Calls Aborted	356	17.1%	350	16.6%	349	16.2%	380	17.8%	398	18.6%	367	17.3%
Calls Lost	38	1.8%	38	1.8%	38	1.8%	55	2.6%	60	2.8%	46	2.2%
Calls Answered < 1 min	876	42.0%	844	40.1%	912	42.3%	782	36.7%	748	35.0%	832	39.2%

EXHIBIT 9–52

Arena Contact Center Edition Smart Files

Sheet CSmart | Chapter 9 Worksheets.xls

Arena Smart files, a collection of small example models that demonstrate a variety of modeling techniques and situations commonly encountered using Arena Contact Center Template

Smart files have been specifically designed for use as a training or reference tool.

These Smart model files are located in the Smarts folder within the main Arena folder:

..\Program Files\Rockwell Software\Arena\Smarts\ContactCenter

Model Name (*.DOE)	Application	Description
CSmart01	Basic	This example shows a basic contact center with a one-week planning horizon Calls enter the center and are queued for a Customer Service Agent If the caller waits for more than 10 minutes, it hangs up (is disconnected)
CSmart02	Abandonment	Call abandonment is illustrated in this example After calls enter the center, they queue for a Customer Service Agent If the call waits for more than its abandon wait time (specified in the Call module), the call will abandon The Call Times and Counts report shows the number of abandoned calls
CSmart03	Transfer	Support calls enter the system and are handled by agents from the general staff Of these calls, 40% are typically transferred either to the advanced support staff or to the sales staff Of these, distribution is split 60% to the advanced support staff and 40% to the sales staff Calls are only transferred to the sales staff if a member of that staff is available If a member of the advanced support staff is not available, the call may leave a message Agent transfer is specified in the call script using the Transfer to Agent module
CSmart04	Conference	In this conference example, twenty-five percent of the support calls that are handled by the general support staff will require a conference with either a member of the advanced support staff or a supervisor If no member of the advanced support staff or a supervisor is available, the conference will not occur

EXHIBIT 9–53

Arena Contact Center Edition Example Model Files

Sheet examples | Chapter 9 Worksheets.xls

Arena Example files, a collection of small example models that demonstrate a variety of modeling techniques and situations commonly encountered using Arena Contact Center Template

Example files have been specifically designed for use as a training or reference tool.

These Example mode files are located in the Examples folder within the main Arena folder:

..\Program Files\Rockwell Software\Arena\Examples\ContactCenter

Model Name (*.DOE)	Description
Bank	This Contact Center example model depicts various transactions and activities at a bank. Specifically three call type activities are modeled: 1. Savings Account Transactions 2. Checking Account Transactions 3. Account Balance Transactions Online statistics are maintained on the number of calls waiting to be answered, as well as the waiting time for each type of transaction.
BaseLineAllSites	Five-Cities National model
Bilingual	The Bilingual example models a call center that serves an English and Spanish population with three types of agents. This model can be used to analyze staffing levels and the value of bilingual agents under different demand forecasts. The types of agents are: 1. English-speaking 2. Spanish-speaking 3. Bilingual The focus of the example is on agent and parent groups, and the call abandonment and call back capabilities.

The basic process of the Arena Contact Center Edition simulation is to generate a stream of arriving contacts, assign them to trunk lines, and route them through the center to an agent. To create a simulation model of a contact center or network of contact centers, the model builder describes the sequence of events that occur as contacts move through the system, from the arrival of the contact at the contact center to successful resolution. The model builder needs to specify information about the contact center itself (trunk line capacity, agent schedules, etc.).

As the Arena Contact Center Edition model is built, it may be helpful to keep in mind the Contact Center Core Process. The basic components of this process are

- Calls
- Call arrival patterns
- Trunk groups
- Routing scripts
- Schedules
- Agents

The relationships between the Arena Contact Center Edition Modeling components are illustrated in Exhibit 9–54.

In addition, the length of the simulation run, *planning horizon,* and granularity of data specification and collection, *time slots,* needs to be specified. Animation and performance measure reporting are also important components of Arena Contact Center Edition models.

**EXHIBIT 9–54   Arena Contact Center Edition Modeling
Components**

Page modeling components | Chapter 9 Drawings.vsd

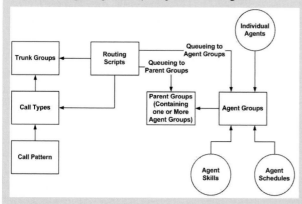

Planning Horizon

The planning horizon is defined as the time period that is being examined by a particular simulation model. The planning horizon is typically one day, one week, two weeks, or one month.

Time Slots

The planning horizon is broken into specific time slots for data specification and collection. These intervals are typically 30 minutes or 1 hour long.

In Arena Contact Center Edition, the minute is the basic unit of time. With the exception of the planning horizon, trunk costs, agent costs, and contact service level, all inputs are in terms of minutes or fractions of minutes.

Call Types

Describing different types of calls is generally the starting point for contact center modeling and analysis. Each call type represents a particular customer request for agent services. The expected talk time, as well as the associated call arrival pattern and the trunk group on which the calls enter the center characterize it. The following more advanced aspects of call behavior may also be modeled in Arena Contact Center Edition:

- Abandonment
- After call work
- Prioritization
- Call back
- Call return
- Outbound calls

Information about call volumes is typically taken from business forecasts and expected talk time is available, either from contact center automated call distribution (ACD) databases or from a call tracking system.

Call Arrival Pattern

Call patterns describe the arrival of calls across the planning horizon by specifying the distribution of calls across each time slot. Within the Call Pattern module, this distribution is specified in terms of expected call counts for each time slot.

The arrival times of calls within the time slot are randomly generated according to a Poisson process with the defined rate. Therefore, the actual number of calls arriving within the time slot may differ from the expected number.

For example, suppose that the planning horizon is one day (24 hours) and the time slots are 60 minutes long. Then, if the call arrival pattern specifies that 240 calls are handled during the 10:00 AM to 11:00 AM time slot, the simulation model would assume 240 expected calls during the 10:00 AM to 11:00 AM time slot. The Poisson arrival rate for the time slot is 0.25 (60/240) or one call every 15 seconds.

Call arrival pattern data is available either from contact center ACD databases or from a call tracking system.

Trunk Groups

Trunk groups represent groups of phone lines that are dedicated to a particular set of call types. A single trunk group can serve multiple call types, but one trunk group can only serve each call type. Trunk groups have an associated capacity (number of lines), cost, and a default routing script and call priority. Any incoming call type assumes the default priority and follows the default routing script unless these attributes are overridden at the call level.

Note that trunk line capacity determines maximum number of calls that the contact center can accommodate simultaneously. If a trunk line is not available when a call attempts to enter the center, the call is blocked and does not gain entry. Otherwise, the call is attached to a trunk line and remains with that particular line until it exits the center or until it is transferred to another trunk line.

A fundamental component of the contact center infrastructure, trunk line organization, and capacity are determined in the phone switching hardware.

Routing Scripts

Routing scripts are sequences of actions that control the flow of calls through the center's phone system. This will result in calls being connected with agents, leaving messages, being disconnected, or abandoning the center.

From a simulation modeling perspective, scripts allow call flow logic to be categorized into six general areas:

1. Time delays (playing announcements, music, doing nothing—waiting)
2. Conditional route branching (caller entered information, center dynamics)
3. Allocation of calls into queues (single or simultaneous) or message ports
4. Call prioritization within queues (ranking)
5. Call flow between queues (movement of calls out of and into queues, overflow)
6. Call flow between scripts

These command sequences are generally referred to as "scripts," although each switch vendor has a different name for their particular variety. These scripts specify the actions, activities, and state that each call undergoes as it attempts to reach an agent.

Agent Skill Sets

Agent skill sets define how particular call types are processed. An agent's repertoire of call handling skills specifies what call types the agent is skilled to handle, the priority (or order) in which the agent will perform available work, and the agent's proficiency in each call type, expressed as a multiplier of average talk time for the call type.

Estimates of call handling proficiency may be obtained from careful study of handle time statistics collected from the ACD database or call tracking system, or based on the expertise of group managers. For example, a group of experienced agents may have a very high proficiency level, while a group of newly hired agents may experience significantly higher handle times.

Similarly, agent transfer and conference data may be available through the ACD database or through a manager's or supervisor's understanding of call handling policies and tendencies.

Schedules

Schedules dictate when agents are available to handle calls. Each schedule specifies on-duty shifts for each day in the planning horizon. In addition to phone time, these schedules can include lunches, breaks, meetings, or other on-duty time that is spent away from the phones.

Agent Groups

Agents are the primary resource of the contact center. An agent group represents a group of agents within the contact center that have the same skill sets and follow the same schedule. From a modeling perspective, an agent group is a set of identical agents. In building a model, the key questions to answer regarding agent groups are the following:

- How many agents are in this group?
- What hours do these agents work?
- What types of calls can an agent of this type handle, and in what priority order?
- How long does it take for these agents to handle each type of call?

The definition of agent groups may depend on the purpose of the simulation study and will not necessarily correspond to the group definition within the organization. However, the agent lists and skill sets maintained by the Human Resources or Planning and Analysis group is a good starting point.

Parent Groups

A parent group is a collection of agent groups. Parent groups are used to

- Implement simultaneous queuing.
- Simplify routing scripts by masking the underlying complexity of agent group definitions (multiple schedules, sites, groups, etc.).
- Collect statistics across agent groups.

Parent groups typically support call routing and their definition may depend on the purpose of the simulation study. However, if a model is being made of current contact center operations, insight into parent groupings may be obtained from an examination of existing routing scripts.

Queues

Call queues are the mechanism by which calls and agents interact in the contact center. Each agent group has a queue associated with it to hold its calls while they wait to be handled. Calls may move from one queue (i.e., one agent group) to another before being serviced, based upon the routing script that is assigned to that call type.

Note that while queues are an important concept to understand, the data and logic associated with call queues is specified in the Agent module and related modules located on the script panel (e.g., Queue for Agent module, Transfer to Agent module, etc.).

Animation

Simulation animation is intended to provide dynamic graphical insight into contact center conditions. A variety of plots, charts, and counters are available to animate specific contact center elements. These animations are often useful for validation and verification of the contact center model.

Performance Measures/Reporting

In addition to default reports covering the entire planning horizon, there are focused reports that collect and report data by user-defined time slot. These results quantify the impact of various changes on contact center operations. Arena Contact Center Edition Crystal Reports are available for

- Call counts
- Call times
- Agent utilization
- Trunk utilization
- Overflow

Arena Contact Center Edition Templates

The Arena Contact Center Edition is supplied by Rockwell Software in the form of two special-purpose template panels: ContactData.tpo and Script.tpo. In addition, two other files must present to use the Arena Contact Center Edition: CSUtil.tpo and callsimrules.dll. All of theses files are normally loaded when Arena is installed.

Template Panel ContactData provides modules for defining the call or contact center being modeled. Template Panel Script provides modules for defining how calls are processed. Exhibit 9–55 lists the first Arena Contact Center Edition Module. Notice that the user can selectively view this worksheet using the Excel filtering tool.

EXHIBIT 9–55

Arena Contact Center Edition Modules

Sheet ACCE modules | Chapter 9 Worksheets.xls

Panel	Module	Main Topic	Remarks
Contact Data	Configuration	The Configuration module's purpose is to specify the layout of the contact center to be simulated. The simulation planning horizon and all trunk groups applicable to the contact center are defined.	One and only one Configuration module must be defined for each simulation model. The Planning Horizon defined within the Configuration module determines the length (in minutes) of the simulation run. The Priorities and Scripts defined at the Trunk Group level are provided as defaults for the Calls using those trunk lines. Overrides of these attributes may be specified at the Call level. The advanced functionality dealing with replications and system initialization is detailed in the Replicate Element. In very large models, the Maximum number of Agent Groups may need to be increased accordingly. The simulation begins at time 0.0, which in calendar time is Monday at midnight.
Contact Data	Schedule	The Schedule module defines schedules to which agents can be assigned. The schedule is based on the planning horizon and timeslot structure, with an agent availability state associated with each timeslot.	By default, all timeslots are initialized to an Off-Duty availability state. Therefore, agent shifts need only be defined for those time intervals that are not Off-Duty.

Exercises

1. Describe a recent personal call center experience. Indicate how your experience might have been improved.

2. Develop a process map for calls entering your place of business or any organization that you are personally familiar with. Indicate how calls are routed or transferred to operators or individuals with more experience or knowledge. Suggest possible process improvements.

3. Envision a new business organization that you plan to start. How could a call center be used to support the business's customer service requirements? How many hours per week would the call center need to be staffed? Could all or part of this operation be contracted to an outside agency?

4. Using model CSC.doe as a starting point, develop a method to determine the number of lost and aborted calls by hour of the day.

5. Use the results determined in exercise 4 to develop at least three alternative staffing patterns and test their effectiveness using model CSC.doe model.

Challenge

6. Using model CSC ACCE.doe as a starting point, develop a method to determine the number lost and aborted calls by hour of the day.

7. Use the results determined in exercise 6 to develop at least three alternative staffing patterns and test their effectiveness using model CSC ACCE.doe.

Process Analysis and Improvement Application: Supply Chain Management

Summary and Learning Objectives

This chapter introduces process analysis and improvement techniques used to study the supply chain for major global organizations and to present a Beer Game simulation model used to demonstrate a multiple-level supply chain.

The learning objectives for this chapter are to

1. Learn how to view a product supply chain from a process perspective.
2. Develop a consumer product supply chain flow model using Visio.
3. Develop and test various what-if business decision scenarios using Beer Game simulation models.

Process Improvement, a Supply Chain Perspective

Many business organizations are involved in establishing the best supply chains for their products. This is part of a campaign to improve and integrate business processes across various business partners forming the chain. New technology has an impact on the selection of an effective product supply chain. A good example is the impact of new printing technology on the book supply chain. New printing technology, such as the DocuTech system, lowers the point of entry for printing on demand.

Today, many books are created, edited, stored, and printed electronically. This means that it is possible to redesign the book supply chain. Instead of printing books in large numbers and distributing them through a network of distributors to retailers, it is possible for the publisher to print on demand in the bookstore or the online retailer's shipping center.

The impact of the supply chain redesign is to increase the product range that can be offered by an individual retailer, but also to reduce the delivery lead time and price—especially for specialty and professional titles. However, printing on demand in the bookstore or in the online retailer's shipping center is simply doing what the conventional supply chain does, only faster and cheaper for a wider range of titles.

Here, one can do much more. One can also change the value offering. McGraw-Hill has used the print-on-demand supply chain to enable instructors of college courses to tailor their own textbooks—textbooks that fit each instructor's personal teaching technique, style, pace, course content, and organization. The new value offering is in addition to the speed and price advantage from print on demand. The textbook is available in the campus bookstore within 10 days, instead of up to 10 weeks for textbooks through the conventional supply chain. The student pays only for text that is required for course study.

Exhibit 10-1 illustrates the custom textbook supply chain provided by Primis Custom Publishing. This supply chain offers the instructor the ability to customize the textbook for each course and to provide the material on a demand basis from the campus bookstore. Students benefit by receiving only the desired course material at a reasonable price.

Holmstrom et al. (1999) use the concept of value engineering to find not only the best supply chain for the product, but also the right value offering for the customer. They state that in a conventional chain, the supplier focuses on winning the customer's purchase, that is, he competes on price, delivery, and product range; whereas successful demand–supply chain shapers have moved beyond only offering products for purchase. For instance, the cost efficiency of Dell's direct model is well-known, but what may be less understood is that the efficiency is enabled by Dell Computer's value-added offerings to the end users in the businesses buying direct. For example, a PC can be delivered directly to an employee's desk in a collaborating customer company and switched on. No PC technician is needed to install company software and configure the PC to the network. Dell has already done this in the assembly plant. In short, business customers reduce their information technology (IT) support cost by sharing openly their system configuration with Dell, and the costs for Dell are reduced by assembling to specific customer demand. This is partly because direct delivery eliminates obsolescence costs, but also because electronic components' prices fall at a quick rate, so purchasing components later significantly lowers the costs of goods sold.

Successful companies do not just add value, but they are able to reinvent it. To succeed in innovating value, a company must abandon the perspective that each supply chain member performs a distinct value-adding task, and instead regard both suppliers and customer as potential coproducers of value. The question here is how do you become your customer's coproducer of value? That is, how do you improve and integrate business processes within a supplier company by recognizing its customer's portion of the supply chain, which is referred to in the literature as the *demand chain?* The demand chain transfers demand from markets to suppliers. For example, *prospecting,* specifying the product and making the purchase is a simple demand chain for a consumer. For a retailer, the demand chain would consist of merchandising, inventory management, and purchasing. This approach enables a company to actively pursue opportunities to improve its own operations by improving its customer's business.

EXHIBIT 10–1
Primis Custom Publishing Textbook Supply Chain
Page Primis Custom Publishing | Chapter 10 Drawings.vsd

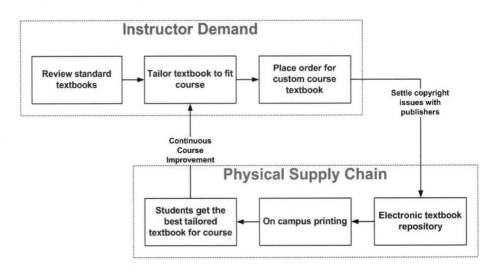

Integrated Supply Chain Management

During the past few years, supply chain–excellence, optimization, and integration have become the focus and goal of many organizations worldwide. This is because progressive firms are focusing on revenue growth instead of merely striving to meet annual cost reduction targets. Strengthening management of the supply chain is perceived by many firms as enhancing customer satisfaction and enabling profitable growth (Advance Manufacturing Research, 1997).

Depending on why and how the supply chain concept has been applied to problem solving, it has come to signify independent evaluation and/or implementation of one or more of the following characteristics:

1. An arrangement of suppliers of products and services.
2. A network for efficient management of demand and flow of products and services.
3. A philosophy of conducting business.
4. A strategy to gain competitive advantage through coordination and synchronization of actions of its members.

This is primarily due to a lack of awareness of techniques available for implementing structural components of a supply chain (such as represented by characteristics 1, 2, and 3 above) with its functional components (such as represented by characteristic 4 above).

The rest of this chapter integrates the basic tenets of supply chain generic structures with common attributes of functional strategies, such as reduction in inventory, lead time, and safety stock. This is the *fundamental change* that we propose in our framework, to an application of the concept of supply chain for problem solving. By taking a historical perspective on supply chains we trace the emergence of this enterprise integration concept. We then describe the supply chain management philosophy derived from an analysis of this perspective. Following this, we present examples of strategies employed for solving supply chain problems, which led to our framework. We note the implications of this research on supply chain management issues. Finally, the chapter demonstrates a supply chain simulation model using the widely known Beer Game.

A Historical Perspective on Supply Chain

In order to understand the significance of changes taking place in supply chain initiatives, it would be prudent to review historical aspects of production and operations management activities (Bruce, 1997; Poirier and Reiter, 1996).

During the period from 1960 to 1975, corporations had vertical organization structures and optimization of activities was focused on functions. Relationships with vendors were win–lose interactions and were often adversarial. Manufacturing systems were focused on Materials Requirements Planning (MRP).

In the time frame of 1975 to 1990, corporations were still vertically aligned, but several were involved in process mapping and analysis to evaluate their operations. Organizations realized the benefit of integrating functions such as product design and manufacturing. Various quality initiatives, such as the Total Quality Management philosophies of Deming, Juran, and Crosby; and ISO Standards for quality measurement were initiated by many organizations. The Malcolm Baldridge Award and Shingo Prize for recognizing excellence in these and other quality initiatives were initiated. Manufacturing systems were focused on MRP II.

Starting in 1990, corporations all over the world have been experiencing increasing national and international competition. Strategic alliances among organizations have been growing. Organization structures are starting to align with processes. Manufacturing systems in organizations have been enhanced with IT tools such as enterprise resource planning, distribution requirements planning, electronic commerce, product data management, and collaborative engineering, among others (Aberdeen, 1996). Design for disassembly, synchronous manufacturing, and agile manufacturing are some of the new paradigms in manufacturing. There has been a growing appreciation in many firms of total cost focus for a product from its source to consumption, as opposed to extracting the lowest price from immediate vendor(s) (Turbide, 1997). There has also been an increased reliance on purchased materials and outside processing with a simultaneous reduction in the number of suppliers and greater sharing of information between vendors and customers. A noticeable shift has taken place in the marketplace from mass production to customized products. This has resulted in an emphasis on greater organizational and process flexibility and coordination of processes across many sites. More and more organizations are promoting employee empowerment and the need for rules-based, real-time decision support systems to attain organizational and process flexibility as well as to respond to competitive pressure to introduce new products more quickly, cheaply, and of improved quality.

The underlying philosophy of managing supply chains has evolved to respond to these changing business trends. Supply chain management phenomenon has received the attention of researchers and practitioners in various topics. In the earlier years, the emphasis was on materials planning, utilizing materials requirements planning techniques, inventory logistics management with one wholesaler multiretailer distribution system, and push-and-pull operation techniques for production systems. In the last few years, however, there has been a renewed interest in designing and implementing integrated systems, such as enterprise resource planning, multi-echelon inventory, and synchronous-flow manufacturing, respectively. A number of factors have contributed to this shift. First, there has been a realization that better planning and management of complex interrelated systems, such as materials planning, inventory management, capacity planning, logistics, and production systems will lead to overall improvement in enterprise productivity. Second, advances in information and communication technologies complemented by sophisticated decision support systems enable designing, implementing, and controlling strategic and tactical strategies essential to the delivery of integrated systems. The availability of such systems has the potential of fundamentally influencing enterprise integration issues. The motivation in presenting this section is to propose a *framework* that enables dealing with such issues in supply chain effectively.

Our approach in utilizing supply chain philosophy for enterprise integration proposes domain-independent problem solving and modeling, and domain-dependent analysis and implementation. The purpose of the approach is to ascertain characteristics of the problem independent of the specific problem environment. Consequently, the approach delivers solution(s) or the solution method that is intrinsic to the problem and not its environment. Analysis methods help to understand characteristics of the solution methodology as well as to provide specific guarantees of effectiveness. Invariably, insights gained from these analyses can be used to develop effective problem-solving tools and techniques for complex enterprise integration problems.

Our objective in this section is to make a case for a supply chain management philosophy utilizing such an approach. The next section provides practical examples of supply chain management philosophies.

Supply Chain Management Philosophy

To balance customers' demands with the need for profitable growth, many firms moved aggressively to improve supply chain management (Advance Manufacturing Research, 1995; Andersen et al., 1997; Copacino, 1997; and Poirier and Reiter, 1996). Their channel integration efforts have focused on following main issues, such as

- Organizational structures and associated relationships.
- Supply chain coordination.
- Inter and intra enterprise communication.
- Sourcing.
- Manufacturing orientation.
- Inventory and cost management.

We describe each of these issues next.

1. Flexible Organizations

An important attribute for any supplier is agility realized through its flexible organization. A flexible organization of a firm supports plant and distribution networks by achieving operational efficiency through quick line changeovers, as well as savings realized as a result of avoiding back hauling, and enhanced product realization.

As firms move to supply chain excellence, they are concerned with both internal and external efficiencies. Internal efficiency, the key driving force to supply chain operational efficiency is agility, rather than economies of size. Investments in plant and distribution equipment are important to maintain an agile organization in a supply chain. Externally, supplier efficiency is extremely critical to supply chain performance.

2. Organizational Relationships

Strategic alliances and partnerships are crucial to the success of a supply chain. Firms are encouraged to focus their attention on the entire supply chain and to reduce the number of suppliers with whom they have to deal. Many firms have developed preferred supplier programs as well as core transport carriers to ensure that a quality product is received where and when it is needed.

A successful strategic alliance or a partnership must be based on extreme trust, loyalty, positive sum game (a win-win relationship), cross-functional teams, sharing common goals and cooperation that includes willingness to assist, and positive negotiations based on fairness.

3. Total Supply Chain Coordination

Each firm may have multiple supply chains and each of these may have potentially different business needs. It is important to employ cross-channel coordination when sharing some of the common resources among different supply chains. This coordination allows supply chains in a company to integrate with each other (Francett, 1996; Fraser, 1997; Gould, 1998; Harlend and Scharlacken, 1997).

Creating supply chain value is important for successful coordination. The most important single factor in creating supply chain value is the ability to predict or forecast demand. The goal for total coordination is to be demand driven, not lot-size driven. This implies that suppliers should supply products according to demand and not lot quotas.

In the past, forecasting was done primarily by utilizing historical data. Firms are moving away from this method and beginning to use point of sale data, which tells them exactly how much was purchased during a certain time frame (Costanza, 1998; Davis, 1993; Fisher et al., 1994; Fraser, 1998).

4. Improved Communications

Both uncertainty and inventory levels are lowered through improved communications "within" and "between" supply chain constituents. A successful customer–vendor relationship is built by the exchanging of information pertaining to product development for new products, product improvements, costs, demand schedules including point-of-sale data, and materials and supplies needed to meet production schedules.

It is crucial to relay information about end-use consumers to manufacturers back through the chain. This results in better product information about customers' needs and improved production operations.

5. Outsourcing Noncore Competencies

Outsourcing will continue to be important for having a cost-effective business (Poirier and Reiter, 1996). Such arrangements place responsibility for logistics or production functions in the supply chain in the hands of the constituent who is most capable of performing them successfully. Many firms are currently outsourcing the distribution process. They are able to track all deliveries through a third-party provider.

6. Build-to-Order Manufacturing Strategy

The economics of build-to-order (BTO) manufacturing strategy transcends industry segments. In the March 1998 issue of *Fortune* magazine it was reported that Ford was migrating to a build-to-order strategy. Their goal was to meet a majority of demand for cars using this manufacturing strategy by the end of 1999. In 1996, the delivery period for a Mustang car from the plant to a dealer was 50 days. Today, it takes only 15 days. A BTO manufacturing strategy and aggressive profit and loss management enabled Dell Computers to minimize its working capital requirements, increase cash flow, and realize a negative five days cash-to-cash conversion cycle.

7. Inventory Management

In the past, carrying inventory in stock was a normal business practice to guard against the risk of unmet demand. Today many firms find that holding inventory is costly and so they try to push the inventory on to someone else in the supply chain. It is a challenge for the constituents to ascertain where inventory should be held in the supply chain. Some firms are demanding that the manufacturer deliver the inventory to private customer warehouses more frequently and in smaller lots.

Some important supply chain inventory issues are shorter delivery times, just-in-time (JIT), point-of-sale data, vendor-managed inventory, and consignment inventory (Mayer, 1996). Shorter delivery times, JIT, and point-of-sale data are complementary to one another. For example, in order to utilize a JIT system, shorter delivery times are needed and point-of-sale data are required to know which products are to be replenished quickly. Information sharing is critical to resolving these issues. Vendor-managed and consignment inventory are becoming important management strategies designed to locate inventory in the supply chain efficiently.

8. Cost Control

Supply chain management must be able to quantify a bottom-line impact. There is a tendency to accept short-term profits as opposed to long-term investments for sustained profits and growth.

It is typical in many firms that the Operation function desires improved product forecasts and longer lead times. On the other hand, the Sales and Marketing function desires more inventories to alleviate the potential for stock out. These demands lead to enhanced production capacity, thus creating excess inventory and consequently higher production costs. Both functions blame this phenomenon on the current process. These activities pull efforts away from doing the basics well, which include sharing information among functions and concentrating on demand management.

Issues 1 to 4 have potential impact on the enterprise at the macro level, whereas 5 to 8 can affect it at the micro level. Channel integration for an enterprise is best achieved when macro- and micro-level issues are resolved in a coordinated manner. It requires integration of generic strategies at the macro level with functional strategies at the micro level. We describe this phenomenon through the Acceleration Principle, a strategy often utilized for solving supply chain problems.

Strategies for Solving Supply Chain Problems

The Acceleration Principle: Lead Time/Safety Stock and Inventory Reduction Syndromes

Numerous articles in recent years have described the desirability of supply chain strategies and the specific steps taken to implement them. One path-breaking example is the use of the Acceleration Principle proposed by Jay Forrester at the Massachusetts Institute of Technology. It is best explained by a management training exercise developed in the 1950s, called the Beer Game (Sherman 1997). It is designed to simulate product and information flows through a multiechelon supply chain. More commonly known as the Production Game, the result of this simulation is what has been called the Forrester's Effect, or the Acceleration Principle. According to this principle, for example, a 10 percent change in the rate of sale at the retail level can result in up to a 40 percent change in demand for the manufacturer. It is a result of slow reaction time and batch-processing time between echelons in the supply chain. Panic starts an overreaction to the current state of inventory, increasing the amplitude of the effect. The effect becomes cyclical, with periods of high backorders switching to periods of high inventory. Players blame each other for lack of success during the game similar to the way departments do within a firm. Yet, it is not the performance of the individual, but the structure of our system that is to blame for failures. The effect can be minimized if retail sales information is shared throughout the supply line. It can potentially reduce the reaction time to respond to fluctuation in demand. First, however, it is appropriate to turn the focus on a business entity within the supply chain. This is where an individual entity has the most leverage and can exercise control. However, each entity must set its own house in order, before all constituent entities can collectively work on supply chain improvements.

Firms deal with two types of flows: material and information (Plossl, 1991). The production process is exposing only the top layer of problems that a manufacturing firm faces today with managing these flows. Functional silos or arbitrary walls within each company affect the flow of information and materials, just as multifirms (echelons) do in the supply chain. Batch processing of information generates effects of the Acceleration Principle within the organization. Distorted demand data and delayed information become commonplace eliciting a reaction typical of purchasing personnel and production planners. This reaction is referred to as the Lead Time (or Safety Stock) syndrome (Plossl, 1991) and is illustrated in Exhibit 10–2. The effect continues to escalate leading up to the undesired capacity increase based on this condition. This capacity increase, however, is not without a corresponding cost increase.

Eventually, the overload is relieved as increased capacity floods the supply chain causing the second effect from distorted demand data. This effect, labeled the Inventory Reduction syndrome, is illustrated in Exhibit 10–3. It is the result of the organization addressing the excess inventory created by the first syndrome. Without process changes, these two syndromes feed each other in a continuous loop.

EXHIBIT 10–2 **Lead Time/Safety Stock Syndrome**

Page lead time syndrome | Chapter 10 Drawings.vsd

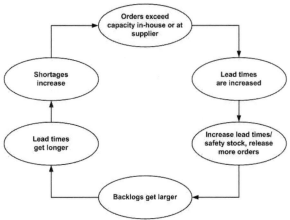

EXHIBIT 10–3 **Inventory Reduction Syndrome**
Page inventory reduction syndrome | Chapter 10
Drawings.vsd

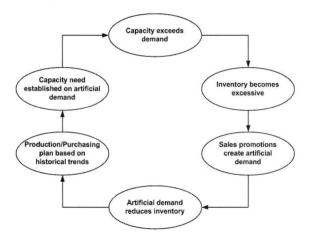

Ultimately, another silo is established in the organization. It is specifically chartered to run promotions in the hope of increasing market share, while targeting reduction in excess inventories. This action is also erroneous.

The firm has now combined perpetual reductions in sales prices from the Inventory Reduction syndrome with increasing production costs from the Lead Time syndrome.

In a growing market, the combination of these two effects is consumed by the growth in demand. Firms can survive and even flourish during this growth period, in spite of the oscillating cycle that focuses on reducing inventory during one time period while expediting product delivery regardless of cost during the next period. When the market experiences a plateau or a decline at this time, the organization can spiral itself right out of existence.

The proposed framework represents the impact of these syndromes in the supply chain as throughput, cycle time, inventory at various stages, and quality of decision making in conjunction with generic structural elements as flexibility, coordination, synchronization, and standardization, to develop a waste-sensitized strategy mix. The next section provides examples of successful supply chain management strategies.

Implementing Effective Supply Chain Management Strategies

The primary purpose in establishing supply chains is to minimize the flow of raw materials and finished products at every point in the pipeline in order to enhance productivity and cost savings (Cohen, 1996; Cooper and Ellram, 1993). Successful supply chain ventures manage critical elements for parts (i.e., individual business unit or a division/function) and/or the whole of the entire supply chain. These critical elements are discussed in the sections that follow.

Manage Inventory Investment in the Chain Each constituent of the supply chain wants to hold no more than its fair share of inventory. For instance, the distributor wants fewer inventories and would like to see inventory held by the manufacturer. As a result, the concept of vendor-managed inventory has become a trend in inventory management. This system allows the inventory to be pushed back to the vendor and as a result lowers the investment and risk for the other chain members (Donovan, 1997; Mayer, 1996).

As product life cycles are shortening, lower inventory investments in the chain have become important. Cycle times are being reduced as a result of a quick response inventory system. The quick response system improves customer service because the customer gets the right amount of product, when and where it is needed (May 1994). Quick response also serves to increase manufacturing inventory turns.

Establish Supplier Relationships It is important to establish strategic partnerships with suppliers for a successful supply chain. Corporations have started to limit the number of suppliers with whom they do business by implementing vendor review programs. These programs strive to find suppliers with operational excellence, so the customer can determine which supplier is serving it better. The ability to have a closer customer-to-supplier relationship is very important because these suppliers are easier to work with.

With the evolution toward a sole supplier relationship, firms need full disclosure of information such as financial, gain sharing, and jointly designed work. They may establish a comparable culture and also implement compatible forecasting and information technology systems. This is because their suppliers must be able to link electronically into the customer's system to obtain shipping, production schedules, and any other needed information (Copacino, 1996; Coyle et al., 1996; Keller, 1995).

Increase Customer Responsiveness   To remain competitive, firms focus on improved supply chain efforts to enhance customer service through increased frequency of reliable product deliveries. Increasing demands on customer service levels is driving partnerships between customers and suppliers. The ability of suppliers to serve their customers with higher levels of quality service, including speedier delivery of products, is vital to partnering efforts. Having a successful relationship with a supplier results in trust and the ability to be customer driven, customer intimate, and customer focused (Willis, 1995).

Build a Competitive Advantage for the Channel   Achieving and maintaining a competitive advantage in an industry is not an easy undertaking for a firm. Many competitive pressures force a firm to remain efficient. Supply chain management is seen by some as a competitive advantage for firms that employ resources to implement the process. It also serves to increase the clout in the channel because these firms are recognized as leading edge and are treated with respect.

Attaining a competitive advantage in the channel comes with top management support for decreased costs and waste, in addition to increased profits. Many firms want to push costs back to their suppliers and take labor costs out of the system. These cost-reducing tactics tend to increase the competitive efficiency of the entire supply chain.

Firms have become more market-channel focused. They are watching how the entire channel's activities affect system operation. In recent times, the channel power has shifted to the retailer. Retailer channel power in the distribution channel is driven by the shift to some large retail firms such as Wal-Mart, Kmart, and Target. The large size of these retailers allows them the power to dictate exactly how they want their suppliers to do business with them. The use of point-of-sales data and increased efficiency of distribution also has been instrumental in improving channel power and competitive advantage (Magretta, 1998; Robinson, 1998; Ross, 1996).

Introduce Supply Chain Management Solutions and Enabling Information Technology
Information is vital to effectively operating the supply chain. The communication capability of an enterprise is enhanced by an information technology system. However, information system compatibility among trading partners can limit the capability to exchange information. An improved IT system that is user friendly, and where partners in the channel have access to common databases that are updated in real time is needed.

These examples plus the research summarized in the preceding sections provide the basis for a new framework for supply chain management.

Supply Chain Management: A Framework for Analysis

This section describes a framework that enables managing supply chain problems. It combines basic tenets of linking generic (structural) strategies with functional (prescriptive) strategies.

Many strategists agree that firms may not be able to rely either on a price leadership role or a differentiation strategy alone to guarantee sustained market strength. To sustain long-term growth, however, combinations of both strategies are needed to operate effectively within constraints imposed by the environment. Such is also the case for a supply chain of products and services offered by a firm. However, since a number of autonomous business entities belong to the supply chain network, it becomes imperative to develop a common mission, goals, and objectives for the group as a whole, while pursuing independent policies at the individual member's level. This scenario offers opportunities for the design, modeling, and implementation of supply chain networks for maximum effectiveness, efficiency, and productivity in a dynamic environment.

As we noted earlier, a supply chain network as depicted in Exhibit 10–4 can be a complex web of systems, subsystems, operations, and activities. Their relationships to one another can also be complex, with entities belonging to its various members, namely, raw material vendors, Tier I and II suppliers, manufacturing plants, distributors, wholesalers, retailers, and consumers.

Notice the two directional flows illustrated in Exhibit 10–4. Demand or informational flow (dashed lines) moves from right to left or up the supply chain. Products or materials flow (solid lines) moves from left to right or down the supply chain. This flow format is used throughout the remainder of this chapter.

The design, modeling, and implementation of such a system, therefore, can be difficult, unless various parts of it are cohesively tied to the whole. Our motivation in proposing a framework to manage a supply chain system is to facilitate integration of its various components through a common set of principles, strategies, policies, and performance metrics throughout its developmental life cycle.

As a special class of network, a supply chain offers unique ways to amalgamate the structural component with functional components of the enterprise. We propose an integrated framework to manage a supply chain network. Its building blocks are availability and supply and demand for inventory; and a planning unit that coordinates marketing and production of inventory. Relationships between these are expressed in traditional "inventory-balance" equations, as follows:

$$Inventory\ level\ +\ Supply\ level\ =\ Demand\ level$$

EXHIBIT 10–4
Supply Chain Network
Page supply chain network | Chapter 10 Drawings.vsd

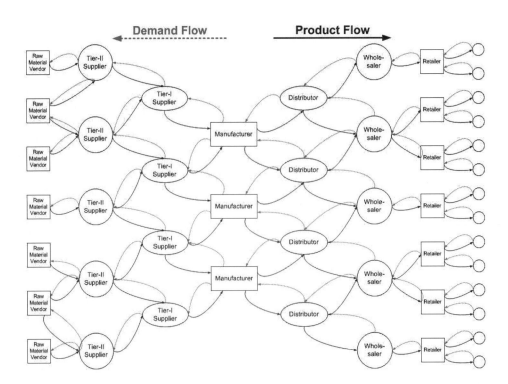

These building blocks and their relationships can be extended and generalized at any level of the supply chain hierarchy.

We describe this architecture in relation to these building blocks, briefly, below:

• Production Operations Management Systems (POMS) manage functional components, such as demand and production functions of individual members of the supply chain enterprise. POMS are concerned with the production of goods and services. In conjunction with other functional systems, these also deal with the management of resources (inputs) and the distribution of finished goods and services to customers (outputs). Operations signify the production of goods and services, the set of value-added activities that transform inputs into outputs. Supply chain as a special class of network offers unique and creative ways of planning and managing complex interrelated systems. Its members realize that designing and implementing various subsystems of POMS, such as materials planning, inventory management, capacity planning, logistics, and production systems utilizing supply chain philosophy will lead to overall improvement in enterprise productivity.

• Integrated Production Planning and Control (IPPC) systems assume the role of coordinator of demand and production functions. IPPC is a combination of philosophies, concepts, and tools and techniques to manage deviations in expectations of the demand and supply functions of a productive system. It is an integrated material-flow-based information system, whose planning and control is based on a feedback loop of control theory. The main approaches to IPPC are push, pull, and synchronous flow production systems. Advances in information and communication technologies complemented by sophisticated decision support systems enable designing, implementing, and controlling strategies essential to the delivery of integrated systems, such as supply chain systems.

An example of a manufacturing supply chain network (Tzafestas and Papsiotis, 1994), depicted in Exhibit 10–5, captures the essence of the proposed framework. It has been derived from the general architecture of a supply chain network depicted in Exhibit 10–4.

This supply chain is made up of a manufacturer and a two-level hierarchy of suppliers. Each subsystem in the supply chain network incurs costs that are to be monitored and controlled. At each level in the supply chain, delay due to procurement activity is incurred, which has the potential of imposing waste, and thus incurring additional costs in the system. This closed loop form of a supply chain system, mandates tight coupling among its components. Our framework adapts this rationale.

We have categorized the supply chain framework elements as follows:

• Goals
• Objectives

EXHIBIT 10–5
Manufacturing Supply Chain Network
Page manufacturing supply chain | Chapter 10 Drawings.vsd

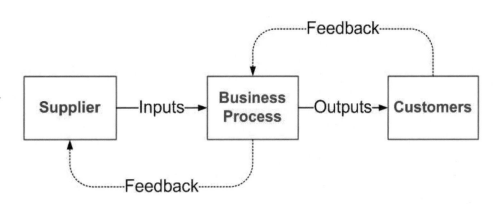

- Modeling principles
- Coordinated strategies
- Implementation

We discuss each of these elements in the context of a manufacturing supply chain network, an example of which is depicted in Exhibit 10–5.

1. **Goals.** Supply chain goals are mutually agreed to between its members in a spirit of cooperation. Members negotiate and compromise with each other in order to arrive at acceptable goals. Goals for supply chains are set at two levels. Members synergize their activities and resources toward accomplishing common goals for the supply chain as a group, goals that aim to benefit all, and not just a few among the group. In addition, members may pursue individual goals that reflect their organizational values and expectations. However, the two sets of goals must be coordinated in order to provide effective performance measures for the supply chain. This may require fine-tuning the individual goals of members so that common supply chain goals can be met.

A common goal for a manufacturing supply chain may be to maintain an industry benchmark of *X percent order-fill-rate within T hours of receipt of customer orders.* On the basis of this common goal, individual members may set their own goals as *achieving K inventory turns, realizing an S percent shipment-fill-rate of within T hours of order,* and so forth.

2. **Objectives.** Supply chain objectives directly support the supply chain's stated goals. As such, they are derived from published goals. For example, a common manufacturing supply chain goal can be *to enhance revenue through eliminating or alleviating bottleneck operations* in the system. Supply chain objectives that directly support this goal can be identified to

- Increase throughput.
- Reduce cycle time.
- Reduce inventory at different stages (raw materials to work-in-process to finished goods).

As can be seen, these objectives are complementary to each other. For example, a primary objective of increased throughput in the supply chain must be supported by a secondary objective to reduce cycle time. A reduction in processing time and setup time will allow smaller batches to be processed faster, thereby lessening congestion in the system and registering shorter cycle time. This will also create increased throughput, and consequently, a higher revenue stream in the supply chain. As a result of this improvement in the supply chain, the tertiary objective of reduced inventory at different stages, which supports both the primary and secondary objectives, can be realized because inventory at different stages will not have to wait for availability of operations for further processing.

Objectives can be set both at the group level for supply chain as well as at the member level for individual members. However, the two sets of objectives ought to be coordinated in order to provide effective performance measures for the supply chain. This may require fine-tuning the individual objectives of members so that common supply chain objectives can be met.

3. **Modeling Principles.** A productive system, such as a supply chain, generates a stream of waste, primarily due to potential structural weaknesses in its design. A manufacturing enterprise may carry potential waste throughout its product and/or service life cycle.

Next, we discuss modeling principles that can be applied to managing waste in the context of the manufacturing supply chain example, described earlier in this section. These principles are generic enough so that the modeler may ascertain characteristics of the problem independent of the specific problem environment. Consequently, the approach delivers solution(s) or the solution method that is intrinsic to the problem and not its environment.

In general, then, the principles described below support the goals and objectives identified earlier in this section for the manufacturing supply chain example. Overall, by applying these principles, we hope to develop waste management models that reduce variability in the supply chain due to product and/or process specifications, out-of-control processes, inefficient logistics, and inefficiencies that are inherently present in any system.

We describe these principles below in the sections that follow:

Principle 1—Reducing the Influence of Lead-Time Variability in the Productive Process

The influence of lead time can be felt in the supply chain at any and/or all stages of its life cycle. The transformation of the product through various stages in its life cycle bring out cycle time in its various manifestations, such as setup time, process time, queue time, wait time, and idle time. One of the primary challenges in modeling waste management in the supply chain is to reduce the variability of these elements of cycle time. This is mainly accomplished by designing coordinating mechanisms through the sharing of information in the form of demand schedules, capacity plans, production schedules, and so forth.

For example,

- Set-up time can be alleviated by ensuring constant demand in the system.
- Process time variations can be reduced and/or eliminated by standardizing methods and procedures.
- Queue time can be eliminated by coordinating schedules between servers so that elapsed time for service can be minimized and server efficiency improved.
- Idle time can be eliminated or alleviated by scheduling maintenance of productive resources.

Principle 2—Reducing the Influence of Inventory Variability at Different Supply Chain Stages and Locations

Inventory variability poses a serious challenge in the management of a supply chain. This is primarily because the material flow in a supply chain takes on many forms through its life cycle and thus assumes various inventory classifications. Let us illustrate this with an example drawn from the textile industry. A garment sold to a consumer at retail has a material flow from fiber, nondyed fabric, dyed fabric, apparel, and finally a finished garment.

Various types of inventories are created throughout the aforementioned above material transformation. Fiber production is a continuous manufacturing process, where batches are introduced in order to achieve economies of scale and/or production efficiencies. However, batches of production cause inventory (or *cycle stock*). Production of textile fabric from fiber may impose sequence dependencies *between* processes, or create goods-in-transit for a multiechelon assembly line setup. *Decoupling stocks* can also be created if, for example, an end product of one process (Greige goods), and a raw material for the next process (fabric coloring) is warehoused to achieve production economies. Material flow at the next stage is in the form of textile fabric components, required to produce apparel. *Anticipation inventories* can be created for apparels with seasonal demand. *Work-in-process inventories* may be created for apparels requiring assembly of various components. Finally, the consumer demand pattern, product characteristics, and customer service levels dictate maintaining *safety stocks* of apparel to avoid stock outs.

Management of inventories at various stages will have to be proposed as part of an overall IPPC philosophy that integrates inventory policies with appropriate procurement policies and scheduling heuristics. Exhibit 10–6 offers details on this.

Textile Sector	Primary Focus	Integrated Production Planning and Control Philosophy
Retailer	High customer service by maintaining reduced levels of inventories	Economic-order-quantity and reorder point
Apparel	Effective coordination of material component and labor needs	Material requirement planning; Quick response
Textile	Minimization of setup times and inventories; High capacity utilization	Just-in-time; Economic-order-quantity
Fiber	High utilization of installed capacity	Multi-stage Economic-order-quantity and reorder point

Principle 3—Reducing the Influence of Batching Effects Variability in the Productive System This principle prescribes that the relationship between lot size and lead time should be closely managed in a manufacturing supply chain. Two types of effects that emerge from this relationship are batching effect and saturation effect (Karmarkar, Kekre, and Freeman, 1985; Graves, Rinnooy Kan, and Zipkin, 1993; Sipper and Bulfin, 1997). We describe these below.

Batching Effect. The rationale behind the batching effect is that an increase in lot size should also increase lead-time. For example, a batch of one unit can immediately move to the next operation as soon as its processing is complete. However, a batch of five units does not move until all five are completed. That is, the first unit waits until the other four units are completed before it moves to the next operation. A doubling of the batch size to 10 units requires the first unit to wait for the processing of remaining nine units. The bottom line is that large batches will cause longer delays of parts waiting for the rest of the batch to be completed.

Saturation Effect. The rationale behind the saturation effect is that it works conversely to the batching effect. That is, when lot sizes decrease, and setup is not reduced, lead time will eventually increase. The reason is that if demand stays the same as lot sizes are reduced, there will be more lots in the shop. This results in more time spent on setups and less time available for processing. As a result, demand becomes a relatively larger proportion of available capacity, and congestion increases.

Since the effects of the two phenomena are opposite, the aggregate behavior of lead time as a function of lot size assumes a convex or a U-shape.

In the final analysis, by making the transfer batch smaller than the production batch, production lead time can be substantially reduced.

Principle 4—Reducing the Influence of Variability Due to Supply Chain Bottlenecked Operations The rationale behind this principle is that rather than balancing capacities, the flow of product through the system should be balanced. That is, the modeling of waste management should be designed to control throughput and work-in-process inventory simultaneously. This will require converting a bottlenecked activity to nonbottlenecked activity in the supply chain. We can achieve this by creating buffers due to time, inventory, lead time, and other variables to allow the bottlenecked activity to be synchronized with the succeeding nonbottlenecked activity. An approach that enables doing so is the drum-buffer-rope (DBR) approach based on the theory of constraint (Cohen, 1988). A bottlenecked operation becomes the control point whose production rate controls the pace of the system. This bottleneck beats the drum that enables execution of policies that create a buffer before the control point so that it gets a leeway to synchronize its actions with downstream operations in the supply chain. A rope in the form of feedback of information from the bottlenecked operation to upstream operations enables the pipeline to maintain its throughput. Implementing the DBR approach is a key element of synchronous manufacturing in a supply chain.

4. **Developing Coordinated Strategies.** The implementation of waste management models for a manufacturing supply chain mandates cohesive strategies that support the goals and objectives of the enterprise. We believe that there is a need for models that describe and implement controls of various subsystems for controlling the total supply chain system. We outline a model that focuses on the dynamic structure of the supply chain and effective coordination of its processes. Such a model enables developing interaction between production and marketing policies, and between supply process of raw materials and production of finished products.

We have built the element of coordination in developing effective strategies for a manufacturing supply chain by incorporating planning and control function as the integration unit. For example, marketing strategies for a supply chain emphasize varying stocking policies to maintain inventory effectiveness while ensuring service levels under varying planning and control scenarios. Exhibit 10–7 depicts various strategic alternatives that can be evaluated for implementation in a supply chain.

Production strategies for a supply chain emphasize varying resource optimization and batching policies to realize production effectiveness while ensuring lead times under varying planning and control scenarios. Exhibit 10–8 depicts various strategic alternatives that can be evaluated for implementation in a supply chain.

EXHIBIT 10–7
Supply Chain Network: Marketing Strategies
Page marketing strategies | Chapter 10 Drawings.vsd

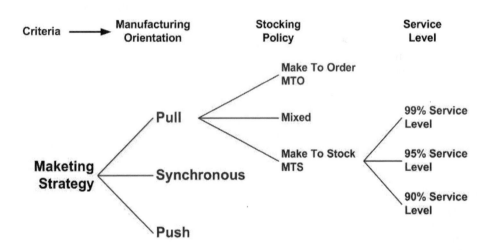

EXHIBIT 10–8
Supply Chain Network: Production Strategies
Page production strategies | Chapter 10 Drawings.vsd

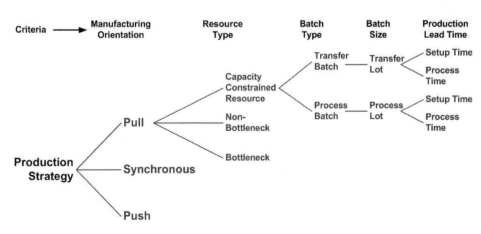

Developing an interaction of marketing and production strategies, however, offers opportunities for modeling coordination and synchronization in a supply chain. Our framework emphasizes such an approach. We highlight below some of the advantages of pursuing coordinated strategies:

1. Maintaining effective inventories while realizing production efficiencies.
2. Achieving integration through synchronization and coordination of various system components.
3. Potentially increasing supply chain payoffs.

Exhibit 10–9 depicts a model that coordinates the demand and supply functions of a manufacturing supply chain.

The two submodels that are designed for separate execution represent independent and autonomous members, offering a distinct product or service in the supply chain. The coordination of the end product (or service) of each of the two submodels, however, is coordinated with the help of a common model that performs the planning and control functions of the supply chain. In this manner, common policies agreed to between various members of the supply chain are implemented. For example, it may be possible to enforce common quotas for capacities, mutually-agreed-to price and cost structures, as well as production schedules, and more.

5. **Implementation.** We illustrate the implementation of the proposed framework with the help of manufacturing supply chain examples from the steel and food industries. Exhibits 10–10 and 10–11 depict these supply chains.

In the case of the food industry, which is depicted in Exhibit 10–10, common objectives between members are used to manage lead time and inventory at various stages in the supply chain. Similarly, lead time and inventory are also managed within a member. Coordination of activities of various entities in the supply chain is achieved through information sharing with feed forward and feedback, in a closed form system. For example, the lead time is negotiated and committed to through a bidding process and plans at various stages are shared through information loops. Due to the usually heavy marketing focus of the food industry, cooperation among functions is modeled to incorporate every facet of the product life cycle, from raw material source to consumer.

EXHIBIT 10–9
Supply Chain Network: Coordinating Strategies
Page coordinating strategies | Chapter 10 Drawings.vsd

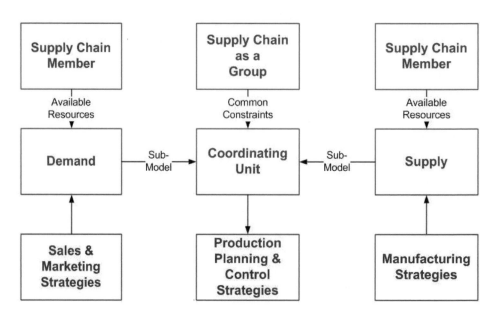

EXHIBIT 10–10 **Supply Chain Network: Food Production Process**

Page food production process | Chapter 10 Drawings.vsd

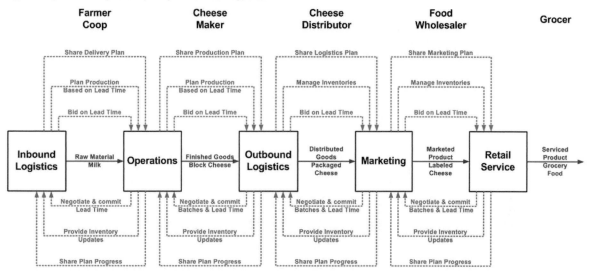

EXHIBIT 10–11 **Supply Chain Network: Steel Production Process**

Page steel production process | Chapter 10 Drawings.vsd

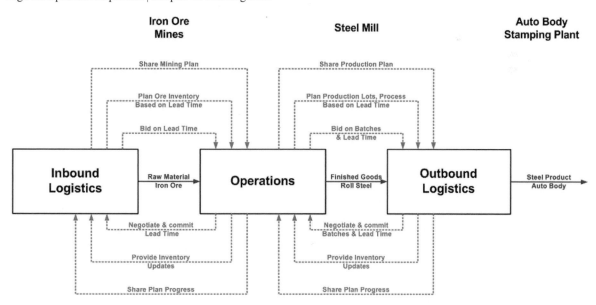

In the steel industry case, depicted in Exhibit 10–11, common objectives between members are to manage production batches, lot sizes, and process and setup times at various stages in the supply chain. Lead time and inventory are managed within a member. Coordination of activities of various entities in the supply chain is achieved through information sharing with feed forward and feedback, in a closed form system. For example, the lead time is negotiated and committed to through a bidding process and plans at various stages are shared through information loops. Due to the usually heavy production focus of the steel industry, cooperation among functions is modeled to emphasize operations and the associated logistics, from raw material source to finished steel.

Thus, while the focus of the two supply chains is different, similarities in approaches to design goals and objectives and model various waste management principles should enable analysts to develop generic solutions to problem solving for these fairly diverse industry environments. For example, the generic marketing and production strategies described in the preceding section can be represented by defining variables for each of the performance metrics, and analyzing various strategic alternatives through the coordination of functional models in the product life cycle.

The long-term success of a firm depends on the success of its suppliers and customers. That is, the entire supply chain must be successful. Poorly performing supply chains are easy to recognize and are generally used to schedule product, using forecasting. These supply chains push product through to the customer, have low overall reliability, and maintain high inventory levels to achieve fulfillment rates. Overtime, expediting premium freight, and inventory obsolescence drives up product costs. A growing number of firms are designing products and operating in an extended multicompany enterprise. They are minimizing non-value-added work and reducing inventory levels across the supply chain. These organizations are also coordinating planning, forecasting, and operating in multicompany context and managing a multitier supplier environment. Many firms are eliminating costs rather than reallocating them. An example of this effort is the outsourcing of materials management function. They are implementing customer pull across multiple boundaries and also treating suppliers as partners rather than as adversaries. What we are experiencing today is a fundamental change in global business philosophy of increasing partnering arrangements.

In order to manage these supply chain arrangements, it is necessary to improve planning and the management of complex interrelated systems, such as materials planning, inventory management, capacity planning, logistics, and production systems and realize overall improvement in enterprise productivity. The availability of information technologies has enabled the delivery of integrated systems for decision making. We have proposed a framework to delivery-integrated systems for supply chain management. Since the proposed approach offers generic solutions for problem solving, it is now possible to address the variety of problems across industries having a similar design and modeling characteristics.

Supply Chain Simulation: The Beer Game

Maximizing customer service and profits by managing each component of the supply chain is explicitly understood. On the other hand, it is not so obvious when it comes to determining the value of taking an integrated approach to managing the entire supply chain.

The Beer Game is a role-playing simulation developed at MIT in the 1960s to clarify the advantages of taking an integrated approach to managing the supply chain. It particularly demonstrates the value of sharing information across various supply chain components. Exhibit 10–12 illustrates the production process model introduced in Chapter 1 and constructed for the Beer Game.

The Beer Game is an exercise that simulates material and information flows in a production distribution system. The activity demonstrates the relationship between nodes on a supply/demand chain with a time delay. It emphasizes the importance of information flow in the multiple echelon systems. In large part, the activity also demonstrates aspects of human nature, specifically the tendency to overreact and overcompensate. As illustrated in Exhibit 10–12 the primary decision or control variables for the Beer Game are the Reorder Points and Reorder Quantity. The Beer Game has an inherent Demand Level and Cost Structure, which might be changeable in the long run but not during the gaming situation. The Beer Game has two sources of random variation, Retail Demand and Lead Times. In the Arena simulation model, we will introduce later how these random variations can be

EXHIBIT 10–12 **Beer Game Production Process Model**

Page Beer Game process model | Chapter 10 Drawings.vsd

Decision Variables

Reorder Point | Reorder Quantity

Inputs

Demand Level

Cost Structure

Supply Chain

Outputs

Holding Cost→

Penalty Cost→

Profit→

Retail Demand | Lead Time

Random Variation

suppressed. The Beer Game supply chain is designed to deliver kegs of beer to retail customers. These sales generate revenue, which when offset by inventory holding and shortage penalty costs, provide a measure of the potential system profitability.

The Beer Game has the following four players or supply chain levels:

1. Retailer
2. Wholesaler
3. Distributor
4. Factory

Customer demand (in kegs of beer) arises at the retailer, which replenishes its inventory from the wholesaler, the wholesaler from the distributor, and the distributor from the factory. In each period, channel members must decide how much, if any, to order from their respective suppliers and the factory must decide how much, if any, to produce. There are transportation lead times in shipping the material from one location to another, and there is a production lead time at the factory. While material flows from upstream to downstream, information flows in the opposite direction through order placements. There is an order processing delay, or information lead time, between when an order is placed and when the order is received by the supplier. The players share a common objective to optimize the systemwide performance or total profit after the exclusion of inventory-related costs.

Exhibit 10–13 shows material and information flows in the supply chain and also gives two kinds of delays at each node or level:

1. Information delay (Order Flow, dashed lines).
2. Transportation delay (Keg Flow, solid lines).

As illustrated in Exhibit 10–13, the lead time between retailer and wholesaler, wholesaler and distributor, and distributor and factory are all four days. The factory's internal lead time is one day. The Arena simulation model permits all of these lead times to be changed and also to be probabilistic.

In the original Beer Game, the customer demand is X kegs per period for the first several periods and then changes to $2X$ kegs per period for the rest of the game. Moreover, the players have no prior knowledge about the demand process. (The demand pattern and the players' lack of information about it are important.) The customer demands in different periods are independent and identically distributed, and all players a priori know the demand distribution.

In our version of the Beer Game, the retail demand level is a random variable drawn from or generated from a Normal distribution with a specified set of parameters, mean, and standard deviation. The value of these parameters can be changed for any simulation run.

EXHIBIT 10–13

Beer Game Supply Chain Flow Model

Page Beer Game flow model | Chapter 10 Drawings.vsd

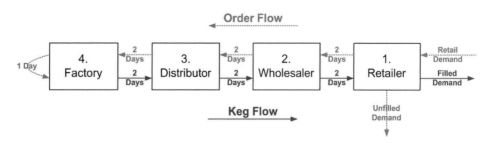

Also during the Arena simulation, the value of the Retail demand mean can be increased or decreased.

Description of the Beer Game

We have developed a simplified Beer Game supply chain model using Arena. The game consists of a single retailer; a single wholesaler, who supplies the retailer; a single distributor that supplies the wholesaler; and a single factory with unlimited raw materials that makes the beer and supplies the distributor. Each node in the supply chain has unlimited storage capacity, and there is a supply lead time and order delay time between each node or level. Material flow travels from upstream to downstream, that is, from the factory to the distributor, then to the wholesaler, and finally to the retailer, whereas information in the form of replenishment orders flows in the opposite direction. Exhibit 10–14 illustrates the flows into and from a typical Beer Game node or level.

Both material and information flows are subject to delays. Customer demand arises at the retail store only. The demands in different periods (days) are independent and identically distributed random variables following the Normal distribution. Holding costs are incurred at each level for their on-hand inventories, and backorder costs are incurred only at the retail store for customer backorders. The goal is to minimize the total holding and backorder costs incurred in the entire supply chain.

Holding costs are assessed at every level for on-hand inventories. Each node must satisfy orders from its downstream participant (or customers) as much as possible. In case of a stockout, the excess demand is backlogged. A penalty cost is assessed for customer backorders at each level reflecting the need to provide good customer service throughout the supply chain.

For the stationary Beer Game, under the objective of minimizing the long-run average total cost in the supply chain, the optimal strategy for each node is to place orders to keep its inventory level at a constant target level, that is, to follow an installation base-stock policy. The installation stock for a node is its on-hand inventory minus its backorders plus its outstanding orders; that is, orders placed but not yet received.

Various business scenarios for the supply chain management can be studied, for example, eliminating the information lead time. Another alternative structure relates to transmitting the customer demand information to upstream participants, that is, when the retailer places an order, it also provides the most recent customer demand.

Beer Game Arena Simulation Model

We have developed an Arena Beer Game simulation model, **Beer Game.doe,** using Arena software. Model Beer Game.doe uses VBA code to read the initial values of input variables from worksheet **Variables** location in Excel workbook, **Beer Game.xls.** Exhibit 10–15 lists the simulation model variables and their initial values used for this text. On the worksheet the user can change all of the data values formatted in red. The simulation model functions by tracking the values of the various variables over time.

EXHIBIT 10–14 **Beer Game Node Model**

Page Beer Game node model | Chapter 10 Drawings.vsd

Model Beer Game.doe Input Variables

Let us review the input variables used in the Beer Game Arena model entered in workbook **Beer Game.xls,** Exhibit 10–15.

1. Daily demand for beer kegs at the Retailer level is assumed to follow a Normal distribution. The illustrated model uses a daily **Demand.Mean** of 25 kegs with a standard deviation of 5 kegs. Setting the value of the

EXHIBIT 10–15
**Model Beer
Game.doe Input
Variables**
Sheet variables | Beer
Game.xls
Sheet single unit |
Chapter 10
Worksheets.xls

Arena Variable Name	New Value	Units
Demand.Mean	25.0	Kegs / Day
Demand.Standard.Deviation	5.0	Kegs / Day
Retail.BackOrders.Allowed	0	0 = no or 1 = yes

Arena Variable Array Name	1 Retailer	2 Wholesaler	3 Distributor	4 Factory	Units
Kegs.OnHand	100	150	200	250	Kegs
Reorder.Point	100	150	200	250	Kegs
Reorder.Quantity	100	150	200	250	Kegs
Order.Days	0	2	2	2	Days
Ship.Days	2	2	2	1	Days
Lead.Time.Standard.Deviation	0.00	0.00	0.00	0.00	Days
Keg.Profit	$4.00	$3.75	$3.50	$3.25	$ / Keg
Holding.Cost	$0.30	$0.25	$0.20	$0.15	$ / Keg Day
Penalty.Cost	$5.00	$2.50	$1.25	$1.00	$ / Keg Day
Order Lead Time	4	4	4	1	Days
Lead Time Demand	100	100	100	25	Kegs
Maximum Inventory Level	200	300	400	500	Kegs

variable **Demand.Standard.Deviation** to zero removes demand variability from the model. The simulation model operates on a daily basis driven by demands at the retailer level. These demands, in turn, may require additional orders from higher levels in the supply chain

2. At the Retailer level, no backorders are allowed if the value of variable **Retail.Backorders.Allowed** is set to 1. If the value of variable **Retail.Backorders.Allowed** is set to 0, customer demand beyond the on-hand inventory level will be lost. No direct cost is associated with this loss of sales other than the potential profit throughout the supply chain.
The following simulation model variables are indexed by supply chain levels (Arena attribute **Level**). Variable values must be specified for each of the four supply chain levels: Retailer, Wholesaler, Distributor, and Factory. The values of these variables may be different for each supply chain level.

3. The initial **Kegs.OnHand** inventory in kegs is used to start the tracking of inventory quantities over the duration of the simulation.

4. The **Reorder.Point** value is used to trigger orders. Orders are placed to the next upstream level when the Kegs.Onhand plus Kegs.Onorder drops to or below the Reorder.Point quantity.

5. The **Reorder.Quantity** represents the fixed order size in kegs.

6. The **Order.Days** indicates the time in days between the order origination at one level and the time that the order arrives at the next upstream level. Retail customers demand that their orders be filled immediately; therefore, the Order.Days for the Retailer level is typically zero.

7. The **Ship.Days** indicates the time in days it takes for a keg shipment to move from one level to next level downstream.

8. The **Lead.Time.Standard.Deviation** indicates the Normal distribution variability or standard deviation for each lead time component. As illustrated in Exhibit 10–15 the lead times can be forced to be deterministic, that is, Lead.Time.Standard.Deviation = 0.0. A large Lead.Time.Standard.Deviation may result in a small or negative lead time. To

prevent this unwanted occurrence the Beer Game.doe model included a variable, **Minimum.Lead.Time.Fraction,** initially set to 0.25 that restricts the lead time random variable value. The simulated lead time is calculated by the simulation model using the following expression:

$$\text{Simulated.Lead.Time} = \text{Max (Mean.Lead.Time} * \text{Minimum.Lead.Time.Fraction,}$$
$$\text{Normal (Mean.Lead.Time, Lead.Time.Standard.Deviation))}$$

9. The **Holding.Cost** represents the cost of holding one keg in inventory for a single period or day.

10. The **Penalty.Cost** represents the cost of being short one keg for a single period or day. The Penalty.Cost at the Retailer level will be active only if the variable Retail.Backorders.Allowed is set to one.

Workbook Beer Game.xls illustrates two sets of values to assist the user in setting up the model data.

1. The *Order Lead Time* is the duration in days from the time the order is placed to the time when the order shipment is expected to be received. If the supplier level does not have stock, this period could be increased.

2. The *Maximum Inventory Level* represents the maximum possible inventory quantity, the Reorder.Point plus the Reorder.Quantity.

Model Beer Game.doe Network Logic Flow

The logic submodel of the Beer Game.doe simulation model developed using Arena simulation software is illustrated Exhibit 10–16. The simulation model is set up to perform 12 replications; each replication is 30 days or one month in length. The Beer Game.doe model is too large to be modified using the Arena academic license. The Beer Game.doe model executes in the Arena run-time mode, which permits variable values to be changed, but no model logic changes.

Various simulation model-processing steps are described below and relate to the labels illustrated in Exhibit 10–16:

1. **Retail Order.** The Arena simulation model starts with triggering the Retailer-level daily demand. It results in the creation of a Retailer customer order. The daily **Demand.Mean** and **Demand.Standard.Deviation** are user-defined variables. Since this

EXHIBIT 10–16
Model Beer Game.doe Network Logic Flow

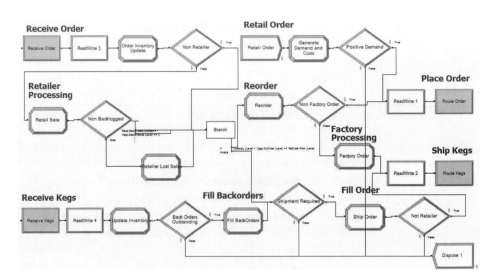

process is performed daily, it is also used to accumulate the inventory holding and penalty cost for each supply chain level. The calculations illustrated in Exhibit 10–17 are performed by the Assign module labeled **Generate Demand and Costs.** Because of the random nature of the daily demand, the value of attribute Kegs.Ordered may be zero. Such order entities are immediately disposed. The attribute **Level** is used throughout the Beer Game.doe model to make the code generic or operative at any level in the supply chain and readily expandable to supply chains with more than four levels.

2. **Place Order.** Positive orders from all but the Factory level are routed to the **Receive Order** station using the Route module illustrated in Exhibit 10–18. The random variable for order lead time is calculated by the following expression:

$$\text{Max (Minimum.Lead.Time.Fraction} * \text{Order.Days (Level), Normal}$$
$$\text{(Order.Days (Level), Lead.Time.Standard.Deviation (Level), 2))}$$

3. **Receive Order.** The Assign Module labeled **Order Inventory Update** illustrated in Exhibit 10–19 is used to determine how many kegs can be shipped, **Kegs.Shipped,** and to update the inventory levels, Inventory, Kegs.OnHand, and Kegs.BackOrdered at the supplier level.

4. **Retail Processing.** A special processing step is required for the Retailer-level entities. The Assign module labeled **Retail Sale Update** illustrated in Exhibit 10–20 accumulates the variable **Kegs.Sold.Retail.**

EXHIBIT 10–17   **Model Beer Game.doe Generate Demand Costs Assign Module**

		Type	Attribute Name	Other	New Value
1		Attribute	Kegs.Ordered	J	max (0, ANINT(Normal (Demand.Mean, Demand.Standard.Deviation, 1)))
2		Attribute	Level	J	LevelRetailer
3		Other	Attribute 3	Cost.Holding (LevelRetailer)	Cost.Holding (LevelRetailer) + Cost Holding (LevelRetailer)
4		Other	Attribute 3	Cost.Holding (LevelWholesaler)	Cost.Holding (LevelWholesaler) + Cost Holding (LevelWholesaler)
5		Other	Attribute 3	Cost.Holding (LevelDistributor)	Cost.Holding (LevelDistributor) + Cost Holding (LevelDistributor)
6		Other	Attribute 3	Cost.Holding (LevelFactory)	Cost.Holding (LevelFactory) + Cost Holding (LevelFactory)
7		Other	Attribute 3	Cost.Penalty (LevelRetailer)	Cost.Penalty (LevelRetailer) + Cost Penalty (LevelRetailer)
8		Other	Attribute 3	Cost.Penalty (LevelWholesaler)	Cost.Penalty (LevelWholesaler) + Cost Penalty (LevelWholesaler)
9		Other	Attribute 3	Cost.Penalty (LevelDistributor)	Cost.Penalty (LevelDistributor) + Cost Penalty (LevelDistributor)
10		Other	Attribute 3	Cost.Penalty (LevelFactory)	Cost.Penalty (LevelFactory) + Cost Penalty (LevelFactory)
11		Other	Attribute 11	Profit (LevelRetailer)	Profit (LevelRetailer) - Cost Holding (LevelRetailer) - Cost Penalty (LevelRetailer)
12		Other	Attribute 12	Profit (LevelWholesaler)	Profit (LevelWholesaler) - Cost Holding (LevelWholesaler) - Cost Penalty (LevelWholesaler)
13		Other	Attribute 13	Profit (LevelDistributor)	Profit (LevelDistributor) - Cost Holding (LevelDistributor) - Cost Penalty (LevelDistributor)
14		Other	Attribute 14	Profit (LevelFactory)	Profit (LevelFactory) - Cost Holding (LevelFactory) - Cost Penalty (LevelFactory)

	Name	Assignments
1	Generate Demand and Costs	14 rows
2	Order Inventory Update	4 rows
3	Reorder	5 rows
4	Ship Order	4 rows
5	Update Inventory	4 rows
6	Fill BackOrders	4 rows
7	Factory Order	3 rows
8	Retailer Lost Sale	3 rows

EXHIBIT 10–18   **Model Beer Game.doe Route Order Module**

	Name	Route Time	Units	Destination Type	Expression
1	Route Order	Max (Minimum.Lead.Time.Fraction * Order.Days (Level), Normal (Order.Days (Level), Lead.Time.Standard.Deviation (Level), 2))	Days	Expression	Receive.Order (Level)

EXHIBIT 10–19   **Model Beer Game.doe Order Inventory Update Assign Module**

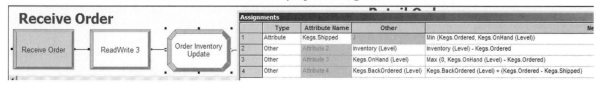

	Type	Attribute Name	Other	Ne
1	Attribute	Kegs.Shipped		Min (Kegs.Ordered, Kegs.OnHand (Level))
2	Other	Attribute 2	Inventory (Level)	Inventory (Level) - Kegs.Ordered
3	Other	Attribute 3	Kegs.OnHand (Level)	Max (0, Kegs.OnHand (Level) - Kegs.Ordered)
4	Other	Attribute 4	Kegs.BackOrdered (Level)	Kegs.BackOrdered (Level) + (Kegs.Ordered - Kegs.Shipped)

EXHIBIT 10–20
Model Beer
Game.doe Retail Sale
Assign Module

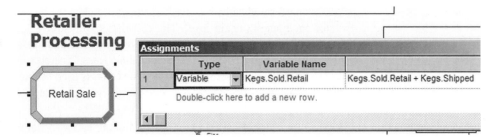

5. Next, a check is made to determine whether retail backorders are allowed. If retail backorders are allowed, then normal processing for backorders takes place. If retail backorders are not allowed, lost sales at the Retailer level are accumulated by the Assign module labeled **Retailer Lost Sale.** The inventory levels are also adjusted as illustrated in Exhibit 10–21.

6. **Reorder.** If the inventory on hand and on order is less than or equal to the inventory reorder point (Level), a new entity is generated to create a new order from the next higher level in the supply chain. The Assign module labeled **Reorder** performs the calculations illustrated in Exhibit 10–22 to complete the placement of a new order. Notice that the entity attribute Level is increased by one to indicate that the order entity is going to the next higher level, for example, Wholesaler to Distributor, and so forth.

7. **Factory Processing.** If the reorder is at the Factory level (Level = 4), special processing is required. Factory orders are routed as a shipment back to the Factory level after a delay of one day per the worksheet illustrated in Exhibit 10–15. The Assign Module labeled **Factory Order** performs the assignments illustrated in Exhibit 10–23 to complete the Factory ordering and shipping operations.

EXHIBIT 10–21 Model Beer Game.doe Retailer Lost Sale Assign Module

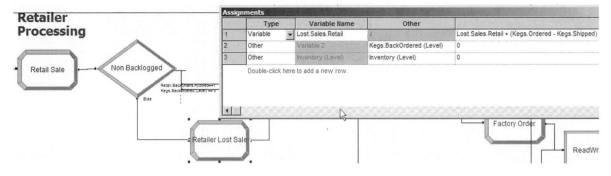

EXHIBIT 10–22 Model Beer Game.doe Reorder Assign Module

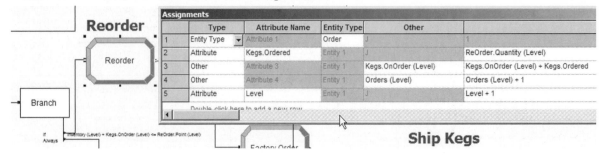

EXHIBIT 10–23
Model Beer
Game.doe Factory
Order Assign Module

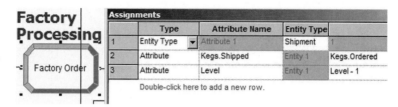

8. **Receive Kegs.** When keg shipments are received, the inventory variables are updated by the Assign module labeled **Update Inventory,** illustrated in Exhibit 10–24.

9. **Fill Backorders.** A check is made to determine if any outstanding backorders remain to be filled at the current level using the expression **Kegs.BackOrdered (Level) > 0.** If so, the Assign module labeled **Fill BackOrders** illustrated in Exhibit 10–25 assigns the available kegs to fill as many backorders as possible using the following. Notice that the fourth assignment only functions at the Retailer level.

10. **Fill Order.** The available onhand quantities are prepared for shipment using the Assign module labeled **Ship Order,** illustrated in Exhibit 10–26.

11. The Decide module labeled **Not Retailer** sends Retailer-level entities to the Dispose module and nonretailer-level entities value of **Kegs.Shipped** is added to the variable **Kegs.Sold.Retail.** Keg shipments are routed from each level with a delay of **Ship.Days,** as illustrated in Exhibit 10–27.

Model Beer Game.doe Display

Exhibit 10–28 illustrates the operation of the Arena model Beer Game.doe. Exhibit 10–28 shows two sets of Arena plots, as well as statistics for the current simulation replication or month. Colors have been used in the development of the Arena model Beer Game.doe to illustrate multiple inventories simultaneously.

EXHIBIT 10–24
Model Beer
Game.doe Update
Inventory Assign
Module

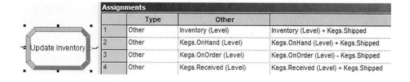

EXHIBIT 10–25 Model Beer Game.doe Fill BackOrders Assign Module

EXHIBIT 10–26 Model Beer Game.doe Ship Order Assign Module

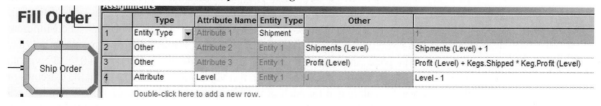

EXHIBIT 10–27   **Model Beer Game.doe Route Kegs Spreadsheet**

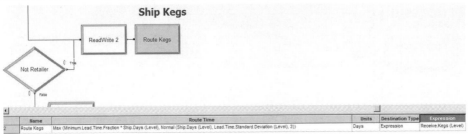

EXHIBIT 10–28   **Model Beer Game.doe Plots**

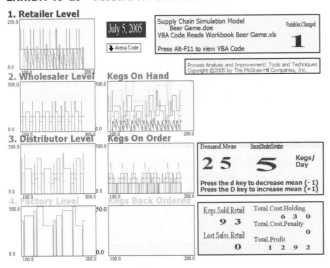

Because these color differences are not distinguishable in the text, the reader is encouraged to run the Arena model Beer Game.doe to fully view and understand the multicolored plots.

The first set of plots (left side) shows line plots for Kegs on Hand (rose), Kegs on Order (red), and Kegs Backordered (green) at each level (Retailer, Wholesaler, Distributor, and Factory). The other set of plots (right side) shows the Kegs on Hand, Kegs on Order, and Kegs Backordered for the four levels: Retailer (blue), Wholesaler (rose), Distributor (red), and Factory (green).

Notice that using the values from the Beer Game workbook (Exhibit 10–15), the Kegs on Hand and Kegs on Order increased with the supply chain level. That is, the Factory level carries more inventory than does the Distributor level.

The information on the right of Exhibit 10–28 indicates the demand level currently being used by the model. The information indicates how it can be changed and current simulation replication statistics: Total Holding Cost, Total Penalty Cost, Retail Sales, Retail Sales Lost, and Total Profit at the current point in the simulation replication and current simulation date, July 5, 2005 or TNOW = 185. The Model Beer Game.doe uses a replication length of 30 or roughly a calendar month. July 5 corresponds to the early part of the seventh simulation replication. At this point for the seventh replication, 93 kegs have been sold by the retailer with no lost sales. The total holding cost accumulated at all four levels is $630 with a total profit of $1,292.

Model Beer Game.doe Crystal Reports

Exhibit 10–29 illustrates the Crystal Reports time-persistent statistics for the complete 12-month simulation run. The Average, Half Width (95 percent Confidence Level), Minimum Average, Maximum Average, Minimum Value, and Maximum Value are illustrated for the Inventory, Kegs Backordered, Kegs on Hand Quantity, and Kegs on Order at each of the four levels. The average values are also plotted at the bottom of Exhibit 10–29. The Minimum Value and the Maximum Value represent the overall extremes for the 12-month or 360-day simulation run. For example, the number of Kegs at the Retailer ranged from 0 to 137 with an average of 61.4. The Minimum Average and the Maximum Average indicate the extremes of the Average value calculated for each of the 12 replications. It appears from Exhibit 10–29 that inventories could be reduced at all levels in the supply chain with the exception of retail.

EXHIBIT 10–29
Model Beer Game.doe Crystal Reports (Time-Persistent Statistics)

Time Persistent

Time Persistent	Average	Half Width	Minimum Average	Maximum Average	Minimum Value	Maximum Value
Inventory Kegs 1 Retailer	61.4139	1.70	56.5667	66.1667	0.00	137.00
Inventory Kegs 2 Wholesaler	158.19	4.81	140.00	165.00	50.0000	300.00
Inventory Kegs 3 Distributor	220.97	7.43	193.33	236.67	50.0000	400.00
Inventory Kegs 4 Factory	373.33	19.28	318.33	420.00	50.0000	500.00
Kegs Backordered 1 Retailer	0.00	0.00	0.00	0.00	0.00	0.00
Kegs Backordered 2 Wholesaler	0.00	0.00	0.00	0.00	0.00	0.00
Kegs Backordered 3 Distributor	0.00	0.00	0.00	0.00	0.00	0.00
Kegs Backordered 4 Factory	0.00	0.00	0.00	0.00	0.00	0.00
Kegs On Hand 1 Retailer	61.4139	1.70	56.5667	66.1667	0.00	137.00
Kegs On Hand 2 Wholesaler	158.19	4.81	140.00	165.00	50.0000	300.00
Kegs On Hand 3 Distributor	220.97	7.43	193.33	236.67	50.0000	400.00
Kegs On Hand 4 Factory	373.33	19.28	318.33	420.00	50.0000	500.00
Kegs On Order 1 Retailer	91.3889	1.91	86.6667	96.6667	0.00	200.00
Kegs On Order 2 Wholesaler	91.6667	5.30	80.0000	100.00	0.00	150.00
Kegs On Order 3 Distributor	93.3333	5.71	80.0000	106.67	0.00	200.00
Kegs On Order 4 Factory	23.6111	3.80	16.6667	33.3333	0.00	250.00

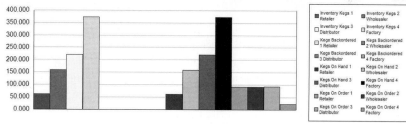

EXHIBIT 10–30   **Model Beer Game.doe Crystal Reports**

Output	Average	Half Width	Minimum Average	Maximum Average
Cost Holding 1 Retailer	553.98	15.10	509.10	595.50
Cost Holding 2 Wholesaler	1184.38	35.38	1050.00	1237.50
Cost Holding 3 Distributor	1392.50	34.39	1280.00	1460.00
Cost Holding 4 Factory	1748.75	81.00	1545.00	1965.00
Cost Holding Total	4879.60	122.43	4430.00	5149.60
Cost Penalty 1 Retailer	0.00	0.00	0.00	0.00
Cost Penalty 2 Wholesaler	0.00	0.00	0.00	0.00
Cost Penalty 3 Distributor	0.00	0.00	0.00	0.00
Cost Penalty 4 Factory	0.00	0.00	0.00	0.00
Cost Penalty Total	0.00	0.00	0.00	0.00
Kegs Received by 1 Retailer	683.33	24.73	600.00	700.00
Kegs Received by 2 Wholesaler	687.50	49.08	600.00	750.00
Kegs Received by 3 Distributor	700.00	66.36	600.00	800.00
Kegs Received by 4 Factory	708.33	114.01	500.00	1000.00
Orders Placed by 1 Retailer	6.9167	0.18	6.0000	7.0000
Orders Placed by 2 Wholesaler	4.5833	0.33	4.0000	5.0000
Orders Placed by 3 Distributor	3.5000	0.33	3.0000	4.0000
Orders Placed by 4 Factory	2.8333	0.60	2.0000	4.0000
Orders Shipped by 1 Retailer	29.5833	0.33	29.0000	30.0000
Orders Shipped by 2 Wholesaler	6.9167	0.33	6.0000	8.0000
Orders Shipped by 3 Distributor	4.7500	0.39	4.0000	6.0000
Orders Shipped by 4 Factory	3.5000	0.33	3.0000	4.0000
Profit 1 Retailer	2192.69	71.35	1981.20	2363.20
Profit 2 Wholesaler	1378.13	100.13	1062.50	1575.00
Profit 3 Distributor	1013.75	187.66	660.00	1345.00
Profit 4 Factory	526.25	251.20	15.0000	1055.00
Profit Total	5110.82	381.69	4369.40	6104.00
Retailer Sales	686.67	16.15	636.00	724.00
Retailer Sales Lost	58.4167	10.43	34.0000	90.0000
Retailer Sales Lost Fraction	0.07807529	0.01	0.04563758	0.1158

Exhibit 10–30 illustrates the Crystal Reports Output Statistics for the complete 12-month simulation run; Average, Half Width (95 percent Confidence Level), Minimum Average, and Maximum Average. The reported Output Statistics include inventory holding cost, backordered penalty cost, number of kegs received, number of orders placed and shipped, and the profit are illustrated for each of the four levels. The total Profit and Retailer Sales in Kegs are also reported.

The goal of this simulation model is profit maximization. The monthly total profit averages $5,111 for the complete 12-month simulation run with a range of $4,369 to $6,104. The 95 percent confidence interval for average total profit is $5,111 ± $382 or a range of $4,729 to $5,493. An average of 687 kegs per month were sold compared to an expected demand of 25 ∗ 30 = 750 kegs. Arena reported average lost sales per month of 58 kegs or about 8 percent of the potential demand. In the next section, we'll run the Arena model with retail backorders allowed. In that case, no lost sales occur but backorder penalty costs might occur.

Challenge

Model Beer Game.doe Output Files

The display illustrated in Exhibit 10–28 can be selected following the Beer Game.doe simulation run using the Arena Output Analyzer. The Arena Output Analyzer reads, processes, and displays data files generated by Arena during the prior simulation run. The saving of output files is controlled by the Sta-

EXHIBIT 10–31   **Model Beer Game.doe Output Files**

Sheet Beer Game output files | Chapter 10 Worksheets

Output Description	Output Filename
Inventory Kegs 1 Retailer	InventoryRetailer.dat
Inventory Kegs 2 Wholesaler	InventoryWholesaler.dat
Inventory Kegs 3 Distributor	InventoryDistributor.dat
Inventory Kegs 4 Factory	InventoryFactory.dat
Kegs Backordered 1 Retailer	KegsBackOrderedRetailer.dat
Kegs Backordered 2 Wholesaler	KegsBackOrderedWholesaler.dat
Kegs Backordered 3 Distributor	KegsBackOrderedDistributor.dat
Kegs Backordered 4 Factory	KegsBackOrderedFactory.dat
Kegs On Hand 1 Retailer	KegsOnHandRetailer.dat
Kegs On Hand 2 Wholesaler	KegsOnHandWholesaler.dat
Kegs On Hand 3 Distributor	KegsOnHandDistributor.dat
Kegs On Hand 4 Factory	KegsOnHandFactory.dat
Kegs On Order 1 Retailer	KegsOnOrderRetailer.dat
Kegs On Order 2 Wholesaler	KegsOnOrderWholesaler.dat
Kegs On Order 3 Distributor	KegsOnOrderDistributor.dat
Kegs On Order 4 Factory	KegsOnOrderFactory.dat

tistic module of the Arena Advance Process Panel. The 16 Arena output files saved during each execution of model Beer Game.doe are listed in Exhibit 10–31. Exhibit 10–32 illustrates a plot of two of these files: InventoryRetailer.dat and KegsOnOrderRetailer.dat for the 11th replication.

Exhibit 10–32 is similar to the plot in the upper left of Exhibit 10–28. The red or saw-toothed plot represents the Retailer inventory in kegs over the period from day 300 to 330. Each day the inventory is decreased by the demand, Normal (25, 5). Whenever the inventory decreases to the reorder point, 100, an order of size 100 is placed to the Wholesaler. This order arrives after a delay of four days. The number of kegs on order is indicated by the dashed or green plot. While the plots illustrated in Exhibit 10–32 aid in the verification of the simulation model, more interesting plots are obtained when the model includes additional variability. The reader is encouraged to run the model Beer Game.doe and analyze its results using the Arena Output Analyzer.

Model Beer Game.doe Optimization Analysis

The Beer Game has many decision variables that may impact total profit. The decision of whether or not to permit retail backorders may have a major impact on the total supply chain profitability. Other potentially key decision variables are the reorder quantities and reorder points for each of the four operating levels. This multi-variable decision problem is ideally suited to OptQuest software included with Arena. Unfortunately, the limited academic version of Arena will not handle a problem of this size. Thus, we have turned to the Arena Process Analyzer (PAN) program to assist our search for a solution that at least appears to maximize total profit.

Because the Arena Process Analyzer program can control the initial setting of model variables, a special version of the original model Beer Game.doe was prepared: Beer Game PAN.doe. This model removed the VBA code and the generation of Arena Output files to speed the model execution.

Because of the potential range of experimentation variables, we elected the following procedure for seeking an optimal Beer Game solution:

1. Base Case Reorder Points, No Retailer Backorders Allowed.

2. Optimize Reorder Points, No Retailer Backorders Allowed.

3. Base Case Reorder Points, Yes Retailer Backorders Allowed.

3a. Optimize Reorder Points, Yes Retailer Backorders Allowed.

4. Base Case Reorder Quantities, No Retailer Backorders Allowed.

4a. Optimize Reorder Quantities, No Retailer Backorders Allowed.

EXHIBIT 10–32

Model Beer Game.doe InventoryRetailedat and KegsOnOrderRetailer.dat

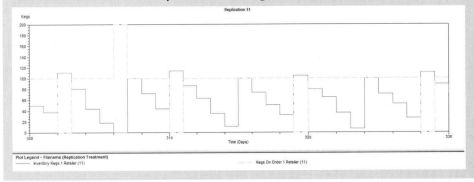

5. Base Case Reorder Quantities, Yes Retailer Backorders Allowed.

5a. Optimize Reorder Quantities, Yes Retailer Backorders Allowed.

Exhibit 10–33 illustrates the Arena Process Analyzer (PAN) program display using the file Beer Game PAN 1. PAN used the Base Case the Reorder Points with no Retailer Backorders Allowed. Eleven scenarios were tested. A base case with the Reorder Points is set at 100, 150, 200, and 250 for the four supply chain levels. Next, each of the Reorder Points were decreased and increased by 50 kegs for each level. Finally, all Reorder Points were decreased by 50 kegs and then increased by 50 kegs. Three responses were reported as Total Profit, Retail Sales, and Retail Sales Lost.

The information in Exhibit 10–33 was transferred to the Excel worksheet PAN 1 to facilitate additional analysis. That worksheet is illustrated in Exhibit 10–34 where it is sorted by total profit.

From Exhibit 10–34 it appears that the profit can be maximized by keeping the reorder point high for the Retailer level and low for the other supply chain levels. Exhibit 10–35 illustrates seven additional scenarios tested based on the finding of the initial Base Case experiments. While this search has been far from exhaustive, it appears that good results can be obtained with reorder points of 150, 100, 150, and 200 for the four supply chain levels. Also notice in Exhibit 10–35 that the total profit is relatively stable over the range of reorder points tested.

We next used the best solution from PAN 2, Exhibit 10–35, to test reorder quantities. The pattern reorder quantities screening from PAN 1 were repeated and illustrated in Exhibit 10–36. Notice the extreme sensitivity of the results to the reorder quantities. For example, the base case generated an average profit of $6,506. Decreasing the Retailer reorder quantity from 100 to 50 greatly increased the number of lost sales and with it the profits became a negative $50,848. Likewise, increasing the Retailer reorder quantity from 100 to 150 greatly increased the number of lost sales and with it the profits became a negative $40,260. Thus, a reorder quantity at or near 100 seems to be a "sweet" spot. In fact, only three of the 11 tested scenarios generated a positive profit. One additional scenario was tested (100, 200, 200, and 300) and found to improve the total profit to $6,888.

Although we cannot say that the "optimal" or maximum profit point has been found, a great many poor solutions have been eliminated by this testing. Exhibits 10–37 and 10–38 illustrate a similar search for the case when retail backorders are allowed.

EXHIBIT 10–33
Model Beer Game PAN.doe Process Analyzer (PAN) Display

S	Name	Program File	Reps	ReOrder Point (1)	ReOrder Point (2)	ReOrder Point (3)	ReOrder Point (4)	Retail BackOrders Allowed	Profit Total	Retailer Sales	Retailer Sales Lost
1	Base Case	1 : BeerGamePAN.p	12	100	150	200	250	0	5111	687	58
2	Low Retailer	1 : BeerGamePAN.p	12	50	150	200	250	0	1661	466	279
3	High Retailer	1 : BeerGamePAN.p	12	150	150	200	250	0	5690	744	1
4	Low Wholesaler	1 : BeerGamePAN.p	12	100	100	200	250	0	5328	687	58
5	High Wholesaler	1 : BeerGamePAN.p	12	100	200	200	250	0	4807	687	58
6	Low Distributor	1 : BeerGamePAN.p	12	100	150	150	250	0	5323	687	58
7	High Distributor	1 : BeerGamePAN.p	12	100	150	250	250	0	4763	687	58
8	Low Factory	1 : BeerGamePAN.p	12	100	150	200	200	0	5336	687	58
9	High Factory	1 : BeerGamePAN.p	12	100	150	200	300	0	4911	687	58
10	Low All	1 : BeerGamePAN.p	12	50	100	150	200	0	2542	466	279
11	High All	1 : BeerGamePAN.p	12	150	200	250	300	0	4864	744	1

EXHIBIT 10–34
Model Beer Game.doe Results, PAN 1
Sheet PAN 1 | Chapter 10 Worksheets.xls

	Beer Game Analysis	Process Analysis and Improvement: Tools and Techniques Copyright ©2005 by The McGraw-Hill Companies, Inc.					Simulation Results 12-Month Averages		
	Search 1	ReOrder Point				Retailer	Goal Maximize	Retailer Sales	
Simulation Number	Scenario	1 Retailer	2 Wholesaler	3 Distributor	4 Factory	Backorders Allowed?	Profit	Completed	Lost
2	Low Retailer	50	150	200	250	0 = No	$1,661	466	279
10	Low All	50	100	150	200	0 = No	$2,542	466	279
7	High Distributor	100	150	250	250	0 = No	$4,763	687	58
5	High Wholesaler	100	200	200	250	0 = No	$4,807	687	58
11	High All	150	200	250	300	0 = No	$4,864	744	1
9	High Factory	100	150	200	300	0 = No	$4,911	687	58
1	Base Case	100	150	200	250	0 = No	$5,111	687	58
6	Low Distributor	100	150	150	250	0 = No	$5,323	687	58
4	Low Wholesaler	100	100	200	250	0 = No	$5,328	687	58
8	Low Factory	100	150	200	200	0 = No	$5,336	687	58
3	High Retailer	150	150	200	250	0 = No	$5,690	744	1

EXHIBIT 10–35
Model Beer Game.doe Results, PAN 2
Sheet PAN 2 |
Chapter 10
Worksheets.xls

Beer Game Analysis		Process Analysis and Improvement: Tools and Techniques Copyright ©2005 by The McGraw-Hill Companies, Inc.					Simulation Results 12-Month Averages		
Search 2		ReOrder Point				Retailer Backorders Allowed?	Goal Maximize Profit	Retailer Sales	
Simulation Number	Scenario	1 Retailer	2 Wholesaler	3 Distributor	4 Factory			Completed	Lost
12	High- Retailer	125	150	200	250	0 = No	$5,750	734	11
13	High Retailer	150	150	200	250	0 = No	$5,690	744	1
14	High+ Retailer	175	150	200	250	0 = No	$5,500	744	1
15	HR Low Wholesale	150	100	200	250	0 = No	$5,960	744	1
16	HR Low Distributor	150	150	150	250	0 = No	$5,833	744	1
17	HR Low Factory	150	150	200	200	0 = No	$5,921	744	1
18	HR Low Others	150	100	150	200	0 = No	$6,506	744	1

EXHIBIT 10–36
Model Beer Game.doe Results, PAN 3
Sheet PAN 3 |
Chapter 10
Worksheets.xls

Beer Game Analysis		Process Analysis and Improvement: Tools and Techniques					Copyright ©2005 by The McGraw-Hill Companies, Inc.				Simulation Results 12-Month Averages		
Search 3		ReOrder Point				Retailer Backorders Allowed?	ReOrder Quantity				Goal Maximize Profit	Retailer Sales	
Simulation Number	Scenario	1 Retailer	2 Wholesaler	3 Distributor	4 Factory		1 Retailer	2 Wholesaler	3 Distributor	4 Factory		Completed	Lost
1	Base Case	150	100	150	200	0 = No	100	150	200	250	$6,506	744	1
2	Low Retailer	150	100	150	200	0 = No	50	150	200	250	-$50,848	79	666
3	High Retailer	150	100	150	200	0 = No	150	150	200	250	-$40,260	54	691
4	Low Wholesaler	150	100	150	200	0 = No	100	100	200	250	-$20,910	29	716
5	High Wholesaler	150	100	150	200	0 = No	100	200	200	250	$6,739	744	1
6	Low Distributor	150	100	150	200	0 = No	100	150	150	250	-$47,656	183	562
7	High Distributor	150	100	150	200	0 = No	100	150	250	250	-$30,083	125	620
8	Low Factory	150	100	150	200	0 = No	100	150	200	200	-$19,430	71	674
9	High Factory	150	100	150	200	0 = No	100	150	200	300	$6,713	744	1
10	Low All	150	100	150	200	0 = No	50	100	150	200	-$47,950	117	628
11	High All	150	100	150	200	0 = No	150	200	250	300	-$32,088	71	674
12	High Wholesaler & Factory	150	100	150	200	0 = No	100	200	200	300	$6,888	744	1

EXHIBIT 10–37
Model Beer Game.doe Results, PAN 4
Sheet PAN 4 |
Chapter 10
Worksheets.xls

Beer Game Analysis		Process Analysis and Improvement: Tools and Techniques Copyright ©2005 by The McGraw-Hill Companies, Inc.					Simulation Results 12-Month Averages		
Search 4		ReOrder Point				Retailer Backorders Allowed?	Goal Maximize Profit	Retailer Sales	
Simulation Number	Scenario	1 Retailer	2 Wholesaler	3 Distributor	4 Factory			Completed	Lost
2	Low Retailer	50	150	200	250	1 = Yes	$4,573	745	0
11	High All	150	200	250	300	1 = Yes	$4,945	745	0
10	Low All	50	100	150	200	1 = Yes	$5,617	745	0
5	High Wholesaler	100	200	200	250	1 = Yes	$5,684	745	0
3	High Retailer	150	150	200	250	1 = Yes	$5,781	745	0
7	High Distributor	100	150	250	250	1 = Yes	$5,800	745	0
9	High Factory	100	150	200	300	1 = Yes	$5,940	745	0
1	Base Case	100	150	200	250	1 = Yes	$6,125	745	0
6	Low Distributor	100	150	150	250	1 = Yes	$6,274	745	0
8	Low Factory	100	150	200	200	1 = Yes	$6,350	745	0
4	Low Wholesaler	100	100	200	250	1 = Yes	$6,380	745	0
12	Retail- Others Low	75	100	150	200	1 = Yes	$6,692	745	0
13	Retail Others Low	100	100	150	200	1 = Yes	$6,885	745	0
14	Retail+ Others Low	125	100	150	200	1 = Yes	$6,698	745	0
15	Retail++ Others Low	150	100	150	200	1 = Yes	$6,492	745	0

EXHIBIT 10–38
Model Beer Game.doe Results, PAN 5
Sheet PAN 5 |
Chapter 10
Worksheets.xls

Beer Game Analysis		Process Analysis and Improvement: Tools and Techniques					Copyright ©2005 by The McGraw-Hill Companies, Inc.				Simulation Results 12-Month Averages		
Search 5		ReOrder Point				Retailer Backorders Allowed?	ReOrder Quantity				Goal Maximize Profit	Retailer Sales	
Simulation Number	Scenario	1 Retailer	2 Wholesaler	3 Distributor	4 Factory		1 Retailer	2 Wholesaler	3 Distributor	4 Factory		Completed	Lost
1	Base Case	100	100	150	200	1 = Yes	100	150	200	250	$6,885	745	0
2	Low Retailer	100	100	150	200	1 = Yes	50	150	200	250	$7,112	745	0
3	High Retailer	100	100	150	200	1 = Yes	150	150	200	250	-$385,477	475	0
4	Low Wholesaler	100	100	150	200	1 = Yes	100	100	200	250	-$463,979	388	0
5	High Wholesaler	100	100	150	200	1 = Yes	100	200	200	250	$6,885	745	0
6	Low Distributor	100	100	150	200	1 = Yes	100	150	150	250	-$368,428	508	0
7	High Distributor	100	100	150	200	1 = Yes	100	150	250	250	-$385,039	475	0
8	Low Factory	100	100	150	200	1 = Yes	100	150	200	200	$7,404	745	0
9	High Factory	100	100	150	200	1 = Yes	100	150	200	300	$6,885	745	0
10	Low All	100	100	150	200	1 = Yes	50	100	150	200	-$620,596	358	0
11	High All	100	100	150	200	1 = Yes	150	200	250	300	-$613,371	329	0
12	Low Retailer & Factory	100	100	150	200	1 = Yes	50	150	200	200	$7,540	745	0

Two Unit Beer Game Model

The Beer Game model presented in the previous section included the four supply chain levels: Retailer, Wholesaler, Distributor, and Factory. The model assumed only a single unit at each level in the supply chain. Normally, the entity at each supply chain level is expected to service the demand from several lower level entities. For example, a single wholesaler may service 10 or more retailers. One distributor may service several wholesalers. To make the Beer Game model more realistic, a second Arena model was developed. Two Units.doe was developed to model the more generalized system illustrated in Exhibit 10–39. This two-unit model requires each supply chain level to service two independent lower level units. Thus, the factory supplies two distributors; each distributor supplies two wholesalers; and so on.

Exhibit 10–40 illustrates the Excel worksheet used to update the variable values for the Two Units.doe model. These variables are similar to the Beer Game.doe variables illustrated in Exhibit 10–15; however, they have been adjusted to more closely match the increased demands placed on each supply chain level.

The overall Arena simulation model logic is very similar between Beer Game.doe and Two Units.doe. The major difference is the added logic to track specific units requesting and being supplied kegs of beer. A second dimension has been added to most variables to track individual units. Because the retailer level has the most units, eight, that value is used for each level. Variable array Index (4, 8) is used to map or locate the specific unit at each level in Exhibit 10–39. For example, Wholesaler 3 services Retailers 5 and 6 and is serviced by Distributor 2.

Exhibit 10–41 illustrates the operation of model Two Units.doe. Compared to Exhibit 10–28, the maximum displayed inventory level has been increased from 500 to 2,000. The

EXHIBIT 10–39
Two Unit Beer Game
Flow Network
Page Two Unit Beer
Game | Chapter 10
Drawings.vsd

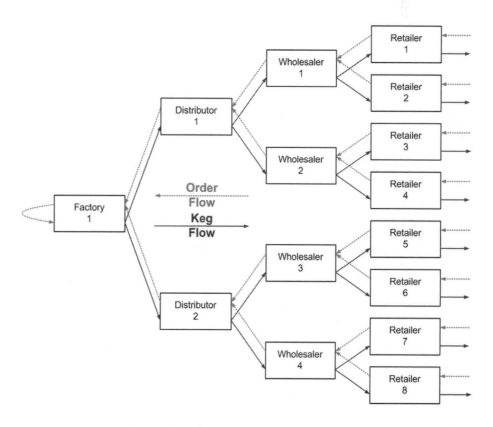

EXHIBIT 10–40

Model Two Units.doe Variables

Sheet Variables | Two Units.xls

Input Multiple Variables Worksheet	Beer Game Workbook	Data in Red May Be Changed		
Process Analysis and Improvement: Tools and Techniques Copyright ©2005 by The McGraw-Hill Companies, Inc.	Two Units per Level		Data Elements are defined in comments	
Retail.BackOrders.Allowed	0	0 = no or 1 = yes		

Arena Variable Array Name	1 Retailer	2 Wholesaler	3 Distributor	4 Factory	Units
Kegs.OnHand	200	600	600	1,000	Kegs
Reorder.Point	125	500	500	800	Kegs
Reorder.Quantity	100	200	400	800	Kegs
Order.Days	0	2	2	2	Days
Ship.Days	2	2	2	1	Days
Lead.Time.Standard.Deviation	0.00	0.00	0.00	0.00	Days
Keg.Profit	$4.00	$3.75	$3.50	$3.25	$ / Keg
Holding.Cost	$0.30	$0.25	$0.20	$0.15	$ / Keg Day
Penalty.Cost	$5.00	$2.50	$1.25	$1.00	$ / Keg Day
Order Lead Time	4	4	4	1	Days
Lead Time Demand	100	200	400	200	Kegs
Maximum Inventory Level	1,800	2,800	1,800	1,600	Kegs
Multiple Units	2	2	2	-	Units
Total Number of Units	8	4	2	1	Units

general level of inventory variability is similar. The most striking difference is the negative total profit generated by the Two Units.doe model. This difference is better illustrated in Exhibit 10–42, which should be compared to Exhibit 10–30.

As indicated in Exhibit 10–42, only the retailer level generated a profit in the Two Units.doe model. The reader is encouraged to alter the inventory control parameters to move this system to profitability.

EXHIBIT 10–41   **Model Two Units.doe Display**

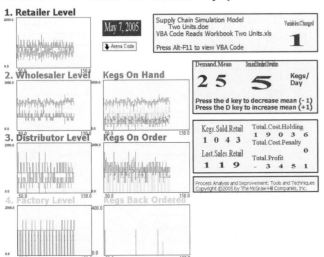

EXHIBIT 10–42
Model Two Units.doe
Crystal Reports

Output	Average	Half Width	Minimum Average	Maximum Average
Cost Holding 1 Retailer	5468.53	464.50	4406.40	6535.20
Cost Holding 2 Wholesaler	32225.00	1,270.97	30100.00	35450.00
Cost Holding 3 Distributor	25603.33	535.48	24360.00	26840.00
Cost Holding 4 Factory	36130.00	234.92	35580.00	36660.00
Cost Holding Total	99426.86	1,588.59	96046.90	103501.90
Cost Penalty 1 Retailer	0.00	0.00	0.00	0.00
Cost Penalty 2 Wholesaler	9645.83	8,810.89	0.00	30000.00
Cost Penalty 3 Distributor	83.3333	103.46	0.00	500.00
Cost Penalty 4 Factory	0.00	0.00	0.00	0.00
Cost Penalty Total	9729.17	8,771.23	0.00	30000.00
Kegs Received by 1 Retailer	5366.67	446.29	4300.00	6200.00
Kegs Received by 2 Wholesaler	5383.33	448.34	4400.00	6200.00
Kegs Received by 3 Distributor	5366.67	490.18	4000.00	6000.00
Kegs Received by 4 Factory	5400.00	490.68	4000.00	6400.00
Orders Placed by 1 Retailer	54.5000	4.36	43.0000	62.0000
Orders Placed by 2 Wholesaler	27.2500	2.20	21.0000	31.0000
Orders Placed by 3 Distributor	13.5833	1.16	10.0000	16.0000
Orders Placed by 4 Factory	6.7500	0.67	5.0000	8.0000
Orders Shipped 1 Retailer	221.00	17.58	180.00	240.00
Orders Shipped 2 Wholesaler	54.0000	4.44	44.0000	61.0000
Orders Shipped 3 Distributor	27.0000	2.30	21.0000	31.0000
Orders Shipped 4 Factory	13.5000	1.17	11.0000	16.0000
Profit 1 Retailer	16387.14	1,315.91	13192.50	18184.50
Profit 2 Wholesaler	-21620.83	11,676.31	-48575	-7975
Profit 3 Distributor	-6786.67	2,099.42	-12060	-2910
Profit 4 Factory	-18580.00	1,697.84	-22360	-14780
Profit Total	-30600.36	16,408.62	-69095	-9192
Retailer Sales	5463.92	436.61	4419.00	6023.00
Retailer Sales Lost	531.33	432.06	32.0000	1553.00
Retailer Sales Lost Fraction	0.08870543	0.07	0.00543478	0.2600

Exercises

1. Comment on the Lead Time syndrome and the Inventory Reduction syndrome as it impacts a product supply chain. Would it benefit businesses if they recognized these syndromes? What would you suggest they should do to improve their operations?

2. Comment on the four principles described in this chapter with regard to how these facilitate product supply chain improvements.

3. Describe how to implement a major supply chain management initiative for a business organization vis-à-vis its trading partners (major customers, major suppliers, logistics providers, and financial institutions) and competitors.

4. Experiment with the Beer Game.doe input variables to find the least total (holding + penalty) cost solution with a mean daily demand of 50 kegs and 100 kegs. Assume that retail backorders are allowed and the demand standard deviation remains at 20 percent of the mean daily demand.

5. Change the lead times between Retailers and Wholesalers; Wholesalers and Distributors; Distributors and Factory and analyze the impact on inventory accumulations, backorder quantities, and various costs at various stages of the supply chain.

6. Change reorder points and reorder quantities for various business entities in the value chain and analyze their impact on inventories, costs, backorder quantities, and so forth.

Student Process Analysis and Improvement Projects

Summary and Learning Objectives

This chapter introduces the readers to four process analysis and improvement projects completed by students utilizing the methodology and application of computer-based tools described in this book. It also shows a general outline of the project plan for any process analysis and improvement study.

The learning objectives for this chapter are to

1. Critique the strengths and weaknesses of process analysis and improvement projects presented in this chapter.
2. Develop a process analysis and improvement project plan.
3. Develop a process analysis and improvement project report outline.
4. Develop a process analysis and improvement project presentation format.

Process Analysis and Improvement Project Course

Project Assignment Description

The student process analysis and improvement project is designed to closely follow the procedures followed in the industry to analyze and improve processes.

Project Objective

The objective of the process analysis and improvement project is to review, analyze, and improve a complete business operation (such as the order fulfillment process, product distribution, product design and development, product manufacturing, production scheduling, etc.) using the tools, techniques, and ideas covered in the Process Analysis and Improvement course taught by the authors. Instructors act as facilitators in the use of tools and any guidance necessary to help complete the student project.

Project Gantt Chart

Exhibit 11–1 illustrates the course project Gantt chart. This Gantt chart was developed in Chapter 3 using Visio. The Gantt chart defines the general sequence of events found to result in a successful process analysis and improvement project. The time frame generally fits a typical college semester.

EXHIBIT 11–1 **Project Gantt Chart**

Page project Gantt chart | Chapter 11 Drawings.vsd

							Sep 2004				Oct 2004				Nov 2004				Dec 2004
Process Analysis and Improvement Project																			
ID	Task Name	Text Chapter	Resource Names	Start	Finish	Duration	9/5	9/12	9/19	9/26	10/3	10/10	10/17	10/24	10/31	11/7	11/14	11/21	11/28	12/5
1	Define Process Analysis and Improvement Project	1 & 11	Instructor	9/8/2004	9/8/2004	1d														
2	Indentify Process Analysis and Improvement Project		Student	9/9/2004	9/12/2004	4d														
3	Interview Project Personnel		Student	9/13/2004	9/15/2004	3d														
4	Present Project Proposal		Student	9/15/2004	9/15/2004	1d														
5	Refine Project Proposal		Joint	9/16/2004	9/22/2004	7d														
6	Visio Instruction	2 & 3	Instructor	9/15/2004	9/28/2004	14d														
7	Develop Visio Process Maps & Layouts		Student	9/16/2004	9/27/2004	12d														
8	Present & Review Process Maps		Joint	9/28/2004	9/28/2004	1d														
9	Excel Instruction	4 & 5	Instructor	9/29/2004	10/12/2004	14d														
10	Collect & Organize Process Data		Student	9/30/2004	10/13/2004	14d														
11	Analysis Process Data		Student	10/14/2004	10/26/2004	13d														
12	Present and Review Process Data		Joint	10/27/2004	10/27/2004	1d														
13	Arena Instruction	6 & 8	Instructor	10/13/2004	11/1/2004	20d														
14	Develop Preliminary Arena Process Model		Student	10/14/2004	10/20/2004	7d														
15	Develop Detailed Arena Process Model		Student	10/21/2004	10/26/2004	6d														
16	Model Verification & Validation		Joint	10/27/2004	10/27/2004	1d														
17	Develop Model Experimentation Plan		Student	10/28/2004	11/3/2004	7d														
18	Conduct Simulation Experiments		Student	11/4/2004	11/17/2004	14d														
19	Develop and Refine Conclusions & Recommendations		Student	11/18/2004	11/24/2004	7d														
20	Document Project Findings & Results	11	Student	11/25/2004	11/30/2004	6d														
21	Present Project Findings & Results		Student	12/1/2004	12/1/2004	1d														
22	Evaluate Project		Instructor	12/2/2004	12/8/2004	7d														

Course Syllabus

Exhibit 11–2 illustrates the 14-week course taught by the authors using the materials developed for this textbook. This course was designed for a student working toward a master's degree in manufacturing engineering.

Project Grading

In their course, the authors assigned 60 percent of the student course grade to the process analysis and improvement project. Various categories for a grading scale breakdown for the process analysis and improvement project include the following:

1. Comprehension of the industry problem.
2. Versatility in the use of computer tools.
3. Conclusions supported by analysis of data and other information.
4. Overall organization with proper headings.
5. Current references.
6. Glossary of terms.

Four Student Process Analysis and Improvement Projects

The following examples of process analysis and/or improvement opportunities are a cross section of successfully completed student projects. Details on each project provide a

EXHIBIT 11–2

Course Syllabus

Sheet course syllabus |
Chapter 11
Worksheets.xls

Week	Text Chapter			Topics Covered
1	1			1. Introduction to Process Analysis and Improvement
				a. Introduction to Computer-Based Tools: Excel, Visio, and Arena
				b. Drive and Eat Case Study
2	11			1. Application of Computer-Based Tools and Techniques: Student Case Studies
				2. Course Project Requirements & Software Problems
3	2			1. Process Improvement Using Visio
				a. Seven Process Improvement Tasks
				b. Process Mapping Symbols and Visio Stencils, Templates, and Shape Sheets
4	3			1. Applications Using Visio
				a. Cause and Effect Diagram
				b. Process Improvement Using Value Analysis
				c. Building an Organization Chart
				b. Creating an Office Layout
5	4			1. Data Management and Analysis Using Excel
				a. Basic Excel Concepts
				b. Advanced Excel Techniques: Data Filters, Pivot Tables, Optimization
6	5			1. Applications using Excel
				a. Quality Function Deployment (QFD)
				b. Technology Function Deployment (TFD)
				c. Six-Sigma
				b. Operating/Repair Cycle
7	6			1. Mid Term Exam
				2. Queuing System Analysis and Process Simulation Using Arena
8	7			1. Applications Using Arena
				a. Manufacturing Simulation Models
				b. Arena Academic Edition Limits
9	7			1. Applications Using Arena Continued
				a. Inspection – Rejection – Rework
				b. Material Handling Equipment
				c. Multiple Product Flows
10	8			1. Computer-Based Tools Integration using VBA
11	9			1. Application of Computer-Based Tools and Techniques
				a. Customer Service Center Case Study
				b. Arena Contact Center Edition
12	10			1. Application of Computer-Based Tools and Techniques: Supply Chain Management
13	12			1. Future Computer-Based Tools for Process Analysis and Improvement
				2. Course Evaluation
14				1. Final Project Presentations

description of the process, data collection and analysis, simulation, and the new or improved process.

The first case study describes the results of modeling a segment of the thin film recording head manufacturing process called the Stack Segment Wafer Process. The objective of the study was to identify bottlenecks in the manufacturing process as well as to predict cycle time, resource requirements, and work in process (WIP) flow. Data collection was organized in Excel and process modeling was carried out using Arena Simulation.

The purpose of the second case study is to construct a pulsed laser weld simulation tool for the cover to case weld in batteries used to power implantable medical devices. The tool was developed to be used as a thermal model during the initial design or redesign stages of a product development project. Ultimately, the goal was to create a system that would allow a user to select a different cover to case weld starting locations for a given thermocouple location and then to simulate the weld while charting the thermal profile of the preselected settings. The project utilized Visio to create the Master layout and Excel to store raw thermocouple data. VBA code was created to interface between Excel and Visio to provide the laser weld simulation.

The third case study relates to improvements in the existing assembly process of the electronic stethoscopes in a large multinational medical products manufacturer. The electronic assembly portion of the manufacturing process was targeted for this study to identify inefficiencies. Visio was used to map the process and data on process timings for electronic assembly were collected in Excel files. Arena simulation of the existing and improved process was carried out to come up with a series of process improvements.

The fourth case study deals with a U.S.-owned and operated semiconductor foundry, which provides foundry services for leading semiconductor suppliers and independent device manufacturers. The company has some challenges with the performance and capacity of the epitaxial area, which is one of the primary constraints in the company's complex manufacturing process. The first objective of the study was to develop a static capacity planning tool using Excel that can be used to assess gross tool requirements for the epitaxial area at various product volumes and mixes. The second objective was to develop a discrete-event simulation model using Arena that can be used to identify the impact of key input variation on epitaxial performance. And the third objective was to offer recommendation to the optimum levels of key process variables. Visio was also used to map existing and improved wafer manufacturing process.

Project A. Stack Segment Wafer Process

Process Description

Stack processing is a segment of the thin film recording head manufacturing process. Recording heads of disc drives read and write magnetic "bits" on the media. The stack-processing segment consists of preparing the substrate for deposition, depositing a complex stack of thin films, and then annealing them in a magnetic field. It is this process of building up structures for recording heads on a substrate that this study endeavors to model. The entire process of building structures on a substrate consists of more than 400 steps. Modeling the entire process is thus impractical and outside the scope of the course that prompted this project. The study was also limited to the production of a single class of product. In reality, many generations of products are manufactured in the factory simultaneously.

Data Collection and Analysis

The data collected was on resource parameters, such as maximum capacity, capacity, typical load, overhead and product load, unload and process times, and availability (MTBF and MTTR). The resources for wafer processing included CVC (a cluster tool used for vacuum deposition and processing of materials on wafers); Annealing oven; Matrix Ash tools; Prometrix (a four-point probe device for measuring sheet resistance); and Looper (a tool used in measuring properties of magnetic materials). The detailed wafer processing resource parameters data were collected and organized in an Excel spreadsheet shown in Exhibit 11A–1.

The wafer manufacturing process at this company was optimized at one time by professional industrial engineers. Continual development and changes to the processes make it unclear as to whether the process remains optimized or whether best practices have become relaxed. The objective of the study was to identify bottlenecks in the wafer manufacturing process, as well as predict cycle time, resource requirements, and WIP flow.

The simulation performed was for a 30-day period of operations. Ten repetitions were performed to acquire enough data for minimal statistics. Resources considered are made up of three types of processing tools, two metrology tools, and two operators. Two operators are used during each 12-hour shift. During any shift, there are never any more than two operators utilized. The same operators are cross-trained for all operations simulated. Failure rates were estimated for each resource except for operators. Batch sizes were modeled to be a normal distribution with a mean of 6.

Simulation

The first simulation performed represented the line load of a single product. The arrival rate associated for this was approximately one batch every 24 hours. The results are

EXHIBIT 11A–1
Wafer Processing Resource Parameters
Sheet resource parameters | Chapter 11A Worksheets.xls

Processing Resource Parameters				Load Time		Unload Time		Process Time		Availability Data	
				Overhead	Product	Overhead	Product	Overhead	Product	MTBF	MTTR
Tool	Maximum Capacity	Model Capacity	Typical Load	Minutes	Minutes / Wafer	Minutes	Minutes / Wafer	Minutes	Minutes / Wafer	Hours	Hours
CVC											
Tool1	12	10	6	1.32	0.50	0.52	0.26	47.80	19.70	148.41	2.00
Anneal											
Tool1	15	14	8	4.22	0.30	1.57	0.32		375.00	292.40	1.80
Tool2	15	14	8	4.22	0.30	1.57	0.32		375.00	292.40	1.80
Tool3	10	9	8	4.22	0.30	1.57	0.32		375.00	122.70	1.78
Average									15.00	235.83	1.79
Matrix Ash											
Tool1M1	12	12	12	0.30	0.07		0.12		2.62		
Tool1M2	12	12	12	0.30	0.07		0.12		2.62		
Tool2M1	12	12	12	0.30	0.07		0.12		2.62		
Tool2M2	12	12	12	0.30	0.07		0.12		2.62		
Tool3M1	12	12	12	0.30	0.07		0.12		2.62		
Tool3M2	12	12	12	0.30	0.07		0.12		2.62		
Tool4M1	12	12	12	0.30	0.07		0.12		2.62		
Tool4M2	12	12	12	0.30	0.07		0.12		2.62		
Average											
Prometrix											
Tool1	1	1	1		0.78		0.38		3.60	64.15	7.00
Tool2	1	1	1		0.78		0.38		3.60	64.15	7.00
Tool3	1	1	1		0.78		0.38		3.60	64.15	7.00
Average										64.15	7.00
Looper											
Tool1	1	1	1		0.183		0.167		6.217	38.79	3.00
Tool2	1	1	1		0.183		0.167		6.217	64.17	3.00
Tool3	1	1	1		0.183		0.167		6.217	85.34	3.00
Average										62.77	3.00

representative of the resource utilization for that single product. Since this product has nearly identical processing paths as a whole class of products, extrapolations can be made for general loading of the process path used in this model. Exhibit 11A–2 illustrates the main logic of Arena simulation model for stack processing.

Single Product Simulation Results One batch arrival every 24 hours is used as input for the single product simulation. The finish time is the average processing time in hours. Wafers out and WIP are average batches of wafers. The resource utilization represents the average number of resources that are busy. A percentage of available resources has been given. The results obtained and shown in Exhibit 11A–3 represented the averages for 10 iterations or replications.

These results showed the amount of the specified resources that were consumed by a single product. An average 10 percent of the Anneal Oven capacity and 14 percent of the CVC capacity was busy with a single product arriving at our simulation every 24 hours. As expected, there was on average no wait time for use of the Ash process. The Ash was the first step in the simulated process and its process time was far less than the arrival time of wafers to the station. These results seemed roughly equivalent to current factory performance data.

EXHIBIT 11A–2 **Arena Simulation Model Case-A. doe for Stack Processing**

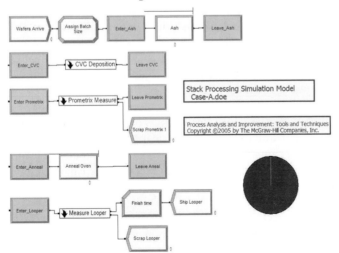

Stack Processing Simulation Model Case-A.doe

Process Analysis and Improvement: Tools and Techniques Copyright ©2005 by The McGraw-Hill Companies, Inc.

EXHIBIT 11A–3   **Single Product Simulation Summary Statistics**

Sheet single product results | Chapter 11A Worksheets.xls

Throughput Statistics

Finish Time in hours	Wafers Out	WIP
26.2	169	1.0014

Resource Statistics

Resource	Number Busy	Utilization	Wait Time
Anneal	0.313	10.43%	0.032
CVC	0.136	13.56%	0.027
Looper	0.004	0.19%	0.265
Matrix Ash	0.014	1.42%	0.000
Operator	0.024	1.20%	
Prometrix	0.006	0.32%	1.424

EXHIBIT 11A–4   **Batch Throughput Statistics and Chart**

Sheet batch throughput | Chapter 11A Worksheets.xls

Throughput Statistics

Start Interval (Hours)	Finish Time (Hours)	Wafers Out	WIP (Batches)
24	26.2	169	1.0
12	26.9	329	2.0
6	26.0	563	3.3
2	92.7	557	12.6

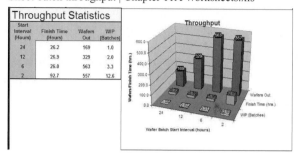

Increased Batch Arrival Comparisons Additional simulations were performed with a single batch arriving at our model once every 12 hours, 6 hours, and 2 hours, respectively. The comparisons of results are shown in Exhibits 11A–4, 11A–5, and 11A–6.

Data Analysis

A comparison of the results showed a rather dramatic change in performance metrics with a decreasing interval between batch arrivals. At two hours between batch arrivals, there appeared to be too much WIP in the system with long queue lines. The system appeared to be full since the number of batches out over 30 days did not increase despite increased starts between a six-hour and two-hour arrival interval. At a two-hour arrival interval the wait in the CVC queue increased dramatically. The amount of WIP in the system significantly increased between six- and two-hour arrival intervals. It appeared that the maximum arrival rate of single batches at the Ash should be between six and two hours apart.

EXHIBIT 11A–5   **Resource Utilization Statistics and Chart**

Sheet resource utilization | Chapter 11A Worksheets.xls

Resource (Utilization)

Start Interval (Hours)	Anneal	CVC	Looper	Matrix Ash	Operator	Prometrix
24	10.4%	13.0%	0.2%	1.4%	1.2%	0.3%
12	20.3%	27.3%	0.0%	2.9%	2.4%	0.6%
6	34.2%	45.1%	0.6%	4.7%	4.0%	1.1%
2	34.2%	44.6%	0.6%	4.6%	3.9%	1.1%

Resource (Number Busy)

Start Interval (Hours)	Anneal	CVC	Looper	Matrix Ash	Operator	Prometrix
24	0.31	0.14	0.00	0.01	0.02	0.01
12	0.61	0.27	0.00	0.03	0.05	0.01
6	1.03	0.45	0.01	0.05	0.08	0.02
2	1.03	0.45	0.01	0.05	0.08	0.02

EXHIBIT 11A–6   **Resource Wait Time Statistics and Chart**

Sheet resource wait time | Chapter 11A Worksheets.xls

Wait Time

Start Interval (Hours)	Looper	Prometrix	Anneal	Matrix Ash	CVC
24	0.27	1.42	0.03	0.00	0.03
12	0.34	1.76	0.11	0.00	0.05
6	0.30	1.24	0.33	0.00	0.20
2	0.47	1.39	1.93	0.00	6.50

Project B. Pulsed Laser Weld Simulation Design

Process Description

This project is about the design of a pulsed laser weld simulation system tool for the cover to case weld in batteries used in implantable medical devices. The system would enable a user to select a different starting location of a battery cover to case weld after selecting different locations in the battery that are thermally sensitive. Subsequently, the system facilitated simulation of the weld while charting the thermal profile of the preselected locations.

Most batteries manufactured by this company are prismatic, single-cell batteries. There are as many as six laser welds per battery cell. Many of the batteries' components are highly sensitive to thermal input. The cover to case weld joint geometries vary in length, width, height, and corner radius. A cover design that minimizes the cover to case gap is generally chosen for qualification. This helps provide a more uniform weld both visually and thermally. The project requirements included a user interface that must be extremely user friendly; simulation tools accessible to all design staff; and a database that must be easy to update and maintain.

Data Collection and Analysis

The three critical procedures that needed to be defined for this project to be successful were

- Database
  - Raw Data Collection
  - Database Arrangement
- Interface
  - Interface Construction
- Simulation
  - Interface and Database Integration

Each of these topics was addressed individually.

Database Data were collected with an omega tempbook/66 thermocouple/voltage measurement system. Type "k" 30 gauge thermocouple wire with a deviation of 0.5 degree Fahrenheit (F) at 399.5 degree F was resistance welded to the case and cover in thermally sensitive locations (for this project, a location on the cover was randomly chosen, shown in Exhibit 11B–1 for thermocouple location). One thousand data points were collected per run at a frequency of 70 hertz (Hz). The data was then arranged in an Excel spreadsheet.

Interface Visio was used as the interface and served as the master. First, a menu page was created and illustrated in Exhibit 11B–2.

The function of the menu page was to provide a starting place for the user. In the middle of the page, a 2-D model of the cover to case weld surface was created. On the weld surface, four different start locations were mapped by numbered circles, which were hyperlinked to their own pages. Pointers displaying the weld joint geometry and thermocouple location were also displayed.

A separate page was constructed for each start location (see Exhibit 11B–3 for the Start Location 1 page).

At the top of the start location pages, four hyperlinks were created for easy transfer between the other start location options and the menu. Below that, three command buttons were developed. The first was a Start Weld button, the second a Reset button, and the third a Results button. In the center of the page, the 2-D model of the weld surface was displayed with the start location and thermocouple locators. An Excel chart was placed on the bottom of the page. The chart was linked to the Excel file containing the raw thermocouple data.

EXHIBIT 11B–1
Thermocouple Location on Battery
Page menu | Chapter 11B Drawings.vsd

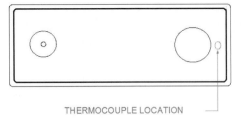

THERMOCOUPLE LOCATION

EXHIBIT 11B–2
Menu Page for the Simulation Tool
Page menu | Chapter 11B Drawings.vsd

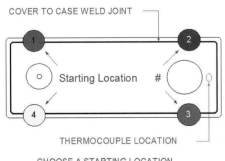

COVER TO CASE WELD JOINT

Starting Location   #

THERMOCOUPLE LOCATION

CHOOSE A STARTING LOCATION

EXHIBIT 11B–3

Separate Page for Each Starting Location

Page Start 1 | Chapter 11B Drawings.vsd

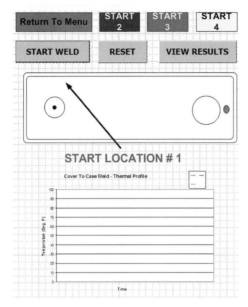

EXHIBIT 11B–4

Shapes Dropped Onto the Weld Joint Template

Page Start 1 | Chapter 11B Drawings.vsd

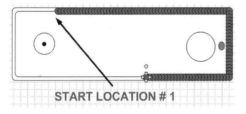

EXHIBIT 11B–5

Thermal Profile of the Weld Generated by Simulation

Sheet Chart 1 | Chapter 11B Worksheets.xls

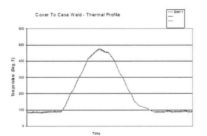

Simulation

For this project, two of the most common battery geometries were modeled and targeted for simulation. Visio VBA code was created to interface between Excel and Visio to provide the laser weld simulation. A master shape was created to imitate a single laser pulse. The blue ball shape was saved as a Visio stencil. The Shape sheet for each pulse was defined in the VBA Code. The shapes were then dropped onto the weld joint template via the VBA code (see Exhibit 11B–4).

The raw thermocouple data in Excel was manipulated with the Visio VBA code so that the Excel chart could plot the thermal profile of the weld as the weld simulation took place (see Exhibit 11B–5).

Designed Process

The simulation is controlled by the three command buttons on the interface. Behind each command button is the VBA code that executes a portion of the simulation. Some general weld parameter information along with the maximum temperature data is displayed when the results button is activated. The maximum temperature results are pulled from the Excel database. A temperature of 0 degree F shows up if the simulation for that given start location has not yet been run. Several safety features were built into the VBA code to make the simulation as user friendly as possible.

In this project, no quantifiable results are available. However, a number of qualitative results were identified. For instance, this simulation system was intended for use during the development stages of a battery and is likely to reduce product development time. It must simply demonstrate approximate thermal profiles in key locations internal to the battery. This tool would guide development engineers when determining material selection and internal component placement so that thermal damage from the weld zone can be avoided. The tool is being used as a technology show piece in the company's science and technology shows. It is also becoming a visual tool for nontechnical people involved in product design and development.

Project C. Medical Product Electronic Assembly

Process and Product Description

This study describes the assembly process of the electronic stethoscopes in a large multinational medical products manufacturer and investigates methods to optimize this process. The electronic stethoscope is assembled solely at a single plant in Minnesota.

Product Description Very similar to a conventional stethoscope, this product allows the user to auscultate low frequency body sounds, such as the heart, as well as high frequency sounds, such as the lungs and stomach. The major advantage is that it can provide adjustable volume for amplification up to 14 times more than conventional scopes. In order to appeal to the existing market, the chestpiece was designed to be very similar in feel and ergonomics to the existing high-end products and emulate the same frequency response as the best conventional stethoscope. Added features include selectable frequency modes, auto-shutoff, and a low battery indicator powered by a standard AAA size battery.

Market The annual projected sales for this product is approximately $4.8 million. Customers include health care professionals such as family practice, general practice, nursing, cardiology, and veterinary practice. Through distribution channels, these stethoscopes can be purchased for the current suggested retail price of $389. This is a very personalized tool, which is primarily purchased by the end users and worn around the neck like jewelry.

Competitors Competition in the area of electronic stethoscopes has grown in the last few years with the growth of electronic devices becoming more readily available in diagnosis and the care of patients. Other current players include Agilent (Hewlett-Packard), Welch Allen, CadiTech, and DRG (Doctor's Research Group). Currently, this product is under constraints primarily in the areas of tight fabrication tolerances in the manufacturing of some components and high factory costs. Demand continues to hold the product in backorder with numbers slightly below projected sales. For this reason, the official launch of the product, including advertising and promotions, will not occur until these issues can be resolved.

While the fabrication tolerance issues are being resolved, the scope of this study was to investigate the entire assembly process including labor functions, which are not clearly known. Discussion with plant personnel made it possible to review the process from receiving to shipment of finished product. Specifics gathered at this time included tasks, time, and associated costs along with the important support of plant personnel.

Suppliers Components of the electronic stethoscopes are also used on the conventional (nonelectronic) product line. These include ear tubes, ear tips, and diaphragms, which are manufactured externally and shipped directly from the conventional stethoscope assembly plant in Massachusetts. Circuit board blanks are fabricated externally, and components used to populate the board blanks are purchased from external suppliers. Tubing is supplied by the same company that supplies the tubing for the Massachusetts plant, but it is shipped directly to the plant in Minnesota because the composition is different from other products. The chestpiece is investment cast stainless steel supplied by a supplier in Arizona. Microphone and speaker wiring assemblies are supplied by a local assembly house.

Data Collection and Analysis

Mapping the entire manufacturing process served as a frame from which to review the process for inefficiencies and areas for cost reduction. For the purposes of this study, detailed information is shown only in the area of electronic assembly. There are other areas of concern in the overall process, but for the purposes of this study, the electronic assembly area was used for simulation and the resulting analysis was used to propose cost reduction changes. Exhibit 11C–1 shows a Visio drawing of the electronic assembly process.

After mapping the process and holding a discussion with the process engineer at the plant, some redundancy was identified that may be beneficial to remove. One of them was the second nonvalue-added inspection procedure occurring after the manual parts insertion. This occurs just after another inspection prior to the ATE testing. The latter inspection could perform the same function as both and potentially reduce labor costs and increase throughput.

EXHIBIT 11C–1   Electronic Assembly Process Flow Diagram

Page electronic assembly | Chapter 11C Drawings.vsd

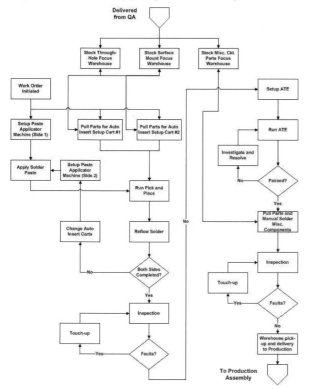

EXHIBIT 11C–2   Electronic Assembly Timing

Sheet electronic assembly timing | Chapter 11C Worksheets.xls

Function Nume	Delay Type	Time in minutes Mean	Standard Deviation
Pull Parts for PWB Auto Insert	Non-Value Added	10	5.00
Setup PWB Paste Applicator	Non-Value Added	5	0.05
Apply Solder Paste	Value Added	3	0.03
Run Pick and Place	Value Added	15	3.00
Setup Pick and Place Cart	Non-Value Added	20	3.00
Reflow Solder 2.0	Value Added	5	0.10
Inspection	Non-Value Added	5	2.00
Touch Up	Value Added	2	0.20
Setup ATE Test	Non-Value Added	5	0.20
Run ATE Test	Value Added	8	0.10
Investigate and Resolve	Value Added	20	5.00
Manual Solder Components	Value Added	7	0.20
Inspection 2	Non-Value Added	2	0.25
Touch Up 2	Value Added	5	2.00
Reflow Solder 1.0	Value Added	5	0.10
Pull Parts	Non-Value Added	15	0.20

The process timing for the electronic assembly area is illustrated in Exhibit 11C–2.

Simulation

Using Arena software, the process flow of the electronic assembly was mapped taking care of resource costs for the inspection steps (Exhibit 11C–3). For comparison, a second model was created with the first inspection process removed (Exhibit 11C–4). The two simulation models were run using the timing in Exhibit 11C–2 and

EXHIBIT 11C–3
Arena Model Case-C Present.doe: Existing Manufacturing Process

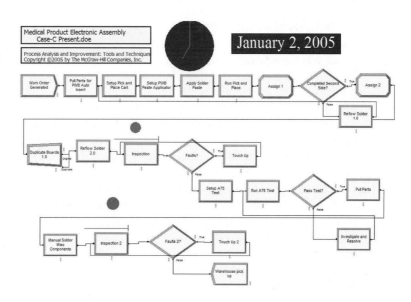

EXHIBIT 11C–4
Arena Model Case-C
Proposed.doe
Proposed
Manufacturing
Process

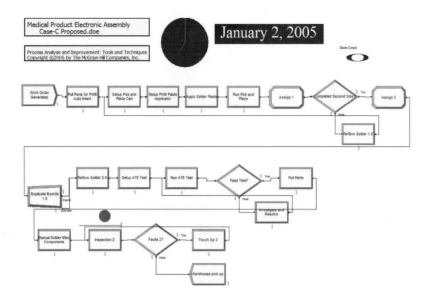

resources for both inspection stations at a rate of $40 per hour. Results pertaining to the existing and proposed processes are shown in Exhibit 11C–5.

Proposed Process

In order to determine if changing the identified inefficiencies would add significantly to justify their implementation, the time, cost, and feasibility of the tasks involved for the system overall would need further analysis. Reviewing the results of the simulation in Exhibit 11C–6 identifies a cost per part change from $4.87 to $3.37 or a potential savings of 30 percent by shifting to new proposed process.

Changing parts of the process and using statistical analysis to see the effects of changing demand, one can determine the possible results of changes to the process. This change alone may not be significant, but with other identified inefficiencies in the process, this could be an effective tool to reduce waste.

Project D. Wafer Fabrication Process Improvement

Current Business Operation

The company is the only U.S.-owned and operated pure-play semiconductor foundry that focuses on foundry services for leading semiconductor suppliers and independent device manufacturers without wafer fabrication facilities. The company has more than 30 years of experience in the semiconductor industry, exclusively in silicon analog and mixed signal applications.

The company originated in the 1970s as part of a major computer manufacturing firm. In 1984, the division was purchased and operated independently, specializing in the manufacture of high-speed integrated circuits. The company has shifted its business focus to pure-play semiconductor foundry services.

The company's ability to respond quickly and effectively to its customers' ever-changing requirements has earned the company recognition as the Flexible Foundry. By providing unparalleled design support, a broad range of process technologies and superior manufacturing methods, the company is able to provide its customers a level of service that is unique in the semiconductor industry.

The key to the company's success is in its ability to minimize the customer's capital investment in expensive manufacturing processes and to help them convert their design into a manufacturable product. Living up to the name *Flexible Foundry* has rewarded the com-

EXHIBIT 11C–5
Process Simulation Statistics
Sheet process simulation statistics | Chapter 11C Worksheets.xls

Simulation Statisitc	Existing Process	Proposed Process
NVA Time	35.6	0.83
Total Time	197.78	3.56
VA Time	28.21	0.73
Wait Time	133.98	2.01
NVA Cost	4.87	3.37
Total Cost	4.87	3.37
Number In	103	250
Number Out	100	250
WIP	16.73	1.24
Number Busy	0.37	N/A
Number Scheduled	1	N/A
Utilization	0.37	N/A
Busy Cost	350.55	N/A
Idle Cost	609.45	N/A
Number Times Used	107	N/A
Scheduled Utilization	0.37	N/A
Number Busy	0.14	0.03
Number Scheduled	1	1
Utilization	0.14	0.03
Busy Cost	136.41	842.38
Idle Cost	823.59	27,957.62
Number Times Used	102	253
Scheduled Utilization	0.14	0.03

EXHIBIT 11C–6
Product Cost Difference Before and After Process Change
Sheet process simulation statistics | Chapter 11C Worksheets.xls

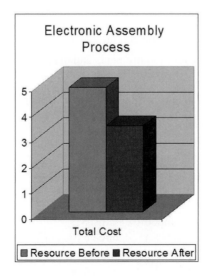

pany with a successful and growing business. What was once a small operation has grown into a company that employs more than 300 people and generates annual revenues in excess of $75 million.

The epitaxial growth process is a means of depositing a thin layer (0.5 to 20 μm) of single crystal material upon the surface of a single crystal substrate. The company uses the epitaxy process to apply a thin film of silicon on a silicon substrate. The vapor phase method (VPE) is utilized because it allows for maximum control of impurity concentration and an optimized crystalline structure.

The main purpose of epitaxy growth is to enhance the electrical performance of bipolar transistors and bipolar integrated circuits. By growing a lightly doped epitaxial layer over a heavily doped silicon substrate, the bipolar device is optimized for high breakdown voltage of the collector-substrate junction while maintaining low collector resistance. The low collector resistance provides for higher device operating speeds at moderate currents. Other advantages of fabricating devices in an epitaxy layer are that the doping concentration of the device can be accurately controlled and the layer can be made free of oxygen and carbon.

Problem Description and Formulation

Company management has expressed concern over the performance and capacity of the epitaxial area. With a significant increase in volume expected later this year and the continued diversification of the product mix, it is unclear if the epitaxial area is capable of meeting throughput and delivery requirements. History has proven that the epitaxial area is one of the primary constraints in the company's complex manufacturing process. It tends to be very sensitive to changes in unit volume and more importantly in product mix.

As the company's focus has shifted to foundry services, the product and process offerings have expanded rapidly. A manufacturing environment that was once characterized by few products produced in long runs is now characterized by many products produced in short runs. For a setup intensive tool such as an epitaxial reactor, this can pose significant problems. Lengthy setup times and demanding tool qualification requirements make it challenging for the epitaxial area to remain productive in an increasingly flexible environment.

Currently the company does not make use of either a static capacity planning tool or a discrete-event simulation model. As a result, the organization reacts to changes in processes or business requirements instead of proactively preparing for their occurrence. Management desires to establish flexible analytical tools to measure and quantify processes, to determine constraint operations, and to improve understanding of the variables that impact business performance. Three key metrics that must be considered are throughput, equipment utilization, and product cycle time.

The objectives and deliverables for the project are briefly outlined below:

1. Develop a static capacity-planning tool using Excel that can be used to assess gross tool requirements for the epitaxial area at various product volumes and mixes. This tool will serve the purpose of good rough-cut production planning.

2. Develop a discrete-event simulation model using Arena that can be used to identify the impact of key input variation on epitaxial performance. This tool will provide the ability to run "what-if" scenarios used to optimize epitaxial processing.

3. Offer recommendations to the optimum levels of the key process variables. These variables include the following:

a. Batch sizing to optimize utilization and product cycle time.

b. Recipe loading to balance tool requirements and maximize throughput.

c. Lot-start logic that minimizes reactor changeovers.

d. Tool qualification requirements to balance quality with productivity.

State of the Art—Factory Modeling in the Semiconductor Industry The detailed analysis of factory performance and resource capacity is vital to business performance in a semiconductor organization. The importance of capacity is related to many distinct factors, which are unique to the industry. However, the use of tools such as static modeling and dynamic simulation for capacity analysis is in the beginning stages for most semiconductor companies. The successful implementation of these tools is critical to the longevity of any organization in this increasingly competitive industry.

Regardless of the specific markets served, three basic performance measurements drive every semiconductor company; throughput, equipment utilization, and product cycle time. Each of these measures is opposed to the others to some degree. To ensure that the required volume and delivery targets are met, a company may add tool capacity to increase productivity. This strategy may accomplish this end but will undoubtedly have an adverse impact on tool utilization. This is a significant issue considering the level of capital commitment required in a semiconductor process. However, if the resource levels are too lean, the company's ability to meet the customer's delivery requirements will be dramatically reduced. The key is to be able to produce more with less without taking longer to do so. This sounds simple but is a substantial challenge for any company that lacks effective production planning tools.

The landscape of the semiconductor industry has changed dramatically over the last several years. There is greater emphasis on customization and make-to-order manufacturing practices. As a result, most companies are experiencing increased product variety, smaller production runs, shorter life cycles, and tougher delivery expectations. This places an immense strain on plant productivity and equipment utilization while making the task of production planning more complex.

The typical semiconductor production planner faces many issues and questions on a daily basis. A few of the common questions are

1. How many lots of which product need to be started each day?
2. What is the cycle time expected for the lot?
3. What is the effect of product mix on equipment utilization?
4. Which lots move next?
5. When should the machine get preventive maintenance?
6. Which lots should be batched together for this operation?
7. What is the impact of expedited lots?

The ability for the planner to use sound logic to answer these questions is critical to the ultimate success of the organization. Without having tools to assist them, the planner will be forced to use experience, intuition, and even guesswork to develop the production plan.

There are basically two types of planning tools used in semiconductor operations today: static capacity models and discrete-event simulation models. Each tool has unique features that address specific elements of the production plan. Essentially, static capacity models determine gross resource requirements (human and machine) and simulation models predict performance levels for such metrics as WIP and product cycle time. Because they both serve different purposes, it is important to incorporate both types of tools into any effective production plan. Given the capital-intensive nature of the semiconductor industry, the successful implementation of these tools can have an immediate impact on bottom-line performance.

"What can be done with fewer is done in vain with more." William of Ockham

Known as Ockham's Razor, this quote describes a common dilemma faced by many semiconductor companies. To achieve an acceptable level of throughput and product cycle time, additional resources are integrated into the process using a "brute-force" approach. This is known as slack capacity and is used to compensate for the lack of process understanding and to ensure delivery requirements are achieved. However, a goal of any organization, particularly in the semiconductor industry, is to maximize return on assets. To add fat to the process may result in improved delivery metrics, but it adds to product cost, erodes profits, and ultimately limits the organization's ability to remain competitive.

To minimize the need for slack capacity, a static capacity model must be developed to determine the appropriate levels of all resources required to meet product demand. The static capacity model is typically a spreadsheet that utilizes key process metrics such as forecasted demand, product routings, standard times, and equipment utilization to determine resource levels. The static model allows an organization to accurately quantify resource requirements, which reduces the need for slack capacity. Certainly it is not possible to eliminate slack capacity completely, but by using a static model it is possible to minimize its application.

Even though static capacity models are useful in quickly performing rough-cut production planning, they are not nearly as effective in determining the impact that process variation has on dynamic measures, such as product cycle time. Static model data is based on averages and expected targets. In most cases, they do not account for process variability. Common sources of variation that are important to consider are tool availability, workflow, product mix, and product demand. The accumulative impact that variation has on both resource requirements and operations performance is beyond the capability of most static capacity tools.

Typically, static capacity models incorporate a minimum buffer capacity of 10 percent to 20 percent to ensure that cycle time targets are met. They do not take into account many complex process elements, which are common in semiconductor manufacturing: batch processing, reentrant flow, rework, sequence-based setups, and time-bound processes, which further facilitate the use of buffer capacity. Static capacity models provide a rough-cut analysis to determine gross tool requirements. However, it is equally important to analyze the dynamic nature of the manufacturing process, which requires a more refined tool.

Discrete-event simulation models are used to determine the effect that process variation has on operations performance. These tools make use of specialized software, utilizing many of the same input parameters as the static capacity model. However, rather than using the average or targeted values for these parameters, distributions are used to integrate variation into the end result. That coupled with the incorporation of complex process elements such as rework, reentrant flow, and batch processing make this tool much more effective at quantifying key performance metrics, such as WIP levels and product cycle time.

Simulation models treat the entire manufacturing process as a unified system. They are useful in managing both constraint and nonconstraint operations. The goals of most dynamic simulation models include the following:

1. Plan and commit to demands based on resource capabilities.
2. Release lots intelligently to minimize queues and cycle time.
3. Predict constraints and manage them.
4. Determine leading cycle time contributors, not always the constraints.
5. Determine optimum dispatching logic.
6. Schedule items such as preventative maintenance events.
7. Balance conflicting demands—overall equipment effectiveness (OEE), quick cycle time, and customer satisfaction.

Along with the dynamic representation of the semiconductor process, simulation models can be used to run experimental scenarios, or "what-ifs." Prior to implementing new process changes, preventative maintenance schedules, or new manufacturing equipment, simulation scenarios can be established and executed to determine the net impact of the proposed change. This increases the likelihood that an optimum decision is made rather than implementing a quick decision based on gut feel and then hoping for the best.

"We are not concerned with local optimums." Jonah, *The Goal*

Oftentimes improvement decisions are made to achieve local optimums. For example, a decision may be made to increase the batch size for a setup intensive process to improve equipment utilization. This may improve this specific operation; however, it may also have an adverse impact on the downstream processes as well as product cycle time. By treating the entire process as a unified system, simulation models seek to determine the impact of the change on the overall process rather than achieve local optimums.

Typically the use of discrete-event simulation models results in a 10 percent to 20 percent increase in realized capacity without adding equipment. This is accomplished by clearly defining and managing the constraint operations to achieve a higher level of production without adversely impacting product cycle time. This is not possible by using sim-

EXHIBIT 11D–1 **Recipe Loading Profile**

Sheet recipe loading profile | Chapter 11D Worksheets.xls

Product	Epi Layer #	Epi Type	Epi 1 Recipe	Epi 2 Recipe	Epi3 Recipe
WHB1P	1	N		7	7
IP50	1	N		7	7
IP70	1	N		7	7
FP30	1	N		205	205
FP22	1	N		203	203
FP23	1	N		203	203
IP80	1	N		207	207
IP80	2	N		208	208
PMOS4/3M	1	P	1		211
PMOS4/3M	2	P	2		210
IP40	2	P	2		210
IP43	2	P	2		210
IP44	2	P	2		210

EXHIBIT 11D–2 **Recipe Parameters**

Sheet recipe parameters | Chapter 11D Worksheets.xls

Recipe	Epi Thickness (um)	Shot Size (wafers)	Epi 1 Time (min.)	Epi 2 Time (min.)	Epi 3 Time (min.)	Avg. Lot Qty.
#1	15	14	82.5			25
#2	3.5	13	67.3			22
#7	1.6	15		57	57	24
#203	7.1	15		62	62	24
#205	7	15		62	62	24.5
#207	2	12		57	57	24
#208	3.5	12		54	54	22
#210	3.5	13			72	22
#211	15	14			93	25
#255	5	NA		61	61	
Etch & Coat	5	NA	130.2	98	98	

EXHIBIT 11D–3 **Demand by Route**

Sheet demand by route | Chapter 11D Worksheets.xls

Route	Weekly Volume	% of Total Volume	# Epi Layers	Total Wafers	% of Total Wafers
WHB1P	1,075	32.0%	1	1,075.0	29.0%
FP30	640	19.1%	1	640.0	17.3%
IP40	340	10.1%	1	340.0	9.2%
FP22	315	9.4%	1	315.0	8.5%
IP50	275	8.2%	1	275.0	7.4%
IP80	240	7.2%	2	480.0	13.0%
IP44	165	4.9%	1	165.0	4.5%
IP43	110	3.3%	1	110.0	3.0%
PMOS4/3M	110	3.3%	2	220.0	5.9%
FP23	45	1.3%	1	45.0	1.2%
IP70	40	1.2%	1	40.0	1.1%
Total	**3,355**	**100%**		**3,705.0**	**100%**

ple static capacity models, which meet cycle time targets by incorporating slack capacity.

It is clear that both the static capacity model and the discrete-event simulation model play unique but equally important roles in the production planning process. Static capacity models are useful in determining gross resource requirements while simulation models quantify the impact of process variation on factory performance metrics, such as product cycle time. To optimize their effectiveness, it is critical to utilize both tools as a part of the production planning process.

Data Collection and Analysis

Three Applied Materials epitaxial reactors are used to process epitaxy:

1. Epi 1 is an AMC 7800 tool dedicated to P-Type epitaxy.
2. Epi 2 is an AMC 7700 tool dedicated to N-Type epitaxy.
3. Epi 3 is an AMC 7700 tool that is plumbed to process both P and N-Type epitaxy.

Seven epi recipes are used to process 11 different product families. The recipe loading profile by product and tool is defined in Exhibit 11D–1.

The key parameters for the seven epi recipes are defined in Exhibit 11D–2.

The forecasted demand and product mix applicable to epi are defined in Exhibit 11D–3.

The impact of operator equipment interference is negligible in comparison to the impact of machine failure, tool setup, and qualification requirements and will not be considered in the study. Five minutes are required to perform a tool setup, which represents load and unload times. The setup time is independent of tool, recipe, product type, or shot size.

Based on the projected volume and product mix, it is assumed that Epi 3 will be dedicated to N-Type epitaxy and will be converted to P-Type epitaxy, only if Epi 1 is down and a minimum of five lots reside in the P-Type queue. This limitation reflects the reality that nearly 100 percent of its services are required to meet N-Type demand and that a substantial situation must exist to justify the tool changeover.

The number of shots required to process a given lot will be calculated by the average lot quantity or maximum shot size. In practice, this may be a slight underestimation since tails exist at the end of a recipe run where the shot size will be less than the maximum. However, considering the forecasted volumes, the impact of this will be negligible relative to other effects. The average lot quantity estimates for each recipe are defined in Exhibit 11D–3.

Although initiating a reactor full clean is based on tool particle levels, it is estimated that a full clean on Epi 1 will be performed after 1500 +/−200 μm of epi and on Epi 2/Epi 3 after 1300 +/−200 μm.

The time required to perform a full clean follows the continuous distribution in Arena format:

$$\text{CONT } (0.70, 24 \text{ hrs}, 0.85, 30 \text{ hrs}, 1.0, 36 \text{ hrs})$$

An etch and coat is required after 150 μm of epi on Epi 1 and after 160 μm on Epi 2/Epi 3.

The number of test shots required to achieve an acceptable measurement follows the discrete distribution in Arena format:

$$\text{DISC } (0.50, 1, 0.95, 2, 1.0, 3)$$

Test shot measurements require 10 minutes of tool time in addition to the run time to account for the wafer measurement.

When converting from high-dope epi to either first or second epi on IP80, recipe 255 or a test shot must be performed prior to running product wafers.

When converting Epi 3 from one epi type to another, an etch and coat and a test shot are required prior to running product wafers.

A test shot and an acceptable measurement are required prior to running product if a good test has not been performed on the recipe in the last 24 hours. It is assumed that an acceptable production run counts as a good test.

Tool downtime, which accounts for all mechanical, engineering, facilities, and daily qualification events is estimated to be 13 percent. The mean time between downtime events (MTBDE) is estimated to be 46.9 hours and the mean time per downtime event (MTDE) is estimated to be 6.4 hours.

Methodology

To gain a clear understanding of the epitaxial process including all of the inputs, outputs, and key process variables, a process map was established using Visio. The lead process engineer for the epitaxial area was interviewed to gather the essential information for the process map illustrated in Exhibits 11D–4 and 11D–5.

EXHIBIT 11D–4

Epi Process Map
Page Epi Process Map | Chapter 11D Drawings.vsd

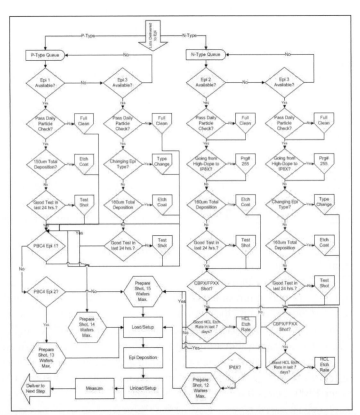

EXHIBIT 11D–5 **Tests / Quals Process Map, Page 2**

Page tests / Quals | Chapter 11D Drawings.vsd

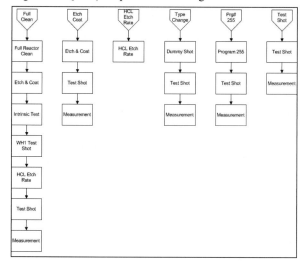

It is apparent from reviewing Exhibit 11D–4 that there are many restrictions and nonvalue-added activities that impact the throughput and flow of product through the epitaxial area. The yellow modules on the process map represent decisions and exceptions that are made prior to running product wafers. These activities are the core focus of this study to determine their effect on the capacity and performance of the epi reactors.

Utilizing Exhibit 11D–1 and Exhibit 11D–3, the forecasted demand by route was converted to forecasted demand by recipe. This demand is defined in Exhibit 11D–6.

Important variables in the dynamic model are the rate of arrivals and the number of lots per arrival. Historical data for the previous six months of production was pulled from the Visio information system and imported into Excel for analysis. See Exhibit 11D–7 for the Epi Arrival Rate Data and Histograms and Exhibit 11D–8 for Epi Arrival Quantity Data and Histograms.

In reviewing the histograms applied to the arrival rate data in Exhibit 11D–7, it is clear that for products of significant volume such as Prg 7 and Prg 205, the data follows an exponential distribution. The higher the volume, the more frequent the arrival of product into the epitaxial area. For lower volume products, such as Prg 203, it is difficult to determine a definitive distribution. However, as volume increases to the level indicated by the forecast, it can be expected that the arrival rate for these products will form an exponential distribution with a mean dependent upon the volume. The distributions recorded in Exhibit 11D–7 are useful in terms of establishing the exponential distribution that will be used to define arrival rate. However, in that the model will represent forecasted demand, the actual mean value of the data cannot be used and must be calculated individually for each recipe.

In reviewing the histograms applied to the arrival quantity data in Exhibit 11D–8, it is clear that several patterns exist depending upon the recipe. It is important to note that each recipe is unique in terms of its relative position in the overall product route, which impacts the expected quantity that will arrive in the epitaxial area. For example, Prg 7 is used on a WH1-type product where the epi step is performed on several masking layers after the lot is started in production. It can be expected that the number of lots per arrival of such a product will follow a random pattern, even though the product may be started in groups of four or more lots. As can be shown in the histogram for Prg 7, this random pattern results in an average of 1.57 lots per arrival.

In contrast, Prg 1/211 is performed very early in the process for the PBC4 type product. It can be expected that the number of lots per arrival will follow a pattern similar to that of the lot starts for PBC4. In that PBC4 product is typically started in groups of four lots, it makes sense that the average arrival quantity of Prg 1/211 into the epi area averages 3.06 lots.

Based on this data, it was decided that for recipes that do not follow a predictable pattern based on their proximity to either lot

EXHIBIT 11D–6

Demand by Recipe

Sheet demand by recipe | Chapter 11D Worksheets.xls

Recipe	Weekly Volume	% of Total Volume
#1/#211	110	3.0%
#2/#210	725	19.6%
#7	1,390	37.5%
#203	360	9.7%
#205	640	17.3%
#207	240	6.5%
#208	240	6.5%
Total	3,705	100%

EXHIBIT 11D–7
Epi Arrival Rate Data and Histograms
Sheet arrival rate data | Chapter 11D Worksheets.xls

Arrival Interval Histogram Data

Interval/Batch	Prg# 7	Prg# 203	Prg# 205	Prg# 207	Prg# 208	Prg# 1/211	Prg#2/210	Total
12	317	0	35	1	1	2	94	450
24	21	0	19	2	2	13	21	78
36	6	0	8	0	0	9	3	26
48	1	0	4	0	0	1	5	11
72	0	0	3	0	2	1	3	9
96	1	0	2	1	0	1	2	7
120	0	0	0	1	2	1	0	4
144	0	1	0	1	1	0	1	4
168	0	0	0	0	0	0	0	0
192	0	4	1	1	2	2	1	11
Sum	346	5	72	7	10	30	130	600
Average	4.76	274.33	22.55	205.75	164.60	53.10	12.56	2.72

Interval/Batch	Prg# 7	Prg# 203	Prg# 205	Prg# 207	Prg# 208	Prg# 1/211	Prg#2/210	Total
12	92%	0%	49%	14%	10%	7%	72%	75%
24	6%	0%	26%	29%	20%	43%	16%	13%
36	2%	0%	11%	0%	0%	30%	2%	4%
48	0%	0%	6%	0%	0%	3%	4%	2%
72	0%	0%	4%	0%	20%	3%	2%	2%
96	0%	0%	3%	14%	0%	3%	2%	1%
120	0%	0%	0%	14%	20%	3%	0%	1%
144	0%	20%	0%	14%	10%	0%	1%	1%
168	0%	0%	0%	0%	0%	0%	0%	0%
192	0%	80%	1%	14%	20%	7%	1%	2%

EXHIBIT 11D–8
Epi Arrival Quantity Data and Histograms
Sheet arrival quantity data | Chapter 11D Worksheets.xls

Batch Size Histogram Data

# Lots in Batch	Prg# 7	Prg# 203	Prg# 205	Prg# 207	Prg# 208	Prg# 1/211	Prg#2/210	Total
1	222	6	5	6	7	1	91	338
2	76	0	6	2	2	11	31	128
3	32	0	7	0	0	6	6	51
4	9	0	51	0	0	12	3	75
5	6	0	1	0	1	0	0	8
6	1	0	0	0	0	1	0	2
7	0	0	0	0	0	0	0	0
8	0	0	3	0	0	0	0	3
9	0	0	0	0	0	0	0	0
10	0	0	0	0	0	0	0	0
Sum	346	6	73	8	10	31	131	605
Average	1.57	1.00	3.71	1.25	1.60	3.06	1.40	1.86

# Lots in Batch	Prg# 7	Prg# 203	Prg# 205	Prg# 207	Prg# 208	Prg# 1/211	Prg#2/210	Total
1	64%	100%	7%	75%	70%	3%	69%	56%
2	22%	0%	8%	25%	20%	35%	24%	21%
3	9%	0%	10%	0%	0%	19%	5%	8%
4	3%	0%	70%	0%	0%	39%	2%	12%
5	2%	0%	1%	0%	10%	0%	0%	1%
6	0%	0%	0%	0%	0%	3%	0%	0%
7	0%	0%	0%	0%	0%	0%	0%	0%
8	0%	0%	4%	0%	0%	0%	0%	0%
9	0%	0%	0%	0%	0%	0%	0%	0%
10	0%	0%	0%	0%	0%	0%	0%	0%

starts or a queuing type operation, the arrival quantity would follow a random pattern similar to that of Prg 7. This assumption was applied to Prg 203, Prg 207, Prg 208, and Prg 2/210. For the remaining recipes, the arrival quantity was based on the histogram data, which reflects its dependence upon nonrandom events.

Even though the epitaxial process is a batch-type process where multiple wafers are processed together, the lot quantity must be determined in that the recipe shot quantity is most often less than the number of wafers in a lot. For example, a WH1-type lot is typically started in lots of 25 wafers. However, the maximum shot quantity for Prg 7 is 15 wafers. Therefore, multiple shots will be required to process the lot.

EXHIBIT 11D–9 **Average Lot Quantities**

Sheet arrival rate data | Chapter 11D Worksheets.xls

Recipe ▾	Data ▾	Total	Average Lot Quantity	Interval Hours
7	Count of Batch Size (L)	346	23.89	4.76
	Max of Batch Size (L)	6		18.22
	Min of Batch Size (L)	1		3.04
	Average of Batch Size (L)	1.566		
	Average of Batch Size (W)	37.43		
203	Count of Batch Size (L)	6	17.50	274.33
	Max of Batch Size (L)	1		274.33
	Min of Batch Size (L)	1		274.33
	Average of Batch Size (L)	1		
	Average of Batch Size (W)	17.5		
205	Count of Batch Size (L)	73	24.40	22.55
	Max of Batch Size (L)	8		48.59
	Min of Batch Size (L)	1		6.07
	Average of Batch Size (L)	3.712		
	Average of Batch Size (W)	90.59		
207	Count of Batch Size (L)	8	16.90	205.75
	Max of Batch Size (L)	2		329.20
	Min of Batch Size (L)	1		164.60
	Average of Batch Size (L)	1.25		
	Average of Batch Size (W)	21.13		
208	Count of Batch Size (L)	10	18.06	164.60
	Max of Batch Size (L)	5		514.38
	Min of Batch Size (L)	1		102.88
	Average of Batch Size (L)	1.6		
	Average of Batch Size (W)	28.9		
1/211	Count of Batch Size (L)	31	25.00	53.10
	Max of Batch Size (L)	6		103.96
	Min of Batch Size (L)	1		17.33
	Average of Batch Size (L)	3.065		
	Average of Batch Size (W)	76.61		
2/210	Count of Batch Size (L)	131	21.35	12.56
	Max of Batch Size (L)	4		35.98
	Min of Batch Size (L)	1		8.99
	Average of Batch Size (L)	1.397		
	Average of Batch Size (W)	29.82		
Total Count of Batch Size (L)		605	23.52	2.72
Total Max of Batch Size (L)		8		11.73
Total Min of Batch Size (L)		0		0.00
Total Average of Batch Size (L)		1.856		
Total Average of Batch Size (W)		43.65		

EXHIBIT 11D–10 **Arrival Data**

Sheet arrival data | Chapter 11D Worksheets.xls

Recipe	MTBA (Hours)	MTBA Distribution	MLPA (Lots)	MLPA Distribution	Average Lot Quantity
#1/#211	116.8	Expo (116.8)	3.1	DISC (0.03, 1, 0.38, 2, 0.57, 3, 0.96, 4, 0.98, 5, 1.0, 6)	25
#2/#210	8.1	Expo (8.1)	1.4	DISC (0.69, 1, 0.93, 2, 0.98, 3, 1.0, 4)	22
#7	4.7	Expo (4.7)	1.6	DISC (0.64, 1, 0.86, 2, 0.95, 3, 0.98, 4, 1.0, 5)	24
#203	18.3	Expo (18.3)	1.6	DISC (0.64, 1, 0.86, 2, 0.95, 3, 0.98, 4, 1.0, 5)	24
#205	23.6	Expo (23.6)	3.6	DISC (0.07, 1, 0.15, 2, 0.25, 3, 0.95, 4, 0.96, 5, 0.98, 6, 0.99, 7, 1.0, 8)	24.5
#207	27.5	Expo (27.5)	1.6	DISC (0.64, 1, 0.86, 2, 0.95, 3, 0.98, 4, 1.0, 5)	24
#208	27.5	Expo (27.5)	1.6	DISC (0.64, 1, 0.86, 2, 0.95, 3, 0.98, 4, 1.0, 5)	22

Historical data from the previous six months was pulled from the Visio system and imported into Excel for analysis. An Excel pivot table was created to summarize the expected number of wafers in a lot for each recipe (see Exhibit 11D–9).

As was the case with the arrival quantity, lot quantity is dependent upon its relative position to the start of the process. The earlier the epi step occurs in the route, the larger the lot quantity. The later it occurs in the route, the smaller the lot quantity as a result of wafer scrap.

The only adjustment that was made to this data was to the lower volume recipes, Prg 203, Prg 207, and Prg 208. The data contained in Exhibit 11D–9 does not represent the expected result once the products that utilize these recipes are processed in larger volumes as indicated in the forecast. The average lot quantities for Prg 203 and Prg 207 were assumed to be similar to Prg 7, or 24 wafer lots. The average lot quantity for Prg 208 was assumed to be similar to Prg 2/210, or 22 wafer lots.

See Exhibit 11D–10 for a summary of the arrival data and average lot quantities by recipe, (MTBA = mean time between arrivals, MLPA = mean number of lots per arrival):

To determine the availability of the epi reactors, tool event data was pulled from the Visio system and analyzed in Excel. Histograms were created to evaluate the mean value and the expected distribution of the mean time between events, as well as the mean time to up the tool. For analytical purposes, the data was summarized into three categories: mechanical failure (mean time between failure [MTBF]; mean time to repair [MTTR]); preventive maintenance (mean time between PMs [MTBPM]; mean time per PM [MTPM]); and downtime event (mean time between downtime event [MTBDE]; mean time per downtime event [MTDE]).

It is clear that the MTBDE and MTDE follow exponential distributions. However, the mean values for the data were adjusted to account for the fact that many of the downtime events captured in this data would be directly incorporated into the simulation model. Items such as etch and coats, full reactor cleans, and various tool qualification events are volume and mix dependent and are important variables to be considered in the model. As a result, the proportion of these items was estimated and eliminated from the historical data summarized in Exhibit 11D–11 for the adjusted availability data.

The input variables that have been defined in the previous seven steps were organized into a static capacity model using Excel and illustrated in Exhibit 11D–12.

The static capacity model essentially establishes a rough-cut plan of the epitaxial resources required to meet a specific demand based on the defined process. The model incorporates the following step-by-step approach:

EXHIBIT 11D–11   **Tool Availability**

Sheet tool availability | Chapter 11D Worksheets.xls

MTBDE (Hours)	MTBDE Distribution	MTDE (Hours)	MTDE Distribution	Availability
46.9	Expo (46.9)	6.4	Expo (6.4)	86.4%

EXHIBIT 11D–12   **Epitaxial Static Capacity Model**

Sheet static capacity model | Chapter 11D Worksheets.xls

Volume Mix Analysis:

Route	Wkly Demand	# Lots	1st Epi Prg.	2nd Epi Prg.	# Epi Layers	Total Wfrs.	Total Lots
WHB1P	1075	43	7		1	1075	43
FP30	640	25.6	205		1	640	25.6
IP40	340	13.6		2	1	340	13.6
FP22	315	12.6	203		1	315	12.6
IP50	275	11	7		1	275	11
IP80	240	9.6	207	208	2	480	19.2
IP44	165	6.6		2	1	165	6.6
IP43	110	4.4		2	1	110	4.4
PMOS4/3M	110	4.4	1	2	2	220	8.8
FP23	45	1.8	203		1	45	1.8
IP70	40	1.6	7		1	40	1.6
Totals	3355	134.2				3705	148.2

Demand by Recipe:

Recipe	# Lots
1	4.4
2	29
7	55.6
203	14.4
205	25.6
207	9.6
208	9.6
Total	148.2

Recipe Information:

Recipe	Type	Thickness	Epi 1 Time	Epi 2 Time	Epi 3 Time	Shot Size	Avg. Lot Qty	Shots/Lot
1	P Type	15.0	82.5		93.0	14	25	1.8
2	P Type	3.5	67.3		72.0	13	22	1.7
7	N Type	1.6		57.0	57.0	15	24	1.6
203	N Type	7.1		62.0	62.0	15	24	1.6
205	N Type	7.0		62.0	62.0	15	24.5	1.6
207	N Type	2.0		57.0	57.0	12	24	2.0
208	N Type	3.5		54.0	54.0	12	22	1.8

- Determine the required volume and product mix (number of lots).

- Convert product volume into recipe volume (number of lots).

- Quantify recipe parameters: process time, thickness, maximum shot quantity.

- Establish the recipe loading by tool, that is, which tools run which recipe.

- Document and quantify the critical constraints: frequency/duration of setups, full cleans, etch and coats, product changeovers, and test shots.

- Based on the input data, determine the total number of events for production shots, full cleans, etch and coats, changeovers, and test shots.

- Convert events into time requirements based on the recipe parameters.

- Distribute the total time to each tool based on the recipe loading.

- Roll up the total time for each tool and compare to both the scheduled time and the available time after downtime is accounted for. The end result is the percent of available tool capacity required to satisfy the forecasted demand.

- The static capacity model provides a very close approximation of the gross tool requirements to meet the forecasted demand. The results obtained from this tool will also help validate results obtained from the discrete-event simulation model.

Simulation Modeling

The final development step of the study was to create simulation models for both the P-Type and N-Type epi processes utilizing Arena. The information that was used to create the static capacity model was used as the key input to the simulation models.

Since both the P-Type and N-Type epi processes make use of a common tool, Epi 3, it would have been desirable to establish a single, integrated model. However, due to the limitations of the student version of Arena, this was not feasible. It was decided that two distinct models would be created with Epi 3 being a resource in each. Reviewing the static capacity model indicated that Epi 3 would be required to assist Epi 1 with P-Type epi approximately 5 percent of the time. Essentially this meant that it would only be needed in emergency situations where Epi 1 was down and the backlog of P-Type epi justified a tool changeover. As a result, the impact of not having a single, integrated model was minimized.

Even after establishing two separate models, it became necessary to make further accommodations to work within the restrictions of the student version of Arena. It became difficult to put together the N-Type model and maintain a maximum level of 100 entities in the system. Based on the volume being processed and the fact that the volume pushed the capacity limits of the tools, it was common for the WIP levels to exceed 100 units. To accommodate the restriction, the entity logic was modified such that each entity represented two lots instead of one. All pertinent metrics such as arrivals, process times, and epi thickness were adjusted accordingly.

EXHIBIT 11D–13
Model Case-D
P-Type.doe P-Type
Simulation Model

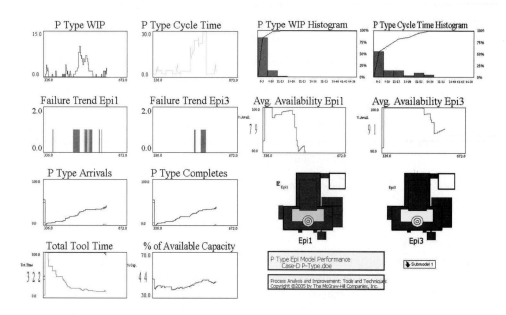

To provide a more detailed analysis of the model status, several charts were established to track the progress of the simulation. The following charts were created for both the P-Type and N-Type models:

- WIP level, including a histogram summarizing the results.
- Average cycle time, including a histogram summarizing the results.
- Failure trend (tracking individual failure frequency/ duration by tool).
- Tool availability (probability of tool downtime).
- Number of entity arrivals.
- Number of entity completions.
- Total tool time per entity (actual recipe time as well as time allocated for nonvalue-added activities such as etch and coats and full cleans).
- Percent of available capacity (total tool time/available time).

The P-Type simulation model is illustrated in Exhibit 11D–13 and the N-Type simulation model is shown in Exhibit 11D–14.

Once the base level simulation models were established and validated against known data, it became possible to run different scenarios to test the sensitivity of the model to changes in key variables. The results of these scenarios provided the basis for the performance improvement recommendations. The following scenarios were run:

N-Type Scenarios

- Effect of product mix, same total volume, but all WH1 products.

- Effect of limited shot size, run all recipes with 15 wafer shots.

- Effect of low volume arrivals, start FP2X and IP80 once per week.

- Effect of changes to the etch and coat and full clean thickness limits, increase etch and coat limit from 160 μm to 180 μm and the full clean limit from 1300 μm to 1450 μm.

- Effect of running IP80; same total volume but no IP80.

• Effect of changes to the test shot restriction, change the restriction from a test shot every 24 hours to one every 48 hours.

• Effect of the Prg 255 requirement for IP80 recipes; eliminate requirement.

• Effect of improvements to machine availability, increase MTBDE by 10 percent and decrease MTDE by 10 percent.

• Combination scenario, all shot quantities equal 15 wafers, start FP2X and IP80 once per week, increase etch and coat and full clean limits, increase test shot requirement to once every 48 hours and improve machine downtime parameters by 10 percent.

P-Type Scenarios

• Effect of changes in PBC4 mix, same total volume but increase volume of PMOS4/3M from 110 wafers per week to 330 wafers per week.

Analysis of Results

The critical results from the base simulation models are summarized in Exhibit 11D–15. In analyzing the results from the base simulation models, it is clear that there is a stark contrast between the performance of the P-Type and N-Type epi processes. Certainly there exists enough tool capacity to accommodate the forecasted demand. However, in the case of N-Type epi, the available tool capacity requirement is quite high at 94 percent. Running at this level, results in an average lot cycle time of nearly two days is unacceptable in an industry that is extremely cycle time conscious. This results from variation contributed from several critical factors: arrival rate, arrival quantity, product mix, and tool availability.

The accumulative effect of variation is the primary contributor to excessively high WIP levels and product cycle time. With only 6 percent, or about 75 minutes, of "cushion" time available per tool per day on the N-Type tools, any unforeseen downtime event that is significant in length is difficult to recover from in a timely fashion. In contrast, the P-Type epi demand consumes a mere 58 percent of the available tool capacity resulting in an average

EXHIBIT 11D–14
Model Case-D
N-Type.doe N-Type
Simulation Model

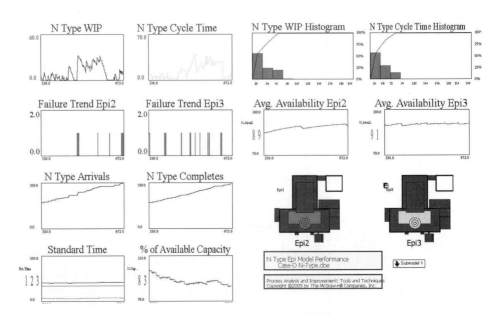

lot cycle time of 10 hours. This tool is much more responsive to recover quickly from after catastrophic downtime events.

It appears that an imbalance of recipe loading exists between the three epi tools. This is a constant dilemma with dedicated tools when the product volume and mix fluctuate. This issue can be attacked using a couple of different strategies. The first strategy would be to leave the recipe loading as it currently exists and address the constraints of the N-Type process. Constraints such as etch and coats, full cleans, test shots, and tool changeovers consume a significant amount of capacity and result in a low tool efficiency of 72 percent. The second strategy, recipe load redistribution, will undoubtedly require tool modifications. This may be the quickest and most cost-effective course of action. However, it may still leave a gross imbalance between the tool loads. To ensure that throughput and cycle time targets are achieved, recipe load redistribution may be a necessity.

The N-Type scenario results are summarized in Exhibit 11D–16. Considering the results from various N-Type scenario runs, it is clear that even small changes in the process inputs and variables can lead to dramatic improvements. The most dramatic result is the impact of product mix. Obviously, there isn't any direct control over the volume or product mix, but it is interesting to see the effect that the foundry business has on epitaxial performance. The second scenario where the same wafer volume was used with all WH1 products revealed that the available tool capacity requirement dropped from 94 percent to 67 percent and the product cycle time dropped from 47 hours to less than 8 hours. The primary reason for this is the greatly reduced number of test shots, changeovers, and qualification runs. To maintain effective utilization of the epi reactors, it will be critical for the frequency and duration of these events to be reduced as the product offering expands.

It is also interesting to note the effect of the IP80 product. Even though it makes up a mere 15 percent of the total N-Type epi requirement, IP80 has a significant impact on the overall performance. The sixth scenario where the same wafer volume is processed without IP80 resulted in a reduction in available tool capacity requirement from 94 percent to 82 percent and in product cycle time from 47 hours to less than 20 hours. The primary reason for this is the requirement of running Prg 255 before converting to IP80. The fact that the demand for IP80 is relatively small only compounds this issue in that it is difficult to justify the substantial setup investment.

The other scenarios have a positive impact on N-Type epi performance, albeit the impact is small in individual significance. However, if a few of these modifications are made in combination, these can result in substantial improvement. The combination scenario defined in the Methodology section resulted in a reduction of available tool capacity requirement from 94 percent to 78 percent and product cycle time from 47 hours to 21 hours.

The feasibility of accomplishing these enhancements is the primary issue. However, the point is clear that the restrictions imposed upon these tools are costly and greatly influence the capability to meet forecasted demand. These restrictions must be the primary focus for improvement as the demand continues to ramp. Certainly the cost to implement these changes is far less than the cost to redistribute the recipe loading or to purchase an additional tool.

For P-Type epi, the scenarios were much simpler. The only significant variable that would greatly impact the performance in

EXHIBIT 11D–15
Base Model Results
Sheet base model results | Chapter 11D Worksheets.xls

Metric	P-Type	N-Type
VA Time (hours)	2.1	1.8
NVA Time (hours)	0.6	0.7
Tool Efficiency	78%	72%
Wait Time (hours)	7.3	44.4
Total Time (hours)	10	46.9
WIP (# lots)	2	34.6
Utilization	51%	83%
Available Capacity Used	58%	94%

this area is the proportion of the P-Type mix made up of PMOS4/3M product. In that this product is the only PBC4 product requiring two layers of epi with the first being a 15 μm layer, any variation one way or the other will have a tremendous impact on the P-Type tool requirement. The P-Type scenario results are summarized in Exhibit 11D–17.

This scenario kept the total volume of wafers constant but increased the number of PMOS4/3M wafers from 110 per week to 330 per week. This resulted in an increase of the available tool capacity requirement from 58 percent to 76 percent and in product cycle time from 10 hours to 18 hours. It is important to consider this sensitivity prior to making any decisions regarding the redistribution of epi recipe loading. What may appear as an under-utilized tool may in fact be pushed to its capacity limit if the PMOS4/3M volume is significantly higher than forecasted.

The final set of scenarios involved the redistribution of recipe loading. It makes sense to evaluate tool recipe distribution since the P-Type epi tool is utilized only 58 percent and the N-Type epi tools are utilized nearly 95 percent. An option considered was to establish one tool dedicated to running N-Type epi and the other two tools equipped, such that they process both types of epi. The intent was to increase tool flexibility and to better distribute demand to improve throughput capabilities as well as cycle time performance.

Exhibit 11D–18 illustrates the recipe redistribution results summary. In reviewing these results, it is clear that the improvement was less than initially predicted. The primary reason is that in order to run both types of epi, the tool must go through a three- to four-hour conversion routine prior to running a different epi type. This results in a very low tool efficiency of 70 percent on Epi 2 and Epi 3. To make this a feasible option would require the staging of product by epi type such that they can be processed in larger batches resulting in fewer tool changes. However, this will have an adverse effect on cycle time and the ability to accommodate changes in demand and priority lots.

Based on the existing forecast, if the P-Type epi product was staged such that it were processed once per day, one of the tools would have to undergo two type changes resulting in a loss of nearly a full eight-hour shift per day. The data summarized in Exhibit 11D–11 was based on this assumption. Even though the improvement was less than expected, this scenario did distribute the work more evenly among the reactors and provided for a more consistent cycle time for all products. However, it did not improve the throughput situation, and a consistent cycle time of 30 hours isn't necessarily acceptable.

Consideration of Alternatives

Based on the data presented in this case, there are essentially four alternatives to consider:

1. Leave things as they are and accept the capacity and cycle time shortcomings.
2. Leverage improvement of the process constraints to address the capacity and cycle time issue.

EXHIBIT 11D–16   **N-Type Scenario Results**

Sheet N-Type results | Chapter 11D Worksheets.xls

#	Scenario	VA Time	NVA Time	Efficiency	Cycle Time	Capacity Use	Scenario Description
1	Current	1.75	0.68	72%	40.9	94%	Current situation as defined by Epi Flowchart.
2	All WH1	1.65	0.11	94%	9.2	67%	Same wafer volume but only running WH1.
3	15 wfr Shots	1.69	0.63	73%	37.9	89%	All shot quantities=15 wafers including IPBX.
4	FP20 & IP80 1/Week	1.75	0.51	77%	40.6	86%	Start FP2X and IP8X 1/week.
5	Increase ECT & FCT Limits 10%	1.75	0.64	73%	36.1	92%	Increase ECT to 180um and FCT to 1450um.
6	No IPBX	1.72	0.41	81%	21.9	82%	Same wafer volume but running no IPBX.
7	48 Hr. Test Shot Limit	1.75	0.60	74%	35.9	90%	Increase test shot requirement from 24hrs. to 48hrs.
8	No R255	1.75	0.53	77%	37.5	89%	Remove requirement of running Prg#255 before IPBX.
9	Improve MTBF & MTTR 10%	1.75	0.68	72%	40.2	90%	Increase MTBF by 10% and reduce MTTR by 10%.
10	Combo1	1.69	0.39	81%	22.9	78%	Combination: #3, #4, #5, #7, #8

EXHIBIT 11D–17   **P-Type Scenario Results**

Sheet P-Type results | Chapter 11D Worksheets.xls

#	Scenario	VA Time	NVA Time	Efficiency	Cycle Time	Capacity Use
1	Current	2.1	0.58	78%	10	58%
2	3x 3122s	2.27	0.83	73%	18.3	76%

3. Redistribute the recipe loading to provide better balance among the epi reactors.

4. Consider purchasing an additional tool to assist in N-Type epi processing.

Option 1. Leave Things As They Are   In an industry where so much emphasis is placed on product cycle time, it is unwise to accept the current situation. Of course, the forecasted demand must be validated before significant time, money, and resources are committed to process improvement. However, if the forecast is valid, the current situation must be addressed.

Most of the products that the company produces have a cycle time requirement of between 40 and 45 days. To absorb nearly two days of that total on a single epi product and four days on a double epi product is too much to bear and still have a reasonable chance at achieving the total cycle time target. Running any tool at 95 percent of available capacity would demand an extremely predictable and consistent process. Neither of these attributes would be used to characterize the current epi environment. An effort must be made to reduce the burden on the N-Type tools to a level of between 80 percent and 85 percent of the available tool capacity without reducing throughput.

Option 2. Constraint Improvement   This is as an enticing option in that it is relatively inexpensive in comparison to the final two options. As is evident with the simulation results, even small changes in the critical inputs can yield remarkable results. It would appear that the "biggest bang for the buck" would be in the area of test shots, etch and coats, tool failure, and the control of low-volume product starts.

The combination scenario described in the "Analysis of Results" section resulted in an available tool capacity requirement of 78 percent and a product cycle time of about 20 hours. If only half of this result was realized, it would certainly be a great improvement over the current situation. This improvement coupled with the relatively low investment makes it an attractive choice and one that should be considered regardless of the final selection.

The largest issue with this option is from an engineering perspective. The feasibility of addressing the current restrictions imposed on the epi tools without hindering the quality of the current process is a significant consideration. Clearly these restrictions were imposed for a reason and can presumably be substantiated with sound engineering data. However, they were imposed during a time when there was far less tool demand than will be required in the future. An economic balance must be struck between quality, productivity, and customer delivery requirements.

Option 3. Redistribution of Recipe Loading   The selection of this option is dependent upon the validity of the forecast as well as the consistency of the projected product mix. Clearly it would not make any sense to commit time and money to convert a tool to a different type of epi only to change it back at some point down the road. However, if this mix is the way of the future, this option deserves considerable attention. Although option 2 buys some time to address the immediate performance concerns, it does not address the obvious imbalance of the P-Type versus N-Type demand requirement.

In order for this scenario to work with the existing tool set, two things would have to occur. Epi 1 would have to be converted to N-Type and Epi 2 would have to be plumbed so that it can do both N-Type and P-Type product. The conversion of Epi 1 is a matter of switch-

EXHIBIT 11D–18   **Recipe Redistribution Results**
Sheet recipe redistribution results | Chapter 11D Worksheets.xls

#	Scenario	VA Time	NVA Time	Efficiency	Cycle Time	Capacity Use
1	Epi 1	1.81	0.92	66%	29.4	85%
2	Epi 2&3	1.90	0.82	70%	32.1	93%

ing the dopant bottle, which carries very little cost. However, there are concerns with Epi 1's top zone thickness uniformity and its overall capability, which must be considered. The conversion of Epi 2 will require approximately $20,000 in parts and two to three shifts of maintenance and tool qualification time.

As was mentioned in the "Methodology" section, there is a significant amount of time lost converting the reactors to a different type of epi. An etch and coat and a good test shot are required prior to the change that, under normal circumstances, consumes nearly four hours of the tool's capacity. Compounding this issue are the concerns that changing the tool from one type to another may result in additional machine failure that will further reduce the gains made by optimizing flexibility.

Option 4. Purchase an Additional epi Reactor The final option to purchase an additional tool is obviously the most expensive and difficult to implement. The immediate concern is the fact that currently no real estate exists for a new piece of equipment in the 6-inch fab. Perhaps there is space in the 8-inch fab, but that space is currently reserved for expansion in the 8-inch technology. The space concerns coupled with the expense of the new tool make this a "last resort" option.

If the decision was made to purchase a new tool, it would require a minimum of six to nine months to locate, procure, install, and qualify the new tool for production. Certainly with the forecasted demand that has been proposed for ramp-up in third quarter 2003, this alternative would not provide immediate assistance to the problem at hand. However, at some point the reality is that additional equipment will be needed to achieve volume growth beyond what is forecast.

Currently there is an epi tool available at another division of the company for a minimal investment. The installation expense is estimated at $80,000 to $100,000. The cost of a used tool on the open market is roughly $250,000 plus the installation expense. These estimates do not reflect the cost to allocate space to the new tool, which currently is unavailable in the 6-inch fab.

Suggestions for Process Improvements

Based on the complexity of implementation, the time frame to implement as well as the overall cost of each proposal, a three-tiered improvement plan is recommended. First, the immediate capacity and cycle time concerns can be addressed utilizing the existing recipe loading profile if the imposed restrictions are addressed. As was clearly shown with several of the simulation scenarios, it does not take a significant improvement in any individual area to make a substantial improvement in epi performance. Considering the impact of this alternative and the low implementation costs, this alternative is a good choice to address immediate concerns.

Second, if the long-term product mix dictates, the recipe loading should be redistributed. Improved recipe balance will increase throughput potential and lower epi cycle time. This option would involve the conversion of Epi 1 to N-Type product and Epi 2 to P- and N-Type product. The conversion would require approximately $20,000 in parts and two to three shifts of tool time to implement. It would be critical to address the changeover time required to convert the reactors from one epi type to another or much of the gains due to enhanced flexibility would be lost to tool conversion time.

Third, a long-term strategy would be a plan to expand capacity in the epi area to account for future volume growth. At best, the three epi reactors combined are running at 85 percent of the available capacity. No significant increase in throughput will be achieved without a major process overhaul or the purchase of additional tools. Currently, an epi tool is available for a minimal investment and would cost $80,000 to $100,000 to install. The purchase of a used tool on the open market would cost approximately $250,000 plus installation. The key issue with this phase would be to find the necessary floor space for the additional tool.

Finally, it is recommended that the company incorporate the use of both static capacity and dynamic simulation modeling tools in the production planning process. The potential benefits that they provide are well documented in industry literature and this study. The study explored the unique concerns facing the epitaxial area and provided recommendations to improve performance. However, this is a local optimum. The decisions that are made in epi will have an impact, positive or negative, on the entire operation.

It is critical to utilize these tools to analyze the entire operation as a unified system to ensure global optimums are achieved. There are perhaps many constraint areas like epi that will limit the successful accommodation of the forecasted demand. Without these tools, these areas may go unnoticed until delivery metrics make it very clear that a problem exists.

The static models would utilize Excel, meaning that no software investment would be required. It is estimated that two to three months of dedicated development time would be required to complete the static model with an ongoing commitment to maintain it.

The simulation models would utilize Arena software or perhaps another package such as Factory Explorer that is tailored to the semiconductor industry. A demo version of Arena was used to develop the models in this study. It is estimated that three to four months of dedicated development time would be required to complete the simulation models. As with the static models, there would be an ongoing commitment to maintain the simulation models.

Glossary of Terms

Availability—The total time that a machine is available to run product net of all downtime events.

Available Tool Capacity—The level of output that a machine can produce in its available time.

Available Tool Capacity Requirement—The proportion of available tool capacity that is consumed to accommodate product demand.

Constraint—Bottleneck or restricting operation in a production system. Typically, excess inventory is found. A constraint limits throughput and product cycle time.

Cycle Time—The total time a product spends in a production system from order entry to shipping.

Discrete-Event Simulation—Utilizing specialized software to model the impact of process variability on factory performance metrics such as throughput, utilization, and product cycle time.

Epitaxy—The means of depositing a thin layer of single crystal material upon the surface of a single crystal substrate. Commonly used to add a layer of silicon to a silicon substrate.

Etch and Coat (ECT)—The process that is used to clean accumulated silicon from the inside of the epi reactor.

Full Clean (FCT)—The process of completely tearing down the epi reactor. Also a thorough cleaning and preventive maintenance activities.

MTBDE—A machine availability term used to describe mean time between all down-time events.

MTBF—A machine availability term used to describe mean time between failures.

MTBPM—A machine availability term used to describe mean time between preventive maintenance events.

MTDE—A machine availability term used to describe mean time of downtime events.

MTPM—A machine availability term used to describe mean time of preventive maintenance events.

MTTR—A machine availability term used to describe mean time to repair.

N-Type Epi—A process of applying silicon to a substrate that has an N-type crystalline structure.

Non-Value-Added (NVA)—Machine processing time that does not add value to the product, such as setup time.

P-Type Epi—A process of applying silicon to a substrate that has a P-type crystalline structure.

Process Map—A flowchart that indicates the inputs, outputs, and the sequence of steps required to perform a process.

Recipe—The name commonly used to describe a machine program or routine in the semiconductor industry.

Recipe Loading—The distribution of recipes across a given tool set; which tools run which recipes.

Reentrant Flow—Workflow where products return to the same operation several times during the production process.

Sequence-Based Setups—Machine setups performed as a result of the sequence that products are processed on the machine.

Shot—The name commonly used to describe a batch or group of material processed together in a machine.

Slack Capacity—Adding extra resources to a process to account for variability, also known as buffer capacity.

Static Capacity—Determining the gross resource requirements to accommodate a desired level of demand.

Test Shots—Running a test sequence on an epi tool so that key product parameters can be measured prior to running good product.

Throughput—The maximum volume that can be produced in a manufacturing system.

Time-Bound Process—A process that must be performed within a fixed period of time or the product must either be reprocessed or be scrapped.

Utilization—The proportion of available machine time used to add value to product.

Value-Added (VA)—Machine processing time that adds value to the product.

Vapor Phase (VPE)—The epitaxy method that utilizes vapor to apply silicon to the substrate.

Work-in-Progress (WIP)—The total level of inventory in a production system at any given time.

Exercises

1. Four process analysis and improvement projects are described in this chapter. Outline the strengths and weaknesses for each project relative to how each problem was analyzed, opportunities for improvements identified, modeling carried out, and the process improvements recommended.

2. Select a potential process analysis and improvement project and develop a project plan using the Visio Gantt chart described in this chapter and in Chapter 3.

3. Develop a report outline for the chosen process analysis and improvement project.

4. Develop a PowerPoint presentation of your process analysis and improvement project analysis and findings for the process stakeholders.

The Future of Computer-Based Tools for Process Analysis and Improvement

Summary and Learning Objectives

The focus of this chapter is to introduce readers to state-of-the-art tools and techniques for enterprise integration. These include composite applications developed by a number of leading software houses; business to business (B2B) collaborative process management using a library of common standard processes and collaborative process managers of participating business entities; dynamic data–driven application systems where data inputs are injected dynamically into simulations and other applications to enhance predictive capabilities of business applications; advanced transaction models for business processes; and business process intelligence utilizing data warehousing and data mining technologies. All of these emerging new tools and techniques are described in this chapter.

The learning objectives for this chapter are to

1. Become informed about the state-of-the-art tools and techniques for enterprise integration.
2. Gain knowledge of evolving tools for business process design and improvement.

Introduction

Over the past decade, there has been a lot of work in developing middleware for integrating and automating enterprise business processes. With the rapid deployment of e-commerce strategies across every aspect of the enterprise and blurring of enterprise boundaries, new business rules have evolved in virtually every function within the enterprise. No one function in an enterprise can be effectively managed without considering the impact on another. The strength of an enterprise now is measured not only by its bottom line, but also by the strength of its supply chain, which is a set of rules that promotes the efficient (profitable) and effective (timely) manufacturing, distribution, and delivery of a product or service to the customer. E-business affects the entire spectrum of processes from the selling side (customer relationship management) operations to the buying side (supply chain management) as shown in Exhibit 12–1. There is renewed interest in business process coordination, especially for interorganizational processes. Such business processes are typically of long duration, involve coordination across many manual and automated tasks, require access to several different databases and the invocation of several applications systems (such as ERP,

EXHIBIT 12–1

Range of Processes in E-Business Supply Chain

Page supply chain | Chapter 12 Drawing.vsd

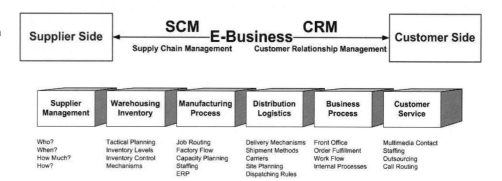

PDM, and more), and are governed by complex business rules. These applications, when used aggregately, form what is called *composite applications systems*.

There has been a lot more research over the last decade in business process modeling, advanced transaction models for business processes, and architectures and implementation techniques for business process management systems, and numerous commercial products have appeared. There is also recent work in interenterprise collaborative business process management, and standards are being introduced by various consortia, such as RosettaNet and ebXML.

Another recent area of research is that of business process intelligence. The motivation for business process automation is to improve operational efficiencies and reduce error, but commercial business process management middleware lacks tools for quantitatively tracking these business metrics. Business process intelligence aims to apply data warehousing, data analysis, and data mining techniques to process execution data, thus enabling the analysis, interpretation, and optimization of business processes. The rest of the chapter provides an overview on a number of areas of interest where development work is currently underway in industry and universities in developing models and systems for business process analysis and improvement.

Composite Applications

Many vendors have developed enterprise software that support complex business processes. They call it **composite applications.** As the concept now stands, composite applications will cut across traditional software boundaries to automate business processes that span multiple functions. By doing so, these applications will more realistically reflect how companies are actually organized and will more uniformly automate the flow of information. They address a decades-old problem in software-related automation: the many disconnected silos of information that have been built over the years in nearly every functional area due to proprietary products and a lack of standards.

Composite applications present the potential to bring together disparate, heterogeneous computing environments into an organized whole by establishing coordination at the business process level. The result can be better, more accurate, and timelier information about what a company does and how it does it. For manufacturers, getting comfortable with the idea of these so-called composite applications would require a significant change in thinking. It means thinking outside of traditional software categories promoted by vendors and analysts and focusing on the business processes they need to automate, the data models and mapping between systems, and the functionality needed to support those processes regardless of the underlying software. Enterprise software that manufacturers have adopted in the past or are now in the process of implementing—product life cycle management (PLM), customer relationship management (CRM), supply chain management (SCM), enterprise resource planning (ERP), business intelligence (BI), and so forth—still provides important functionality, but the shift in the thinking required will result in applying software in a very different way than in the past. By their very nature, traditional software categories imply business and information silos that don't promote or encourage information sharing within an organization. Composite applications aim to change all that.

Enterprise software vendors such as SAP AG (Walldorf, Germany), Baan (Barneveldt, Netherlands), Rockwell Software's Factory Analyzer, PeopleSoft Inc. (Pleasanton, CA), Siebel Systems Inc. (San Mateo, CA), Oracle Corporation (Redwood City, CA), IFS AB (Linkoping, Sweden), and Commerce One Inc. (Pleasanton, CA) all have initiatives underway to deliver prebuilt composite applications to the market.

Manufacturers would be well advised to begin thinking through what composite applications are and what they can do for their businesses. Thinking about business processes requires putting business sequences and interactions first in the thought process about automation. Technology (and how it is applied) becomes secondary and truly assumes the role of an enabling factor. Taking full advantage of composite applications will require organizations to ignore individual application boundaries. In the case of the life cycle of a design document, to use one example, the thought process must extend through the request for proposal (RFP), contract, purchase order, invoice, and settlement stages. Organizations also have to be willing to dismantle the walls between their internal divisions and functions so business processes can move forward unimpeded.

Baan, a unit of Invensys plc, is one of a number of enterprise software vendors on the move with the new wave of boundary-spanning software applications. In most cases, branding has preceded delivery, and each of them has called their initiatives with a mix of technical and business-sounding names. SAP AG, for example, has its xApps, while PeopleSoft has AppConnect, Oracle has Business Flow Accelerators, Siebel Systems has its Universal Application Network (UAN), Commerce One offers Conductor, IFS Group has labeled its initiative Composite Applications, and Baan is calling its eventual product line Value Apps.

Baan introduced its Value Apps strategy in the fall of 2002; applications include supplier collaboration, configuration and commitment, and engineering design collaboration. These applications are to be built on a platform Baan calls OpenWorldX, which consists of its OpenWorld, B2B Server, and Business Intelligence Server products. Both OpenWorldX and Value Apps are part of its RealTime Enterprise Framework, described by Baan as a three-tiered, process-driven architecture that manages collaboration among people, applications, and devices.

In their efforts to build the new composite applications, most ERP vendors are focused on providing common horizontal processes before moving onto industry-specific processes.

Many observers of the composite applications trend expect early adopters to fit the profile of those focusing on linking applications from a particular vendor's suite. But the real test of the promise of composite applications will come from manufacturers who need to integrate applications from multiple vendors into business processes.

One of the keys to making composite applications possible is improved integration technologies like Web services, XML, and adapters. Each vendor's strategy must include a way to track and manage data and data-model mapping between applications so changes can be made quickly, easily, and only once and then populated out to the affected systems. Not all of these facilities are available today. The jury may still be out on composite applications, but the biggest benefit to manufacturers will likely come out of the move on the part of enterprise software vendors to the open, standards-based technologies used to develop them. Proprietary systems are being reworked to support standards to enable companies to more easily connect other vendors' applications as well as home-grown legacy applications into business processes. As they do this, enterprise vendors will theoretically make it easier for customers to pick and choose the extended functionality they need from multiple vendor applications as well as stitch that functionality together from other vendors' offerings.

For those businesses that can change their thinking to prioritize business processes, there will be tools and components available that will make it easier to both create processes and integrate applications and data from various systems. Only time will tell whether the new generation of composite applications now coming to market are indeed the ones manufacturers hope for or only the first shot in an integration campaign that will continue for some time to come.

Inter-enterprise (B2B) Collaborative Business Process Management

The potential business value of streamlining interenterprise business processes has fueled a renewed interest in process management technologies. However, the conventional intraenterprise process management architecture faces a number of challenges. First of all, a mechanism must exist to allow participating enterprises to reach agreement on the business process description and the data to be exchanged during process execution. To allow scalable B2B interoperation and alleviate the burden of pairwise negotiation of integration points, a library of common, standard processes must exist so that by binding to a common, standard process, an enterprise achieves the ability of collaborating with a large number of partners' processes. Second, the process management function needs to be carried out as collaboration among multiple distributed process managers. In essence, in crossing enterprise boundaries, the technologies traditionally suited for central coordination and integration need to be fundamentally reworked. The CrossFlow project is one research effort aimed at collaborative business process management. It enables provision of high-level support of workflows in dynamically formed virtual organizations. High-level support is obtained by abstracting services and offering advanced cooperation support. Virtual organizations are dynamically formed by contract-based matchmaking between service providers and consumers. CrossFlow developments are driven by requirements from real-world scenarios. At this time, seven European institutions are part of the CrossFlow ESPRIT project.

The collaborative process framework proposed in the literature can extend the centralized process management technology as shown in Exhibit 12–2.

A collaborative process involves multiple parties, each playing a role in the process. Two aspects distinguish the collaborative process model from the conventional centralized process model:

- The process definition is based on a commonly agreed business interaction protocol, such as the protocol for online purchase or auction.
- The process execution is not performed by a centralized workflow engine but by multiple engines collaboratively.

In the collaborative process framework, the common business process definitions drive the definition and development of a process-compliant service at an enterprise. This is illustrated in the two Role Spec boxes in Exhibit 12–2. An enterprise determines the role(s) it wishes to play in a process, and develops the role process specifications and the corresponding internal execution control, including invocation or dispatching of local services. Once the process-compliant role specification is developed, it can be published as a Web service. Local services are accessed indirectly through the local collaborative process manager.

As shown in Exhibit 12–2, each execution of a collaborative process, or a logical process instance, consists of a set of peer process instances run by the Collaborative Process Managers (CPMs) of participating parties. These peer instances conform in behavior to the

EXHIBIT 12–2
Collaborative Process Framework
Page collaborative |
Chapter 12
Drawing.vsd

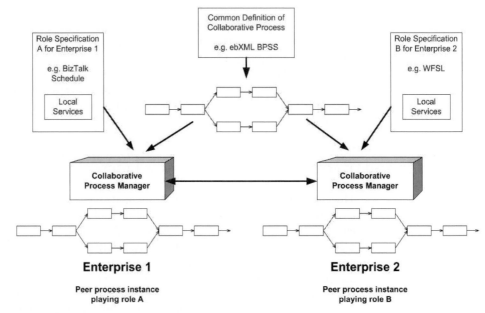

specification of the role set forth in the common process definition but may have private process data and subprocesses. The CPM of each party is used to schedule, dispatch, and control the tasks that that party is responsible for, and the CPMs interoperate through an inter-CPM protocol to exchange the process data (or documents) and to inform each other on the progress of the process execution.

Many challenging research issues remain in interenterprise collaborative business processes. They include the ability to express and support transactional semantics, exception handling, and quality of services in the common process description; methods and tools conducive to achieving a library of reusable and composable common business documents and processes; efficient registration and searching/matching mechanisms; efficient and reliable inter-CPM execution protocols; and end-to-end process monitoring and analysis in a distributed environment.

Dynamic Data–Driven Application Systems

Typically, applications and simulations we use today only allow data inputs that are fixed when the application/simulation is launched. Traditionally, these processes are disjointed and serialized, not synchronized and cooperative. This lack of ability to inject data dynamically into simulations and other applications as these applications execute, limits the analysis and predictive capabilities of these applications. Needs for such dynamic applications are already emerging in business, engineering, and scientific processes, analysis, and design.

Many researchers are currently working on the creation and enablement of a new generation of dynamic/adaptive applications. The novel capabilities to be created are application simulations that can dynamically accept and respond to online field data and measurements and/or can control such measurements. This synergistic and symbiotic feedback control loop between applications/simulations, and measurements are a novel technical direction that can open new domains in the capabilities of simulations with a high potential payoff, and create applications with new and enhanced capabilities. It has the potential to transform the way science and engineering are done, and induce a major beneficial impact in the way many functions in our society are conducted, such as manufacturing, commerce, transportation, hazard prediction/management, and medicine, to name a few.

Characteristics of a Dynamic Data–Driven Application System (DDDAS)

Pictorially the new paradigm is shown below in Exhibit 12–3. The intent is to show the new and tight (feedback and control) interaction between the ongoing computations and the measurements (or field-data collections processes).

Exhibit 12–3 identifies three primary modes of interaction for a DDDAS environment: Human and Computation Interaction; Model or Computation Interaction with Physical System; and Computation and Computational Infrastructure Interaction. While the DDDAS paradigm emphasizes the new technologies that need to be developed for modes 2 and 3, the program will be imbalanced if mode 1 is ignored. In fact, by providing much more accurate information for the human in the loop, DDDAS will result in enhancing mode 1 also.

Physical systems (for example, prosthetic legs, chemical plants, and active wings of an aircraft) operate at widely varying rates. Cosmologic and geologic rates are extremely slow relative to the timescale of subatomic events that happen very fast. Physical processes can also produce and consume widely varying data volumes. In many cases, a computation may be able to interact directly with a physical system via some set of sensors and actuators (for example, a prosthetic leg that can sense the terrain and apply the necessary forces to complete a walking motion). High-energy physics experiments provide another example.

For the purposes of explanation of how this paradigm can affect other than engineering/scientific applications, we provide here the following supply chain management example from the e-business world (commercial/manufacturing and finance sectors): Businesses have increasingly become global but, at the same time, have become more specialized in order to concentrate on core competencies. As a result, the path from raw material to finished product delivered to a customer has become highly complex in terms of geographic scope, number of organizations involved, and technological depth. Organizations have broadly adopted enterprise resource planning (ERP) and supply chain management (SCM) systems in an attempt to better control and manage their dispersed operations. While these systems typically do well at collecting and integrating transaction data and at providing support for planning decisions, they are not effective at supporting real-time decision making, particularly with respect to unplanned incidents. Research is currently underway into the modeling of the interactions among supply chain entities and the manner in which major events impact overall supply chain operations. Research is also taking place as to how to

EXHIBIT 12–3
DDDAS Interactions
Page DDDAS
Interactions | Chapter
12 Drawing.vsd

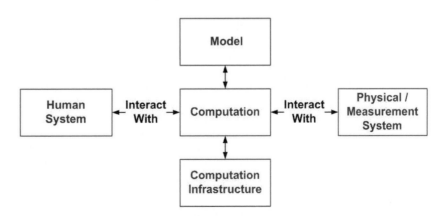

interface such models with the currently available data collection mechanisms. Under a DDDAS approach, a simulation would receive real-time data from ERP and SCM systems in order to maintain an accurate current picture of the supply chain. Decision makers would employ the simulation to project the impact of decision options. Of particular significance would be the analysis of ways to mitigate the impact of major disruptive events, such as emergency customer orders, plant breakdowns, missed shipments, and so forth. This environment has several distinguished characteristics, including the wide range and magnitude of data sources, the fact that a variety of organizations own and/or generate the data, and the dependence of system behavior on humans (decision makers and customers).

The use of continuous data streams presents an additional challenge for data–driven simulations since the results vary based on the sampling rate and the discretization scheme used. In other cases, dynamic data assimilation or interpolation might be necessary to provide feedback to experimental design/control. DDDAS algorithms also need to dynamically assimilate new data at mid-simulation as the data arrives, necessitating warm restart capabilities.

Data inputs to the dynamic data–driven applications may be in the form of continuous data streams in addition to discrete data sets. Incorporating discrete data inputs during execution of an application itself presents several challenges, such as the ability to warm start the algorithm when new data arrives or to guide the search using new information. The use of continuous streaming data requires the algorithms to use appropriate data discretization methods to use the available information. The issues of optimally discretizing continuous data and providing feedback to the data generation process—either sensors or computation code—to change the sampling frequency are inherently interesting research issues. Moreover, data–driven applications will not always receive data from known sources with well-defined structure and semantics. The ability to handle different data structures and elicit appropriate semantic information is crucial to a robust DDDAS.

Advanced Transaction Models (ATM) for Business Processes

An important contribution that the database community has made to business process management is to link transactional concepts with workflows. When most database programmers refer to a transaction, they are referring to an ACID transaction. These transactions (logical unit of work) are designed for short-lived decisions, usually lasting under a few seconds. *ACID* is an acronym, where *A* stands for Atomic—Transactions are atomic (all or none); *C* stands for Consistency—A consistent state of the database may be expected at all times; *I* stands for Isolation—Transactions are isolated from another; and *D* stands for Durable—Once a transaction commits, its updates survive even if the system goes down.

Quite early on, it was recognized that business processes contained activities that accessed shared, persistent data resources, and so had to be subject to transactional semantics. In particular, the properties of atomicity and isolation could be usefully applied to business processes (or at least to part of a business process). For example, one might want to declare that the payment of an invoice and crediting the payee's account were part of an atomic unit of work. However, it was also recognized that it would be overkill to treat an entire business process as a single ACID transaction. First, since business processes typically are of long duration, treating an entire process as a transaction would require locking resources for long periods of time. Second, since business processes typically involve many independent database and application systems, enforcing ACID properties across the entire process would require expensive coordination among these systems. Third, since business processes almost always have external effects, ensuring atomicity using conventional transactional rollback mechanisms is infeasible and may not even be semantically desirable. It became apparent that the existing database transaction models would have to be extended.

Several models for long-running transactions have been developed to allow the definition of ACID-like properties at the business process level and to handle task failures.

The Activity-Transaction Model (ATM) allows long-running transactions to be both nested and chained. Nesting allows concurrency within a transaction (for example, tasks that were triggered by some event occurring in a parent transaction could execute in concurrent subtransactions) and also provide hierarchical control for failure and exception handling. Ideas similar to those in ATM also exist in other transactional workflow models. The basic ideas of transactional bracketing of parts of a business process, attaching compensation and contingency activities to the activities of the process, declaring some of the activities to be vital (or critical), and defining points in the process up to which rollback occurs on failure, followed by forward execution (roll forward) permeate many of the transactional models. These models typically differ in how much flexibility the process designer has in specifying the backward compensation and forward execution process.

Business Process Intelligence

Organizations automate their business processes with the objectives of improving operational efficiency, reducing costs, improving the quality of service offered to their customers, and reducing human error. However, apart from graphical tools for designing business processes and some simulation tools for detecting performance bottlenecks, business process management systems today provide few, if any, analytic tools to quantify performance against specific business metrics.

There has been some research on defining formal Petri Net-based execution semantics for business processes. In these approaches, the process definition graph is translated into some form of Petri Net, enabling formal properties, such as termination and freedom from deadlock, to be proved. Other approaches use formal logic to specify and reason about workflows and transactions. However, these approaches are focused on verifying process definitions, not on analyzing or optimizing process executions.

The emerging area of business process intelligence is aimed at applying data warehousing and data mining technologies to analyzing and optimizing business processes.

Business process management systems today collect a lot of data about process executions. They log significant events that occur during process execution, such as the start and completion times of activities, the input and output data of each activity, failure events or other exceptions, and the assignment of resources to each activity. The log data is typically stored in a relational database, which can be queried to produce basic reports such as the number of workflow instances executed in a given time period, the average execution time, resource utilization statistics, and so forth. Traditional graphical querying and reporting tools are used for this purpose. However, these tools are limited in the types of analysis supported.

A more promising approach is to build a business process data warehouse, which can be loaded with the log data suitably cleaned, transformed, and aggregated, and perhaps integrated with data from other data source. The data in the warehouse can be analyzed using multidimensional (OLAP) analysis tools and data mining tools to answer questions that a business manager or process analyst may be interested in in order to:

• Analyze the performance and quality of resources. For example, resources of type A take 50 percent longer than average to execute activity B when the activity is initiated on Friday afternoons.

• Understand and predict exceptions. For example, what factors are strongly correlated with missed deadlines or other violations of service level agreements?

• Discover conditions under which paths or subgraphs of the process are executed, so that the process can be redefined.

• Optimize process execution time and quality through optimal configuration of the system, assignment of resources, and dynamic adaptation of the process.

Exactly how to answer these questions is a ripe area for research. There are challenges in designing a process data warehouse to support these kinds of analysis and the application of data mining techniques for understanding, predicting, and preventing exceptions.

Another area of great interest is business process discovery, where the goal is to learn the structure of a business process from workflow log data. This would be especially useful for semistructured and unstructured business activities where the process is not defined a priori. Such a process is usually implemented via rules triggered by events, such as the start and completion of tasks. In some situations, there may be a latent structure that occurs regularly and that can be discerned by analyzing the history of events and rules.

This learned structure could then be scripted and implemented efficiently as a business process. For enterprise business processes in particular, it is very unlikely that a complete business process that spans activities in different enterprises will be easily defined and agreed to by all the participants. In such situations, it may be possible to learn the underlying process by analyzing the sequences of interactions among the participants.

Conclusion

Business process integration and automation have become high priorities for enterprises to achieve operational efficiency. With the burgeoning of e-commerce, there is a renewed interest in technologies for coordinating and automating intra- and interenterprise business processes. We have reviewed the progress that has been made in the last decade and the state of the art today, in research and commercial products. We identified research issues, especially in collaborative, interenterprise process management through composite applications, dynamic data–driven application systems, transaction models for business processes, and in the emerging area of business process intelligence.

Exercises

1. Industry and academia are actively involved in developing new techniques, protocols, and software tools for business systems integration. Research the state-of-the-art techniques and tools in progress for enterprise integration and develop a report of your findings.
2. Develop a short motivational presentation on data warehousing and data mining and how these technologies can be applied to optimize business processes.
3. Develop a PowerPoint presentation on state-of-the-art, dynamic data–driven application systems.
4. Present your research and analysis on composite applications.

A

Aberdeen Group. (1996). Advanced planning engine technologies: Can capital generating technology change the face of manufacturing? February. (White Paper).

Albright, S. Christian. (2001). *VBA for Modelers: Developing Decision Support Systems Using Management Science.* Stamford, CT: Brooks/Cole.

Aldowaisan, Tariq A. (1999). Business process reengineering: An approach for process mapping. *Omega, 27*(5), 515.

Advance Manufacturing Research. (1995). *The Supply Chain Primer.* Boston, MA: AMR Reports.

Advance Manufacturing Research. (1997). The AMR report on supply chain management. *AMR Report,* May–December.

Andersen, D. L., Britt, F. E., and Favre, D. J. (1997). The seven principles of supply chain management. Available: www.manufacturing.net.

Anderson, R. E. (1997). Phased product development: Friend or foe. *The Journal of Product Innovation Management, 14*(3), 225–306.

Anonymous. (2002). IIE Transactions special issues of operations engineering: Advances in large-scale optimization for logistics, production and manufacturing systems. *IIE Transactions, 34*(9), V.

Anonymous. (2002). The ABCs of Six Sigma. *Aviation Week & Space Technology, 157*(14), 56.

B

Banks, J., Nicol, D. M., Carson, J. S., and Nelson, B. L. (2000). *Discrete-Event System Simulation.* Upper Saddle River, NJ: Pearson Education.

Baylis, D. (1998). Fab planning: Trading in your spreadsheet. Available from Semipark site: http://www.semipark.co.kr/upload1/Fabplanning-trading.pdf.

Birnbaum, Duane, and Andy Harris. (2002). *Microsoft Excel VBA Programming for the Absolute Beginner.* Indianapolis, IN: Premier Press.

Bisgaard, S. (1992). Industrial use of statistically designed experiments: Case study references and some historical anecdotes, *Quality Engineering, 4*(4), 547–62.

Bisson, Barbara, and Folk, Valerie. (2000). Case study: How to do business process improvement. *The Journal of Quality and Participation, 23*(1), 58–63.

Bond, T. C. (1999). Systems analysis and business process mapping: a symbiosis. *Business Process Management Journal, 5*(2), 164.

Bonner, A. (1999). Workflow, Transactions, and Datalog. *Proceedings of the International Conference on Principles of Database Systems,* May.

Box, G. E. P., Hunter, W. G., and Hunter, J. S. (1978). *Statistics for Experimenters.* New York: John Wiley.

Bruce, H. (1997). Demand chain management: The future paradigm for the 21st century. *International Conference Proceedings.* American Production and Control Society.

C

Carraway, R., Cummins, J., and Freeland, J. (2000). Solving spreadsheet-based integer programming models: An example from international telecommunications. *Decision Sciences, 21*(4), 808–24.

Chen, Q., and Hsu, M. (2001). Inter-enterprise collaborative business process management. *Proceedings of the International Conference on Data Engineering (ICDE),* Germany.

Cohen, O. (1988). The Drum-Buffer-Rope (DBR) approach to logistics. In A. Rolstadas (Ed.), *Computer-Aided Production Management.* New York: Springer-Verlag.

Cohen, S. (1996). Supply chain council introduces the supply-chain operations reference model. *PRTM Insight, 8*(3).

Cole, R. E. (1989). Large-scale change and the quality resolution. In A. M. Mohrman, S. A. Mohrman, G. E. Ledford, T. G. Cummings, E. E. Lawler III, and Associates, *Large Scale Organizational Change.* San Francisco: Jossey-Bass.

Cooper, M. C., and Ellram, L. M. (1993). Characteristics of supply chain management and the implications for purchasing and logistics strategy. *The International Journal of Logistics Management. 4*(2), 13–24.

Copacino, W. C. (1996). Why you should synchronize logistics and manufacturing. *Logistics Management, 35*(11), 63.

Copacino, W. C., (1997). *Supply chain management: The basics and beyond.* Boca Raton, FL: St. Lucie Press.

Costanza, J. R. (1998). The flow revolution. *Manufacturing Systems,* April, p. 10.

Course Technology Staff. (2000). *Course IIt: Visio Professional Student.* Karen Jacot (Ed.), ISBN: 0619014245, Course Technology, Inc., September.

Coyle, J. J., Bardi, E. J., and Langley, C. J. (1996). *The management of business logistics* (6th ed.). St. Paul, MN: West Publishing.

Cummings, Steve. (1998). *VBA for dummies.* San Mateo, CA: IDG Books.

D

Damelio, Robert. (1996). *The basics of process mapping.* New York: Quality Resources.

Dano, S. (1974). *Linear programming in industry* (4th ed.). Wien: Springer-Verlag.

Davenport, T. H. (1993). *Process innovation.* Boston, MA: Harvard Business School Press.

Davenport, T. H., and Short, J. E. (1990). The new industrial engineering: Information technology and business process redesign. *Sloan Management Review,* Summer, pp. 11–27.

Davis, T. (1993). Effective supply chain management. *Sloan Management Review,* Summer, pp. 35–46.

Dayal, U., Hsu, M., Ladin, R. (1991). A transactional model for long-running activities. *Proceedings from the 17th Conference on Very Large Data Bases,* September.

Del Franco, Mark. (2001). Case study: PC connection. *Catalog Age,* February, pp. 52–4.

Demers, Julie. (2002). The lean philosophy. *CMA Management, 76*(7), 31–3.

Deming, W. E. (1993). *The New Economics.* Cambridge, MA: MIT Center for Advanced Engineering Study.

DocuTech 6135 Publisher, Xerox (1999). Available: http://www.xerox.com.

Domaschke, J., Brown, S., Leibl, F., Robinson, J. (1998). Effective implementation of cycle time reduction strategies for semiconductor back-end manufacturing. Available from FabTime site: http://www.fabtime.com/abs_Siem98.shtml.

Donovan, M. R. (1997). Reduce inventories and improve business performance. *Midrange ERP,* July/August, pp. 62–4.

Dornier, P. P., Ernst, R., Fender, M., and Kouvelis, P. (1998). *Global Operations and Logistics.* New York: John Wiley & Sons, pp. 251–57.

E

Eaton, Nanette J. (2001). *Microsoft Visio Version 2002 Inside Out.* Redmond, VA: Microsoft Press.

Eder, J., and Liebhart, W. (1995). The workflow activity model WAMO. *Proceedings of the 3rd International Conference on Cooperative Information Systems;* Vienna, Austria, May.

Eder, J., and Liebhart, W. (1998). Contributions to exception handling in workflow management. *Proceedings of the Sixth International Conference on Extending Database Technology;* Valencia, Spain, March.

Edson, David. (1999). *Professional development with Visio.* Indianapolis: Sams.

Elmagarmid, A. K. (1992). *Database transaction models for advanced applications.* San Francisco: Morgan-Kaufmann.

Enabling a Global Electronic Market, ebXML http://www.ebxml.org/

F

Finn, Widget. (2002). Know your assets: Part one: Knowledge management. *Director, 55*(11), 80–85.

Fisher, M. L., Hammond, J. H., Obermeyer, W. R., and Raman, A. (1994). Making supply meet demand in an uncertain world. *Harvard Business Review,* May–June.

Fishman, George S. (2001). *Discrete event simulation.* Berlin: Springer-Verlag.

Foster, William F. (2002). Managing six sigma, quality progress. *Milwaukee, 35*(8), 110.

Francett, B. (1996). The synchronized supply chain: From connectivity to commerce. *Software Magazine,* December, pp. 113–16.

Fraser, J. (1997). Synchronization: More than a buzzword. *The Performance Advantage,* April, p. 76.

Fraser, J. (1998). Demand management works even if the forecast is wrong. *Midrange ERP,* March/April, pp. 58–60.

G

Gander, Mary. (2002). The importance of improved design. *Quality Progress, 35*(12), 112–14.

Gass, Saul L. (1985). *Linear programming* (5th ed.), New York: McGraw Hill.

Getz, Ken, and Mike Gilbert. (1998). *VBA Developer's Handbook.* Alameda, CA: Sybex.

Giglio, R., Robinson, J. K. (1999). Capacity planning for semiconductor wafer fabrication with time constraints between operations. Available: http://www.fabtime.com/abs_TBS99.shtml.

Gilbreth, Frank B., and Lillian M. Gilbreth. (1921). Process charts. *Transactions of the ASME,* 43, Paper 1818, 1029–50.

Goddard, Walter E. (1986). Capacity planning: Ten steps to better operating control. *Industrial Management, 10*(4), 22–27.

Gould, L. (1998). Rethinking supply chains. *Managing Automation,* March, pp. 35–46.

Grabowski, Ralph. (2001a). *Learn Microsoft Visio 2002.* Plano, TX: Wordware Publishing.

Grabowski, Ralph. (2001b). *Learn to diagram with Microsoft Visio 2002.* Plano, TX: Wordware Publishing.

Grauer, Robert T., and Barber, Maryann. (2001). *Exploring Microsoft Excel XP.* Upper Saddle River, NJ: Prentice Hall Professional Technical Reference.

Graves, S. C., Rinnooy Kan, A. H. G., and Zipkin, P. H. (Eds.). (1993). *Logistics of production and inventory.* Amsterdam: North Holland.

Green, J., Rosenberg, R., and Bullen, S. (2001). *Excel XP VBA programmer's reference.* Indianapolis, IN: Wrox Press.

Greenfield, Mathew. (2002). Process mapping's next step, quality progress. *Milwaukee, 35*(9), 50–55.

Grefen, P., Vonk, J., Boertjes, E., and Apers, P. (1997). Two-layer transaction management for workflow management applications. *Proceedings of the Eighth International Conference on Database and Expert Systems Administration,* Toulouse, France.

Grewal, N. S., Wulf, T. M., Bruska, A. C., and Robinson, J. K. (1998). Integrating targeted cycle-time reduction into the capital planning process. Available: http://www.fabtime.com/abs_Sea98.shtml.

Griffin, A. (1992). Evaluating QFD's use in U.S. firms as a process for developing products. *Journal of Product Innovation Management, 9,* 171–87.

H

Harbour, Jerry L. (1996a). Cycle time reduction: Designing and streamlining work for high performance. *Quality Resources.*

Harbour, Jerry L. (1996b). Flow time reduction: Designing and streamlining work for high performance. *Quality Resources.*

Harlend, D., and Scharlacken, J. W. (1997). Global supply chain planning: Synchronizing operations and logistics with the pulse of the international marketplace. *Conference Proceedings of the American Production and Inventory Control Society.*

Harrell, C., Bowden, R., and Ghosh, B. K. (2002). *Simulation using ProModel.* New York: McGraw-Hill.

Harrington, H. James. (1991). Flowcharting: Drawing a process picture. In *Business process improvement.* New York: McGraw-Hill.

Harvard Business School Case Study 9-696-023. (1999). *Process Fundaments,* April 20, pp. 1–17.

Hauser, J. R., and Clausing, D. (1988). The House of Quality. *Harvard Business Review,* June, pp. 63–73.

Hedtke, J. V., and Knottingham, E. (1999). *Visio: The official guide.* Emeryville, CA: Osborne McGraw-Hill.

Hoi An Le Thi. (2002). Combination between global and local methods for solving an optimization problem over the efficient set. *European Journal of Operational Research, 142*(2), 258.

Holmstrom, J., Hoover Jr., W. E., Eloranta, E., and Vasara, A. (1999). Using value engineering to implement breakthrough solutions for customers. *The International Journal of Logistics Management, 10*(2), 1–12.

Hutchinson, T. P. (2000). ANOVA applied to examination scores. *Work Study, 49*(3), 104.

J

Jacobson, Reed. (2001). *Microsoft Excel 2002 Visual Basic for Applications step by step.* Redmond, WA: Microsoft Press.

Jajodia, S., and Kerschberg, S. (1997). *Advanced transaction models and architectures.* New York: Kluwer Academic Publishers.

Jelen, F. C. (1970). *Cost and optimization engineering.* New York: McGraw-Hill.

Jolly, Karen. (2002). *Excel 2002 for Windows XP.* El Granada, CA: Scott/Jones Publisher.

Jones, Jack William, McLeod, Raymond, Jr. (1986). The structure of executive information systems: An exploratory analysis. *Decision Sciences, 17*(2), 220–49.

Juran, J. M., and Gryna, F. M. (1988). *Juran's quality control handbook* (4th ed.). New York: McGraw Hill.

K

Kamath, M., and Ramamritham, K. (1998). Failure handling and coordinated execution of concurrent workflows. *Proceedings of the 14th International Conference on Data Engineering,* Orlando, FL, February.

Karmarkar, U. S., Kekre, S., and Freeman, S. (1985). Lot sizing and lead time performance in manufacturing cell. *Interfaces, 15*(2), 1–9.

Keller, E. L. (1995). Creating concurrent business processes across the supply chain (White Paper). Stamford, CT: Gartner Group.

Kelton, W. D., Sturrock, D. T., and Sadowski, R. P. (2003). *Simulation with Arena* (3rd ed.). New York: McGraw Hill.

Kesner, Richard M. (2001). Preparing for knowledge management: Part 1, process mapping. *Information Strategy, 18*(1).

King, B. (1989). *Better designs in half the time.* Methuen, MA: Goal/QPC.

King, David. (2002). Back to basics: Use process mapping. *Logistics and Transport Focus, 4*(3), 42.

Klungle, Roger. (1999). Simulation of a claims call center: A success and a failure. In Farrington, P. A., Nembhard, H. B, Sturrock, D. T., and Evans, G. W. (Eds.), *Proceedings of the 1999 Winter Simulation Conference* (1648–1653). Piscataway, NJ: Institute of Electrical and Electronics Engineers.

Knottingham, Elisabeth. (2001). *How to do everything with Microsoft Visio 2002.* Emeryville, CA: McGraw-Hill Osborne.

Kofler, Michael. (2003). *Definitive guide to Excel VBA.* Berkeley, CA: APress L. P.

Konz, Stephan. (1994). *Facility design* (2nd ed.). Scottsdale, AZ: Publishing Horizons.

L

Labovitz, George, and Rosansky, Victor. (1997). *The Power of Alignment: How Great Companies Stay Centered and Accomplish Extraordinary Things.* New York: John Wiley & Sons.

Law, Averill M. (1990a). Models of random machine downtimes for simulation. *Industrial Engineering, 22*(8), 58–59.

Law, Averill M. (1990b). Models of random machine downtimes for simulation. *Industrial Engineering, 22*(9), 22–23.

Law, Averill M., and Kelton, W. David. (1999). *Simulation modeling and analysis* (3rd ed.). New York: McGraw Hill.

Lawton, Thomas C., and Michaels, Kevin P. (2001). Advancing to the virtual value chain: Learning from the Dell model. *The Irish Journal of Management, 22*(1), 91–112.

Lee, H. L., and Billington, C. (1993). Material management in decentralized supply chains. *Operations Research, 41*(5), 835–47.

Lomax, Paul. (1998). *VB and VBA in a nutshell: The language.* Sebastopol, CA: O'Reilly & Associates.

M

Magretta, J. (1998). Fast, global, and entrepreneurial: Supply chain management, Hong Kong style: An interview with Victor Fung. *Harvard Business Review,* September/October, pp. 103–14.

Magretta, Joan. (1998). The power of virtual integration: An interview with Dell Computer's Michael Dell. *Harvard Business Review,* March/April, pp. 73–84.

Mangelli and Klein. (1994). *The reengineering handbook.* New York: AMACOM Books.

Mason, R. L., Gunst, R. F., and Hess, J. L. (1989). *Statistical design and analysis of experiments, with applications to engineering and science.* New York: John Wiley and Sons.

May, N. P. (1994). Quick response systems. *1994 Conference Proceedings of the American Production and Inventory Control Society.*

Mayer, J. H. (1996). Supply chain tools cut inventory fat. *Software Magazine,* May, pp. 77–90.

McCann, Todd. (1999). Watch out for informal systems. *Manufacturing Engineering, 123*(4), 128–30.

McKinnon, A. (2002). *Course IIt: Visio 2002 Professional: Basic.* Boston: Course Technology.

Microsoft Corporation. (2001). *Developing Microsoft Visio solutions.* Redmond, WA: Microsoft Press.

Middleton, Michael R. (2003). *Data analysis using Microsoft Excel: Updated for Office XP.* Belmont, CA: Duxbury.

Miller, Katherine, and Bapat, Vivek. (1999). Case study: Simulation of the call center environment for comparing competing call routing technologies for business case ROI projection. In Farrington, P. A., Nembhard, H. B, Sturrock, D. T., and Evans, G. W. (Eds.), *Proceedings of the 1999 Winter Simulation Conference* (1694–170). Piscataway, NJ: Institute of Electrical and Electronics Engineers.

Montgomery, D. C. (1991). *Design and analysis of experiments* (3rd ed.). New York: John Wiley.

N

Nemhauser, G. L., and Wolsey, L. A. (1988). *Integer and combinatorial optimization.* New York: John Wiley and Sons, 1988.

Norman, Richard, and Ramirez. R. (1993). From value chain to value constellation: Designing interactive strategy. *Harvard Business Review,* July/August, pp. 65–77.

NSF Workshop on Dynamic Data Driven Application Systems. (2000). Creating a dynamic and symbiotic coupling of application/simulations with measurements/experiments, Arlington, VA, March 8–10.

P

Parsons, S. J., Oja, D., Ageloff, R., and Carey, P. (2001). *New Perspectives on Microsoft Excel XP.* Boston: Course Technology.

Peace, Glen S. (1993). *Taguchi methods, a hands-on approach to quality engineering.* Reading, MA: Addison-Wesley.

Pegden, C. Dennis, Shannon, Robert E., and Sadowski, Randall P. (1995). *Introduction to simulation using SIMAN* (2nd ed.). Boston: McGraw Hill.

Perspection, Inc. (2001). *Microsoft Visio Version 2002 step by step.* Redmond, WA: Microsoft Press.

Plossl, G. W. (1991). *Managing in the new world of manufacturing.* Englewood Cliffs, NJ: Prentice Hall.

Poirier, C. C., and Reiter, S. E. (1996). *Supply chain optimization.* San Francisco, CA: Berrett-Koehler Publishers.

Powell, Keith. (2002). *Special edition using Microsoft Visio 2002.* Indianapolis: Que.

Prasad, B. (2002). *Concurrent engineering fundamentals: Integrated product and process organization,* Vol. I. Upper Saddle River, NJ: Prentice Hall.

Primis Custom Publishing. (1999). McGraw-Hill. Available: http://www.mhhe.com/primis.

R

Ravichandran, T., and Rai, Arun. (2000). Quality management in systems development: An organizational system perspective. *MIS Quarterly, 24*(3), 381–415.

Robinson, T. (1998). Weaving a supply chain web. *Managing Automation,* April, pp. 22–28.

Rockwell Software. (2004a). *Arena basic edition user's guide* (Available on Arena CD-ROM).

Rockwell Software. (2004b). *Arena contact center edition on line documentation* (Available on Arena CD-ROM).

Rockwell Software. (2004c). *Arena standard edition user's guide* (Available on Arena CD-ROM).

Rockwell Software. (2004d). *Arena variables guide* (Available on Arena CD-ROM).

Rockwell Software. (2004-5). *OptQuest for Arena* (Available on Arena CD-ROM).

Roman, Steven A. (2002). *Writing Excel Macros with VBA* (2nd ed.). Sebastopol, CA: O'Reilly & Associates.

Ross, D. (1996). Meeting the challenge of supply chain management. *APICS—The Performance Advantage,* September, pp. 38–49.

Ross, Sheldon M. (2002). *Simulation* (3rd ed.). New York: Academic Press.

Rotella, Mark. (2002). The power of design for Six Sigma. *Publishers Weekly, 249*(43), 63

Rummler, G. A., and Brache, A. P. (1995). *Improving performance: How to manage the white space on the organization chart.* San Francisco: Jossey-Bass Publishers.

S

Saccomano, Ann. (1999). Dell Computer builds service. *Traffic World,* July 26, pp. 26–27.

Savory, Paul, and Olson, John. (2001). Guidelines for using process mapping to aid improvement efforts. *Hospital Material Management Quarterly, 22*(3), 10–16.

Selander, Jeffrey P. (1999). Process redesign: Is it worth it? *Government Finance Review, 15*(4), 23–27.

Selander, J. P., and Cross, K. F. (1999). Process redesign: Is it worth it? *Management Accounting* (January): 40–44. London.

Seppanen, M. S. (1992). Automatic animation generation for special purpose simulators. In W. Krug and A. Lehmann (Eds.), *Proceedings of the 1992 European Simulation Symposium* (285–289). Dresden, Germany: Society for Computer Simulation International.

Seppanen, M. S. (1995). Developing industrial strength simulation models. In C. Alexopoulos, K. Kang, W. R. Lilegdon, and D. Goldsman (Eds.), *Proceedings of the 1995 Winter Simulation Conference* (936–39). Arlington, VA: Institute of Electrical and Electronics Engineers.

Seppanen, M. S. (1996). A database approach to simulation modeling. In A. Javor, A. Lehmann, and I. Molnar (Eds.), *Proceedings of the 1996 European Simulation Symposium* (332–35). Budapest, Hungary: Society for Computer Simulation International.

Sherman, R. (1997). First establish demand. *Manufacturing Systems, 15*(8), 68–72.

Sipper, D., and Bulfin, R. L., Jr. (1997). *Production: planning, control, and integration.* New York: McGraw-Hill.

SonicAir. (2004). A UPS logistics group company. Available: http://www.pandaexpress.ups.com/unusual/memor.html.

Sterman, John. (1992). Teaching takes off, flight simulators for management education. *OR/MS Today,* October, pp. 40–44.

Sule, D. R. (1994). *Manufacturing facilities—Location, planning, and design* (2nd ed.). Boston: PWS Publishing.

Swaminathan, J. M., Smith, S. F., and Sadeh, N. M. (1996). A multi-agent framework for modeling supply chain dynamics. *Proceedings of the Artificial Intelligence and Manufacturing Research Planning Workshop,* Albuquerque, New Mexico, June 24–26, pp. 210–238.

T

Tanir, Oryal, and Booth, Richard J. (1999). Call center simulation in Bell Canada. In Farrington, P. A., Nembhard, H. B, Sturrock, D. T., and Evans, G. W. (Eds.), *Proceedings of the 1999 Winter Simulation Conference* (1640–1647). Piscataway, NJ: Institute of Electrical and Electronics Engineers.

Tehrani, Rich. (2002). Rising to the challenge at the Merrill Lynch Contact Center. *Customer Interaction Solutions,* June, pp. 12, 14.

Tompkins, J. A., White, J. A., Bozer, Y. A., Frazelle, E. H., Tanchoco, JMA, and Trevino, J. (1966). *Facilities planning* (2nd ed.). New York: John Wiley & Sons.

Turbide, D. (1997). The new world of procurement. *Midrange ERP,* July/August, pp. 12–16.

Tzafestas, S., and Papsiotis, G. (1994). Coordinated control of manufacturing/supply chains using multi-level techniques. *Computer Integrated Manufacturing Systems, 10*(3), 206–12.

V

Vander Alst, W. M. P. (1998). The application of petri nets to workflow management. *Journal of Circuits, Systems, and Computers, 8*(1).

Vollman, Thomas. (1996). *The transformation imperative, achieving market dominance through radical change.* Boston, MA: Harvard Business School Press.

W

Walkenbach, John. (1999). *Microsoft Excel 2000 bible.* New York: Hungry Minds, Inc.

Walkenbach, John. (2001). *Excel 2002 power programming with VBA.* New York: John Wiley & Sons.

Wells, Eric. (1995). *Developing Microsoft Excel 95 solution with Visual Basic for Applications,* Redmond, WA: Microsoft Press.

Wideman, Graham. (2001). *Visio 2002 developer's survival pack.* Victoria, BC: Trafford Publishing.

Wilbur, Randa A. (1999). Making changes the right way. *Workforce,* March, pp. 12–13.

Willis, A. K. (1995). Customer delight and demand management: Can they be integrated? *1995 Conference Proceedings of the American Production and Inventory Control Society.*

Wolf, S., and Tauber, R. N. (1986). Silicon processing for the VLSI era, Vol. 1, *Process Technology.* Sunset Beach, CA: Lattice Press.

Z

Zavacki, John. (2002). Six sigma deployment, quality progress. *Milwaukee, 35*(10), 112.

Zygmont, Jeffrey. (1988). Why plant automation fails. *High Technology Business, 8*(11), 26–29.

INDEX

Exhibits are indicated by (exh.).